THE CAMBRIDGE HISTORY OF ISLAM

IN TWO VOLUMES

Volume I

THE CAMBRIDGE HISTORY OF ISLAM

Volume 1

THE CENTRAL ISLAMIC LANDS

edited by
P. M. HOLT
Professor of Arab History in the University of London
ANN K. S. LAMBTON
Professor of Persian in the University of London
BERNARD LEWIS
Professor of the History of the Near and Middle East in the University of London

CAMBRIDGE
AT THE UNIVERSITY PRESS
1970

Published by the Syndics of the Cambridge University Press
Bentley House, 200 Euston Road, London N.W.1
American Branch: 32 East 57th Street, New York, N.Y. 10022

Library of Congress Catalogue Card Number: 73-77291

Standard Book Number: 521 07567 X

Printed in Great Britain
Spottiswoode, Ballantyne & Co. Ltd.
London and Colchester

CONTENTS

LIST OF MAPS

EDITORS' NOTE

The editors wish to state that they were responsible for the corrections made to the first proof, and co-operated in revising the second proof with the Cambridge University Press, which took responsibility for correcting it.

PREFACE

The aim of these volumes is to present the history of Islam as a cultural whole. It is hoped that in a single concise work the reader will be able to follow all the main threads: political, theological, philosophical, economic, scientific, military, artistic. But *The Cambridge history of Islam* is not a repository of facts, names and dates; it is not intended primarily for reference, but as a book for continuous reading. The editors believe that, while it will not be despised by the expert orientalist, it will be useful to students in other fields of history, and particularly to university students of oriental subjects, and will also appeal to those who read history for intellectual pleasure.

A standardized system of translation has been employed for proper names and technical terms in the three principal Islamic languages—Arabic, Persian and Turkish. Some anomalies have, however, been inevitable, and place-names which have a widely accepted conventional spelling have been given in that form. Dates before the nineteenth century have normally been given according to both the Islamic (*Hijrī*) and Christian eras. Footnotes have been used sparingly; principally to give references for quotations or authority for conclusions in the text. The bibliographies are not intended as an exhaustive documentation of the subjects to which they refer, but as a guide to further reading. For this reason, and to avoid extensive repetition of titles, many of the bibliographies have been consolidated to cover two or more related contributions.

The Editors are responsible for the planning and organization of the work as a whole. They have tried to avoid gaps and overlaps, and have given general guidance to contributors, designed to secure some consistency of form and presentation. The individual authors are, of course, responsible for their own opinions and interpretations.

The Editors wish to express their thanks to all who have assisted in the preparation of this work. They are particularly grateful to those who undertook the translation of contributions or gave advice and sub-editorial assistance, especially Mr J. G. Burton-Page, Professor C. D. Cowan, Dr J. F. P. Hopkins, Dr A. I. Sabra, Professor H. R. Tinker, Col. Geoffrey Wheeler and Dr D. T. Whiteside. They would also like to thank members of the staff of the Cambridge University Press for their invariable patience and helpfulness.

THE EDITORS

INTRODUCTION

P. M. HOLT[1]

A reader taking up a work entitled *The Cambridge history of Islam* may reasonably ask, 'What is Islam? In what sense is Islam an appropriate field for historical enquiry?' Primarily, of course, Islam is, like Christianity, a religion, the antecedents, origin and development of which may, without prejudice to its transcendental aspects, be a legitimate concern of historians. Religious history in the narrow sense is not, however, the only, or even the main, concern of the contributors to these volumes. For the faith of Islam has, again like Christianity, been a great synthesizing agent. From its earliest days it displayed features of kinship with the earlier monotheisms of Judaism and Christianity. Implanted in the former provinces of the Byzantine and Sasanian empires, it was compelled to maintain and define its autonomy against older and more developed faiths. Like Judaism and Christianity before it, it met the challenge of Greek philosophy, and adopted the conceptual and logical tools of this opponent to expand, to deepen, and to render articulate its self-consciousness. In this connexion, the first three centuries of Islam, like the first three centuries of Christianity, were critical for establishing the norms of belief and practice, and for embodying them in a tradition which was, or which purported to be, historical.

The Islamic synthesis did not stop at this stage. The external frontier of Islam has continued to move until our own day. For the most part, this movement has been one of expansion—into Central Asia, into the Indian sub-continent and south-east Asia, and into trans-Saharan Africa—but there have also been phases of retreat and withdrawal, notably in Spain, and in central and south-eastern Europe. But besides this external frontier, which has largely been the creation of conquering armies, (although with important exceptions in Central and south-east Asia and Africa) there has also been throughout Islamic history an internal frontier—the invisible line of division between Muslim and non-Muslim. Here also over the centuries there has been an expansion of Islam, so that, for example, in the former Byzantine and Sasanian lands the Christian and Zoroastrian communities were reduced to numerical insignificance, and became minority-groups like the Jews. This twofold

[1] I should like to thank my co-editors, Professors Lambton and Lewis, for reading and commenting on this Introduction in draft.

expansion has brought new elements into the Islamic synthesis, some permanent and widely accepted, others more transient or local in their effects.

The process of synthesization has not gone forward in a political vacuum. Unlike the early Christian Church, the Islamic *Umma*, or community of believers, achieved political power from the outset, and was organized for mutual support in the maintenance of the faith. This concern of the community for the faith survived the break-up of the caliphate and the emergence of new and often transitory régimes. It has taken various forms. Two of the principal institutions of Islam, *Sharīʿa* and *Jihād,* the Holy Law and the Holy War, are expressions of the concern in its conservative and militant aspects respectively—aspects moreover which are not wholly distinct, since the Holy War is fought in defence of the Holy Law against its external and internal enemies. In political matters as in others, Islam adopted and incorporated contributions from many sources. The successors of the Prophet as heads of his community drew on the customs of Arab tribal leadership, as well as the usages of the Meccan trading oligarchy. They inherited the legacy of Byzantine administration, as well as the traditions of the Sasanian monarchy. Later rulers were influenced by other political concepts: those brought into the medieval Islamic world by Turkish and Mongol immigrants from the steppes, and in the latest age the constitutional and legal doctrines of liberal Europe, followed by the seductive panaceas of totalitarianism.

Islam, then, as it will be examined in the following chapters, is a complex cultural synthesis, centred in a distinctive religious faith, and necessarily set in the framework of a continuing political life. The religion, the culture, and the political structures alike present many features which seem familiar to an observer whose own background is that of Christian Europe. It could hardly be otherwise, since elements derived from Judaism and Hellenism are common to both the Islamic and the Christian syntheses; since, furthermore, the histories of the Islamic community and of Christendom have touched so often and at so many points. But consciousness of the similarities must always be balanced by an awareness of the characteristic and substantial differences. Like Christianity, Islam is a monotheism with an historical founder and a sacred book; although its theology in regard to both differs essentially from Christian theology. There is also a perceptible difference in the criteria of membership of the community. Whereas in Christianity acceptance of the catholic creeds has been the basic criterion, in Islam credal theology has been of less relative importance; adherence to the Holy Law is the characteristic manifestation of faith, and hence orthopraxy rather than orthodoxy has been the usual token of membership. Another difference is that Islam has no equivalent to the Christian sacraments (although certain practices, notably the Fast of Ramaḍān and the Pilgrimage, appear to have an unacknowledged quasi-sacramental character), and no priesthood, although the '*ulamā*' (the religious scholars) and the leaders of the Ṣūfī orders (two groups at some times and in some places closely interconnected) have often played a part in Muslim societies analogous to that of the clergy amongst Christians. The absence of a sacerdotal hierarchy, or of any conciliar system, to define the faith, linked with the primacy ascribed to orthopraxy, has made Islam more tolerant of variations of belief than Christianity. It is in general true to say that heresy (to use a term not quite appropriate in Islam) has been repressed only when it has been manifested as political subversion: it is also true to say that, since Islam is both a religious and a political community, the distinction between religious and political dissent is not clearcut.

Another question which the reader of this work may ask is, 'What are the sources on which knowledge of the history of Islam is based?' The Islamic civilization of the first three centuries (in this as in other respects the seminal period) evolved two characteristic types of historical writing. The first of these was the chronicle, of which the outstanding example is that composed by al-Ṭabarī (d. 310/923). But behind the chronicle lay diverse historiographical elements—the sagas and genealogies of the pre-Islamic Arab tribes, the semi-legendary narratives of the Persian kings, and, serving as the central theme to which all others were subservient, the career of the Prophet and the vicissitudes of the *Umma* which he founded. The early historians were primarily religious scholars: the traditions which they recorded were in part Traditions in the technical Islamic sense, i.e. *Ḥadīth,* the memorials of the alleged acts and sayings of the Prophet, as transmitted by a chain of informants. There was no formal distinction between the historical *Ḥadīth* and the main body of Traditions which formed a principal element in the elaboration of the Holy Law; indeed, it is clear that many items ostensibly of an historical nature had in fact legal and social purposes. There is also a fundamental problem of criticism; namely, the difficulty of establishing how much of this copious *Ḥadīth* material is a veritable record of Muḥammad's activities, and how much is of subsequent and extraneous origin, assimilated in this form into Islam. The early Muslim scholars were keenly aware of the problem, although the criteria they adopted for discriminating between the authentic and the feigned Traditions seem artificial and insufficiently rigorous by modern standards of historical investigation. The whole subject is highly controversial at the present day, with, on the whole, non-Muslim scholars adopting a more radical, and Muslim scholars a more conservative attitude in *Ḥadīth* criticism.

Thus the motive which led to the development of Islamic historiography was primarily religious. In nothing does Islam so clearly demonstrate its kinship with Judaism and Christianity as in its sense of, and attitude towards, history; its consciousness of the existence of the world under a divine dispensation, and its emphasis on the significance of human lives and acts. Muḥammad saw himself as the last in a sequence of prophets who were God's apostles to mankind. The Qur'ān abounds in references to sacred history. Hence Islamic historiography assumes as axiomatic the pattern already evolved in Judaeo-Christian thought: a succession of events in time, opening with the creation, culminating in a point of supreme divine revelation (when, in effect, there is a new creation of a holy community), and looking prospectively to a Last Day and the end of history. In this connexion, it is significant that, in spite of the contacts between Islamic and late Hellenistic civilization, and of the Muslim reception of much of the Graeco-Roman cultural heritage, the Islamic historians were almost totally uninterested in their Classical predecessors, whether as sources of information, or as models of historiography. The Roman Empire played no part in the *praeparatio evangelica* for Islam as it did for Christianity.

This conception of Islamic history as sacred history was a factor in the development of the second characteristic type of historical writing, a type original in Islam—the biographical dictionary. The earliest of these to survive is a collection of lives of Companions of the Prophet, and, in the words of Sir Hamilton Gibb:

> it is clear that the conception that underlies the oldest biographical dictionaries is that the history of the Islamic Community is essentially the contribution of individual men and women to the building up and transmission of its specific culture; that it is these persons (rather than the political governors) who represent or reflect the active forces in Muslim society in their respective spheres; and that their individual contributions are worthy of being recorded for future generations.[1]

[1] H. A. R. Gibb, 'Islamic biographical literature', in *Historians of the Middle East,* ed. B. Lewis and P. M. Holt (London, 1962), p. 54.

Although both the chronicle and the biographical dictionary changed and developed as, after the third Islamic century, historical writing ceased to be the special field of the religious scholars, as the caliphate was fragmented, and as new states and dynasties arose, the two persisted as the standard forms of historical writing until recent times. From Arabic they were carried over into the Persian and Turkish literatures, and from the heartlands of the Middle East to the fringes of Islam. Only during the last century, and partly at least in consequence of the reception of Western historical objectives and techniques by Muslim scholars, have they become moribund.

One important class of source-material, familiar to the student of Western history, is almost completely lacking for the history of Islam—namely, archives. Certain documents are to be found transcribed in chronicles, as well as in collections of model letters and the encyclopaedic handbooks written for the guidance of government officials, but these are at least at one remove from their originals, and as isolated pieces are of diminished evidential value. Climatic conditions in Egypt, and chancery practice in Europe, have preserved some documents, more or less at random, but only with the records of the Ottoman Empire does a rich and systematically maintained government archive become available. With the nineteenth century, archival material increases. As in other fields of historical study, important contributions have been made by the auxiliary sciences of archaeology, epigraphy, palaeography, diplomatic and numismatics.

The modern study of Islamic history goes back to developments in Europe during the sixteenth and seventeenth centuries. Throughout the previous millennium, the peoples in the lands of Western Christendom and Islam had remained in almost total ignorance of each others' history; but whereas the Muslims almost without exception chose to ignore events which seemed to them extraneous and irrelevant, the Christian writers elaborated what has rightly been called a 'deformed image' of Islam and its founder.[1] In the sixteenth and seventeenth centuries, this came to be challenged. The contacts of trade and diplomacy were increasing between Muslim and Christian states. The study of Arabic was established in European universities for a variety of reasons, not least that it was seen to be the key to the writings of the Muslim philosophers and scientists, hitherto known only in imperfect medieval Latin translations. A knowledge of Arabic was also important in the

[1] See N. Daniel, *Islam and the West: the making of an image* (Edinburgh, 1960).

study of the Hebrew Bible—a study which flourished in the age of the Renaissance and the Reformation. During the same period in Western Europe, the foundations of critical historical enquiry were being laid: ancient texts were being published, old documents were being brought out of neglected archives. The motive behind much of this activity was ardently polemic; nevertheless, controversialists both in Britain and on the Continent were fashioning the instruments and devising the methods of modern research.

A new approach to the study of Islam was one aspect of this 'historical revolution', as it has been called.[1] It was demonstrated in two principal respects. The first of these was the publication of texts. Here the initiative was taken by Dutch scholars, Erpenius and Golius, in the first half of the seventeenth century, to be followed shortly by the Englishman, Edward Pococke (1604–91). The greatness of Pococke, however, lies mainly in a second respect. He had for his time an unrivalled knowledge of Muslim history and Arab antiquities, of which he gave an exposition in a short but very influential work, *Specimen historiae Arabum* (1650). The book remained authoritative for a century and a half, during which time it served as a quarry for a succession of writers. Resting on an encyclopaedic range of Arabic sources, the *Specimen*, implicitly by its scholarship, as well as by the occasional explicit comment, prepared the way for a more accurate and dispassionate view of Islam than the 'deformed image', which was still commonly accepted—and indeed lingered for two centuries. A later generation of orientalists extended the new understanding of Islam, and, by writing in modern languages, conveyed it to a less academic readership. Three highly important works in this connexion were the *Bibliothèque orientale* (1697) of Bartholomé d'Herbelot, *The history of the Saracens* (1708, 1718) of Simon Ockley, and George Sale's Preliminary Discourse to his translation of the Qur'ān (1734). Besides the information thus made available on the Islamic (and especially the Arab) past, there was in the same period a growing body of literature on the contemporary Muslim powers, especially the Ottomans and the Safavids. Through such publications, as well as others which were works of controversy rather than of scholarship, Islamic history became more familiar to educated Europeans, and was established beside ancient and modern history as an accepted field of study. This expansion of the world-view of European historians is

[1] See F. S. Fussner, *The historical revolution: English historical writing and thought, 1580–1640* (London, 1962).

demonstrated by Edward Gibbon, who, in his *Decline and fall of the Roman Empire* (1776–88) devoted nine out of seventy-one chapters to Islamic history, ranging from Arabia in the time of the Prophet to the Mongol and Ottoman conquests, and viewed its course with the same ironical detachment as he did the establishment of Christianity and the barbarian invasions of the West.

In the space of nearly two hundred years that have elapsed since Gibbon wrote, the Renaissance, the Reformation and the Enlightenment have themselves passed into history, and new forces have emerged in the development of European society. Political, social and economic change, the new ideologies of liberalism, nationalism and Marxism, have contributed to form the outlook and to define the preoccupations of historians in the nineteenth and twentieth centuries. At the same time, the methods of historical study have continued to evolve. The source-materials available for research have immensely increased, and the range of techniques at the historian's disposal has been extended. The aims of the historian have changed in response to both of these factors. Where the pioneers in the field sought primarily to construct, from the best sources they could find, the essential framework of political history, and to chronicle as accurately as possible the acts of rulers, historians today are more conscious of the need to evaluate their materials—a critique all the more important in Islamic history since the control supplied by archives is so largely deficient. They seek to penetrate the dynastic screen, to trace the real sites and shifts of power in the capitals and the camps, and to identify, not merely the leaders and figure-heads, but the ethnic, religious, social or economic groups of anonymous individuals who supported constituted authority or promoted subversion. It is no longer possible, therefore, to segregate the political history of Islam from its social and economic history—although in the latter field especially materials are notably sparse over wide regions and long periods. As the study of Islamic history is now developing, many of the apparent certainties of the older Western historiography (often reflecting the assertions and interpretations of the Muslim traditional historians) have dissolved, and it is only gradually through detailed research that a truer understanding of the past may be attained. At the same time, the range of investigation has been extended from its older foci, the heyday of classical Islam, the great dynastic empires, and the areas of confrontation with Christendom, to other periods and regions, which as recently as ten or twenty years ago aroused little interest among serious historians.

The Cambridge history of Islam cannot therefore pretend to supply a definitive conspectus of its field: it seeks rather to offer an authoritative guide to the state of knowledge at the present day, and to provide a sound foundation on which to build. The majority of its chapters are devoted to political history—this is inevitable in view of the relative abundance of source-material, and of the comparatively large amount of work that has been done here. Similar reasons explain the generous proportion of space allotted to the Muslim lands of the Middle East—which were, moreover, the region in which the classical Islamic synthesis evolved. Yet the picture which the work as a whole seeks to present is of the great and diversified community of Islam, evolving and expanding throughout thirteen centuries, creating its characteristic religious, political and social institutions, and making through its philosophy, literature and art a notable contribution to civilizations outside its own household of faith.

PART I

THE RISE AND DOMINATION OF THE ARABS

CHAPTER I

PRE-ISLAMIC ARABIA

In the history of the ancient world, Arabia has a place not unlike that of two other peninsulas in the Mediterranean region—Italy and the Balkans. It owes this place to its being the homeland of the Semitic peoples who developed a civilization which, alongside the Hellenic and the Roman, was to be a constituent in the tripartite structure of the cultural synthesis which the Mediterranean world witnessed in the early centuries of the Christian era. But this place is rather uncertain as far as the ancient world is concerned not so much because Arabia, after all, may not have been the 'original homeland' of the Semites, but because Semitic civilization in its highest forms was developed not within Arabia but outside its confines, in the semi-circle known as the Fertile Crescent. Be that as it may for the Arabia of the ancient Near East, there is no doubt whatsoever that Arabia is both the homeland of the *Arabs* and the cradle of *Islam*. The term 'pre-Islamic Arabia' is thus a fortunate and a significant one, reflecting as it does the decisive role which Islam played in changing its character, both as a religion which appeared within its boundaries, and as a movement which launched the Arabs on the paths of world conquest. It is, therefore, from this angle that this chapter on pre-Islamic Arabia has been written, as the last in the history of the ancient Semitic Near East and the introduction to the history of the medieval Islamic world.

Of all the factors which have shaped the history of the Arabian peninsula, geography has been the most decisive. Most of Arabia is the victim of *natura maligna*. The geological process is responsible for its shape and outline, a huge quadrilateral placed between two continents. Although surrounded by five seas, it has hardly any adjacent islands to diminish its inaccessibility and isolation; no good harbours with the exception of Aden; no hospitable coasts, but forbidding and narrow stretches; while the seas which surround it from east and west are plagued either by coral reefs as the Red Sea, or by shoals as the Persian Gulf. Its internal configuration is also unfortunate. In the whole of this huge land mass, with the exception of Ḥajar in the south, there is not a single river to facilitate transport and communication through the vast expanses of sun-scorched deserts and steppes as those in its eastern half (the relatively recent sedimentary area), or the rugged mountainous regions, especially the ancient shield of igneous rocks in the west; hence the importance of the major *wādīs,* the four principal ones of which connect the various parts of the peninsula: Sirḥān, Rumma, Dawāsir, and Ḥaḍramawt. But it is not so much the geological process as the terrestrial climate that has decisively shaped the history of Arabia. Of this climatic environmental complex, water, or lack of it, is the most important factor. Atmospheric precipitation there is on the outskirts of the peninsula, and in the monsoon area to the south-west it becomes ample rain, but the remaining greater part of the peninsula is arid, having no lakes or rivers, its hydrosphere consisting mainly of wells, torrents, and flashfloods.

Water then is the most decisive of all geographic determinants in the human story in Arabia, and it is the principle which divides the peninsula into two distinct parts: the rain-fed area of the outer parts, particularly the south-west; and the arid area of the centre or the inner regions. The peninsula, thus, is a land of strident contrasts which contains within its frontiers the two extremes side by side, as in the case of the fertile and luxuriant south, blessed by soil and climate, a Garden of Eden, and the adjacent area to the north-east, a veritable hell on earth known as the Empty Quarter, the most savage part of the arid area and the most extensive body of continuous sand in the whole world. The coexistence of these two extremes within the confines of one peninsula enables the features and characteristics of the human adaptation and response in each of the two areas to be clearly discerned and boldly drawn, which in its turn illuminates this first phase in the historico-cultural process in Arabia and contributes substantially towards redrawing the ethnographic map of the peninsula.

The arid area with its various degrees of aridity witnesses remarkable adaptations to the hard facts of physical geography. The classical examples of its plant, animal, and human ecology are the date-palm, the camel, and the bedouin, respectively, all examples of hardiness and endurance. Important as the date-palm is, it is less important than the camel, the *sine qua non* of bedouin life in the arid area, whose domestication in Arabia turned out to be a major event in the *anthropology* of the peninsula. The bedouin is truly 'the parasite of the camel' just as the camel is truly 'the ship of the desert'. The human adaptation or type is the bedouin; hard, enduring, and resourceful. He is necessarily a pastoralist, shepherd and herder, constantly moving, but his mobility is patterned by climatic conditions and related to pasturing his flocks and herds. His life is a competitive struggle for existence, hence war is a natural institution waged by tribes to which the individual bedouin must belong if he is to survive at all. On the outskirts of the arid area, there is a ring of oases where some form of sedentary life develops, made possible by the perennial springs of the oases which in their turn give rise to a form of agriculture, the basis of sedentary life and political aggregation. But these centres of settled life in the arid area remain what in fact they are, oases, subject to the law of generation and decay which governs the desert ephemerals, exposed to the unwelcome attention of the bedouins, and floating in a sea of sand. The bedouins of the desert and the sedentarized nomads of the oases are the two main representatives of the arid area-dwellers in the north.

The rain-fed area in the south is the nursling of *natura benigna,* and witnesses equally remarkable adaptations to the clement facts of physical geography. The complementary resources of soil and climate explain the fact that it is the flora, not the fauna, which is the key to understanding its life and history. It is a veritable cornucopia, where the vegetation is luxuriantly abundant, strikingly diversified, and comprehensively representative of all levels of use and need from the necessities of life to its luxuries. The symbol of the southern flora which reflects the luxuriant and luxurious tone of its vegetation is the frankincense tree, contrasting sharply with the date-palm of the arid area. The same sharp contrast applies to the human type. He is a sedentary, essentially an agriculturalist, and he is a mountaineer whose concern is the flora of his land, for the sake of which he transforms the terrain into a landscape of terraces and dams, symbols of intensive irrigated agriculture and the central position of hydrography in his scheme of things. The economy of the south, unlike the familial and tribal one in the north, is territorially based. The south is a land of towns and cities solidly established, unlike the centres of habitation in the north, whether the portable tents of the nomad or the oases whose sedentarized nomads are liable to revert to nomadism in special circumstances. The towns are close to one another, and so the region is thickly populated, a spatio-temporal human continuum, unlike the sand-girt oases of the arid area which spread sporadically and sometimes ephemerally, separated by vast distances. The south has all the elements necessary for the rise of a developed form of political life and a high material culture.

This clear division in the ecological order of the Arabian peninsula has its counterpart in ethnography. The inhabitants of the peninsula are clearly divisible into two major groups, closely related but quite distinct from each other. The process of differentiation between the two groups which started at the basic ecological level was carried further by other factors which completed the process of differentiation, a fact most clearly discernible on the linguistic level. In ethnographic terms, the peninsula then is divided between the peoples of the south, who speak a Semitic language of their own which has its dialectal variations, and the Arabs of the arid area and the oases of its outskirts, whose language is Arabic, the *ʿarabiyya,* which also has its own dialectal variations. But just as Sabaic is not Arabic or a dialect of Arabic, so are the Sabaeans and other peoples of the south not Arabs, although the two languages and the two peoples are closely related within the wider framework of Semitic. A grasp of these linguistic and ethnographic distinctions is indispensable for constructing the necessary framework within which the history of pre-Islamic Arabia must be set, if it is to be an intelligible field of historical study.

In concrete topographical terms, the Semites of the south are the peoples of Maʿīn, Saba', Qatabān, and Ḥaḍramawt, who inhabit the triangular area in the south-western part of the peninsula, and who may be called the Sabaeans or the Himyarites, following the practice of calling the whole by the name of the part, or may possibly be called the Yemenites, from a Sabaic word which denotes the south, and so would be a convenient term, had it not been for its medieval and modern associations. Those of the arid area and its oases, the Arabs, live mostly in the northern half, e.g. in Ḥijāz, Najd, and Yamāma, both as nomads of the steppe and as sedentaries in the ring of caravan-cities which surrounds the arid area. But the two groups are constantly in touch with each other; there are Arabs who live in the south, and there are Maʿinite and Sabaean colonies and communities in the north.

Such is the linguistic and ethnographic map of Arabia in the first millennium B.C. with its two major Semitic groups and languages. The historic migrations from the peninsula, or most of them, had already taken place. The centre of interest of Semitic history is not the peninsula but the Fertile Crescent, where the Semites develop their civilization. Arabia recedes into the background. In spite of the prosperous region to the south-west, it is mostly a forbidding and inhospitable region made more so by its inaccessibility and geographical isolation. And it would probably have remained so, had it not been for the southern Arabians, the Ma'inites and the Sabaeans in particular, who exhumed Arabia from obscurity. It was the Sabaeans who developed a high-level material Semitic culture within the peninsula and it was they who by their enterprise gave it an important though peculiar place in the history of the ancient Near East and of international relations. The south, then, is the region of dominance in pre-Islamic Arabia, and the Arabs of the north move in the orbit of the powerful south. It is, therefore, to the peoples and states of the south that first place in this chapter is given for a brief description of their history in the millennium or so before the rise of Islam.

Of the various city-states of the south, four may be mentioned as the most important. They are, as they lie from north to south-west, Ma'īn, Saba', Qatabān, and Ḥaḍramawt, whose capitals are Qarnaw, Ma'rib, Tamna', and Shabwa, respectively. Early in their history these peoples are ruled by *mukarribs,* a term of uncertain vocalization and signification, generally translated as 'priest-kings'. The rule of the *mukarribs* is followed by that of kings, and the monarchical institution becomes firmly rooted. This transition from the rule of *mukarrib* to *malik* (king) could indicate a process of partial secularization in the political life of the south. The monarchy is hereditary, and the principle of co-regency is sometimes applied, as when the reigning king associates with himself a brother or a son in the exercise of his kingly duties. Military power is in his hands but he has around him the powerful chiefs, the famous *qayls*. The social units which the *qayls* head are the tribes (*ash'b*). But the tribe in the south is to be distinguished from that of the north which is composed of a number of families linked by blood-ties. It is a sedentary unit, a territorially based organization bound by commercial and labour ties, and its members are recruited from the various classes of society, even the serfs. But nomadic tribes of the arid area are not unknown in the south. Royal charters, known as *watf,* record their presence and give a glimpse of how they were sedentarized in the south by a grant of land in return for military service and garrison duties. Slavery was a well-established institution, and the serfs were one of the props of economic life.

Religion was an important fact in the history of the south and its peoples. This would be most clearly evidenced by the rule of the *mukarribs* if the term really meant 'priest-kings'; however, the formula by which the state of Saba' was denoted, namely, 'Ilmaqah—the name of the *mukarrib*—Saba'', supports the religious connotation which can be

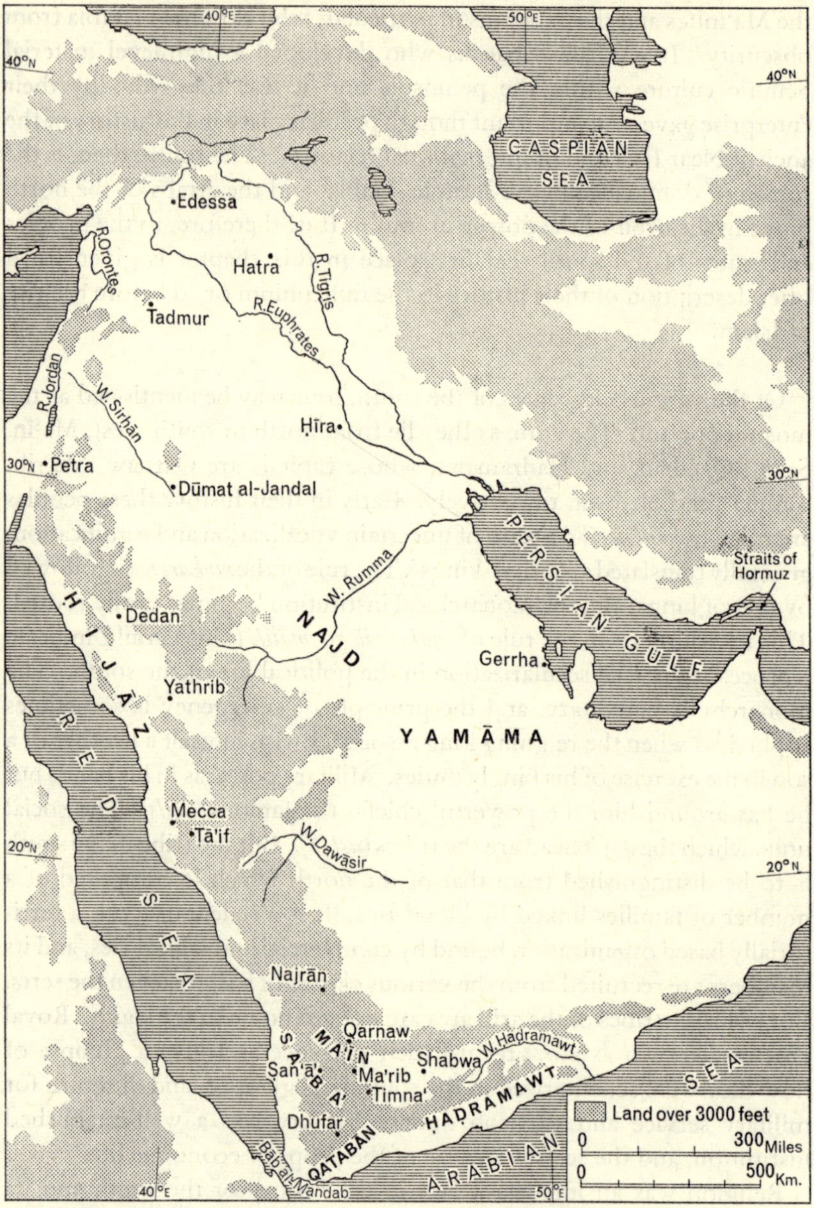

Map 1. Pre-Islamic Arabia and the Fertile Crescent.

imparted to the term *mukarrib,* and points to the theocratic basis upon which the Sabaean state was founded. The religious pantheon of the south is characterized by an astral triad composed of the Sun (Shams), the

Star-god ('Athtar), and the Moon, known as Ilmaqah in Saba', Wadd in Ma'īn, 'Amm in Qatabān, and Sīn in Ḥaḍramawt. Theophoric names abound, another indication of the close relationship which obtained between man and deity in the life of the south.

It will have been noticed from the constant reference to the 'peoples' of the south that the region was not a political unit, but was divided into a number of political entities. This fragmentation is a feature of its political life, almost a permanent one in spite of attempts to unify it. This is evident from the royal titulary of its late kings, which suggests a confederation of states rather than a truly unified and centralized realm. Of the four important kingdoms of the south, Ma'īn, Saba', Qatabān, and Ḥaḍramawt, it is Saba' which merits most attention. Just as the south is the region of dominance in the peninsula, so is Saba' the dominant state in that region. It is the most dynamic of all its states, and its military enterprise and political dominance enable the south to be viewed as a unitary region in spite of its division into a number of small states; its absorptive and expansionist policies enable the history of the south to be understood in terms of phases, as each territorial annexation ushers in a new phase. Within the thousand years or so before the rise of Islam, the following phases may be distinguished, reflected, with the exception of one, in the royal titulary: (a) Saba' absorbs the oldest of the kingdoms of the south, Ma'īn; (b) the royal titulary of the Sabaean king includes Dhū Raydān, a term variously interpreted as referring either to the state of Qatabān or to Ḥimyar; this second expansion is associated with the name of King Ilsharaḥ Yaḥḍub; (c) around A.D. 300, a great warrior-king, Shammar Yuhar'ish, annexes two more regions, Ḥaḍramawt and Yamanat; (d) around A.D. 400 the royal title of King Abkarib As'ad includes 'and their Arabs in Ṭawd and Tihāmat' (or in the highlands and the lowlands) a phrase which, in spite of inconclusive interpretations, does reflect the addition of a new sphere of influence for the Sabaean kings and which remains as part of the titulary until the sixth century. These four phases reveal a trend in the evolution of southern Arabian history, namely, the tendency towards larger political aggregation which finds its climax around A.D. 300 with the union of all the kingdoms of the south.

Important as all these aspects of Sabaean history happen to be, it is their economic history which is most noteworthy. It was economic facts and factors which moulded their own internal history, determined their development of the Arabian peninsula, and gave them their place in international relations. Not the fauna but the flora of their 'good earth', that was the basis of their economic prosperity. Of the flora, it was the articles of luxury that mattered, and that made of Sabaean Ma'rib the Paris of the ancient world, creating that romantic image of Arabia in the minds of Classical authors who called it *Felix* long before the time of the Arabian Nights. Of the luxury articles, the most important were frankincense and myrrh, which made possible a more precise description of Arabia Felix, namely, *Arabia Odorifera* 'Fragrant Arabia', the presumed kingdom of the queen who 'heard of the fame of Solomon' and visited him in Jerusalem, and whose articles of luxury, which certainly included 'gold, and frankincense, and myrrh', could have figured at the Adoration in Bethlehem at the end of that millennium. Southern Arabia was the sole supplier of frankincense in the Near East and the Mediterranean region. The plant grew in Ḥaḍramawt and in the transmarine colonies, Socotra and Somalia. South Arabia was not only the producer of luxury articles, but was also the importer of others from two other major areas of production in Asia and Africa, namely, India and Somalia. To their own sub-tropical luxuries the southern Arabians now added the tropical *exotica* of these two regions. Just as climate and soil in their homeland favoured them in becoming the producers of certain luxury articles, so did their privileged geographical location make them the entrepreneurs of the products of the Indian Ocean region, part of which they colonized in Socotra and Somalia. As a result of this expansion, the southern Arabian commercial empire consisted of two parts, the one complementing the other. The southern half was naval, its commercial lines connecting the two sides of the Indian Ocean with Arabia and thus making of Qana' (rather than Aden) the great naval station of the Indian Ocean. The northern part was the Arabian peninsula with overland trade routes carrying the products and imports of the south to the Fertile Crescent and the Mediterranean region. This made Ma'rib the great commercial capital of the ancient world in its southern parts, the centre of a vast network of trade-routes which reached it from the south-west and the south-east and which forked out from it to the north-east and the north-west.

The efficient working of this intricate and complex commercial organization required a high degree of vigilance and control which involved the three parts of its tripartite structure. In the Indian Ocean it was necessary to keep secret whatever geographical discoveries had been made, and to control the straits of Hormuz and Aden, lest the Indian and African trade should slip into other hands and be diverted from southern Arabia. Internally, the peaceful coexistence of the city-states was necessary for promoting the indigenous products, some of which, such as frankincense, entailed a high degree of skill in cultivating and harvesting, and for the smooth passage of the caravans from one state to another on their way to the north. In the peninsula, it was necessary to open up its expanses for trade-routes, to organize the caravans and ensure their safe conduct until they reached their termini in the Fertile Crescent. The history of the Arabian south consists largely of attempts to perpetuate these conditions in the three segments of its vast commercial network. In spite of the obvious difficulties which attend all complex operations, the southern Arabians were for a long time successful in their system of monopolistic control. They had no serious rivals in the Indian Ocean, which became a kind of *mare nostrum* for them. Within the peninsula they were able not only to control the nomads of the arid area but also to enlist the bedouin and harness his camel in the service of their trade. The hostility of the powers in the north did not seriously menace their existence. Southern Arabia was a sea-girt and a sand-girt fortress, far removed from the historic routes of world conquerors, and protected by inhospitable seas, scorching deserts, and forbidding distances. Its geographical location was its best ally, and is also the key to its remarkable longevity in spite of constant internecine wars and general political instability.

But the law of change and the emergence of new forces in the dynamics of Near Eastern history overtook the southern Arabians. Their system was inherently fragile by its very complexity and its precarious dependence upon so many external factors beyond their control, so that a single major factor, adversely operative, might throw it out of joint. How much of the collapse was due to internal disintegration or external pressure is difficult to determine. The internal process of decline, whether in the south itself or in the rest of the peninsula, is traceable: the political division of the country among feuding city-states is chronic, and it enables foreign powers to ally themselves with one state against the other; the national psychology or *ethos* is that of an affluent society whose prosperity is built on articles of luxury, and whose drift towards effeteness is difficult to check, sharply contrasting with that of their virile neighbours to the north, who heighten their martial spirit by breeding a new animal, the horse, which in its turn contributes to the feudalization of the south and to an appreciable rise in the power of the *qayls,* all new and disturbing factors. As for the rest of the peninsula, the Arabs increase their interference in the affairs of the south starting from the second century A.D.; the bedouin is no longer only a cameleer but also a horseman, a dangerous foe and a valuable ally; some of the old Ma'inite and Sabaean colonies, as Dedan, assert their independence, and the northern termini of the 'spice route' are now powerful Arab caravan-cities, such as Petra and Palmyra, and these move in the political orbits of new masters for the Fertile Crescent who pursue economic policies not calculated to advantage the Arabian south.

External factors, however, are more noticeable as they contribute to the decline and fall of southern Arabia. It has been observed that it was geography that favoured the south with its impregnable and inaccessible position. But the privileges of geography were soon to be withdrawn from the south as its heel of Achilles was discovered, and the region became vulnerable. It was not the Semitic empires of the Fertile Crescent but the Indo-European ones that began to menace southern Arabia's existence; not so much the Persians or the Romans but the Macedonians, especially the Ptolemies of Egypt, who effectively challenged the power of the south. Theirs was an aggressive, enterprising, naval state which succeeded in converting the northern half of the Red Sea into a Ptolemaic lake, and after Hippalus finally unlocked the secret of the monsoons towards the end of the second century B.C. they were able to establish a direct trade route between Egypt and India. The Ptolemies were a Red Sea power, sharing the Erythrean with the Sabaeans, and thus militarily were within striking distance of southern Arabia, unlike mightier but more distant empires, such as that of Rome, whose ill-starred expedition in 24 B.C. was shattered by the harsh facts of physical and human geography. Even more deadly than the Ptolemies were the Abyssinians of Axum who were closer to southern Arabia than the Ptolemies. Semites, like the southern Arabians to whom they were related, they were thoroughly familiar with the latter's political divisions and alignments. Separated from them only by Bāb al-Mandab and in possession of a beach-head on the Arabian mainland itself, the Axumites were most dangerously poised to administer a fatal blow.

Such was the situation in the Red Sea area around A.D. 300. Soon after, more adverse factors become operative when a new Near East comes into being with the *translatio imperii* from Rome to Constantinople and the conversion of Constantine. A new force, namely religion, enters into the dynamics of Near Eastern history, and continues to acquire momentum throughout the whole of this period from the fourth to the seventh centuries. The peninsula is now surrounded by vigorous, newly rejuvenated states, and each of the two contestants for supremacy, Christian Byzantium and Zoroastrian Persia, has definite religious and economic policies which operate to the disadvantage of southern Arabia. The conversion of the Ethiopian negus, ʿĒzānā, to Christianity brings Byzantium and Ethiopia even closer, and closes the ring around the south. These changes in the international scene, both in the Red Sea area and the Near East in general, do not fail to produce repercussions in the peninsula, particularly in the part most sensitive to such changes, namely, the south.

In the political sphere, the peninsula as a whole assumes even greater importance for the south. This is reflected in major military operations conducted by Shammar Yuharʿish *c.* A.D. 300, which take him far, to the north-east, to the Sasanid frontier. The increasing importance of the Arabs in the military history of the south is reflected by the addition of 'and their *Aʿrāb*' to the royal titulary. Just as the camel, domesticated by the Arabs, made possible the long-distance Sabaean caravan trade, so the Arab horse now plays a similarly important role in the militarization of the south and the campaigns of the southern Arabian kings, as Shammar Yuharʿish and Abkarib Asʿad in the third and fifth centuries. To this period in the history of the north may be traced the settlement of many of the southern Arab tribes, whose presence in the north could thus be attributed to their participation as auxiliaries in the armies of the Himyaritic kings during the latter's north peninsular campaigns; but the breaking of the famous dam of Ma'rib could have also been a contributory factor, however indirect. To the same period in the history of the south may be traced the levelling of the distinctions between the Himyarites and the Arabs, and the gradual arabization of the south, a process which was accelerated in the sixth century and completed with the Arab conquest of the south and the islamization of the country in the seventh century. The new decisive factor in the Near East, religion, soon involves Arabia, and the peninsula's involvement in it is most vividly reflected by its new image in the outside world, no longer 'happy' (*Felix*) or 'fragrant' (*Odorifera*) but 'the breeding ground of heresies', *Arabia haeresium ferax*. Christianity with its universalistic claims could not overlook much longer the evangelization of Arabia, while its adoption as the state religion by both Byzantium and Ethiopia, two states which had always schemed against the south, added a political tone or dimension to its universalistic claims. But Arabia had already been penetrated by another monotheistic religion—Judaism; the peninsula had begun to assume great importance for that religion after the destruction of the Temple in A.D. 70 and the christianization of the Roman Empire in the fourth century. Hence the complication of the religious issue by a competition between the two religions of the Old and the New Testaments which might be described as 'the struggle for Arabia'. The south was naturally more disposed towards Judaism, since Christianity was associated with its two traditional enemies, Byzantium and Ethiopia. Through the mission of Theophilus Indus in the fourth century, Christianity had succeeded in establishing churches at Ẓafār and Aden. In the fifth century Judaism gained the upper hand with the judaization of the kings of the south, but Christianity continued to make progress in the outlying areas such as Ḥaḍramawt, and particularly in the now arabized city of Najrān, which had strong ties with Monophysite Syriac Christianity in the Fertile Crescent. The struggle came to a head in the first quarter of the sixth century, when the judaizing king of Ḥimyar, Yūsuf As'ar, tried systematically to spread Judaism in the south. Clashes with Christianity were inevitable, and they culminated in the famous massacre of the Christians of Najrān, which proved to be a turning-point in the history of the south and the peninsula. Around A.D. 520 an Ethiopian expedition crossed Bāb al-Mandab with the blessings of Byzantium and the Monophysite world, destroyed the power of the last judaizing king of Ḥimyar, and made the country an Ethiopian protectorate. The victory of the Ethiopian negus, Ella Aṣbeḥa, brought to a close the final phase of Himyaritic history which lasted for more than two centuries, starting with the campaigns of Shammar Yuharʿish, during which the south braced itself to great military efforts which spread its influence throughout the Arabian peninsula.

The Ethiopian invasion ushered in a century of anarchy and political upheavals which left the south politically prostrate. The Ethiopian occupation lasted for about half a century, punctuated by the revolt of Abraha, an Ethiopian soldier of fortune who killed the Himyaritic viceroy of the negus, and asserted his virtual independence. Various activities are associated with his name as the building of a famous church in Ṣanʿāʾ, *al-Qalīs* (*ecclesia*), but more celebrated is his expedition against Mecca which, if proved historical in its important details, would be a contemporary testimony to the rising power of that caravan-city and the

Arab area. In the last quarter of the sixth century, the south is under new masters, this time the Persians who were called in by a *qayl* of the Dhū Yaz'an family, the same that played such an important role in the history of the south throughout the sixth century. The Persian occupation lasts for about half a century, and is terminated by the third and final invasion of the south, that by the Arabs under the banner of Islam.

The continual dislocations which left the country politically prostrate did not leave it entirely devoid of interest. Indeed, the beginnings of a cultural awakening are discernible in the south, and the great stimulant is religion. The country which for centuries resisted cultural assimilation in its religious form is now wide open to a bewildering variety of religious currents which run in the wake of each foreign invasion. The Ethiopian occupation gives a strong impetus to Monophysite Christianity, while the Persian occupation enables Judaism and possibly Nestorian Christianity to regain strength and admits an Indo-European form of religious experience, Iranian Zoroastrianism, into this old Semitic stronghold. The wave of the Arab conquest in the seventh century brings in Islam, the last and most powerful ray in this richly diversified religious spectrum. The sixth century witnessed the emergence of Najrān as the great Christian centre in the south, a holy city, sanctified by its martyrs, whose chief, al-Ḥārith b. Ka'b (St Arethas), was canonized, and made famous like Ṣan'ā', by its church, *Ka'bat Najrān*. The strong religious colour of the south with its conflicting faiths creates a new conception of southern Arabia in the consciousness of the outside world. In Classical times it had been a favourite of geographers, fascinated by its aromatic and exotic products; in the sixth century and after, it became a region of intense religious passions, attractive to hagiographers and other ecclesiastical writers of the period and of later times. For Orthodox Byzantium the country was the beneficiary of a new code, the *Laws of St Gregentius*; for the Ethiopians, it was the scene of their great crusade under Negus Kāleb, and thus takes an honoured place in their national epic, the *Kebra Nagast*; for Syriac Christianity, it was the *martyrium* of their Monophysite co-religionists, symbolizing the triumph of the persecuted Monophysite church in the sixth century; for the medieval Islamic world, it was the homeland of Sayf b. Dhī Yazan, the hero of a famous *sīra,* who fought for the true religion against the godless and heathen Ethiopians. All these literary remains and the religious currents they reflect are of importance for the history of the south in the sixth century, but they are even more important for the history of ideas in the north during the same period, and for a better understanding of the peculiar history of the Yemen in Islamic times.

The fall of the Himyaritic kingdom in the sixth century was an historic event of the first order, not fully appreciated at the time except in ecclesiastical writings, but even these, quite understandably, take a narrowly focused view of its significance. Before its fall, the Arabian south had endured as the dominant region in the southern parts of the Near East for at least a millennium, during which it made its mark in the history of the ancient world, of the Semites, and of the Arabian peninsula.

In the history of the ancient world, the southern Arabians were responsible for what might be termed the commercial revolution in the Near East. They brought together the world of the Indian Ocean and that of the Mediterranean Sea by laying out a long trade-route extending from India and Somalia to the Fertile Crescent, which formed with another major trade-route in the Mediterranean also laid out by a Semitic people, the Phoenicians, the longest trade-route in the history of the world until the advent of the Oceanic Age. They may not have discovered India themselves, but they advertised its products to the world of the Mediterranean, and thus introduced into international politics the first phase of the Eastern Question, a drama to which Hippalus contributed a chapter, Columbus another, Vasco da Gama a third, and which finally found epic literary expression in *Os Lusíadas*.

In the history of the Semites, they represent the southern wing of Semitic civilization, balancing the northern one in the Fertile Crescent. In their political divisions and constant feuding, they were more akin to the Semites of Syro-Palaestina than to those of Mesopotamia, coming closest to the Phoenicians; indeed, they were the Phoenicians of the south. Like these, they were the great traders of the ancient world and the colonizers of the African mainland. But, unlike the overexposed Semites of Syro-Palaestina, they enjoyed a sheltered existence owing to their geographical isolation which, however, was not an unmixed blessing. Although this enabled them to develop a variety of Semitic civilization relatively free from foreign cultural penetration, in spite of their early contacts with Hellenic and other influences, it might partially explain the complexion of their cultural achievement—intellectually, spiritually, and artistically, rather pale compared to that of the northern Semites. Theirs was a business culture, and their ideal was materialistic, the acquisition of wealth, which they relentlessly pursued, as the

Carthaginians did, with similar results. The remains of their material culture are uninspiring, more interesting archeologically than artistically, lacking that significant form which differentiates an artefact from a work of art. A splendid exception to this is the *musnad,* their elegant and graceful script. But the very same isolation which possibly operated to their disadvantage in the cultural sphere was their salvation politically; in the context of Semitic history, theirs was the only state which maintained the political presence of the Semites in western Asia for a millennium after the fall of Babylon to Cyrus in 539 B.C. and the inauguration of the Indo-European interregnum in the Semitic Near East. Their millennial political existence thus forms the middle period in the history of the Semites between the ancient one which was terminated by the fall of the Fertile Crescent to the Persians, and the medieval one which began with the mission of Muḥammad and the rise of Islam.

In the history of Arabia, the peoples of the south were able to develop a civilization *within* its confines and thus relieved it of its character as a mere 'Semitic homeland' or an 'ethnic reservoir'. In so doing they deeply influenced the fortunes of the Arab area. By the same spirit of enterprise with which they sailed the southern seas, they now opened up the deserts of the north. The north ceases to be only an arid expanse, but becomes a transit area through which pass the commercial arteries of world trade. Its landscape is transformed by new functions given to some of its constituents—the *wādī,* the camel, the horse, the bedouin, and the oasis. The *wādī* becomes a trade-route, a segment of a longer commercial artery, threaded by the camel, now 'the ship of the desert', not merely a domesticated animal for bedouin use, but a constituent member of the southern caravan. The horse is also harnessed as part of a cavalry unit in the regular armies of the south. The bedouin, in addition to his function in the auxiliary troops of the southern armies, is also a guard and a guide for the southern caravan. Thus the south raised to a higher power or level of function those constituents of the desert scene, and introduced a measure of organization in the life of the bedouin and a degree of purposefulness in his mobility. Of all the contributions of the south to the Arab area, it was the impetus it gave to the urbanization of western Arabia that proved to be the most decisive. The oasis is no longer a cluster of date-palms or a 'sunny spot of greenery', but a station on a trade-route—a new type of urban settlement—the caravan-city; this in its turn gives rise to a new type of community among the Arabs—the community of traders. Important as the bedouin were to be in the Arab conquests, it was not they but the urban communities settled in caravan-cities who initiated the historic movement of the seventh century. Those near the Byzantine and Persian borders played little or no part in that movement; it was the communities in Inner Arabia on the 'incense route' which did, and these owed their development to the initiative and enterprise of the south. In this sense the history of the south which as an independent region was brought to an inglorious and almost pathetic end in the sixth century, became a *Praeparatio Arabica* or *Islamica*. To the Arabs who were to sponsor Islam and spread it, the next part of this chapter is devoted.

The history of the Arabs in the arid area of the north presents a spectacle which contrasts with that of their Semitic neighbours to the south. Unlike the fairly homogeneous society of the south, theirs is heterogeneous, divided into nomads and sedentaries. The area of their habitation, unlike the compact triangle of the southern Arabians, is vast and far-flung, where the nomads roam in its central and north-eastern parts while the sedentaries dwell in the oases which dot the peripheral regions. The centres of sedentary life also display among themselves some cultural and social heterogeneity, and their political life is fitful and intermittent. But beneath all this diversity within the Arab scene lies the ethnological fact which informs all this seeming diversity with essential unity, namely that of the Arabs as one people, who remain recognizably Arab in spite of the various forms of political, social, and cultural life which they adopt, as they respond to the challenges of their environmental complex and the laws which govern their historic evolution.

The most important feature of their history is its dualistic structure—the existence side by side, among the same people, and within the same area, of two groups at different degrees of evolution—the nomads of the desert and the sedentaries of the oases. This fact is the key to understanding the dynamics of Arab history as it unfolded itself in pre-Islamic times.

The bedouin are a permanent factor in the Arab area. The unfavourable facts of physical geography within the peninsula and of political history outside it forced upon them a perpetual struggle for existence or subsistence, which in its turn created that military tension within the peninsula and without it in the area of their penetration. This is reflected in the inscriptions of the neighbouring powers in the north and in the south, who, however, were able to contain their onslaughts and to harness them (and their fauna, the horse and camel) as auxiliaries in their armies or their caravans. In the first millennium before the rise of Islam, the bedouin could not effect major breakthroughs similar to the ones they had effected in previous times, since the Fertile Crescent was now under powerful masters, whether Semitic or Indo-European. Hence they were a more important factor within the peninsula both in the north and in the south. With the decline and eventual downfall of the south, it was their relationship with the Arab sedentaries of the north which assumed greater importance; and it was the stabilization of this relationship in the sixth Christian century which finally channelled the energies of this restless human mass who were to play in the seventh century an historic role of the first order. Until then, the bedouin remained on a primitive level of evolution, and their history, recorded incidentally and intermittently by their neighbours, displays a uniformity of pattern almost monotonous. It is, therefore, the sedentaries of the Arab area who deserve most attention.

The sedentaries are former bedouin who were able, during their search for better living conditions, to possess themselves of many oases within the peninsula and sometimes to penetrate, not too deeply, the neighbouring regions, overcoming oases already inhabited by other Semitic peoples. Their centrifugal migrations are reflected graphically by the chain of settled establishments which dot a huge arc on the periphery of the arid area, from the Persian Gulf, to the Fertile Crescent, to Western Arabia, such as Gerrha, Qaṭīf, Ḥīra, Ḥaḍr, Tadmur, Petra, Dedan, Mecca, Ṭā'if, and Najrān. This is roughly the extent of the Arab expansion in this millennium.

The rise, decline, and fall of these sedentary establishments follow the laws which govern the life of settlements on the frontier between the Desert and the Sown and which derive from the political and the economic life of the ancient Near East. *Politically,* the stronger the Fertile Crescent and southern Arabia are, the more difficult it is for the bedouin to effect deep penetration and establish themselves in these areas as sedentaries. During most of the first millennium before Christ, the Arabs had to face a Fertile Crescent united by the military might of the Assyrians, a unity which was maintained by the neo-Babylonians and the Persians. But in the second century B.C. this unity was broken, and the Crescent remained divided between hostile groups, the Parthians and the Seleucids, the Parthians and the Romans, and finally the Sasanids and the Byzantines. *Economically,* these Arab establishments owe their prosperity to the fact that they are stations on the vital west Arabian and Mesopotamian trade-routes. Hence the continued prosperity of this or that establishment is dependent upon the prosperity of the particular trade-route on which it is a station. The rise and fall of Arab sedentary establishments is, therefore, determined to a great extent by changes which affect the fortunes of these routes.

In spite of striking similarities among these Arab establishments of the periphery, considerable diversities obtain, which derive from a number of factors and circumstances. Some of these settlements have an agricultural basis, as Yathrib and Najrān, others a purely strategic position on the trade-route, as Petra and Palmyra. They become more complex and diversified as the original character of the establishments changes with the assumption of new functions, e.g. those of the caravan-city. The process of acculturation is another factor which contributes to diversity as each establishment takes on a complexion which reflects that of the orbit in which it happens to be moving. During the centuries of the Christian era there were three such orbits, the Persian, the Roman, and the Sabaean; hence the arc of the Arab establishments is culturally divisible into three segments. In the north-east, under Persian influence, grow the cities of Ḥīra and Ḥaḍr; under Hellenistic and Roman influence are such Arab establishments as Petra; while Palmyra, because of its intermediate position between Persia and Rome, is influenced by both; lastly, most of the cities of western Arabia, e.g. Dedan, are in the Sabaean orbit. All these establishments, however, develop on Semitic soil and in a Semitic ambiance, particularly those of the third segment. Important as the Persian, Hellenistic, and Roman contacts were for these establishments, it was Semitic soil and ambiance which deeply influenced the Arabs in the cultural sphere: Aramaean in the north and Sabaean in the south, with the Aramaean influence eventually prevailing over the Sabaean, even in the latter's cultural orbit. Perhaps the most concrete manifestation of the Aramaean influence is its script which in its late Nabatean form established itself as the script of Classical Arabic, sweeping away centuries of Sabaean influence, represented by the *musnad*. The progress of monotheistic ideas among the Arabs is another illustration of the importance of the Semitic factor. Although Christianity was championed by Byzantium, it remained to the Arabs a Semitic religion, preached to them by Eastern ecclesiastics, whose liturgical language was Semitic, and whose two great centres, Ḥīra and later Najrān, were dominated by Syriac culture.

All these establishments, powerful as some of them came to be, enjoyed no independent existence, but one dependent upon political and economic factors over which they had no control, and which were determined by the powerful empires surrounding them. For this reason their history is divisible chronologically into the same periods as those of the major supremacies in the Fertile Crescent, starting from that of the Assyrians. The inscriptions of the latter provide information on campaigns against the Arabs and their fortress Adumu (Dūmat al-Jandal) and refer to a series of Arab queens, thus evidencing a matriarchal period in the history of the Arabs, which was to recur a thousand years later with the more celebrated queens, Zenobia and Mavia. The unification of the Fertile Crescent effected by the Assyrians and the continuation of this unity by the neo-Babylonians and the Persians, was broken in the second century B.C., when the Parthians ejected the Seleucids west of the Euphrates, and thus created a new political structure in the Crescent favourable to the Arabs. With the decay of the power of the Seleucids, the Arabs deepened their penetration of Syria, which was practically possessed by Arab dynasties when the Romans appeared and annexed Syria. It was during the Roman period that Petra and Palmyra developed in the western half of the Crescent, and they afford the best illustration of the precariousness of the life of these military establishments. In A.D. 106 Trajan annexed Petra whose territories thus became *Provincia Arabia*. In A.D. 272 Aurelian destroyed Palmyra, whose military thrusts under Zenobia had brought the Arabs to the shores of the Mediterranean, and whose conquest of Egypt and Asia Minor represents the climax of all Arab military and political history in ancient times. Its fall is, therefore, a landmark which makes the third century a dividing line in the pre-Islamic history of the Arabs, particularly since the same century witnessed the fall of two other Arab military establishments, Hatra at the hands of Shāpūr, and Edessa at the hands of Gordian, thus bringing to a close this long period which was characterized by the rise of powerful caravan-cities on the borders of the Fertile Crescent.

The dismantling of the Arab military establishment in the third century opens a new historical period in the evolution of the Arabs which lasts for some three centuries until the rise of Islam. A new Near East emerges, partitioned among the three great powers, Persia, Byzantium, and Himyar, in which religion is the new decisive factor. The Arabs are surrounded by these three powerful states of the Near East, in whose wars they play an important part as clients and auxiliaries, the Lakhmids for the Persians, the Ghassanids for Byzantium, and Kinda for Ḥimyar. All the three groups are influenced culturally by the various orbits within which they move, and the most significant of all these cultural influences is religion. This is the period during which Christianity, and to a lesser degree Judaism, spread among the Arabs, and during which Ḥīra and Najrān emerged as great centres which were diffusing Christianity among the Arabs. These three Arab groups, Kinda, Lakhm, and Ghassān, now occupy the stage of Arab history and play an important part in the wars of the period especially during the reigns of their illustrious kings, the Kindite al-Ḥārith b. ʿAmr (d. 528), the Lakhmid al-Mundhir b. al-Nuʿmān (503–54), and the Ghassanid, al-Ḥārith b. Jabala (529–69). Their history is vividly remembered by the pre-Islamic Arab poets whom the Lakhmid and Ghassanid dynasts in particular patronized. In spite of their power and military efficiency, these groups remained what in fact they were, clients to the great powers, dependent upon their support, and collapsible when these decide to bring about their downfall. And so it was with the Ghassanids and the Lakhmids, whose power their Byzantine and Sasanid masters reduced towards the end of the sixth century. Kinda, too, which played a significant role in Inner Arabia and the life of its bedouin disintegrated in the same century and withdrew to the south, whence it had issued. The period of the Arab client-kingdoms which followed that of the Arab caravan-cities of the north, represented by Palmyra in the third century, thus comes to a close. The client-kingdoms fall, victims to the operation of the laws which govern the life of all such political ephemerals in the history of the Arabian peninsula.

Simultaneously with the rise and fall of the Arab client-kingdoms, another world was coming into being, representing an entirely new departure in the evolution of Arab history. It is the world of Inner Arabia, composed of bedouin moving in the orbit of the sedentaries of the Ḥijāz, particularly those of Mecca. This city, which was growing silently in the sheltered segment of the western Arabian route, was, in conjunction with the bedouin of Najd, to rebuild Arab strength, and bring about the second and greater climax in the history of the Arabs since the fall of Palmyra.

The bedouin of central Arabia, who had been consigned to a state of arrested development, were soon to experience a cultural explosion which remains one of the curiosities of Semitic history. This is the period of their great militancy as riders of saddled horses; it is the heroic age of pre-Islamic Arabia, the age of *Ayyām al-ʿArab* and the famed *equus caballus*. The peculiarly Arab concept of *murūʾa* (cf. *vir-tus*) reaches its maturity in this period, which also witnesses the emergence of a more celebrated concept, that of chivalry. But more basic and significant was their perfection of a literary *koinê*, Classical Arabic, the elaboration of a complex metrical system, and the composition of a highly artistic poetry, unique in the literary history of the Semites. Significant as this artistic outburst is in the history of comparative and Semitic literature, its greater significance was extra-literary, as its linguistic medium, *al-ʿarabiyya*, enhanced the Arabs' awareness of their unity and identity and contributed to the rise of a strong Arab national sentiment.

The bedouin achievement might conceivably have dissipated itself had it not been for the rise of a new cultural orbit within the peninsula into which the bedouin were drawn, i.e. that of the newly rising caravan-city of western Arabia, Mecca. After centuries of uneasy association with foreign powers or Arab clients of foreign powers, the bedouin are now associated with the Arabs of Mecca, who are independent of foreign rule, and whose indigenous Arab culture provides a sympathetic context for bedouin achievement.

As part of western Arabia through which the *via odorifera* passed, the Ḥijāz had always been in a strategically advantageous position. And this position became even more advantageous in this period which, after the fall of Palmyra, witnessed a gradual shift in world commerce from the Mesopotamian to the west Arabian route. Culturally, too, the Ḥijāz was to benefit from this position, open as it was to the two main religious influences which were dominant in the peninsula, Judaism and Christianity, with strongholds at Yathrib and Najrān, respectively. The geographical position of Mecca on the spice route, half-way between Jewish Yathrib and Christian Najrān, naturally exposed it to the two currents of economic and religious life which were running in western Arabia. Inevitably it became a confluence of these two currents, which remained inseparable in the history of pre-Islamic Mecca, at one and the same time a caravan-station and a holy city. Although it had probably long combined the two features of a religious and commercial centre (judging from its Classical name, *Makorba,* temple?) it was in the sixth century that this combination reached arresting dimensions, after the tribe of Quraysh had possessed itself of the city through the enterprise of

Quṣayy (*c.* 500?) undoubtedly an historical figure. It was Quṣayy who laid the foundation for the prosperity of Mecca as the great 'commercial republic' of Arabia in the sixth century. What is not clear or certain is his contribution to its religious life which was unmistakably that of idolatry and polytheism, and the significant feature of which was a pantheon, composed of a triad of goddesses, al-Lāt, al-'Uzzā, and Manāt, the daughters of Allāh, either the Judaeo-Christian God or another Semitic deity. The traditional accounts credit Quṣayy and Quraysh with the restoration of the monotheistic biblical tradition to Meccan religious life, which had become adulterated by pagan practices. This is not incredible. Biblical religious conceptions were not unknown to the pre-Islamic Arabs of the Ḥijāz as the appearance of the mysterious and so-called *ḥanīfs* could argue. One of these biblical conceptions was of particular significance to the Arabs, namely their descent from Ishmael, and through Ishmael from Abraham. The eponymate of Ishmael and the patrimony of Abraham were to remain central in Arab religious life. Syncretistic and uninspiring, spiritually or aesthetically, the Meccan religious system was, however, of crucial importance to the success of the new experiment in inter-Arab relations. The primacy of Mecca as well as the unity of the Arabs was reflected and promoted annually during the Sacred Months when the Arabs would flock to Mecca and the neighbouring region, where a complex of three places and many activities were involved: 'Ukāẓ, the fair and scene of poetic contests; Mecca, the Holy City with its *Ḥaram,* the sacred precinct, and its Ka'ba, the temple; and 'Arafāt, the Holy Mountain of the pilgrimage. The concept of *Arabia Sacra* was slowly emerging in the sixth century. Mecca's character as a holy city, and that of Quraysh, as the descendants of Ishmael and the custodians of the Ka'ba, assumed a central position in the success of the new symbiosis whereby the complementary resources of Arab nomad and sedentary were brought nearer to each other, the tensions which inevitably arise within a heterogeneous social structure were partially resolved, and the Arab area within the peninsula was integrated in a manner and to a degree it had never attained before. This was Mecca's achievement. But Mecca's achievement as well as its prosperity was made possible by the operation of one of the factors which governed the evolution of Arab history, namely the overwhelming power of its foreign neighbours, which was now operating to Mecca's advantage. The sixth century witnessed the outbreak of international wars which brought about the fall of Ḥimyar in the south, and which considerably weakened the two main contestants in the north, Persia and Byzantium, including their clients, Lakhm and Ghassān, thus enabling Mecca's power to grow unnoticed and unmolested. It was in the prosperous metropolis of sixth-century Arabia that a prophet, a lineal descendant of Quṣayy, was born *c.* A.D. 570. With the birth of Muḥammad, Arabia became 'the Cradle of Islam'.

It will have become clear that the evolution of Arab history in pre-Islamic times was conditioned and circumscribed by two adverse factors, which made the Arabs the most disinherited of the 'sons of Shem'. Geographical conditions within the peninsula forced them to be constantly occupied with the struggle for existence and kept their area underdeveloped, while the political situation in the Fertile Crescent and southern Arabia placed a term to their expansion into areas where they could have developed a higher form of political life and culture, as other cognate Semitic groups had done. From the operation of these two adverse factors, the place of the Arabs in the ancient Near East clearly emerges. Just as the area of their evolution as sedentaries is geographically peripheral, so is their role in the Near East historically marginal. The exception which proves the rule is Palmyra, and the achievement of the Palmyrene Odenathus and that of his widow, Queen Zenobia, is more telling for Arab history than that of Philip the Arab whose elevation to the Roman imperial purple is purely episodic, and more significant for Roman than for Arab history. As for their contribution to the life of the Near East, it was principally in the area of material culture. Their domestication of the camel rather than their breeding of their celebrated horse was their more important achievement, since the camel performed a basic function for them and their neighbours, while the horse was and has remained a luxury article. The camel, without which their very life in the desert would have been inconceivable, was also their contribution to the economic life of the Near East as the more advanced south discovered its value for caravan trade, which in its turn gave the Arabs an important economic function. By participating in the conduct and the protection of the caravans, they contributed to the economic revolution in the ancient Near East brought about by the Sabaeans, and also created the image of the desert Arab as a cameleer and a caravaneer.

The extraordinary events of the seventh century completely reversed the role of the Arabs and changed the nature of their contribution. From a peninsular people who had played a marginal and subordinate role in history, they develop into an imperial race, and succeed in terminating the Indo-European interregnum in the Near East, reasserting Semitic political presence in the region, and carrying the Semitic political factor into the medieval world by the foundation of a universal state. After centuries of association with their celebrated breed and domesticate, and with the winding caravans of the ancient trade-routes, all of which stamped their contribution as one related to material culture, the Arabs now ride out of their peninsula as Muslims, inspired and animated by the ideals of the new faith, and establish a theocratic state within which develops a civilization, religious in spirit and manifestation, that of medieval Islam.

The mission of Muḥammad and the Arab conquests are the climax of all previous Arab history and for this reason they are especially relevant to this account of the history of pre-Islamic Arabia. The conquests are the classical example that illustrates the law which had governed Arab penetration of the Fertile Crescent in pre-Islamic times; they took place at an incredibly propitious moment in the *peripeteia* of Near Eastern history, when, after twenty years of continuous warfare and Pyrrhic victories, the fortunes of their adversaries in the Fertile Crescent had reached their lowest ebb. The subsequent development of Islamic civilization, not within the peninsula but outside it, in the fairer regions of the Fertile Crescent, witnesses to the continued operativeness of the adverse geographical factor which had prevented the Arab area from developing a higher form of cultural life. It is only in the twentieth century that this adverse factor has become less operative, as the forces of technology are neutralizing it in one of the most forsaken parts of the peninsula. The military victories which attended the conquests, prove in the most conclusive manner that, as in pre-Islamic times, it was the sedentaries and not the nomads who effectively shaped Arab history. Just as it had been a city, Mecca, which in the sixth century was able to achieve that measure of integration within the Arab area, so it was again a city-dweller, Muḥammad, who by bringing into being the *Umma,* the Islamic community, was able to raise to the highest level of integration the Meccan achievement; and it was the three cities of the Ḥijāz, Mecca, Medina, and Ṭā'if, which produced the generals and administrators of the nascent Islamic state.

In one important respect, however, the conquests represent a sharp departure from the pattern of earlier Arab expansion and penetration.

In spite of military necessities, of economic factors and imperial instincts which did not fail to assert themselves, there is no doubt that the original impulse in Islam as an expansionist movement is not to be sought in the material order, but in that of religious thought. Rooted in a spiritual soil, Islam was able to survive as a civilization after the collapse of its Arab political structure. A hundred years before the *Hijra,* a kingdom of grey antiquity, that of the Himyarites, fell to pieces, and with its fall perished a whole civilization, materially prosperous but spiritually dead, as that of Carthage had perished before. The same fate would probably have awaited the 'commercial republic' of western Arabia, which as a caravan-city had developed along lines similar to those of the trading centres of the south. Herein lies the significance of Islam's spiritual foundation for pre-Islamic Arab history. Although as a revolt and a protest against the pre-Islamic past it rejected much of it, it did, however, accept some of it and integrated it in its structure. The integration was mutually beneficial; these integrated constituents of the pre-Islamic scene contributed substantially and decisively to the success of Islam as a revealed religion, a political institution, an expansionist movement, and a cultural expression. Islam for its part ensured the survival of these pre-Islamic constituents, endowed them with a universal significance, and provided them with a context within which they have enjoyed a most remarkable longevity. Some of these significant constituents, nomadic and sedentary, the pre-Islamic roots which have formed the persistent heritage, deserve to be noted and discussed.

The pre-Islamic Pilgrimage in its essential features survives, indeed is built into the very structure of Islam as one of its Five Pillars of Faith. Of these Five Pillars, it is the one relevant to the pre-Islamic scene and to pre-Islamic Arabia. It has ensured for the latter a permanent and privileged place in the consciousness of the Muslim world, particularly important to a peninsula which was slipping and receding into the background of the Islamic scene, as the centre of political power shifted from Medina to Damascus and later to Baghdād. After thirteen centuries, Muslims from the four corners of the earth still flock to the Ḥijāz for the Pilgrimage, to the same places that the Arabs used to visit in pre-Islamic times.

The pre-Islamic tribe of Quraysh, which had made Mecca the metropolis of the Arab area, provided Islam, as it developed into a political institution, with its leaders, generals, and administrators, and above all with its caliphs. Islam has enhanced the primacy of Quraysh, and has contributed to the perpetuation of that primacy throughout the ages. Even after the political eclipse of the Arabs, the House of Hāshim has remained a force in Arab history, and as the *Sharīfs* of Mecca, they played a major role in the re-emergence of the Arabs in the twentieth century.

Although the camel had been the more important animal in pre-Islamic Arabia, it was the horse that occupied the scene of Arab history when it unfolded under the banner of Islam. It was the cavalry units under their bedouin riders, the armoured divisions of the Arab armies and the sinews of the 'Semitic backlash', which effected the historic breakthroughs in the Fertile Crescent. With the conquest of North Africa and Spain the Arab horse entered the southern and western parts of the Mediterranean region. It was accompanied by the pre-Islamic concept of chivalry which was to figure so prominently in medieval love, romance, and poetry. The Arab horse is still very much alive today, associated with aristocratic pleasures and pastimes and has for an illustrious blood relation the Anglo-Arab thoroughbred.

The common literary idiom perfected by the poets of pre-Islamic Arabia proved to be indispensable for the mission of Muḥammad and for Islam throughout the ages. It became the linguistic medium of the Qur'anic revelation, and the basis of the doctrine of the Arabic Qur'ān. In the evolution of Islamic culture, Arabic played a major role: the study of the Arabic language in its various aspects represents the first stage in the rise of Arabic Islamic culture, while the poetry expressed through it in pre-Islamic times became the model of Islamic poetic composition, making literature the most important constituent in the structure of Islamic civilization. Islam for its part rendered it inestimable services. Without it, Arabic might have remained an obscure Semitic language in *Arabia Deserta*. As the language of the new dispensation it acquired a new character; it became a sacred language for the Muslim peoples. With the expansion of Islam and the foundation of the Arab empire, it became a world language and the language of medieval Islamic civilization, the Latin of the Muslim world. But the most remarkable result of its association with the Qur'ān has been the maintenance of its original structure throughout this long period of thirteen centuries, a linguistic feature which has had far-reaching extra-linguistic consequences in Arab history. It proved to be the single most important factor in the rise of Arab nationalism in the nineteenth century, and has functioned, particularly after the secularization of Arab society and the political fragmentation of the Arab world, as the most objective element in Arab nationalism. Thus, of all the constituents of the pre-Islamic scene relevant to Arab history, the one which has proved the most vital and durable of all has undoubtedly been the linguistic medium of pre-Islamic poetry, the seemingly indestructible *al-ʿarabiyya*.

CHAPTER 2

MUḤAMMAD

For the occidental reader there are grave difficulties in attaining a balanced understanding of the historical role of Muḥammad. The most serious of these is that the dominant conception of religion as a private and individual matter leads men to expect that a religious leader will be a certain kind of man; and it is disconcerting to find that Muḥammad does not conform to this expectation. He was undoubtedly a religious leader; but for him religion was the total response of his personality to the total situation in which he found himself. He was responding not merely to what the occidental would call the religious and intellectual aspects of the situation, but also to the economic, social and political pressures to which contemporary Mecca was subject. Because he was great as a leader his influence was important in all these spheres, and it is impossible for any occidental to distinguish within his achievement between what is religious and what is non-religious or secular.

Another difficulty is that some occidental readers are still not completely free from the prejudices inherited from their medieval ancestors. In the bitterness of the Crusades and other wars against the Saracens, they came to regard the Muslims, and in particular Muḥammad, as the incarnation of all that was evil, and the continuing effect of the propaganda of that period has not yet been completely removed from occidental thinking about Islam. It is still much commoner to find good spoken about Buddhism than about Islam.

There are also some of the difficulties usually attendant on the historical study of remote periods. Thus it is not easy to find the kernel of fact in the legends about Muḥammad's birth, childhood, and early manhood. For his public career there is indeed the Qur'ān, which is universally accepted as a contemporary record; but it is silent on many points about which the historian would like information, and such historical material as it has is not always easy to date or interpret. Despite these difficulties, however, some progress is being made towards a more adequate appreciation of Muḥammad and his career.[1]

[1] A fuller exposition of the view of Muḥammad presented here will be found in the author's *Muhammad Prophet and Statesman* (London, Oxford University Press, 1961). Detailed references are in *Muhammad at Mecca* and *Muhammad at Medina* (Oxford, Clarendon Press, 1953, 1956).

LAUNCHING A NEW RELIGION

About A.D. 610 a citizen of Mecca, then aged about forty, began to tell relatives and acquaintances of certain experiences which had come to him. Some three years later he began to speak more publicly. A number of his fellow-citizens were attracted by his words, and professed themselves his followers in the way of life he was teaching. For a time a successful movement seemed to be developing, but eventually opposition and hostility made their appearance. What was the nature of the movement and of Muḥammad's teaching in this early period before opposition was provoked?

The religious movement may be said to have begun with two visions experienced by Muḥammad and briefly described in *Sūra* 53 of the Qur'ān, verses 1–18. There are also Traditions[1] which appear to refer to the visions, but have not the same authority as the Qur'ān. At first Muḥammad may have interpreted these experiences as visions of God himself, but he later regarded the wonderful being he had seen as an angel from God. As a result of the visions, Muḥammad came to a deep conviction that he had been specially commissioned as the 'messenger of God' (*rasūl Allāh*). In the later stages of Muḥammad's career, this came to be interpreted as some kind of agent on behalf of God, but to begin with the 'messenger' was simply the carrier of a message.

Either in the course of the visions or shortly afterwards, Muḥammad began to receive 'messages' or 'revelations' from God. Sometimes he may have heard the words being spoken to him, but for the most part he seems simply to have 'found them in his heart'. Whatever the precise 'manner of revelation'—and several different 'manners' were listed by Muslim scholars—the important point is that the message was not the product of Muḥammad's conscious mind. He believed that he could easily distinguish between his own thinking and these revelations. His sincerity in this belief must be accepted by the modern historian, for this alone makes credible the development of a great religion. The further question, however, whether the messages came from Muḥammad's unconscious, or the collective unconscious functioning in him, or from some divine source, is beyond the competence of the historian.

The messages which thus came to Muḥammad from beyond his conscious mind were at first fairly short, and consisted of short verses

[1] Arabic singular, *Ḥadīth*: a technical term for anecdotes about Muḥammad, at first transmitted orally.

ending in a common rhyme or assonance. They were committed to memory by Muḥammad and his followers, and recited as part of their common worship. Muḥammad continued to receive the messages at intervals until his death. In his closing years the revelations tended to be longer, to have much longer verses and to deal with the affairs of the community of Muslims at Medina. All, or at least many, of the revelations were probably written down during Muḥammad's lifetime by his secretaries. The whole collection of 'revealed' material was given its definitive form by a body of scholars working under the instructions of the Caliph 'Uthmān (23–35/644–56), and this is the Qur'ān as we now have it. There is no detailed agreement about the dates at which the various passages were revealed, and each *sūra* or 'chapter' may contain passages from different dates. It is generally held, however, that most of the short *sūras* towards the end of the Qur'ān are early, and in other respects there is a rough agreement about dating.

If now we examine the passages generally regarded as belonging to the earliest period, especially those where no hostility or opposition to Muḥammad is implied or asserted, we find that their contents may be summarized under five heads.

(1) God[1] is good and all-powerful. Various natural phenomena are described and asserted to be signs of God's goodness and power, since they contribute to the maintenance and well-being of mankind. The development of a human being from an embryo is regarded as specially wonderful.

(2) God will bring all men back to himself on the Last Day for judgment, and will then assign them for eternity either to heaven (the Garden) or hell (the Fire). In some of the early passages this is spoken of as a judgment on the individual, but in somewhat later passages whole communities seem to be judged together.

(3) In the world thus created by God and controlled by Him in the present, man's appropriate attitude is to be grateful to Him and to worship Him. Worship is essentially an acknowledgment of God's might and majesty, and of man's relative weakness and lack of power.

(4) God also expects man to be generous with his wealth and not niggardly. This is one of the chief points to be considered in the judgment. In particular the rich are expected to take steps to help the poor and unfortunate.

[1] It is appropriate to use the word 'God' rather than the transliteration 'Allah'. For one thing it cannot be denied that Islam is an offshoot of the Judaeo-Christian tradition, and for another the Christian Arabs of today have no other word for 'God' than *Allāh*.

(5) Muḥammad has a special vocation as a 'messenger' from God to his own people and as a 'warner' to them about judgment and punishment.

The message of the Qur'ān, both in this early form and in its later developments, has sometimes been regarded by Christian and Jewish scholars as a pale reflection of some points in the teaching of the Old and New Testaments. To emphasize such dependence, however, even if there were more justification for the assertions than there is, diverts attention from a proper understanding of the beginnings of the Islamic religion in its historical context. In a sense we can say that the ideas of the early passages of the Qur'ān were accepted by Muḥammad and his followers because they thought they were true; but this does not explain why certain ideas were selected for emphasis. When a modern scholar looks at the relation of these ideas to the historical situation in Mecca in the years from 610 onwards, he sees that they are specially appropriate and relevant. They are, in fact, dealing with the religious aspect of the contemporary economic, social, and political tensions, and are capable of guiding and directing at all levels men's response to these tensions.

In the sphere of economics, which is fundamental in that it deals with the things that are necessary for human survival, the important feature of the age was that Mecca had won control of the caravan trade up the west coast of Arabia from the Yemen in the south to Damascus and Gaza in the north. Southwards, the trade-routes continued into Ethiopia and by the use of the monsoons to India. Northwards, the eastern Roman empire or Byzantine empire was eager for the products of the Orient. Perhaps the struggle between the Byzantines and the Persians had diverted trade from the Persian Gulf to western Arabia. Certainly by 610 the trade through Mecca had become very lucrative, the chief entrepreneurs had become wealthy merchants, and most of the town shared in the prosperity. This dominant position of Mecca had not been attained without unscrupulous dealings to discourage merchants from the Yemen coming to Mecca, while rivals in the neighbouring town of Ṭā'if had been forced to submit to Mecca after defeat in battle. By 610 the people of Mecca were gaining their livelihood almost exclusively through this mercantile economy.

The social tensions present in Mecca about 610 appear to have been mainly due to the conflict between the attitudes fostered by the new mercantile economy and the residual attitudes derived from the previous nomadic economy. Commerce encouraged the acceptance of material values and an individualistic spirit. The great merchant naturally thought chiefly about making the largest possible profit for himself. The capital on which his operations had originally been based had often been the common property of the clan; but he conveniently forgot this. He associated with other merchants whom he regarded as useful business partners, rather than with members of his clan whose business acumen might be inferior. From the Qur'ān it appears that the great merchants, who were often also heads of clans, were no longer willing to use their wealth to help the poor and unfortunate among their fellow-clansmen. This indicates a breaking up of the tribal solidarity which had been a prominent feature of nomadic society. Nomadic conceptions of honour hardly applied in the circumstances of commercial life, and so these merchants could be niggardly and selfish without being exposed to obloquy.

To this state of affairs the Qur'anic call to generosity and care for the unfortunate was directly relevant. Nomadic attitudes based on the *lex talionis* were still sufficiently strong to ensure the preservation of public order, that is, the avoidance of homicide, bodily injury, and theft. The more serious moral problem was thus the care of the unfortunate who for some reason or other were unable to share in the general prosperity. Not merely did the Qur'ān urge men to show care and concern for the needy, but in its teaching about the Last Day it asserted the existence of a sanction applicable to men as individuals in matters where their selfishness was no longer restrained by nomadic ideas of dishonour.

The teaching of the Qur'ān is not so obviously relevant to the internal politics of Mecca. The tensions here were due to the growth of commerce. There is no trace of a distinction between aristocrats and plebeians such as is found elsewhere. Those referred to as 'weak' were not plebeians but persons without effective protection from a clan. Nearly all the inhabitants of Mecca belonged to the tribe of Quraysh, and acknowledged a common ancestry. The tribe was divided into clans which varied in importance, partly according to numbers, and partly according to the degree of success or failure in commercial ventures. The leading men of the more powerful clans were great merchants who had gained a monopolistic hold over some aspects of the trade of Mecca. Muḥammad's clan, that of Hāshim, had failed to maintain a place among the leaders, but had become head of a league of less strong clans which opposed the monopolists. Because Qur'anic teaching was directed against the monopolists or great merchants, the clan of Hāshim, though mostly not approving of Muḥammad's religion, was willing for several years to give him full support against the great merchants who were hostile to his movement.

In the external politics of Mecca the dominant fact was the titanic struggle between the Byzantine and Persian empires which had already lasted for nearly half a century when Muḥammad began to preach. Meccan trade dictated a policy of neutrality, for it connected the Persian-held Yemen in the south with Byzantine Syria in the north, and had also links with 'Irāq, the effective centre of the Persian empire, and with Ethiopia, friendly to the Byzantines. The Byzantines and Ethiopians were definitely Christian; the Persian empire was officially Zoroastrian, but it seems also to have given some support to Judaism, while there was a strong element of Nestorian Christianity, which was bitterly hostile to the forms of Christianity prevailing in the Byzantine and Ethiopian empires. Thus it would have been difficult for the Meccans to maintain political neutrality, had they adopted any of these forms of monotheism. The Qur'ān offered the Arabs a monotheism comparable to Judaism and Christianity but without their political ties. This may be described as the external political relevance of Muḥammad's claim to be the messenger of God.

One may also speak of a specifically religious aspect in the malaise of Mecca about 610. Material prosperity had led to an excessive valuation of wealth and power and to a belief that human planning could achieve almost anything. The great merchants were chiefly affected, but similar attitudes were found among those who were dependent on them or who tried to copy them. Against this the Qur'ān insisted on the omnipotence of God and his punishment of evildoers, including wealthy men who refuse to help the needy; this punishment might be either in this world, or in the life to come, or in both. The nomadic Arabs had believed that human planning was overruled not by a deity but by the operation of an impersonal Time or Fate; but the Qur'ān combated any residue of this belief among its hearers by insisting that God was not only all-powerful but also good and merciful. All the people of Mecca were called on to worship God, the Lord of their Ka'ba or sanctuary, in gratitude to him for their prosperity (*Sūra* 106). This was essentially a call to acknowledge that human life was determined by a power which was fundamentally benevolent.

Since the teaching of the earlier passages of the Qur'ān was thus relevant to the situation in Mecca about 610, it is not surprising to find that those who accepted this teaching and professed themselves followers of Muḥammad were men who had been affected in particular ways by that situation. Three groups may be distinguished among the early Muslims. Firstly, there were younger brothers and sons of the great merchants themselves; secondly, there were more important men from clans which had fallen out of the first rank or failed to attain it; and thirdly, there were a few reckoned 'weak'—mostly foreigners who had not found any clan willing to give them effective protection. No doubt all these men followed Muḥammad because they thought the teaching of the Qur'ān was true. When we look at the facts as external observers, however, we note that all three groups had suffered in some way from the selfishness and unscrupulous dealing of the great merchants, and had therefore presumably seen in the ideas of the Qur'ān a possible way out of their tensions and troubles. Muḥammad himself as a posthumous child, unable by Arab custom to receive any of his father's property, and yet aware of his great administrative ability, must have been specially conscious of the unenviable position of those excluded from the inner circle of great merchants. Muḥammad must have experienced great hardship until, when he was twenty-five, a wealthy woman, Khadīja, first employed him as steward of her merchandise and then married him. After his marriage he was in comfortable circumstances, but the memory of the early years of hardship doubtless remained with him.

OPPOSITION AND PERSECUTION

Despite the initial successes of Muḥammad's religious movement it did not gain the support of any of the great merchants. Two reasons may be suggested for their coolness and subsequent hostility. They may have felt that Muḥammad was criticizing business practices which they deemed essential to the successful conduct of commercial operations, and more generally may have resented the Qur'anic attitude to the values by which they lived. In the second place they may have felt that Muḥammad's claim to receive messages from God would make ordinary people think he had a superior wisdom, so that, should he ever aspire to become ruler of Mecca, he would have much popular support.

Whatever thoughts may have been most prominent in the minds of particular men, the great merchants as a whole certainly came to be opposed to Muḥammad. They tried to come to some arrangement with him; if he would abandon his preaching, he would be admitted into the inner circle of merchants, and his position there established by an advantageous marriage; but Muḥammad would have none of this. They tried to get the clan of Hāshim to bring pressure to bear on him to stop preaching; but honour, perhaps combined with interest in opposing monopolies, led the chief of the clan, his uncle Abū Ṭālib, to continue to give him support. Even when the whole clan of Hāshim was subjected to a kind of boycott, it went on supporting Muḥammad.

The hostility between Muḥammad and the great merchants became an open breach after the incident of the 'satanic verses'. This incident is so strange that it cannot be sheer invention, though the motives alleged may have been altered by the story-tellers. The Qur'ān (22. 52/1) implies that on at least one occasion 'Satan had interposed' something in the revelation Muḥammad received, and this probably refers to the incident to be described. The story is that, while Muḥammad was hoping for some accommodation with the great merchants, he received a revelation mentioning the goddesses al-Lāt, al-'Uzzā, and Manāt (53. 19, 20 as now found), but continuing with other two (or three) verses sanctioning intercession to these deities. At some later date Muḥammad received a further revelation abrogating the latter verses, but retaining the names of the goddesses, and saying it was unfair that God should have only daughters while human beings had sons.

It is impossible that any later Muslim could have depicted Muḥammad as thus appearing to tolerate polytheism. The deities mentioned were specially connected with shrines at Ṭā'if and two other spots in the region of Mecca. The Arabic phrase 'daughters of God' (*banāt Allāh*), which is sometimes used, expressed only an abstract relationship and means something like 'divine or semi-divine beings'; there is no suggestion of families of gods and goddesses as in Greek mythology. Presumably Muḥammad, in accepting worship at these shrines on the basis of the 'satanic verses', thought of it as addressed to some kind of angelic being subordinate to God. He may not originally have regarded the permission to worship at these shrines as a compromise; but in the course of time he must have come to realize that toleration of such worship was bound to jeopardize the important aspects of his teaching, and make his new religion indistinguishable from paganism.

After the revelation abrogating the 'satanic verses' the breach between Muḥammad and the great merchants was an open one. It seems unlikely that the merchants themselves had any profound belief in the old pagan religion, but they were prepared to make use of its remaining influence over the common people, for example, by carrying images of al-Lāt and al-'Uzzā into battle against the Muslims at Uḥud. The Qur'ān, on the other hand, vigorously attacks polytheism; sometimes it allows a supernatural reality short of divinity to the beings worshipped but holds that they will repudiate their worshippers, while at other times it asserts that they are merely names to which no reality corresponds. From this time onwards the insistence that God is one and unique is characteristic of Islam.

From the refutations in the Qur'ān we can also learn some of the arguments used by the opponents to discredit Muḥammad. They thought that in pointing to mouldering bodies they had a good argument against resurrection and judgment; but the Qur'ān counters by emphasizing that it is God who creates man in the first place 'when he is nothing', and that it is no more difficult to restore life to what is left of his body. The opponents also made attacks on Muḥammad personally: he was too unimportant a person to be a messenger from God; his alleged revelations were communicated to him by a human assistant; his teaching was an innovation and a departure from ancestral custom—and this latter was a very serious fault in Arab eyes. Sometimes the Qur'ān denied the charges outright. In a sense, however, its more general reply was in its frequent references to former prophets, biblical and other. These stories and allusions helped to create the image of a noble spiritual ancestry for Muḥammad and the Muslims.

In addition to the verbal criticisms, there was a certain amount of physical persecution. The extent of this is difficult to determine. Because of the *lex talionis* and the clan system there was little that even the most powerful man could do against a member of another clan, so long as the latter's clan was ready to protect him. Sharp business practices, of course, were outside the purview of the *lex talionis*; and the great merchants doubtless brought about the commercial ruin of any merchant who openly supported Muḥammad. They had also much power within the clan, and some young relatives of the leading merchants suffered considerably at their hands. The 'weak' persons without clan protection were most vulnerable, and there are stories of the hardships they underwent. Muḥammad himself, at least until about 619, was protected by his clan, and only met with minor insults, such as having garbage dumped at his door. At a comparatively early date a number of Muḥammad's followers are said to have gone to Abyssinia to avoid persecution; but since some of these stayed on until 628 they may have had other motives.

The situation changed for the worse about 619 with the death of Abū Ṭālib, Muḥammad's uncle and chief of the clan of Hāshim. He was succeeded as chief of the clan by another uncle, Abū Lahab, who was prospering commercially, and had close business relationships with some of the great merchants. These induced Abū Lahab to get Muḥammad to admit that his grandfather as a pagan was in hell; and Abū Lahab seems to have made this disrespect towards a former chief of the clan the ground for denying full clan protection. The sources tend to pass over this feature, which later members of Hāshim would regard as disgraceful, but it is implicit in other statements in the sources.

Presumably at first Abū Lahab merely threatened to withdraw protection from Muḥammad if he went on preaching his religion. We hear of Muḥammad making approaches to various nomadic tribes, and then visiting the town of Ṭā'if in hopes, it would seem, of finding a base there. This visit was a disastrous failure, and on his return Muḥammad was unable to enter Mecca until he found the chief of another clan willing to give him protection. The outlook for Muḥammad and the Muslims was extremely gloomy when, at the Pilgrimage in the summer of 620, he met six men from Medina (Yathrib) who began to discuss the possibility of his going there.

THE *Hijra* OR EMIGRATION TO MEDINA

Medina is a fertile oasis, somewhat more than two hundred miles north of Mecca. The inhabitants were mainly pagan Arabs, but there were also a number of Jews. The Jews probably differed little racially and culturally from their Arab neighbours, and were only marked off by religion. They seem to have pioneered the agricultural development of the oasis, and for a time had been dominant politically, but now were declining in power. The Jews were divided into three major clans and some minor groups; eight large clans are distinguished among the Arabs, but some of these had important subdivisions.

For nearly a hundred years before 620 there had been fighting in the oasis. At first it had been between single clans; then clans had joined together in ever larger groups. The Jewish clans combined with the others, and were sometimes on opposing sides. Finally, about 618, there had been a great battle at a spot called Bu'āth, in which nearly all the clans of the oasis had been involved. In this battle there had been heavy slaughter, and, though the fighting had ceased, there had been no agreement about the resulting claims for blood, or blood-money. It was becoming obvious that the conception of the blood-feud and the *lex talionis*, though useful for maintaining a degree of public order in desert conditions, were unworkable in the confined space of an oasis unless there was one man with authority to adjudicate in disputed cases. One of the most powerful men in the oasis, ʿAbd Allāh b. Ubayy, had along with his clan remained neutral at Buʿāth, presumably in the hope of becoming such an adjudicator acceptable to all. It was said that, but for the arrival of Muḥammad, he would have become prince of Medina.

Contact with the Jews had familiarized the Arabs of Medina with the conception of an inspired religious leader, perhaps even with the expectation of a Messiah. Thus among the six men who met Muḥammad in 620 there would be a degree of readiness to accept his claims at the religious level. At the same time they could not but be aware that a neutral outsider to Medina like Muḥammad, with authority based on religious claims, would be in a better position to act as impartial arbiter than any inhabitant of Medina. The six were so impressed by Muḥammad that at the Pilgrimage of 621 five of them came back to Mecca with seven others to have further discussions with Muḥammad. The twelve represented the most important clans, and expressed their readiness to accept Muḥammad as prophet and to avoid certain sins. This is known as the First Pledge of al-ʿAqaba.

Muḥammad must have been delighted, but after his failure at Ṭā'if he proceeded with care and circumspection. He sent an agent to Medina, ostensibly to instruct the people of Medina in his religion, but presumably also to observe at first hand the internal politics of the community. Things went well, however, and at the Pilgrimage of June 622 seventy-five persons came to Mecca, and not merely repeated the former promise, but also pledged themselves to fight on behalf of Muḥammad. This was the Second Pledge of al-ʿAqaba or the Pledge of War. Relying on this support from Medina, Muḥammad began to encourage his followers in Mecca to emigrate, and they set out in small parties, possibly unnoticed by the great merchants of Mecca. By September about seventy had reached Medina and been given hospitality by Muḥammad's supporters there. None willing to make the journey remained in Mecca apart from Muḥammad, Abū Bakr, his chief adviser, and ʿAlī, his cousin and son-in-law, together with their families.

One need not believe all the stories which have grown round Muḥammad's own emigration, or *Hijra*—the word means primarily a severing of relationships. His opponents may tardily have realized what was afoot. It is likely, however, that he was still safe so long as he remained in Mecca and kept quiet. The danger would be during the course of the journey, after he had abandoned whatever protection he had in Mecca by leaving the town, and before he reached Medina and the protection pledged to him there. He therefore slipped away by night, leaving ʿAlī sleeping on his bed. Along with Abū Bakr he hid for three days in a cave near Mecca. Then, after the Meccan pursuers had wearied, the two of them with a servant and a camel-man made their way by little-used routes to Medina. After about nine days' travelling they reached the outskirts of the oasis of Medina on 24 September 622. This is the *Hijra* which is the basis of Islamic chronology, but reckoning commences with the first day of the Arab year in which the emigration took place, viz. 16 July 622.

A document, sometimes called the Constitution of Medina, has been preserved in the earliest life of Muḥammad. In the form in which we have it, this document seems to be conflated from two or more separate documents, and to be not earlier than the year 5/627. Yet presumably there was some such agreement when Muḥammad went to Medina, and this is doubtless reflected in the present form of the document. In essentials the Constitution establishes a kind of alliance or federation between nine different groups, eight clans from Medina and the 'clan' of Emigrants (*Muhājirūn*) from the Quraysh of Mecca. It is presupposed that all these groups have accepted Muḥammad as the messenger of God. Some non-Muslim groups, Jews or pagans, have a subordinate place in the federation as allies of the main participants. Apart from having his religious claims recognized, Muḥammad simply functions as head of one of the nine groups and has no special power or authority, except that disputes endangering the peace of the oasis are to be referred to him. He was thus far from being ruler of the new polity set up at Medina.

AGAINST MECCA AND AGAINST THE JEWS

The occidental conception of a religious leader would suggest that, when Muḥammad and his Meccan followers went to Medina, they would settle down to earn their living by honest hard work as law-abiding citizens. A consideration of how Muḥammad might have expected his followers to gain a livelihood indicates that he had very different ones. The oasis had numerous palm-trees and grew some cereal crops, and there was still some land capable of being made fertile; but it seems most unlikely that Muḥammad expected his followers to become agriculturalists. He cannot have intended that they should permanently depend on the hospitality of the Muslims of Medina. Such skill as they had was chiefly in commerce, but, if they organized long-distance caravans to Syria, they were bound to come into conflict with the Meccans. It is hard to resist the conclusion that, perhaps even before the *Hijra,* Muḥammad realized that fighting against the Meccans was inevitable. He may not have said much about this, however, to the Muslims of Medina.

The assumption that Muḥammad deliberately moved towards open hostility with the Meccans explains what became a feature of the Medinan period of his career, viz. the sending out of expeditions. The raid or razzia (Ar. *ghazwa,* etc., pl. *maghāzī*) was a normal occupation of the nomadic Arab male, indeed almost a kind of sport. A common aim was the carrying off of the sheep or camels of rival groups. Severe fighting was usually avoided, for the favourite tactic was to pounce unexpectedly on an isolated party of herdsmen with force so overwhelming that resistance was pointless. After some six months in Medina, Muḥammad began to send out razzias with the special aim of intercepting and capturing Meccan caravans on the way to or from Syria. None of the first expeditions was successful in this primary aim, but they managed to establish friendly relations between the Muslims and nomadic tribes already in alliance with some of the clans of Medina. The reason for the failures was probably that Muḥammad's opponents in Medina alerted the Meccans.

Eventually about Rajab 2/January 624 Muḥammad sent out an expedition of a dozen men or less with sealed orders; in this way there was no chance of their destination being betrayed to the enemy. They set off eastwards, and only opened their orders after a day's march. To the dismay of one or two of them, they found that they were expected to go south to the neighbourhood of Mecca and intercept a caravan approaching Mecca from the Yemen. The most likely version of what subsequently happened is that the party of Muslims, pretending to be pilgrims, fraternized with the four guards of the caravan they hoped to attack. This was easy because they were still in the sacred month, when bloodshed was forbidden; but it became apparent that the caravan would enter the sacred territory of Mecca before the end of the month, and the would-be attackers were therefore in a dilemma—unless they gave up their plan, they must violate either the sacred month or the sacred territory. They decided to act during the sacred month, and quickly overpowered the guards, killing one and taking two prisoners. They seem to have had no difficulty in reaching Medina with the captured caravan and the prisoners.

Muḥammad appeared to be surprised at some of the reactions in Medina to this event. There was delight among the Emigrants and some of the Muslims of Medina at this first success after a run of failures. Others, however, expressed dismay at the profanation of the sacred month, and Muḥammad is said to have hesitated before acknowledging the raid by accepting a fifth of the booty (which came to be recognized as the appropriate share for him). Doubtless the dismay was due not so much to the breaking of the taboo on bloodshed (which was really pagan, though later ascribed to God by the Qur'ān), as to the dangers from the Meccans seeking blood-revenge. A revelation was received (2. 217/4) to the effect that, while fighting in the sacred month was sinful, the persecution of the Muslims by the pagan Meccans had been even more sinful. This was followed by a general acknowledgment of the raid to Nakhla, as it was called, together with readiness to accept the consequences.

Muḥammad may well have foreseen that many of the Muslims of Medina would hesitate before deliberately incurring the active hostility of the Meccans, but he must have judged that the time was now opportune to go ahead with his plans, and gently to push his more reluctant, and perhaps nominal, followers into full support of his policy. About the same time other important decisions were made. Up to this point it was probably only Meccan Emigrants who had taken part in the razzias from Medina; but about this time one of the leading men of Medina, Sa'd b. Mu'ādh (reckoned head of the group of clans constituting the 'tribe' of the Aws), decided to support Muḥammad to the extent of taking part in razzias. It was doubtless this decision by Sa'd which made it possible for Muḥammad to contemplate more active operations against the Meccans, and notably the raid which led to the battle of Badr.

About the same time another change in policy was made. Before he went to Medina and during the early months there Muḥammad had shown himself anxious to be accepted as a prophet by the Jews of Medina. From the first, it would seem, he had regarded the message he had to convey to the Arabs as identical with that brought to the Jews by Moses and to the Christians by Jesus; and he naturally supposed that the Jews of Medina would welcome him gladly and recognize him as a prophet, at least to the Arabs. Many of the Jews, however, had close links with 'Abd Allāh b. Ubayy, the potential prince of Medina, and may have hoped to increase their influence if he became ruler. Besides that, Jews would normally be unwilling to admit that a non-Jew could be a prophet. So instead of welcoming Muḥammad to Medina, they began to criticize. Since they were able to say, for example, that some passages in the Qur'ān contradicted their own ancient scriptures, they were in a position to make some men doubt whether Muḥammad was a prophet receiving messages from God; and such doubts threatened Muḥammad's whole religious movement.

The Qur'ān met these intellectual criticisms by developing the conception of the religion of Abraham. While the knowledge of Abraham came from the Old Testament and material based on that, Abraham could be regarded as the ancestor of the Arabs through Ishmael. It was also an undeniable fact that he was not a Jew or a Christian, since the Jews are either to be taken as the followers of Moses or as the descendants of Abraham's grandson, Jacob. At the same time Abraham had stood for the worship of God alone. The Qur'ān therefore claimed that it was restoring the pure monotheism of Abraham which had been corrupted in various, not clearly specified, ways by Jews and Christians.

On 15 Ṣafar 2/11 February 624 an event is said to have taken place which symbolized the Muslims' break with the Jews. Muḥammad was conducting the prayers or worship in a place of prayer belonging to the clan of Salima. They began all facing Jerusalem as had been customary; and this itself was a mark of Muḥammad's desire to be accepted by the Jews. As they prayed, however, he received a revelation bidding him take Mecca as his *qibla,* that is, face in the direction of Mecca; and he and those praying with him at once turned round. This break with the Jews meant that from this time onwards no attempt was made to win them by the acceptance of Jewish practices. On the contrary, Islam was now developed as a separate religion, superior to Judaism and Christianity, and specially connected with the Arabs and Mecca. What appears to be chiefly a religious decision probably also had political aspects. It seems to be closely bound up with the decision to rely on the support of Sa'd b. Mu'ādh and dispense with that of 'Abd Allāh b. Ubayy; the latter was in alliance with some of the Jewish clans, whereas there are traces of anti-Jewish feelings among some of the associates of Sa'd.

THE BATTLES AGAINST THE MECCANS

The Meccans must have been infuriated at the capture of their caravan almost from under their noses, as it were. The prestige and honour of

Mecca required a clear demonstration that such things could not be done with impunity. The various changes of policy at Medina in the two months after the expedition of Nakhla amounted to a reaffirmation of what was implicit in that razzia, namely, a throwing down of the gauntlet to the Meccans. In consequence it is not surprising that Muḥammad and the Muslims stepped up the scale of their operations.

About a month after the change of *qibla,* it became known that a large and rich Meccan caravan was to pass near Medina on its return from Gaza. There were said to be a thousand camels and merchandise worth 50,000 dinars. Muḥammad decided on a razzia to intercept this caravan, and with the help of Sa'd b. Mu'ādh was able to collect a force of about 320 men, of whom just over a quarter were Emigrants and nearly three-quarters Muslims of Medina, who came to be known as *Anṣār,* or Helpers. The raiding party set out in good time, some five days before the caravan was due to pass Badr, the point at which its route lay closest to Medina. The leader of the caravan, Abū Sufyān, however, was aware of the threat, and by forced marches and a slight change of route eluded the Muslims. Meanwhile a force of perhaps 900 men had been collected in Mecca and had marched north to protect the caravan.

According to the usual Arab ideas, a force of 300 men would never have thought of attacking a force of 900; it would have tried to avoid the superior force, yet without giving the impression of running away from it; and in normal circumstances even the 900 might not have felt their superiority sufficiently overwhelming to justify an attack on 300. The Meccan commander, Abū Jahl, however, was bent on teaching a lesson to the impudent upstarts in Medina, and did not immediately return home on hearing that the caravan was safe. Muḥammad, for his part, having got the *Anṣār* to come so far, may have wanted to see them more fully committed, and Sa'd b. Mu'ādh may have acquiesced in this. What is certain is that both forces found themselves in a position from which honour made it impossible to withdraw without fighting. The Muslims had occupied the wells of Badr and, when they learnt of the proximity of the enemy, stopped up all the wells except the one nearest the enemy. The Meccans, hidden for a time behind a hill, would have been disgraced if they had not made an effort to get water. So on 19 Ramaḍān 2/15 March 624 a battle took place.

Little can be said about the course of the battle except that it began with single combats. The result was complete victory for the Muslims. Some fifty or more of the Meccans were killed, and nearly seventy taken prisoner. The dead included Abū Jahl and at least a dozen of the leading men of Mecca, whose administrative and commercial skills could hardly be replaced. The Muslims, on the other hand, had only fourteen dead. The chief reason for the victory was doubtless the greater confidence of the Muslims as a result of their religious faith, though it has been suggested that the agriculturalists of Medina were physically stronger than the townsmen of Mecca. There was much booty, which was divided equally among the participants, but the ransoms accepted for most of the prisoners usually went to the individual captor.

The significance of Badr is both political and religious. Politically, it made it clear that Muḥammad was a serious threat to Mecca. Meccan prestige was greatly diminished by the defeat even though the numbers involved in the battle had been relatively small. The potential threat to Meccan commerce was also considerable. Thus the Meccans were bound to exert all their strength to destroy Muḥammad, or at the very least to drive him out of Medina. On the political level, then, the events of the next few years may be understood as the Meccan effort to meet the challenge from Muḥammad to their very existence as a commercial state. On the religious side, again, the victory of Badr appeared to Muḥammad and the Muslims as God's vindication of their cause after all the hardships they had undergone, and as a proof of the truth of Muḥammad's mission.

After the battle of Badr, Muḥammad doubtless realized that the Meccans would prosecute the war against him more vigorously, and did what he could to consolidate his position in Medina. There were three political assassinations of persons who had used their poetical gifts in the war of ideas against him, and, while he may not have encouraged or even connived at these acts, he did not in any way punish the perpetrators. A few weeks after Badr he took advantage of a quarrel between Muslims and some Jews of the clan of Qaynuqāʿ to besiege the clan in their forts or keeps. After fifteen days, when their ally ʿAbd Allāh b. Ubayy had proved unable to help them, they surrendered and were expelled from Medina. They had been armourers and goldsmiths, besides conducting a local market; the Emigrants probably took over the market activities, while the arms and metal-working tools which they had to leave behind would benefit all the Muslims. The incident as a whole is in line with the new complex of policies associated with the 'break with the Jews'.

At Mecca everyone had been stunned at the magnitude of the loss of life. Abū Sufyān, who had commanded the caravan, took the lead in rallying the spirits of the Meccans and setting about the repair of the damage. Ten weeks after Badr he led 200 men in a razzia into the Medinan oasis—a typical nomadic Arab gesture—but after burning a couple of houses retired before Muḥammad could intercept him. To avoid dissipating Meccan energies, Abū Sufyān allowed no caravans to go to Syria; and one which attempted to reach Iraq in Jumādā II 3/November 624 was captured by the Muslims. Nevertheless by March 625 Abū Sufyān had collected a force of 3,000 'infantry' with a camel each, and 200 cavalry, and set out for Medina. They reached Medina in ten days, and entered the oasis from the north-west, camping with the hill of Uḥud a little to the north, and the main settlements rather farther to the south.

Muḥammad was forced to fight, rather against his will, by the fact that the Meccan horses were eating or trampling down some of the cereal crops near the camp. By a night march, he was able to take up a strong position on the lower slopes of the hill of Uḥud. At the last moment 'Abd Allāh b. Ubayy and his followers withdrew, leaving Muḥammad with only about 700 men. The battle began on the morning of 7 Shawwāl 3/23 March 625. The main Meccan force advanced on the Muslims, but was soon thrown back in disorder. Meanwhile, however, the Meccan cavalry (commanded by Khālid b. al-Walīd) took advantage of some disarray among the advancing Muslims to launch a flank attack. One party of Muslims tried to reach the nearest forts to the south, but was mostly cut down. Muḥammad, though he received a wound, was able to withdraw most of his men to their original position on Uḥud, where they were safe from the cavalry. Perhaps to the surprise of the Muslims, the Meccans now slowly collected their forces, and marched away along the road to Mecca.

The battle of Uḥud has sometimes been presented by occidental scholars as a serious defeat for the Muslims. This is certainly not so. It is indeed true that some seventy-five Muslims had been killed as against twenty-seven Meccans; but this barely gave the Meccans a life for a life when the losses at Badr are added, whereas they had boasted they would make the Muslims pay several times over. More important, they had completely failed in their strategic aim of destroying Muḥammad. That they withdrew when they did was an admission of weakness. For Muḥammad, then, though the loss of life was serious, the military result was not altogether unsatisfactory; the supremacy of his infantry had been clearly demonstrated. For him and the Muslims, however, the battle had also a religious aspect. They had regarded the victory of Badr as given to them by God in sign of his approval; and they had come to think of themselves as, with God's help, virtually invincible. The question for the Muslims was: had their view of Badr been correct, and was God really supporting them, for, if he were, how could he allow them to suffer such a misfortune?

The religious problem was solved by a revelation (3. 152/45f.) blaming the reverse on the Muslims' disobedience and desire for booty. In other ways Muḥammad went on steadily consolidating his strength. Razzias in various directions made the nomads realize that Muḥammad could not be trifled with, though two small expeditions ended in disaster through treachery or an ambush. Some of the razzias brought in booty, and this attracted other nomads to become followers of Muḥammad and share in the razzias. In Rabīʿ I 4/August 625 a second Jewish clan was expelled, al-Naḍīr, which owned numerous palm-trees. While these events were taking place a new Islamic conception of the family was developing. To provide for the widows made by Uḥud, Muslim men were encouraged to take up to four wives. This appears to have replaced not monogamy, but various marital arrangements based on matrilineal kinship, and often involving polyandry. Thus in various ways the strength of Muḥammad and his community grew in the two years following Uḥud.

These two years had been spent by the Meccans in preparations for a supreme effort to destroy the Muslims. Abū Sufyān had no longer an undisputed position of command, and some dissension among the leaders did not help their war effort. Nevertheless, by arming as many as possible of themselves and their immediate confederates, and by using various inducements to interest nomadic tribes in the expedition, they managed to collect from 7,000 to 10,000 men, including 600 cavalry. To meet this large force, Muḥammad had only about 3,000 men and no more than a dozen or two horses. His infantry would no doubt be more than a match for the opponents, but their cavalry was a serious threat. To counter it he employed a device said to have been suggested by a Persian convert, namely, the digging of a trench, or *khandaq,* across the open part of the north side of the oasis—the other sides were protected by lava flows. Muḥammad also saw to it that the cereal crops in the region to the north of the trench were harvested in good time.

The Meccans and their confederates reached Medina on 8 Dhu'l-Qaʿda 5/31 March 627, and began what was in effect a siege. The trench proved an effective barrier to the Meccan cavalry. A few managed to cross, but the defenders were able to concentrate in sufficient numbers to thrust them back with loss. A siege was outside the normal tradition of Arab fighting, and the men soon became restive. Intrigues between the different groups, skilfully fomented by Muḥammad's agents, lowered morale further, and, when the weather became exceptionally cold and there was a severe storm of wind, the vast confederacy faded away overnight. The siege had lasted about a fortnight. The remaining large Jewish group in Medina, the clan of Qurayẓa, had been overtly correct in its behaviour during the siege, but had almost certainly been in contact with the enemy, and would have attacked Muḥammad in the rear had there been an opportunity. As soon as the Meccans had departed, Muḥammad attacked this clan in their forts. When they eventually surrendered, the men were all killed, and the women and children sold. In Arab eyes this was not barbarous but a mark of strength, since it showed that the Muslims were not afraid of blood reprisals.

The failure of the siege was a great victory for Muḥammad. The Meccans had committed all their resources to this effort to dislodge or destroy him, and there was no more they could do. Their prestige was gone, and their trade with Syria virtually ruined by the Muslim attacks. Some began to wonder whether they might not have a brighter future as followers of Muḥammad and his religion.

THE WINNING OF THE MECCANS

Long before the siege of Medina, Muḥammad may have pondered future possibilities. After the siege these could be discerned more clearly, and he must have begun to take the decisions which shaped the future course of his own career, and indeed of the Muslim community after his death. Once again, however, we find religion and politics intermingled in a way which it is difficult for an occidental to understand. Muḥammad thought of himself as a 'messenger of God' and as one sent specially to the Arabs. Thus he had a religious motive for summoning men to acknowledge God throughout Arabia. After the siege of Medina, however, he had also great political power. Just before the siege 'Abd Allāh b. Ubayy and other opponents attacked him through an incident which seemed to involve his wife 'Ā'isha (daughter of Abū Bakr) in scandal, but when it came to a showdown it was evident that they were now relatively weak. After the siege, for several years there is no mention of any opposition in Medina. Thus Muḥammad was head of what was in some sense a state, even though it had an unusual form of polity; and many nomads and townsmen doubtless attached themselves to this state for 'political' or non-religious reasons, such as desire for booty.

After the siege it was not unreasonable for Muḥammad to expect that a large proportion of the Arabs would accept his religion and become his followers. He naturally assumed that his followers would live at peace with one another; but, since much of the energy of the Arabs was expended on razzias against other tribes, an alternative outlet for this energy had to be found. This was already to hand in the conception of the *jihād* or 'holy war', which was basically a razzia, might include the capturing of booty, but had to be against non-Muslims and came to an end with the opponents' profession of Islam. In the new perspective after the failure of the siege, it cannot have been too difficult to see that in a few years' time there might be few non-Muslims left in Arabia, and that therefore the *jihād* would have to be directed outside Arabia into Iraq and Syria. It may also have been apparent to Muḥammad that large-scale operations would be involved, requiring men with administrative abilities. The obvious source of such men was Mecca, where there had been experience of large commercial undertakings.

Certainly from about the time of the siege, Muḥammad's aim ceased to be the destruction of the Meccans. He did all he could to avoid antagonizing them further, and instead tried to win them to his side. He continued to harry their trade with Syria, but made no preparations for a direct assault on Mecca. He also strengthened himself by alliances with various nomadic tribes. In Dhu'l-Qa'da 6/spring 628, presumably to show his power to the Meccans and also his good will, and to test their feeling, he decided to perform the Lesser Pilgrimage or *'Umra*. He was disappointed in the response of the nomadic allies, but was able to set out with about 1,500 townsmen and animals for slaughter. The Meccans stopped him, however, on the edge of the sacred territory of Mecca at a spot called al-Ḥudaybiya. Here, after days of parleying, a treaty was signed. The Muslims were not to be allowed to enter Mecca in this year, but it would be evacuated for them for three days in the following year. There were also provisions about allies and about minors adhering to Islam.

The mere signing of a treaty as an equal was a triumph for Muḥammad. His followers, who had perhaps been disappointed of booty, were led on a successful expedition a month or two later against the Jews of the oasis of Khaybar, and the capture of Khaybar may be said to have inaugurated the Islamic empire in that the inhabitants were allowed to go on cultivating their lands, provided they gave a proportion of the fruits to the Muslims. In the following year, Muḥammad and his followers made the Pilgrimage as arranged, and no doubt impressed the Meccans by their orderliness. The treaty, though superficially more favourable to the Meccans, allowed the attraction of the Islamic religion and the material inducements of the *jihād* to build up the strength of Muḥammad's state.

When an incident between allies of the two sides strained relations to breaking-point, Muḥammad was ready to act effectively. Abū Sufyān, probably relying on Muḥammad's marriage to a daughter of his (herself a Muslim and widow of a Muslim), headed a deputation to Medina seeking some compromise over the incident, but Muḥammad persuaded him to work for the peaceful surrender of Mecca; this is not clear in the sources because they are mostly biased against Abū Sufyān as the ancestor of the Umayyad caliphs. Next, Muḥammad with a measure of secrecy quickly collected 10,000 men and set out for Mecca. The Meccans were overawed. Abū Sufyān was able to lead out a deputation to make a formal submission. Muḥammad agreed that all who claimed Abū Sufyān's protection, or closed their houses and remained indoors, should be unmolested. His troops then entered Mecca in four columns, of which only one met resistance; but that was soon overcome. Two Muslims died, and twenty-eight on the Meccan side. Thus virtually without bloodshed Muḥammad entered his native town in triumph. The date was about 20 Ramaḍān 8/11 January 630.

Muḥammad remained in Mecca from two to three weeks, making arrangements for the future administration of the town and the surrounding region. Of a dozen or so persons specifically excluded from the general amnesty, several were pardoned. Muḥammad's treatment of the Meccans as a whole was so generous that, when a new danger threatening them all appeared in the east, 2,000 of them joined his army as he marched out to deal with the situation.

THE UNIFYING OF THE ARABS

The danger came from Hawāzin, a group of tribes with which was associated Thaqīf, the tribe inhabiting Ṭā'if. It is not clear whether their concentration at Ḥunayn, an unidentified spot east of Mecca, was aimed primarily against the Muslims or against the Meccans, or whether the leaders hoped to take advantage of the confusion after the expected battle between the two. Whatever the motives of Hawāzin, Muḥammad decided to oppose them. They were reputed to have 20,000 men against his 12,000. The battle was hotly contested, and for a time a large part of the Muslim army was in flight. Muḥammad himself, however, and a few seasoned veterans of the Emigrants and Helpers stood firm, and soon the enemy was fleeing in disarray. Their women and children had been stationed just behind the army, and all these were now captured by the Muslims, as well as vast spoils. The Muslims attempted to besiege the Thaqīf in Ṭā'if, but, when it was seen that there would be no speedy surrender, Muḥammad called off the siege. The booty was then divided, but Hawāzin were given their women and children back in return for a special payment.

The victory of Ḥunayn meant that, with the exception of tribes on the frontiers of Syria and Iraq, there was no group of tribes in Arabia capable of assembling a force sufficiently strong to meet Muḥammad with any prospect of success. In other words he was the strongest man in Arabia. The Arabs have always admired strength, and there now took place what may be described as a rush to climb on the band-waggon. Most of the Arab tribes (with roughly the same exceptions as above) sent deputations to Medina seeking alliance with Muḥammad.

From an early date in the Medinan period, Muḥammad had contracted alliances of different kinds with nomadic tribes. At first some were merely pacts of non-aggression, since Muḥammad was in no position to give effective help to tribes close to Mecca. As his strength grew, however, he could both offer more, and also make greater demands in return for the privilege of alliance with himself. In particular he came to demand acceptance of Islam, that is, acknowledgment of his own prophethood, performance of the prayer or worship, and payment of a kind of tithe, the 'legal alms' or *zakāt*. This was probably required of all tribes entering into alliance after the treaty of al-Ḥudaybiya, and certainly after the conquest of Mecca, though an exception may have been made of some of the strong tribes in the north-east.

The polity which thus developed out of the 'city-state' of Medina was, according to Arab ideas, a federation of tribes. This explains why for over a century after Muḥammad's death non-Arabs on becoming Muslims had to be attached as 'clients' (*mawālī*) to an Arab tribe. The polity had also a religious basis in that all the members of the constituent tribes or clans were supposed to be Muslims; but for a long time this religious basis seems to have been secondary in the actual functioning of the polity.

It is impossible to say definitely how much of Arabia was under the *pax Islamica,* as the system might be called. The sources report deputations from most of the tribes, but some deputations may have represented only a small section of a tribe. Where there were rival factions in a tribe, one of them would try to steal a march on the other by gaining Muḥammad's support for itself. It seems probable that most of the tribes in the Ḥijāz and Najd supported Muḥammad in their entirety. On the Persian Gulf and the south coast, a faction in each place was in alliance with Muḥammad, but this may have been less than half the population. The tribes towards 'Irāq were in alliance with Muḥammad, but may not have been Muslims, while those on the Syrian frontier still professed allegiance to the Byzantine empire.

The reason for the position on the east and south coasts was that in the various towns there Persian influence had kept a pro-Persian faction in power. About 614 Persia had overrun Syria, Egypt, and other parts of the Byzantine empire, but Heraclius had fought back with grim determination and recovered much ground. In February 628 the Persian emperor died, and succession difficulties led in a few years to the complete collapse of the Persian empire. As the need for support from some other source became clear to these pro-Persian factions, they seem to have turned to Muḥammad and Islam.

Apart from this development of the polity, a feature of Muḥammad's last years is the reconnaissance and perhaps softening-up of the routes for expansion beyond Arabia. From the numbers reported as taking part in his earlier expeditions along the route to Syria, the high importance he attached to the route may be inferred, though little is said about the results of the expeditions. Along this route from Rajab to Ramaḍān 9/October to December 630, Muḥammad led the greatest of all his expeditions, the expedition of Tabūk, allegedly comprising 30,000 men and 10,000 horses. This can only properly be understood as a preliminary to the later conquests; and it is also significant that during the expedition treaties were made with Jewish and Christian communities which set the pattern for the later *dhimmī* system of the Islamic empire.

What happened along the road to 'Irāq is not so clear. There were strong tribes there, notably Bakr b. Wā'il and Taghlib, both partly Christian, and both capable of sending large forces on raids into 'Irāq. It seems probable that at first Muḥammad had alliances with them on equal terms, that is to say, without insisting that they should become Muslims. This arrangement secured the presence of Muslims in the advance into 'Irāq, and gave them an opening for expansion in this direction, while the conception of the *jihād* transformed what would have been tribal raids for booty into a war of conquest.

The continued presence in Arabia of opposition to the *pax Islamica* is shown by the so-called 'wars of apostasy' (or *ridda*) which occupied most of the caliphate of Abū Bakr. These had begun, however, before Muḥammad's death. Early in 632 or perhaps before that a man called Musaylima had come forward in the largely Christian tribe of Ḥanīfa in the centre of Arabia, claiming to be a prophet and to receive revelations like Muḥammad. About Dhu'l-Ḥijja 10/March 632 there was another 'prophet' in the Yemen, al-Aswad. The very fact that they claimed to be prophets is a tribute to the soundness of Muḥammad's method of transcending the tribal system and dealing with contemporary tensions.

The last two and a half years of Muḥammad's life were thus occupied in dealing with the vast new problems created by his successes. There were also difficulties in his family life, and great grief at the death of the little son borne to him by his Coptic concubine, Māriya. In March 632 he led the Greater Pilgrimage or *Ḥajj* to Mecca, and thereby completed the incorporation into Islam of a complex of pre-Islamic ceremonies. From this time onwards he was in poor health. He ceased to attend to business about the beginning of June, retired to 'Ā'isha's apartment, and there died on 13 Rabī' I 11/8 June 632. Abū Bakr had been appointed to lead the worship in Muḥammad's absence, but otherwise there were no arrangements for the succession. For a moment it looked as if the Islamic state might break up, but vigorous action by 'Umar b. al-Khaṭṭāb led to the acceptance of Abū Bakr as *khalīfat Rasūl Allāh*, 'successor (or, caliph) of the Messenger of God'.

MUḤAMMAD'S ACHIEVEMENT

In attempting to assess what Muḥammad achieved, one must take into account not only the events of his lifetime but also the contribution made by these events to subsequent history, and indeed their continuing influence at the present time. In particular one must consider the rapid expansion of the Arab and Islamic state. From a wide historical perspective, it is clear that this expansion was made possible by various factors operative in the world of the Mediterranean and the Middle East.

Two were specially important: firstly, the power-vacuum following the collapse of the Persian empire and the exhaustion of the Byzantine; and secondly, the rising tide of feeling against Hellenism and the Byzantine Greeks among the peoples of Syria, Egypt, and other provinces. These factors made it certain that, once expansion had begun, it would rapidly spread over a wide area. These two factors, however, even in conjunction with the ever-present desire of the nomad for the comforts and luxuries of the Sown, would not have produced the Arab empire but for the unification of the Arabs achieved by Muḥammad. Such unification was in no sense inevitable. It only occurred because Muḥammad had a rare combination of gifts.

In the first place he had what might be termed the gifts of a seer. He was aware of the deep religious roots of the social tensions and malaise at Mecca, and he produced a set of ideas which, by placing the squabbles of Mecca in a wider frame, made it possible to resolve them to some degree. The ideas he proclaimed eventually gave him a position of leadership, with an authority not based on tribal status but on 'religion'. Because of his position and the nature of his authority, clans and tribes which were rivals in secular matters could all accept him as leader. This in turn created a community whose members were all at peace with one another. To prevent their warlike energies from disrupting the community the conception of the *jihād* or 'Holy War' directed these energies outwards against non-Muslims. Thus internal peace and external expansion were complementary. Internal peace gave the Arabs the unified army and unified command needed for effective expansion, while the expansion was required in order to maintain internal peace.

In working out these ideas in actual events and institutions Muḥammad showed great gifts as a statesman. He had shrewd insight into the important aspects of any situation, and concentrated on these. He knew when men were ready to accept a decision if it was imposed on them with the help of a little pressure from outside. Altogether he gradually evolved a coherent set of policies, and built up viable institutions which continued to function after his death.

Another gift was his great tact and charm in the handling of men, and he was able to smooth over many difficulties among his followers. Their trust in his judgment in itself removed many tensions. In his choice of men for various tasks he showed much wisdom, being aware of the capabilities of each and always ready with the word of encouragement when needed.

All in all, the rapid Arab expansion, with the ensuing spread of Islam and growth of Islamic culture, was the outcome of a complex of historical factors; but the set of ideas and the body of men capable of giving a unified direction to the expansion would not have existed but for the unique combination of gifts in Muḥammad himself.

CHAPTER 3

THE PATRIARCHAL AND UMAYYAD CALIPHATES

THE INSTITUTION OF THE CALIPHATE AND THE *Ridda*

There was great consternation in Medina when Muḥammad died (13 Rabīʿ I 11/8 June 632). Nevertheless, the Muslims realized at once that they would have to choose a successor to the dead man. His successor could not be another prophet, since it was known by divine revelation that Muḥammad was the Seal of the Prophets, but it was urgently necessary to choose a new head of the community. So, while the relatives, including his cousin and son-in-law ʿAlī, kept vigil by the body and made preparations for the burial—curiously enough, in the room where it lay—a numerous group of Companions gathered in a roofed enclosure, the *saqīfa* of the Banū Sāʿida, to decide what should be done. The discussion was animated, and at times even violent, for the old antagonism between Medinese Helpers (*Anṣār*) and Meccan Emigrants (*Muhājirūn*) flared up afresh, and the idea had been mooted that there should be one Medinese and one Meccan head, with consequences that would have spelt disaster for Islam. During a momentary pause, however, ʿUmar paid homage to Abū Bakr, Muḥammad's intimate friend and collaborator, by grasping his hand as was the custom when a pact was concluded, and his example was followed by others. Abū Bakr thus became the successor (*khalīfa*) of the Messenger of God and in this way the caliphate was founded, an institution which had no equivalent—and was destined never to have any—outside the Muslim world. The caliphate lasted for centuries, and many things were subsequently changed, but the idea that the appointment of the caliph was a kind of contract imposing reciprocal obligations on the man elected and on his subjects gained ground, and became a fundamental concept once the Muslims had developed a juridical mentality. The fortuitous circumstances that the first man to be elected to this high office was a Qurayshite became, for all except the heterodox, a principle—the caliph had to be a member of the Prophet's tribe, and the Prophet was a Qurayshite. Since the men who elected Abū Bakr, while the populace waited outside to hear the result, had been Muḥammad's closest associates, it became the privilege of the leading figures in the community (the 'men who release and bind') to have the right of choosing, and the populace had only to ratify their decision.

To show that for him the will of the Messenger of God was law, Abū Bakr's first act as head of the state was to dispatch the expedition organized by Muḥammad to avenge the defeat which the Muslims had suffered in Byzantine territory. In the meantime, as soon as they heard of the Prophet's death, the Arab tribes revolted, and there was grave danger that the Muslim state would disintegrate. In four of the six centres of the insurrection, the rebels rallied around men who claimed to be prophets. The movement, which the Muslims called 'the apostasy' (*al-ridda*), thus acquired a certain religious character—though nobody thought of restoring paganism—but it was in reality mainly political. The Arabs in most parts of the peninsula had acknowledged the authority of the Messenger of God, but had no intention of remaining longer subject to Medina, or paying tithe to the caliph. The various tribes had to be subdued one by one by the troops, who in the meantime had returned from Byzantine territory, with the aid of other contingents. Much of their success was due to a brilliant commander and famous strategist, Khālid b. al-Walīd, on whom Muḥammad had conferred the title of 'The Sword of Allāh', which, in subsequent operations of even greater importance, he showed that he deserved.

THE EARLY MUSLIM CONQUESTS

As soon as the rebellion in Arabia had been suppressed, Abū Bakr sent the tribes he had just subdued to carry war into the lands beyond the borders. He obtained his first successes in 'Irāq[1] by exploiting the warlike spirit of a tribe living on the margins of this territory, the Bakr b. Wā'il, whose chieftain was the valorous al-Muthannā, and later he sent Khālid b. al-Walīd there to take over command, at the same time dispatching other troops to wage war in Byzantine territory. It was then that a remarkable thing happened, which the Muslims consider to be a great credit to Islam. For centuries bedouin tribes had been fighting one another all over the peninsula, carrying on feuds to which only exhaustion or the intervention of certain chieftains could put a stop, but now they placed themselves obediently under the orders of Ḥijāzī commanders, and their advance beyond the frontiers was irresistible. It was undoubtedly favoured by the fact that previously, owing perhaps to the

[1] The 'Irāq (*al-'Irāq*) was the southern part of the Tigris-Euphrates basin, and was hence of much more limited extent than the modern state of Iraq.

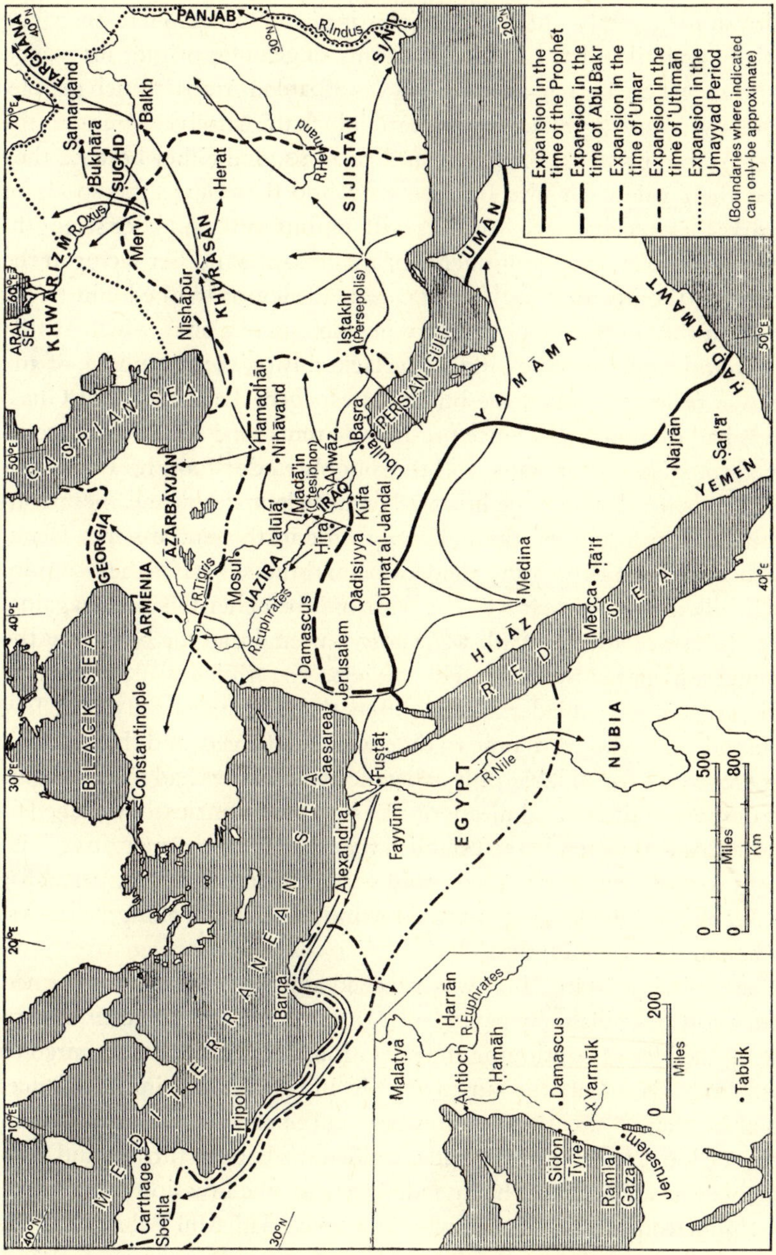

Map 2. The Arab conquests.

rapid increase of the population in Arabia, there had been a steady infiltration of Arabs into Syria, Palestine, and 'Irāq. Here they had partially assimilated the local inhabitants of Semitic origin, for which reason they were known as *musta'riba*, 'self-styled Arabs'. Such people, even if they were of mixed origin, certainly felt themselves bound to the 'pure Arabs' by ties of language and customs, and either because they hated their rulers, or else because they hoped to share the spoils of victory, they received the invaders with enthusiasm, and later strengthened their forces with contingents of their own. Another factor in the success of the invaders was the innate tendency of the bedouin to lay hands on the property of sedentary peoples—a tendency which at that time found ample scope owing to the lack, during the first phase, of any effective resistance, since the buffer states of the Lakhmids and Ghassanids had disappeared. Since pre-Islamic times, the Arabs were accustomed to organize caravans, and thoroughly understood how to equip their bands for distant expeditions. Nevertheless, despite all these concomitant circumstances, the decisive factor in this success was Islam, which was the co-ordinating element behind the efforts of the bedouin, and instilled into the hearts of the warriors the belief that a war against the followers of another faith was a holy war, and that the booty was the recompense offered by God to His soldiers. The armies were not hordes, as those of other invaders were; often they consisted only of a few thousand men who from time to time were reinforced, and they became numerous and formidable only when decisive battles had to be fought. The desert was their usual means of access to the countries they wished to conquer, and they tended to establish themselves on the margins of the desert, so that if necessary they could withdraw into it and disperse, for the Arabs had long been accustomed to moving rapidly along its tracks, and across its vast solitudes.

The capital of 'Irāq, Ḥīra, was attacked, and saved itself from armed occupation and pillage by paying a large sum. Khālid, however, had to give up the idea of continuing the operation, because he was required to hasten to Syria, where the fate of the Muslim armies was in the balance, and al-Muthannā was thus left to carry on the campaign alone. But an energetic king, Yazdigird III, had ascended the Persian throne, and, as it soon became evident that he intended to resist the invasion by raising a more numerous army, 'Umar, who had succeeded Abū Bakr as caliph, despatched reinforcements. The Muslims suffered a severe defeat (13/634) known as the Battle of the Bridge (because al-Muthannā saved the army from complete disaster by putting up a heroic resistance at a bridge over the Euphrates), but a victory at Buwayb (14/635) restored their fortunes. The decisive battle of the campaign was fought near the modern Najaf, at Qādisiyya (15/636).[1] The commander of the Persian army was an imperial marshal, the nobleman Rustam, while 'Umar sent one of the Companions, Sa'd b. Abī Waqqāṣ, who had taken part in many of Muḥammad's expeditions, to lead the Arab forces. Stricken by illness, Sa'd directed the movements of his troops from a distance—this being a novelty for the Arabs. The Persians were heavily defeated, and the result was that the Muslims gained control over the whole of 'Irāq. As the road to Ctesiphon, the winter capital of the Sasanids, not far from ancient Babylon was now open, they soon reached that coveted goal. Arab chroniclers of later centuries, living in highly civilized and refined surroundings, relate with amusement a number of episodes illustrating the crudeness and ignorance of the bedouin conquerors; a wonderful carpet encrusted with precious stones was torn to pieces and divided among the soldiers; dogs were given their food on gold plates; camphor was mistaken for salt, and used to flavour soups.

After their disastrous defeat at Qādisiyya the only hope for the Persians was to retire up the slopes of the Zagros, and attempt a counter-attack from there. But all their efforts were frustrated. After occupying the Jazīra (i.e. Mesopotamia, now northern Iraq), the Muslims pursued them across the Iranian plateau, and entered Ahwāz, the main city of Khūzistān. In the neighbourhood of Nihāvand, to the south-west of Hamadhān, a battle was fought which sealed the fate of the Persian empire and was therefore called by the Muslims 'the Victory of Victories' (21/642). After this the Persians were unable to offer any effective resistance. As the invaders advanced—slowly, because the distances were great, the population hostile, and towns and fortresses had to be captured one by one—King Yazdigird retreated first to Iṣfahān, and then to Iṣṭakhr, the ancient Persepolis, the summer capital of the Sasanids. Finally he took refuge in Khurāsān. Here, abandoned by all except a few faithful followers, he was assassinated by a local satrap (31/651–2). The memory of his romantic life and his sad end still lives in the minds of his countrymen, to such an extent that the Parsees

[1] The dates of many of the battles fought about this time are rather uncertain; according to some sources the battle of Qādisiyya took place in 15/636. In his *Annali dell'Islam*, under the year 16 H., 1–2, Leone Caetani supports the dating in the sixteenth year of the *Hijra*.

who emigrated to India, but remained true to the religion and traditions of their country of origin, date the beginning of their era from the day on which he mounted the throne (16 June 632).

While this campaign in 'Irāq was still in progress, the Muslims also took the offensive against Syria and Palestine. Two columns of Arabs entered Transjordan, and another, led by a general who was later to become famous, 'Amr b. al-'Āṣ, penetrated into south-eastern Palestine. Hearing that the Emperor Heraclius was equipping a large army, Abū Bakr ordered Khālid b. al-Walīd to hasten from 'Irāq to Syria, and with a few hundred men he crossed the Syrian desert, a feat which in those days was considered a miracle of audacity and organization (winter 12/633–4). His arrival in Syria was providential. He inspired the troops with fresh courage, and in a series of battles defeated the army of Heraclius, and occupied Damascus (Rajab 14/September 635). Heraclius, however, refused to admit that he was beaten, and raised a formidable new army; whereupon the Muslims withdrew to the Yarmūk, an affluent of the left bank of the Jordan, into which it flows south of Lake Tiberias. This was the scene of a pitched battle on 15 August 636, which resulted in practically the whole of Syria falling into Muslim hands. One city after another fell, the only one to offer some resistance being Qinnasrīn, at that time an important centre of trade, not far from Aleppo. In the meantime Abū Bakr had died, and 'Umar succeeded to the caliphate. The most important episodes of the subsequent operations in Palestine were the occupation of Jerusalem (17/638), and, after the Muslims had recovered from the effects of a terrible outbreak of plague, the fall of Caesarea (19/641). When the surrender of Jerusalem seemed to be imminent, 'Umar went to Syria and concluded a treaty with the notables of the city on very generous terms. Christians were to be given protection, and to have freedom of worship, paying a tax which in comparison was less heavy than that which in the past they had paid to Byzantium. Khālid had previously made a similar treaty with the inhabitants of Damascus. Arab historians relate with pride how 'Umar made his entry into Jerusalem after the surrender, clad in a coarse mantle, and thus causing astonishment among the populace accustomed to Byzantine splendour. He went up to the terrace, reduced to a rubbish-heap, where the Temple of Solomon had once stood, and ordered that the debris should be cleared away, and a mosque built on the site—a very modest edifice, it is true, and not to be confused with the magnificent building to which his name is often wrongly applied, the Dome of the Rock.

The Muslim advance to the north was stopped by the inaccessible Mount Amanus in northern Lebanon, but continued towards the east in the Jazīra (639–41) and thence into Armenia (640–3), and south-west towards Egypt.

When 'Amr b. al-'Āṣ marched into Egypt, with or without the authorization of 'Umar, he did not make straight for the capital, Alexandria, but advanced through the desert towards the Fayyūm. After ravaging this area, he encountered near Heliopolis (Rajab 19/July 640) the Byzantine forces which he had cleverly lured away from the fortress of Babylon (Bābilyūn), where they had assembled. He defeated them; and the Patriarch Cyrus, who was also the civil governor of the country, seeing that the situation was becoming critical, began negotiations for peace, and then went to Byzantium to obtain approval of his conduct. The Emperor Heraclius, however, refused to believe that the position was so serious, and looked upon Cyrus as a traitor. It was only after the death of the emperor, on 11 February 641, that Cyrus was able to conclude peace, after the surrender of Babylon (Rabī' 21 20/9 April 641), and the failure of Byzantium to send help, because of internal troubles and the war in Italy. The conditions of peace were severe for the Byzantines, who were compelled to abandon this rich province, but the Christian and Jewish population obtained the usual lenient treatment regularly accorded to the People of the Book. The Byzantines departed, and although they landed again at Alexandria shortly afterwards, and were warmly received by the Grecophile inhabitants, their success was a brief one, and they were soon driven out again by 'Amr, this time for good.

Raids along the coast of North Africa had begun after the first occupation of the Egyptian capital. Pentapolis (Cyrenaica, called Barqa by the Arabs) was more or less overrun, but it was not until the year 27/647 that a strong army destroyed the forces of the Patrician Gregory at Sufetula (the modern Sbeitla, in Tunisia). Even this victory did not give the Muslims complete control of Byzantine Africa, and fearing a counter-offensive, they withdrew. They returned to Ifrīqiya (corresponding to modern Tunisia and part of Algeria) when the situation in their own empire, torn by civil wars, had improved.

'UMAR AND THE ORGANIZATION OF THE EMPIRE

Before his death in 13/634, Abū Bakr urged the Companions to elect 'Umar as his successor, and since they were well aware of his many virtues, not least among which were his energy and talent for organization, they followed this advice. Their expectations were not disappointed, for if an isolated episode in Arab history, such as Islam was before the death of the Prophet, was transformed into an event of world-wide importance, and the foundations were laid of a Muslim empire which civil wars, lack of unity, and attacks from abroad might shake, but could not destroy, the chief credit for these things must be attributed to the political gifts of ʿUmar.

As a result of the conquests begun under Abū Bakr and continued under ʿUmar, the empire increased enormously in extent. Since it covered areas inhabited by people of different races, customs, degrees of civilization, and types of government, ʿUmar allowed the local administrators of occupied countries to carry on and confined himself to appointing a commander or governor (*amīr*) with full powers, sometimes assisted by an agent (*ʿāmil*) responsible directly to Medina to look after financial matters. By keeping a tight rein on these lieutenants, and compelling them to follow his directives, he gave a certain unity to the empire. Later writers attribute the whole organization of the Muslim state to him, but this is not true, and there is reason to believe that it was the fruit of a gradual process in which various successors of ʿUmar, assisted by experts, had their share. He was, however, undoubtedly responsible for the solution of a number of important problems that needed immediate attention.

First of these was that of the lands belonging to inhabitants of the vanquished countries. If the population surrendered to the invaders under the terms of a treaty, this was a simple matter, since the Holy Law laid down that treaties must be respected; but if they resisted until they were overwhelmed, the question was more complicated, since in such cases the victors had the right to treat the vanquished as they liked. Realizing that the land must be cultivated in the interests of all—his bedouin could not be transformed into peasants in a day—ʿUmar left it in the hands of the previous owners. Subsequently, Muslim jurists argued as to what right they had to it, and could find no satisfactory reply. It is obvious that ʿUmar acted empirically but wisely as he was a far-seeing man. Another problem was that of the lands left without owners, for example crown lands and estates abandoned by Byzantine or Persian functionaries, or those of which the owners had fled or could not be found. ʿUmar confiscated such lands, instead of dividing them among his soldiers and others who had deserved well of Islam. We know, however, that certain Muslims did become owners of large properties in the conquered countries, but it is not clear whether these were uncultivated lands which they reclaimed by employing slaves, at that time very numerous, or whether some of them secured allotments of fertile public lands, or, being extremely rich, purchased large estates in the country. According to old sources, 'Umar was opposed to Arabs having any interests outside Arabia, but the facts do not support this, and it may be that his wishes were not always carried out.

The taxes on lands left in the hands of their owners, and the rents from those which had been confiscated, together with sundry other items of revenue (the tithe paid by Muslims, one-fifth of the value of booty, the tribute and personal taxes paid by the vanquished) supplied the public treasury (*bayt al-māl*). Another merit of 'Umar was that he realized the need of a stable fiscal system, which could meet the present and future requirements of the state. To satisfy the soldiers and keep their morale high, he thought of the expedient of reserving to the state the duty of compensating them, and founding a *dīwān,* i.e. a register of pensioners. The list of those entitled to pensions was headed by the name of 'Ā'isha, who had been the Prophet's favourite wife; next, with smaller pensions, came the relatives of Muḥammad, those who had deserved well of Islam and those who knew the Qur'ān well; and lastly, the soldiers with their wives and children. By establishing the principle that it was the state's duty to provide for such people, 'Umar was thinking more of the public interest than of the momentary satisfaction of individual or collective claims. It would not appear that anyone protested against this during 'Umar's lifetime, perhaps because too short a time elapsed between the institution of the *dīwān* and his death, or because he obtained approval for his measures in a great assembly of military commanders at Jābiya near Damascus, or else because his authority was so great that none dared to oppose him.

In territories which had been definitely conquered, 'Umar endeavoured to set up efficient administrations, and in such cases he replaced the military commanders by men with more experience in the organization of civil affairs. For example, he employed 'Amr b. al-'Āṣ in Egypt as long as the military situation demanded it, but as soon as the circumstances allowed, he appointed 'Abd Allāh b. Sa'd b. Abī Sarḥ, and to Syria he sent a much esteemed Companion, Abū 'Ubayda, to replace Khālid b. al-Walīd.

To prevent the troops having too close contacts with the native population, and to keep them prepared for every emergency, since it was also their duty to maintain internal order, 'Umar founded two camp-towns (*amṣār*) in 'Irāq, Baṣra and Kūfa, which quickly became important urban centres and capitals of districts. The soldiers and their families were quartered according to their tribes, so that the tribal system continued to prevail even when, by mingling all the elements which flowed in from Arabia (a measure not taken until later) it would have been possible to eliminate some of its disadvantages, to the benefit of Islamic unity. The tribal system was, however, useful to the governors, who employed heads of tribes to transmit their orders, and see that they were obeyed.

'Umar raised one army after another in order to break the intensified resistance of his enemies, to make good the mistakes due to the rashness of commanders, or to keep the rhythm of conquest going, as he occupied more and more distant territories; and it is an astonishing fact that he never seems to have lost control over his generals. His ability was also revealed in his diplomacy, the aim of which was to appease quarrels and restrain the ambitions of some of the less tractable among the Companions.

Another important step taken by 'Umar was the fixing, for administrative reasons, of the beginning of a new era. The choice of the initial date fell on the first day of the lunar year during which Muḥammad had emigrated to Medina. In Arabic, the word *Hijra* was used to denote that Emigration, and was also applied to the new era. The first day of the first month (*Muḥarram*) of that lunar year corresponded to 15 or 16 July 622 in the Julian calendar, whereas Muḥammad had emigrated in September. The choice was determined by the realization that the Emigration was of prime importance for the fortunes of Islam; moreover, the date was precise, whereas there has always been doubt as to the exact year of the Prophet's birth, and the day on which he was summoned by God to accomplish his mission.

Physically, 'Umar was a giant with a long beard. His very appearance inspired respect. He was of a harsh disposition, as severe with himself as he was with others. Tradition relates that he used to wear coarse clothing, often patched, that he ate plain food in order to conform with the Prophet's example, and that he was fond of walking about the streets of Medina with a hide whip in his hand, which he did not hesitate to apply to the shoulders of those who infringed the law. He was more feared than loved.

THE OPPOSITION TO ʿUTHMĀN AND THE FIRST CIVIL WAR

ʿUmar had been on the throne only ten years and was still in the prime of life—he was fifty-three years old—when he was mortally wounded, because of a personal grudge, by a slave of Persian origin (26 Dhu'l-Ḥijja 23/3 November 644). One of his sons believed that someone had instigated the crime; his suspicions fell on a Persian general named Hurmuzān, who had been brought to Medina as a slave, and in an access of anger he slew him.

As he lay dying, ʿUmar was anxious about the succession and he appointed a committee of six, all Qurayshites, whose duty it should be to choose one of their number as caliph. The inhabitants of Medina no longer had any share in the election of the head of the state. The two most favoured candidates were ʿUthmān, an Umayyad and Muḥammad's father-in-law, and ʿAlī, who, as we have already said, was the Prophet's cousin and son-in-law. The choice eventually fell upon the former, probably because it was thought that he would continue the policy of ʿUmar. ʿAlī, inspired by a rigorous pietism, was not convinced that all the measures taken by the preceding caliphs were in conformity with the precepts of the Qur'ān or with the actions of Muḥammad. It is thus possible that he intended, if he were elected caliph, to make changes which would have prejudiced certain well-established interests. In any case it is certain that he was viewed with mistrust in most quarters, and that from the very first hours of ʿUthmān's caliphate he joined the ranks of the opposition. Immediately after the election he and other Companions demanded that the *lex talionis* should be applied to the son of ʿUmar who had killed Hurmuzān, and it was only with some difficulty that the new caliph managed to save the unfortunate man from death.

During the twelve years of ʿUthmān's reign, the opposition gradually increased its numbers, and ʿAlī was one of its leading members. The caliph was accused of nepotism, favouritism, and the encouragement of abuses. But this was not all; he was also charged with introducing into the Muslim rites, and the administration of state property, certain reprehensible innovations which found no justification in the Qur'ān or in the practice of Muḥammad. By insisting that the innovations were of this kind, the accusers gave a religious colouring to protests which in reality were based on economic motives. It is, in fact, not quite clear what the aims of the opposition really were; there may have been conflicting trends among them, ranging from moderation to extremism. The most violent recriminations came from the soldiers, over the question of lands conquered by force of arms, and in particular those confiscated by the treasury. The soldiers claimed that these ought to be allotted to them, or at least that the revenue received should be divided among them. So long as the booty captured on the field of battle had been plentiful, their discontent had had no reason to become vocal, nor was there any trouble in Syria, where the provincial administration was well managed (as Byzantine methods had not been changed), and pensions were paid regularly and in full. But with the passage of time, the *dīwān* instituted by 'Umar revealed itself for what it really was—an expedient to counter the exorbitant claims of those who had deserved well of Islam. Equally evident was the contrast between the hard life of the soldiers and that of those Muslims who, far away from the battle-fields, enjoyed luxurious existence, and became rich, thanks to privileges of all kinds and more generous pensions. During the reign of 'Uthmān one of the Companions, Abū Dharr al-Ghifārī, stirred up such a violent campaign against the wealthy that the caliph deemed it prudent to banish him.

The historians attribute the intensification of unrest partly to the fact that 'Uthmān was a weak man, but some of his actions, for example his firm opposition to a proposal that he should abdicate, and his dignified behaviour in the face of death, seem to contradict this assumption. It has also been maintained that he had not received the requisite training to enable him to govern an empire, since he had never previously held government posts. He had, however, the assistance of his able kinsman and secretary, Marwān, as well as of a sort of advisory council, composed of Companions of the Prophet. It is more probable that the troubles which afflicted the closing years of his caliphate had deep and ineradicable roots; for which reason, despite promises to change his policy, he was unable to rectify the situation. An economic crisis certainly existed, and it may be assumed that this affected both victors and vanquished, though the information we possess reveals its repercussions only among the former, and particularly among the soldiers, since the other grumblers, so far as we know, confined themselves to vague requests for the replacement of functionaries and the elimination of abuses. Public finance was undoubtedly in a parlous state, since the administration, apart from Syria, was generally badly managed, and war was less profitable when it was waged in poor and distant lands. One specific fact may well have contributed to the situation, and this was the immigration into 'Irāq and Egypt of too many bedouin, who offered themselves for military service in the hope of getting good pay. The government could not refuse to accept them, despite the increasing gravity of the financial situation.

'Uthmān did his utmost to find a remedy, not only by reducing expenditure, but also by conquering still more territory, and in fact the policy of military expansion was continued during his reign. But did all the profits reach Medina? The normal administrative procedure was that the provincial governments were authorized to meet local and military expenditure out of revenue, only the balance being remitted to the central government, and it is thus legitimate to suppose that this was often subject to drastic reductions. It was not without reason that the agent in charge of finance, if one existed, took his orders directly from Medina, and not from the local governor.

It was in Egypt and 'Irāq that the greatest anxiety was felt. In the end, groups of malcontents made their way from Egypt to Medina. There they demanded, and were promised, reforms, whereupon they departed. We are told that, on their way home, they intercepted a courier carrying a letter from Marwān, in which he ordered the governor of Egypt to punish the most violent and dangerous among them, and so they returned once more to Medina. But since in the meantime the unrest in that city had continued (it being evident that neither the caliph nor his functionaries had any intention of enforcing the reforms), and a riot took place in the mosque, during which stones were thrown at 'Uthmān himself, it is more probable that they were recalled to the city by their comrades in the struggle, who at the same time persuaded other malcontents to come from 'Irāq to Medina. The rioters laid siege to the caliph's house and cut off supplies of food and water. Later, when news arrived from the provinces that help for the beleaguered caliph was on its way, the more desperate among the rioters broke into the house and pitilessly slew the venerable old man as he was reading the Qur'ān (end 35/June 656). 'Umar, too, had died a tragic death; but in his case the crime was committed by a foreigner, driven by hatred, whereas the murderers of 'Uthmān were his coreligionists, among them even a son of the Caliph Abū Bakr. The scandal in the Muslim world was enormous.

While 'Uthmān's household and his supporters hastened to flee from Medina, 'Alī, who had kept aloof during the siege, and, instead of defending the caliph, had sometimes acted as spokesman for the rebels, was chosen to be head of the state. Almost all the notables then in Medina paid him homage; at that time he was the leading figure among the Companions of the Prophet and moreover he had given his support to

'Uthmān's opponents. Who, therefore, would dare oppose him? Nevertheless, after only a short time Ṭalḥa and al-Zubayr broke away from him and went to Mecca, where they found 'Ā'isha, the Prophet's widow, and the three of them decided on open rebellion. They announced that the law of retaliation should be respected and the caliph's murderers should pay the penalty for their crime. When the three insurgents proceeded to 'Irāq, where they hoped to find supporters and arms, 'Alī followed them, but failed to stop them. A battle took place near Baṣra between the forces which 'Alī had raised in Medina, on his way and at Kūfa, and the army of the insurgents which in the meantime had grown in numbers. 'Ā'isha watched it from a palanquin on the back of a camel and for this reason it was called the Battle of the Camel. Ṭalḥa and al-Zubayr were killed, and 'Alī was victorious. 'Ā'isha, with all due respect, was sent back to Medina. But this did not put an end to the civil war.

Ever since his election 'Alī had been trying to persuade the Umayyad governor of Syria, Muʿāwiya, to pay him homage, but the latter had refused to do this. Now, as a relative of 'Uthmān, he demanded that the murderers of the caliph should be handed over to him, so that vengeance might be done, in accordance with the right granted by the Qur'ān to the next-of-kin of any man who had been 'unjustly' killed (17. 35/33).

'Alī marched out to enforce obedience to his order, and Muʿāwiya went to meet him. The two armies faced each other for several months at Ṣiffīn, near the great bend of the Euphrates, and there at last one of the most famous battles in the history of Islam was fought. When things were beginning to go badly for Muʿāwiya, 'Amr b. al-ʿĀṣ, who had rallied to his side, advised him to hoist copies of the Qur'ān on lances, as an invitation to the enemy to settle the question, not by force of arms, but by arbitration. 'Alī's more fanatical supporters forced him to accept this proposal, and they were so convinced that right was on their side that they insisted on having a neutral, Abū Mūsā al-Ashʿarī, as their arbiter. For his part, Muʿāwiya chose 'Amr. The task of the arbiters was to establish whether 'Uthmān had been killed 'unjustly', or whether his death at the hands of the infuriated populace had been caused by his own reprehensible innovations, in which case the killers would have been merely executioners, and the next-of-kin would have no claim against them.[1]

[1] On the question of the arbiters' functions and other controversial points, see Laura Veccia Vaglieri, 'Il conflitto 'Alī-Muʿāwiya e la secessione khārigita riesaminati alla luce di fonti ibadite' in *Annali dell'Istituto Universitario Orientale di Napoli,* N.S., IV, 1–94, and Appendix, *ibid.,* N.S., V, 1–98.

The two armies drew apart, and waited for the verdict of the arbiters. It would seem that, after studying the matter for months, they met at the oasis of Dūmat al-Jandal (the modern al-Jawf) and decided against ʿAlī, but the latter protested that the verdict was not in accordance with the Qur'ān and the practice (*Sunna*) of the Prophet, and he intended to resume his campaign against Muʿāwiya. In the meantime, however, something had happened, the importance of which could only be measured later. Some of ʿAlī's supporters at Ṣiffīn thought that the acceptance of arbitration was wrong, because the right of judging belongs to God alone and not to men, since in His revelation in the Qur'ān He has laid down that rebels must be fought until they return to obedience (49. 9). As Muʿāwiya and his followers had undoubtedly rebelled against ʿAlī, it must be wrong to come to terms with them. The number of dissidents grew, and those who shared their opinion felt that they could no longer follow ʿAlī. They therefore withdrew to a place called Nahrawān. From the verb *kharaja* meaning 'to go out', but also used in the sense of 'to rebel', they are known as Kharijites (*Khawārij*, in the singular, *Khārijī*). Before taking action against Muʿāwiya, ʿAlī decided to crush this agitation, and, since the dissidents refused to listen to his appeals, he massacred them. They were all pious Muslims, much given to prayer, and were convinced that they were obeying God, whereas ʿAlī, according to them, had committed an act of disobedience. The killing of these men therefore caused great indignation. Other Muslims criticized the fact that ʿAlī, after accepting arbitration as the means of settling the dispute, had not submitted to the verdict. As a result, when he resumed his advance against Muʿāwiya, there were so many desertions from his forces that he had to abandon his project, and return to Kūfa. A few months later, at Adhruḥ in Transjordan, a large number of Muslims assembled to choose a new caliph. The possibility that ʿAlī, disqualified by the verdict and by his subsequent conduct, might be confirmed as caliph, was not even taken into consideration during the discussions that followed. The final decision was left to the two arbiters, who, however, were unable to reach an agreement. ʿAmr thought that Muʿāwiya ought to be chosen for his outstanding qualities, but Abū Mūsā al-Ashʿarī, seeing no other solution, wished to refer the election of a caliph to a committee. In the end, all those who were present assembled to hear what the arbiters had decided, whereupon there was a sensational development. From the platform Abū Mūsā announced that neither ʿAlī nor Muʿāwiya (who in the meantime had been proclaimed caliph by his own supporters) would be elected, and proposed that the whole matter should be postponed, though he let it be seen that he himself was in favour of 'Abd Allāh, a son of 'Umar. After 'Amr had declared that he supported the candidature of Mu'āwiya, the meeting broke up in disorder without any decision having been reached. 'Alī continued to govern the area over which he still had control, and Mu'āwiya, who in the meantime had occupied Egypt, took good care not to attack him. He played for time, confining himself to marginal operations which had only a nuisance value, his aim being to disrupt 'Alī's party by means of a subtle policy of persuasion among the malcontents and the lukewarm. Then one day 'Alī was stabbed to death in the mosque of Kūfa, the victim of a Kharijite's hatred. After inducing 'Alī's son, al-Ḥasan, to forgo his claim to the throne, Mu'āwiya was recognized as caliph by the great majority of Muslims.

The events we have just described may seem to be mere episodes against the vast background of history, but in reality this is not so. Ever since those days, the Muslim community has been split into three politico-religious sects, which in the course of time accentuated their religious aspect, so that Islam was divided into a majority, which considered itself orthodox, and two schismatic groups. The party of Mu'āwiya, which soon found numerous adherents, became *ahl al-Sunna,* the Sunnīs, not because its adherents were more attached than the others to the *Sunna,* since all Muslims agree as to its value,[1] but because they claimed to be the depositaries of correct and orthodox theory and practice. *Shī'at 'Alī,* the party of 'Alī, became the Shī'a, and its doctrine is generally known to occidental scholars as Shi'ism. The Khawārij also evolved a doctrine of their own, which Western scholars call Kharijism.

POETRY AND CULTURE DURING THE PATRIARCHAL CALIPHATE

The vitality which poetry had displayed in pre-Islamic times soon died away after the advent of the new Faith. Neither religious feeling, nor the stirring events which took place under the first caliphs, provided the poets with new motifs, and they continued to follow in the path of their predecessors. A few poets emerged, however; for example Ḥassān b. Thābit, who had been the Prophet's official bard and outlived him by

[1] The term *Sunna* here means the practice of the Prophet as related in very numerous Traditions (sing., *Ḥadīth*).

many years (d. 54/674), Abū Miḥjan and al-Ḥuṭay'a, but these all remained faithful to the world of bygone days, to the old conventional subjects and styles of pagan times, except for fleeting references to the events of which they had been witnesses or participants. In general, the poetry of those days was occasional and extempore. When it touched on current events, it was concerned only with details, to which the poet brought the mentality of a bedouin with limited horizons, who could neither understand them nor reflect their grandeur. Prose must have been extensively cultivated at that time, since it was called upon to fulfil new functions, among the reasons being that a type of oratory came into use which was destined for the masses; correspondence between the central government and provincial functionaries became necessary; and the wording of treaties and regulations involved the use of legal phraseology, or at all events of clearly defined terms. Unfortunately, the numerous speeches of leaders, in the form in which they have been handed down to us by historians, are no guarantee that such words were ever spoken, since they were written down long after the event; while epistles could be considered authentic only if we were certain that they had been preserved in archives, and documents reveal such a number of variants that we are led to think they cannot have been accurately copied from one and the same original. From the days of the Companions date, as it is claimed, thousands of Traditions (sing., *Ḥadīth*; pl., *Aḥādīth*), purporting to reproduce the words and deeds of the Prophet, set in a framework describing the circumstances. Whether such words were actually uttered by Muḥammad, or such deeds accomplished by him, is a question that does not concern us here. It should, however, be noted that the halting, crude and summary prose of these *Ḥadīth,* because of these very characteristics, justifies the assumption that many of them are very old, especially those in which the lack of any tendentiousness is evident.

The days of the first caliphs saw the beginnings of an attentive study of the divine revelations constituting the Qur'ān, and a category of *qurrā'* (reciters) arose to spread the knowledge of the sacred Book. Different readings and variants in the wording began to appear here and there in the revelations. The Caliph 'Uthmān therefore decided to have the exact and definitive Qur'anic text established by a committee of experts. When this had been done, copies were sent to the provincial capitals (*amṣār*) and orders were given to destroy all other collections of texts from the Qur'ān, whether complete or fragmentary. For this reason the Qur'anic text which has come down to us has not undergone any modifications since those days. The study of these divine revelations, which for the Muslims are the Word of God, naturally led to reflections on the language of the Qur'ān as an aid to better comprehension, to a study of the meanings that might be attached to words and phrases, and to investigation of the circumstances in which each revelation was made. At first the result was a mass of disconnected observations, notes, comparisons, and interpretations, and only later did a systematic exegesis and kindred sciences emerge from this mass.

During the thirty years of the Patriarchal Caliphate, some prominent persons became famous for their knowledge of the Qur'ān, among them 'Alī, Ibn 'Abbās and Abū Mūsā al-Ash'arī, and even in those days controversies arose as to the interpretation of many passages in the sacred Book, and the application of these by analogy to the new situations which arose. At the same time the manner of life and habits (*Sunna*) of the Prophet were studied, since they were held to have been inspired by God and to reflect His will. In the days of 'Alī and 'Uthmān, as we have already seen, differences of interpretation regarding passages of the Qur'ān and the *Sunna,* were invoked to justify political actions.

CHARACTERISTICS OF THE UMAYYAD CALIPHATE

With the accession of Mu'āwiya the Patriarchal Caliphate came to an end and a new era began, in which the head of the state became conscious of his own position as ruler of an empire and determined to make everyone —his own co-religionists as well as the conquered peoples—realize his importance. To achieve this end, even in external matters, he abandoned the simple life and the paternalistic methods of bygone days, and set a distance between himself and the people. He surrounded himself with a court, instituted ceremonial practices, appeared at public prayer on Fridays escorted by guards, and indulged in a certain pomp.

Other more concrete differences distinguished the Umayyad caliphs from their four predecessors, who are comprehensively distinguished by the epithet *al-Rāshidūn,* 'the rightly guided'.

Towards the end of his reign, Mu'āwiya, using all his diplomatic skill, managed to persuade the notables of the empire to recognize his son Yazīd as heir to the throne, leaving untouched the rule that homage must be paid at the moment of succession. In this way he achieved a compromise. Theoretically, the will of the electors was respected, since it was admitted that they could reject the heir appointed by the reigning sovereign (in actual fact, only four or five notables refused to accede to Mu'āwiya's request), but in reality it implied the abolition of the elective system, which had been the cause of so much trouble in the past, and introduced hereditary succession. Mu'āwiya's innovation was followed by all the caliphs who came after him, and enabled the Umayyads to retain power for ninety years, and the 'Abbasids for five centuries. The same system was introduced in the Muslim states which came into being within the territories or on the margin of the caliphate, whether under its aegis or as independent polities, as generally in these also hereditary dynasties reigned for longer or shorter periods. Nevertheless, wars of succession were not completely eliminated. Often on the death of a caliph pretenders arose, who claimed that they had recognized the heir to the throne under duress, or else they revolted, profiting by the fact that the new caliph was still very young. Since pre-Islamic days the Arabs had always favoured the principle of seniority.

A real theocracy had been established when Muḥammad transmitted the Word of God as His Messenger, and acted as the vicegerent of God on earth. After his death there had been a kind of second theocracy, since the Patriarchal Caliphs had felt obliged to take the precepts of the Qur'ān as a standard for their own actions, and to model their behaviour on that of the Prophet. Animated by fear of error, before taking a decision, they would, if they were in doubt, make enquiries of anyone who had listened to these precepts, and was well acquainted with that behaviour, by having lived at the side of the Prophet. If they acted on their own initiative, public opinion soon recalled them to their duty. When, after the deaths of 'Alī and many other old Companions, that category of men disappeared who might have availed themselves of their intimacy with Muḥammad in order to protest, the caliphs no longer had any obstacle to surmount. It is true that a class of scholars devoted to the study of the Qur'ān was gradually being formed, but it had not yet acquired sufficient authority to assume the task of establishing what was right, because it conformed with the sacred Book, or what was wrong, because it was arbitrary. In time, however, these scholars began to make their voices heard, and then a chorus of protests was raised. It should be added that there were far too many spurious *Ḥadīth* in circulation—the expurgation of these and the collecting of the more reliable came later, under the 'Abbasids. Consequently, even as regards the practice of Muḥammad, the caliph could find alleged precedents when it came to making new laws. Indeed, despite the fact that God was supposed to be the Muslim community's only lawgiver, even 'Umar had assumed certain legislative powers, and after him 'Uthmān had done the same, because neither the Qur'ān nor the *Sunna* contained rules applicable to all the vicissitudes of life. Strictly speaking, no distinction can be drawn between the Patriarchal Caliphs and the Umayyads in this respect, but there is no doubt that it was Mu'āwiya, who, without encountering serious opposition, accentuated the evolution of government towards a greater freedom of decision, and took a broader view of the question of making laws. Under his successors an increasing secularization of government can be clearly discerned. The Muslims perceived this and maintained that the Umayyad era was not a caliphate, but a 'kingdom' (*mulk*), since it had betrayed the theocratic spirit of the early days of Islam, and, in contrast with the democratic tendencies of Arab society, and the systems in vogue under the first caliphs, had adopted a form of autocratic government, and an organization of the state bearing the marks of foreign origin. We used the word 'secularization', but by that we do not mean that the Umayyad régime was a secular government. Although various caliphs were criticized for their personal lack of attachment to religion, they never ceased to enforce obedience to the law of God. Religion still remained the basic criterion for discrimination between subjects, although superimposed on this was the question of whether they belonged to the Arab race or not.

Another feature of the Umayyad régime was indeed the concession of privileges to the Arabs, on the grounds that they were the people chosen by God, who had sent one of them as a prophet to reveal His truth in the Arabic language. Not without reason did Wellhausen call his book on the Umayyad era *Das arabische Reich und sein Sturz*. But here it is permissible to ask ourselves a question. Did the Arabs bring their nationalistic sentiments with them when they left their deserts, and invaded the bordering countries; or were these sentiments a reaction on the part of the ruling class to the hosts of new converts, who demanded equal rights, and of arabized peoples, who felt that they were just as good as the pure Arabs? Our doubts are based on the fact that the Arabs lacked solidarity, and did not feel that they were members of one race. On the contrary, hatred drove those belonging to different tribes to wage war on one another. In any case the shield of Arabism behind which the governing class took refuge in order to defend itself against its formidable host, revealed its fragility when the 'Abbasids, advancing, shattered the Umayyad dynasty by promising justice in the name of Islam.

The centre of gravity of the empire shifted to Syria. Even in 'Alī's day, Medina had ceased to be the capital, and Kūfa had taken its place. Now the former seat of the Patriarchal Caliphs definitely declined to the status of a provincial centre, and all attempts to restore it to its earlier function proved vain. The transfer of the capital to Damascus also aroused the envy of the 'Irāqīs, and the desire to do away with the Syrian hegemony was a cause of various risings. Another result was that the Umayyads started a vigorous policy of expansion in the Mediterranean, which continued even after they had disappeared, for when the 'Abbasids removed the capital of the empire to 'Irāq, this policy was carried on by the Muslim polities on the shores of the Inland Sea.

The accession to power of an aristocratic Meccan family which, except for 'Uthmān, had answered Muḥammad's call only after his success, was a grave blow to the Muslims of old standing; hence the hostility of their descendants towards the Umayyads, a hostility soon transformed into accusations—not always justified—of lukewarm faith or even of unbelief. These raised the much discussed question whether a verbal profession of faith was sufficient proof that an individual was a Muslim, or whether a firm conviction of his sincerity was not equally necessary; or again, whether this should not be accompanied by practice of the rites. This was a very serious problem, for if the ruler were not a true Muslim, his subjects could refuse to obey him.

THE RULE OF THE SUFYANIDS[1]

For the Islamic empire, Mu'āwiya's accession to power marked the beginning of twenty years of internal peace, prosperity, and military conquests. Various factors contributed to the progress of Syria. First of these was a good administration, based on the well-tried Byzantine system, which Mu'āwiya was intelligent enough to retain and improve by availing himself of the services of able advisers. In financial matters, these were Christians. Another factor was the higher degree of civilization reached by the Arabs who had immigrated into the territory before the days of Islam, and were consequently orderly and accustomed to a centralized form of government. Furthermore, peaceful relations existed, despite the diversity of religion, between the native population

[1] The first three Umayyad caliphs are called Sufyanids, from the name of Abū Sufyān, the father of Mu'āwiya.

and the Arabs, who arrived with the conquest but were not kept segregated in camp-towns, the tolerance of the caliph himself furnishing an example and an incentive. Other contributory factors included the transfer of the capital to Damascus, and probably the revival of trade after the opening of the roads to the east, when the frontiers between the Byzantine and the Persian empires were eliminated.

Muʿāwiya also deserves credit for raising an army of Syrian soldiers which, owing to the good treatment its members received, and the training provided by frequent large-scale attacks on the Byzantines, achieved a high degree of efficiency, and gave valuable support to the dynasty on many occasions when danger threatened.

Muʿāwiya ensured the maintenance of order in ʿIrāq by appointing men of outstanding ability to be governors of Kūfa and Baṣra, for among his many gifts was that of knowing how to choose collaborators. For several years al-Mughīra b. Shuʿba was governor of Kūfa, a town which it had always been difficult to keep quiet, while Ziyād b. Abīhi governed Baṣra from 45/665, and, after the death of al-Mughīra, Kūfa as well. Appreciating the great ability of this young man, Muʿāwiya, instead of reproaching him for having served under ʿAlī, and for his stubborn resistance in Persia, induced him to come over to his side, and finally obtained his complete adherence by giving him satisfaction in a matter of personal pride. Ziyād was called 'ibn Abīhi', which means 'son of his father', because there was some doubt as to his paternity; disregarding any possible criticism Muʿāwiya declared him to be the son of Abū Sufyān, and therefore his own half-brother. In Baṣra there were several turbulent factions, not least among them being the Kharijites; in reality the town was in the hands of the mob. As soon as Ziyād arrived to take over office, he made a speech in the course of which, without beating about the bush, he announced his programme for restoring order: '...Many heads do I see tottering; let each man see to it that his own remains on his shoulders'. By giving a few examples of severity at the beginning of his period of office, he won the respect of the Basrans, and a hitherto unknown tranquillity reigned, not only in the city, but also in the Persian provinces, and even in the Arabian desert. It was Ziyād who, in order to keep a better hold on the warriors of Kūfa, divided them into four groups formed from different tribes, each with a leader chosen, not by them, but by the government, and, to avoid trouble, he also sent fifty thousand bedouin away to Khurāsān.

Although the eastern provinces had governors of their own, they were under the jurisdiction of the two 'Irāqī cities, part of whose duty it was to raise and direct the armies required for the conquest of other territories in Asia. Two bodies of troops were organized; one of them marched from Khurāsān to the valley of the Indus, and sent a flying column as far as Lahore (44/664); the other reached the north-east frontier of Khurāsān, which was then the Oxus, the modern Amu Darya; in this way they came into contact for the first time with the Turkish peoples living on the far side of the river, which for centuries had been the natural frontier of Persia.

To Egypt Mu'āwiya sent 'Amr b. al-'Āṣ, who had consented to take his side in the war against 'Alī on the express condition that this province should be assigned to him. 'Amr, however, died shortly afterwards (43/663) and was succeeded in Egypt by various governors. A region where few changes in the government were made was the Maghrib, as, except for a period of disgrace, the famous 'Uqba b. Nāfi' was active there from 43/662 to 55/675, and from 62/682 to his death.

Having established a military base at Qayrawān (50/670), 'Uqba conquered Ifrīqiya, and, as he was deeply religious, he did his utmost to convert it to Islam. After his return to that province, he led a daring raid as far as the Atlantic coast, and tradition records that he rode his horse into the waves of the ocean, calling God to witness that he had kept his oath to carry Islam to the extreme limits of the world. On his way back from this expedition he divided his troops into small detachments, keeping only a weak escort for his own person, and in 63/683 he was surrounded by rebellious natives and slain. Ever since prehistoric times North Africa had been inhabited by Hamitic peoples known collectively as Berbers, who had given much trouble to all invaders of their country, including the Romans. The ambush into which 'Uqba fell was organized by Kusayla, one of their chieftains and a kind of seventh-century Jugurtha. Ifrīqiya remained under his rule for some years, since the situation in the east had deteriorated, and the caliphs had other things on their minds.

Mu'āwiya had a powerful fleet, which had already given a good account of itself in raids on various islands (Cyprus in 28/648; Rhodes and Crete in 53/672–3) and in naval engagements, for instance defeating the Byzantines during the *Ghazwat al-Ṣawārī* (Expedition of the Mainmasts) off the coast of Lycia (34/655), and attacking Sicilian and African ports. In 52/672 Mu'āwiya thought the time had come to strike a great blow against Byzantium. He established a base on the peninsula of Cyzicus, where his forces could winter, and in 54/674 attacked Constantinople from the land side as well as from the sea; but it was defended by a double circle of walls, and Greek fire, used here perhaps for the first time, inflicted grave damage on his ships. After three years of fruitless attacks, the siege was raised in 57/677. We are told that the Muslims left 30,000 dead before the walls of the city in a last vain attempt to storm it, after which, 'with great shame and grief', as Theophanes says, the fleet sailed for home. A violent gale, and an attack by the Byzantine squadron, completed its discomfiture.

Although the enterprise against Constantinople ended disastrously, Muʿāwiya had a great success in the diplomatic action which he took to wipe out the last traces of the long preceding crisis in the Muslim community, and this must undoubtedly be attributed to his own personal skill. A typical feature in his character was *ḥilm,* an Arabic word denoting leniency towards opponents, and in his case the tolerance with which he forgot, or pretended to forget, the hostile acts of the ʿAlid faction, the smiling indifference with which he took even severe blows to his *amour propre* and disarmed his adversaries, and his intelligent generosity, the aim of which was to bind his enemies with golden chains. To one who criticized his lavishness, he remarked that war cost far more. He was also conspicuous for the cunning way in which he relegated his relatives to the background or avoided keeping them too long in office, his eloquence and the keenness of mind with which he fascinated his adversaries, his affable treatment of visitors which made him seem more like the *sayyid* of an Arab tribe than a sovereign, and the firmness with which he reduced the crushing burden of pensions, and insisted that the balance of provincial revenue should be remitted to the central government in fixed quotas. Of him it was said that, had he been shut up behind seven doors, he would have found a way to smash all seven locks.

Muʿāwiya died at the age of eighty in the year 60/April 680, and though the tombs of the other Umayyads were violated after the advent of the ʿAbbasids, his and that of one of his successors, the pious ʿUmar II were respected.

When Yazīd I assumed the reins of power, the opposition, which his father had kept in check, rose against him. The pro-ʿAlid faction in Kūfa plotted his overthrow, the Medinese or *Anṣār* (a term which now also included the descendants of the *Muhājirūn*) revolted; and around ʿAbd Allāh b. al-Zubayr, a claimant to the throne who lived in Mecca, all those Muslims rallied who considered it an affront to the sanctity of religion that a family should remain in power whose adherence to Islam had been the subject of so much criticism. At the same time the Kharijites reorganized their party, and prepared to enter the struggle. The outbreaks of trouble in various parts of the empire were not always due to the same cause, but they had certain factors in common—the dislike of a strong government which had reduced its subjects to disciplined obsequiousness, envy of Syria because it had become the centre of the empire, and the belief that things would go better if a rigidly theocratic form of government were to be restored. All these revolts were cloaked in religious motives, and so, for that matter, were the subsequent movements organized by the Kharijites, the scholars, the Zaydites, and lastly the ʿAlids and the ʿAbbasids, who joined forces in their efforts to overthrow the Umayyad régime. All of them asserted that it was the duty of Muslims to observe the precepts of the Book of God and the *Sunna* of His Prophet.

What happened was this. Immediately after his accession Yazīd ordered his governor in Medina to compel ʿAlī's son, al-Ḥusayn, Ibn al-Zubayr, and ʿAbd Allāh, a son of ʿUmar, who had been reluctant to recognize him as heir to the throne, to pay him homage. The first two persisted in their refusal and fled to Mecca, where they felt safer, and ʿAbd Allāh was the only one of the three who consented to follow the majority of Muslims. Some months later, al-Ḥusayn was persuaded by emissaries of the pro-ʿAlid party in Kūfa to put himself at the head of a revolt. He sent a cousin of his to prepare the ground, and, after receiving a favourable report, went to Kūfa with his harem and a small escort of relatives and supporters. In the meantime, the plot had been discovered, and the governor of that city, ʿUbayd Allāh, son of the famous Ziyād, got rid of al-Ḥusayn's cousin, and set detachments of cavalry to watch the moves of this son of ʿAlī and persuade him to desist from the enterprise. When al-Ḥusayn refused, ʿUbayd Allāh's forces stopped the advance of the rebels at Karbalā', and after a final summons attacked the little group of ʿAlids and their supporters. As these made a fanatical resistance, they went on to slay all the fighters, and eventually killed al-Ḥusayn, who had watched the battle from a distance (10 Muḥarram 61/10 October 680). In the eyes of the Sunnīs this killing of a grandson of the Prophet was not a very serious offence, for, since al-Ḥusayn had rebelled, he was deemed to be an outlaw; but for the Shīʿa, and for Islam in general, it had most serious consequences. In fact, it deepened the rift between the Shīʿa and other Muslims, and in the eyes of the former, al-Ḥusayn became a martyr who had spontaneously given his life for the people. In Shīʿī lands, the anniversary of the tragedy of Karbalāʾ is still commemorated by ceremonies, and, if they are not forbidden by the authorities, by the performance of sacred plays in which the episodes of the conflict are reproduced in symbolic form.

Yazīd later tried to placate the hostile Medinese, but although he bestowed largesse upon a deputation which went to his court from Medina, its members returned with horrifying stories about his conduct, saying that he had surrounded himself with evil companions, drank wine and owned hounds. Egged on by these informers, the Medinese broke into open revolt (63/682–3), which they symbolized by a curious ceremony. Assembling in the mosque, they threw down their turbans, mantles, and sandals, signifying in this way that they were deposing Yazīd. They then drove the Umayyads resident in Medina, and their supporters, out of the city and the caliph was obliged to send an army of Syrians to restore order. Since no one else was willing to undertake this thankless task, he entrusted it to a faithful henchman, Muslim b. ʿUqba, despite the fact that he was old and sick. A battle took place on the plain strewn with volcanic rocks known as al-Ḥarra; the Medinese were defeated, and the city was given over to pillage for three days.

The Syrian troops then marched on Mecca, and laid siege to this city under the command of another general, Muslim having died on the way. Without the least scruple they shot stones from catapults on to the sanctuary, and during the fighting the Kaʿba was destroyed by fire. Suddenly, however, news arrived that Yazīd was dead (63/683). The besiegers no longer knew for whom they were fighting, since it was doubtful whether Yazīd's son, still an adolescent, would be recognized as sovereign. Their general wanted to proclaim Ibn al-Zubayr caliph, on condition, however, that he should go to Syria, but this was not in accordance with Ibn al-Zubayr's plans, and he refused. Yazīd's son, Muʿāwiya II, was proclaimed caliph, but not unanimously. He died shortly afterwards, and chaos ensued.

THE SECOND CIVIL WAR AND THE ESTABLISHMENT OF MARWANID POWER

The eleven succeeding Umayyad caliphs are known as Marwanids, from the name of the first member of the family to ascend the throne, Marwān b. al-Ḥakam, whom we have already had occasion to mention as the

Caliph 'Uthmān's right-hand man. When Mu'āwiya II died, Marwān was the most prominent member of the family, but he was not elected unanimously, because many Muslims were averse to having yet another Umayyad on the throne.

The Arab tribes, who had emigrated in waves from their original homes, were scattered all over the conquered lands, and had often grouped themselves into confederacies and leagues. Two such groups, formed in Syria, had taken the names of tribes already living there, the Banū Qays and the Banū Kalb, and in the course of time had become two mutually hostile factions, either for economic and social reasons which are difficult to define, or else because of the age-long hatred between the tribes of northern and southern Arabia. The former of these two groups is known as the Qaysites, and the latter as the Kalbites, nowadays often called Yemenites. These two factions had been skilfully held at bay by Mu'āwiya I, but they came into conflict when a new caliph had to be chosen after the death of Mu'āwiya II, because the Kalbites wanted Marwān b. al-Ḥakam, whereas the Qaysites would have preferred Ibn al-Zubayr. They thus reverted to those tribal conflicts, which had been usual in Arabia in the pre-Islamic period, and which Islam had tried to eliminate. The battle between them lasted twenty days, with heavy losses on both sides. It took place at Marj Rāhiṭ near Damascus (end of 64/July 684), and the Kalbites were victorious. Marwān I therefore ascended the throne, but this did not put an end to the revolt of Ibn al-Zubayr, or to the antagonism between Qaysites and Kalbites, which in fact became even more acute. The blood that had been shed cried for vengeance, hatred became more deeply rooted, and the struggle continued both in Syria, where the various Umayyad caliphs sought the support of one or the other faction, and for centuries elsewhere, for example in Africa, Spain, and Sicily. The names given to the parties in the various territories frequently differ (we find mention of 'Adnanites fighting Qahtanites, Ma'addites or Mudarites at war with Yemenites, Tamīm with Azd, and so on), but generally speaking it was always a matter of Arabs from northern Arabia fighting against those from the Yemen and neighbouring districts.

Marwān reconquered Egypt, but he could not devote himself to the reorganization of the State, because he died in 65/685, a few months after the battle of Marj Rāhiṭ. The task of completing the reunification of the empire was left to his able son, 'Abd al-Malik, and this was no easy matter, for the situation was still chaotic. Ibn al-Zubayr, at all events nominally, was still master of Arabia and part of ʿIrāq; Kūfa had fallen into the hands of a clever adventurer named al-Mukhtār, who had begun his revolt as a Shīʿī. When he failed in his attempt to have ʿAlī's son, Ibn al-Ḥanafiyya (at that time the leading ʿAlid) made head of the movement, he continued it on his own account, spreading strange ideas which added to his prestige, and defending the rights of the oppressed, especially the newly converted, who complained bitterly of not being treated as well as the Muslims of long standing. As the possessor of Kūfa, al-Mukhtār was in a position to appoint governors of his own choice in Persia, Mesopotamia and Āzarbāyjān. ʿAbd al-Malik attacked him, but with little success, and he was eventually defeated and killed by Muṣʿab, brother of Ibn al-Zubayr and governor of Baṣra (67/687).

When al-Mukhtār had thus been disposed of, the two claimants to the caliphate, the Umayyad and the Zubayrid, found themselves face to face, since the latter had caused himself to be proclaimed caliph while the civil war in Syria was still raging. But before giving battle, each of them had to attend to restoring order in his own territory. Ibn al-Zubayr had to deal with the Kharijites, some of whom had occupied whole areas of Arabia (Baḥrayn, Yemen, Ḥaḍramawt) and were intercepting the caravans, while others, still more fanatical, controlled ʿIrāq, whither Ibn al-Zubayr dispatched one of his best generals, al-Muhallab. ʿAbd al-Malik had to reduce to obedience rebels of every species, and also to resist the Byzantines, who had become very enterprising. Nevertheless, passing from one success to another, he restored order in his domains, and concluded an armistice with the Byzantines in order to safeguard his rear. He then took the field against Ibn al-Zubayr. First he defeated Muṣʿab and then (72/691) he dispatched a Syrian army against Mecca under the command of a faithful adherent, al-Ḥajjāj. After a siege of several months (73/692), during which he bombarded the Kaʿba with catapults, disregarding its sanctity, al-Ḥajjāj stormed the city. Ibn al-Zubayr fell on the field of battle, and so there disappeared from the political scene this veteran of many battles, the champion of the old faith who had resisted three caliphs (or four, if we include his refusal to do homage to Yazīd when summoned by Muʿāwiya). Many of the sources describe him as a model of piety, but according to other reports he was of a mean, jealous, and spiteful disposition.

Having destroyed the Kharijites of Arabia after a campaign lasting about two years, and being now master of the whole peninsula, al-Ḥajjāj entered 'Irāq. He arrived in Kūfa unexpectedly at the head of only a few men. Entering the mosque and mounting to the pulpit, he tore away the veil concealing his face, and to the astonished crowd made a speech even more menacing than that of Ziyād:

I see heads ripe for cutting. People of 'Irāq, I shall not let myself be crushed like a soft fig... The Commander of the Faithful has drawn the arrows from his quiver and tested the wood, and has found that I am the hardest... And so, by Allah, I will strip you as men strip the bark from trees... I will beat you as straying camels are beaten...

From that moment al-Ḥajjāj became governor of 'Irāq and ruled the people with an iron hand. He re-established the authority of the government even in the eastern provinces, resisted and, after some trouble, finally crushed the revolt of one of his generals, Ibn al-Ash'ath, who had been sent to fight on the frontiers of Sijistān, but came back a rebel at the head of his whole army and the garrisons of many towns, and also had the support of the inhabitants of Baṣra and Kūfa. After this, al-Ḥajjāj established his abode in the citadel of Wāsiṭ, which he had built half-way between Baṣra and Kūfa for reasons of security. Here he stationed his faithful Syrian militia, under the pretext that they must not be allowed to disturb the life of the *amṣār*, and from that time on he may be said to have governed without serious opposition until his death in 95/714, towards the end of the caliphate of the son and successor of 'Abd al-Malik, al-Walīd, who had taken good care not to send any other governor in his place. Profiting by this peace imposed by force, al-Ḥajjāj contrived to heal the wounds caused by war, encouraged agriculture by reclaiming land and various other measures, and being himself a cultured man, did all he could to promote education. He also undertook new conquests. The strange thing is that, instead of stressing these merits, the old Arab sources speak at great length of his harshness, arrogance, cruelty, and impiousness. This last accusation was due not so much to his sacrilegious assault on Mecca as to the measures he took against the newly converted—a subject to which we shall return later.

The son and heir of 'Abd al-Malik, al-Walīd I, reaped the fruits of his father's labours. There was an intensified expansion of military power, the empire attained its maximum extent, and the Umayyad dynasty its climax. The caliph was able to gratify his passion for building, and by erecting the magnificent mosque named after the Umayyads in Damascus—how much more imposing it must have been before fire destroyed its decorations!—he left an imperishable monument to himself in the history of Islamic art. But to carry out all his plans—the erection of that great mosque in the capital, restorations and rebuildings, the construction of new mosques in the provinces—a passion for art and internal peace were not enough, for these things cost money. Al-Walīd had money, because the financial policy of his father had been prudent, and the revenue as a result of the new conquests was enormous, while Syria and Egypt prospered, thanks to the prevailing tranquillity. On the other hand, in the eastern provinces revenue was declining. To restore it to its former level was the task of al-Ḥajjāj, with his harsh methods that had only one aim—the welfare of the state and of the reigning dynasty.

Armies had been carefully trained and equipped by al-Ḥajjāj. One of these, under Qutayba b. Muslim set out for Transoxania and Farghānā (87–96/706–15) and may have got as far as Kashgar in Chinese Turkistan. Others, under Muḥammad b. al-Qāsim, transformed into a definite conquest the first incursions into the valley of the Indus (91–4/710–13).

While these expeditions were occupying Asiatic territory, others were organized in Egypt with a view to driving the Byzantines out of Ifrīqiya, as they had profited by the departure of the Arabs to re-establish their rule in most of that region. Under the command of Ḥassān b. al-Nu'mān they succeeded in occupying Carthage (79/698) and other towns on the coast, but they were forced to withdraw owing to a revolt of the Berbers under a woman called al-Kāhina, 'the Priestess' or 'the Prophetess', because it was said that she had received the gift of prophecy. Fortunately for the Muslims, al-Kāhina alienated her followers by deciding to lay waste the country, in order to make a return of the invaders more difficult. Despite this, the Muslims returned and reoccupied Carthage, slew al-Kāhina and after the year 86/705 extended their dominion as far as the Atlantic coast, this time under the command of Mūsā b. Nuṣayr, their governor in Ifrīqiya. After establishing themselves firmly in the western Maghrib, and incorporating into their ranks the Berbers, who were born fighters, they turned their eager gaze towards the Iberian peninsula.

The force of only 7,000 men which crossed the strait was commanded by a freedman of Mūsā b. Nuṣayr named Ṭāriq (whence the name of Gibraltar: Jabal Ṭāriq, the Mount of Ṭāriq). After landing and receiving reinforcements of a few more thousand men, Ṭāriq, in a battle near the

Janda lagoon, defeated the Visigothic King Roderick, who had hastened thither at the head of an army said to have consisted of 100,000—though by the time it came to the battle he had been deserted by many of his men, who were supporters of a pretender to the throne. This battle sealed the fate of the Visigothic régime in Spain. After a series of successes Ṭāriq reached the capital, Toledo, which he occupied without encountering resistance. Mūsā b. Nuṣayr then crossed the strait, in order, it is said, that his freedman should not have all the credit for this enterprise, and after successful attacks against a number of fortified cities he too reached Toledo, where he compelled Ṭāriq to hand over the fabulous treasures found in the royal palaces, or confiscated from churches. Mūsā b. Nuṣayr ordered coinage to be struck, engraved in Latin with the formula of the Muslim faith. The Visigothic kingdom collapsed like a pack of cards, and the road to the north lay open to the invaders.

Mūsā set out once more on the path of conquest, but when he had occupied Saragossa and was about to achieve fresh successes, the caliph ordered both him and Ṭāriq to return to Damascus. After completing the occupation of the Cantabrian massif and the neighbouring districts, Mūsā decided to comply with this order. The long march back was a slow one, because he was followed by a host of Arab chieftains, Berbers, and Visigothic nobles whom he had taken prisoner, and also because the column was encumbered with spoils. At Damascus, the Caliph al-Walīd received the victors with all due ceremony in the courtyard of the Umayyad mosque—an occasion which was long remembered. But Mūsā did not enjoy his triumph for long. He fell into disgrace during the reign of Sulaymān, al-Walīd's brother and successor, and was subjected to the most grievous humiliations. Ṭāriq, too, ended his life in obscurity in the east.

ISLAMIZATION OF THE CONQUERED PEOPLES AND THE PROBLEM OF THE *Mawālī*

The chroniclers and historians who wrote in Arabic are our best sources on the Muslim world, for those who wrote in other languages tell us very little. Although we are fairly well informed as to events concerning the Muslims in the two chief cities of ʻIrāq, we know far less about what happened in Syria, despite the fact that it was the seat of the empire. We know something about the situation in Khurāsān, which was important as a starting-point for military expeditions, and something too, thanks to the papyri, about the situation in Egypt, but very little about the remaining provinces. As to the condition of the native populations and their evolution, the sources provide us only with scanty information, or merely reflect the reactions of the conquerors to certain movements.

The Arabs who had emigrated to the provinces from their peninsula retained, at all events to begin with, their privileges as well as the burdens deriving from military service, which was incumbent on them alone. The natives continued to devote themselves to agriculture or to the exercise of their crafts and professions as builders, cultivators, physicians, and teachers, while they also obtained employment in the administrative offices, built ships for the conquerors, and offered their services as sailors. This was because the Arabs despised work in the fields, and scorned certain crafts, for example the weaving of textiles, or lacked the necessary training; because they were afraid of the sea, and in the government service could occupy only those posts which required no previous experience. From the fact that the conquerors needed the conquered in order to carry on many activities, we may infer that the latter, once they had a profession or trade in their hands, did not fare so badly. In addition to this, the non-Muslim communities enjoyed considerable autonomy, and, owing to their numbers and their social status, they must have represented a force which was not to be underrated. Mu'āwiya's tolerance towards Christians can also be explained as due to his awareness of their strength. To this must be added the kinship resulting from marriages between the conquerors and women of the vanquished races, which contributed to forge bonds of affection. Only the agricultural labourers must at times have felt that their lot was a hard one, and in fact they soon began to desert the fields and flock to the towns, obviously in the hope of earning more. This phenomenon of urbanization assumed such alarming proportions that in 'Irāq, al-Ḥajjāj had to take drastic steps, and, without listening to explanations, he sent the immigrants back to the fields whence they had come. If we ask ourselves why agricultural work did not provide sufficient rewards for the peasants in a fertile country like 'Irāq, we can only make guesses. Was land too heavily taxed? Could the big estate-owners, who employed slaves or labourers—who in any case were virtually slaves—to cultivate their own lands, sell their produce at prices so low that the small farmer obtained no profit by bringing his to market? Was the demand for labour in the towns so great as to constitute an irresistible inducement to migrate? In any case, the influx into the towns of masses of people who a few days before had been working on the land, and had no other skills, must have contributed to the formation of a turbulent proletariat, ready to answer the first summons to rise in revolt.

In short, we know so little that it is difficult to form an idea of how the natives lived under the Umayyad Caliphate. For example, a pall of silence descended upon most of Persia for several centuries after the Muslim conquest. The monuments of the Umayyad period and the objects spared by the ravages of time are our only means of discovering how the local craftsmen and artisans worked, following the traditional methods of building and decorating, though not to such an extent as during the Sasanid era.

About one thing, the increasing frequency of conversions, we know more, because it influenced the policy of caliphs and governors. The first conquerors did not trouble to convert the inhabitants of the countries they occupied, a proof of this being found in treaties whereby they allowed them to keep their religion, and authorized their leaders—bishops, rabbis, or, in Persia, *dihqāns* (who owned landed estates)—to administer the private affairs of their coreligionists, and to act as judges in litigation. They felt it to be their duty to strengthen Islam, but devoted their attention only to the religious education of the Arabs who poured into the conquered territories. Preachers and reciters of the Qur'ān followed in the wake of the advancing armies, judges were appointed in the camp-towns, so that in these the administration of the Holy Law might be exemplary. Nevertheless, despite the indifference of the government to the propagation of Islam, large numbers of non-Muslims embraced the faith of their conquerors. A truly surprising phenomenon was the light-hearted abandonment of the old beliefs in territories coming under Muslim rule. How can this be explained? One reason was certainly eagerness to come nearer to the new masters, and to share the advantages the latter enjoyed, not least among which was that of being far less heavily taxed. After such a lapse of time, it is difficult to estimate the part played by Muslims fired with missionary zeal; or by the ingenuous belief among the vanquished that the conquerors must have had divine aid in achieving their successes; and, in certain circles, by the idea that Islam was a syncretist faith which, thanks to its simplicity and tolerance, excluded all disputes—unlike their own religions in which too many schisms had developed, invariably followed by persecution and strife.

Once converted, the subject peoples naturally expected to receive the same treatment as the Muslims of long standing, but this right was granted them only in the early days, when their numbers were still small. If they fought like the others for the cause of Islam, why should they not be inscribed in the *dīwān* and be entitled to pensions? And above all, why should they not be treated like Muslims and pay only the tithe?

To explain the situation which was gradually evolving is a complicated matter. There had been a custom in Arabia since pre-Islamic times whereby an individual might attach himself to a tribe as a *jār* (literally, 'neighbour'). A non-Arab subject in the conquered territories would avail himself of this custom: he would become a client (Arabic, *mawlā*; pl. *mawālī*) of an Arab, and usually of a powerful person, thus obtaining his protection, and (through group-solidarity) that of his family and tribe. In this way a bond was established between protector and protected, by which on occasion the latter aided his protector, by going out to fight with him, and sharing his fate. Since conversion to Islam preceded the request for clientship, new converts were called *mawālī*. Islamic scholars use this term and speak of a '*mawālī* problem'. We will now examine this problem in so far as it concerns taxation.

After a conquest, there was no hesitation on one point, namely that non-Muslims would have to pay to the Muslim community, in return for protection (*dhimma,* hence the term *dhimmī* applied to the protected person), the taxes that they had paid to the preceding government. The fiscal system resulting from the application of this principle, however, differed from one conquered country to another, since in many cases special agreements were made between the invaders and the leaders of the conquered communities. This occurred in Syria and Palestine in particular. Elsewhere other decisions were reached; or else the new rulers were simply accustomed to retain the existing system, which, however, differed in the various countries, and concerning these differences we know very little.

A distinction between property-tax and poll-tax existed in Sasanid times; in the Byzantine world the position was more complex, but here too there was a personal tax, payable at all events by tenant-farmers and by non-Christians, as well as a general tax payable by all. Generally speaking, therefore, from the earliest days of Muslim rule there must have been a property-tax and a poll-tax, but to confuse the issue in the early period Arab writers while using *jizya* used *kharāj* indifferently for either form of taxation, and only later was a distinction drawn between the two; the latter being used to denote property-tax and the former for poll-tax. Under the Sasanids, the Persian aristocracy, consisting of the big landowners, was exempt from property-tax, and they soon realized the advantage of becoming Muslims in order to retain this privilege. But did they pay tithe? That we do not know.

In any case, conversions were not confined to the aristocracy, but became more and more frequent both in the territories of the former Persian empire and elsewhere. This gave rise to another problem: whether to exempt new converts from taxation, taking into account their change of status; and, if this were done, how to balance the budget, since revenue would thus be considerably reduced. The government, or rather the various local governments, took different measures in the various territories, all of which, however, had the same basic aim—to make new converts pay taxes. Sometimes they drew a distinction between property-tax and poll-tax, making the former an incident of land tenure, no matter whether the owner had changed his religion or not, and exempting the convert only from the latter. Sometimes they demanded that each individual should pay his taxes personally, and at other times they made the community or the local notables responsible for payment. All these things seemed to the *mawālī* to be mere trickery. Consequently they resorted to agitation and became a valuable asset for the opposition.

In pietist circles, in particular, they found people who agreed with them, because they did not wish to stop the flow of conversions. The Caliph ʿUmar II, who had grown up in pietistic surroundings at Medina, tried to find a remedy, as we shall see below. But after his death everything reverted to what it had been before, and the problem of the *mawālī* was a constant worry to the government, which in self-defence took refuge in Arabism, in the hope of obtaining the support of the Arabs.

The progress of islamization was accompanied by that of arabization; although the latter proceeded more slowly, was less extensive, and differed in character in each country. It was naturally easier in Syria and Palestine, where the population spoke a Semitic language akin to Arabic in its grammatical structure, and containing many similar words. On the other hand, in Egypt, Coptic, a language very different from Arabic, was overwhelmed only during the third century of the *Hijra* by the language of the conquerors, perhaps because Arab tribes had established themselves there a hundred years earlier. At Baṣra and Kūfa, founded as settlements for Arab warriors, there had been an influx of non-Arab merchants, artisans and slaves, which resulted in the formation of a kind of *lingua franca,* with a much simplified grammar and vocabulary. The same phenomenon occurred in other centres where there were Arab colonies, and also in the armed forces, for similar reasons. From the towns, this Arabic reduced to basic essentials spread to the countryside, and sufficed for the needs of the masses. But Baṣra, Kūfa and other towns quickly became centres of intellectual life, where students devoted themselves to the study of the newborn Islamic sciences, and these relied on the language of the Qur'ān. Consequently, the conquered peoples, notwithstanding their cultural superiority, failed to impose their languages on the conquerors, and Arabic became the means of culture even in countries like Persia, where the population continued to speak its own tongue. Ultimately, a grave blow was inflicted on Greek and Pahlavi by the decrees of 'Abd al-Malik and al-Walīd II, ordering that the registers of the administration should be kept in Arabic, and official correspondence conducted in that language. To keep their posts, the functionaries had to adapt themselves, and learn thoroughly the language of their conquerors.

THE LATER MARWANIDS

The long reigns of 'Abd al-Malik (65–86/685–705) and al-Walīd I (86–96/705–15) were followed by two short ones, those of Sulaymān (a little more than two and a half years) and 'Umar II (barely two and a half years), and then by a longer one (nearly four years) of Yazīd II, who lacked the necessary qualities of a ruler.

Sulaymān began his reign by persecuting the relatives and friends of the defunct al-Ḥajjāj (d. 95/714), for whom he and the new governor of 'Irāq, a son of the general al-Muhallab, named Yazīd, had a profound dislike. Among the victims of this persecution were the two great conquerors of Transoxania and Sind, Qutayba b. Muslim and Muḥammad b. al-Qāsim; the former indirectly, because, foreseeing his dismissal, he organized an unsuccessful rebellion; the latter directly, since he was thrown into prison, and executed soon afterwards. The outstanding event in the reign of Sulaymān, however, was the expedition against the Byzantines, of which we shall speak later.

Important for the Muslims of that time, as well as for modern historians of Islam, was the caliphate of 'Umar II. Even the way he came to the throne was unusual. The theologian Rajā persuaded Sulaymān as he lay on his deathbed to appoint 'Umar as his successor, instead of a nearer relative. It may well be that the opposition had become so vociferous that the caliph himself thought it better to grant this request. 'Umar was born in Medina, and had been brought up there by pietists, and whereas Sulaymān was addicted to gluttony and vice (in his presence the talk was only of good food and women), 'Umar was almost an ascetic, and his whole policy was dominated by a desire to remedy defects, and suppress abuses—or rather, to amend those measures of his predecessors which in the eyes of the pietists were defects and abuses. He therefore decided to encourage conversions instead of regarding them with distrust; and he introduced a fiscal reform, which, if it did not grant complete exemption from taxation to new converts, at least appeared to eliminate the disproportion between their liability and that of the Muslims of long standing. In order to expand his frontiers by peaceful means instead of by war, he offered his enemies (Soghdians and Berbers) exemption from the payment of the tribute provided they became Muslims. To the *mawālī* who fought in the Arab armies he gave pensions. He admitted that the *dhimmīs* had been badly treated and sought to improve their status, though he still forbade them to build new churches and synagogues and subjected them to humiliating discrimination, as, in fact, he had a right to do according to the principles of Islam. He showed his desire for justice and for the scrupulous observance of Islamic laws, replacing the governors then in office by men on whose rectitude and religious sentiments he could rely. He treated theologians and jurists with respect, and gave more independence to judges. To allay internal disorder, he forced himself to be impartial between the Qaysites and Kalbites, and he prohibited the cursing of 'Alī from the pulpit. Although his successors were to suppress his fiscal reforms as uneconomic, and other measures introduced by him were soon forgotten, his policy found general approval, while his reputation for integrity and his piety were never disputed. The disrepute into which the other Umayyads fell never affected his noble figure.

A serious rebellion, which can be considered as the aftermath of the persecution of followers of al-Ḥajjāj and as an episode in the struggle between Qaysites and Kalbites, marred the early years of the reign of Yazīd II. It was instigated by Yazīd b. al-Muhallab, who had had a large share in that persecution, and now feared the vengeance of the new caliph, who was a relative of al-Ḥajjāj. The rebellion was suppressed, Yazīd b. al-Muhallab was slain, and his whole family stricken; the adults either fell in battle or were executed; the women and children, in defiance of the principles of Islam, were enslaved and sold. Fortunately for them, a high functionary of the Umayyads courageously and magnanimously redeemed them.

Yazīd II tried to imitate his predecessor, but his character was very different. He loved sport and music; he allowed two young female singers to acquire great influence at his court; and he was so afflicted by the death of one of them, his beloved Ḥabāba, due to his involuntary fault, that he died a week later, or so at least we are told.

In the days of the Caliph Sulaymān, the Muslims launched another great attack against the Byzantine capital. An army, said to have numbered 80,000 men, and a fleet of 1,800 ships besieged Constantinople for a whole year under the command of Maslama, a son of ʿAbd al-Malik and half-brother of the reigning sovereign (99–100/August 717–August 718). Leo III the Isaurian defended the city vigorously, and Sulaymān himself, or his successor, ʿUmar II, perceiving that there was no hope of success, ordered the expedition to withdraw to its bases. This was the last full-scale attempt made by the Arabs to destroy the capital of an enemy, who, if occasion offered, was always a danger to the very core of their empire, and frustrated their maritime enterprises. Henceforth the wars between Muslims and Byzantines reverted to what they had previously been, that is to say they were marked by temporary successes of one or the other side; frontier fortresses changed hands according to which of the two adversaries was in a position to take the offensive, but after a time the line was re-established on positions generally determined by the nature of the terrain.

On the other frontiers in the east there was also, on the whole, a pause in the days of al-Walīd's successors, sometimes accompanied by withdrawals. Conversely, in Spain there was a period of consolidation, which, however, met with some opposition, while at the same time the Muslims advanced into France, established military bases there, and carried out a series of naval raids in the western Mediterranean. In this sector, although the governors were appointed by the central government, they enjoyed almost complete independence, and military operations were directed from the chief base at Qayrawān with the aid of Berbers recruited in North Africa. The Maghrib already tended to become a world cut off militarily and politically from the East.[1]

As we have already seen, the conquest of the Iberian peninsula had

[1] For further information on developments in the Maghrib, see Vol. 2, part VII.

been rapid but incomplete, and for many years a state of instability persisted. At Cavadonga, probably in 718, a gallant Asturian, Pelayo, had stopped the advance of the Muslims, for which reason the name of the town acquired glory in Spanish history and legend as the scene of the first Christian victory over the Muslims. Centres of resistance were formed here and there, one or two cities were recaptured by the Spaniards as the result of local risings and, except in the south, the general situation remained fluid. This general instability was aggravated by quarrels among the conquerors. The Berbers were incensed with their comrades-in-arms because they thought that they had not received the reward they deserved, and the Arabs were at loggerheads with one another because of a recrudescence of the old rivalry between Qaysites and Yemenites. Despite this the conquest of France was begun.

In 99/717 a first expedition had already crossed the Pyrenees under the command of the *Amīr* al-Ḥurr al-Thaqafī. One is tempted to ask whether some of the Muslim commanders had wild hopes of reaching Constantinople overland, and in view of the ignorance of geography prevalent at the time this is quite possible. In any case, the first aim of the invaders was the pillaging of churches and convents. In 101/719–20 Muslim forces under the *Amīr* al-Samḥ captured Narbonne, which they converted into a base for future operations. Shortly after this they were severely defeated near Toulouse (102/721) by Eudo, duke of Aquitaine, and this induced them to diverge in the direction of the Rhone valley. Here they carried out raids, without making any permanent gains, probably because the area presented too many natural obstacles. A few years later they crossed the Pyrenees again with a large army under the *Amīr* ʿAbd al-Raḥmān al-Ghāfiqī (114/732), who, after defeating Eudo between the Garonne and the Dordogne, pursued him almost as far as Tours, at that time the chief religious centre in France. Here, however, Fortune turned her back on him. Eudo summoned to his aid Charles Martel, who marched against the Muslims in time to save Tours and the treasures of its cathedral from pillage. Between Tours and Poitiers took place the famous battle which is known under the names of both towns. For seven days the troops of the Frankish prince and those of the *amīr* faced one another without giving battle. Then the *amīr* took the offensive, but his cavalry could do nothing against the Franks, who, shoulder to shoulder, formed a square at the crucial moment of the battle. When darkness fell the two armies disengaged, and great was the surprise of the Franks when they discovered at dawn on the following day that the Muslims had abandoned their camp and all their baggage. Poitiers was the furthest point reached by the Muslims in the course of their military forays in Europe, and that is why its name has remained so famous, despite the fact that the battle did not definitely decide the outcome of the war. In any case the Muslims would have been compelled to withdraw, for dissension between Berbers and Arabs had flared up again in their rear and there was thus no hope of receiving reinforcements. They therefore confined themselves to carrying out raids, usually with the assistance of Provençal nobles, until Charles Martel made up his mind to drive them out of Languedoc for good. A few years later, in 142/759, the Muslims evacuated Narbonne, their last citadel to the north of the Pyrenees.

In 105/724 Hishām, the fourth son of ʿAbd al-Malik, was elected caliph, and in the course of his twenty years' reign the empire recovered from the depression into which it had fallen. The north-western frontiers were consolidated, Muslim rule was re-established in territories which had been given up for lost—Transoxania, invaded by the Turks, and the Maghrib, where the Berbers had revolted. Although he was not a soldier, Hishām was careful to keep his armies up to strength; and to ensure a much needed improvement in the financial situation, he did not hesitate to adopt a harsh fiscal policy, which brought him the reputation of being a greedy man, out for profit. The governor of ʿIrāq and the eastern provinces, Khālid al-Qasrī, was a stout collaborator of Hishām for fifteen years until he fell into disgrace. After Ziyād and al-Ḥajjāj, Khālid can be considered the best of the Muslim viceroys; he administered the territories entrusted to his care extremely well, ensuring tranquillity and security and organizing grandiose schemes for the reclamation of land. But against him he had the Qaysites; rumour spread that he was an unbeliever, and he was accused of illicit speculations. On being brought to trial, Khālid behaved with dignity and courage. No sooner had he left his post than a Shīʿī revolt broke out, led by the Husaynid, Zayd, a great-grandson of ʿAlī, and the son of a slave-woman. The revolt was promptly suppressed, but the movement which took its name from Zayd was not extinguished. Zaydites took part in the anti-Umayyad campaign, organized rebellions, and finally, in the ninth century, created an independent state in the mountains to the south of the Caspian, while in the closing years of that century they conquered the Yemen. Zaydism has a theological doctrine of its own, and is the most moderate type of Shiʿism.

LITERATURE, CULTURE AND ART IN THE UMAYYAD PERIOD

During the Umayyad Caliphate poetry explored new paths. One school remained firmly attached to the old subject-matter and the now antiquated vocabulary of pre-Islamic times, for which reason it was contemptuously called 'camel poetry'; but another, while still remaining faithful to classical tradition, took care not to exaggerate the archaic forms, and found, in the changed circumstances, simpler means of expression. This latter trend was represented by the famous trio consisting of al-Akhtal—a Christian decidedly averse to accepting Islam, but nevertheless a panegyrist of the Umayyads—Farazdaq and Jarīr, these two being known chiefly for their ferocious satires. A third school freed itself from conventionalism by singing the praises of love and wine as independent themes, not, that is to say, incorporated in a traditional ode (*qaṣīda*), and used simple language in verses suitable for setting to music. Outstanding among the poets of this school was the bedouin, Jamīl, who sang the joys of chaste love in what are known as 'Udhrite poems, because the writers who produced verses of this kind belonged to the Banū 'Udhra. These poets were so romantic that it was said that 'when they love, they die'. Other representatives of this school were 'Umar b. Abī Rabī'a, malicious, sometimes licentious, but never coarse; and al-Walīd b. Yazīd, who specialized in the Bacchic genre with a levity and spontaneity heralding the 'new style' of the 'Abbasid era. During the Umayyad Caliphate, poetry, hitherto the preserve of the Arabs alone, was also practised by non-Arabs, who by now had mastered the language of their conquerors. It is noteworthy that Mecca and Medina, despite their sacred character and the presence in both of numerous pious men, became centres of music and song—arts which were frowned upon by the bigots. As a result there was much indulgence in wine and in the other pleasures of life in both these cities.

Prose continued its evolution in obedience to the needs of a higher standard of cultural life, to which the conquered peoples made a large contribution. A proof that it had now become a malleable means of expression is provided by the reform introduced by 'Abd al-Malik, substituting Arabic for Greek and Pahlavi as the official language. There are, however, other proofs. Among the sciences, perhaps the first to avail itself of the written language for the production of books, and not of mere notes, was historiography; about this time collections of traditions regarding certain events were made, and these, which are veritable monographs, have for the most part come down to us incorporated in the writings of 'Abbasid authors. Explanations of passages in the Qur'ān given by old exegetes were also put into writing, and were included in the commentaries (*tafsīr*) of later date. But although we may lack contemporary written proofs of the use of prose, we must give the scholars of the Umayyad period credit for having laid the foundations of the Islamic sciences in the wider sense of the term (including theology, jurisprudence and philology), and for making spoken Arabic a suitable vehicle for narrative, commentaries and discussions of cultural problems; in short, for having placed it on the first rung in its ascent to the status of a world language. For example, during the Umayyad Caliphate there was a school at Baṣra in which religious questions were discussed. One of its most famous teachers was Ḥasan al-Baṣrī, who died in 110/728. No written records of these discussions have been preserved, but the formulation of many problems which were later discussed in writing goes back to them.

It was during the Umayyad era that the great problem arose as to how a Muslim who violated the law of God was to be treated. Should he be deemed guilty of a grave sin, and therefore as an unbeliever (*kāfir*) suffer serious legal consequences, as the Kharijites demanded? Or should the task of judging him be left to God, and his formal profession of faith and adherence to the prescribed rites be considered acceptable? This was what the Murji'ites maintained, since they feared that undue severity would prejudice the unity and the very existence of the Muslim community. At the same time, as a result of the activities of two disciples of Ḥasan al-Baṣrī, there arose the Mu'tazilite movement, which advocated a compromise between these conflicting opinions concerning a Muslim guilty of grave offences; according to them he was hovering between faith and unbelief, and was therefore neither *kāfir* nor *muslim*, but *fāsiq* (i.e., impious), in a state, that is to say, from which he could redeem himself by repentance. To this theory, born of a desire to placate political disputes, Mu'tazilites added others of a more purely theological nature, and Mu'tazilism became an important doctrine during the 'Abbasid period.

Until the last years of Umayyad rule, there was no prose which deserves to be called literary. About that time Marwān II's secretary, 'Abd al-Ḥamīd (d. 132/750), a *mawlā* of Persian origin, wrote an epistle on the secretary's art, the form of which, with its abundance of synonyms, the balanced structure of its sentences and its clarity of expression, shows how the language had developed, and how, at all events in epistolography, it was tending towards artificiality. About the same time Ibn al-Muqaffa' (d. 142/759), a Zoroastrian who had embraced, though not sincerely, the Islamic faith, made an admirable translation from Pahlavi, adapted to the needs of the Islamic world, of a collection of fables originally written in Sanskrit and entitled, in the Arabic translation, *Kalīla wa-Dimna,* from the names of two jackals who play leading roles. Thanks to this work Ibn al-Muqaffa' is often called the creator of Arabic prose, an assertion which must naturally be taken with a grain of salt.

When Muḥammad built his house in Medina he provided it with a spacious courtyard, to be used for domestic purposes and for meetings of his followers. He planted two tree-trunks in the manner of columns close to one of the perimeter walls, to show worshippers the direction towards which they should turn their faces during prayer; and on one side he built a low shelter as a hospice for the poorest Emigrants.

After the foundation of Baṣra and Kūfa, among the reed huts of the soldiers, two rough buildings were erected in the middle of these camp-towns, one as a dwelling for the governor, and the other for use as a mosque. Both these edifices were naturally very primitive. The mosque was used for communal prayer, and for meetings of the populace at which the chieftains made speeches. In the early days, therefore, its function was not exclusively religious; for a long time it was used as a tribunal for the judges, as a hall in which teachers gave lessons, as a place where travellers could spend the night, or where anyone could transact his private business. The mosque at Kūfa consisted of a spacious square court and a prayer-hall; the latter supported, it would seem, by five rows of columns which had been brought from Ḥīra. It was unpaved and had neither minaret nor pulpit (*minbar*), not even a *miḥrāb.*[1] Was the design of the prayer-hall inspired by the shelter which Muḥammad built in his courtyard? This is quite possible, though there would also be a natural desire on the part of those present at meetings to be shaded from the scorching rays of the sun. By the time 'Uthmān became caliph, the design of the mosques in Mecca and Medina had already been modified, the shelters built of palm-trunks and branches being replaced by arcades supported by columns; but these mosques were still primitive.

Not until the days of 'Abd al-Malik and al-Walīd do we find caliphs with a passion for architecture, anxious to give dignity to mosques. To

[1] The *miḥrāb* is a niche indicating the *qibla,* or direction of prayer.

these two we owe the Dome of the Rock in Jerusalem and the Mosque of the Umayyads in Damascus, the latter so called because the successors of al-Walīd also contributed towards its construction and decoration. Both these edifices were of a type distinct from the previous mosques, and one which has become general in all countries having a hot climate, namely a spacious courtyard with the prayer-hall opening on to one side of it. One of the finest examples of this type is the mosque at Qayrawān, which, however, in its present form dates from the ʿAbbasid era. The Dome of the Rock is octagonal, the bare, irregular surface of the great rock sacred to the Jews in the centre, contrasting with the sumptuous decorations of the dome, and of the double arcade surrounding it. This arcade served for the ritual walks similar to those which pilgrims had to make round the Kaʿba, for ʿAbd al-Malik hoped to divert pilgrims from Mecca, then in the hands of Ibn al-Zubayr, to Jerusalem. The Mosque of the Umayyads in Damascus is a very different building. The site had been occupied through the centuries by pagan temples and then by the church of St John the Baptist. The architects employed by al-Walīd demolished the church, but preserved the perimeter wall with the four square towers at the corners, the propylaeum and three gates of the Roman temple, and built the mosque to fit in with these already existing elements. For this reason, and also because they had before their eyes buildings of the basilica type, they gave the mosque some of the same characteristics. Therefore a new type of mosque was designed, with the roof of the prayer-hall resting on colonnades, instead of on equidistant supports, and with an axial nave wider than the side-aisles and the *miḥrāb* at the far end. A fine example of this new style is al-Masjid al-Aqṣā in Jerusalem, built on the same terrace as the Dome of the Rock, a site sacred to Muslims because they believe that it was from this terrace that the Prophet ascended into Heaven after a miraculous nocturnal journey.

To the Umayyads we also owe the idea of another type of building. With few exceptions, they did not like living in the capital, which they visited only when, for example, solemn functions made their presence necessary. In the deserts of Transjordan and Syria they had old Roman forts converted into residences, or else they built entirely new hunting lodges. The desert probably attracted them because of their innate love of a free life in its boundless immensity, where the air was pure, and they could practise their beloved pastimes of hunting and riding. The plans of these buildings differed widely, ranging from simple constructions with a bath and a living-room for the guests encamped in the open, to large comfortable residences with apartments, a mosque, baths and gardens, to which water was brought from neighbouring *wādīs* by means of canals. The decorations also differed, some being almost without ornamentation, while others were elaborately adorned with sculptures, paintings and mosaics. Remarkable for its paintings, undoubtedly the work of Syrian or Byzantine artists, was Quṣayr 'Amr discovered by Musil in the heart of the desert, and today we are still amazed by Khirbat al-Mafjar near Jericho, the restoration of which is revealing its richness. Spacious and architecturally the most beautiful of all is the Mushattā, or 'winter camp', though we do not know for certain whether it was built during the Umayyad period or later, since the vogue for hunting lodges and residences in the desert continued under the 'Abbasids.

THE COLLAPSE OF THE UMAYYAD DYNASTY

After the death of Hishām in 125/743, the last phase of Umayyad rule was little more than a succession of rebellions due to the general discontent. The Kharijites revolted again at Mosul, and in the surrounding district. They arose *en masse,* and succeeded in occupying Kūfa, while other parties also entered the struggle. The financial crisis, for which Hishām had tried to find a remedy, may have become more serious, or else the unrest may have been caused by other reasons.[1] In any case, an ideology, as we should call it nowadays, was the underlying reason of all, or nearly all, the movements against the Umayyads, and its application was believed to be a panacea for all ills. This ideology proclaimed the necessity of returning to the right observance of the Qur'ān and the *Sunna* of the Prophet, as in primitive Islam. From this principle many opponents of the régime drew the consequence that all Muslims ought to enjoy the same rights, without any discrimination based on their origin, or the date of their conversion. As for non-Muslims, they ought to be treated justly.

The movement which succeeded in undermining the authority of the dynasty was that of the 'Alids and 'Abbasids, the latter being descendants of al-'Abbās, the Prophet's paternal uncle. It had a religious tinge, and accused the Umayyads of betraying the real Islam; at the same time it

[1] Yazīd III's speech when he was receiving homage in 126/744 throws an indirect light on the accusations made against the government of wasting funds on building and land-reclamation, demanding money from the provinces that should have been spent locally, and exacting such heavy taxes from non-Muslims that they were reduced to despair.

pressed for reforms, whereby privileges would be abolished, and the oppressed given satisfaction. It maintained, however, that only if power were entrusted to a relative of the Prophet could order and justice be restored.

The last of the Umayyads, Marwān II (127–32/744–50), had gained military experience during the campaign in the Caucasus, and his unusual energy had earned him the nickname of *al-Ḥimār* ('the Wild Ass'). He had almost succeeded in mastering the situation when a violent insurrection, which had been brewing for a long time, broke out in Khurāsān, and against this his efforts proved unsuccessful. At this point, however, before we conclude, we must open a parenthesis and go back a few years.

With the consent of the 'Abbasids, their confederates in the struggle, the 'Alids had some time before secretly chosen as heir-presumptive to the throne a Hasanid member of their family named Muḥammad, afterwards known as 'the Pure Soul' (*al-Nafs al-Zakiyya*). But at the very last moment it became known that in Khurāsān homage—the *bay'a*—had been rendered, not to the man they had chosen, but to an 'Abbasid, who, for reasons into which we need not enter, had taken the control of the insurrectionary movement in that region into his hands. The 'Alids had to make the best of a bad job. The credit for the sudden change in the fortunes of the 'Abbasids was due to a freedman named Abū Muslim, who at Merv hoisted the black flags of the revolution, considered in eschatological prophecies to be symbols of the coming of a messianic deliverer. A battle on the Great Zāb, an affluent of the Tigris, sealed the fate of the reigning dynasty (132/750). Marwān II fled, and was murdered a few months later in Egypt. By means of a ferocious massacre of Umayyads, the 'Abbasid, Abu'l-'Abbās eliminated all danger of a recovery.

The Umayyads, especially the last caliphs of the line, certainly made many mistakes. They had destroyed each other in their individual lust for power, instead of forming a solid block against their adversaries. They had stirred up tribal antagonisms among the Arab elements, alternately seeking the support of the Qaysite and Kalbite factions. They had persisted in the ill-omened policy of granting privileges to the Arabs, and it was perhaps a misfortune for the dynasty that one of its caliphs, Yazīd III, who promised reforms designed to satisfy, at least in part, the claims of the malcontents, should have remained on the throne for only five months. The fall of the Umayyads was not due, however, to their mistakes, or to the scandal caused by the private lives of some of their sovereigns. The ideology of a restoration of primitive Islam, with variants reflecting different trends, had conquered the masses, and, with the support of a majority of the learned men, became part of the programme of all, or nearly all, the leaders of parties. It triumphed when the 'Abbasids adopted it as their slogan.

CHAPTER 4

THE 'ABBASID CALIPHATE

The 'Abbasid dynasty, known to its supporters as the 'blessed dynasty', which imposed its authority on the Islamic empire in 132/750, claimed to inaugurate a new era of justice, piety and happiness. Its sovereigns, all members of Muḥammad's family, proclaimed that they alone had been designated to lead the community; all of them endeavoured to show, by means of the throne-names which they adopted, that they had the blessing of divine support. This second dynasty of Islam was thus characterized by a new moral trend, though in fact it pursued a policy which differed little from that of its predecessors. Indeed, throughout its period of domination, it suffered the consequences of the circumstances which had raised it to power; it was obliged to face the social disturbances, both economic and religious in origin, which the Umayyad caliphs had exhausted themselves in trying to suppress with their Syrian forces and it was confronted by the same difficulties as the last representatives of the fallen dynasty without having acquired any really new means of resolving them. The prestige of the new rulers was, however, to be buttressed by two tendencies, in some ways contradictory, which continued to become more pronounced over the years: on the one hand by the development of religious feeling, and on the other by the ever-increasing pomp and luxury of the caliphate.

Although linked with their predecessors by the very nature of the loosely constructed imperial state of which they had become the masters, the 'Abbasids had formerly, during that period of more or less violent disturbances which is usually referred to as the 'Abbasid revolution, been radically opposed to the Umayyads, whom they regarded as impious usurpers. They had even profited, though it is not yet easy to say how much, from the support of the Shī'ī movements, composed of implacable enemies of the Umayyads, which had not ceased to dazzle the eyes of their initiates with aspirations quite contrary to the principles of the government then in power.

The active propaganda of the 'Abbasids appears to have begun with the efforts of Muḥammad b. 'Alī, great-grandson of al-'Abbās, the uncle of the Prophet. Although his father, 'Alī b. 'Abd Allāh, had rallied to the side of the Umayyads from the time of 'Abd al-Malik, whom he had supported against Ibn al-Zubayr, Muḥammad, after becoming leader of the Hashimite clan which was settled at Ḥumayma, an oasis situated on the borders of Transjordan and Arabia, laid claim to the caliphate and took advantage, according to tradition, of the will which Abū Hāshim, son of Muḥammad b. al-Ḥanafiyya, had made in his favour. It was in the year 100/718, in the reign of 'Umar II, that he sent his first 'missionaries' into the Persian provinces where, it is said, the people were more inclined to support action in favour of the family of the Prophet and where, moreover, local popular discontent and the distance from the capital prevented the Umayyad government from forcibly exerting its influence. Until 126/743, the year of Muḥammad's death, his propaganda, under the direction of a non-Arab native of Sijistān named Bukayr b. Māhān, suffered a series of reverses: most of the missionaries were seized and put to death by the Umayyad governor. One of them, Khidāsh, who had adopted the very heterodox ideas of the Khurramiyya, combining an appeal for social reform with a belief in metempsychosis and in the successive incarnations of the holy spirit in the personality of various prophets, was even, after his execution in 118/736, disavowed publicly by the 'Abbasid claimant and it was consequently difficult for Bukayr to secure the adherence of his supporters in Khurāsān.

Under the *Imām* Ibrāhīm, however, who assumed the leadership of the party on the death of his father, Muḥammad, in 126/743, propaganda was intensified and the movement met with increasing success. The two principal exponents of the policy at that time were Abū Salama, the successor to Bukayr who had died in 127/744, and the celebrated Abū Muslim, a former slave of Persian origin, also recruited by Bukayr, who had already been in the service of the secret Kaysānī movement, working for the successors of Muḥammad b. al-Ḥanafiyya. Abū Salama acted as the link between the *imām*, who still resided at Ḥumayma, and his supporters in Khurāsān, who for their part were organized by Abū Muslim. Open revolt broke out in Khurāsān in 130/747; the black standards which were the emblems of the movement were unfurled and a military attack under the leadership of an Arab named Qaḥṭaba was launched against the Umayyads, who were denounced as enemies of the family of the Prophet.

This violent insurrection, instigated in the name of the Qur'ān and of the *Sunna* in favour of an *imām*, who, though not designated, must be the best representative of the Hashimites (comprising the descendants both of 'Alī and of al-'Abbās), promised to protect the weak against their oppressors, and succeeded in gaining the support of the majority of the opponents of the Umayyad régime. The armies of Qaḥṭaba, making use of a considerable secret organization already in existence, seized Merv at the outset and the whole of Khurāsān; thence they advanced as far as Rayy and on to Nihāvand, which laid open the way to 'Irāq. They once more defeated the Umayyad troops near Kūfa, in a battle in which Qaḥṭaba met his death, and entered Kūfa in Muḥarram 132/September 749. The sons of Qaḥṭaba thereupon handed the power to Abū Salama as representative (*wazīr*) of the family of the Prophet. He proclaimed the Hashimite imamate, without disclosing the name of the *imām* who was to succeed Ibrāhīm; the latter had in fact meanwhile been taken and executed on the orders of the Umayyad Caliph Marwān II.

Another 'Abbasid army, commanded by Abū 'Awn, then flung itself against the main body of the Umayyad forces in Upper Mesopotamia. With the help of reinforcements from Kūfa, it was victorious in the battle of the Great Zāb, in Jumādā II 132/February 750, over the troops mustered by Marwān, who fled into Syria, then into Egypt where he was eventually killed. The members of the Umayyad family were nearly all massacred in Syria, where they had been lured into an ambush by the orders of the new 'Abbasid caliph. The Umayyad governor of Wāsiṭ, Ibn Hubayra, who had surrendered on being promised a safeconduct, was nevertheless also executed. By these means the 'Abbasid movement endeavoured to eliminate all notable representatives of the attainted régime who might later have become a serious danger to the development of the future dynasty.

Although the armies had thus been successful in routing the Umayyad forces, the seizure of power by the new caliph at Kūfa was not so easy: according to a tradition which appears to be trustworthy, the *wazīr* Abū Salama would have liked to confer the caliphate on an 'Alid, a descendant of al-Ḥusayn or of al-Ḥasan, but none of the possible claimants made any response to his overtures. Meanwhile certain leaders of the movement succeeded in discovering the hiding-place at Kūfa of the 'Abbasid princes, among whom was the brother of Ibrāhīm, the future Abu'l-'Abbās al-Saffāḥ. The latter was then proclaimed caliph in the absence of his *wazīr* in Jumādā I 132/December 749, and he immediately delivered an address in the great mosque in which he described the outlines of the new régime and appeared to pardon Abū Salama for his earlier vacillations. Some weeks later, however, in Rajab 132/February 750, he nevertheless had him assassinated with the agreement of Abū Muslim, who lost no time in eliminating the agents formerly appointed by the *wazīr* in the eastern provinces.

This episode, combined with the dubious methods previously used in promoting the 'Abbasid propaganda, has not failed to arouse criticism of various kinds, and to create doubts regarding both the orthodoxy of the caliphate's new masters and their sincerity. Thus some historians are of the opinion that they were the authentic leaders of the Hāshimiyya Shī'ī movement within the wider movement of the Kaysāniyya, leaders who must in some degree have betrayed their former allies immediately after their accession to power, and then abandoned the doctrine of the party. Others, on the contrary, refuse to see in the former claims of the 'Abbasids the least trace of genuine heterodoxy, and perceive in them only the desire for vengeance on the part of members of the family who had been displaced by the Umayyad usurpers. Others finally consider that the 'Abbasid propaganda first developed 'in coexistence with the Kaysānī ideology without renouncing any of its own ultimate beliefs' (H. Laoust).[1]

This last view is seemingly the most in accordance with the facts, for the problem of heterodoxy must have arisen much more at the level of the followers than among the *imāms* themselves, who were only concerned, whatever their party, with the conquest of power. Moreover, it now appears that the Kaysānī party, made use of by the 'Abbasids, itself admitted various offshoots of the disputed doctrines, while preserving as its principal characteristic the custom of putting forward a representative of the *imām* rather than this personage himself. There was thus nothing to prevent the 'Abbasids from partially belonging to it and making use of its revolutionary methods, while turning to their own account the practice of establishing an adoptive link between the *imām* and his representative and thus benefiting from the attitude of groups, particularly in Persia, in which doctrines of a messianic character were circulated (symbolized by the adoption of the black standards),[2] without going so far as to give total acceptance to such doctrines. With regard to their most effective supporters, it was possible for them too, like the celebrated Abū Muslim, to have been impregnated in their youth with the same beliefs and yet to rally later without reserve to the purely

[1] H. Laoust, *Les schismes dans l'Islam*, 56–7 (Paris, 1965); see B. Lewis, *EI*², under 'ABBĀSIDS; Cl. Cahen, in *Revue Historique*, fasc. 468 (1963), 295–338.

[2] On the significance of the black standards, see E. Tyan, *Institutions du droit public musulman*, I, *Le califat*, 502–7, and B. Lewis, *EI*², under 'ABBĀSIDS.

political programme of the ʿAbbasids. In any case it remains clear that the new sovereign, by the terms of the address which he delivered in Kūfa at the time of his accession to the caliphate, offered himself as being the most suitable representative of the Hashimite family, thus in fact, though not necessarily in law, sweeping aside the claims of the descendants of ʿAlī.

Finally it should be added that the seizure of power by the ʿAbbasids has often been regarded as an actual revolution in the history of Islam, a revolution consisting notably of the victory of Iranianism over Semitic Arabism. This interpretation was more or less directly inspired by the theories, now discarded, of Gobineau, which may fittingly be reduced to more modest proportions. Certainly one of the characteristics of the ʿAbbasid movement, as previously of the Kaysānī movement which it succeeded, was the use of some client-converts (*mawālī*) of Persian origin in important positions, and this trend was continued under the first ʿAbbasid caliphs, who for preference chose Persians as their aides. But it must not be forgotten that numerous Arabs, mostly of Yemenite origin, also took part in the revolutionary movement, and even provided some of the leaders of the victorious armies, and that, in consequence, the Arab element always retained legal prerogatives which rendered the position of the *mawālī* very insecure. On the other hand, the tendency to allow the *mawālī* a higher status in society and at court had already been perceptibly initiated by the end of the Umayyad period. The ʿAbbasid revolution, if it is permissible to use such a term, consisted chiefly in the replacement of the Syrian *mawālī* in the entourage of the sovereign by ʿIrāqī and Persian *mawālī*. It was thus not only the Iranians who were successful, but also the ʿIrāqīs, and the arrival of these newcomers in administrative posts from which they had previously been excluded cannot be regarded as more than a qualified triumph for Iranianism.[1]

At all events it is likely that the numerical and economic superiority of these Persian-ʿIrāqī elements had a direct bearing on the transformation of the Islamic empire into an empire which was more Asian than Mediterranean, a transformation which became apparent at this period and coincided with the ascendancy of its new centre of gravity, ʿIrāq. Indeed, although the caliphs continued, chiefly for reasons of prestige, to make war on the Byzantines, they effectively ceased to extend their domination over the eastern basin of the Mediterranean and gave up henceforward all attempts at a direct attack on Constantinople.

[1] On this question see the arguments of B. Lewis, *EI*², under ʿABBĀSIDS.

The twofold claim of the new government to have liberated the oppressed eastern peoples and to have restored the authority of the family of the Prophet, which had previously been ousted, did not prevent it from being challenged, in its turn, with varying degrees of success, by renewed Shī'ī revolts, dynastic disturbances, secessionist attempts in the provinces, administrative and financial difficulties, and foreign wars.

The first two reigns, those of Abu'l-'Abbās, surnamed al-Saffāḥ (an ancient name which must originally have meant 'the generous one' but to which the meaning of 'bloody' was given after the victory), lasting from 132/750 to 136/754, and of his brother Abū Ja'far al-Manṣūr, 'he who receives victorious succour from God', which lasted longer, from 136/754 to 158/775, served to consolidate the régime and to determine its orientation. Al-Saffāḥ governed with the support of his brother, to whom fell the delicate responsibility of extracting the oath of allegiance from the powerful Abū Muslim; the latter had remained at Merv, where he acted as governor of Khurāsān, and Abū Ja'far had to make a special visit to him for the purpose of ensuring his obedience. It was also necessary for the sovereign to pay the greatest attention to the views of this same Abū Muslim, who took advantage of the 'treason' and subsequent elimination of Abū Salama to extend his own influence. Although al-Saffāḥ had begun by acquiring a *mawlā* secretary, Khālid b. Barmak, to whom he entrusted control of the administration, he also continued to rely upon members of his own family, particularly his uncles, for numerous confidential missions to the provinces.

The accession of al-Manṣūr was to precipitate a development which had already begun to take shape. The first acts of the caliph were designed to reinforce his personal authority, which had been somewhat impaired. Indeed, at the very outset he encountered the rivalry of his uncle 'Abd Allāh b. 'Alī who, whether rightly or wrongly is not known, claimed to have been appointed by al-Saffāḥ as his successor, and in order to defeat this rival he was obliged to have recourse to the services of Abū Muslim. In consequence Abū Muslim, whose relations with Abū Ja'far appear always to have been strained, became a dangerous person who was also suitable for elimination; this was in fact achieved shortly afterwards, when the caliph succeeded in luring the governor to his court without his escort (Sha'bān 137/February 755). The murder of Abū Muslim did not fail to cause some disturbances among the peoples of Khurāsān who were loyal to him, at times almost to the point of idolatry. A means was found, however, of calming these local storms and of curbing any fresh desires for independence by the execution of the new governor, 'Abd al-Jabbār, in 141/758.

In order to consolidate his authority, al-Manṣūr also deprived his uncles, the Banū 'Alī, of all their important offices, and ordered the execution of the most competent of their secretaries, the celebrated Ibn al-Muqaffa', who was also a bold thinker and whose Arabic adaptation of the tales of *Kalīla wa-Dimna* assured him an enduring literary fame. The members of the caliph's family in his immediate entourage, who were suspected of having designs on the supreme power, which was subject to no definite rules of succession, were gradually disposed of, and replaced by menials of obscure origin, often liberated slaves, such as the Persian secretary, Abū Ayyūb, and the chamberlain al-Rabī' b. Yūnus, not to mention such persons as Khālid b. Barmak, who was put in charge of important provinces, or Abū 'Ubayd Allāh Mu'āwiya, who became tutor to the sovereign's son.

Meanwhile al-Manṣūr was obliged, from the very beginning of his reign, to take action against the Shī'īs. It appears that no great importance need be attached to the demonstration of certain members of the caliph's guard, belonging to the sect known as the Rāwandiyya, who in 141/758 besieged the sovereign in his residence at Hāshimiyya and desired to regard him as a divine incarnation. The intervention of certain loyal leaders, such as Ma'n b. Zā'ida, was sufficient to disperse these over-zealous supporters, some of whom were put to death. The incident demonstrated nevertheless that feelings were then still at boiling-point and that some people were not satisfied with the religious and political orientation of the régime.

The revolt at the same period of two claimants, both Shī'ī descendants of al-Ḥasan b. 'Alī, was more serious. The first, Muḥammad, called *al-Nafs al-Zakiyya,* 'the Pure Soul', a great-grandson of al-Ḥasan, had not given his oath to al-Saffāḥ and had remained in hiding since the accession of the 'Abbasids. Al-Manṣūr, being unsuccessful in discovering his hiding-place and that of his brother Ibrāhīm, had their father, 'Abd Allāh, imprisoned, followed by all the descendants of al-Ḥasan living in Medina. Muḥammad was thus induced to come out in open rebellion at Medina and to denounce al-Manṣūr as a tyrant who did not respect Islamic law. Notwithstanding the support he received from certain religious scholars, he was unable to rally a sufficiently large number of adherents and was quickly crushed by the caliph's troops in Ramaḍān 145/December 762, when his brother Ibrāhīm had also just revolted in the region of Baṣra. For a time Ibrāhīm constituted a serious threat to the towns of 'Irāq, but he too was soon defeated by al-Manṣūr's general, his cousin 'Isā b. Mūsā. The suppression of these two 'Alid revolts, although securing several years of peace for the caliph, set him definitely among the enemies of the family of the Prophet.

The atmosphere of struggle and repressive police measures which surrounded the first years of the reign partly explains the decision taken by al-Manṣūr to choose a new residence for himself, and also the nature of his choice. He and his brother had indeed originally made their abode in the neighbourhood of Kūfa, and al-Manṣūr had actually built in this region a castle called Hāshimiyya, the site of which has not so far been identified, where he had met the onset of the Rāwandiyya. As a result of this attack he certainly had no intention of leaving 'Irāq, which was the centre of the new Asian empire, but he wished to move away from the already crowded cities abounding in seditious elements. He also wished to found a citadel which might be a symbol of power for the new dynasty, while at the same time providing him with a secure residence.

It appears that his attention was soon drawn to the site of Baghdād, which must have appealed to him on account of its climate, the ease with which it could be provisioned, and its strategic advantage. He accordingly founded a royal citadel there which bore the name of the City of Peace (*Madīnat al-Salām*), and remained famous above all for its circular shape. It was situated at the point where the Tigris and the Euphrates are closest to each other, and are linked by a series of canals which can serve as a natural defence against potential aggressors. The work of building, which was decided upon in Rabī' 141/July–August 758, was halted for a time during the twofold 'Alid revolt, but was resumed afterwards with increased vigour, and in 145/762 the caliph took up residence in his new palace, next to the great mosque and in the middle of an impressive open square. Around it rose the houses of his dignitaries, the guards' barracks and essential shops, while a double enclosure wall pierced by four monumental gates surrounded the entire compound.

It was not long before this fortified residence, which had been intended primarily as a dwelling for the caliph and his entourage, became the hub of an important city; after some years the merchants were ejected from the so-called 'Round City' and settled outside in a new quarter which continued to develop. The caliph's son in turn built a residence on the other bank of the Tigris, where he settled his own army; this residence was to become the centre of the future quarter of Ruṣāfa. The caliph himself also had a new palace built outside the Round City, on the bank of the river and opposite the bridge of boats, by which it could then be crossed.

No less important in one way than the foundation of Baghdād was the decision of al-Manṣūr to have his son Muḥammad, who took the surname al-Mahdī, 'the well-directed' (by God), recognized as the heir apparent. For this purpose it was necessary to obtain the resignation of his cousin, 'Isā b. Mūsā, whom al-Saffāḥ had designated as second heir after al-Manṣūr himself. So the caliph followed the lead already given by the Umayyads, who had endeavoured by means of the anticipatory oath to assure the continuance in power of their direct descendants. Thereby, moreover, within the Hashimite clan, the rights of the descendants of 'Alī, who were flatly opposed by al-Manṣūr, as is emphasized by the Shī'ī chroniclers, were once and for all subordinated to the rights of the posterity of al-'Abbās. Inside the 'Abbasid family, however, no principle governing the succession was laid down, so that there was the same unremitting contention for power as there had been in the Umayyad period.

At all events, by the end of al-Manṣūr's reign the régime had become firmly established and the unity of the empire safeguarded in all essential respects. Only in Spain had the central government been unable to prevent an Umayyad prince who had escaped from the massacre from founding an amirate over which Baghdād retained no control. It had also been unable to quell the revolts which had broken out at the end of the Umayyad period in the Berber Maghrib, which remained, apart from a narrow strip of Ifrīqiya, secure from expeditions arriving from the East.

Al-Manṣūr died in the course of a pilgrimage to Mecca, in Dhu'l-Ḥijja 158/October 775, leaving behind him the reputation of having been an energetic, but unscrupulous and untrustworthy ruler, sparing with public funds, and jealous of his own authority. Whatever judgment may be passed on his political outlook, it cannot be denied that his reign contributed substantially to the strengthening of the régime, and to the definition of a policy which, despite temporary vacillations and the subsequent ventures of al-Ma'mūn, was to be continued until the end of the third/ninth century.

The reign of al-Mahdī (158–69/775–85) to whom the oath of allegiance was administered actually at Mecca, through the offices of the chamberlain al-Rabīʿ, before the death of al-Manṣūr had become known—a fact which shows how precarious the authority of al-Manṣūr still was over the members of the Hashimite family—was dominated by two main problems; the problem of Shiʿism, which remained absorbing, and the new problem of the Iranian influence which was disseminated by the *mawālī* from the eastern provinces. Nor did the caliph lack other difficulties elsewhere. The war against the Byzantines was continued and the Muslim armies met with some success. A revolution broke out in Persia, under the leadership of a former secretary of Abū Muslim, known by the name of al-Muqannaʿ, 'the veiled one', who claimed to be the final incarnation of the holy spirit; and this rebellion, which was inspired by an extremist Shīʿī ideology, and was at the same time allied to movements voicing social demands, caused a disturbance which could not be subdued for a long time (159–63/776–80). However, the chief anxieties of al-Mahdī were over other matters.

He decided therefore at the outset of his reign to make his peace with the Shīʿīs, at least with those of them who did not profess extremist doctrines, while at the same time setting ʿAbbasid legitimism on a new foundation: the designation of al-ʿAbbās himself by the Prophet. For this purpose he granted a liberal amnesty to all the former supporters of the Hasanid rebels who had been imprisoned by al-Manṣūr and even went so far as to admit into his close entourage one of them, Yaʿqūb b. Dāwūd, who promised to help him to meet the ʿAlid leaders of the day. He then made Yaʿqūb his *wazīr*, after having declared him to be his 'brother in God', that is to say, having created between Yaʿqūb and himself a spiritual relationship of a sacred character analogous to that which formerly existed between the *imāms* and their missionaries. This step did not, however, have the expected results: Yaʿqūb, who was regarded as a traitor by his former allies, did not render the services to the sovereign which the latter had hoped for and was finally disgraced. Even more serious perhaps was the fact that al-Mahdī, in order to take Yaʿqūb as a counsellor, had been obliged to dispose of Abū ʿUbayd Allāh Muʿāwiya, whom his father had given him as tutor and who had subsequently become minister, perhaps with the title of *wazīr*. Al-Mahdī thus deprived himself, without any compensating gain, of the services of a man whose administrative ability and intelligence had greatly assisted him in his youth.

Although he had been conciliatory, to little effect, towards the moderate Shīʿīs, al-Mahdī was very much less so with that class of persons known as the *zindīqs,* from an Iranian word which appears, under the Sasanid empire, to have signified the Manichaeans who opposed the official religion. The question arose at this time of individuals who, it was alleged, after undergoing a superficial conversion had retained their former Manichaean convictions and were even working for this religion in order to destroy Islam. A great obscurity shrouds the nature of this movement, the *zandaqa,* which was in evidence at the beginning of the ʿAbbasid period. Certainly, among persons who incurred such suspicion, there were very few true Manichaeans, and the proceedings directed by the caliph, or by his representative specially appointed for the purpose, involved many of the *mawālī* whom it was desired, for various reasons, to eliminate. It is no less true that this *zandaqa* amounted to a genuine movement, denounced as such by the chroniclers, with the object, if not of destroying Islam, at least of curtailing the range of its influence, and of keeping alive Persian cultural traditions. The danger was thus a real one for Islam, which constituted an indivisible whole, and it was inevitable that the caliph should wish to combat it.

On the other hand, al-Mahdī is considered to have introduced into his court Iranian fashions and luxurious habits which were clearly borrowed from abroad. The caliph no longer led the austere life that al-Manṣūr had done in the midst of his intimate friends, but a gilded existence largely given over to entertainment. Meanwhile the government officers kept a closer control on the financial system, which they improved; while there is evidence that al-Khayzurān, the wife of the caliph, tried to intervene in the problem of the succession; it was the beginning of the influence exercised by women on political life within the ʿAbbasid court.

The brevity of the following reign, that of al-Hādī (169–70/785–6), is directly attributable to the rivalry which then existed between the two sons of al-Mahdī. Mūsā al-Hādī, the heir designate, whom his father during the last few months of his reign wanted to compel to give up his rights, was acknowledged as caliph, but he in his turn wanted his brother Hārūn to renounce his rights as the next heir, and did not hesitate to resort to force in order to achieve his object. The result of his behaviour was to arouse the antagonism of al-Khayzurān, the mother of Hārūn, who had the new caliph poisoned. Al-Hādī has remained famous in history chiefly for the massacre of the ʿAlid princes after an unsuccessful rising which took place near Mecca at Fakhkh (169/786). He had no other opportunity of displaying the feelings which inspired him, nor of taking action in respect of truly political questions.

It was consequently a heavy inheritance which Hārūn, called al-Rashīd, who reigned from 170/786 to 193/809, received at the age of twenty-three. The brutally repressive measures of al-Hādī had been far from resolving the Shī'ī problem; the Persian provinces remained on the point of revolt; the Maghrib was always unstable; and the Byzantines continued to threaten the northern frontiers of the empire, in which, though the economy was prosperous enough, opposing ideological tendencies were beginning to confront one another. Being indebted for the caliphate, and perhaps for his personal safety, to his secretary and tutor, Yaḥyā, son of Khālid b. Barmak, Hārūn entrusted him with the conduct of affairs. Thus began that period, renowned in history, of the Barmecide rule; the father and two of his sons appear to have governed the empire for seventeen years, until the day of their cruel and unexpected downfall, which caught the imagination both of their contemporaries and of the chroniclers, more interested in this tragedy than in the genuine problems of the period.

In fact the power of the Barmecides was not so great as has sometimes been imagined, and the relationship between the caliph and his ministers —to whom the title of *wazīr* has often been attributed, although only Yaḥyā bore it officially—were very soon clouded by disagreements arising over fundamental issues. Thus one of the sons of Yaḥyā, al-Faḍl, found himself twice disowned, the second time publicly, because of his attitude with regard to the 'Alid pretenders; Yaḥyā himself was suspected of favouring possible rebels. Such incidents amounted to more than occasional friction, and appear, on the contrary, to have resulted in prolonged conflicts, both political and religious in character.

It seems likely indeed that the Barmecides may have sought to improve the conditions of the peoples of their own native Iranian provinces, and may also have been in favour of an attempt at compromise which would have made it possible for the 'Abbasids and the 'Alids to be reconciled. Similarly they took an interest in the various philosophical movements which were flourishing at this period, and encouraged free discussion on a great variety of subjects, theological, philosophical and political. The caliph, on the other hand, was suspicious by nature and imbued with his own eminent superiority over his non-Arab ministers. Being in close touch with the devout men of his day, and himself well versed, it is said, in religious studies, he did not imagine that the régime which he embodied could be maintained otherwise than by the use of violence against possible rivals, and by adherence to traditional theological beliefs. Moreover, he regarded his role of sovereign more seriously than is sometimes stated, endeavouring by turns to lead the Pilgrimage to Mecca, on which he was accompanied by jurists, and military expeditions against the Byzantines, who in his time suffered several heavy defeats. It was during his reign that the frontier regions (*ʿawāṣim*) of Syria, henceforward detached from the normal provincial administration, were organized on autonomous lines, and that fortified posts (*ribāṭ*) were established at various points along the Mediterranean coast.

The differences of opinion which thus became apparent between the sovereign and his ministers (among whom the two sons of Yaḥyā had been entrusted with the education of the hereditary princes, the sons of the caliph, and so found themselves designated to be in control of the government one day) explain why al-Rashīd should finally have decided to dispense with these auxiliaries who, after fifteen years in power, had gathered around themselves a considerable body of dependants or devoted partisans. The one element which is still really obscure in their disgrace, which came upon them in Muḥarram 187/January 803, is the reason for the particularly cruel fate reserved for Jaʿfar, the second son of Yaḥyā. This person who, unlike his brother, had become the intimate friend of the caliph and his boon-companion, was in fact put mercilessly to death, while Yaḥyā and al-Faḍl were merely thrown into prison, where they later perished.

The powers conferred by al-Rashīd on the successor to the Barmecides, al-Faḍl b. al-Rabīʿ, son of the chamberlain of al-Manṣūr, were much less extensive. However, the advent of these famous ministers had brought to light both the extent and the weakness of the power of the caliph at that time. Since he was in effect unable to govern the state without the help of administrators who had been trained in problems of government, and who belonged inevitably to the class of the *mawālī* from which all the secretaries were recruited, the sovereign could only preserve his freedom of action at the cost of brutal reactions and emergency measures, which he was obliged to have carried out by loyal servants. Thus there appears to have been in the palace staff at this time a succession of freedmen of Turkish origin, whose principal merit must have been an unwavering loyalty and devotion to the person of the caliph.

With or without the support of the Barmecides, Hārūn al-Rashīd in the course of his reign took a certain number of measures which indicated its orientation. The 'Alids were persecuted. Yaḥyā b. 'Abd Allāh, a brother of Muḥammad *al-Nafs al-Zakiyya,* who had succeeded in leading a number of his supporters to Ṭabaristān and settling there, was ultimately obliged to accept the safeconduct offered him by the caliph; he was brought back to Baghdād, and shortly afterwards, in spite of the promise which had been made to him, was thrown into prison where he died. A little later the Husaynid, Mūsā al-Kāẓim, who had been accused by the caliph of plotting against the régime, was recalled from Medina where he lived, imprisoned in his turn, and put to death (183/799). The Shī'is were not spared, and the poet al-Sayyid al-Ḥimyarī, who was guilty of having insulted the Companions of the Prophet, was denied burial. The Mu'tazilites, whose doctrine appears to have been formed at this period, were not able to profess their principles publicly since they were opposed to the traditional beliefs. Even the Christians were harassed by the caliph, who wished to impose upon them, at least in Baghdād, the observance of certain ancient prohibitions which had fallen into disuse.

The results of al-Rashīd's policy towards the 'Alids remain difficult to assess. There are, on the other hand, good grounds for stating that the decisions which he took on Khurāsān, against the advice of Yaḥyā, were unfortunate: he allowed himself in fact to be deceived by the governor whom he had chosen himself, and who sent a succession of presents to the court while at the same time oppressing the people. In consequence there was a rising which was sufficiently serious for the caliph to feel obliged to set off in person at the head of his troops. It was in the course of this expedition that he was taken ill and died, in the Persian town of Ṭūs, where he was buried.

Khurāsān had not, however, been the only province to cause the caliph concern. Somewhat earlier, Syria had appeared so disturbed that al-Rashīd had been obliged to charge Ja'far with the task of restoring order in that country, where ancestral tribal feuds had broken out afresh and where an anti-'Abbasid movement was always liable to occur. In Egypt too it had been necessary to recall, not without some difficulty, a governor with leanings to independence.

Finally the distant Maghrib had become completely detached from the 'Abbasid empire. The Hasanid Idrīs, who had escaped the massacre of Fakhkh, had sought refuge in Africa and had founded, in 172/788, the Idrisid kingdom, the capital of which had been established near the site of the former Roman town of Volubilis. This little state existed side by side with the Rustamid kingdom set up in 144/761 round about Tahert, to the south of present-day Algiers. In Ifrīqiya there was no lack of problems either. As a result of various disturbances, the caliph had appointed the *amīr* Ibrāhīm b. al-Aghlab governor in 184/800 and he was shortly afterwards favoured with a privileged status, an innovation under the empire: the caliph, while reserving the right to confirm the appointment of governors and exacting the payment of tribute, granted him the privilege of handing down the power to his descendants. In this way a dynasty which was autonomous while remaining obedient to Baghdād was established within the boundaries of the empire.

The 'Abbasid caliph was nevertheless one of the most powerful princes reigning at this period. Although the precise object is not known of the two embassies which were sent to Hārūn al-Rashīd by the Emperor Charlemagne, and which appear to have had at least the result of obtaining the grant of certain privileges to the Latin clergy in Jerusalem,[1] relation existed between the two sovereigns, both of whom were hostile to the *amīrs* of Spain. These embassies provided the caliph with the opportunity of bestowing on the emperor of the Franks sumptuous presents of a kind unknown in the West. Indeed the economy of the Muslim countries was flourishing at the end of the second/eighth century, and the 'Abbasid ruler, in his grandiose palaces, led a singularly luxurious existence which was emulated by his courtiers. The riches accumulated around him at that time in the shape of jewels and precious stones appear to have been truly remarkable, if the descriptions of contemporary chroniclers are to be believed.

The unity and prosperity of the empire were soon to be jeopardized, however, by the sudden death of al-Rashīd, and by the decisions which he had taken several years earlier regarding the succession. The caliph had in fact been undecided which to choose of his two elder sons; one of whom, Muḥammad, was the son of an Arab wife of Hashimite origin named Zubayda, while the other, 'Abd Allāh, who apparently showed more aptitude for the task of government, was the son of a Persian concubine. In 175/792 he made Muḥammad, called al-Amīn, his successor and subsequently designated 'Abd Allāh, called al-Ma'mūn, as next heir in 183/799. The succession was not finally settled until 186/802, when he stated specifically that al-Ma'mūn was to retain the government of Khurāsān now conferred upon him, when his brother acceded to the

[1] See particularly S. Runciman, 'Charlemagne and Palestine', in *English Historical Review*, L (1935), 606 seq., and, more recently, G. Musca, *Carlo Magno ed Harun al-Rashid* (Bari, 1963).

throne. By two solemn acts, affixed to the walls of the Ka'ba in the course of a pilgrimage made by the caliph in this year, the two brothers were then pledged to respect the decisions of their father.

Matters came to a head when al-Rashīd, after leading the 'Irāqī army to Ṭūs, died there in Jumādā II 193/March 809. While al-Ma'mūn established himself at Merv, and took over the government of Khurāsān which he had hitherto exercised only nominally, al-Amīn was proclaimed caliph at Baghdād, and the *wazīr* al-Faḍl b. al-Rabī' ordered the army to return to Baghdād, an order which, according to al-Ma'mūn, was contrary to certain contingent arrangements made by the deceased caliph. The disagreement which arose from this initial incident only increased in the course of the succeeding months. The result was that al-Ma'mūn, supported by his Persian counsellor al-Faḍl b. Sahl, formerly a protégé of the Barmecides, resisted the demands of his brother, who wanted either to control his actions inside Khurāsān or to compel him to come to Baghdād, and who finally (early 195/late 810) declared that al-Ma'mūn had been deprived of his rights of succession, and conferred them on his own son.

This rivalry did not, however, remain for long confined to words. Shortly afterwards, under the influence of his *wazīr* al-Faḍl b. al-Rabī', al-Amīn sent troops to fight against his brother who, for his part, had just subdued the rebel Rāfi' b. al-Layth. In spite of its small numbers the army of al-Ma'mūn, under the command of Ṭāhir, achieved victory, by means of a bold manoeuvre, over the 'Irāqī forces in their first encounter (Jumādā II 195/March 811); emboldened, they then continued their advance and occupied the region of Jibāl, resisting fresh forces sent by the caliph and finally laying siege to Baghdād (Dhu'l-Ḥijja 196/August 812). This siege remained memorable as the most arduous which the city had to endure. The supporters of the caliph defended themselves inch by inch, supported by an improvized popular militia, which, although short of arms, fought fiercely against the besieging forces and showed a valour which exacted the admiration even of those chroniclers who were least favourable to al-Amīn. It appears that the population of Baghdād, apart from the rich merchants of Karkh who desired a speedy peace, particularly dreaded the victory of al-Ma'mūn. The city, which was badly damaged, was taken after a siege of more than a year; al-Amīn was captured and put to death by one of the generals, against the wishes, it is said, of al-Ma'mūn, who was then universally accepted as caliph (Muḥarram 198/September 813). A year earlier al-Amīn had been declared 'deprived' (*makhlūʿ*), the name by which the chroniclers were henceforth to refer to him, and by degrees the western provinces rallied to the side of al-Ma'mūn.

The civil war between al-Amīn and al-Ma'mūn, in the course of which troops from Khurāsān had set out, as they had done sixty years before, to perpetrate an attack on the caliph and the invasion of ʿIrāq, has sometimes been regarded by modern historians as an encounter between Iranianism, championed by al-Ma'mūn, and Arabism, represented by al-Amīn, the son of a Hashimite mother. It is true that al-Ma'mūn, son of the 'Persian woman', who was surrounded by newly converted Persians like al-Faḍl b. Sahl, had been obliged to take conciliatory measures in order to win over the peoples of the eastern provinces which constituted his domain. But persons of Arab origin were also included in his entourage and it was not until the final stages of the struggle that al-Amīn sought to appeal to the Arab sentiments of some of his leaders. If therefore it is necessary to look for deeper causes in this ostensibly dynastic quarrel, it is in the realm of religious ideas that they are most likely to be found. There is indeed no doubt that the entourage of al-Ma'mūn was imbued with those political and religious ideas which had been favoured by the Barmecides, and which shocked the representatives of traditional Islam. The desire to oppose such tendencies certainly played a considerable part in the attitude of al-Amīn and of his entourage.

Al-Amīn, a weak and frivolous personage, whom the Arab historians usually accuse of having neglected the government so as to pass his time in amusements, and of leaving the political initiative to bad counsellors, was therefore succeeded by al-Ma'mūn, who was to make his mark on the history of the ʿAbbasid régime, in spite of the setbacks which were to be encountered by his new religious policy (198–218/813–33).

Al-Ma'mūn, who appears to have had a strong personality and wide intellectual interests, took the line, as he had done in his earliest clashes with his brother, of being a reformer. Following the example of some Shīʿī claimants, or even of his ʿAbbasid ancestors, he stated that he wished to apply in their entirety the precepts of the Qur'ān and of the *Sunna* of the Prophet. After the breach with Baghdād he took the title of *imām*, which the caliphs had no longer borne officially since the successful ʿAbbasid revolution, and he identified his policy with a religious propaganda (*daʿwa*) for which his counsellor al-Faḍl b. Sahl was responsible.

Once master of the caliphate, he seemed henceforth to shrink from contact with Baghdād society and remained settled at Merv, entrusting the government of 'Irāq to one of his trusted men, al-Ḥasan b. Sahl, the brother of al-Faḍl, who was faced almost at once with a serious Shī'ī revolt, that of Abu'l-Sarāyā, who in Jumādā II 199/January 815 sent out a call to arms from Kūfa in support of the Hasanid Ibn Ṭabāṭabā. The revolt was difficult to suppress, and al-Ḥasan b. Sahl was obliged to call in the troops of the Khurāsānī general, Harthama, before Abu'l-Sarāyā could finally be vanquished and killed (Rabī' I 200/October 815). No doubt this fresh act of aggression by Shī'ī partisans made a deep impression on the caliph, and partly explains the decision which he took in Ramaḍān 201/March 817 to designate as heir an 'Alid prince of the Husaynid line, 'Alī al-Riḍā, whom he summoned immediately to Merv from Medina. In the act of appointment, al-Ma'mūn justified his choice by maintaining that the 'Alid was the most suitable person to fulfil the functions of caliph after himself, but no mention was made of rules governing the succession for the future. The 'Abbasids were thus not *a priori* excluded from power, but al-Ma'mūn seems to have been trying to put into effect a new system by which the descendants of 'Alī or of al-'Abbās might indiscriminately, by virtue of personal merit alone, be elevated to the caliphate. Such an interpretation finds confirmation in the writings of an author like al-Jāḥiẓ who, being impregnated with the Mu'tazilite ideas (professed also by al-Ma'mūn), regarded the imamate as depending entirely on personal merit, a doctrine which was to be taken up and completed a little later by Shī'ī theoreticians of Zaydite leanings. It may be thought that the existence of this doctrine induced al-Ma'mūn to take a decision which was at first sight surprising; it was supplemented by a policy of matrimonial alliances, the sovereign giving one of his daughters in marriage to 'Alī al-Riḍā, and promising another daughter to the latter's son, who was still a boy.

The attempt ultimately resulted in failure. The caliph no doubt succeeded in his immediate object of rallying to his cause several 'Alids and nearly all the Zaydite partisans, but he did not carry 'Irāqī public opinion, which he could not afford to ignore. The 'Irāqīs, who were loyally devoted to 'Abbasid legitimism, did not understand the new policy, and saw in it a manoeuvre of the *wazīr* al-Faḍl b. Sahl designed to establish Persian domination over the whole of the empire. They therefore had no hesitation in proclaiming a brother of al-Rashīd, Ibrāhīm b. al-Mahdī, caliph in Muḥarram 202/July 817, while in

Baghdād the popular militia roamed through the city demanding a return to the Qur'ān and the *Sunna*.

In ʿIrāq there were military engagements between Baghdād, Kūfa and Wāsiṭ, bringing the forces loyal to al-Ma'mūn to grips with the supporters of the anti-caliph, who were themselves much harassed by financial difficulties and problems of commissariat, but these events were at first concealed from al-Ma'mūn, from whom it was kept secret that his uncle had taken the title of caliph. When he eventually learned of it as the result of an indiscretion, he abruptly took the decision to return to Baghdād with his court. He set out half way through the year 202/beginning of 818 and the journey lasted for several months. Two events occurred in the course of it, the responsibility for which will always remain uncertain, and which induced, or at least facilitated, the abandonment by al-Ma'mūn of his original policy. Firstly there was the assassination at Sarakhs, in Shaʿbān 202/February 818, of the *wazīr* al-Faḍl b. Sahl by four *mamlūks* of the caliph's suite, who were seized and executed, but not before they had declared that they had been acting on the orders of their master. There followed at Ṭūs, in Ṣafar 203/September 818, the death of ʿAlī al-Riḍā, who was poisoned in mysterious circumstances. A year later, in Ṣafar 204/August 819, al-Ma'mūn made his entry into Baghdād, Ibrāhīm b. al-Mahdī having disappeared from the city several weeks earlier.

The return to Baghdād marked the end of what has often been called the pro-Shīʿa policy of al-Ma'mūn, and was in fact followed by the discarding of the colour green which had been substituted at Merv for the traditional black of the ʿAbbasids. Green was not, in any case, the emblem of the ʿAlids, who at this period sported white; it rather symbolized the era of reconciliation which the caliph had vainly wished to introduce.

Al-Ma'mūn, who towards the end of his reign was faced with numerous problems, governed with the help of counsellors on whom he did not deign to confer the title of *wazīr*. It was necessary for him to restore order in Egypt where, since the arrival of refugees from Cordova in 182/798, there had been continuous disturbances, and where an unduly severe system of taxation appeared to be conducive to a series of revolts. The last of these, among the Copts of the Delta, was the most difficult to suppress and was the cause of the most murderous expeditions. It was at this juncture that the caliph, then in Syria, thought it necessary to go to Egypt in person in order to clear up a situation which his lieutenants had been unable to control (Muḥarram 217/February 832). In addition he found himself involved in defending the frontiers of Islam against the Byzantines, from whom he succeeded in recapturing Heraclea; he was to be again in conflict with them when he was attacked by the illness from which he died.

In the eastern provinces his authority was on the whole more fully recognized, with the exception of the relatively limited territory remaining in the hands of Bābak, a rebel who, allied to the sect of the Khurramiyya, revolted in Āẕarbāyjān in 201/816, and from his mountain-retreats resisted all the expeditions sent against him by the central power. Al-Ma'mūn had appointed as governor of Khurāsān his former general Ṭāhir, who had defeated al-Amīn. According to tradition, Ṭāhir's leanings towards autonomy caused his abrupt end (207/822), perhaps as a result of precautions taken by the caliph or by his counsellor, but the government of the province remained in the hands of his descendants, some of whom were to assume the administration of Khurāsān, others the prefecture of the Baghdād police over several decades.

Al-Ma'mūn, who was thus in his turn occupied in preserving the unity and the peace of the empire, had not given up his attempts to reconcile the two hostile groups who divided the Islamic community. It was apparently in order to try to give the community a basic doctrine acceptable to all that he undertook to impose Mu'tazilism, while at the same time taking various measures designed to win the favour of the Shī'īs. Mu'tazilism, the concept of which had been developed in the time of al-Rashīd on five principles which enabled its members to regard themselves as an entity, manifested itself not only as a theological movement for the defence of Islam against foreign doctrines, but also as a faction which put forward an original solution of political problems by emphasizing the pre-eminence of the leader of the community, and the qualities which were to be expected from him. Its doctrine of the created Qur'ān also made it possible to restrict the part played by the religious teachers, who at that time regarded themselves as the sole interpreters of the sacred text. In 212/827 al-Ma'mūn officially declared his adherence to the dogma of the created Qur'ān; at the same time he proclaimed the superiority of 'Alī over the other Companions and contemplated various modifications of the law and ritual which were inspired by Shī'ī practices. Then in 218/833, when he himself was at Raqqa in Syria, engaged in despatching expeditions against the Byzantines, he decided to submit the jurists and the religious teachers to an actual inquisition, known in the Sunnī annals by the name of *miḥna,* 'ordeal'.

In spite of the efforts of the Baghdād police, whose task it was to examine the *qāḍīs* and the Traditionists, the caliph's policy met with stiff resistance. The majority of the persons interrogated ended by acquiescing, most frequently under the influence of threats, and paying lip-service to the doctrine set forth by the caliph in official letters, wherein he violently attacked the jurists who had been guilty of leading the people astray. Two of them, however, including the celebrated Ibn Ḥanbal, refused to comply in any way and were sent under escort to al-Ma'mūn. The death of the caliph at Tarsus, which occurred in the midst of these events (Rajab 218/August 833), made it possible for Ibn Ḥanbal to return to Baghdād.

On this occasion al-Ma'mūn appears to have underestimated the opposition of the religious teachers. He nevertheless charged his brother and heir, al-Mu'taṣim, with the prosecution of this policy, which seemed to him well-suited to satisfy the whole of the community, while allowing the caliph to strengthen his authority in matters of doctrine.[1] Al-Ma'mūn had indeed done all he could to encourage the development of the Mu'tazilite school and in particular he had founded, on the advice of a well-known Mu'tazilite, the famous House of Wisdom (*Bayt al-Ḥikma*), dedicated to the translation of those Greek philosophical works from which the Mu'tazilites derived their methods of reasoning and sometimes their inspiration, while at the same time he encouraged astronomical research by providing Baghdād and Damascus with important observatories.

After his death the Mu'tazilite policy was continued during the reign of al-Mu'taṣim (218–27/833–42) and also during the reign of al-Wāthiq (227–32/842–7). It was the great *qāḍī,* Aḥmad b. Abī Du'ād, who was made chiefly responsible for instituting the new dogma. Certainly Ibn Ḥanbal, who had continued to put up an obstinate resistance when submitted to severe interrogation, had been eventually set free and thereafter lived in retirement, but the *miḥna* appears to have been resumed even more violently under al-Wāthiq, which explains the attempt at a popular revolt made in Baghdād in the name of an eminent Traditionist, Aḥmad b. Naṣr al-Khuzā'ī. The rising failed; Ibn Naṣr

[1] On the policy of al-Ma'mūn see particularly D. Sourdel, in *Revue des Etudes Islamiques,* XXX (1962), 27–48; W. Montgomery Watt, 'The Political Attitudes of the Mu'tazila', in *Journal of the Royal Asiatic Society* (1963), 38–57; H. Laoust, *Les schismes dans l'Islam,* 98–111.

was arrested and interrogated by the caliph, before whom he refused categorically to confess the new articles of faith. He was condemned and executed, his head being exposed on the gibbet in the middle of the city as an example to others (Sha'bān 231/April 846).

Three other serious risings took place during al-Mu'taṣim's caliphate: those of the Zuṭṭ (gipsies) of Lower 'Irāq; of Bābak, whom al-Ma'mūn had not succeeded in crushing; and finally of Mazyār, a local chieftain of Ṭabaristān, against whom the caliph sent the Turkish general Afshīn, the conqueror of Bābak. This caliphate also witnessed the defeat of the Byzantines outside Amorium, which was conquered by the Muslim forces. Above all it was to remain famous in history for the introduction of Turks into the caliph's army, and for the foundation of a new capital at Sāmarrā.

The civil war between al-Amīn and al-Ma'mūn had demonstrated the need for the caliph to have at his disposal an armed force which was completely loyal to him and which was outside religious quarrels. For this reason al-Mu'taṣim, even during the lifetime of al-Ma'mūn, and especially when he was appointed to important governorships, formed his own guard of 4,000 Turks of servile origin. After becoming caliph he considerably increased the number of these slaves, who included, in addition to Turks bought in Transoxania, known for their skill as horsemen and archers, Slavs and even Berbers. Within a short time, it is said, the caliph's army had grown to nearly 70,000 slave mercenaries, and the Khurāsānīs of Persian or Arab origin, who had represented under the earlier 'Abbasids the core of the Muslim forces, were gradually eliminated. This transformation must have had grave consequences for the régime, for the slaves enrolled in the army were often emancipated in reward for their services, and promoted to high office in the palace of the caliph and even within the government itself.

The formation of these contingents of Turkish mercenaries was, according to the chroniclers, the direct cause of al-Mu'taṣim's departure from Baghdād. In fact the population of this city, where both Shī'ī and Hanbalite elements were violently opposed to the Mu'tazilite policy, had become very rebellious at this time, and incidents which occurred between local inhabitants and Turkish horsemen only served to bring matters to a head. Moreover, there was the well-known appetite of Muslim sovereigns for new residences to symbolize their power; al-Rashīd, for example, had abandoned Baghdād for several years in the middle of his reign in order to settle at Raqqa, a town founded by al-Manṣūr in Upper Mesopotamia, on the banks of the Euphrates.

Al-Mu'taṣim, after exploring the sites on the banks of the Tigris north of Baghdād, chose the locality of Sāmarrā, sixty miles from the old capital. He ordered the construction of a collection of buildings there which at first constituted essentially a royal residence designed to house the caliph, his family, his army, the dignitaries of the court and the ministries of the central administration. Its most important elements were the palace, the great mosque, the dwellings of important personages, the offices and the barracks. As a royal residence, Sāmarrā was not fortified like the Round City at Baghdād, and extended at length along the banks of the Tigris. The rapidity with which enormous plots of land were distributed and then built upon did not prevent the caliph from indulging his taste for vast and luxurious edifices in this new capital, the battered ruins of which still strike the imagination by their colossal size. The mercenaries were housed in separate quarters according to their units and places of origin and they were forbidden to mix with the local population or to take any other wives than the young Turkish girls bought by the caliph for that purpose.

With the accession of al-Mutawakkil (232–47/847–61), who succeeded his brother al-Wāthiq, the caliphate entered on a new phase, which is generally regarded as a period of decline. The authority of the caliph was indeed diminishing, despite real but short-lived efforts to reaffirm it, while the officers and bureaucrats, competing among themselves, interfered increasingly in the conduct of affairs.

Under the caliphate of al-Mutawakkil the Mu'tazilite policy was at once abandoned and no 'Abbasid caliph ever attempted to return to it subsequently. From the beginning of his reign, the new caliph put a stop to persecution, and he allowed the burial of Ibn Naṣr al-Khuzā'ī. He then prohibited belief in the created Qur'ān, and forbade all discussion of the traditional articles of faith, thus condemning that dogmatic theology (*kalām*) which had been advocated by the Mu'tazilites. By way of making the struggle against error more effective, the sovereign invited a certain number of religious teachers to refute from the pulpit the doctrines of the Mu'tazilites or of the partisans of free-will.

The reaction against Mu'tazilism was accompanied by measures against the Shī'īs: the mausoleum of al-Ḥusayn at Karbalā' was demolished and razed to the ground in 236/851; the tenth *imām*, 'Alī al-Hādī, was brought from Medina to Sāmarrā, where he was allocated a residence and lived until his death; finally the caliph did not hesitate to impose the penalty of death by flagellation on any person who might insult the Companions or the wives of the Prophet. Moreover, in 235/850 and 239/853 al-Mutawakkil issued decrees designed to ensure the strict application to Christians and Jews of the discriminatory status which was imposed on them by Muslim society but often disregarded. They were forbidden in particular to hold office under the administration, or to send their children to schools where they would learn Arabic, the object being to keep Christians and Jews strictly segregated from Muslims, while at the same time guaranteeing to them the liberties which they had enjoyed since the early days of Islam. In fact, so far as the Christians were concerned, it is said that the decrees of al-Mutawakkil were applied very unevenly, for although the Copt in charge of the Cairo Nilometer is known to have been dismissed at the end of the reign, it is also understood that the management of a canal in 'Irāq was in the same period entrusted to a Christian, and that the caliph kept in his household a Christian major-domo.

Although al-Mutawakkil adopted a religious policy at variance with that of his immediate predecessors, he nevertheless retained their taste for magnificent buildings. At Sāmarrā, after building close to the former caliphal palace a great mosque which was of immense size and remarkable for its minaret with a spiral ramp, he abandoned at the end of his reign the complex built by al-Mu'taṣim in order to found a new city further north, called, from his personal name, Ja'fariyya. It contained a new caliphal palace, a great mosque, dwellings and barracks. He also built for his sons, luxurious palaces some of which were situated to the south of the former complex. An enormous city nearly twenty miles long thus resulted from his activities as a builder, which accounted for the considerable expenditure recorded by the chroniclers.

In these palaces banquets were given which came to be remembered as displays of incomparable luxury. The most famous of them was organized to celebrate the circumcision of the young prince al-Mu'tazz. Even the solemn audiences, which, in accordance with ancient custom, were regularly given, also followed an increasingly complicated ceremonial, which was designed to emphasize still further the majesty of the ruler. It was at this period that rules appear to have been fixed for strict observance by the court; among them was the requirement of court dress, consisting of a short tunic in black.

Al-Mutawakkil, who took his dignity as a ruler very seriously, also governed in a very authoritarian fashion. He was one of the few 'Abbasid caliphs who for several years refrained from making use of the services of a *wazīr,* and attended personally to affairs. There were in his entourage, however, side by side with the Turkish chiefs who occupied the post of chamberlain, influential favourites or secretaries, also of Turkish origin, such as the famous al-Fatḥ b. Khāqān and also the skilful administrator who effected the restoration of the office of *wazīr,* 'Ubayd Allāh b. Yaḥyā b. Khāqān by name.

The position occupied by the Turkish chiefs at the court, together with the rivalries which divided the sons of the caliph, accounts for the tragic death of a ruler who was one of the strongest personalities of the 'Abbasid dynasty. In Shawwāl 247/December 861 he was assassinated by Turkish officers who had championed the cause of one of his sons, who was about to be deprived of his rights to the succession. The assassination marked the beginning of a period of anarchy, in the course of which the caliphs were made or unmade by Turkish *amīrs*; of the four princes who succeeded him, three were likewise assassinated by Turkish guards, as a result of struggles for power combined with the effects of political and religious divergencies. Al-Muntaṣir, the immediate successor to al-Mutawakkil, was induced to repeal the anti-Shī'ī measures of his father, while the third in succession, the other son, al-Mu'tazz, chose to adopt a policy of inflexibility very similar to his own. This disturbed period, which lasted for nearly ten years, was marked by exactions of all kinds, chiefly imposed by the *amīrs* on the secretaries, from whom they wished to extort money. It also witnessed another siege of Baghdād, sustained by the Caliph al-Musta'īn who had been dethroned at Sāmarrā by officers supporting al-Mu'tazz. This siege, which continued for nearly a year (251/865–6) gave the besieged an opportunity of fortifying the city, especially the eastern sector, where a wall was built surrounding the most important districts. Meanwhile the complicity of a governor made it possible for a Zaydite Shī'ī amirate to be created in Ṭabaristān; its leader was soon compelled to take flight, but in 261/875 he finally succeeded in founding an independent Shī'ī state.

The last of the caliphs to reside at Sāmarrā was al-Mu'tamid, another son of al-Mutawakkil, who, after being proclaimed caliph in 256/870, returned to settle in Baghdād in 278/892, in an attempt to shake off the yoke of his brother and regent al-Muwaffaq some months before his death. His reign had been dominated by the power of this brother and colleague, who, in his capacity as governor of the eastern provinces, had strengthened the defences of the régime against its various adversaries and attempted, for the benefit of his own descendants, to restore the authority of the caliph, since al-Muʿtamid himself was incapable of commanding respect. Serious insurrection had broken out in Lower ʿIrāq, which for fourteen years was a source of danger to the caliphate; it resulted from peculiar social difficulties which had not hitherto aroused any concern. In this region rich landowners possessed large domains given over to the cultivation of sugar-cane, on which the labour for tilling the soil was provided by large numbers of Zanj—black slaves, natives of east Africa, who existed in wretched conditions. In 254/868 a man named ʿAlī who claimed to be of ʿAlid origin set himself at the head of a rebellion, which was the more difficult to suppress because in that part of the country all military activity was obstructed by canals. The Zanj were thus able to make raids on Khūzistān, massacring and laying waste as they went, to intercept trade between Baghdād and Baṣra, even to pillage Baṣra and to threaten Wāsiṭ. It was necessary for the caliph to take drastic steps to destroy the capital of the Zanj, a fortress called Manīʿa constructed to the south of Baṣra (269/883). The triumph over the Zanj was celebrated as a great victory and the regent received or assumed on this occasion the honorific of *al-Nāṣir li-dīn Allāh,* 'he who upholds the religion of God', while his right-hand man, the secretary Sāʿid b. Makhlad, received the title of *Dhu'l-wizāratayn,* 'the holder of two wazirates'.

At the same time, however, separatist movements were occurring in the Persian provinces of Khurāsān, Transoxania and Sijistān, that of the Saffarids in Sijistān being the most troublesome to the central government. In 247/861 a former craftsman, the coppersmith Yaʿqūb al-Ṣaffār, leader of one of the groups for urban self-defence which were endeavouring to maintain order in the face of local risings fomented by the Kharijites, succeeded in imposing his authority on the small province of Sijistān, which at that time formed part of the domain of the Tahirids. Emboldened by the weakness of these governors, who were then chiefly preoccupied with intrigues at court, he enlarged his territory and succeeded in gaining recognition by the caliph as governor of Fārs. His claims nevertheless brought him into conflict with the caliphal forces, and al-Muwaffaq, who was engaged in the war against the Zanj, achieved some successes against him. Yaʿqūb then extended his domination over Khurāsān, seizing Nīshāpūr and destroying the Tahirid power in 259/873, so that by 262/876 the government of the whole of the eastern provinces had been acquired by this ambitious person, who attempted to storm Baghdād in order to gain official recognition. Further intervention by al-Muwaffaq's army was necessary to force him to withdraw. Ya'qūb died shortly afterwards in 265/879, but his brothers succeeded him and the dynasty was to last for a further thirty years.

This same period also witnessed an attempt at autonomy in the province of Egypt, which from the time of the Caliph al-Mu'tazz had been governed in practice by Aḥmad b. Ṭūlūn, the son of a Turkish slave in the caliphal guard at Sāmarrā and the lieutenant of the nominal governor, who remained at court. Ibn Ṭūlūn, having in 258/871 secured the recall of the financial administrator representing the central power, himself assumed control of expenditure. While recognizing the authority of the caliph, he succeeded by means of the financial independence which he had obtained, in raising an army of servile mercenaries similar to that of the caliphs. At the same time he had undertaken the construction near Fusṭāṭ of a new residence designed to rival the edifices of Sāmarrā, and called Qaṭā'i' from the Arabic term for the assignment of land allowed to army officers. He behaved, moreover, from 268/882 onwards, as an independent governor, having his name inscribed on the coinage, below or by the side of the names of the caliph and his son. At this time he also intervened in the dissensions of the central power by taking the side of the Caliph al-Mu'tamid, and resisting the regent, who had attempted during the war against the Zanj to obtain a special contribution from him in money and in men and had then tried to remove him from office. Considering that the regent had overstepped his rights, Ibn Ṭūlūn invaded Syria where he had already had for some years a right of inspection, being responsible for securing the defences of the frontier-regions. He attempted to deprive al-Muwaffaq of his privileges and encouraged the Caliph al-Mu'tamid in a plan for escape (269/883). The failure of this venture did not discourage Ibn Ṭūlūn, who somewhat later urged that a group of religious teachers assembled at Damascus should announce that al-Mu'tamid, who was held a prisoner by his brother, no longer had any freedom of action, and that al-Muwaffaq ought to be deprived of his succession rights. In this project he again met with failure and died shortly afterwards, but in 273/886 his son, Khumārawayh, after several military engagements with the caliph's forces, succeeded in gaining recognition as governor of Egypt and of Syria for thirty years, on condition that the name of al-Muwaffaq was mentioned in the *khuṭba*. The conflict begun by Ibn Ṭūlūn was concluded with this agreement, which was imposed on the caliphate against its will, as the events of succeeding years were to show.

In 'Irāq, as in Persia, Egypt and Syria, the general situation was therefore showing definite signs of improvement in 278/892, on the eve of the death of al-Muwaffaq, although the revenues were at their lowest ebb and the same political and religious problems continued to recur. No doubt the position of the Shī'is was considerably affected by the death (in 260/873-74) of the eleventh *Imām*, and the disappearance shortly afterwards of the twelfth. These occurred at Sāmarrā, where they had been residing under supervision. Since the line was now at an end, their supporters, the Twelver Shī'is, were obliged to resort to the theory of 'occultation' (*ghayba*), by virtue of which the last *imām* would return one day as *mahdī* to establish the reign of justice. This new state of affairs, which henceforward prevented the Twelver or Imāmī Shī'is from seizing power by force, but allowed them to play an active part in a society in which many of them were influential administrators and bankers, had nevertheless failed to turn them into loyal servants of the caliphate. From the time when they first appeared on the governmental scene at the end of the reign of al-Mu'tamid, to defend him against the claims of his regent-brother, these ambitious and unscrupulous financiers had sought only to enrich themselves at the expense of the régime, into which they introduced a new element of disorder.

To assist him in the work of government, the regent al-Muwaffaq had similarly made particular use of the services of a secretary, Sā'id b. Makhlad, who was a convert of Christian origin, and he too plotted, so that his former co-religionists might acquire an improved legal status. Although this Islamo-Christian policy of the Nestorian scribes ultimately failed, and Sā'id paid for his intervention by disgrace, the secretaries concerned, many of whom had been recruited by the Turkish *amīrs* who valued their competence and their devotion, continued nevertheless to aspire to the highest administrative functions apart from that of *wazīr*.

In these circumstances the task which devolved on al-Mu'taḍid, the son of al-Muwaffaq, whose designation as heir had been secured by his father before the death of al-Mu'tamid, was particularly difficult. The treasury was once again empty and the authority of the caliphate was not firmly established over the provinces. The new caliph, who reigned from 279/892 to 289/902, made an effort to restore the financial situation and to pacify the religious conflicts by measures of appeasement. In order to obtain advances of money, and, first, to pay the salaries of the various government and court functionaries, he appealed to a member of the corps of Shīʿī secretaries, a certain Aḥmad b. al-Furāt, whom he rescued from the prison into which he had been thrown at the end of the previous reign; this was the only man who, thanks to his relations with various governors, was in a position to obtain the necessary funds. With the help also of a competent *wazīr,* ʿUbayd Allāh b. Sulaymān, and of a remarkable chief of staff, his freedman Badr, al-Muʿtaḍid suppressed the attempts at insurrection which had broken out in Persia, where a certain Rāfiʿ was championing the cause of the ʿAlids of Ṭabaristān. He was successful in recovering control over the lands in Fārs where the descendants of Abū Dulaf had, since the beginning of the century, formed a small independent principality. He was also able, through the reconquest of Āmid (286/899), to parry the attacks of the Byzantines, who were trying to take advantage of the difficulties of the caliphate in order to infiltrate into Islamic territory.

Above all, however, he applied himself to improving the internal situation. First he took a definite stand on the side of traditional beliefs, and prohibited from the outset of his reign the spread of works dealing with dogmatic theology, while at the same time abolishing the office for property in escheat, regarded by the Hanbalites as illegal. He managed, however, not to offend the ʿAlid pretenders, and sought to remain on good terms with the leaders of the Zaydite state of Ṭabaristān. For this purpose he even considered having the memory of Muʿāwiya officially cursed, a gesture which would certainly have gratified the Shīʿīs, and he only refrained from doing so at the last moment, on the advice of his close assistants, for fear of the disturbances which such a declaration might provoke. The fact remains that at the end of his reign the second Zaydite state, that of the Yemen, was founded in 288/901.

There became apparent at the same period the first signs of the Carmathian movement, which was to be a source of danger to the régime for many years. This movement appears at first to have been associated with the Ismāʿīlī movement, and to have represented an aspect of it which Sunnī Muslim authors call *al-daʿwa al-bāṭiniyya* (the esoteric propaganda), but its origins remain obscure. It apparently owed its name to the founder of the sect, Ḥamdān Qarmaṭ, some of whose successors settled in Syria, while others attempted to stir up revolts in ʿIrāq and in Arabia, particularly in Baḥrayn. Thus in 287/900 a rising occurred in the neighbourhood of Baṣra, and in the following year the

Carmathians spread into the region of Kūfa, inflicting reverses on the forces of the central government.

In the following reign, that of al-Muktafī (289–95/902–8), Carmathian bands became still more menacing in both Arabia and Syria. It is not known exactly by what ties they were linked, and it is possible that from then onwards the rebels operating in Syria enjoyed complete independence and no longer maintained any connexion with the future founders of the Fatimid state nor with their rivals of Baḥrayn, where a small state was actually organized on a communal basis. Their attempts at sedition were in any case vigorously suppressed, and after a state of insurrection had prevailed in Syria between 288/901 and 290/903, followed by the occupation of several important cities including Damascus, order was restored by the caliph's forces. The Carmathian leader, the *ṣāḥib al-khāl,* after being seized and made a prisoner, was tortured in Baghdād as a public spectacle. Carmathian action in consequence recurred only very intermittently in this region. Moreover, this intervention made it possible to bring to an end the independence of the Tulunids, who were accused of having been unable to check the revolt in a province for which they were responsible, and in 292/905 a speedy campaign brought Egypt once again under the control of Baghdād.

Al-Muktafī also attempted, in the course of his brief reign, to strengthen the governmental machine. He achieved his object through the agency of a *wazīr,* al-Qāsim b. 'Ubayd Allāh, who has left behind him an enduring reputation for brutality. Al-Qāsim's first concern was to dispose of the commander-in-chief Badr, whom he replaced by a former secretary for army affairs. The influence of the *amīrs* was thus appreciably reduced and military operations were brought under the control of the *wazīr,* who, as aide and counsellor to the caliph, had authority over the army as well as over the reorganized administration. The ministries were collectively administered from a centre called the Palace Office, where all letters and requests were received, and whence the appropriate instructions were conveyed to the specialized departments responsible for putting them into effect. The financial offices, rearranged to represent the eastern and western provinces respectively, assured the healthiest possible system of taxation, and the caliph's treasury contained adequate resources. One shadow nevertheless remained: there existed at the head of financial affairs those Shī'ī secretaries to whom al-Mu'taḍid had been obliged to have recourse, and against whom the *wazīr* now opened hostilities. Although he succeeded in removing several of them, sometimes by forcible means, he was unable to touch the powerful Aḥmad b. al-Furāt, and had to wait until after he was dead in order to inculpate his brother, ʿAlī b. al-Furāt, whom he tried to ruin by demanding from him a strict rendering of accounts. He himself died, however, before he had been able to achieve his object, and his successor, al-ʿAbbās, was outwitted by Ibn al-Furāt, who thus ended by retaining all his authority.

The death of al-Muktafī marked the beginning of a new period of crisis for the régime. The question of the succession, for which he had made no provision, gave rise to animated discussions among the secretaries of state, on whom at this time the responsibility effectively devolved for appointing a new caliph. The fundamental differences of opinion which divided the two principal groups in the administration were brought into the open and the *wazīr* al-ʿAbbās had in fact to choose between two courses of action, advocated respectively by ʿAlī b. ʿĪsā and by Ibn al-Furāt, who represented two different views regarding the power. The first consisted of setting aside Jaʿfar, the son of the dying sovereign, who was only thirteen years old, in favour of a man of experience, the grandson of al-Mutawakkil, who was known by the name of Ibn al-Muʿtazz. This prince was skilled in political matters, and ready to continue al-Muktafī's efforts to combat dissident elements, and some of the secretaries believed that they would be able to co-operate with him effectively to restore the authority of the shaken régime. According to the second proposal the young Jaʿfar was to be proclaimed caliph, despite the objections raised on account of his age, so that in future it would be the *wazīrs* who really exercised power, and the Shīʿī movement would be allowed to develop freely.

In the end the second proposal prevailed. Jaʿfar, whose throne-name was al-Muqtadir, was proclaimed caliph in Dhu'l-Qaʿda 295/September 908, and took as *wazīr* al-ʿAbbās, with ʿAlī b. al-Furāt as his assistant. However, it was not long before the arrogant behaviour of the minister and the dissatisfaction of the *Amīr* al-Ḥusayn b. Ḥamdān led to the formation of a conspiracy such as the Sunnī secretaries desired. Its aim was the replacement of al-Muqtadir by Ibn al-Muʿtazz. The blow struck on 20 Rabīʿ I 296/17 December 908 by al-Ḥusayn was only partially successful; after twenty-four hours the supporters of Ibn al-Muʿtazz were compelled to abandon him; he was consequently known as the 'One-day Caliph', and was seized and executed. Since al-ʿAbbās had been killed at the very beginning of the fighting, his right-hand man, Ibn al-Furāt, became *wazīr*, with powers which were practically unlimited.

His dictatorship did not last for long, however, and the caliphate of al-Muqtadir, which was to continue for twenty-four years (295–320/908–32), was a period of very unstable government. Although the caliph, who at first was assisted by a kind of regency council composed of his mother, one of his uncles, and various high-ranking eunuchs of the court, allowed his *wazīr* great freedom of action in all matters, he reserved the right to dismiss him, and, if necessary, to bring him to trial when the *wazīr*'s policy ceased to please him—a right which he both used and abused. The result was that during his reign there were no fewer than fourteen wazirates; and certain personages, such as Ibn al-Furāt and 'Alī b. 'Īsā, occupied this office several times.

The *wazīrs* of this period had all been well trained in administration and were originally financial experts. As such, they endeavoured to exercise a strict control over the raising of taxes in those provinces which came directly under the caliphate—for a long time Khurāsān and Transoxania, which were in the hands of the Samanids after their victory over the Saffarid 'Amr b. al-Layth in 287/900, had been practically independent. In order to balance the budget, the *wazīrs* resorted to devious methods, especially loans obtained from financiers who belonged to their own families. They were also in charge of such military operations as might be required by events and usually took precedence over the army leaders. Diplomacy was likewise in their hands, and it was they who actually negotiated with the foreign ambassadors, especially the Byzantines, whom the caliph received at his court with dazzling splendour.

The *wazīrs* were of different religious and political persuasions. Ibn al-Furāt was a confirmed Shī'ī, choosing for preference the services of those who belonged to the same clandestine movement as himself, and having no compunction with regard to misappropriation. 'Alī b. 'Īsā, on the other hand, strove not only to balance the budget by imposing on the court an economy programme which was in general not very well received, but to abolish the extraordinary taxes which it had been customary to levy on various occasions. In spite of being a convinced Sunnī, he nevertheless disapproved of the risings fomented by Hanbalites. Al-Khāqānī, by contrast, supported these latter elements and actively persecuted the Shī'ī groups which gathered together in certain quarters of the capital.

Despite these contradictory tendencies, all three endeavoured to defend the régime, to which they were equally attached, even when, like Ibn al-Furāt, they did not acknowledge its legitimacy. In a period, therefore, when the caliph's authority was constantly being disputed by the various governors, they all worked with equal energy. Ibn al-Furāt was obliged to send two successive armies to Fārs, first to secure the person of a Saffarid who claimed to be occupying this province, and then to obtain the submission of the governor in charge of it, who refused to pay over the sums demanded of him. In his time too an expedition was sent to Egypt with the object of repelling the first attack of the Fatimid al-Mahdī, who had established himself in Ifrīqiya. It then became necessary to call to order other governors who had been granted a degree of autonomy—for example Ibn Abi'l-Sāj in Āẕarbāyjān, for the central power was only too often persuaded to grant to its deputies the farming of taxes in their provinces. If regular and effective control over them were not maintained, such persons were encouraged to make themselves lords of their territories. Finally there were always the attacks of the Carmathians to be held in check; they had at that time organized a state in Baḥrayn from which the armies of the caliph were powerless to dislodge them, and they asserted themselves by repeated attacks on caravans of pilgrims proceeding to Mecca. A little later they were to become so bold in their attacks as to pillage Baṣra (312/924), to threaten Baghdād (315/927), and to remove the Black Stone from the Ka'ba (317/930). All the *wazīrs* took up the struggle against them, but some, such as 'Alī b. 'Īsā, preferred negotiation to costly military expeditions, a point of view which was severely criticized at the time. There were indeed many who regarded the Carmathians not merely as schismatics but as actual infidels.

One result of the Carmathian threat was the development among the people of Baghdād of a fear-psychosis, which explains the bitterness of the religious struggles during the first part of al-Muqtadir's reign, and more particularly the course taken by the trial of the celebrated mystic al-Ḥallāj. After being prosecuted by Ibn al-Furāt in 296/908 for having taken the side of the conspirators against al-Muqtadir, this preacher, who was intoxicated with divine love, was arrested in 301/913 and accused of claiming divinity. When at last judgment was given in 309/922, he was condemned, after long disputations, on the advice of one of the *qāḍīs* of Baghdād and executed as a heretic. The political and religious atmosphere of the period explains why this mystic, whose chief offence had been the desire to preach moral reform among the people, while at the same time professing doctrines which it was difficult for the common herd to understand, should have been accused by some of extremist Shi'ism or of Carmathianism, regarded by others as a charlatan or a trouble-maker, and finally abandoned, for reasons of expediency, by 'Alī b. 'Īsā, the only man who could have defended him effectively, at that time assistant to the *wazīr* Ḥāmid, whom he did not wish to displease.

The year 312/924 marks a turning-point in the history of the reign, for the difficulties created by the attacks of the Carmathians obliged Ibn al-Furāt, then *wazīr* for the third time, to recall the *Amīr* Mu'nis whom he had recently banished from the capital. The situation was so serious that Ibn al-Furāt himself went to meet the *amīr* on his return to Baghdād. The civil power represented by the *wazīr* was then superseded by the military power, which it had previously succeeded in dominating since the end of the previous century. The *wazīrs* continued to follow one another in rapid succession, but not one of them was able to reassert his pre-eminence over the *amīr*, who was prefect of police and commander-in-chief, nor to solve the financial crisis which was becoming more serious all the time. The fact was that the persistent disturbances in the provinces, even within quite a short distance of the capital, the incessant wars, fraud and misappropriation constituted a perpetual drain on the resources of the treasury, while at the same time the caliph maintained a luxurious court with servants and guards whose number is estimated at several thousands. These difficulties were the underlying cause of the delays which frequently occurred in the payment of the troops, and consequently of the mutinies, which became more numerous in the capital during the latter half of the reign. One such rising led to the temporary deposition of al-Muqtadir in Muḥarram 317/March 929. Three years later the *Amīr* Mu'nis, after playing an equivocal part in the events of 317/929, openly revolted against the caliph, who left the capital at the head of the troops which had remained loyal in order to resist him, and met his death in the ensuing battle.

The two reigns which followed, of al-Qāhir (320–2/932–4) and of al-Rāḍī (322–9/934–40) represented an effort at stiffening the power of the caliphate, followed by an abrupt decline. External affairs at this period faded into the background, although the behaviour of the governors of nearby provinces had a definite influence on the course of events. More important were the intrigues which sundry personages commanding varying degrees of support or financial resources, wove around the caliphs in an effort to divest them of their remaining powers.

At first the *Amīr* Mu'nis appeared to have the upper hand. He nominated as *wazīr* whomsoever he fancied and allowed great freedom of action to the new chamberlain, Ibn Yalbaq. The latter undertook to launch an attack on the Caliph al-Qāhir, and desired to show his authority by ordering the name of Mu'āwiya to be publicly cursed, and by putting the Hanbalite leaders into prison. The caliph, however, reacted forcefully: he ordered the arrest and then the execution of Mu'nis, his deputy Ibn Yalbaq, and his son, but in the end he too met his downfall, being the victim of a plot devised by the former *wazīr* Ibn Muqla. He was at first imprisoned, but he refused to abdicate and was then blinded.

After the proclamation of his successor, al-Rāḍī, the real power fell into the hands of a new military leader, the chamberlain Ibn Yāqūt, who was appointed commander-in-chief and at the same time succeeded in gaining control of the financial administration also, in place of the *wazīr*. His ascendancy was, however, short; al-Rāḍī recovered himself, and re-established Ibn Muqla in his office of *wazīr*. He then tried to restore peaceful conditions, while at the same time persecuting the Shī'ī extremists and the Hanbalites. Increasing financial difficulties, however, proved too much for the authority of the caliphate.

It was indeed at this period that the Persian provinces nearest to the capital began in their turn to fall under the domination of local leaders, who succeeded in gaining recognition from the caliph. After the revolt of Mardāvīj, the Daylamite 'Alī b. Buwayh (Būyeh) settled at Fārs, while Ibn Ilyās occupied Kirmān; they were both in control of the finances and continually postponed making the payments to which they were committed. Even in the eastern Fertile Crescent, governors or tax-farmers were joining forces to refuse to pay over to the central government monies owing to it; the Hamdanid *amīr* of Mosul, the Banu'l-Barīdī in Ahwāz and Ibn Rā'iq at Baṣra, all acted in this way. It became impossible for the state to meet its expenses, so long, at least, as the caliph did not accede to the proposals of Ibn Rā'iq, who was ready to supply the treasury in return for control of the army and of finance.

Al-Rāḍī therefore, being abandoned by all, decided to confer for the first time on Ibn Rā'iq the title of 'chief *amīr*' (*amīr al-umarā'*), and to order that his name should be mentioned after his own in the *khuṭba*. In Dhu'l-Ḥijja 324/November 936 Ibn Rā'iq made his entry into Baghdād, where henceforward it was to be an *amīr* who really exercised the power, in the name of a titular caliph.

The effacement of the caliph served in fact to sanction the parcelling-out of the Arab-Muslim empire, with the development of new centres, both political and intellectual, and the reappearance of local cultures. A new epoch began in which Arabic, while retaining its pre-eminence as the sacred language and medium for religious studies, ceased to be the literary language of the empire. Moreover, the western provinces were increasingly detached as separate units, while the Iranian and Turkish elements made preparations for the complete domination of the political life of those Muslim countries east of the Syro-Mesopotamian steppe.

PART II

THE COMING OF THE STEPPE PEOPLES

CHAPTER I

THE DISINTEGRATION OF THE CALIPHATE IN THE EAST

THE PERIOD OF THE BUYIDS, SAMANIDS AND GHAZNAVIDS

The many disorders in the government, the deposition of caliphs and *wazīrs,* the arbitrary attitudes of the Turks, the quarrels between the different sects and theological schools, all prepared the way for new political changes in the eastern Fertile Crescent. Once again the foreign conquerors came from the east, as they did at the time of the 'Abbasid revolution. They were from the Daylam area to the south-west of the Caspian Sea, and were led by a ruling family called, from their eponym, the Buyids (also Buwayhids, from the Arabic form of the name). Within a few years from 320/932 they had risen to greater importance than their Daylamite predecessors with their few petty dominions in what is now Āẕarbāyjān and in Māzandarān. In 334/945 they occupied Baghdād, installed a new caliph, al-Muṭī', and took over the secular government of the country. Thereby the Commander of the Faithful was subordinated to a family that did not in fact recognize the religious basis of his dignity, but refrained from attacking it in order to prevent the caliphs from settling elsewhere outside their sphere of influence, and thus becoming more dangerous. However, the caliphs found themselves in a very awkward situation. It was indeed alleviated to some extent by the fact that the members of the Buyid house were often at enmity with one another, so that the individual provinces of western Persia under their dominion were usually in the hands of various members of the dynasty; a real Buyid central authority existed only under 'Aḍud al-Dawla from 366/976 to 372/983. In addition, the Turkish mercenaries had by no means been eliminated, and being Sunnīs, they served—as did also a number of local rulers who theoretically accepted the caliph's suzerainty—as a counterpoise against the arbitrary acts of the Shī'ī rulers, and therefore in some degree as a protection for the caliphate. Among these petty dynasties, the Marwanids at the end of the fourth/tenth century superseded the Hamdanids in the region of Diyār Bakr; they had a certain cultural importance as patrons of a number of poets and men of letters. In spite of struggles with their neighbours and internal strife they survived until well into the Seljuk period (477/1085). The same is true of the ʿUqaylids, who held Mosul from 380/991 to 489/1096.

The Shīʿa could now raise their heads more freely in ʿIrāq—not only the Zaydīs but also the Twelvers, who now for the first time attained considerable importance in the Islamic world. But the Buyids, like the caliph's court, were always strongly averse to the Ismāʿīlīs—an attitude reinforced by the instinct of self-preservation. Thus there ensued a shift of the internal balance of power in the eastern Fertile Crescent which became, especially in the fifth/eleventh century, an urgent danger to the caliphate. Again, the Christian sects, the Nestorians and Jacobites (Monophysites)—then incomparably more numerous than today—could also develop more freely and live under less oppressive conditions where the Muslim majority was split into religious factions openly contending or secretly intriguing against one another. This was to the advantage of the Muslims themselves, who even in the fourth/tenth century were still taking over much Hellenistic learning through Christian channels and had no inhibitions about using Christians as their teachers. The position of the Jews reached a significant intellectual and economic peak at this time, so that they were better off here and in Muslim Spain than in the contemporary West.

The central authorities at Baghdād and the caliphs themselves were thus largely restricted in their freedom of action. Even before the end of the fourth/tenth century the Buyids had, in the main, to be content with maintaining the essentials of their own internal and external security. Persia thus rose to ever greater importance. A vast majority of its population had meanwhile embraced Islam; most of the syncretist sects had been suppressed. Unlike the inhabitants of the Nile valley, North Africa, Mesopotamia and Syria, where Arabic had increasingly superseded the native dialects, the Persians had, in the stubborn literary battles of the *Shuʿūbiyya,* been able to maintain prestige equally with the Arabs, and to preserve their national language. Meanwhile on the Persian plateau, besides a number of local rulers in the east and north-west and on the southern edge of the Caspian Sea, the dynasty of the Samanids had risen to power from 261/874 onwards, on the break-up of the Tahirids (259/873) and the Saffarids (287/900). The Samanids were the descendants of a Zoroastrian priestly family from Sāmān in the district of Balkh, but were themselves convinced Sunnīs and zealous adherents of the caliphate. Although the Samanids held fast to Arabic in their chancery

—as a token of the unity of the caliphate—they nevertheless made it possible for a number of Persian poets such as Rūdakī (d. 329/940–1) and Daqīqī (*c.* 325–70/935-80) to be the first to write in a form of their native language, evolved from various native dialects. This was accepted at court, eventually gained currency as 'New Persian', and has, with some phonetic changes, survived to the present day. New Persian was written in Arabic characters and adopted more and more Arabic words; this was to some extent a concession to the universal victorious progress of Islam.

After the Arabs had overwhelmed the country in the first/seventh century the Persian language had been banished from public use for nearly three hundred years. Any Persians significant in intellectual life used Arabic to express their ideas. The number of Persians writing Arabic in those centuries was extraordinarily large, and the so-called 'Arabic literature' was largely the work of Persians. Among them were the most important Arabic grammarian, Sībawayh (d. *c.* 184/800), the historian and Qur'anic commentator, al-Ṭabarī (224–310/839–923), the antiquarian 'Abd al-Malik al-Tha'ālibī (350–430/961–1038), and by reason of his culture also the philosopher al-Fārābī—who was almost certainly of Turkish descent—as well as countless others. In the fourth/tenth century, however, as a result of the *Shu'ūbiyya,* the Persian people had so thoroughly established themselves in the framework of Islam that their native language came back into written use. It was admittedly not yet used in the administrative sphere, and for the time being hardly at all in historical writings (if we leave out of account Bal'amī's translation and revision of al-Ṭabarī in 352/963), and not at all in theology, which for centuries remained the exclusive preserve of Arabic. Arabic is still used to some extent by modern Persian Shī'ī theologians. The real blossoming in the fourth/tenth century came in poetry; the epic *Shāh-nāma* by Firdawsī (d. 411/1020) immediately reached a degree of perfection never again equalled in this genre.

This achievement also became important in a cultural and political sense. Not only did the Persian people find in the *Shāh-nāma* a mirror of itself and its ideals against the background of pre-Islamic history, but it also became the basis of the language and general direction of New Persian literature. No single book did more to strengthen and support the Persian language, as a rival to Arabic, than Firdawsī's life-work. Moreover, it rapidly reduced the Persian dialects and a number of minor Iranian languages to the level of mere media of oral communication, and over large areas superseded them altogether. Finally the *Shāh-nāma* assigned to the Persian people their proper position in the struggle now beginning against the advancing powers of Central Asia—a struggle which it transposed into mythical times as the battle between Īrān and Tūrān.

The *Shāh-nāma* was only possible because the Persian provinces of the caliph's empire were, from the later third/ninth century onwards, largely united in the hands of the native dynasty of the Samanids. Its founder, Naṣr I (261–79/874–92), and a number of other important rulers had succeeded in ensuring a period of comparative tranquillity for the Persians, though admittedly not everywhere or at all times. The stability of the country was endangered by attempts to re-establish a polity of pre-Islamic pattern, made by the Ziyarid Mardāvīj (316–23/928–35), and also by the religious extravagance of the magnificent Samanid Naṣr II (301–31/913–42), who in later life went over to the Ismāʿīlīs and thereby set himself in opposition to the caliphate, which in fact formed the theoretical mainstay of the dynasty. However, even before the fall of the Samanids was presaged by their struggle with the influential land-owning families (*dihqāns*) and individual families of officials, also by quarrels within the ruling family, and finally by the spread of Buyid power in west and south-west Persia, a development began on the north-east fringe of its sphere of influence which was to change the whole face of the Islamic world from the fifth/eleventh century onwards. For a long time 'warriors for the faith' had carried the burden of defensive warfare on the borders of the Byzantine empire and also taken part in the advances made into Buyid territory almost every year—the 'Summer Raids' as they were called—but without achieving any great successes for Islam among the orthodox population of Anatolia. In Transoxania and on the edge of the Farghānā valley there had also been skirmishes with non-Islamic neighbours. The only major gain made by the Samanids in the struggle with their neighbours was the occupation of Ṭarāz (Talās) in 280/893. The neighbours in question were the dynasty of the Kara-Khanids or Ilig-Khanids (both names from the titles they bore); these ruled over the Turkish people of the Qarluqs. Their empire had come into being after the collapse of the second Kök-Türk empire, but very soon disintegrated into several member-states whose relations with one another were not always amicable.

The generally stable situation on the northern frontier of the Samanid state, where bloody affrays were much less frequent than in Anatolia, allowed the numerous march-warriors to turn to missionary tasks, in which there was considerable Ṣūfī and Shīʿī influence. Whereas the Greeks—even down to the present day—have shown themselves almost completely immune to Islam, the Turks living on the Samanid borders—largely shamanists with a very small Christian element and therefore not members of a world religion—were with no great difficulty won over to Islam by peaceful methods. Of course the backing given to the missionaries and march-warriors by the Samanid state was an important factor; without this support the development could hardly have happened as it did. In this, as well as in the encouragement of Persian literature and in securing peace for large parts of Persia, the Samanids again played an important role in world history. The Islamic world owed it largely to them that the Turks were won over to Islam, which in the following centuries was to become the religion of practically all the Turkish peoples. At the same time it followed from the Samanids' close attachment to Sunnī Islam that this spread among the Turks, which subsequently helped this sect to attain an ever-growing predominance within Islam. However, in spite of all their religious merits, the Samanids dug their own grave by islamizing the Turks. The Qarluqs were soon pressing in upon Samanid Transoxania. The *'ulamā'*, however, summoned by the rulers to support their cause, declared that the advancing Turks were also good Muslims and that a holy war (*jihād*) against them was out of the question. Thus the Samanid state was unable to put up any sustained resistance and collapsed in the years 389–94/999–1004, and the dynasty perished. The lands north of the Oxus came under the dominion of the Kara-Khanids. South of the river their inheritance was taken over by the Ghaznavids, who were descended from a Turkish mercenary leader; their name was derived from their capital town, Ghazna, in what is today Afghanistan. At that period they were represented by Maḥmūd of Ghazna (388–421/998–1030), one of the great figures of Islamic history, a convinced Sunnī—as were also the Kara-Khanids—and ruler while Firdawsī was writing his *Shāh-nāma*. One of the effects of the renaissance of the Persian spirit evoked by this work was that the Ghaznavids were also persianized and thereby became a Persian dynasty.

Firdawsī's spiteful remarks about Maḥmūd, who had rewarded him for the *Shāh-nāma* less generously than he expected, should not blind us to the fact that Maḥmūd did not squander the money at his disposal but used it largely for an undertaking that is, seen in historical perspective, entirely comparable with the establishment of Persian as a cultural language of Islam. Almost every year Maḥmūd made advances into the Indus valley, and he largely succeeded in subduing it; other parts of India also acknowledged his supremacy. This opened the way into India for Islam. The two petty Islamic states around Mūltān that had emerged since 92/711 had no effect on the surrounding areas, and their long-standing inclination towards Carmathian ideas prevented them from getting any support from Baghdād or the Persians; for this reason Maḥmūd emphatically and forcefully encouraged the spread of Islam in its Sunnī form. Thus, a few decades after winning over the Turks, Islam was given the opportunity of converting yet another people. No longer merely the property of Arabs or arabized peoples, Islam became an expanding world religion.

It would, however, be erroneous to see this merely in its military or even missionary aspects. Very early in their history the Muslims were already concerned about their neighbours, acquired some knowledge of them and collected it together in the geographical literature that flourished among them at that time and reached its first peak with al-Muqaddasī (*c.* 375/985). This knowledge definitely did not influence the rhythm of Muslim life; they did not borrow from it, as they did from the heritage of later antiquity, and they continued to feel consciously that they belonged to the Mediterranean world. The Muslim world-view is linked with the man who was probably the most comprehensive scholar Islam ever produced, namely Abū Rayḥān Muḥammad al-Bīrūnī (362–*c.* 442/973–*c.* 1050) from Khwārazm and for the greater part of his life a subject of the great Ghaznavid sultan. Besides his writings on natural science, mathematics, astronomy and chronology, the most astonishing part of his work was his description of India, precisely that country whose gates had been opened to him by Maḥmūd's advance. Bīrūnī studied Sanskrit in order to get really close to Indian knowledge. Thus his book about this country (written in 421/1030) displays information of an extent and depth which makes it even today an important source for us. It shows how Muslims, looking outward disinterestedly from their own geographical and cultural mid-point, made scholarly inferences that rank with the heroic achievements of the human spirit.

Maḥmūd's empire, which was in essence just as much an oriental despotism as all the other Islamic states of that age, was nevertheless also to become important for Persia itself. In the lands south of the Oxus, which had come into the hands of the Ghaznavids in 389/999, Maḥmūd had a safe base from which to extend westwards and steadily force back the power of the Buyids, whom the strict Sunnī hated because of their Shīʿī beliefs. In the year before his death he gained Rayy; Khurāsān and Iṣfahān had already fallen into his hands. It seemed likely that the Ghaznavids would very soon be able to eliminate the Buyid state, which was already unsettled by all kinds of internal strife, by religious extravagance (such as a temporary inclination towards the Ismāʿīliyya), and also by the caliphs' increasing independence of outlook.

THE SELJUKS AND THEIR SUCCESSORS

However, Maḥmūd's son and successor, Masʿūd I (421–32/1030–40) did not succeed in following the road marked out for him. He was not prevented from doing so by the struggles in the Indus valley, which he inherited from his father. The real hindrance was caused by parties of Turks on the other side of the Oxus, who—having quarrelled with the Kara-Khanid rulers—had crossed the river and established themselves south of it in the years after 416/1025. Being mobile nomads, they were able to hold their own quite easily against the settled population of Khurāsān and to bring up reinforcements. They were led by the descendants of a chieftain, Seljük (in Arabic, Saljūq), and were therefore called the Seljuks. They proved ever more insistent disturbers of the peace. Masʿūd was compelled to take military action against them. A battle ensued in 431/1040 at Dandānqān; Masʿūd was defeated and the way to the Persian plateau was opened decisively to the Seljuk Turks. Very shortly afterwards they flooded into Persia, and the Ghaznavids were confined to the eastern fringe of this region (substantially what is now Afghanistan). They retained indeed their conquests in the Indus valley, the Panjāb (Persian, 'the land of the five rivers'). Thus it was not the Ghaznavids but the Seljuks, equally strict Sunnīs, who eliminated the remnants of Buyid dominion, and in 447/1055 made a triumphant entry into Baghdād, to free the caliph at last from the supremacy of the Shīʿī sectarians.

At that period it was no longer predominantly the Zaydīs or the Twelver Shīʿīs who harassed the caliph most persistently and caused them various anxieties. It was rather the Ismāʿīlīs who had become a real danger, since they had from 358/969 possessed a base in Egypt, whence a dynamic propaganda was directed by the Fatimids. From this source all the Fertile Crescent, and above all, Persia, were covered with a network of Ismāʿīlī strongpoints. Their recruiting agents appeared everywhere, and were to meet with a lasting response. The Ismāʿīlīs might well have gained the upper hand, if the Seljuks had not appeared and ruthlessly imposed the *Sunna*. The Seljuks did not halt in Persia and the eastern Fertile Crescent. They thrust forward to Syria, took Jerusalem in 463/1071 and Damascus in 468/1076, and thereby triggered off the Crusades. But this was not all; after several preparatory incursions they succeeded in 463/1071 in destroying a strong Byzantine army at Manzikert (Malāzgird), north-west of Lake Van, and in penetrating into the interior of Anatolia, which henceforward began to become a land of Turkish speech and Islamic faith—in short, 'Turkey'.

The Seljuk empire, firmly established by Alp Arslan (455–65/1063–72) became under Malik-Shāh (465–85/1072–92) the ruling power in the lands of the eastern caliphate. It meant the dawn of a new era in the history of Islam. For the first time a Turkish people dominated most of south-west Asia and thereby had political mastery over the caliphate. At the same time it was fortunate for the ʿAbbasids that the Seljuks were, and remained, faithful Sunnīs and therefore hastened to co-operate closely with the caliphs—though they naturally got the lion's share of power—and put down the Ismāʿīlī conspirators with an iron hand. But that was not all. Like the Ghaznavids before them, the Seljuks and their Turkish warriors soon succumbed to the spell of that Persian culture which had just been brought to its peak by Firdawsī. They rapidly adopted Persian as the language of the educated, and soon also as the language of daily life. They, and not the Persians themselves, gave this language a prestige that spread far beyond the Persian plateau and was destined to give Turkish culture a characteristic stamp, leaving its traces down to the present day. In this they were supported by one of the greatest ministers in Islamic history, the Persian Niẓām al-Mulk (408–85/1018–92), who impressed his own personality on his ruler Malik-Shāh and made the Seljuk empire into a strong cultural, military and organizing power in the Near East—naturally to the dismay of the Shīʿa, as he, like his ruler, was prepared for a merciless battle against them. This pressure inevitably evoked a counter-pressure. It was impossible to prevent a branch of the Ismāʿīlīs, at enmity with the Fatimid line for dogmatic reasons, from settling under their leader Ḥasan-i Ṣabbāḥ (d. 518/1124) in the wild mountain country of Alamūt, north-west of what is now Tehran. From their base in Alamūt this community, who recognized as rightful *imāms* the Fatimid prince Nizār and his successors, were able to spread terror among the Muslims from the last years of the fifth/eleventh century onwards. They used emissaries called *fidā'īs*, 'the self-sacrificers', who were pliant instruments of the grand master of Alamūt. The community did not shrink from the murder of religious opponents. One of the first victims of their revenge was Niẓām al-Mulk.[1]

The advance of the Crusaders affected mainly the Fatimids and Byzantium, but it hardly touched the Seljuks, and remained a marginal event for Islam in general. Much greater disruptive factors were the Ismā'īlīs, and the dissolution of the Great Seljuk empire into separate territories, caused by the quarrels over the succession that soon broke out after the death of Malik-Shāh in 485/1092. Of these territories, only Kirmān (433–583/1041–1186) gained anything more than local importance. The splitting off of the Seljuk state of Rūm in Anatolia created favourable conditions for the gradual emergence of an Ottoman-Turkish nationhood. In the central area of Syria, Mesopotamia and Persia, Muḥammad (498–511/1105–18) came to power after the death of his father Malik-Shāh. Finally, in the east Sanjar (511–52/1118–57) vigorously reunited the Seljuk empire; he had already administered Khurāsān since 492/1098.

The Seljuk domination was certainly not a phase of complete peace for the eastern half of the 'Abbasid caliphate. However, the periods of internal disorder and struggles for the throne were intermittent and lasted only a few years. Thus the material prosperity that had largely been destroyed in the constant struggles of the fourth/tenth and early fifth/eleventh centuries was now restored, and also permitted a full development of cultural life, above all in Persia. We have already seen that the Seljuks were the first to give supra-national prestige to the culture of the Persian nation. This also gradually showed itself in the names chosen for members of this Turkish dynasty; such names were now taken from Persian heroic legends, especially among the Seljuks of Rūm. It must also be reckoned to the credit of this dynasty that it suppressed the underground activities of the Ismā'īlīs. The Twelvers now replaced the Ismā'īlīs as the most important group of Shī'a. A large number of other branches had meanwhile become completely or nearly extinct; these had come into being through repeated groupings of supporters around some pretender or other from the numerous descendants of the Prophet's daughter Fāṭima and his cousin 'Alī. As

[1] The community came to be known by Western Europeans as the Assassins. For the origin and significance of this term, see Bernard Lewis, *The Assassins* (London, 1967), 1–19.

against these, the Twelver Shīʿīs had the advantage that for them the twelfth *Imām* (from whom they took their name) Muḥammad al-Mahdī was a child of some five years of age when he went into concealment in 260/873-4 at Sāmarrā, and he was not to emerge again until the end of time. Until 329/940, during the 'Lesser Occultation', he directed the fortunes of the community through the agency of four successive 'deputies'. Subsequently, during the 'Greater Occultation', they were left to themselves without the leadership of any *Imām* living among them; therefore no dissensions about any particular person could arise. The Twelvers were more moderate than the Ismāʿīlīs and less extreme in their interpretation of the Qur'ān—the Ismāʿīlīs had found secret ideas in every word of the Holy Book. They were therefore able to attach more firmly to themselves those classes of the population who were devoted to the Prophet's family and to survive the difficult times they experienced under the Seljuks. At the same time the Shīʿīs were aided by the right of any member of their community, when in danger, to escape persecution by a temporary denial of his faith (*taqiyya*). In any case the Seljuk domination decided the issue; the Sunnī creed prevailed in the Asian part of Islam for the time being; the Shīʿa could not take over completely until considerably later, and then only in particular areas: Persia, Āẕarbāyjān and southern Iraq.

In the Seljuk period Sunnī orthodoxy now found the form that was characteristic of it until the attempted reforms in the last hundred years. The gradual repression of the Muʿtazila from the fourth/tenth century onwards by means of the dialectic (*kalām*) that they themselves had developed had in fact ended the development of orthodox Sunnī dogma. However, Ṣūfī mysticism—to which large parts of the population were receptive—had at this time not yet had its full effect. It manifested itself in various ways: in the shape of pantheistic speculations that found a grandiose synthesis with Ibn al-ʿArabī but gradually came to nothing; in the first beginnings of groups around individual mystics and in the development of schools and associations which (mainly in the seventh/thirteenth and eighth/fourteenth centuries) became the germ-cells of the dervish orders. However, the strongest tendency was the desire to fit certain fundamental concerns of mysticism—above all the cultivation of individual piety, spiritual and devotional life, and the exercise of charity—into Sunnī orthodoxy in such a way that they could find a place in it without disturbing dogma and cult. This process was completed under the Seljuks by the life-work of a Persian, Abū Ḥāmid

Muḥammad al-Ghazālī (450–505/1058–1111). He experienced in his own person the inadequate satisfaction obtainable from a legalistic Islam that was confined to the mere fulfilment of duties. He therefore abandoned his celebrated teaching activities at the Niẓāmiyya, a citadel of orthodoxy founded at Baghdād in 459/1067 by Niẓām al-Mulk as a counterblast to al-Azhar, then an Ismā'īlī propaganda-centre. In long years of wandering and self-communion he came to realize the importance of direct dialogue with God, personal prayer and practical charity; to this he devoted the remaining years of his relatively short life. He tried above all in his voluminous chief work, *Iḥyā' 'ulūm al-dīn* ('The revival of the religious sciences') to formulate his ideas. He thus seemed to his disciples to be the 'reviver of religion' (*muḥyī al-dīn*) who was supposed to appear at the end of every Islamic century. His ideas and reasoning, as they became known from this work, were at first bitterly opposed by the strictly orthodox theologians of the Islamic West, especially the Mālikī *madhhab*, but they took firm hold and became the basis of a revived Sunnī Islam, which has kept its validity down to the present day. The 'Revival' has acquired almost canonical authority, and its author has long been regarded as the greatest Sunnī theologian.

It was always characteristic of the Turkish states that they kept a tight hold on administrative affairs and also integrated foreign peoples implacably into their own system, even though they learned from them in cultural matters and acknowledged their occasional intellectual superiority; this was for centuries especially evident in their relations with the Persians. The administrative successes of the Turks were largely due to the strict discipline of their armies, which the Seljuks were always concerned to maintain. The early Islamic administrative pattern of the caliphate, with its payment of pensions to predominantly Arab warriors as defenders and extenders of the empire, had finally collapsed in the late second/early ninth century; thereafter the army was infiltrated with ever greater numbers of Turks. The most urgent need was to satisfy the financial demands of the Turkish officers, and now, at a time when booty from external campaigns was rare, the yield from taxes was insufficient for this purpose. Thus even in Buyid times, and subsequently to an ever-increasing degree in Seljuk times (from 479/1087 onwards) the caliphs and their *wazīrs* (who were generally Arabs and Persians and only rarely Turks) were forced to compensate officers, and soon also subordinate commanders and soldiers, by means of tax-farms and allocations of land. This granting of assignments (sing., *iqṭā'*) has only a remote resemblance to the feudal system of the Western world. Islam knew nothing of the principles of ethically-based obligation to mutual loyalty and the hereditary cession of defined territories which characterize the Western system. Certainly the officers were often sufficiently interested in the land granted to them—not infrequently far distant from 'Irāq—to take good care of it and to increase, or at least maintain, its productivity. Subordinate commanders and soldiers, on the other hand, merely sought to squeeze out everything possible; thereafter they gave back their exhausted land, and demanded other more productive estates in exchange. The tax-farmers also were naturally only interested in making the taxes that accrued to them show the greatest possible profit on the sums they themselves had paid out to the state. These sharp practices ruined the economic development of the country, and especially agriculture, the very basis of its existence, and in 'Irāq they caused the rapid decay of the vital irrigation system.

On the other hand the urban notables—at this period in the eastern Fertile Crescent (unlike, for example, Persia) still largely non-Muslims and mostly Nestorian or Jacobite Christians or else Jews—were generally able to evade the economic recession by being doctors, lawyers or religious functionaries; or else, as merchants, bankers or money-changers, they were able to make some profit from the situation. It was common practice to obtain a loan on a draft on an *iqṭā'*, in order to be free from the trouble of a long journey and the collection of revenues. For these reasons the money economy—which even in early 'Abbasid times was probably more extensive than that of the contemporary Western world—continued to flourish.

In the eastern Fertile Crescent the power of the Seljuks dwindled more rapidly than in Persia. After the death of Sultan Muḥammad in 511/1118 the petty dominions were on the rise, especially in the northern part of the country. Artukids had, partly as helpers of the Seljuks and partly through struggles with them, established a dynasty in northern Syria; its influence was, however, soon restricted by constant divisions of the inheritance. After 511/1118 they held out in the area around Mardin and Diyār Bakr. In Mosul, however, they were superseded in 521/1127 by the *atabeg* 'Imād al-Dīn Zangī; Aleppo also fell into his hands in the following year. Neither of the two dynasties made any real attempt to reach out southwards from the Jazīra. The situation was rather that their sphere of influence in the seventh/twelfth century was involved with events in Syria, which in their turn were bound up with

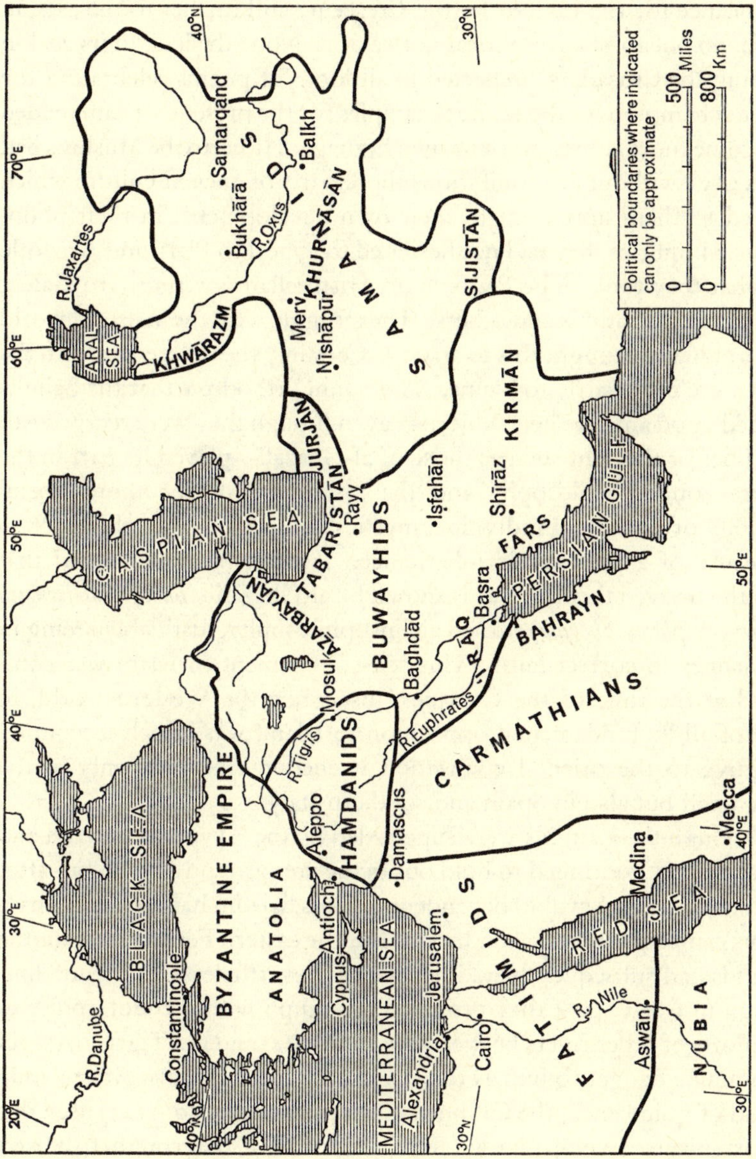

Map 3. The central Islamic lands in the late fourth/tenth century.

the Crusaders' advance into this area. The intervention of the 'Franks' in the struggle between Fatimids, Seljuks and native dynasties had no significance for the eastern Fertile Crescent; still further to the east, in Persia, no one took any political notice of it. None the less, in its zeal in resisting the Crusaders—reflected in all kinds of poems celebrating the ancient champions of the faith as examples for the present—Islam tended to become more conscious of its own heritage. Hitherto the Muslims had taken over without any inhibitions those parts of ancient culture which seemed to them important to their own development; in their philosophical inquiries they had not hesitated to appeal to Plato and Aristotle (or what they took to be Platonic or Aristotelian doctrines), to Galen, Hippocrates, Plotinus and others. The struggle with the Western world now gradually brought this to an end. Certainly the differences with the West were only partly to blame. The Sunnī orthodoxy that the Seljuks insisted upon among their subjects—even though they were receptive to new lines of thought such as those of al-Ghazālī—played its part in the suppression of philosophy and the restriction of the more liberal theology of important individual mystics, and also in the reluctance to make use of a pre-Islamic inheritance. It must be remembered that even the revived theology, as is shown by al-Ghazālī's *Tahāfut al-falāsifa* (*Destructio philosophorum*) turned against philosophy, justifiably seeing in it a danger to correct faith. This self-confinement of Islam was completed at the time of the Crusades, just when the Western world, in spite of all its fundamental opposition to Islam, was largely becoming receptive to the oriental civilization it encountered, not only in the Holy Land but also in Spain and southern Italy.

Although the Zangids were superseded by the Ayyubids in Syria and Palestine they continued to hold out in the area around Mosul, but after 583/1187 only as Ayyubid dependents. Thus Saladin had here too a base for his campaign in Syria and Egypt. For the eastern Fertile Crescent the Zangids had subsequently no importance; nevertheless until their elimination in 631/1233–4 they provided the caliph with a counterpoise to the efforts of other rulers between the Euphrates and the Tigris, without becoming a danger to him as they were convinced Sunnīs. After a long period of quiescence, the Caliph al-Nāṣir (575–622/1180–1225) used this opportunity to develop his own activities. In doing so he sought to bolster up his own position by co-operating with a movement of obscure origins that had begun at that time concurrently with the emergence of the Ṣūfī orders and apparently united mainly craftsmen and guild-members on a more secular and humanitarian basis—namely the *futuwwa*. In this movement the widespread devotion to the Prophet's family was reflected in adoration of 'Alī. 'Alī figured as the protector of the corporation. After an elaborate admission ceremony the initiate was bound to obey a master (*pīr*); the members met regularly under the direction of the master for social gatherings and probably also for spiritual exercises. They also provided hospitality for travelling members. The Caliph al-Nāṣir now took over as protector of the *futuwwa*, emphasized above all its sporting aspects, such as archery, and also invited foreign princes to join it, in order to form a kind of association for the revival of Islamic life under the caliph. His appeal had in fact some measure of success. Throughout the seventh/thirteenth century there is evidence here and there of the activities of this peculiar association, even as far afield as the Nile valley. However, the *futuwwa* never became a real prop to the caliphate. It still played an important role in Anatolia at the beginning of the eighth/fourteenth century and had a lasting influence on the spirit and ethical alignment of the guilds there; but soon after this the *futuwwa* ceased to exist as an independent institution.

In Persia, Sanjar had been master of the situation until after the middle of the sixth/twelfth century. He had succeeded in maintaining his supremacy over the Khwārazm region south of the Aral Sea, even though a local dynasty, founded by a governor of Turkish descent, caused him all kinds of difficulties. The dynasty had assumed the old title of the princes of this region, Khwārazm-Shāh. The son of its founder, Atsız (521–51/1128–56), had finally, after various attempted rebellions, had to resign himself to dependence on Sanjar. Developments in Central Asia were more ominous. After the fall of the Liao dynasty, which had ruled northern China from 916 to 1125, a part of the Khitay (in Chinese K'i-tan) people supporting the dynasty split off westwards under the prince Ye-Lü Ta-shi and, after various struggles, subjugated the state of the so-called 'Western Uigurs' in the neighbourhood of Turfan and Kucha as well as the empire of the Kara-Khanids east of the Aral Sea. The Khitay proper reserved to themselves the area between the River Chu and Semirech'ye south of Lake Balkhash with its capital city Balāsāghūn. Known as the 'Western Khitay' (Kara-Khitay), they were strongly influenced by Chinese culture and wrote their language—which was possibly somewhat akin to Mongolian—in a script with characters patterned on the Chinese system, which have not yet been properly deciphered. They largely professed Buddhism. Obviously incited by the Khwārazm-Shāh, they attacked Transoxania. On 25–6 Muḥarram 536/9–10 September 1141 Sanjar confronted them on a plain north of Samarqand, but was defeated. This victory of a non-Islamic army over Islam's champion in the east apparently first gave rise to the legend of 'Prester John' as the helper soon to come to the aid of the hard-pressed Christians of the Near East. The ruler of the Kara-Khitay in fact bore the title of *kürkhan* (in Persian, *gūrkhān*), which Western pronunciation distorted into Johannes or John. Sanjar recovered from this setback, and was on the whole able to maintain his possessions in Khurāsān. However, the Oghuz (Ghuzz), set on by the Kara-Khitay, invaded his territories in 548/1153; this cost him three years of captivity, during which time the Khwārazm-Shāh Atsız had full freedom of action. Sanjar died in 552/1157, a year after his release, and then the Seljuk domination of Persia was practically at an end. Its inheritance passed to the new Khwārazm-Shāh Il Arslan, who succeeded his father on the throne in 551/1156.

A new period of unrest now closed in on Persia. If the Khwārazm-Shāhs had been content to extend their influence over the Seljuks and to push forward into central and western Persia, the population would not have been greatly affected by this change of overlord; the Khwārazm-Shāhs were in any case just as good Sunnīs as the Seljuks. But after the death of Il Arslan in 567/1172 his two sons wasted their energies for nineteen years in a struggle for predominance. Their mother also intervened, and brought about further intrigues and additional unrest. All this, however, was insignificant in comparison with the advent of one of the worst monsters the Islamic world has ever seen, the prince 'Alā' al-Dīn Ḥusayn of the Ghurids, so named after the inaccessible mountain district of Ghūr between Herat and Hilmand. Enraged at the treacherous execution of two of his brothers by the Ghaznavids, 'Alā' al-Dīn fell upon the town of Ghazna in 545/1150 and had its entire population slaughtered after luring them from their hiding-places by the call to prayer. With good reason 'Alā' al-Dīn was thereafter called *Jahānsūz* ('Burner of the World'), a nickname that endured among the people of Persia until after the Mongol period. The Ghaznavids were soon able to retake the ruins of Ghazna and to hold out there for the time being, as the Ghurids were held in check by Sanjar and later by the Oghuz. In 557/1162 two nephews of 'Alā' al-Dīn united in joint rule over their uncle's heritage; in the following year they forced the last Ghaznavid to withdraw from Ghazna to Lahore in the Panjāb, where he eventually, in 583/1187, became the victim of further Ghurid expansion.

In these same years the Ghurids also reached out westwards and involved the Khwārazm-Shāhs in embittered struggles. In this situation the latter found it a relief when the last Seljuk, Ṭughrul III (nominally from 570/1175), who eventually possessed the area around Hamadān and Iṣfahān, met his death in battle with them in 590/1194. Not until 601/1204 did the Khwārazm-Shāh Muḥammad II (from 596/1200) win a decisive victory over the Ghurids, who were almost wiped out by the Kara-Khitay during their retreat. After the Ghurid Muʿizz al-Dīn was murdered in India in 603/1206 the dynasty was no longer a danger to its neighbours.

The Ismāʿīlīs in Alamūt were also in the sixth/twelfth century no longer a threat to the population. They had little opportunity to reach out beyond their mountain castles, though meanwhile their offshoot in Syria was much more active. The rulers of Alamūt were now increasingly preoccupied with theological questions. One of them indeed declared in 559/1164 that the great Resurrection had begun, and that the *Sharīʿa* was abrogated. It was only in 607/1210 that this fiction was publicly renounced and the *Sharīʿa* proclaimed valid again. At the same time, an accommodation was sought with the Sunnīs, although this policy was abandoned in 618/1221 after a change of ruler.

After 601/1204 the Khwārazm-Shāh Muḥammad II no longer had any serious opponents in the Persian area. He could therefore aim at restoring the old connexion between Persia and Transoxania as it had existed for centuries and finally under the Samanids. The Kara-Khitay state had maintained itself in the territories won by its founder—partly under the rule of women, whose position in this Buddhist community was much freer than in Islam—but had not attempted any expansion in the direction of the Persian plateau. Its military power gradually decayed. The last ruler was deposed in 608/1211 by his son-in-law Küchlüg, who was the son of the chief of the Mongol tribe of the Naiman, and had fled from the east. Küchlüg presumably went over from Nestorianism to Buddhism in order to secure his power as *kürkhan*. However, he worked himself up into an insane hatred of the Muslims, whom he exposed to all kinds of oppression. This inevitably aroused the anger of Muḥammad II. But the limit was reached when in 609/1212 the suzerain of the Kara-Khitay, the Kara-Khanid ruler ʿO͟smān, ordered the murder of all the Khwarazmians living there. Muḥammad II put him out of action by a rapid advance, and thereby went over to the offensive against Transoxania. In the following year he tried to subjugate a Mongol tribe settled in the west, the Kipchaks; this led to an indecisive battle, which for the time being brought the Khwārazm-Shāh to a halt.

The cautiousness of the Khwarazmians was moreover due to the fact that Muḥammad was also waging war in the south-west. In Mosul and in Āẕarbāyjān and its neighbourhood major-domos (the *atabegs*) had established themselves here and there as guardians of young princes and in some places as actual rulers; they found support in the active policy of the Caliph al-Nāṣir. Muḥammad II was often at odds with the most important of them, Özbeg in Tabrīz (607–22/1210–25), and this led to disputes with the caliph. The Khwārazm-Shāh sought to get the better of him by setting up an 'Alid anti-caliph—a hitherto unheard-of proceeding. He prepared for a campaign against Baghdād in the hope of getting the position that the Seljuks had occupied there. An early winter hindered the advance over the Zagros mountains, and when spring came the Khwārazm-Shāh had quite different anxieties. He was called to battle with the most formidable opponent that Islam had ever had to face in the whole of its existence.

THE MONGOLS

This was not the first time that east Asian peoples had reached out towards Central Asia and beyond it. Only the Seljuks, however, had found their way to the Persian plateau and beyond it to the Near East. But they were already Muslims at the moment of this advance; they were therefore rapidly assimilated to the culture of their subjects and even became zealous admirers and promoters of it. With the Mongols—whom numerous Turks had joined from the very beginning—the situation was entirely different. Several of their tribes had already embraced Nestorian Christianity in the eleventh century, for example the Keräit and the Merkit and also parts of the Naiman ('eight', i.e. the Eight Clans). Others were shamanists or possibly adherents of nature religions. Monotheism was, of course, widespread even among such peoples. Living northwards and eastwards of the Kirghiz, the Khitay and the Jurchen, the Mongols were to the greatest possible extent cut off from Chinese culture and civilization and also from Buddhism. In addition, the domination of northern China down to the south of Peking by the Khitay (916–1125) and the Jurchen (1125–1215) had saved them from a Chinese thrust into their homeland. Thus the son of a petty chieftain,

Temujin ('the smith') was able, without foreign intervention, to assert himself among the tribes, and eventually to gain sovereignty over them. In the course of this development many a friend and helper of his early days became his enemy, and had to flee before him or fell a victim to his attacking troops. Finally—probably in 1206—Temujin had become so powerful that an assembly of the people acknowledged him as supreme lord of the Mongols and gave him the title of distinction Chingiz Khān—the meaning of this title is still in dispute, but it may possibly be 'Ocean-like Khān'. The Buddhist Uigurs around Turfan put themselves under his rule in 1209; so also did many Muslims in Central Asia who felt embarrassed by the religious policy of Küchlüg, the Naiman prince who, after the defeat of his father, had fled westward from Chingiz Khān. This protected Chingiz Khān's line of retreat, and in 1215 he was able to wrest northern China from the Jurchen without excessively severe fighting. Now he had to see how he could secure the south-west flank of his possessions in Inner Asia.

There is no indication that Chingiz Khān had at that time any intention of coming to grips with an opponent like the Khwārazm-Shāh, whose power must seem significant even to one so favourably situated. Thus even a clash between his troops and Muḥammad's, when the latter attacked the Kipchaks, was not regarded by either side as likely to have serious consequences. However, the Mongol khan now sent a delegation of merchants to gather information about conditions in the empire of the Khwārazm-Shāh. It may well be that they were intended not only to establish business contacts but also, on their return, to report on what they had seen and heard. For this particular reason he may well have chosen as his envoys Muslims who knew the Persian language. Muḥammad II obviously regarded them as spies and simply had them executed. A similar fate befell a second Mongol delegation who demanded expiation.

Chingiz Khān was bound to regard this proceeding as sufficient cause for action against Muḥammad II and his breach of the rights of envoys. Later historians inform us that the Caliph al-Nāṣir—hard pressed by the Khwārazm-Shāh, as we have already seen—on his part also tried to arrange an attack on Muḥammad's rear by sending a delegation to Chingiz Khān. This had been a frequent political move by the caliphs throughout past centuries, and therefore the report seems quite credible in itself; it cannot, however, be confirmed from contemporary sources. In any case the caliph could not have anticipated that on this occasion an old-established procedure would have dreadful consequences and even bring about the downfall of his house.

At all events it rapidly became evident that the power of Muḥammad II had very shaky foundations. The Mongols soon forced him and his troops back over the Oxus. Samarqand and Bukhārā, and subsequently Khwārazm, fell into their hands in 617/1220–1 and were cruelly devastated. Those inhabitants who could not be used as forced levies were put to the sword. When the Mongols crossed the Oxus, Muḥammad's state collapsed like a house of cards. Many of his Turkish soldiers deserted to the Mongols, since these already had numerous Turks in their ranks. The ruler was just able to take refuge on an island off the Caspian coast, where he died shortly after. His son Jalāl al-Dīn Mengübirdi held on to his claim to the succession, but had reason to congratulate himself on being able to escape southwards at the head of a small band of faithful warriors and eventually to save his life by swimming alone across the Indus. Meanwhile the Mongols, without encountering any significant resistance, ranged through northern Persia and left it again through the Caucasian Gate near Darband in 620/1223. Jalāl al-Dīn, returning from India and now no more than a *condottiere,* tried to intervene against some occupation troops who had been left behind; he inflicted minor losses on the Mongols in some places. When he was murdered by a Kurdish robber in 628/1231 the dynasty of the Khwārazm-Shāhs finally disappeared.

For the moment the storm was at an end for Persia and for Russia. Only the border regions north of the Oxus were still firmly held by the intruders from the east. The intellectual wealth and the economic importance of this area were extinguished for centuries to come. Transoxania, even though it later recovered to some degree, was never able to regain the central position it had hitherto enjoyed in Islamic and even Persian intellectual life.

The minor dynasties in southern Persia, which had maintained themselves in face of the Khwārazm-Shāhs and could now breathe more freely again, remained in existence, as did also the caliphate. The skilful and wise Caliph al-Nāṣir died in 622/1225, shortly after the storm. His successors were insignificant and imprudent men, who were unable to alter the course of events when the situation once more became critical. Chingiz Khān died in 624/1227, far away in the east. His son and successor Ögedei turned his attention to China and especially to the far west—first towards Russia, which in 633–8/1236–41 was conquered for Batu, a son of Chingiz Khān's eldest son Jochi who died shortly before his father. Seljuk Anatolia also shortly after (641/1243) fell into the hands of the Mongols, and the sultans there had to take an oath of fidelity to the khans. On the other hand, the regions further to the south remained unaffected until a generation later, after the Mongol internal troubles over the succession had been settled by the election of Möngke in 649/1251. When one of Möngke's brothers, Kubilay, was preparing to take over northern China and from thence to invade southern China—which he succeeded in doing in 678/1279–80—another brother, Hülegü (Hūlāgū), was brought into action with a considerable army drawn from all the states of the Mongol empire to advance upon the Near East. On 30 Dhu'l-Qa'da 653/1 January 1256 he crossed the Oxus at the head of some 129,000 warriors and occupied the northern Persian plateau almost without resistance. Only the Ismā'īlīs in Alamūt entrenched themselves in their inaccessible retreats, but in the end they were unable to hold out. The last *imām* shortly afterwards met a violent death, and thus, to the relief of all the neighbouring peoples, this long-standing scourge of the Islamic world was eliminated. Various petty princes in the Zagros mountains, in Fārs and in Kirmān, subjected themselves voluntarily to the new rulers and remained unmolested within their own territories. Here, as also in Central Asia, the Mongols were in no way concerned to extirpate all the native princely houses and take over direct administration everywhere. Anyone who voluntarily surrendered to them had little to fear, but he had to receive a Mongol resident and pay tribute. The Mongols also left unmolested for the time being some territories which had not submitted to them; either because of the inaccessible terrain—as the Kart principality around Herat—or because of the hot damp climate along the southern coast of the Caspian Sea and the northern coast of the Persian Gulf, which made it impossible for the Mongols to stay there for any length of time.

Hülegü continued his thrust westwards. The fumbling policy of the 'Abbasid Caliph al-Musta'ṣim (640–56/1242–58) and his *wazīr* made a peaceful agreement impossible. Baghdād fell into the hands of the Mongols on 4 Ṣafar 656/10 February 1258, and was plundered for several days. The Sunnīs living there found themselves in an unpleasant situation in comparison with the Shī'īs and the still very numerous Christians. The Christians were especially able to bask in the favour of the Mongol ruler, whose principal wife was a Nestorian. The Twelvers enjoyed the protection of the scholar Naṣīr al-Dīn Ṭūsī (d. 672/1274), who was held in the highest esteem by Hülegü. Naṣīr had been liberated from the hands of the Ismā'īlīs in Alamūt. He was a significant figure as the ruler's adviser and above all as one of the most important astronomers of the Middle Ages; his records of astronomical observations made in his observatory at Marāgha in Āẕarbāyjān were important for centuries. The caliph himself was put to death after a few days. After more than five hundred years the 'Abbasid caliphate was at an end, even though 'Abbasid shadow-caliphs resided in Egypt until 923/1517.

On its way from Baghdād to the Mediterranean coast, the Mongol army passed through the Jazīra and the southern slopes of Transcaucasia. A number of local rulers, in part very energetic personalities, were subdued by force and consequently lost their territories. Others, such as the Artukids and similarly the Seljuks of Rūm, were able to save themselves by skilful manoeuvring. All this took up most of the year 657/1259; Hülegü had to go to Central Asia for the election of a new great khan, as his brother Möngke had died just at this time.

In his absence, the year 658/1260 was to set a limit to Mongol expansion in the west, and thereby to bring about a decision that altered the course of world history, and was of especial import for the future of Islam. The towns of Syria had fallen somewhat easily into the hands of the conquerors from the east; only a few castles by the sea, among them some belonging to Crusaders, had held out. Then, on 3 September 1260, the Mongol forces met the army of the Egyptian Mamluks at the Spring of Goliath ('Ayn Jālūt) north of Jerusalem. The Mongol army contained a large admixture of Turks. The ethnic composition of the Mamluk army was very similar, in that it was mostly recruited from Turkish and Caucasian slaves, who had been purchased, trained and emancipated, whence the name: *mamlūk,* 'possessed'. The Mamluks were acquainted with the fighting technique of the intruders—who were generally mounted—and could meet them on equal terms. They were victorious. For the first time the Mongols were decisively beaten, and they were forced to withdraw from Syria. Now that Egyptian rule had been restored, the Christians of various denominations, including the Armenians in the towns, found themselves in an unenviable position as actual or supposed partisans of the enemy.

The Mamluks retained their hold on the Syrian-Palestinian glacis, vital for the defence of the Nile valley, and also dislodged the Crusaders; the continued existence of their state was therefore assured. Even some later attacks by the Mongols from bases in Mesopotamia could do nothing to alter this situation. Certainly Persia and the eastern Fertile Crescent were not so thoroughly devastated during Hülegü's campaign as Transoxania had been a generation before. However, there was now a marked decline in the importance of the Islamic centres in this area. Above all, Baghdād rapidly sank to the level of a small provincial town. On the other hand, in the Nile valley the towns remained undamaged, the population was not decimated, and consequently the Coptic faith was not wiped out. The teaching institutions of Islam, especially al-Azhar, which had become a Sunnī *madrasa,* were now able to continue their activities undisturbed and to make the Nile valley the spiritual centre of Arabic Islam for centuries to come; its influence was felt all over North Africa. Admittedly there was now a Persian Islam side by side and on equal terms with Arabic Islam, and even in Anatolia and India Islamic cultural centres of similar standing were soon to arise. All this led to a marked shift of relative importance in the Islamic world; Cairo, however, never became as important as Baghdād had been in its day.

However, even in the east the continued existence of Islam as a religion was not endangered. Admittedly the supremacy of non-Muslims in these parts was a completely new and odious experience for Muslims. Yet it soon became apparent that the Islamic territories, unlike Russia and the Golden Horde, could not be ruled by the adherents of an alien faith. Before this was generally realized, the rulers of Persia and the eastern Fertile Crescent inclined more and more towards Buddhism, and some had openly embraced it. In many places a Buddhist temple stood beside the mosque, though there are admittedly no indications that there were any convinced Buddhists among the Persians themselves.

Hülegü died in 663/1265. His successors, called the Īl-Khāns (i.e. 'viceroys'), neglected the country badly, even though peace from internal struggles gave the inhabitants time to breathe. On the Oxus and in Caucasia there were indeed various conflicts with the sister-kingdom of the Golden Horde, in which Berke, a convert to Islam, held sway for ten years (655–65/1257–67). When Baghdād was conquered by Hülegü and the caliph was killed, he quarrelled with his cousin, and shortly afterwards he entered into an alliance with Egypt and, for a time, with the Byzantine emperor; the co-operation with the Mamluks in particular lasted for decades. In the area around Khwārazm, which had fallen into the hands of the rulers of the so-called 'White Horde' (a collateral line of the khans of the Golden Horde), there were repeated hostilities, especially in the years after 657/1259 when Kubilay and his brother

Arıq Böge were contending with one another for the Great Khanate. On this occasion the two rulers of ancient civilized countries, Kubilay in China and Hülegü in Persia, had united against the lords of nomadic areas, Arıq Böge in Mongolia and Berke in the Golden Horde. Even after the defeat of Arıq Böge in 663/1264 there was still a struggle for the line of the Oxus, all the more because the Kart dynasty in Herat found temporary support from the Mongols of Central Asia in their fight against the Īl-Khāns and about 1300 offered them an operational base from which they could also ravage northern India for a decade.

Nevertheless the Mongol rulers of Persia succeeded in stopping any large-scale penetration from the north-east or from Caucasia. Furthermore, a number of the hitherto sovereign states of southern Persia gradually accepted the Mongols as their overlords: Fārs in 662/1264, Kirmān in 702/1303. The Mongols were striving for pasture-land, the Persian farmers were trying to keep their ploughland; this opposition caused all kinds of friction and forced many farmers to flee to the mountains and join robber-bands. Mongol troops, left leaderless, became uncontrolled bands who made large areas of the country unsafe. Then in 693/1294, an *īl-khān* intoduced paper money on the Chinese model; the population had no experience of such a currency and no understanding of its economic presuppositions; an economic collapse ensued and was followed by a year of struggles between three candidates for the throne. Eventually the twenty-four-year-old Prince Ghāzān, a great-grandson of Hülegü, won (694/1295). Advised by a very able *wazīr*, the former physician Rashīd al-Dīn (who was obviously of Jewish origin and had been converted to Islam), the new *īl-khān* had an earnest desire to bring peace and order to his country. He created the most important step towards this by an entirely personal act; a few days after he came to the throne he abandoned Buddhism and embraced Sunnī Islam; he thereby gave the signal for most of the Mongols to come over immediately to this religion, if they had not already done so. Buddhism, in Persia a very artificial growth, was soon extinguished; the Buddhist temples were evidently transformed into mosques, though there is no trace of them today. Thus in the religious field the distinction between ruler and subject, between oriental intruders and natives, had disappeared. All the same, the sectarian distinctions within Islam continued to make themselves felt. It was possible to repel an attack by the Golden Horde in Caucasia; an advance on Syria failed. However, this was less significant than the programme of reform that Ghāzān initiated with the aim of achieving internal stability. The finances were to be put in order; the nuisance of banditry was to be checked; the encroachments of government officials and state emissaries were to be restrained, and morality and public order were to be encouraged. It did in fact prove possible to subdue the worst excesses and to revive the economic life that had collapsed because of the paper money. However, the plan had no final success, as Ghāzān died in 703/1304 in his thirty-second year; he too was probably carried off by alcoholism, the family failing of the Īl-Khāns. After the death of Ghāzān his brother Öljeitü strove to continue his work in the same spirit under the guidance of the experienced minister Rashīd al-Dīn; under this *īl-khān* conditions remained fairly stable. He built a new capital in Sulṭāniyya west of Qazvīn—its impressive ruins are still to be seen today—and tried to do justice to the growing importance of the Shī'a in his territories by attaching himself to them about 709/1310. However, when he died in 716/1316 and was succeeded by his twelve-year-old son Abū Sa'īd—now once more a Sunnī—the decay of the state could no longer be arrested. Within two years Rashīd al-Dīn was executed. In the reign of Abū Sa'īd, the minister 'Alī Shāh died a natural death in 724/1324 while still in office—the sources do not fail to give due prominence to this remarkable occurrence—but nevertheless internal stability was rapidly shattered by palace and harem intrigues, revolts, tribal feuds, and possibly also by ethnic antagonism between the Persians on the one hand and on the other hand the Turks and Mongols, who were at that time coalescing with one another in Persia because of a common adherence to Islam and the use of Turkish as their colloquial language. Ghāzān's reforms came to nothing. Everywhere in the provinces there were strong tendencies to secession. Anatolia and Georgia slipped away from their control. In the eastern Fertile Crescent the descendants of a Mongol *amīr* established from 740/1340 the Jalayirid dynasty. In Fārs the Muzaffarids, after all kinds of disorder, succeeded in establishing themselves by 754/1353 with a government that was at first strictly Sunnī. Abū Sa'īd had died in 736/1335; after eighteen further years of fluctuating civil war the last pretender to the throne of the Īl-Khāns disappeared. He was the only one to bear a pure Persian name, Nūshirvān. The sources do not even tell us what eventually became of him.

The role of the Īl-Khāns had bound together in one bloc of states the Persian plateau, the eastern Fertile Crescent, the Rūm Seljuk region, Lesser Armenia (Cilicia) and Georgia, but it had also created sharply defined frontiers with Syria and Egypt. Their antagonism to the Egyptian rulers, at that time the main adversary of the French during the last Crusades, had caused the Īl-Khāns to enter into relations with European states. Ambassadors went repeatedly to and fro between them and the pope, the king of France and the king of England. When the Golden Horde allowed the Genoese to set up a trading post at Kaffa in the Crimea in 664/1266, it was only natural that the Venetians should receive in return freedom of movement at the court of the Īl-Khāns in Tabrīz. The Īl-Khāns, who for a long time were non-Muslims and therefore had to look for counterpoises to their Muslim subjects, had repeatedly made friendly approaches to the Christians of various denominations; even the Georgians enjoyed a certain measure of popularity with them. This policy made them acceptable allies to the Crusaders, who were now fighting desperately in their last coastal fortresses. The West now saw in their troops the hosts of Prester John, who was expected to deliver Jerusalem from the Mamluk yoke. All this promoted trading-relations between East and West, while the Mediterranean progressively regained its function as the link between the states on its shores. The Mamluks similarly encouraged the exchange of goods, which they on their part had organized as a state monopoly.

Intellectual life was also maintained, if not encouraged, by the Mongols, as for instance historical writing in Persian, which naturally had above all to serve the glory of themselves and their ancestors but yet produced independent achievements that are significant even today. In this connexion we must above all remember the extensive work *Jāmiʿ al-tawārīkh* ('The assembly of histories') left by the *wazīr* Rashīd al-Dīn; he used materials collected by a number of collaborators, and wrote in the very readable colloquial Persian of his day, with a considerable admixture of Turkish and Mongol words. The work also contains large sections on the history of the Mongols, of India and of Europe (based on Martin of Troppau). This was a first attempt to survey the history of the Christian West, with which the Orient now had various relations, and was undertaken at a time when no European historical work had yet attempted such a presentation of the Islamic world. Epic and didactic poetry also reached its peak at that time with Saʿdī of Shīrāz (d. 690/1291). A revealing picture of the religious and social condition of Persia can be deduced from allusions and sceptical comments made by the poet.

We must also not forget the work of Jalāl al-Dīn Rūmī (604–72/1207–

73), probably the greatest mystic poet and thinker to write in Persian, even though he lived at the court of the Seljuks of Rūm and was only indirectly under Īl-Khān rule. His *Masnavī* conquered the Persian-speaking world as rapidly as the *Shāh-nāma* had done centuries before. Rūmī represents the end of the period of the free-lance mystics, who sought unhindered, direct ways to God. He and many of his contemporaries, mainly between the sixth/twelfth and eighth/fourteenth centuries, concentrated in the ever-more numerous Ṣūfī orders, that mystical movement which had been incorporated into Sunnī orthodoxy by al-Ghazālī. These confraternities of mystics chiefly spread over the Turkish and Arabic linguistic areas. Among the Persians they were opposed by the powerful—and later dominant—Shī'ī movement, which does not admit immediate access to God without the mediation of the *imāms*. Nevertheless, in the course of time the favourable attitude to 'Alī of many Ṣūfī orders brought about a *rapprochement* between the two points of view, and thus associations of Ṣūfīs arose even in Persia.

Much of the intellectual upsurge that Persia had lately experienced under the Īl-Khāns was lost again in the disorders of the second half of the eighth/fourteenth century. Various dynasties and rulers struggled against one another with varying success. In the east in Sabzavār and the neighbourhood the Shī'ī robber-state of the 'Gallows-Birds' (*Sarbadār*) was able to subsist from about 758/1357 to 781/1379–80. The Kart dynasty continued in Herat and its neighbourhood until 791/1389; some individual rulers also retained their position in Khūzistān and Āzarbāyjān. The only state of real importance was that of the Muzaffarids in Fārs, with Shīrāz as its capital. There, under the son of the founder of the dynasty, Shāh Shujā' (759–86/1358–84), the government showed some tolerance in religious matters; this permitted a flowering of intellectual life which is best known to posterity through the *ghazals* written by the great poet Ḥāfiẓ (*c.* 720–92/1320–90). In many quarters his poems have been taken to be purely secular, and any mystical interpretation of them has been regarded as artificial. Whether this is correct, or whether their scintillating ambiguity also conceals religious ideas which might, with the poet as with other men, depend on changing moods, is a question to which there is no certain answer.

Persia and the Near East were to experience yet another huge Mongol invasion. We must therefore take a brief look at Central Asia, where the descendants of Chingiz Khān's third son Chaghatay had since 709/1309 gained complete supremacy over the descendants of the Great Khan

Ögedei. The territory in which they ruled—Transoxania, Semirech'ye, the Tarim Basin and Jungaria (Dzungaria)—split into two halves in the eighth/fourteenth century. The eastern half was at that time called Mughulistān, because a shamanist Mongol culture had survived in the language and nomadic way of life of large parts of it. On the other hand, since about 731/1330 the rulers in the area west of the Issıq Köl had been Muslims; soon, however, they succumbed to an aristocracy of four leading families which took over the administration. They were in the long run unable to hold out against the rulers of Mughulistān, who were thrusting at them from the east, and had in the meanwhile become Muslims. About 767/1365, Chaghatay's inheritance seems to have become united under the rulers of Mughulistān. Then the major-domo of the reigning prince in Samarqand, Tīmūr (properly Temür, the Turkish word for 'iron'), shook off his allegiance to his master in 771/1369 and made himself the actual ruler, though only with the title of *beg*, i.e. *amīr*. Crippled early on—probably by a war wound—he is known to history as Tīmūr-i Lang (Tīmūr the Lame; the europeanized form of the name is Tamerlane). At that time Tīmūr was about thirty-three. In the remaining thirty-five years of his life, in continual campaigns conducted with indefatigable energy, he subjugated the whole of Persia (from 781/1379), Caucasia (787–9/1385–7), the eastern Fertile Crescent, also in 781/1379 Khwārazm (which had become independent after the beginning of civil wars in the Golden Horde in 760/1359), and in addition the Golden Horde itself (793/1391 and 797/1395). Towards the end of his life he ruled, at least temporarily, over northern India (801/1398), Syria (803/1400) and Anatolia (804/1402)—or rather, he plundered and massacred relentlessly throughout these countries. In spite of his bigoted and ostentatious Sunnī piety, he was one of the worst enemies to whom Islamic civilization ever fell a victim; moreover he systematically decimated the Christians, with the result that since then the Nestorians and Jacobites of Mesopotamia have been only a shadow of their former selves. In the course of his campaigns he slaughtered countless thousands and built pyramids of their skulls. Innumerable towns were devastated and their inhabitants pillaged. Islamic learning and art suffered damage from which they took long to recover, and in some areas never recovered at all. Tīmūr's only aesthetic interest was the embellishment of his capital, Samarqand, which was effected by artists and craftsmen gathered from afar; many of his buildings have survived to the present day, through the care of his successors and subsequent restoration. He put an end to the dynasties of the Karts (791/1389) and the Muzaffarids (795/1393). The Jalayirids in the eastern Fertile Crescent were able to save themselves by flight; the Ottomans were indeed hard hit by the battle of Ankara in 804/1402 but did not go under completely.

Tīmūr spread universal destruction; he undermined Islamic civilization and its power of resistance, but he never created a stable empire and thus in no way gave his subjects the protection of a settled government. He died in Sha'bān 807/January 1405 at Utrār on the Jaxartes just as he was on the point of marching on China. Within two years his empire had fallen asunder. In Anatolia, 'Irāq and northern India the old dynasties returned. For the time being Persia and Transoxania did in fact remain in the hands of his descendants; these repaired much of the damage done by their ancestor—so far as such repair is ever possible.

Tīmūr's fourth son, Shāh-Rukh, who had—side by side, of course, with a number of other sons and grandsons of Tīmūr in various places—gained power in 809/1407 in the greater part of Persia, especially in Khurāsān and Transoxania, proved in contrast to be a peaceful ruler and a protector of religion, scholars and poets; under his rule most of Persia regained peace and orderly economic conditions after many decades of internal disorder. He had nevertheless a good deal of trouble with a popular shaykh, Khwāja Aḥrār, who was backed by numerous adherents and possessed powerful economic interests. Shāh-Rukh's son, Ulugh Beg, ruled as his father's viceroy in Transoxania; he too was a promoter of scholarship and science, but it became apparent after Shāh-Rukh's death in 850/1447 that he was not a very able ruler when deprived of his father's help. He was murdered two years later. In another three years Shāh-Rukh's great-nephew, Abū Sa'īd (855–73/1452–69), came to power, and controlled Persia from the borders of Mesopotamia to Transoxania.

Meanwhile two opponents had arisen against the Timurids. In Mesopotamia the Turcoman horde of the 'Black Sheep' (Kara-Koyunlu) had ruled Mosul from about 776/1375 under Jalayirid sovereignty; under their vigorous leader Kara Yūsuf (from 792/1390) they had, although Shī'īs, succeeded in surviving the storm of Tīmūr's time. Their former Jalayirid overlords were indeed able to supersede Tīmūr's grandsons in 'Irāq after his death, but they had not sufficient forces to hold out against the Kara-Koyunlu; in 813/1410 they lost Baghdād and in 824/1421 Shūshtar was taken from them. The dominion of the Artukids also came to an end in 814/1412 after lasting for three centuries. The result was that the eastern Fertile Crescent was now for the first time subject to a Turkish dynasty. In spite of seventeen years of disputes over the succession after the death of Kara Yūsuf in 823/1420, this dynasty was able to hold out against the Timurids, though with some loss of territory. Mīrzā Jāhān-Shāh from 841/1437 achieved a tolerable understanding with the Timurids, who had helped him against his brother, and this endured until Abū Sa'īd came to the throne in 855/1452. He snatched from Abū Sa'īd a number of districts in western and southern Persia; of these, however, only Jibāl and Kirmān remained in his possession in 860/1456. Meanwhile his rule was repeatedly threatened by revolts on the part of his sons. In 871/1466 he died in battle against the Ak-Koyunlu; two years later his entire territory fell into their hands.

In contrast to the 'Black Sheep', the Turcomans of the 'White Sheep' (Ak-Koyunlu) were Sunnīs. Their rule proved even more dangerous to the Timurids than that of their predecessors and rivals. The Ak-Koyunlu had had frequent brushes with the Kara-Koyunlu in Eastern Anatolia since the beginning of the eighth/fourteenth century; they had been overpowered by these and were largely eliminated by the division of their territories among several rivals. Uzun Ḥasan ('Tall Ḥasan') did not rise to power within the Ak-Koyunlu until 853/1449. It was he who gradually extended its sphere of influence and eliminated the Kara-Koyunlu in 871–3/1466–8. Then he advanced against Abū Sa'īd, defeated him at Tabrīz in 873/1469 and had him executed immediately afterwards. For western and southern Persia (Jibāl, Iṣfahān, Fārs and Kirmān) this meant the end of Timurid domination. Uzun Ḥasan did not venture to attack eastern Persia; he felt increasingly threatened by the Ottomans, who between 871/1466 and 873/1468 had conquered the emirates of Karaman and Kastamonu and thereby removed the chief bulwarks of Uzun Ḥasan. He tried to obtain the co-operation of the Venetians against them, but this led to no practical military action and did not save him from several defeats by the Ottomans in 877–8/1472–3. After his death in 883/1478 his empire was divided up among several of his sons and was thus no longer a danger to either the Ottomans or the Timurids, even though the dynasty lasted on in Baghdād until 921/1515. One of the Timurids, Ḥusayn Baykara, a great-great-grandson of the founder of the dynasty and from a hitherto unimportant line of the family, had to fight for several years from 873/1469 before he superseded other competitors in the east of the Persian plateau. He set up his capital in Herat and during a long reign, under the guidance of his *wazīr,* ʿAlī Shīr Navāʾī (*c.* 843–907/1440–1502), gave it major cultural importance. The last of Persia's seven classic poets, Jāmī (817–98/1414–92), lived in the vicinity of his court, and the historian Mīrkhwānd (836–903/1433–98) wrote a 'History of the world', which determined the Muslim view of history for centuries on end; together with the work of his grandson, Khwāndamīr (*c.* 880–942/1475–1536) it also, through a number of partial translations in the nineteenth century, had a lasting influence on the picture of the history of Islam as seen by the Western nations. ʿAlī Shīr Navāʾī, himself a skilful Persian writer, was at the same time fighting for equal recognition of his native Chaghatay Turkish with Persian. He, together with Bābur in his memoirs, brought about the definite acceptance of this branch of Turkish as a literary language. Simultaneously with Ḥusayn Baykara, the four sons of Abū Saʿīd held sway over Transoxania with Farghānā and also what is today central Afghanistan around Kābul and Ghazna; they did not, however, play a political or even cultural role equal to that of the sultan of Herat.

Ḥusayn Baykara was plagued with gout in his old age and became malevolent. When he died in 911/1506 forces had already come into being that were to destroy his son and heir in the following year. At first it was not at all certain which of the two forces would finally be victorious. In the course of the ninth/fifteenth century the Özbegs, a Turkic people, had gained steadily increasing importance. They took their name from a leader of the Golden Horde. After the death of Tīmūr in 807/1405 they had, in several advances, thrust forward from the area east of the central and southern Urals to the mouth of the Jaxartes on the Aral Sea; they established themselves there in 831/1428 and in Khwārazm in 833–6/1430–2. Gradually the whole northern bank of the Jaxartes up to the Farghānā valley came into the hands of their ruler Abu'l-Khayr al-Shaybānī, i.e. the descendant of Chingiz Khān's grandson, Shiban (arabicized as Shaybān), whence his dynasty is known as the Shaybanids. However, the resistance of the Timurids and the defection of part of his subjects—who thereby became 'deserters' (*Kazakhs*)—prevented him from advancing further towards the Persian plateau. Abu'l-Khayr fell in 873/1468 in an attempt to subdue the deserters.

The Özbeg danger was thereby held in check for a generation. Nothing further happened until, after 900/1495, the dead ruler's grandson Muḥammad Shaybānī started fresh activities from the town of Yası (now the town of Turkistān). Within a few years he drove Abū Sa'īd's sons out of Transoxania, and after the death of Ḥusayn Baykara he seized the opportunity to put an end to this dynasty in eastern Persia as well (912/1507). In 913/1508 he was also able to secure his country against the rulers of Mughulistān; one of them was executed by his command.

Just as under Tīmūr a full century before, the foundations now seemed to have been laid for a great new empire, the central point of which would again have been situated in Transoxania. But now Muḥammad Shaybānī was opposed by Shāh Ismā'īl, the representative of a new political force, who set out to unite Persia principally on the basis of the Twelver Shi'ism. From 906/1500 onwards he had from Āẕarbāyjān succeeded in subjugating extensive stretches of Persia. The question was now which of these two rivals would control the fate of the country. The matter was soon decided when Ismā'īl disputed Muḥammad's right to the fruits of his victory over the Timurids and attacked him in Khurāsān. Muḥammad Shaybānī fell in battle near Merv in Ramaḍān 916/December 1510.

Ismā'īl did not, however, succeed in incorporating Transoxania into his empire and thus maintaining the union of the lands south and north of the Oxus that had been restored by the Timurids. This union was in fact now ended for ever. With the intention of annexing Transoxania, Ismā'īl found an ally against Muḥammad Shaybānī's successor in Bābur, a scion of the fallen Timurid dynasty, the son of the former ruler of Farghānā. This ally had some initial successes, but he suffered a defeat north of Bukhārā in 918/1512 and eventually was unable to hold out even in Samarqand, as the Sunnīs there objected to his collaboration with the champion of the Shī'a. Nevertheless, he was to be the founder of the empire of the Great Mughals in India.

The empire founded by Bābur was one of the three great Muslim empires that gave Islam its characteristic stamp from the ninth/fifteenth and tenth/sixteenth centuries onwards. The second, increasingly differentiated from the others by its Shī'ī faith, was Safavid Persia, bordered on its westward side by the Ottoman Empire. This division of the Near East, and the consequent cutting off of Central Asia from the mainstream of world politics, ushered in an epoch in the history of the Islamic peoples that was largely determined by these three powers.

CHAPTER 2

EGYPT AND SYRIA

TO THE END OF THE FATIMID CALIPHATE

For more than two centuries after the Arab conquest, Egypt was a province of the Islamic empire. Her capital was Fusṭāṭ, a garrison centre established by the conquerors; her rulers were a line of Arab governors, sent by the caliphs in the East. Though the main centres of the empire lay in Asia, the province of Egypt was not unimportant. Her rich corn harvest helped to supply the needs of hungry Arabia; her revenues enriched the imperial exchequer; her ports, her camps, her marts and her schools were the bases from which the fleets and armies, the merchants and missionaries of Islam drove westward and southward, by the Mediterranean and the Red Sea, and far into Africa. Though divided into administrative and fiscal sub-districts, Egypt was highly centralized. The unified valley of a great river, she was easily controlled, and kept firmly under the authority of the central, imperial power.

The Syrian lands, stretching from Sinai to the foothills of Taurus, present a different picture. At first, like Egypt, a conquered province of the Medina caliphate, Syria herself became the seat of empire under the Umayyads—only to revert to provincial status after their fall, and the transfer of the imperial capital to ʿIrāq. But here there was no centralized unity like that of Egypt. In the Syrian lands, a broken landscape of mountains, valleys, rivers, plains and deserts, with ancient and distinctive cities, held a population of great diversity, and imposed a fragmentation of government—a division into widely separated districts and regions, ruled by different authorities and often by different means. Even during the Umayyad century of imperial glory, the effective political unification of Syria was rarely achieved. Under the ʿAbbasids, the processes of political fragmentation were accelerated. In marked contrast with the unity and continuity of Egyptian political life, that of Syria in the Middle Ages is characterized by separatism, regionalism and particularism—a pattern of recurring diversity and conflict.

During the first centuries of Muslim rule, the Hellenistic era in Egypt and Syria came to an end. The Greek language, so long and so firmly established in both countries, died out and was forgotten. Even the indigenous Coptic and Aramaic languages ceased to be spoken or understood by the great mass of the population, and survived only in dialects, in scholarship and in Christian liturgies. In time most of the people of these countries accepted the Muslim faith and the Arabic language. Even the minorities who, rejecting the faith of the conqueror, remained Christians or Jews, adopted his language and, with it, much of his culture, outlook, and way of life.

A primary factor in the arabization of the two countries was the massive movement of Arabs from Arabia. In Syria and Palestine, this had begun, by peaceful immigration, long before the advent of Islam and continued for long after it. In Egypt Arab settlement began with the conquest; at first unorganised and mainly Yemeni, it was given a new direction when in 109/727 the Caliph Hishām authorized the planned migration and settlement of several thousand Qaysī Arabs in the Nile valley. The process of Arab colonization in Egypt continued during the second/eighth and third/ninth centuries.

The settlement of Arabs was not the only instrument of arabization—indeed, when the movement of migration and colonization had spent itself, persons of Arabian origin can still have been only a minority in the conquered provinces. Another was the arabization of the existing inhabitants, with or without their conversion to Islam. This was fostered by the universal use of the Arabic language as the medium of government, culture and commerce. The Syrians and Copts, long accustomed to alien domination, seem to have had no national feeling like that which sustained the separate identity of the Persians even after their conversion to Islam. The Coptic risings against Arab rule were occasional, spasmodic and unorganized, concerned only with local grievances against oppressive taxation, or rather tax-collection, and were not accompanied by any signs of religious or national revival or even awareness. Their failure and discouragement prepared them for assimilation, which was made easier by the simultaneous decline in the political and economic status of the once-privileged Arab settlers themselves.

In the rising of 216/831, following the strains of the civil war between al-Amīn and al-Ma'mūn, Copts and Arabs made common cause, and suffered a common fate. In 217/832 the Caliph al-Ma'mūn visited Egypt—the first caliph ever to do so—and established a Khurāsānī army there. He inaugurated a new system by giving the province of Egypt as an appanage to his Khurāsānī general, 'Abd Allāh b. Ṭāhir. 'Abd Allāh himself named the governor, who was his and not the caliph's agent. He was the first of a series of such officers, most of them Turkish, who held

Egypt as an appanage from the caliph, with brief intervals of direct rule. The last Arab governor, ʿAnbasa, ruled from 238/852 to 242/856.

The transfer of the capital to ʿIrāq lessened the interest and weakened the influence of the central imperial government in the Mediterranean provinces. The Syrians, resentful of their lost power and diminished status, rose in frequent revolt and were subject, as long as feasible, to strict surveillance. Egypt, further away from the centre, was left on a looser rein. During the ninety years of the Umayyad caliphate, twenty-two governors ruled over Egypt; in the first ninety years of the ʿAbbasid caliphate there were fifty-four, of whom no less than sixteen were in the ten years following the accession of al-Ma'mūn—a sure sign of slackening authority.

So far as can be judged from revenue figures available to us, the same period saw an accelerating economic decline. The figures for the revenue and tribute of Egypt given in the Arabic sources are variously defined and therefore difficult to compare. The general picture that emerges, however, is clearly one of falling revenue, accompanied by efforts to maintain it by increasing rigour and severity in assessment and collection. Thus, the papyri of the first half of the third/ninth century show the rate of the land-tax increasing in stages from 1 dinar per feddan of wheat to 1½, 2, 2½ and, in a document of 254/868, 4 dinars. At the same time new taxes and imposts—many of them restorations of old Roman practices not sanctioned by the fiscal provisions of the *Sharīʿa*—were introduced, and several state monopolies established.[1] This new and oppressive fiscal order is associated with the name of Aḥmad b. al-Mudabbir, sent from Baghdād as financial administrator of Egypt in 247/861. Described by al-Maqrīzī as 'a crafty man and a devil of an official',[2] he is credited with having devised and installed the whole system of imposts and monopolies which, despite repeated attempts at reform and abolition, remained characteristic of medieval Muslim Egypt.

Oppressive agrarian policies and the resultant decline of the Coptic peasantry combined to produce a sharp fall in revenue, which in turn led to severer and more oppressive taxation—and so to further decline in yield. While the income from the land-tax was reduced by maladministration, corruption, and flight, that from the poll-tax dwindled as

[1] On these questions see C. N. Becker, *Beiträge zur Geschichte Ägyptens unter dem Islam*, 2 parts (Strasburg, 1902–3); *idem, Islamstudien*, i (Leipzig, 1924); D. C. Dennett, *Conversion and the poll-tax in early Islam* (Cambridge Mass., 1950); C. Cahen, ḌARĪBA, in *EI*[2] (where further references are given).

[2] *Khiṭaṭ*, (Būlāq), i, 103; cf. Becker, *Beiträge*, 143.

more and more Copts found refuge in conversion to Islam. The vicious circle was aggravated by the frequent changes of governor and financial intendant, culminating in the appanage system installed by al-Ma'mūn. The drain of revenue to Baghdād, the costly separation between military and financial authority, the ruthless extortion practised by rulers with only a short-term interest in a maximum immediate return, combined to ruin Egyptian agriculture and bring the economy of the country to the verge of collapse. The manifest disarray of Egyptian affairs brought other dangers, as the Byzantines were tempted to start raiding the weakly defended shores. There must have been many in Egypt who were ready to give a welcome and support to a new régime able to bring the country strong government, financial independence, and reasonable protection and encouragement for economic activities.

A new era in the history of Muslim Egypt begins with the arrival in Fusṭāṭ, on 23 Ramaḍān 254/15 September 868, of Aḥmad b. Ṭūlūn, as governor on behalf of his step-father Bāyakbak, a chamberlain in Baghdād to whom the Caliph al-Mu'tazz had granted Egypt as appanage. His powers were at first strictly limited. The effective separation of powers, in medieval Islam, was in provincial administration—between the three divisions of military affairs, finance, and communications. Its purpose was to maintain the ultimate control of the imperial government, and prevent the emergence of provincial autonomies. When Ibn Ṭūlūn arrived in Fusṭāṭ, he found two officials appointed by and responsible to Baghdād—the financial intendant, Ibn al-Mudabbir, and the postmaster, Shukayr. His own financial powers were very limited, and in addition Alexandria and the western frontier marches were excluded from his jurisdiction.

Dislike and distrust between the new governor and his colleagues were mutual and immediate. A sharp political struggle, fought both in Fusṭāṭ and Baghdād, ended in the final defeat of Ibn al-Mudabbir, who was transferred to Syria, and the deposition of Shukayr, who died shortly after. Aḥmad b. Ṭūlūn now had financial independence in Egypt, and controlled the network of posts and intelligence. These were essential steps on the way to full independence. Meanwhile Bāyakbak had died, and the appanage of Egypt been transferred to Ibn Ṭūlūn's father-in-law, Yarjūkh. He confirmed Ibn Ṭūlūn as governor of Egypt and indeed added to his powers by giving him Alexandria and the marches. On Yarjūkh's death in 259/873 Egypt, with the other western provinces, was placed under the authority of the caliph's son, Ja'far al-Mufawwaḍ, in whose name Ibn Ṭūlūn now ruled. The Caliph al-Muʿtamid, who had succeeded in 256/870, had divided the empire, giving the West to his young son Jaʿfar al-Mufawwaḍ, and the East to his brother al-Muwaffaq, in effect as regent. The resulting struggles aided Ibn Ṭūlūn in establishing himself—but made inevitable an eventual clash with al-Muwaffaq, representing the central imperial power.

By 263/877, when the clash began, Ibn Ṭūlūn had accomplished a great deal. By halting the drain of revenue to Baghdād—or rather, by reducing it to a regular and limited tribute—he had accumulated great wealth. With it, he had built himself a new capital, the fortress-palace-city of Qaṭāʾiʿ, and had also, profiting from various opportunities, built up a strong, well-trained and well-equipped army of Turkish, Greek and Sudanese slaves.

The clash began when the regent al-Muwaffaq, hard pressed in his fight against the Zanj and Saffarid rebels in the East, wrote to Ibn Ṭūlūn to ask for money. This was not strictly within his rights, since Egypt came under the jurisdiction of his co-dominus Jaʿfar al-Mufawwaḍ; the caliph, fearing al-Muwaffaq, himself wrote to Ibn Ṭūlūn asking him not to send money, and warning him of al-Muwaffaq's hostile intentions.

Ibn Ṭūlūn compromised, sending the sum of 1,200,000 dinars to al-Muwaffaq, who seems to have considered it inadequate. The regent remonstrated, and, receiving an insolent reply from Ibn Ṭūlūn, decided to remove and replace him. To accomplish this, he appointed the somewhat reluctant Amājūr, the governor of Syria, as governor of Egypt also, and sent an army from ʿIrāq to enforce this decision. It failed to do so. Ibn Ṭūlūn put Egypt in a state of defence, and the imperial army broke up and returned home without accomplishing anything. The death of Amājūr shortly afterwards gave Ibn Ṭūlūn the opportunity to occupy Syria, which he did, without difficulty, in 264/878. Already in 256/870 Ibn Ṭūlūn had set out to conquer Syria from a rebel governor, ostensibly in the name of the caliph, but had been ordered back by the caliph. This time he was more successful, and was able to make Syria a dependency of his Egyptian principality.

A new crisis began in 269/882 when, after the desertion of a Tulunid governor in Syria to al-Muwaffaq, Ibn Ṭūlūn invited the caliph to come and join him, possibly in the hope of acquiring the regency and making his Syro-Egyptian state the centre of the whole empire. The caliph, chafing under the regent's authority, accepted and set out, but was intercepted by al-Muwaffaq's men and sent back ignominiously to

Sāmarrā. A war of proclamations and curses now broke out between Ibn Tūlūn and al-Muwaffaq, each claiming to be the caliph's protector and denouncing the other as a rebel. Peace negotiations were just beginning when Ibn Ṭūlūn died on 10 Dhu'l-Qa'da 270/10 May 884.

At once imperial troops invaded Syria, which they quickly overran. But the political structure created by Ibn Ṭūlūn was strong enough to survive his death. In Egypt, his twenty-year-old son Khumārawayh succeeded without legal title but with popular and general support—a new and significant assertion of the principle of locally based hereditary rule. Aḥmad b. Ṭūlūn had come as an appointed governor from the East, and had striven to maintain some semblance of legality in his dealings with the imperial power. Khumārawayh succeeded as his father's heir in the government of Egypt and in open defiance of the imperial power, which had nominated a new 'legal' governor. In Ṣafar 271/August 884 the Tulunid generals defeated and drove out the imperial troops, and reoccupied Palestine and southern Syria. A quarrel among the imperial generals enabled them to advance as far as the Euphrates. Khumārawayh, moderate in victory, was content with an agreement with al-Muwaffaq whereby Egypt, Syria and adjoining areas were granted to him and his descendants for a period of thirty years. The pact was renewed by al-Muwaffaq's son, who succeeded as caliph in 279/892 with the title of al-Mu'taḍid, and sealed by the marriage of Khumārawayh's daughter to the caliph. This marriage was celebrated with ruinous pomp. The Tulunid territories now included Cilicia and most of Mesopotamia; the tribute was fixed at 300,000 dinars a year—the amount previously paid by Aḥmad b. Ṭūlūn for Egypt alone.

Khumārawayh lived in peace and luxury, until he was murdered by his own slaves in Damascus, in Dhu'l Ḥijja 282/January–February 896. The Tulunid governor of Damascus and the troops at once swore allegiance to Khumārawayh's fourteen-year-old son, Abu'l-'Asākir Jaysh. Khumārawayh was indolent and extravagant, but could act swiftly and effectively in an emergency. His sons represent a more advanced stage of degeneration, and the dynasty foundered under their headstrong and incompetent rule. Jaysh ruled for barely nine months, during which he alienated most of his father's generals and counsellors. Deposed and murdered, he was succeeded by his equally incompetent younger brother Hārūn, under the regency of Muḥammad b. Abba. The last years of the Tulunid dynasty were a period of weakness, quarrels, intrigues, and rapidly increasing imperial intervention in the affairs of Egypt. A new treaty with the caliph in 286/899—the third—reduced the territories of the Tulunid principality, and increased its annual tribute to 450,000 dinars. Finally, in 292/904–5, the ravages of the Carmathians in Syria provided a pretext for direct intervention by imperial troops. From Syria the victorious imperial general mounted a joint land and sea attack on Egypt. On 19 Ṣafar 292/31 December 904 the drunken and debauched Hārūn was murdered in obscure circumstances, and was succeeded by his uncle Shaybān, who tried to rally the Tulunid forces for defence. It was too late, and on 2 Rabīʿ I 292/12 January 905 the imperial troops entered Fusṭāṭ. The Tulunid state was at an end, and the surviving male members of the family were sent in chains to Baghdād. A new governor was appointed to rule Egypt as representative of the caliph.

In the next thirty years Egypt was again under the direct but ineffectual control of the central government, and was ruled by a series of military governors. The real masters of the country were the intendants of finances, most of them members of the great bureaucratic clan of the Madhārā'īs, a family of ʿIrāqī Persian origin which had risen to prominence in Egypt under the Tulunids. Imperial rule in Egypt continued to be both ineffectual and oppressive. The economic decline, the signs of which had already reappeared under the later Tulunids, was once again aggravated by extortionate taxation. A pro-Tulunid rising was suppressed with difficulty. The Byzantines resumed their raids on the coasts and, most menacing of all, the new imperial power in the West, the Fatimid caliphs in Tunisia, sent invading forces to Egypt in 301–2/913–15 and again in 307–9/919–21, and came within an ace of conquering the country; they remained in possession of Barqa (Cyrenaica), on the western border of Egypt.

Once again the problems of Egypt demanded a strong and independent government. Moreover, the international situation was now far more favourable than it had been in the time of Aḥmad b. Ṭūlūn. Egypt was now between two imperial centres, in east and west, contending for the headship of the whole Islamic world—and even the caliphal government in Baghdād would see merit in a strong, self-reliant state in Egypt which could act as a barrier against the advance of the Fatimids from the west and, later, as a check on the new bedouin dynasties rising in Syria.

The beneficiary from this situation was Muḥammad b. Ṭughj, who arrived in Fusṭāṭ as governor in the summer of 323/935. He is usually known as the Ikhshīd, the title given to him by the caliph two years later.

His first tasks were to repel a Fatimid invasion and set the affairs of Egypt in order. Like Ibn Ṭūlūn, he had to contend with a powerful financial intendant—Abū Bakr Muḥammad al-Madhārā'ī. Unlike him, he took his defeated opponent into his own service, and found him a capable and efficient organizer of his economic affairs. Another difference is that the Ikhshīd enjoyed caliphal support from the start. His relations with Baghdād were friendly; his enemies were the Fatimids and the now independent ruler of northern Syria. In these struggles he was successful, but wisely contented himself with holding central and southern Syria as an Egyptian frontier march, leaving Ibn Rā'iq and, later, the Hamdanids in possession of northern Syria—and of the Byzantine and Mesopotamian frontier.

On his death in 334/946 he was nominally succeeded by his two sons, but the real ruler was their tutor, a Nubian eunuch known as Abu'l-Misk Kāfūr. On the death of the second son in 355/966 Kāfūr was confirmed by Baghdād as ruler in name as well as in fact. A modest but talented ruler, he continued the Ikhshīd's policies of friendship with Baghdād, peace with the Hamdanids, and firm and efficient government at home. His death in 357/968 was the signal for the Fatimid advance to the conquest of Egypt.

The establishment of the Tulunid state, and its revival and continuance by the Ikhshīd and Kāfūr, marks the rise of a new power in Islam. This was a period of political fragmentation, of the growth of regional autonomies, in the vast empire of the caliphs. But there are significant differences of origin and character among the new principalities. The aims of Ibn Ṭūlūn and the Ikhshīd were personal and dynastic, and were both politically and territorially limited. Unlike the Umayyad and Idrisid dynasties that had seized power in Spain and Morocco in the second/eighth century, they did not seek to withdraw from the Islamic oecumene headed by the caliph in Baghdād; still less did they desire, like the Fatimids in Tunisia, to challenge the 'Abbasids for the possession of the caliphate itself. Ibn Ṭūlūn and his successors were orthodox Sunnī Muslims, loyal to the principle of Islamic unity; their purpose was to carve out an autonomous and hereditary principality under loose caliphal suzerainty, rather than to acquire complete independence. They did not emerge from any sectarian religious movement, such as brought the Fatimids to power in North Africa; though they were patrons of letters and of the arts, their rise was not supported or followed by any national or cultural revival, such as accompanied the parallel rise of autonomous states in Persia. Ibn Ṭūlūn and the Ikhshīd were Central Asians, Kāfūr a Nubian. Their armies consisted of Turks and Greeks, Sudanese and Negroes; even their upper civilian bureaucrats were for the most part imported from ʿIrāq. In their art and architecture, the influence of the imperial style of ʿIrāq becomes greater and not less—clear evidence of the continued cultural subordination of Egypt to the metropolitan centres in the East.

Yet, in spite of these limitations, the Tulunids and Ikhshidids inaugurate the separate history of Muslim Egypt, follow recognizably Egyptian policies, and win strong Egyptian support. First, they brought the country security and prosperity. Aḥmad b. Ṭūlūn created a large and powerful army, with excellent discipline sustained by prompt payment and regular rations. This was his great advantage over his opponents, who were constantly hampered by military mutinies and discontents. It is the measure of Ibn Ṭūlūn's success that when he bequeathed his army to Khumārawayh it had never yet fought a war—though it had been used very effectively as an instrument of political warfare. Under Khumārawayh and still more under his sons, with irregular pay and relaxed discipline, the army deteriorated into roving bands of robbers. Under the Ikhshīd it again became an efficient and disciplined force—probably the largest in the Islamic world.

The size and good discipline of the Tulunid and Ikhshidid armies presuppose an efficient fiscal organization with a high yield. Though details are lacking, it is clear that the government was well supplied with money and the country prosperous. The collective memory, as reflected by the Egyptian historians, regarded the Tulunid state as a model of good government. Under Ibn al-Mudabbir, we are told, the revenue from the land-tax had fallen to 800,000 dinars; Ibn Ṭūlūn raised it to 4,300,000—almost the high watermark of Egyptian revenue. This was not achieved by extortion—certain taxes were in fact remitted—but by wise agrarian policies, inducing a higher yield, and by the elimination of abuses. Ibn Ṭūlūn gave greater security of land tenure, increased the cultivated area by new grants, removed uneconomic taxes, and reformed the apparatus of administration. Prices and tax-rates are both reported as being very low in his time. A major factor in this new prosperity was certainly the retention and expenditure in Egypt of great sums previously drained away to Baghdād. After his death his new order declined and collapsed, but was restored and expanded by the Ikhshidids. An interesting feature of this time is the insistence on administrative probity. The Ikhshīd seems to have been the first to establish regular, fixed salaries for civil servants, with close financial supervision. This administrative order was taken over with little change by the Fatimids.

Until the coming of Ibn Ṭūlūn, Egypt had been a subject province of a great empire with its centre elsewhere; under him and his successors it became, for the first time since the Ptolemies, the seat of a separate military and political power, with independent policies and a growing role in the affairs of the Middle East as a whole.

This role was vastly increased with the coming of the Fatimids, who conquered Egypt in 358/969. These new masters of Egypt were more than insubordinate governors with dynastic ambitions. They were the heads of a great religious movement, the Ismāʿīlī Shīʿa; as such they rejected even the nominal sovereignty of the Sunnī ʿAbbasid caliphs, whom they regarded as usurpers. By descent and by divine choice, so they claimed, they were the sole rightful heirs to the caliphate of all Islam, which they intended to take from the ʿAbbasids as the ʿAbbasids had taken it from the Umayyads. Following the ʿAbbasid precedent, they began their work in remote areas—first in the Yemen, and then in North Africa, where they established and proclaimed themselves as caliphs. The first three Fatimid caliphs ruled in the west only, but the fourth, al-Muʿizz, was able to accomplish the long-planned and carefully prepared conquest of Egypt, thus bringing the Fatimid Caliphate into the Islamic heartlands of the Middle East.

On 11 Shaʿbān 358/30 June 969 the Fatimid general Jawhar overwhelmed the last feeble resistance of the Ikhshidid forces near Jīza, and on the following day entered Fusṭāṭ. A week later he gave orders for the founding of a new city, outside Fusṭāṭ, to house his troops. The sources tell us that the conquerors chose a site and pegged out a vast square, with bells hung on ropes from pole to pole. These were to give the signal for the work to commence, when the Moorish astrologers whom al-Muʿizz had brought from Africa had determined the most auspicious moment. But a raven, perching on a rope, anticipated their calculations.[1] The bells rang, the waiting labourers swung their mattocks, and the city was founded—under the baleful ascendancy of the planet Mars, in Arabic *al-Qāhir,* the subduer. To avert the evil influence, the city itself was named after the red planet, and called *al-Qāhira*—in English

[1] It should, however, be noted that al-Masʿūdī (d. 956) tells more or less the same story about the foundation of Alexandria by Alexander (Maçoudi, *Les prairies d'or,* ed. C. Barbier de Meynard and translated by Pavet de Courteille, ii (Paris, 1914), 423–4; rev. Ch. Pellat, ii (Paris, 1965), 313–14).

corrupted into Cairo. The new city—and caliphate—required a new cathedral mosque. On 24 Jumādā I 359/4 April 970 Jawhar laid the foundation stone of the great mosque, to be known as al-Azhar, probably in honour of the daughter of the Prophet and ancestress of the dynasty, Fāṭima al-Zahrā'. The first service was held there on 7 Ramaḍān 361/22 June 971.

Egypt was now not merely an independent principality, but the centre of a vast empire, which at its peak comprised North Africa, Sicily, Palestine, Syria, the Red Sea coast of Africa, the Yemen and the Ḥijāz. The latter included the holy cities of Mecca and Medina, possession of which conferred enormous prestige on a Muslim sovereign—and the power to use the potent weapon of the Pilgrimage to his advantage. Cairo was the seat of a caliph, the head of a religion as well as the sovereign of an empire. Al-Azhar was its intellectual centre, where scholars and teachers elaborated the doctrines of the Ismā'īlī faith, and trained the *dā'īs*—missionaries—who were to preach it to the unconverted at home and abroad.

Al-Mu'izz (341–65/952–75) was well served by two remarkable men—his general, Jawhar, and his minister, Ya'qūb b. Killis. Jawhar, a slave of European origin, was the real conqueror of Egypt and the architect of Fatimid military power. Ya'qūb b. Killis was an islamized Jew of Baghdādī origin, who had been in the service of Kāfūr. A man of great ability, he is credited with having organized the fiscal and administrative system which lasted for much of the Fatimid period. His powers were confirmed and extended by al-'Azīz (365–86/975–96), the second Fatimid caliph in Egypt.

In a poem by Ibn Hāni', the Ismā'īlī panegyrist of al-Mu'izz, the poet depicts a vision of the Fatimid caliph entering Baghdād, and sees before him, open and unimpeded, the ancient Persian imperial highway to Khurāsān and the East. In his vision the poet, himself an Andalusian from the far west of Islam, gives vivid expression to the oecumenical ambitions of the Fatimids—to their determination to establish their imamate and their Ismā'īlī faith in the whole world of Islam.[1]

For more than a century, Fatimid activities were directed largely towards this objective. Sometimes by war, sometimes by diplomacy, they sought to extend their sway into Syria, Arabia, and even 'Irāq—

[1] Ibn Hāni', *Dīwān*, ed. Zāhid 'Alī, (1356 A.H.), 408; cit. M. Canard, 'L'impérialisme des Fatimides et leur propagande', in *Annales de l'Institut d'Études Orientales* (Algiers), vi (1942–7), 185.

though with only intermittent success. Besides their political and military resources, they commanded a great army of missionaries, agents and followers in the ʿAbbasid dominions, under the supreme direction of the *dāʿī al-duʿāt* (chief missionary) in Cairo. Linked with their missionary work was a great commercial expansion, and a skilful economic policy aimed at diverting the sea-born trade with Asia from the Persian Gulf to the Red Sea, and thus at the same time strengthening Egypt and weakening ʿIrāq.[1] In pursuit of this objective, the Fatimids extended their sway down both shores of the Red Sea, established themselves in the Yemen, and engaged in extensive missionary work in India and Afghanistan, on the far side of the ʿAbbasid dominions.

In the end, their great bid for leadership failed. The Ghaznavid ruler of the East, whom they had wooed intensively, threw in his lot with Sunnism, of which he became a weighty support. The Shīʿī Buwayhid (Buyid) in ʿIrāq, whom they had tried to persuade to transfer his allegiance to them as rightful ʿAlid *imāms*, refused and questioned their descent, thus splitting the Shīʿī forces at a crucial moment. Worst of all, they never really succeeded in solving the Syrian problem, and their position in that country was always insecure, subject to attack and overthrow by local leaders, bedouin chieftains, Carmathians from the east and Byzantines from the north. Syria was perhaps the most important stumbling-block in the way of their further expansion eastwards. The high watermark of their expansion came in the years 448–51/1057–9, when a dissident Turkish general in ʿIrāq called Arslan al-Basāsīrī went over to the Fatimid allegiance and proclaimed the Fatimid caliph first in Mosul and then, for a year, in Baghdād itself. The government in Cairo was, however, unable to provide effective support, and the Seljuks drove al-Basāsīrī out of Baghdād in what proved to be a final defeat of the Ismāʿīlī Fatimid cause.

The Fatimids had thus failed to complete the ʿAbbasid pattern of triumphal progress from the periphery to the centre, from revolution to universal empire. They followed, however, at an accelerated pace, on the ʿAbbasid road to disorder and ruin. The first three caliphs in Egypt, al-Muʿizz, al-ʿAzīz, and al-Ḥākim, retained full personal control of government. As the infallible *imām* of the Ismāʿīlīs, the caliph was an absolute monarch, exercising a spiritual—not merely religious—supremacy transmitted by the divine will through a divinely ordained

[1] B. Lewis, 'The Fatimids and the route to India', in *Revue de la Faculté des Sciences economiques de l'Université d'Istanbul,* xi (1949–50), 50–4.

family. As such, he presided with equal authority over the three great branches of government—the bureaucracy, the religious hierarchy, and the army.

It was in the army that, as in Baghdād, the first signs of trouble appeared. The backbone of the army of the conquest had been the Berber regiments, who, like the Khurāsānī troops of the early ʿAbbasids, provided the military basis of Fatimid power. In a sense, the Fatimid Caliphate was for a while a North African ascendancy in the Middle East, as evidenced by the Berber garrisons in Cairo, Damascus and other cities, and by the prominent role of North African merchants in the expanding commerce of Fatimid Egypt—with India as well as Europe. Together with the Berbers, there were a number of *mamlūks* of European—Greek, Slavonic or Italian—origin.

As early as the reign of al-ʿAzīz, it was found necessary to form regiments of Turkish *mamlūks,* of the type already familiar in the east. These were followed by units of Daylamī infantrymen, and the crystallization of rival blocks of Easterners (*Mashāriqa*) and Westerners (*Maghāriba*). With the weakening of civilian control, their quarrels and conflicts brought disorder and ruin to the cities of the empire. Later, the formation of regiments of black slaves, recruited by purchase from Nubia and the Sudan, added a third force to the racial struggle. At first, the Sudanese supported the easterners against the Berber ascendancy. In a trial of strength at the end of the fourth/tenth century the Berbers were defeated, and never really recovered their position. Later, with the loss of North Africa to the Fatimids, the Berbers became less important, and the main struggle was between Turks and Sudanese, with the former—often with Berber support—gaining the upper hand.

Military disturbances first became a serious factor during the minority of al-Ḥākim, who succeeded in 386/996 at the age of eleven. Despite his own reassertion of personal control, his reign marks the decline of caliphal authority and the emergence of the military factions to political significance. The personal and religious authority of the caliph, paramount under his predecessors, began to decline—partly no doubt as a result of his own highly eccentric behaviour. The process was accelerated under his successors who became little more than puppets in the hands of conflicting military cliques.

In 411/1021, al-Ḥākim disappeared in mysterious circumstances, during a period of grave discontent. He is said to have been murdered with the connivance of his sister, the Sitt al-Mulk, who became the real ruler of Egypt as regent for her sixteen-year-old nephew al-Ẓāhir. She ruled competently and vigorously until her death in 415/1027; effective rule then passed into the hands of the *wazīr* Aḥmad al-Jarjarā'ī, who governed Egypt for nearly twenty years.

Al-Ẓāhir died in 427/1036, without ever having shown any interest in politics, and was succeeded by another minor, his seven-year-old son al-Mustanṣir. Already during the reign of al-Ẓāhir the civilian rule of the Sitt al-Mulk and al-Jarjarā'ī was increasingly challenged by military insubordination. Civilian, bureaucratic government was breaking up, commerce was in decline, and fiscal extortion made its appearance again, as the tax-collectors struggled to make good the fall in revenue. In 414–15/1023–5 Egypt suffered a terrible famine, when the people killed and ate their domestic animals, and even the beasts set aside for the Feast of Sacrifices (*'Īd al-Aḍḥā*) were seized. It was not the last such famine.

For the first nine years of al-Mustanṣir's reign, final authority in Egypt was still with his father's *wazīr*, al-Jarjarā'ī. On the latter's death in 436/1045, it passed to the caliph's mother, a Sudanese slave, who exercised it through a succession of ministers and agents. Notable among them were her former master, Abū Sa'd al-Tustarī, a Persian Jewish banker, converted to Islam, who was murdered in 429/1047, and the *qāḍī* Abū Muḥammad Ḥasan al-Yāzūrī, who became *wazīr* in 442/1050 and held the office until his execution in 450/1058.

He was the last civilian minister to exercise any real control. After him, the *wazīrs* were mere puppets, and real power was with the military cliques, whose conflicts and misgovernment brought the country to complete ruin. The vast empire over which al-Mustanṣir reigned in his early years was whittled away. In North Africa, the Zirid rulers, whom the Fatimids themselves had appointed, became independent and transferred their allegiance from the Fatimid to the 'Abbasid caliph; Syria was lost to local dynasts and Seljuk invaders; even the Ḥijāz, so important to the religious pretensions of the dynasty, refused to share the Egyptian famine and turned away to Baghdād.

Inside Egypt, things went from bad to worse. Administrative, fiscal and economic breakdown culminated in a series of terrible famines. Already in 446/1054–5 the caliph had to appeal to the Byzantine Emperor Constantine Monomachus to send food to Egypt. Between 457/1065 and 464/1072, the famine was so bad that men were reduced to eating dogs and cats, and, according to al-Maqrīzī, even human flesh. Meanwhile, in 454/1062 and again in 459/1067, the struggle between the

Turkish and Sudanese soldiery deteriorated into open warfare, ending in a victory for the Turks and their Berber allies. The caliph, deprived of the last shreds of authority, had to sell his treasures to meet their demands.

The end came in 465/1073, when the despairing caliph sent a secret message to Badr al-Jamālī, the governor of Acre, inviting him to come to Egypt and take control. Badr responded swiftly. Originally an Armenian slave of the Syrian *amīr,* Jamāl al-Dīn b. ʿAmmār, he had had a successful career as soldier and governor in Syria. His Armenian body-guard and his army were loyal and reliable—and he insisted on taking them with him to Egypt. Sailing from Acre in mid-winter, he landed at Damietta, and entered Cairo with his body-guard on 28 Jumādā I 466/29 January 1074. The ruling cliques, who had no knowledge of his coming or of its purpose, were taken completely by surprise; in one night, his officers rounded up the leading Turkish generals and Egyptian officials, with their associates, and had them all put to death. Badr was soon master of Egypt, with the triple title, conferred by the caliph, of commander of the armies (*amīr al-juyūsh*), director of the missionaries (*hādī al-duʿāt*), and *wazīr,* signifying his leadership of the military, religious and bureaucratic establishments. It is by the first of these titles that he is usually known.

Egypt was now governed by a military autocracy, headed by the *amīr al-juyūsh* and maintained by his troops. The post became a permanency, in which Badr al-Jamālī was succeeded by his son and then by a series of other military autocrats, who kept the Fatimid caliphs in the same kind of tutelage as had already been endured by the ʿAbbasid caliphs at the hands of the *amīr al-umarā'* in Baghdād. And just as the Sunnī caliphs had been subjected to the domination of the Shīʿī Buwayhids, so now the Ismāʿīlī *imāms* had to suffer the humiliation of control by military *wazīrs* who were not Ismāʿīlis, but Twelver Shīʿīs or even Sunnīs. It was a sad decline for a dynasty that had once claimed the spiritual and political headship of all Islam.

The swift and energetic action of Badr al-Jamālī brought peace and security to Egypt, and even some measure of prosperity—the annual revenue, we are told, was increased from about 2,000,000 to about 3,000,000 dinars; his military and administrative reorganization postponed the collapse of the Fatimid state for nearly a century. At first he even revived the universal claims of the Fatimid Caliphate and, responding to the Seljuk challenge in the East, launched a new campaign of military and political action and religious militancy in Syria, Arabia and India. But these efforts failed, and were abandoned by his successors. On the death of Badr in 487/1094, he was succeeded as *amīr al-juyūsh* by his son al-Afḍal; on the death of the Caliph al-Mustanṣir a few months later it was al-Afḍal who chose the next caliph. His choice was significant. Al-Mustanṣir's elder son, Nizār, had already been nominated by the dead caliph as heir, and was known and accepted by the Ismā'īlī leaders. The younger son, al-Musta'lī, was a youth without allies, or supporters, who would be entirely dependent on al-Afḍal. In marrying al-Musta'lī to his own sister and forcing his succession, al-Afḍal split the Ismā'īlī sect from top to bottom. Even in Egypt there were movements of opposition to this nomination and succession; in the east, the Ismā'īlī sect, revived and redirected under the inspired leadership of Ḥasan-i Ṣabbāḥ, refused to recognize the new caliph, and broke off all relations with the shrunken Fatimid missionary organization (*da'wa*) in Cairo. The divergence between the interests of the state and the revolution had appeared more than once during the Fatimid adventure. It was now complete. By choosing al-Musta'lī, al-Afḍal had, perhaps intentionally, alienated the militant Ismā'īlīs in the east, and dissociated the Egyptian state from their revolutionary doctrines and terrorist actions. Even those Ismā'īlīs who accepted al-Musta'lī broke away a little later. On the death of al-Musta'lī's son, al-Āmir, in 524/1130, most of the remaining faithful outside Egypt refused to recognize his cousin al-Ḥāfiẓ as caliph, but instead claimed that al-Āmir had left an infant son, who was the awaited and expected *imām*. The descendants of al-Mu'izz had become a local Egyptian dynasty, secularized, militarized —and in rapid decline.

The first century of Fatimid rule represents, in many ways, the high watermark of medieval Egypt. The administration, taken over from the Ikhshidids, was reorganized and expanded, and functioned with admirable efficiency. Ibn Killis abolished tax-farming, and he and his successors enforced strict probity and regularity in the assessment and collection of taxes. The revenues of Egypt were high, and instead of being drained by a tribute to an imperial capital elsewhere were now augmented by the incoming tribute of subject provinces. It was also an age of great commercial and industrial efflorescence. From the first, Fatimid governments realized the importance of trade both for the prosperity of Egypt and for the extension of Fatimid influence, and devoted great efforts to its encouragement. The pre-Fatimid trade of Egypt had been limited and meagre—mostly with neighbouring Muslim countries, together with a few exchanges with Constantinople. The Fatimids brought great changes. Inside Egypt, they fostered both agriculture and industry, and developed an important export trade of Egyptian products. Abroad, they developed a wide net of commercial relations, notably with Europe and India—two areas with which Egyptian contacts had previously been almost nil. In Europe, Egyptian ships sailed to Sicily and Spain, Egyptian fleets controlled the eastern Mediterranean, and close relations were established with the Italian city-states, especially Amalfi and Pisa. The two great harbours of Alexandria in Egypt and Tripoli in Syria became marts of world trade. In the east, the Fatimids gradually extended their sovereignty over the ports and outlets of the Red Sea, developed a great seaport at ʿAydhāb, for the trade with India and South-East Asia, and tried to win power or at least influence on the shores of the Indian Ocean. Like some other aspirants to world dominion, the Fatimids tried to use trade both to weaken their rivals and strengthen their own position. In lands far beyond the reach of Fatimid arms, the Ismāʿīlī *dāʿī* and the Egyptian or North African merchant went side by side.

It was, however, on their doorstep, in Palestine and Syria, that the Fatimids suffered their most grievous defeats, and encountered their greatest difficulties—which, aggravated by the subsequent economic collapse of Egypt, brought about the ultimate failure of their bid for Islamic supremacy. It was in Syria that their drive to the east was delayed and halted; from Syria again that the forces emerged which finally destroyed them.

The rise of Aḥmad b. Ṭūlūn had opened a new era in the history of Syria as of Egypt—though in a different way. The emergence of a new centre of power in Egypt made Syria-Palestine a borderland—sometimes a buffer and sometimes a battlefield in the struggles between the rival powers based on the valleys of the Nile and of the Tigris-Euphrates.

Syria was important to both of them. To the rulers of both ʿIrāq and Egypt, the revenues and, to some extent, the manpower of Syria was worth having; still more attractive were her products—foodstuffs, and above all minerals and timber, lacking in both ʿIrāq and Egypt, which Syria could at that time supply. To Egypt especially the natural products of Syria were important, making the two countries, in some measure, economically complementary.

Syria was also important by virtue of her position and communications. In the south, she offered a route to the Ḥijāz, with all that the control of the Holy Cities and of the Pilgrimage could mean to a Muslim monarch with aspirations. To the north lay the fortified Byzantine border—a place of danger and responsibility, and for 'Irāq a vital extension of her own Mesopotamian frontier. For Egypt, Syria lay across the land-routes to Asia—to 'Irāq and Arabia, Persia and the further Orient; for the rulers of the East, Syria was the road to the Mediterranean and to Africa—more specifically, the road into Egypt.

Of all the frontiers of Egypt, that in the north-east has always been the most challenging—and the most vulnerable. To the west lies a vast and daunting desert—a discouragement to the adventurer, and an obstacle to the invader. Only the first Arab conquerors successfully invaded North Africa from Egypt; only the Fatimids conquered Egypt from North Africa—and then only at the fourth attempt, against a collapsing and almost unresisting régime. To the south lay Nubia and the Sudan. In medieval times they offered no serious danger, since despite their fierce and dreaded warriors, they housed no power capable of mounting an assault; nor, for the rulers of Egypt, was there any incentive to invade these torrid and inhospitable lands, since their principal interest there—the acquisition of slaves—could be secured more easily and more effectively by other arrangements. The northern coast needed defence against raids, but presented great difficulties to an invader. There was no successful invasion of Egypt from the sea between Caesar and Bonaparte.

It was from the north-east, through Palestine and Sinai, that Egypt has been most often and most easily invaded—indeed, it may be said that her medieval history begins and ends with the Arab and Turkish conquests. It was by the same route that, in the course of the millennia, many armies set out from Egypt on the road to empire. On the western and southern frontiers, Egyptian governments usually tried to hold or dominate Cyrenaica and Nubia, but hardly ever attempted to press any further. In the same way, the rulers of Egypt have usually tried to maintain a defensive bridgehead on the far side of Sinai and, if possible, in southern Palestine. When they have felt strong enough, they have tried to advance further—to Damascus, to Aleppo, to Taurus and the Euphrates, against the rival powers based in Anatolia or in 'Irāq. When conquest was not feasible, they tried to procure subservient or at least friendly governments in Syria—to protect their own approaches, and to deny the use of the Syrian corridor to their enemies.

Aḥmad b. Ṭūlūn's first and abortive attempt to expand into Syria occurred in 256/870, barely two years after his arrival in Egypt. He tried again, this time more successfully, in 264/878, and in the course of their struggles with Baghdād he and his successor Khumārawayh carried Egyptian power as far as Cilicia and Mesopotamia. The fall of the Tulunids brought a restoration of ʿAbbasid control—but it was of brief duration. The rise of the Ikhshīd once again made northern Syria and Mesopotamia a borderland between the powers, and permitted the emergence of new forces independent of any of them. Ibn Rāʾiq, a dispossessed *amīr al-umarāʾ* who had been given the governorship of the upper Euphrates area, had the idea of seizing Syria and Egypt. In 328/939 his armies clashed with those of the Ikhshīd, and seem to have suffered a serious but not decisive setback. After an exchange of compliments an agreement was reached whereby the Ikhshīd held southern Palestine as far as Ramla, and Ibn Rāʾiq ruled the rest of Palestine and Syria. Ibn Rāʾiq now turned his attention eastward again; on his death in 330/942 the Ikhshīd peacefully reoccupied Syria.

In his expansion from Mesopotamia into Syria, and his attempt to create a state independent of both Baghdād and Egypt, Ibn Rāʾiq set an example which others were to follow—some of them with greater and more lasting success. The first, and in some ways the most important of the dynasties that flourished in the Syrian no man's land was that of the Hamdanids, a family of bedouin origin. Their career is typical of the resurgence of the nomadic and semi-nomadic tribesmen that occurred whenever the weakness or differences of the settled powers gave them the opportunity and encouragement. Descended from the great Arabian tribe of Taghlib, the Hamdanids took their name from an ancestor called Ḥamdān b. Ḥamdūn who flourished in the middle of the third/ninth century. He and his sons rose to greatness through caliphal favour, and managed to build up what was in effect a family principality based on Mosul. In 333/944 the Hamdanid Sayf al-Dawla ʿAlī captured Aleppo and Ḥimṣ from the Ikhshidids, and set up a new principality based on northern Syria, ruling with great *éclat* until his death in 356/967. Sayf al-Dawla is famous in Arabic literature and legend as prince, warrior and patron. His reputation as a patron of poets and scholars is well justified—but it is their efforts, rather than his own, that sustain his reputation as a ruler and as a fighter in the Holy Wars. Hamdanid government presents a picture of extortion coupled with incapacity; enormous revenues were extracted, draining and weakening the country—and squandered on display and on military adventures. These last were all ultimately unsuccessful. Sayf al-Dawla was defeated again and again by the Ikhshidids, and stayed where he was only because they found it convenient to keep him there. He was defeated when he turned east, by the Turkish generals Tuzun and Bajkam, defeated again, in the end, when he turned his arms against the Byzantines, in a loudly proclaimed resumption of the Holy War for Islam. His greatest achievement was to survive, and to maintain some order among the anarchic nomads at a time when imperial government from either side was manifestly unable to do so. In this, he embodied in some measure a bedouin knightly ideal—but the rest of his reputation is a timeless triumph of public relations. His harrying of the Byzantine frontier in fact did great disservice to the Muslim cause. While the damage he did to a vastly stronger enemy was inevitably limited, he drained and exhausted the powers of resistance of the Muslim border provinces, and finally provoked a devastating Byzantine counter-offensive. In 358/969 the Byzantines began their great southward advance, aimed at nothing less than the reconquest of Syria, lost by Heraclius to the Muslim Arabs more than three centuries earlier. In Aleppo, Sayf al-Dawla's son and successor, Sa'd al-Dawla, became a Byzantine vassal; while Nicephorus Phocas, with the main army, advanced almost to Damascus, Byzantine forces entered Ba'albakk and Beirut, and raided almost as far as Jerusalem. They were stopped in the south only by the Fatimids, and remained in control of the north until 387/997, when a treaty was signed between the Fatimid Caliph al-Ḥākim, and the Byzantine Emperor Basil, establishing Fatimid supremacy in Syria. The Hamdanids now transferred their allegiance to Cairo, and their lands were absorbed into the Fatimid empire shortly afterwards.

Despite the pro-Shī'ī and even pro-Ismā'īlī sympathies of part of the population, the Fatimids were never really able to establish themselves firmly in Syria. Their difficulties began with their arrival, when al-Mu'izz's armies, advancing from Egypt, had to deal with the bedouin Jarrahids in Palestine, Carmathian raiders from the east, the adventurer Alptekin in Damascus, and the Hamdanids in the north. By the death of al-'Azīz they had made some limited progress. Fatimid rule was rather shakily established in the south, while the Hamdanids were made to recognize Fatimid suzerainty. But new dangers threatened, notably the Byzantine offensive under Nicephorus Phocas, John Tzimisces and Basil, which was finally halted by al-Ḥākim. Under his successor al-Ẓāhir new troubles appeared in Syria. In the north, a bedouin Arab called Ṣāliḥ b. Mirdās took possession of Aleppo in 414/1023, and founded a dynasty which, with interruptions, ruled the city until they lost it to another bedouin dynasty, the 'Uqaylids of Mosul. Even in Palestine, Fatimid rule was shaken by the intrigues and ambitions of the Jarrahids, sometimes in alliance with other bedouin dynasties further north, sometimes even with the Byzantines. During the long and feeble reign of al-Mustanṣir, Fatimid rule in Syria was further weakened, and was finally ended with the coming of the Seljuks from the east.

The first Turcoman bands are reported to have entered Syria in 456/1064; others followed, at first as allies or auxiliaries of rival Arab chiefs. In 463/1071 a freebooting Turcoman chieftain called Atsız, coming in response to a Fatimid invitation, seized Jerusalem and overran Palestine, and in 468/1076 captured Damascus from its Fatimid Berber garrison. Failing to enter Egypt, he managed with difficulty to repel two Fatimid counter-attacks, and appealed to the Great Seljuk Sultan Malik-Shāh for help. The sultan sent his brother Tutush, with a Seljuk army and a grant of authority over as much territory as he could seize. Atsız handed Damascus over to him, and was shortly after removed by assassination. Apart from the coastal strip, which remained under loose Fatimid control, Palestine, central and southern Syria were now a Seljuk appanage, ruled by Tutush from Damascus; in the north, the 'Uqaylids, who had captured Aleppo in 472/1079, held it as Seljuk vassals. A victory for Tutush over his Seljuk rival Süleymān b. Kutalmısh in Anatolia enabled him to dislodge the 'Uqaylids, and establish Turkish military governors in Aleppo, Antioch and Edessa.

In 488/1095, Tutush was defeated and killed in a battle near Rayy, in a bid for the succession to the Great Seljuk Sultanate. His Syrian kingdom at once disintegrated, and the interrupted fragmentation of the country was resumed, this time into Seljuk and Turkish units. Two sons of Tutush, Riḍwān and Duqāq, ruled in Aleppo and Damascus. Various Seljuk *amīrs* and *atabegs* held the other cities of Syria, supporting one or the other in a complicated system of feuds and rivalries. It was at this moment that the Crusaders entered Syria from the north, and the Fatimid *Amīr al-juyūsh* al-Afḍal, profiting from the confusion, moved in from the south and recaptured Jerusalem from its Seljuk lord Sokman b. Artuk (Ramaḍān 491/August 1098).

They did not hold it for long. The Frankish Crusaders, after defeating the Anatolian Seljuks, advanced rapidly through Syria, where there was no power capable of offering them any serious resistance. The larger cities were held and garrisoned by Seljuk princes and officers; the smaller were mostly in the hands of turbulent and ambitious Arab chieftains, such as had risen to prominence in the interregnum before the coming of the Seljuks. Rival Seljuk armies, and Turcoman and Arab tribes, were scattered through the country, dominating a population which was itself deeply divided, including large Christian communities and many heretical Muslims who, at times, seem to have hated the Sunnī more than the infidel. In the far south, the Fatimids were watching for any opportunity that might offer—but had ceased to be a serious military power. Far from resisting the Crusaders, they were at first ready to co-operate with them—having presumably calculated that a precariously maintained Crusading state in Syria would be a less dangerous neighbour than the Great Seljuk Sultanate.

This co-operation did not last long. Fatimid envoys came to the camp of the Crusaders late in 1097, while they were still beseiging Antioch, and appear to have proposed a partition of Syria and a working understanding against the common Seljuk enemy. William of Tyre remarks that the Fatimids were always friendlier to the Franks than were the Sunnī Muslims, and notes the glee of the Fatimid envoys on hearing of the Seljuk defeat at Nicaea. The envoys stayed until March 1098, after which a Frankish return mission was sent to Cairo. But in the meantime the situation was changing. The southward advance of the Crusaders brought them in May to the region of Beirut, and to their first encounters with Fatimid garrisons. It was becoming clear that the Franks would not be content with lands in northern or central Syria, but were aiming at Palestine—an area which the Fatimids regarded as their own sphere of influence. The Frankish envoys in Cairo were detained, and then released with an offer of free access to and facilities in the Holy Places, provided the Crusaders gave up the idea of invading Fatimid possessions —that is to say, renounced the purpose for which they had come from Europe.

The offer was rejected, and on 22 Shaʿbān 492/15 July 1099, after a siege of five weeks, the Crusaders captured Jerusalem from the Fatimid—Arab and Sudanese—garrison. In return for the surrender of the Tower of David in the citadel and a great sum of money, the Egyptian commandant and his body-guard were permitted to withdraw; the rest of the Muslim and Jewish population of the city, men, women and children, were massacred by the victorious Crusaders. By next day Jerusalem was a Christian city.

The fanaticism and ferocity of the Crusaders represented something new and unfamiliar in the Islamic Orient, where men of different religions had long lived peacefully side by side. But the immediate impact was slight, and the reaction only slowly gathered force. Ibn al-Athīr, in a vivid passage, describes how the first refugees from Syria arrived in Baghdād in the month of Ramaḍān, and 'made a speech in the *dīwān* which brought tears to the eye and pain to the heart. On Friday they rose up in the cathedral mosque and begged for help, weeping and making others weep as they told of what the Muslims had suffered in that place of great sanctity...'.[1]

But all this had little practical effect, and no help was forthcoming even from Syria or Egypt, let alone from far away Baghdād. Only one new force entered Syria from the Muslim East—a branch of the dreaded Assassins of Persia. Fanatical Ismā'īlīs, working for the creation of a new Fatimid Caliphate in the line of Nizār, they seized and fortified a string of mountain strongholds, and from these waged a war of terror against the Sunnī princes of Syria. For some time they showed little interest in the Crusades. Indeed, the Muslims generally were slow to realize the nature of the new force that confronted them. It is noteworthy that in the vast Arabic literature of the period of the Crusades, the terms Crusade and Crusader are missing, and indeed seem to have no Arabic equivalents. For the Muslim historians, the Crusaders are always 'the Franks', who at first came as barbarian auxiliaries of the Byzantines, and then branched out on their own. The process was familiar enough. An 'Irāqī poet, lamenting the fall of Jerusalem and the failure of the Muslims to rally to the defence, even speaks of the conquerors as *Rūm*—Byzantines.[2] At worst, the Frankish advance could be seen as a renewal of the Byzantine offensive of the fourth/tenth century; in fact the new invaders, like the Turcomans and Seljuks from the East, seemed to be settling down in their new principalities, and to be ready to join in the complex and multipartite game of Syrian politics.

By their swift advance down the coastal plains, from Cilicia almost to Sinai, the Crusaders created four feudal Latin states, based on Edessa, Antioch, Tripoli and Jerusalem. Except for the Holy City, they never penetrated the interior; the ruined Frankish castles in the mountains still show the high watermark of their advance, which left the great inland cities of Aleppo, Ḥamāh, Ḥimṣ and Damascus firmly in Muslim hands. Even the Latin kingdom of Jerusalem had its main strength on the coast, and was held and supplied from the sea. With the fall of Tyre

[1] Ibn al-Athīr, *Kāmil*, ed. Tornberg, x, 192–3 (*anno* 492).
[2] Ibn al-Athīr, *loc. cit.*

in 518/1124 the coastline was entirely in their hands; save only for the little port of Ascalon ('Asqalān), which was held by the Egyptians despite their loss of Jerusalem. For a century and a half it was a frontier city and a key military objective in the struggles between the Crusaders and the Muslim rulers of Egypt.

During the first period, when the disunited Muslim states of Syria lacked the capacity—apparently even the desire—to eject the Crusaders, the newcomers had ample scope for their own feuds and intrigues. The Muslim states too became involved in the tangled skein of their relations with one another and with Byzantium. According to Ibn al-Athīr, the Crusaders, while advancing into Syria, wrote to the lords of Aleppo and Damascus to say that they were only fighting for the recovery of the lost Byzantine lands.[1] Certainly the later working alliance between Latin Jerusalem and Muslim Damascus was a reality. From the beginning the Crusaders were ready to use diplomatic as well as military methods. The four new states soon found their place in the Syrian balance of power—and at times Muslim and Christian are allied against Muslim and Christian.

This was a time of colonization, settlement and assimilation. The conquerors and those who followed them—pilgrims, merchants, adventurers—settled in Syria, adopting local customs and often intermarrying with native Christians or even baptized Muslims. They came as masters. 'Every day', wrote Fulcher of Chartres in about 1124, 'our relations and friends follow us, willingly abandoning whatever they possessed in the West. For those who were poor there, God has made rich here. Those who had a few pence there, have numberless gold pieces here; he who had not a village there possesses, with God as giver, a whole town here. Why then return to the West, when the East suits us so well?'[2] And while the feudal lords and knights found themselves new fiefs and manors, the merchants settled in the coastal cities, reproducing and adapting the organization and privileges of the Italian communes.

The dominant groups in the Crusading states were the Franks—that is, Catholics of varied European origin, constituting the three main groups of barons, clergy and merchants. Under them was the mass of the population, consisting of Muslims, non-Catholic Christians and some Jews. During the conquest the Muslim population of the captured

[1] Ibn al-Athīr, x, 188 (*anno* 491).
[2] *Historia Hierosolymitana*, Bk. iii, Ch. 37. Ed. Migne, *Patrologia*, clv, 925.

towns was decimated by mass slaughter. The villages, however, remained, and once their initial fury was spent, the Franks, adapting themselves to local custom, allowed their subjects a status akin to that of the

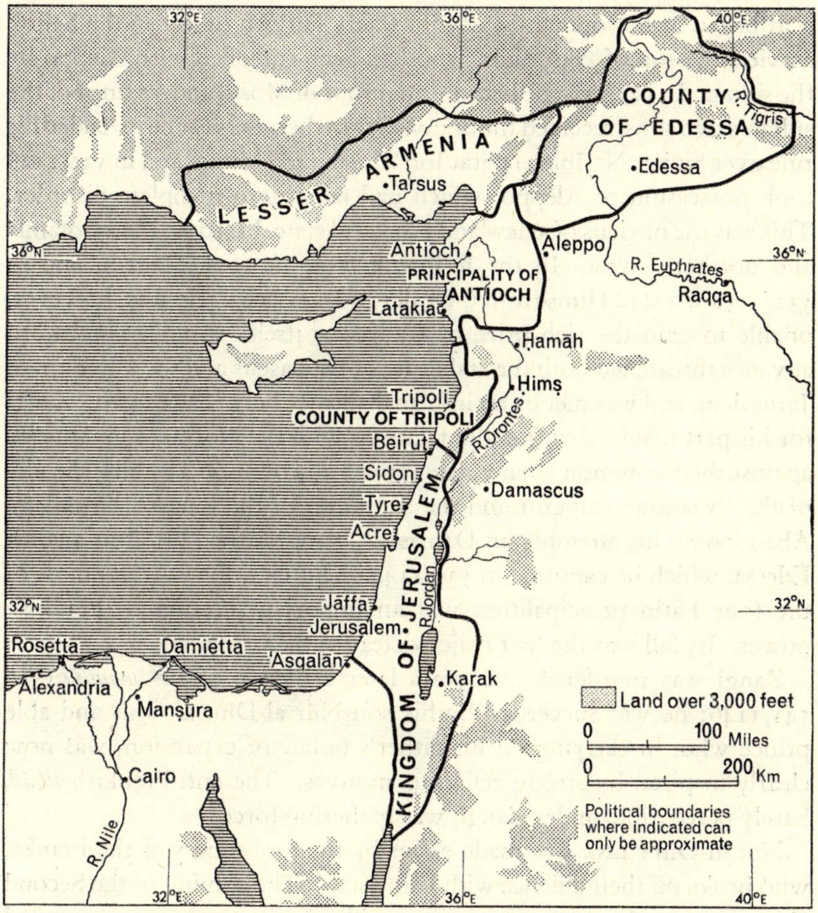

Map 4. Syria and Egypt in the period of the Crusades.

dhimmīs in the Muslim states. By 580/1184 the Spanish Muslim traveller Ibn Jubayr records, as the common opinion, that Muslim peasants were far better treated under Frankish than under Muslim rule.[1]

But in the meantime a new power had arisen in Syria, which was to transform the relationship between Muslims and Crusaders. Its

[1] Ibn Jubayr, *Travels*, ed. W. Wright, revised M. J. de Goeje (Leiden, 1907), 301–2.

emergence can be measured in three phases, corresponding to the careers of ʿImād al-Dīn Zangī, Nūr al-Dīn and Saladin (Ṣalāḥ al-Dīn al-Ayyūbī)—three names that score the gathering crescendo of the Muslim counter-Crusade, the Holy War for Islam.

It began in Mesopotamia. Zangī was a Turkish officer in the Seljuk service, the son of Aksunkur, who had been enfeoffed with Aleppo by the sultan. In 521/1127 he became governor of Mosul and, as tutor of the sultan's two sons, received the title *atabeg*. In the same year he extended his rule over Sinjar, Naṣībīn, Jazīrat Ibn ʿUmar and Ḥarrān, and in 522/1128 took possession of Aleppo, which had fallen into complete disorder. This was the nucleus of a new and powerful state, based on Mesopotamia and northern Syria. In the following year he took Ḥamāh, and in 532/1138 wrested Ḥimṣ from the ruler of Damascus. He was, however, unable to gain the rich prize of Damascus itself. Zangī's southward advance threatened both the atabegate of Damascus and the kingdom of Jerusalem, and was met by an informal alliance between the two. Zangī for his part maintained friendly relations with the Normans in Antioch against their common enemy, the Provençal count of Tripoli—the ally of the Byzantine emperor and the supporter of the king of Jerusalem. Abandoning his attempts on Damascus, Zangī turned his arms against Edessa, which he captured in 539/1144. This city, the northernmost of the four Latin principalities, was an important bastion of Frankish power. Its fall was the first major defeat of the Crusaders.

Zangī was murdered two years later by some of his *mamlūks*, in 541/1146; he was succeeded by his son Nūr al-Dīn, a pious and able prince who, in carrying on his father's policy of expansion, was now clearly inspired by strong religious motives. The anti-Frankish *jihād*, barely perceptible under Zangī, was gathering force.

Nūr al-Dīn's task was made easier by the foolishness of the Franks, who broke off their alliance with Damascus. The coming of the Second Crusade in 1148 made matters worse. The newcomers, not acquainted with local conditions and politics, and contemptuous of those who were, set off to strike a blow for Christendom against the nearest infidel stronghold—the city of Damascus. Their unsuccessful siege of the city deprived the Latin kingdom of its nearest ally. Jerusalem now turned for help to Constantinople, and acknowledged the emperor as suzerain; in return he served to some extent as a check on Nūr al-Dīn's advance. Instead, the *atabeg* turned against Damascus, which he captured in 549/1154. For the first time the Crusaders confronted a united and powerful Muslim state in Syria and Mesopotamia—one increasingly affected by the new mood of Holy War against the Christian invaders.

In Syria, Franks and Muslims faced one another on approximately equal terms—neither side strong enough to gain the upper hand. The key was now to be found in Egypt, where the Fatimid caliphate was tottering to its end. For the first time since the Arab conquest, events in Syria and forces from Syria were to decide the fate of Egypt.

THE AYYUBIDS AND THE MAMLUK SULTANATE

For more than half a century after the coming of the Crusaders, the Egyptians held on to their bridgehead at Ascalon, using it as a base for raids into Palestine. With its population swollen by refugees from the Frankish-held lands, and its garrison regularly reinforced and supplied from Egypt, it became an important military centre. After the Frankish capture of Tyre in 518/1124 the position of Ascalon was much weakened, and a period of inactivity followed.

A new phase began in 545/1150, when the *wazīr* in Cairo, Ibn al-Sallār, entered into an agreement with Nūr al-Dīn, and launched the Egyptian fleet against the traffic of the Frankish ports. The Crusaders retaliated against Ascalon. In 548/1153, after a siege of seven months, Baldwin III captured the port by a combined assault from the land and the sea. In Crusading hands, Ascalon now became the springboard for Frankish political and military adventures in Egypt.

In Egypt there was disorder, and in 549/1154 the Caliph al-Ẓāfir was murdered. A new strong man, Ṭalā'i' b. Ruzzīk, emerged and took control. Appointed *wazīr* to the child Caliph al-Fā'iz, he had continued the attack against the Franks, and was victorious at Gaza and Hebron in 553/1158. Without support from Nūr al-Dīn, and weakened by troubles at home, he was unable to pursue his advantage. His murder, at the instigation of the Fatimid caliph, in 556/1161, and that of his son and successor, Ruzzīk, two years later, opened the way to a struggle for the wazirate between two rival aspirants, Shāwar and Ḍirghām. At first successful, Shāwar was driven out by Ḍirghām, and fled to Nūr al-Dīn, who welcomed the opportunity to intervene as his protector. Shāwar now returned to Egypt with a Syrian army, commanded by the Kurdish general Shīrkūh; the latter was accompanied by his nephew Ṣalāḥ al-Dīn b. Ayyūb, known in the West as Saladin. In return for this help, Shāwar undertook to hand over a third of the revenues of Egypt. Ḍirghām was defeated and killed, and Shāwar resumed the wazirate—

only to fall into the immediate and inevitable conflict with Shīrkūh. For protection against his Syrian protectors Shāwar now turned to the only remaining power—the Latin king of Jerusalem. Amalric had already raided into Egypt in 556/1161 and 557/1162, and exacted tribute. He was more than willing to accept this new opportunity to intervene in Egyptian affairs. Shīrkūh, hard pressed by the Franks and the Egyptians, accepted an offer of a free passage back to Syria; Amalric, alarmed by Nūr al-Dīn's power in the north, also withdrew his forces, and for the moment Egypt was free from both groups of invaders.

But not for long. In 562/1167 Shīrkūh again invaded Egypt, with units of Nūr al-Dīn's army; Shāwar again accepted, after some hesitation, the support of the Franks, with whom he concluded a treaty. In addition to the annual tribute previously agreed, he was to pay them 400,000 gold pieces, half at once, in return for their undertaking to destroy or expel Shīrkūh and his army from Egypt. Despite initial victories, Shīrkūh was again obliged to make terms. Both armies were to withdraw from Egypt, leaving Shāwar in possession—but with a Frankish commissioner, with some troops, in Cairo.

Relations between Shāwar and the Franks now deteriorated, and in Muḥarram 564/October 1168 the Frankish army again took the road to Egypt. On 4 November they captured Bilbays, and celebrated their victory with a massacre of Muslims and even Copts. On 13 November they began the siege of Cairo, but raised it after exacting money and promises from Shāwar. Meanwhile Shīrkūh arrived in Egypt, for the third time, and the Franks hastily withdrew to Bilbays and from there back to Palestine. Shīrkūh marched on Cairo, where he was welcomed by the caliph and the people. Shāwar was ambushed and assassinated, and Shīrkūh himself became *wazīr* to the Fatimid caliph, while remaining in the service of Nūr al-Dīn. On his death two months later he was succeeded by his nephew Saladin.

The Franks were not yet ready to abandon their plans in Egypt. In October 1169, with Byzantine help, they advanced from Ascalon into Egypt, and got as far as Damietta; failing to capture it, they withdrew and returned to Ascalon in December. By the following winter Saladin was attacking Dārūm and Gaza, and in Rabīʿ I 463/December 1170 captured Ayla. The Frankish adventure in Egypt was at an end; the Crusaders now faced a new and perilous situation, with a single Muslim power in control of both Egypt and Syria. The encirclement of the Latin states had begun.

Saladin was now the master of Egypt, nominally as *wazīr* to the Fatimid caliph and at the same time as representative of Nūr al-Dīn. In 567/1171 he clarified his position in the first though not in the second respect. As the last Fatimid caliph, al-'Āḍid, lay dying, Saladin, possibly on orders from Nūr al-Dīn, allowed a preacher to recite the *khuṭba* in the name of the 'Abbasid caliph. The Fatimid Caliphate, already dead as a religious force, was now formally abolished. After more than two centuries, Egypt had returned to orthodoxy and the Islamic fold—with Saladin in undivided control.

His next problem was that of his relations with Nūr al-Dīn. For the *atabeg,* the main task was the war in Syria against the Crusaders; Saladin was in Egypt as his servant, to settle the affairs of that country and mobilize its resources for this purpose. Pressed to give help to his suzerain, Saladin temporized, sending treasure which was found insufficient, and giving some military support which was judged dilatory and inadequate. While building up his own army, he justified his failure to support Nūr al-Dīn by the need to defend Egypt against Frankish attack and Fatimid resurgence. Though both sides avoided a breach, Nūr al-Dīn was suspicious enough to send an auditor to Cairo in 569/1173–4 to check Saladin's finances; Saladin was resentful, but submitted to this demand. He gave orders for accounts to be prepared and presented to the auditor; he also gave him access to the army payrolls, showing the strength and costs of the forces, with the amounts of their fiefs and the figures of pay and allowances.[1]

Saladin was still temporizing when Nūr al-Dīn died, on 11 Shawwāl 569/15 May 1174, leaving his young son al-Malik al-Ṣāliḥ Ismā'īl in Damascus as his heir. His Syro-Mesopotamian kingdom at once disintegrated. In Mosul a nephew of Nūr al-Dīn made himself independent and created a new, separate Zangid principality, including the Mesopotamian territories. In Damascus there were plots against the heir, who was removed to Aleppo, leaving the city in the hands of his *atabeg*; the latter promptly made a truce with Jerusalem. In Aleppo, power was seized by the eunuch Gümüshtekin, who, ostensibly acting as guardian of Nūr al-Dīn's son, placed most of Nūr al-Dīn's senior officers under arrest.

It was in this situation that Saladin began his series of moves to extend his power from Egypt to Syria. The Muslim historians present two radically different pictures of his activities. For those reflecting the

[1] Abū Shāma, *Rawḍatayn*², ed. Muḥ. Ḥilmī Muḥ. Aḥmad (Cairo, 1956), i/2, 558.

Zangid point of view, he was a ruthless and ambitious adventurer, bent on personal aggrandisement. To achieve this, he used both cunning and force against the Zangids, in order to deprive the heirs of his master Nūr al-Dīn of their inheritance, and to seize it for himself. For his own spokesmen, and those of his successors, he was a champion of Islam, who had to reunite the Muslim lands as an essential preliminary to his Holy War against the Crusaders.

For a dozen years Saladin's wars were in fact chiefly against Muslim adversaries, with only an occasional skirmish with the Franks. And then, with Muslim Syria as well as Egypt firmly in his hands, he was ready to unleash the Holy War. It began in 582/1187, as the result of an act of brigandage by the notorious freebooter and buccaneer, Raynald of Châtillon. The Muslim troops advanced rapidly and, winning a decisive victory at the battle of Ḥaṭṭīn, captured Jerusalem, together with a number of other Crusading outposts. The Franks were now confined to the coastal strip, with the three main centres of Antioch, Tripoli, and Tyre, which could be maintained from the sea.

The fall of Jerusalem made a tremendous impact in both Islam and Christendom. From Europe it brought the Third Crusade, and a mighty but vain effort to recover what had been lost. The Crusaders began well, by recapturing Acre—a considerable military achievement. They were, however, unable to advance any further. After hard fighting and protracted negotiations the two sides came to terms on 22-3 Sha'bān 588/2-3 September 1192. The peace recognized Saladin's gains. All Palestine, save a coastal strip, was now Muslim, the Crusaders reserving only the right of unarmed pilgrimage to the holy places. Saladin had broken the back of the Latin kingdom, the leader of the Crusading states, and had established land communication between his Syrian and Egyptian realms. A few months later, in Ṣafar 589/February 1193, he died peacefully in Damascus.

The career of Saladin meant more than the defeat of the Crusaders—who after all were still to remain in the Levant for another century. His rise to power in Egypt, and his use of Egyptian resources to gain power in Syria, mark the restoration of Egypt as a political force—as the main base of Muslim strength in the eastern Mediterranean. Even though his Syrian dominions broke up after his death into a mosaic of small principalities, ruled by his sons, nephews and cousins, Egypt remained a single, unified realm, and its ruler enjoyed an acknowledged primacy among the many branches of the Ayyubid house.

While creating a new political power in Egypt, Saladin was at the same time restoring and tightening the bonds that bound Egypt to eastern Islam. A devout Sunnī, he ended the two centuries of schism inaugurated by the Fatimids, and reincorporated Egypt in the Sunnī oecumene headed by the ʿAbbasid caliph in Baghdād. This was more than a formality; at a time when the caliph was struggling to free himself from Seljuk tutelage and recover some of his lost power and authority, Saladin brought him valuable if somewhat unappreciated support. At the same time, Egypt was opened to the new social changes and intellectual movements that had been emerging in the East. When Saladin deposed the Fatimids, he dispersed their great libraries of Ismāʿīlī literature, and introduced into Egypt the *madrasa*—the intellectual heart of the Sunnī revival. Many *madrasas* were opened in Cairo and other cities under Saladin and his successors, and even al-Azhar, founded as an Ismāʿīlī seminary, became a centre—in time *the* centre—of Islamic orthodoxy.

Saladin's army, though based on Egypt, was not an Egyptian army but was as alien as the Turkish, Berber, Sudanese and other forces of his predecessors. Himself a Kurd, he established a régime and an army of Turkish type, along the lines laid down by the Seljuks and *atabegs* in the East. Inevitably, these lines were modified in accordance with Egyptian conditions and the surviving traditions of the Fatimids. When Saladin arrived in Egypt with Turkish and Turcoman contingents of the Zangid army, he found a Fatimid army, consisting of some 30,000 Sudanese infantry and regiments of white cavalry. The former he broke and drove out of Egypt; the latter he seems to have incorporated in his own forces, eventually relegating them to an inferior position. The mainstay of the armies which he built up in both his Egyptian and his Syro-Mesopotamian possessions were the heavily armed Kurdish and Turkish cavalrymen. Under his successors the latter—especially the Mamluks—began to predominate.

With the new army came the social and economic order on which it was based. Already in late Fatimid times a kind of *iqṭāʿ*, or feudal grant, had become the usual way of paying the officers of the army. The Seljuk conquest of Syria extended to that country the characteristic *iqṭāʿ* system of the East; Saladin carried it to Egypt, where, however, it was modified by the centralist and authoritarian traditions of that country. The Ayyubid fief was notably more feudal than that of the Fatimids; at the same time the Ayyubid fief-holder in Egypt lacked the seigneurial rights and privileges of his colleagues in Syria and the East. His grant was a limited and revocable assignment of revenues, carrying no manorial jurisdiction, or even administrative function.

Economically, the Ayyubid period was one of growth and prosperity. Peace with the Franks brought a resumption—and indeed an extension—of commercial relations. The Italian—later also French and Catalan—merchants continued to operate in the ports under Ayyubid control as well as those still in Frankish hands; Saladin was careful not to discourage this profitable trade, the advantages of which he defended in a letter to the caliph.[1] Egyptian products, notably alum, for which there seems to have been a great demand were exported to Europe; Egypt also profited from the transit trade from the east. It was in this period that the great Kārimī guild of merchants, established in Fatimid times, played a major role in the trade of the Red Sea and Indian Ocean, from which the Frankish merchants were rigorously excluded. Like the Fatimids before him, Saladin had brought the Yemen under his control, thus securing both ends of the Red Sea, and an important point of commercial—and also strategic—advantage. It is significant that one measure of Ayyubid rule in Yemen was to align the Yemeni currency and weights and measures with those of Egypt.

In Syria too the Ayyubid principalities, though divided, maintained a measure of family co-operation in striking contrast with the regional squabbling of earlier times. A period of relative peace and security, and the consequent improvement of both trade and agriculture, helped to swell their revenues. Their intervention in economic life was, however, less direct and less active than that of the rulers of Egypt, where, as in earlier periods, important sectors of both production and commerce—such as sugar-cultivation, mines and forests, and the trade in metals and timber—were under state control or even ownership. A government official writing during the disorders of the early—seventh/thirteenth century laments the damage done by private intervention in state enterprises and by the peculations of government officials when control is relaxed.[2]

Culturally too the Ayyubid period was one of great activity. First Syria, and then Egypt, became centres of Arab scholarship and literature, and acquired that primacy, within the Arabic-speaking portion of the

[1] Abū Shāma, *Rawḍatayn*[2], i/2, 621 f (*anno* 570/1174–5).

[2] Abū ʿAmr ʿUthmān al-Nābulusi, *K. Lumaʿ al-qawānīn,* ed. C. Becker and C. Cahen, in *Bulletin d'Etudes Orientales* (Damascus), xvi (1958–60), especially chapters iv and v.

Islamic world, that they retained until modern times. The prosperity of the cities, the patronage of the Ayyubid princes, the stimulus of the counter-Crusade and the Sunnī revival all have their share in this silver age of Arabic letters.

The second architect of the Ayyubid state was Saladin's brother al-Malik al-ʿĀdil Ṣafā' al-Dīn, known to the Crusaders as Saphadin. A capable, honourable and energetic man, he took control in Egypt, of which he formally became sovereign in 596/1199. Within a few years he had done much to reconstruct Saladin's shattered Syro-Egyptian empire, ruling Egypt and sometimes Damascus directly, and exercising a rather vague suzerainty over his kinsmen in Syria. On his death in 619/1218 he was succeeded by his son al-Malik al-Kāmil, another able and energetic ruler, who governed successfully until his death in 635/1238. Thereafter the dynasty declined rapidly to its end in Egypt, though some branches managed to hang on for some time longer in Syria.

The death of al-Malik al-Kāmil was followed by a new struggle for power among the Ayyubid princes, in which some of them were not averse to seeking the aid of the Crusaders against their rival kinsmen. In 637/1240 al-Malik al-Ṣāliḥ Ayyūb was established as sultan in Egypt, where he reigned until 647/1249. His energies were largely occupied in a complicated struggle with the states of Syria and the East. In these struggles the Latin states in the Levant, and new Crusades from Europe, played a secondary but not unimportant part.

Saladin had come to Egypt from Syria, as a representative of the new power that had arisen in the north. Syria was the scene of his own great political and military actions—the object towards which Egypt herself was only, for him, a stepping-stone. But the Mamluk army of Egypt and, still more, the economic resources of Egypt, contributed in no small measure to his victories. Under his successors, it became clear that the centre of gravity had returned to Egypt, which had once again become the chief bastion of Muslim power in the eastern Mediterranean. This fact was recognized by the Crusaders, who realized that their only hope of achieving final success in Palestine and Syria lay in the destruction of the new power that had emerged in Egypt. In 1215, at the Fourth Lateran Council, Pope Innocent III announced a new Crusade, and demanded, in preparation for it, a ban on all trade with the Muslim states. The object of the attack was to be Egypt; the strategy was to capture Damietta, in the eastern Delta of the Nile, and advance from there to Cairo. A large army assembled at Acre; in Rabīʿ I 615/May 1218 they landed in Egypt and, under the command of the papal legate, Pelagius, laid siege to Damietta, which they finally captured on 25 Sha'bān 616/5 November 1219. They then waited long and in vain for the Emperor Frederick II, whose arrival, with his army, was expected in 1221. The Crusaders advanced as far as the Egyptian fortress later known as Manṣūra, and encamped there at the end of July. Al-Malik al-Kāmil, alarmed at their progress, offered very favourable terms—the return of most of Saladin's conquests in the Latin kingdom, the release of captives, the restoration of the Holy Cross captured by Saladin in Jerusalem. The king of Jerusalem was anxious to accept this offer; the papal legate held out for an indemnity—and the negotiations collapsed. Al-Malik al-Kāmil now prepared for war, and by Jumādā II 618/August 1221 had driven the Crusaders back to Damietta. By this time the best terms that Pelagius could get were a free withdrawal and the restoration of the Cross, in exchange for the surrender of Damietta. A treaty was signed, for a term of eight years, with the proviso that it could be broken only by an emperor or king coming to the East.

In 625/1228 the emperor came on a Crusade cursed by the pope—an excommunicated Crusader, whose success in entering Jerusalem brought the Holy City itself under the papal interdict. The Crusade of Frederick II was conducted by diplomatic, not military means. By negotiation with al-Malik al-Kāmil, the emperor was able to procure a ten-year agreement—the treaty of 22 Rabī' I 626/18 February 1229—by which the sultan ceded Nazareth, Bethlehem and Jerusalem to the Latin kingdom, with a corridor of land linking Jerusalem with the Latin port of Acre. This success was short-lived. Frederick remained involved in the great struggles of empire and papacy; the barons of the Latin kingdom reasserted their power against the monarchy—and in the summer of 642/1244 a force of 10,000 Khwārazmian horsemen ravaged Palestine and captured Jerusalem. Profiting from the discomfiture of the Latins and their local allies, an army from Egypt, commanded by a young Mamluk officer called Baybars, advanced into Palestine. With Khwārazmian support, they won a great victory over the Latins near Gaza on 13 Jumādā I 642/17 October 1244; they occupied and fortified Jerusalem and, in 645/1247, captured Ascalon; the Ayyubid sovereign of Egypt was on the way to establishing his rule in much of Palestine and his supremacy over the Ayyubid *amīrs* of Syria. The surviving remnant of the Latin kingdom was in grave danger.

In response to its need, a new Crusade was launched—led by the sainted French king, Louis IX. Again the objective was Egypt; again the Crusaders landed near Damietta, which they captured without difficulty on 21 Ṣafar 647/5 June 1249. Like the legate Pelagius in 1221, King Louis led his army towards Cairo; like him too he halted before Manṣūra in Rajab 647/December 1249. The sultan offered terms—Jerusalem for Damietta; the king refused—he had come to fight, not to bargain with the enemy. For more than three months the two armies faced one another, skirmishing, foraying, and then waiting—waiting, that is, on the outcome of the struggle for power in Cairo following the death of al-Malik al-Ṣāliḥ on 14 Sha'bān 647/22 November 1249. But the Muslim state and army held firm. The dead sultan's concubine, Shajar al-Durr, concealed the news of his death and, by issuing orders in his name, held both together until the arrival of his son, Tūrān-Shāh, from Mesopotamia in Dhu'l-Qa'da 647/February 1250. By April the king's position had become critical—and the sultan knew it. Now the king offered terms—Damietta for Jerusalem; and the sultan refused. On 11 Muḥarram 649/5 April 1250 the Crusaders struck camp and began to retreat. The Mamluks swiftly followed, and within a few days the Crusading army was surrounded, defeated and made captive. King Louis ransomed himself and some of his army by surrendering Damietta and paying a vast indemnity.

The army of al-Malik al-Ṣāliḥ had acquitted itself well. Despite the shock and uncertainty following his death, it had remained a disciplined and effective fighting force, and had inflicted a decisive defeat on a powerful and dangerous enemy. In this victory the Baḥrī Mamluks, commanded by Baybars, had played a crucial part. The recruitment of Turkish *mamlūks* was already a long-established practice in Egypt. Al-Malik al-Ṣāliḥ was, however, the first of the Egyptian Ayyubids to acquire them in large numbers, and to make them the mainstay of his military power. Already during his struggle for power, the loyalty of his Mamluks was in striking contrast with the unreliability of his Kurdish and other troops, who transferred their allegiance to rival contenders. After his accession, he imported great numbers of them from the Turkish lands conquered by the Mongols, and created a powerful Mamluk army. They were stationed in barracks on Rawḍa island in the River Nile—in Arabic, *Baḥr al-Nīl*—whence they came to be known as the Baḥrīs. Devoted to the sultan's person, they helped him to establish and maintain a personal military ascendancy markedly different from the dynastic leadership of the other Ayyubids. By the time of al-Malik al-Ṣāliḥ's death they formed a well-organized *corps d'élite*, with its own traditions and loyalties, personal, regimental and military rather than dynastic.

The arrival of Tūrān-Shāh with his own Mamluks from Mesopotamia thus provoked a crisis. The fears of the Baḥrīs that they were about to be ousted were confirmed when Tūrān-Shāh promoted his own officers to high positions and made threats and accusations against Shajar al-Durr, to whom the Baḥrīs transferred the allegiance they had owed to al-Malik al-Ṣāliḥ. On Monday 28 Muḥarram 648/2 May 1250 a group of Baḥrī officers led by Baybars murdered Tūrān-Shāh. In his place, the Mamluks proclaimed Shajar al-Durr as sultan[1]—ostensibly as widow of al-Malik al-Ṣāliḥ and mother of his deceased son.

This gesture towards Ayyubid legitimism did not reconcile the Ayyubid princes of Syria to the extinction of their house in Egypt, and Shajar al-Durr soon found herself confronted by a coalition of virtually all of them, seeking her overthrow. Even the caliph in Baghdād, al-Musta'ṣim, did not relish the enthronement of a woman—a former inmate of his own harem, whom he had sent as a gift to al-Malik al-Ṣāliḥ. He gave his support to the Syrians, and ordered the Egyptian Mamluks to choose a sultan. 'If there is not a man left among you whom you can appoint', he is said to have written, 'tell us and we will send you one.'[2]

Shajar al-Durr was a woman of remarkable ability, but she could not wage war. In this emergency she appointed a commander-in-chief—the *Amīr* Aybeg, who promptly consolidated his position by marrying her and becoming sultan. To pacify the legitimists and the Baḥrīs, a ten-year-old Ayyubid prince was found and proclaimed—for a short time—as joint ruler. Though he achieved some military success in warding off the Syrian attack, Aybeg managed to alienate both the Baḥrī Mamluks, many of whom fled to the courts of his Syrian enemies, and also his redoubtable wife and co-sovereign Shajar al-Durr, who arranged his murder on 25 Rabī' I 655/12 April 1257. She herself was murdered three days later.

What followed set the pattern of Mamluk political succession for some time to come. On Aybeg's death, his son 'Alī was accepted as successor—without real power, without effective tenure, but simply as a stop-gap, to maintain legitimacy while the real successor emerged from the play of Mamluk politics. He was then peacefully deposed, and sent to exile or retirement. The real successor this time was the com-

[1] A feminine form, sultana, does not exist in Arabic: the title *sulṭān* appears on Shajar al-Durr's only extant coin. Her name is often wrongly given as Shajarat al-Durr by later writers. See S. Lane-Poole, *A history of Egypt in the Middle Ages* (London, 1901), 255, n.1.

[2] Al-Suyūṭī, *Ḥusn al-muḥāḍara fi akhbār Miṣr wa'l-Qāhira*, ii (Cairo, 1321), 39.

mander of Aybeg's Mamluks, Quṭuz, who was proclaimed sultan on 17 Dhu'l Qa'da 657/12 November 1259. The exiled Baḥrī Mamluks returned to Egypt, where the new sultan received them with open arms and restored them to their place in the army of Egypt. There was work for them to do.

The crisis of the Ayyubids had begun with an attack from the West—the last despairing efforts of the Crusaders to recover and maintain their hold in Palestine and Syria. It ended with an attack from the East—the far greater menace of the new power that had arisen in eastern Asia.

The invasion of the Levant by the steppe peoples began in the mid-fifth/eleventh century, when the first Turcoman bands entered Syria. It continued with the coming of the Seljuks; it reached its climax with the great Mongol conquests of the seventh/thirteenth century.

The terror of the Mongols preceded them. Scattered tribes and broken armies, fleeing before the Mongol invaders of the Muslim East, had begun to move westward—as raiders, as freebooters and as *condottieri* willing to serve any prince who would hire them. Such bands, loosely designated Khwārazmians, invaded and ravaged Syria during the second quarter of the seventh/thirteenth century, for a while as allies of al-Malik al-Ṣāliḥ against his Ayyubid and Frankish enemies. The alliance did not last. In 644/1246 Syrian Ayyubid forces, now with the encouragement of Cairo, inflicted a crushing defeat on the Khwarazmian bands outside Ḥimṣ, ending their threat to Syria.

But worse was to come. In 640/1242–3 Mongol forces under Bayju Noyon had invaded the lands of the Anatolian Seljuks, and established a Mongol suzerainty immediately to the north of Syria. Even after their withdrawal from Anatolia, they continued to harass Mesopotamia from their bases in Persia. The Armenian prince of Cilicia, Hethoum, sought and obtained a Mongol alliance. In 645/1247 he sent his brother on a mission to Mongolia, and in 652/1254 himself took the long road to Karakorum, where he arrived just when the Great Khan Möngke was planning a new and final expedition against the empires of Islam. He was well received, and given promises both for his own kingdom and for the Christians in general. There were some who entertained vaster hopes of an alliance between the Mongols and Christendom, for a joint attack from East and West against the common Muslim enemy. Envoys travelled between Mongol camps and Christian courts, exploring the possibilities of co-operation—but with little tangible result.

The Armenian-Mongol alliance, however, was a reality of some importance in the great Mongol offensive. Immediately after the fall of Baghdād in 656/1258, the Mongol commander Hülegü (Hūlāgū) advanced on Mesopotamia, where he was joined by Hethoum. Crossing the Euphrates, the Mongols and their allies swiftly occupied northern Syria, and, after a siege of only a week, captured Aleppo on 9 Ṣafar 658/25 January 1260. They then advanced swiftly southwards and on 17 Rabīʿ I 658/2 March 1260 the Mongol forces entered the undefended city of Damascus. Their commander was Kitbuga Noyon, a Turk by origin and a Nestorian Christian by religion. With him rode two other Christian princes—Hethoum of Armenia and his Frankish son-in-law Bohemond of Antioch—who was later excommunicated by the pope for allying himself with the Mongols. Dark days had come for Islam. The caliphate was dead; Aleppo and Damascus, the great Muslim cities of Syria, had fallen like Baghdād to the infidel conqueror. Of the old heartlands of Islam, only Egypt and Arabia remained inviolate—and the way seemed open for the Mongols, firmly established in Damascus, to continue their irresistible advance.

In the spring of 658/1260 Mongol detachments occupied Nābulus and Gaza, while others administered a sharp correction to the Franks of the Latin kingdom, who did not seem disposed to follow their northern coreligionists into the Mongol alliance. A Mongol ambassador went to Cairo to demand the submission of the sultan to the khan. Quṭuz refused the demand and defiantly put the ambassador to death. An Egyptian embassy went to Acre to seek the help or at least the acquiescence of the Latin kingdom for an Egyptian advance through Palestine—and by now found them ready to listen. The Franks drew back from a full military alliance, but agreed to allow free passage and supplies of food to the Mamluk army, which advanced northwards along the Palestine coast, and camped in the neighbourhood of Acre in August. Some of the Mamluk commanders, including Baybars, visited the Latin capital as guests. Meanwhile Kitbuga Noyon, with his Mongol troops and his Armenian and Georgian auxiliaries, had crossed the Jordan into Galilee. The Mamluks turned south-east to meet them, and the two armies clashed at a place called ʿAyn Jālūt, 'the Spring of Goliath', a village between Baysān and Nābulus. In this famous battle, the Mamluks won a decisive victory. Luring the enemy into a trap, they destroyed the Mongol army, captured its commander and put him to death. This was the first time that a Mongol army suffered defeat in pitched battle—that the unconquerable had been conquered. The day was Friday, 25 Ramaḍān 658/3 September 1260.

Egypt was saved from the Mongols. The captured cities of Syria at once rose against their Mongol garrisons, and welcomed the victorious Mamluks. In Damascus, the Sunnī population celebrated their release by attacking the Shī'īs, Christians and Jews—all accused of collaboration with the conqueror. A Mongol punitive expedition briefly reoccupied Aleppo in December, but was defeated by the princes of Ḥimṣ and Ḥamāh and driven out of Syria. Meanwhile the victorious Mamluk army returned to Egypt. On Saturday, 15 Dhu'l-Qa'da 658/23 October 1260, Sultan Quṭuz went hawking with some of his chief Mamluks, including Baybars. When they were about to return Baybars approached the sultan and asked him for the gift of a captive Mongol girl. The sultan agreed, and Baybars kissed his hand. On this prearranged signal the Mamluks fell upon him and killed him. He had reigned for eleven months and seventeen days. Returning to the camp, the murderers informed Aqṭāy the *atabeg,* who was in the royal tent, of their deed. 'Which of you killed him?' asked Aqṭāy. 'I did', replied Baybars. 'Then sit on the throne in his place', said Aqṭāy.[1] Baybars sat on the throne, and the other Mamluks pledged allegiance to him as sultan. The kingdom that was saved at 'Ayn Jālūt had a new master.

Not surprisingly, later generations have seen in the battle of 'Ayn Jālūt one of the decisive moments of history—the victory that saved Egypt, Islam, and perhaps more from final destruction by the Mongols. The outcome cannot have seemed so certain at the time. The Mongol force at 'Ayn Jālūt was hardly more than a detachment, numbering perhaps 10,000 men—overwhelmingly outnumbered by the great army assembled by Quṭuz. That the Mongols did not take swift reprisals was due to causes other than the strength of the Mamluks—to the inner struggle within the Mongol empire following the death of Möngke Khān in September 1259, which obliged Hülegü to return to east Asia, taking many of his troops with him. The victory did not end the danger from the Mongols, who continued to hold both Persia and Mesopotamia, and to threaten Syria from both north and east. In the event, however, 'Ayn Jālūt was the high watermark of the Mongol advance; despite the long confrontation which now began between the Mongol power based on Persia and the new sultanate in Egypt, the Mongols were never again able to threaten Egypt.

[1] Ibn Taghrī-Birdī, *al-Nujūm al-zāhira,* vii (Cairo, 1928), 83–4.

There was another aspect to the battle of ʿAyn Jālūt, which did not escape the notice of some contemporary observers. The army of Kitbuga Noyon was an army from the steppe, and its advance marks the limit reached by the great steppe empires. But the Muslim army from Egypt which defeated them was also composed of men from the steppe—of Turkish and other Mamluks commanded by such leaders as the Khwarazmian Quṭuz and the Kipchak Baybars. 'It is a remarkable thing', says the thirteenth-century Damascene historian, Abū Shāma, 'that the Tatars were defeated and destroyed by men of their own kind, who were Turks...'[1] More than a century later the great Arab historian, Ibn Khaldūn, saw the benign providence of God in the coming of these men from the steppe, who gave the Muslim world new strength and vigour at a time of weakness and degeneration, and thus enabled it to meet and overcome the great dangers that threatened it.[2] The role of the Turkish *mamlūks* in Islamic government and society had been growing steadily for a long time. In the new state and order that emerged in Egypt and Syria in the seventh/thirteenth century, they achieved final control. The state which they established is known to scholarship as the Mamluk Sultanate; contemporaries called it *dawlat al-Atrāk*—the empire of the Turks.

Most though not all of the Mamluks were indeed Turks, chiefly from the lands to the north of the Black Sea and the Caspian, and from peoples who had been broken up or displaced by the advance and domination of the Mongols. Besides those who were imported, as bought slaves, there were many who came into the territories of the Mamluk Sultanate as exiles or refugees—often still in their own tribal units. These included Turks, Kurds, and even a sizeable number of Mongols, who for one reason or another fled or were driven from the Mongol lands, or were attracted by the flesh-pots of Egypt. Though Turks and Mongols are probably not related peoples, they had a great deal of shared background and experience; the immense prestige of Mongol arms will have assured some welcome to these Mongol deserters, exiles and adventurers who chose to throw in their lot with the Egyptian sultanate. Numbers of them came during the reign of Baybars, and assisted him in his task of modernizing the Mamluk army—that is to say, of imitating and adopting the methods of the most successful military

[1] Abū Shāma, *Tarājim al-qarnayn al-sādis wa'l-tāsiʿ*, ed. Muḥammad Zāhid al-Kawtharī (Cairo, 1366/1947), 208.

[2] Ibn Khaldūn, *Kitāb al-ʿIbar*, v (Cairo, 1857), 371.

power of the day, the Mongols. Many more came during the reign of al-ʿĀdil Kitbuga, himself a Mongol of the Oirat tribe. By this time their welcome was beginning to wear rather thin.

The Egyptian chroniclers count Baybars (658–76/1260–77) as fourth of the Turkish Mamluk sultans, after Aybeg, his son ʿAlī, and Quṭuz. Yet he must be counted as one of the founders of this new order, which was to endure for two and a half centuries. He came to power by a hard route, with two regicides on his conscience—those of Tūrān-Shāh and Quṭuz. But his toughness and ruthlessness were of service to the state in the difficult times in which he reigned, and his achievements in power have overshadowed the methods by which he attained it.

His career as sultan suggests certain obvious parallels with that of Saladin. Both met and overcame a great foreign menace to Islam; both created, as their base, a united Syro-Egyptian monarchy; both tried to preserve and strengthen that base by introducing great changes in the social order; both tried, in different ways, to reaffirm the principle of Islamic unity as personified in the caliphate.

The manifold activities of Baybars were all consistent, directed to the supreme objective of containing the Mongol attack that still menaced the very heart of the Islamic East. Throughout the early, formative period of the Mamluk sultanate, the dominating fact of life was the presence of a hostile heathen power in Central and south-west Asia, which had conquered half the world of Islam, and seemed poised to conquer the other half. This threat to Islam from the east came from an enemy that was immensely more powerful, more alien, and more terrible than the Crusaders even at their most fanatical and their most ambitious. To meet it, more than ordinary measures were needed.

Against the Mongols a bridgehead in southern Palestine was not enough; all Syria was needed. So Baybars made war against the Ayyubid principalities, bringing most of them under his control or influence; against the Franks, whose possessions he reduced, by a series of offensives, to a narrow strip of coast; against the Assassins, whose dangerous dissidence he ended by capturing their mountain strongholds; against the Armenians, the allies of the Mongols, devastating their lands and sacking their cities. The Egyptian base, too, had to be made strong and secure; other campaigns in Nubia and Libya, against the African neighbours of Egypt, served the same great imperial purpose.

Baybars used diplomacy as well as war. The old Egyptian understanding with Constantinople was renewed, this time to the disadvantage of the Franks in Syria. A split in the Mongol camp enabled him to form an alliance with the Mongol khans of the Golden Horde, since some time converted to Islam, against the Īl-Khāns of Persia. Even in Christian Europe the sultan sought and found associates. In 659/1261 the Syrian historian Ibn Wāṣil went on an embassy from Baybars to the Sicilian king Manfred, the son of Frederick II and an enemy of the papacy; other embassies to Italy followed, and in 662/1264 Charles of Anjou, the papal candidate for the succession to the Swabians, himself sent an embassy with letters and gifts to Cairo—a remarkable recognition of the sultan's strength. Commercial treaties were concluded with Aragon and, later, with several Italian states. The *débâcle* of the Crusaders in Syria, and the concurrent negotiations for a Mongol-Christian alliance, did not prevent the Franks and Muslims from proceeding with these mutually advantageous commercial arrangements.

Meanwhile a brilliant stroke of policy had confirmed the status and prestige of the Egyptian sultanate as the chief bulwark of Islam. For nearly three and a half years, after the destruction of the Baghdād caliphate by the Mongols, the Muslims had been without a caliph. Despite its loss of effective power, the caliphate was still held in great veneration by Muslims as the supreme expression of Muslim unity and legality; its destruction was a shattering blow, which left a dangerous hiatus. Baybars found a way to fill it. In Rajab 659/June 1261 an 'Abbasid prince who had fled from Baghdād was solemnly proclaimed in Cairo as caliph, with the regnal name of al-Mustanṣir. The sultan sent letters to the cities of the empire announcing the new accession, and gave orders to mention the new caliph's name in the Friday prayer and inscribe it on the coinage. An important consequence was the allegiance of the *sharīf* of Mecca, Abū Numayy, who had previously given his support to the Hafsid ruler of Tunisia. The Ḥijāz had for some time past moved from the orbit of 'Irāq into that of Egypt, with some periods of independence under a line of Sharifian rulers. The Mongol conquests had cut off the Pilgrimage and other links with 'Irāq and the East, making the Ḥijāz economically dependent on pilgrims and supplies from Egypt and, through Egypt, from the Muslim West. Despite an occasional show of independence by the *sharīf*, the Ḥijāz now became in effect a dependency of the Mamluk empire, which thus gained all the advantages, in prestige and influence, accruing from the protection of the Holy Places and the control of the Pilgrimage. A new title, *khādim al-ḥaramayn*, 'servant of the two Holy Places', symbolized this authority.

Used by Saladin in an inscription in recaptured Jerusalem,[1] it was adopted by Baybars and his successors to proclaim their custodianship of the central sanctuaries of Islam and thus, by implication, their primacy among Muslim states. Significantly, the title belonged not to the caliph but to the sultan, the real ruler.

In this age of constant and terrible menace, it was essential that the last bulwark of Islam should, at all times, be commanded by an able and vigorous ruler. It was no doubt this pressing need that drove the Mamluks away from the familiar hereditary principle of succession to something new. The change was gradual—even reluctant. The Mamluk sultanate began with a semblance of succession to the Ayyubids. Aybeg was succeeded briefly by his son 'Alī; Baybars too was succeeded by his son Berke Khān, who after a year was deposed in favour of his seven-year-old younger brother Salāmish. But the real ruler was the new strong man, the Mamluk Qalawun (Qalā'ūn), and after a few months, in 678/1279, he added the titles and trappings to the realities of power. His first task was to defeat a rival claimant, Sunqur al-Ashqar, nominated by the Mamluk troops in Syria with support from the sons of Baybars and from local bedouin. Sunqur appealed to the Mongols for help, but, appalled by the forces he had summoned, he made his peace with Qalawun, who was thus left free to defeat and expel the Mongols and their Georgian and Armenian allies.

In general, Qalawun followed the policies of Baybars. To counter the Mongol threat, he sought allies and friends in both Christendom and Islam, exchanging embassies with both the Byzantine and the Holy Roman emperors, concluding agreements with Genoa, Castile and Sicily, and bestowing a title and escutcheon on a Kipchak prince newly converted to Islam. On the other side, missions to the Yemen and to Ceylon show the revival of Egyptian interest in the East and in the routes leading to it. Of crucial importance was the position in Syria, where the sultanate was directly threatened by the Mongols and weakened by the surviving footholds of the Crusaders. To strengthen his grasp on Syria, Qalawun extended and confirmed his control over the Muslim states. During the Mongol invasion, he had made a truce with the Crusaders; with the Mongols safely out of the way, he broke the truce and attacked the Frankish lands, achieving a notable success with the capture, in 688/1289, of the great fortified port of Tripoli—the largest town still in Frankish hands. He died in the following year, while preparing to besiege Acre.

[1] *Repertoire chronologique de l'épigraphie arabe*, ix, no. 3464, inscription of 587/1191.

This unfinished task was taken up by his son and successor, al-Malik al-Ashraf Khalīl, who led a vast army, with nearly a hundred siege engines, to attack the last capital of the Latin kingdom of Jerusalem. On 3 Rabī' II 690/5 April 1291 the Muslim army encamped under the walls of Acre. The siege began next day, and on Friday, 17 Jumādā I/18 May the sultan launched the final assault. By the end of the day the city was in Muslim hands. The remaining Frankish possessions—Beirut, Sidon, Tyre, Athlīth, Haifa—were surrendered or captured with little resistance. The long interlude of Crusader rule in the Levant was at an end. In Damascus festivities continued for one month to celebrate the final departure of the invaders. On the coasts, the Mamluks, like the Ayyubids, destroyed the castles and laid waste the cities they had captured, to discourage the Crusaders from returning: as a further precaution, they settled warlike peoples there—Kurds, Turks and even Mongols—to meet them if they tried.

More fortunate than Baybars, Qalawun founded a dynasty, which reigned, with interruptions, for about a century. Succession was not always from father to son; sometimes it went by what was becoming the more important bond between a master and his slave or freedman—but the last of the line, Ḥājjī, was Qalawun's descendant in the fifth generation. The best known among them was al-Malik al-Nāṣir Muḥammad, the son of Qalawun by a Mongol princess. His long reign lasted, with two interruptions of rule by Mamluks, from 693/1293 to 741/1340, and he is remembered as an able and determined ruler who gave Egypt security and prosperity.

The main problems confronting the rulers of Egypt during the so-called Baḥrī period remained much the same; so too did the methods of dealing with them. The chief enemy was the Mongols in Persia, who remained the rivals of the Mamluks even after their conversion to Islam —a change which was slow to bring improvement in Mongol-Mamluk relations. Mongol forces continued to menace the Mamluk realms, and to seek the help of both local and distant Christian rulers. In Rabī' I 699/December 1299 the *Īl-Khān* Ghāzān, a newly converted Muslim, crossed the Euphrates with a great army; within a short time he was able to occupy Aleppo, defeat the Mamluks near Ḥimṣ, and capture Damascus. On his return to Persia the Mamluks recovered most of Syria, and, after abortive peace negotiations, Ghāzān launched a new offensive. A letter from the Muslim *il-khān* to Pope Boniface VIII, dated 12 April 1302, invited the pope to organize and mobilize a European alliance and attack the Mamluks from the west, while he did so from the east. In the spring of 702/1303 a new Mongol army crossed the Euphrates in what proved the last great Mongol assault on Syria. On 2–3 Ramaḍān/20–21 April the Mamluks met them on the plain of Marj al-Ṣuffār, near Damascus, and won a decisive victory. With the death of Ghāzān shortly afterwards, the danger from the Īl-Khāns was at an end. A few years later, the decline of the Mongol power and menace found symbolic expression in an act of the Egyptian sultan. During the time of the great Mongol conquests, the Muslim sultans and Mamluks, even in Egypt, had adopted Mongol-style dress and accoutrements, and had let their hair grow long in the Mongol fashion instead of cropping their heads in the Muslim way. In 714/1315, after a sickness, the sultan decided to revert to the old Muslim custom. 'He went to the bath', says al-Maqrīzī, 'and shaved his whole head, and every one of the Nāṣirī *amīrs* and *mamlūks* did likewise; and from that time the soldiers ceased to wear their hair long, and so it has continued until today.'[1]

Towards Christendom, Mamluk policy was one of ruthless war against the Christian states in the Levant, coupled with the development of commercial and even political relations with Byzantium and Europe. The destruction of the last Frankish authority in Syria and Palestine was followed by attacks on Cyprus and Armenia—neither of which hindered the growth of mutually convenient relations with the commercial states of southern Europe. At the same time, the Mamluks extended their control or influence on both sides of the Red Sea, in Nubia, the Ḥijāz and the Yemen, and fostered their sea-borne commerce with south and east Asia.

Muḥammad b. Qalawun was followed as sultan by a series of his descendants—most of them incompetent and ineffectual. Finally, the last of them, Ḥājjī, was swept away by an able Mamluk, the Circassian Barqūq, who in 784/1382 ended the Baḥrī sultanate and inaugurated the second series of Mamluk sultans. They are known as the Burjīs—from the *Burj*, tower (of the citadel of Cairo) or as the Circassians, since all but two of them were of that people. The Burjiyya regiment, mainly of Circassian *mamlūks*, had been founded by Qalawun.

The eighth/fourteenth century was on the whole a period of tranquillity and peace. No major foreign enemy threatened the Mamluk realms, and the flourishing trade with both East and West brought great wealth to Egypt and ample revenues to the treasury.

[1] Al-Maqrīzī, *Sulūk*, ii/I (Cairo, 1941), 148.

A new time of troubles began with the rise of Tīmūr in the east—a new world-conqueror who was soon to offer a major threat to the Mamluk Sultanate. By 789/1387 Tīmūr's forces were already in Asia Minor and Mesopotamia, on the borders of Syria; a series of risings against Barqūq by the Mamluk governors of Syria may not have been unconnected with their presence. The sultan of Baghdād sought refuge in Cairo; Tīmūr sent an envoy to Barqūq to demand his return. According to a Persian source favourable to Tīmūr, he also sent a letter offering friendship, an exchange of embassies, and agreement for freedom of commerce between their two realms.[1] Barqūq responded by putting Tīmūr's ambassador to death, and accepting a proposal from the Ottoman Sultan Bāyezīd I for an alliance. The danger was for the moment averted.

The real crisis came after Barqūq's death in 801/1399, during the reign of his son and successor Faraj. Syria was once again in disorder, with the Mamluk *amīrs* in revolt against the new sultan. The alliance with the Ottomans had ended when Bāyezīd briefly occupied Malaṭya on the death of Barqūq. With the new offensive by Tīmūr, the Ottoman ruler again sought an alliance with Cairo. The *amīrs* met in council and decided to reject his overtures. '"He is no friend of ours", they said, "Let him fight for his lands, and we shall fight for our lands and our subjects."...They wrote in this sense to Bāyezīd...and after they had done so not one of the Egyptian *amīrs* made any preparations to fight Tīmūr, or gave any attention to this, for the chief concern of every one of them was how to attain the sultanate of Egypt and eliminate the others...'[2]

As a result of this short-sighted decision, Tīmūr was able to deal with the Ottomans and the Mamluks separately. On 25 Muḥarram 803/15 September 1400 he captured Malaṭya, and entered the Mamluk dominions. Within a few months he had captured and sacked Aleppo, Ḥāmah, Ḥimṣ, Ba'albakk and Damascus—where he exacted a *fatwā* from the *'ulamā'* approving his actions. Among those who went to meet the conqueror was the seventy-two-year-old historian Ibn Khaldūn, who had accompanied the sultan to Damascus and had remained there after his withdrawal. This meeting between the greatest conqueror and the greatest historian of the age is recorded by the latter.[3]

[1] Sharaf al-Dīn 'Alī Yazdī, *Ẓafarnāma*, i, 643.
[2] Ibn Taghrī-Birdī, *Nujūm*, xii (Cairo, 1956), 217–18.
[3] W. J. Fischel, *Ibn Khaldūn and Tamerlane* (Berkeley and Los Angeles, 1952).

Syria was lost, and Egypt ripe for conquest—but fortunately Tīmūr and his armies turned east. He had, however, done irreparable damage, which was aggravated by the depredations of the unleashed bedouin, the quarrels of rebellious *amīrs*, by locusts, famine and pestilence. Syria was devastated, her cities sacked, her craftsmen deported in great numbers to distant Samarqand. Besides the economic ruination of Syria, the war with Tīmūr also imposed great strains on the economy of Egypt. To pay for the war, the government in Cairo resorted to new and heavy taxes, to special levies, and to the depreciation of the currency. The harmful effects of these measures were soon felt; they were accentuated by the famine of 806/1403. An exceptionally low Nile left many lands dry and barren. This was followed by scarcity, high prices and plague. 'This year', says Ibn Taghrī-Birdī, 'was the first of the years of trials and troubles which ruined most of the land of Egypt and her provinces, because of low Niles, discord, changes of governors in the provinces, and other causes.'[1] Egypt had known pestilence during the eighth/fourteenth century, notably in 749/1348, when the Black Death decimated both the Mamluk army and the Egyptian population. During the ninth/fifteenth century pestilence and famine became regular visitors to Egypt, with cumulatively far greater effect. If famine chiefly affected the native Egyptians, the plague struck hardest against the unacclimatized foreigners—above all against the Mamluks themselves. In recurring outbreaks the Mamluks of the royal household especially suffered heavy losses. They were difficult and expensive to replace.

The military situation allowed of no respite. Even after the death of Tīmūr, the Mamluk possessions in Egypt were still menaced by internal disorder, and by enemies beyond the frontier—the Timurids, the Turcoman dynasties, and the new, rising power of the Ottomans. From the west, European pirates raided the Syrian coast and even the port of Alexandria. The new sultan, al-Mu'ayyad Shaykh—who had succeeded Faraj after a six months' interval during which the 'Abbasid Caliph al-Musta'īn reigned as stop-gap—restored the situation on the frontiers, and even extended Mamluk control into Anatolia; but his victories brought little permanent gain. Their cost helped to swell the deficit of the Cairo treasury, and therefore to augment the already crushing fiscal pressure. The economy of Egypt was in disarray, and could not provide the necessary funds. The government, in desperation, turned to

[1] Ibn Taghrī-Birdī, *Nujūm*, xii (Cairo, 1956), 301.

new methods of raising money—to the corrosive practice of selling offices and even exemption from military duties, and to the creation of state monopolies in trade.

Barqūq had been succeeded as effective sultan by his son Faraj. This was the last hereditary succession. Thereafter the sultanate was held by the strongest *amīr*. On the death of a sultan, his son followed him, as a formality, to preside over an interregnum during which the real succession was decided. The son was then peacefully retired, and the new sultan took office. The system had the advantage of providing powerful and effective rulers. It had the disadvantage of stimulating strife among the Mamluks. In the Burjī system the allegiance of the royal slave household was not automatically transferred from one ruler to the next. Each sultan based his authority on his own corps of Mamluks, who rose to power with him, were reinforced and entrenched by him—and were in due course ousted, and often ruthlessly repressed, by the personal Mamluks of his successor. This gave rise to constant intrigues and conflicts between rival groups, particularly between the royal Mamluks and the surviving Mamluks of previous sultans. These latter were of course heterogeneous, and frequently at odds among themselves. Such conflicts added to the not inconsiderable troubles already confronting the Circassian sultans.

In 825/1422 the new sultan was Bārsbāy, a former Mamluk of Barqūq, who reigned until 841/1438. The economic difficulties that confronted him were grave, but there were also political and military problems requiring immediate attention and action. In the Mediterranean, European pirates and privateers, mostly based on Cyprus, had for some time been plaguing the Muslim shores. Bārsbāy built coastal defences and launched a fleet. A peace treaty had been signed in 772/1370 between Egypt and a group of Christian states, including Cyprus; the island kingdom had, however, continued to serve as a base for piratical raids, in which even the king's galleys sometimes took part. By a treaty of 817/1414, the king of Cyprus undertook not to encourage piracy; this had only limited effect, and Bārsbāy decided on a punitive expedition. After some exploratory raids, he sent a fleet and army against the island, in 830/1427. The expedition was completely successful. The Mamluks defeated the Cypriots on land and sea, devastated the island, and returned to Egypt with great booty and many captives, including the king himself. He was released after eight months, having agreed to recognize the sultan as his suzerain, and to pay an annual tribute.

There were problems in Asia too. The Turcoman principalities of the north and north-east, situated between the Ottoman, Timurid, and Mamluk powers, had begun to play an important role, often reflecting the warring interests and policies of their great neighbour. Bārsbāy sent an army to Mesopotamia, which achieved some initial successes; his war against an Ak-Koyunlu prince ended, however, in a stalemate, and a dangerously undisciplined withdrawal by a large part of the Mamluk army. Relations with the Ottomans were on the whole friendly. Further east, the Timurid sovereign of Persia, Shāh-Rukh, while avoiding open conflict, carried on the old feud against the Mamluk Sultanate by indirect means—through his Turcoman allies in the north, and by seeking to gain influence in Arabia. This is no doubt the meaning of the request to the sultan in Cairo for permission to provide a veil (*kiswa*) to cover the Ka'ba, 'if only for one day'. The request was refused, on the grounds that the privilege of providing the *kiswa* belonged by ancient custom to the rulers of Egypt, who had established great *waqfs* for this purpose.

Bārsbāy had good reason for not wishing to grant his rival a foothold, however tenuous, in the Ḥijāz. Like his predecessors, Bārsbāy was interested in the custodianship of the Holy Places, the direction of the Pilgrimage, and the control of the Red Sea and its ports. The troubles in Egypt had encouraged the *sharīfs* of the Ḥijāz to adopt a more independent position, and to try and use the rivalry between the Muslim powers in the east and west to their own advantage. This the sultans were not prepared to tolerate. By military and other methods they brought the insubordinate *sharīfs* to heel and, while leaving them substantial autonomy in internal affairs, maintained effective Egyptian control. This was reinforced by Bārsbāy, who stationed a permanent Mamluk garrison in Mecca, and gave particular attention to the Ḥijāzī ports.

Since Fatimid times, the governments of Egypt had been interested in the Red Sea and eastern trade, which brought precious commodities—spices, silks, aromatic and other woods—to Egypt for local use and for profitable resale, and great revenues to the Egyptian exchequer. The merchants too, organized on a vast scale and operating with very large capital investments, required the protection of a strong government, to safeguard their land and sea communications from brigandage and piracy and to maintain security and confidence. The value of this trade was recognized by the enemies of Egypt—such as the *Īl-Khān* Arghūn, who in the seventh/thirteenth century invited Genoese shipwrights to Baghdād, and launched two galleys in the Indian Ocean to blockade Aden and cut the Egyptian route to India. It was recognized too by the sultans of Egypt, who made great efforts to attract the eastern merchants to their realms. Thus, a circular letter of 687/1288, to the merchants of Yemen, Sind, India and China, invites them to bring their goods to Egypt and Syria, promising them favourable conditions, security, justice, ready markets, and high profits.[1] One of the highest civilian officials, the intendant of the domain, was responsible for the encouragement of the eastern and western merchants. The encyclopaedia of administrative practice of al-Qalqashandī (d. 821/1418) cites a brevet of appointment to this office:

> He will welcome the Kārim merchants coming from the Yemen, seeking their goodwill, showing them courtesy, dealing with them justly, so that they may find a felicity (*yumn*) which they have not found in Arabia Felix (Yemen); likewise the merchants who came from the West... both Muslim and Frankish. Let him receive them kindly, and treat them justly, for the profits... accruing from them... are very great.[2]

The question of tempting merchants from the Yemen to Egypt was an important one. Under the Rasulids, a dynasty founded in the seventh/thirteenth century after the collapse of Ayyubid rule, the Yemen entered on a period of expansion and prosperity. The Rasulids pursued a vigorous policy in Arabia, sent missions to India, Ceylon and China, and revived the port of Aden, which became one of the great emporia of the eastern trade. The sultan of Egypt had an obvious interest in diverting this trade to ports under his control—particularly when, in the early fifteenth century, Chinese junks began to sail as far as the Red Sea. Under the Ming emperors, China had entered on a new era of commercial prosperity, and sought new outlets in the west. Efforts to reopen the overland routes through Persia came to nothing, and the Chinese directed their main efforts to the Red Sea, where they exchanged embassies with the Yemen.

A period of upheaval and extortion in the Yemen, coinciding with the consolidation of Egyptian control in the Ḥijāz, gave Bārsbāy his opportunity. Rather than face the exactions and uncertainties of Aden, the

[1] Ibn al-Furāt, *Ta'rikh*, ed. C. K. Zurayk and Najla Izzedin, viii (Beirut, 1939), 65 ff; cf. G. Wiet, 'Les marchands d'épices sous les sultans mamlouks', in *Cahiers d'histoire égyptienne* (1955), 90 ff.

[2] *Ṣubḥ*, xi (Cairo, 1917), 320; cf. G. Wiet, *op. cit.*, 96.

eastern merchants sailed right past the southern port, and made for Jedda, where the Egyptians tried to create conditions attractive to them. As Aden declined, Jedda rose, becoming one of the main commercial ports of the Mamluk empire. From 825/1425 the Egyptians took over the control of the customs of Jedda from the *sharīfs,* though sometimes allowing them a share of the proceeds. As well as substantial revenue, this brought the business of the port under direct Egyptian authority. From 828/1424 a boat service linked Jedda with Ṭūr, which was becoming the main eastern port of entry on the Egyptian mainland.

In the same year Bārsbāy placed a ban on the circulation of European gold coins in the Mamluk realms. Because of the inferiority and irregularity of Mamluk dinars, they could be used only by weight in commercial transactions. The Venetian ducat, a piece of fixed weight and undisputed purity, was in general circulation in Egypt and Syria as a unit of currency—even in government departments. Bārsbāy called them in and issued his own gold pieces, no doubt at a profit. This, following on other measures, was a serious blow to the European traders, and was probably intended as such. It was not, however, permanent. Later, the ducat reappeared, and remained in circulation until Ottoman times. Bārsbāy also attempted other currency manipulations to the detriment of both Egyptian and foreign merchants, as well as of his own army, whom he paid in dirhams at an artificially low rate.

Bārsbāy's Red Sea policies gave him greater control of commerce, and a great increase in customs revenue from Jedda and from the Egyptian ports on the African side. 'Every year', says a near contemporary author, 'more than a hundred ships call at Jedda, some of them with seven sails, and provide an average annual revenue of 200,000 dinars.'[1]

But it was not enough. If the state could gain so much merely by taxing the profits of the traders, surely it could gain still more by taking over the trade entirely. In pursuit of this reasoning, Bārsbāy began in 826/1423 by making sugar a state monopoly. All private sugar-refineries were closed, and all confectioners, pastry-cooks and other consumers of sugar ordered to buy from the state at a fixed price greatly in excess of current commercial prices. A special government department was set up to deal with the sugar monopoly, which, after a brief relaxation, was extended and strengthened during the

[1] Khalīl al-Ẓāhirī, *Zubdat kashf al-mamālik,* ed. P. Ravaisse (Paris, 1894), 14.

following years. All traffic and manufacture except by the sultan's agents was forbidden, and existing stocks compulsorily acquired. Even the cultivation of sugar-cane was banned except on the sultan's domain estates. The application of these rules in both Syria and Egypt, according to the historians, brought soaring prices and general distress. Other measures of a monopolistic or restrictive nature were applied to cereals and meat, though these were not taken over as fully as sugar. In 837/1433–4 the sultan ordered a survey of the looms of Alexandria, then a great textile centre—no doubt as a preliminary to some fiscal or monopolistic measure. It showed only 800 looms—as against 14,000 in 790/1388. Ibn Taghrī-Birdī, who reports these figures, blames the decline on the tyranny and incompetence of officials.[1]

The monopolization of internal production and trade produced disappointing results. The rich spice trade, linking East and West through an exclusively Egyptian route, promised richer pickings. Bārsbāy began with pepper. A decree of 832/1429 prohibited the sale of pepper to European merchants by private individuals. Instead they were to buy it from the sultan, who had purchased all that the eastern merchants had brought. He bought it cheaply, since no Egyptian merchant would dare to outbid him, and sold it dear, since he was the only seller. In the first year the price required from the European merchants rose from 80 to 120 dinars a load; in the second year to 130. Despite some subsequent fall, prices remained high, and the merchants protested vigorously—but without effect. Other monopolies followed, and the practices of Bārsbāy were carried on by several of his successors, notably by Khushqadam (865–72/1461–7) and Qā'it Bāy (873–901/1468–95). Under the latter the economic collapse of the empire was already far advanced. The position was precariously maintained by drastic and violent taxation, such as the capital levy of 895/1490, by currency depreciation, and by the exploitation—at once ruthless and ineffectual—of the trading community. It could not last.

While the economy was disintegrating, the distinctive social, military and political order of the Mamluk state was also declining, to the point when it was no longer able to withstand the blows that were to fall.

The Mamluk system was a logical development of the Seljuk feudal order brought into Egypt by the Ayyubids. A military officer received a grant of land in lieu of pay, and on condition of maintaining a certain number of men-at-arms, varying from five to five hundred according to

[1] *Nujūm*, ed. Popper, vi (Berkeley, 1915-23), 714.

his rank. These grants were for life or for some lesser period. The grantee did not normally reside in his fief, but in Cairo or in the chief town of the district in which his fief was situated. His concern was with revenue rather than with possession, and most of the affairs of his fief were administered by the army office in Cairo. The system therefore developed no seigneurial powers or jurisdiction of the Western or late Seljuk type. There was no subinfeudation, and even the territorial division of the country into fiefs was subject to rearrangement. Grants were not hereditary, though there were attempts to make them so. The system required that the Egyptian- or Syrian-born children of the Mamluks be evicted to make way for newly imported Mamluks, who alone were eligible for full membership of Mamluk military society.

The Mamluks themselves were bought slaves, brought to Egypt as children or adolescents. They were of non-Muslim birth, and retained a non-Arab name, even after conversion, as a mark of superior status. After a long and careful training and education, they were formally manumitted, receiving their manumission certificates, with their horses and accoutrements, at a passing-out parade. The adult Mamluk was thus a freedman, not a slave of his master or patron. To his master and to other Mamluks of the same master he owed complete loyalty. Through merit, he might hope to advance to the highest offices, even to the sultanate itself. At first the Mamluks were mainly Kipchak Turks, from the northern shores of the Black Sea; they included, however, men of many other races—Turks of various tribes, Kurds, Mongol deserters, Caucasians, Greeks and even some Europeans. Under the Burjī sultans the Circassians became the dominant power in the state. This change was partly due to difficulties of recruitment in the Kipchak steppe, partly to the deliberate policy of the Circassian sultans, who favoured men of their own race at the expense of others and in defiance of the Mamluk system of promotion by merit and seniority.

The children of the Mamluks, free-born and Muslim, could not enter the exclusive but non-hereditary ruling caste to which their fathers had belonged. They could serve in the socially and militarily inferior corps of the *ḥalqa,* but even there could rarely rise to high rank. Some found a career in religion and in the civil administration, where they played a not unimportant part. A few joined the great Syrian and Egyptian official and religious families, the *noblesse de robe*[1] whose skill and devotion, as

[1] The analogy is that of K. S. Salibi, 'The Banū Jamā'a: a dynasty of Shāfi'ite jurists in the Mamluk period', in *Studia Islamica,* ix (1958), 97 ff.

well as the military prowess of the Mamluks, served to maintain the Mamluk Sultanate for two and a half centuries—a régime without equal for longevity and stability in the annals of medieval Islam.

The Mamluks rose to power in a time of great changes in the world of Islam, comparable with the upheavals that ended the Roman empire in the West. The role of the Egyptian sultanate in this age was one of retrenchment and conservation—of an Islamic Byzantium. While the ancient polity and society of Islam were shattered by barbarian conquest, the Mamluks in Egypt, though themselves of barbarian origin, stood firm and saved the Nile valley from invasion. In the north and east, new states and societies were arising, based on the plateaux of Anatolia and Iran, among the Turks and Persians who had taken over the political and cultural leadership of Islam, and a new civilization was developing, expressed mainly in the Persian and Turkish languages. In Egypt, despite great influences from the East, the older order survived, and Islamic culture in its Arabic form entered on its long Byzantine age. Mamluk soldiers, Egyptian and Syrian administrators, defended and maintained the state; Egyptian and Syrian scholars preserved, interpreted and enriched the heritage of classical Islam.

The decline of the Mamluk Sultanate was due to a complex of causes, both internal and external—among them the devastations of Tīmūr, the effects of recurring drought, plague and famine, financial malpractice and economic dislocation, the depletion of the army through falling recruitment, the disruption of the Mamluk order and discipline by Barqūq and his successors.

The final blows came from outside. The first was economic—the coming of the Portuguese to the East. Portuguese fleets, built for the Atlantic, were superior in structure, armament and navigational qualities to the Muslim fleets, and were soon able to establish naval supremacy in Eastern waters. By opening a direct sea-route from India to Europe, the Portuguese deprived Egypt of her exclusive control of the spice trade, and dealt a heavy blow at her commerce. The long-term effects of this were not as great as was at one time believed, and the tenth/sixteenth century saw a considerable revival of the Levant trade.[1] The immediate effects were, however, very serious, and presented Sultan Qānṣawh al-Ghawrī (906–22/1500–16) with an urgent problem of falling trade and revenue. With Venetian encouragement he resolved on war,

[1] F. Braudel, *La Mediterranée et le monde méditerranéen à l'époque de Philippe II* (Paris, 1949), 423–37; Halil Inalcık, 'Türkiye'nin iktisadî vaziyeti...', in *Belleten* (Ankara), xv (1951), 662 ff.

and in 914/1508 sent an Egyptian fleet to India. After some initial successes they were defeated by the Portuguese, who embarked on a systematic destruction of Muslim merchant shipping in the Indian Ocean, and even sent their ships to the Persian Gulf and the Red Sea.

The second, and decisive blow came from the north. Relations between the Mamluk and Ottoman Sultanates had for long been reasonably friendly. They deteriorated during the second half of the ninth/sixteenth century, mainly because of disputes over the Turcoman border-principalities, partly also because of such minor irritants as Egyptian hospitality to fugitive Ottoman princes, and Egyptian confiscation of gifts sent to the Ottoman sultan from India. Between 890/1485 and 896/1490 the two states fought an inconclusive war, in which the Mamluks had on the whole the upper hand.

The military balance was, however, changing rapidly in favour of the Ottomans. The crucial factor was the introduction of firearms—handguns and cannon—which the Ottomans adopted readily, extensively, and with great effect. The Mamluks, on the other hand, were reluctant to adopt this new weapon. Unlike the Ottoman Empire, the Mamluk territories were poor in metals, which had to be imported from elsewhere. But more serious than the economic obstacle was the social and psychological attitude of the Mamluk ruling caste, who clung to the 'lawful' and 'honourable' weapons and tactics of the past, and despised firearms and those who used them as unworthy and inferior. Some desultory efforts were made to introduce firearms, which were given to units consisting of black slaves, the native-born sons of the Mamluks, and even a kind of militia including locally recruited artisans and miscellaneous foreigners. Not surprisingly, they had little effect, and the mounted lancers, swordsmen, and bowmen who were the flower of the Mamluk army were hopelessly outclassed by the musket-armed Ottoman infantry. The Egyptian chronicles vividly depict the contempt of the knightly Mamluks for this base weapon, 'with which even a woman could stop a number of men',[1] and the terrible destruction which it wrought among them.

In the spring of 922/1516 Sultan Selīm I led his army into Asia Minor, ostensibly on the way to Persia; Qānṣawh al-Ghawrī left Cairo in May and marched with his army towards the northern borders, allegedly to mediate between Selīm and the Persian shah. Neither side was

[1] Ibn Zunbul, *Fatḥ Miṣr* (Cairo, 1278 A.H.), 37–9; cf. D. Ayalon, *Gunpowder and firearms in the Mamluk kingdom* (London, 1956), 94.

convinced, and battle was joined on the plain of Marj Dābiq, north of Aleppo, on Sunday, 25 Rajab 922/24 August 1516. The Mamluks suffered a total defeat, in which their sultan died. While the Ottomans advanced southward through Syria, the Mamluks in Cairo chose a new sultan, Tūmān-Bāy. There was little he could do. On 29 Dhu'l-Ḥijja 922/23 January 1517, the Ottomans defeated the Mamluks at Raydāniyya, near Cairo, and, despite a brief rally, Selīm himself entered the city some days later. Tūmān-Bāy was betrayed and hanged; the last of the caliphs, al-Mutawakkil, was sent to Istanbul, from where he returned as a private citizen some years later.[1] Egypt, Syria and their dependencies were part of the Ottoman empire.

[1] The legend of the transfer of the caliphate by al-Mutawakkil to Selīm does not appear until the late eighteenth century, see below pp. 320–3.

CHAPTER 3

ANATOLIA IN THE PERIOD OF THE SELJUKS AND THE *BEYLIKS*

The foundation of the Great Seljuk empire and the domination of the Islamic world by the Turks is a turning point in the history of Islamic civilization and the Muslim peoples. At a time when the Muslim world was suffering from both external and internal crisis, the Seljuks with their fresh power, restored its political unity; with the new elements and institutions which they brought, they endowed Islamic civilization with a new vitality, and started it on a new phase. One of the basic changes brought about by the foundation of the Great Seljuk empire was, without doubt, the conquest and turkification of the Near East, and especially of Anatolia. Anatolia had been the homeland of many peoples, the scene of many civilizations, and had served them as a bridge between three continents; now for the first time in its history, in spite of the continuing local influences, Anatolia underwent a radical transformation from the ethnic, religious, linguistic, cultural, and artistic points of view. If the foundation of the Great Seljuk empire presents an important phase of Islamic civilization and Turkish history, the turkification of Anatolia is of equal importance, in the period after the fall of this empire and its successors, both in preserving Islamic civilization and the Muslim peoples, and in determining the future of certain Muslim and Christian nations. The origins and the historical role of the Ottoman empire prove this point. In spite of its importance, however, the history of the Seljuks has remained obscure, and it is only in our time that its historical significance has begun to be understood.

TURKISH MIGRATION AND FIRST RAIDS ON ANATOLIA

The Seljuk state in Anatolia came into existence in 1075, thirty-five years after the foundation of the Great Seljuk empire in Persia. This event, following the victory at Manzikert in 463/1071, resulted from the migration of a large population of Turks. The Oghuz raids on Anatolia, which began in 409/1018 and lasted until 433/1040, were mere reconnaissances, and had no historical significance. On the other hand, the battles which took place during the thirty years' period between the foundation of the empire and the battle of Manzikert played a decisive role in breaking Byzantine resistance, and preparing the way for the Turkish settlement in Anatolia.

One of the problems which the Seljuk empire had to deal with since its foundation was to find land and subsistence for the great number of Turcoman emigrants. The Great Seljuk sultans like Ṭughrul Beg (429–55/1038–63), Alp Arslan (455–65/1063–72) and Malik-Shāh (465–85/1072–92) considered the Turcomans a threat to the law and order of the state, and, by sending them on raids into Anatolia, they not only prevented depredations in Muslim territories, but also increased their own power against the Byzantine empire, as well as providing land and livelihood for the Turcomans. The conquest and turkification of Anatolia came about as a result of this policy and these needs, although Muslim rulers, ignorant of the nature of the Turkish state and of Turkish nomadic feudalism, held Ṭughrul Beg, as the Turkish and Muslim sultan, responsible for the Turcoman raids and pillaging in their territories, and complained to him.

As a result of the Seljuk policy of directing the Turcoman migration towards Anatolia, this region was a prey to Turkish attacks and pressure for a period of thirty years. The Turcomans, who were occasionally supported by the Seljuks, but mostly under the leadership of their own beys, started their raids from Āẕarbāyjān and penetrated as far as the eastern, central and western towns of Anatolia. As a result of these long and continuous raids and battles they captured not only the plains and plateaus but also the towns of Erzurum in 440/1048, Kars in 446/1054, Malaṭya (Melitene) in 449/1057, Sivas (Sebastia) in 451/1059, Kayseri (Caesarea) in 459/1067, Niksar (Neocaesarea), Konya (Iconium) and ʿAmmūriyya (Amorium) in 460/1068, Honas (Khonae) in 461/1069. In spite of this expansion, which lasted until the victory of Manzikert, Anatolia was still far from being a safe place for the Turks to settle in, because a great number of fortified castles and cities remained, and the Turcomans were closely pursued by the Byzantine forces. For this reason the Turcomans used to go back to Āẕarbāyjān after their attacks and conquests.

THE SETTLEMENT OF THE TURKS IN ANATOLIA

When Byzantine resistance was broken as a result of the victory at Manzikert in Dhu'l-Qaʿda 463/26 August 1071, the Turcomans began to spread and settle in Anatolia. Conscious of their role as defenders of Islam and champions of a universal Turkish domination, the first Seljuk sultans made good their claim to supremacy over Byzantium, and thus at the same time set about solving the problem of Turkish migration. When, as a result of his defeat, the Emperor Romanus Diogenes was deposed, and the peace he had agreed to was broken, Alp Arslan sent a message to him saying that he would himself go to Anatolia to avenge him. His death in 465/1072 during the Turkistan campaign prevented him from carrying out his threat. Nevertheless he had told his commanders before the campaign that the peace with Byzantium was over, and they had his orders to conquer the Christian countries (i.e. Anatolia).

After the battle of Manzikert, there were swift and sudden changes in the ethnic features of Anatolia. Because the great Turkish migration and colonization were neither studied nor understood, the process of turkification in Anatolia remained an enigma, and some historians ascribed these changes to the annihilation or mass conversion to Islam of the local population. While there were indeed conversions and losses of population on both sides, the inaccuracy of such conjectures, which fail to take account of migration and ethnic changes, is shown even by a general picture of events as drawn above.[1]

Although the victory of Manzikert was followed by a considerable flow of population into Anatolia, the transformation of this land into a wholly Turkish territory took some centuries more. The Turks who fled before the Mongols from Central Asia and Persia formed the second great migration, and the process of turkification spread from central Anatolia to the coasts and was completed during the seventh/thirteenth and eighth/fourteenth centuries. This movement of population was essentially based on the nomadic elements, but, with the foundation of the western Seljuk state, peasants, tradesmen, artisans, and religious leaders came to Anatolia as part of the migrations. Here is a very brief description of how Anatolia was settled by the Turks.

THE FOUNDATION OF THE SELJUK STATE OF RŪM

The Seljuk state of Rūm was founded after, and because of, the movement of a large number of Turcoman tribes to Anatolia. But the founder of

[1] The view according to which the Turks in 473/1080, seven years after reaching the Straits, could easily have been driven away, since they had neither settled nor founded a state, is erroneous and arises from ignorance of Turkish history and Oriental sources. It is sufficient to point out that the Great Seljuk empire was in existence, that a nomadic tribe does not necessarily have to adopt a settled life, and that there was no homeland to which these Turcomans could return. Another mistaken view, due to ignorance of Seljuk policy in regard to conquest and settlement in Anatolia, claims on the basis of an isolated event (Alp Arslan's Syrian expedition) that the Seljuk sultans had no intention of conquering Anatolia.

this state, Süleymān, the son of Kutalmısh (the grandson of Seljük and son of Arslan Yabgu) was not among the commanders who were sent to conquer Anatolia by Alp Arslan after the victory of Manzikert. Indeed, among the conquerors mentioned by the later sources as founders of the state only Artuk Bey can be verified. In 464/1072, Artuk Bey defeated a Byzantine army commanded by Isaac Comnenus, taking him prisoner, and then went to the banks of the Sakarya, leaving central Anatolia behind. When the rebellion of John Ducas created a more dangerous situation, the emperor made an agreement with Artuk and asked for his help. In this way the Turks reached the bay of Izmit. Because of the struggle for the succession after Alp Arslan's death, Artuk Bey was called back to Rayy, the capital of the Great Seljuk empire, and helped Malik-Shāh to overcome his uncle.

Such events as Süleymān's campaign in Anatolia, Alp Arslan's death, Artuk's return to the capital and the struggle for the succession to the throne are closely linked. When Kutalmısh was defeated and killed in 456/1064, at the end of his fight for the throne against Alp Arslan, his sons had been banished to the Byzantine frontiers. These princelings without any power started organizing the Anatolian Turcomans around them after Artuk Bey's departure. And some of these Turcomans were no other than the Yabgulu (Yavkiyya, Yavgiyan), the tribes who had rebelled against Ṭughrul Beg and Alp Arslan, and fled to Anatolia.[1] They now needed a Seljuk prince to lead them. The earliest authenticated appearance on the scene of Kutalmısh's sons was in 467/1074, when they were involved in a battle in Syria against the Turcoman (Yavkiyya) bey, Atsız, who had accepted service under Malik-Shāh, and also when they tried to establish relations with the Fatimid caliph in Egypt. After failing to win this battle, Süleymān entered Anatolia, having besieged Aleppo and Antioch on his way. He went on to take over Konya and its region from its Greek rulers, conquered Iznik (Nicaea) without any resistance and proclaimed it his capital in 467/1075. It is also probable that Tutak, who had marched as far as Bithynia at the head of 100,000 men after Artuk's return, also joined him.

The Byzantine empire was in such a state, and its relations with Anatolia were so cut off, that the conquest of a city like Iznik, which played an important part in the history of Christianity, and which was very near Constantinople, passed unremarked in the Byzantine sources.

[1] This name, which is used for the rebellious Turcomans who were the followers of Arslan Yabgu, has been mistaken for that of the Yiva tribe.

It was only mentioned, on the occasion of Nicephorus III Botaniates's succession in 1078, as belonging to Süleymān, which shows that the conquest must have taken place before that date. This is confirmed by the statement of some Muslim authors that, in spite of the distance, Iznik was conquered by Süleymān in 467/1075.[1] When Seljük's great-grandson founded a state in this newly conquered land, the Anatolian Turcomans accepted his sovereignty, and the nomadic tribes who heard of this emigrated to this land in greater numbers. There is a connexion between the great migration in 1080 and the foundation of this state.

In February 1074 the Emperor Michael VII had appealed to Pope Gregory VII for aid, and in return had promised the unification of the Orthodox Church with the Catholic Church. The pope welcomed this approach and summoned certain European kings and the whole of Christendom to a crusade against the Turks, who had conquered the territories of the Byzantine empire as far as the walls of Constantinople. But the conflict between the papacy and the Holy Roman empire delayed the organization of the crusade for twenty years. When the emperor despaired of any help from Europe in 1074, he sent an ambassador with priceless gifts to Malik-Shāh, but all these attempts had no practical results.

Süleymān increased the power of his state by intervening in dynastic disputes in Constantinople, and by helping Nicephorus III Botaniates's succession to the throne. In this way he enlarged his frontiers, and his army made its headquarters in Üsküdar (Chrysopolis) in 471/1078. Later, by supporting Nicephorus Melissenus, he annexed those parts of Phrygia and western Anatolia which he had not yet conquered. In 473/1080 the Seljuks defeated a Byzantine army sent towards Iznik in 1080, and entrenched themselves on the Asian shore of the Bosphorus, where they established customs-houses and began to control shipping. As they had no fleet, the sea prevented them from attacking Constantinople. When Alexius Comnenus became emperor in 1081, the first thing he did was to make peace with Süleymān in order to defend the Balkans against the shamanistic Turkish peoples north of the Danube. This treaty enabled the Seljuk sultan to extend his power in the east.

While Byzantine rule was in decline in Anatolia, a number of Armenian leaders appeared on the shores of the Euphrates and in Cilicia. One of these Armenians, called Philaretos, supported by the governor of Malaṭya, Gabriel, cut communications between Anatolia and the eastern and the southern Muslim countries. In 475/1082, Süleymān marched

[1] Until recently the dates given were 1077, 1078, 1080 and 1081.

eastwards, and, by conquering Adana, Tarsus, Masisa and Anazarba in 476/1083 established his control over all Cilicia. To save his kingdom, Philaretos went to Malik-Shāh, and adopted Islam; the Christian population of Antioch, in order to escape from his tyranny, secretly invited Süleymān on 15 Sha'bān 477/17 December 1084, and gave the city over to him. Because of this conquest he quarrelled with the 'Uqaylid *amīr* Sharaf al-Dawla Muslim, defeated his army, and killed him (478/1085). As a result of his expansionist policy and siege of Aleppo, Süleymān had to fight against the brother of Malik-Shāh, Tutush, the governor of Damascus, and lost his life and his army on 20 Ṣafar 479/6 June 1086.

In the course of ten years, Süleymān had not merely conquered a vast territory. The Armenians, the Syrian Christians and the heretical Paulicians, who hated the religious pressure and the assimilationist policy of Byzantium, found under Süleymān's administration the religious freedom they sought. Thanks to the characteristically Turkish religious freedom and just administration, fully applied by Süleymān's successors, the Seljuk state won the loyalty of the local people and grew stronger. The 'Abbasid caliph recognized Süleymān's sultanate by sending the appropriate emblems, such as a robe of honour, a diploma and a standard. He thus became Süleymān-Shāh and this frontier-state of the *ghāzīs* was saved from Shī'ī influence. Nevertheless, as early as 467/1074, in opposition to his cousins in Persia, he had communicated with the Fatimid caliph in Egypt; and, after he had conquered Tarsus, he did not hesitate to request the Shī'ī ruler of Tripoli in Syria, to find him judges and religious officers. In this connexion, it is appropriate to point out that the view which claims that Süleymān was sent to Anatolia by Malik-Shāh, and was declared its ruler, is nothing but a myth. The same is true of the Byzantine sources which, characteristically, portray him as a vassal of the empire, while in fact he had held their emperors at his mercy.

ANATOLIA AFTER SÜLEYMĀN

After Süleymān's death, his sons who were with him were sent to Malik-Shāh; for a period of time, 479–85/1086–92, the throne of Iznik was vacant, and the political unity of Anatolia was broken. In 477/1084 the founder of the central Anatolian Danishmendid state, Gümüshtekin Aḥmed Ghāzī, as a vassal of Süleymān, and complementing to the latter's operations, attacked the governor of Malaṭya, Gabriel. In 478/1085 the conqueror of Chankırı and Kastamonu, Karatekin, took

Sinop, and in the same year *Emīr* Buldajı invaded the upper regions of the Jayḥān. Another principality, founded by Mengüchek Ghāzī between Erzinjan and Divrigi, fought the Greeks on the Black Sea coast in collaboration with the Danishmendids. There was also another state founded in Izmir (Smyrna) by a brave and intelligent Turkish bey named Chaka. He had been taken prisoner by the Byzantines in one of the Anatolian battles, and educated in the imperial palace. In 474/1081 he ran away to Izmir, and gathered all the Turks in those regions under his command. He also succeeded in creating a navy by recruiting Greeks on the coasts, and was thus able to establish his power over the Aegean islands. This state lasted till the end of the First Crusade. One of the other early principalities which appeared in Anatolia was founded in Erzurum by *Emīr* Saltuk, who recognized the Seljuks of Persia as his sovereigns. The Artukid states, which were to include Diyār Bakr, Mardin and Kharput, and the Sökmenli state near Lake Van were still not in existence, and they would not appear until ten years later.[1] These regions were ruled by Seljuk governors in that period. Apart from the territories of Philaretos and Gabriel, which were greatly reduced by Süleymān and the Danishmendid Gümüshtekin, the only part of Anatolia which was not in Turkish hands was the eastern Black Sea region. In Trebizond, which was taken back from the Turks in 1075, a Greek dukedom had been founded. The successors of the duke remained independent of the Byzantine emperors and occasionally formed alliances with the Turks.

Abu'l-Qāsim, whom Süleymān left as his deputy in Iznik when he went on his campaign to Cilicia and Antioch, not only held the Seljuk state after Süleymān's death, but also advanced as far as the Straits. Malik-Shāh first sent *Emīr* Porsuk to take the Anatolian Seljuks under his control, and had Süleymān's brother killed in 471/1078. He then sent an army to Iznik under the command of *Emīr* Bozan. Faced with the danger of Malik-Shāh's army, Abu'l-Qāsim and Alexius formed an alliance. But Malik-Shāh's death in 485/1092, when Bozan was besieging Iznik, brought an end to the Great Seljuk pressure on Anatolia; and when disputes over the succession started as a result of his death, Süleymān's son, Kılıj Arslan, was released, and went to Iznik in 1092. The Turks welcomed him with great joy, and raised him to the throne. The young Kılıj Arslan I reorganized his state, rebuilt his capital, and appointed governors and commanders. He also drove away the

[1] The formation of the first Anatolian *beyliks* (principalities) is still a controversial subject.

Byzantines who were trying to settle on the shores of Marmara. By accepting the co-operation of the Byzantine emperor, he disposed of his rival, Chaka Bey, who was advancing in the direction of the Dardanelles, and increasing his power. In consequence of his treaty with Byzantium, he felt free to turn eastward for expansion. In 489/1096 he besieged Malaṭya; but although the people of the city, especially the Syrian Christians, offered to surrender the city to him in order to save themselves from Gabriel, who had been converted to Orthodox Christianity and was opposing them, Kılıj Arslan was compelled to return to defend his capital against the Crusaders.

The first party of the Crusaders, who had come with Peter the Hermit, was easily destroyed, but it was difficult to resist the great organized army which followed. The Crusaders besieged Iznik, and, although Kılıj Arslan had hastened back, he was unable to enter the city. On 19 June 1097 the defenders of Iznik, by agreement surrendered to the army of the emperor. These Turks, the sultan's treasures, and his wife, who was Chaka's daughter, were all sent to Constantinople. Kılıj Arslan, taking the Danishmendid Gümüshtekin and the *emīr* of Cappadocia, Ḥasan Bey, as allies, met the Crusaders in Eskishehir, where, on 17 Rajab 490/1 July 1097, a great battle took place. Both armies fought valiantly, and there was a great deal of bloodshed. A chronicler among the Crusaders described how the Seljuks fought in these words: 'If Turks had been Christians nobody could have been their equals in battle and valour.' But the Crusaders had an overwhelming superiority over the Turks. For this reason Kılıj Arslan retreated, in order not to reduce his army by further losses. Although he fought the Crusaders again with Gümüshtekin and Ḥasan Bey at his side at Ereghli near Konya, he suffered very heavy losses, and had to retreat. A mountain was named after *Emīr* Ḥasan (Ḥasan-dagh) as a great number of his soldiers were killed there, and later shrines came into existence in that area in his memory.

Although great losses were sustained by the Anatolian Turks, both in land and manpower, as a result of the First Crusade, they soon recovered. In Ramaḍān 493/July 1100 Gümüshtekin Aḥmed Ghāzī met the Crusaders advancing from Syria, and defeated them at Malaṭya, taking Bohemond and other leading princes as prisoner. In 1100 also, he and Kılıj Arslan completely annihilated two great armies of the Crusaders, one near Amasya, and the other at Ereghli, while they were fighting to set free the Crusaders imprisoned in Niksar. These victories improved the morale of Kılıj Arslan and the Anatolian Turks, which had previously suffered at the hands of the Crusaders. After the fall of Iznik, Kılıj Arslan made Konya his capital. By making an agreement with the emperor against the Crusaders, he was able to turn to conquer the east, as his father had done. He first defeated the Danishmendids, and took them under his suzerainty. In 496/1103 he captured Malaṭya from Gümüshtekin, who had conquered it in 494/1101, and established there his own administration. He then turned his attention to the principalities of eastern Anatolia, and made them recognize him as their overlord. In traditional rivalry with the Great Seljuks, he annexed Mosul. But he was involved in violent battle on the Khābūr river against a strong army sent by the Great Seljuk Sultan Muḥammad, and, like his father, he lost his life as a result of this rivalry (9 Shawwāl 500/3 July 1107). Although the Rūm Seljuk state had declined seriously as a result of his father's death and the attacks of the Crusaders, it revived and became stronger than ever under his leadership; but it suffered an even greater crisis with his own death.

THE PERIOD OF CRISIS AND THE RETREAT OF THE TURKS TO CENTRAL ANATOLIA

Like his father, Kılıj Arslan left the throne in Konya without an owner when he died. His eldest son, Shāhānshāh, then the governor of Mosul, was taken to Iṣfahān as a prisoner, and was not able to go back to Konya, to become sultan, until 504/1110. Profiting from this period of crisis, the Byzantines took the initiative to attack all the coastal areas of Anatolia. Everywhere the Turks prepared to move to the central Anatolian plateau. But their retreat cost them great losses. A great crowd of Turks who were camping near Ulubad (Lopadion), on their way to central Anatolia, were attacked by the Byzantines. Most of them, including women and children, were massacred. In spite of a few successful counter-attacks by the *Emīr* Ḥasan of Cappadocia and Shāhānshāh who ruled in Konya, the general retreat could not be stopped. Alexius and his successor, John II, either expelled the Turks from western Anatolia and the northern and southern coastal areas, or destroyed them.

The Danishmendid ruler, the *Emīr* Ghāzī (449–529/1105–34), the son of Gümüshtekin, helped his son-in-law Mas'ūd to take over the throne in Konya from his brother Shāhānshāh in 510/1116, and thus the Seljuk state was reduced to a small kingdom, limited to the environs of Konya, under Danishmendid protection. Under these circumstances, the Emperor

John II (1118–43) continued his attacks, defeated the Turks and occupied the towns of Denizli (Laodicaea) and Uluborlu (Sozopolis). But in 514/1120, *Emīr* Ghāzī, profiting from the Byzantine operations in the Balkans and with the support of the Artukids, defeated the duke of Trebizond, and his ally, the Mengüchek ruler, at Shiran. Although the sultanate was in the hands of the Seljuks, the real rulers of Anatolia now were the Danishmendids. When Sultan Mas'ūd's other brother, 'Arab, who had settled in Ankara and Kastamonu, marched towards Konya to capture the Seljuk throne in 520/1126, Mas'ūd formed an alliance with the emperor, and defeated his brother, forcing him to take refuge in Cilicia. This enabled the Byzantines to occupy Kastamonu. But the emperor's expedition to Cilicia, and later his brother's attempts to capture the throne, helped *Emīr* Ghāzī to drive away the Byzantines and occupy the Black Sea coast. Sultan Mas'ūd, on the other hand, started advancing in western Anatolia. *Emīr* Ghāzī then entered Cilicia, and defeated the advancing Crusaders. In a short period he became the ruler of all the Anatolian provinces between the Sakarya and the Euphrates. The caliph and Sultan Sanjar conferred on him the title of *malik* (king) and sent him a drum and a standard as emblems of sovereignty, he being the most powerful ruler of Anatolia.

Upon *Malik* Ghāzī's death in 529/1134, Sultan Mas'ūd, who was up to that time under his protection, became the ally and the equal of his protector's son, *Malik* Meḥmed. While the Emperor John punished the Armenians in Cilicia, and quarrelled with the Crusaders, the Seljuks and the Danishmendids had no difficulty in extending their boundaries against the Byzantines. This caused the emperor to march in 534/1140 towards the Danishmendid capital, Niksar, with a great army, in order to destroy the Anatolian Turks. He was also determined to dispose of Theodore Gabras, the duke of Trebizond. He reached Niksar after suffering great losses in northern Anatolia, and besieged the town. During the siege, long and violent battles took place between the Turks and the Greeks. The prolongation of the siege caused disturbances in the Byzantine army, and one of the imperial princes, John, took refuge in Sultan Mas'ūd's camp. The desertion of the prince, who became a Muslim and settled in Konya after marrying the sultan's daughter, forced the emperor to return quietly to Constantinople by the Black Sea in 1141. The failure of this great campaign, which had started so ambitiously, opened up possibilities for new Turkish conquests, and Sultan Mas'ūd advanced as far as the Antalya region.

When the Danishmendids started quarrelling among themselves for the kingship upon *Malik* Meḥmed's death in 536/1142, Sultan Mas'ūd defeated the Danishmendid *malik* of Sivas, Yaghı-Basan, besieged Malaṭya and annexed the Jayḥān region of his territory. With this sudden development, the domination of Anatolia passed again from the Danishmendids to the Seljuks. While the Seljuk sultan was expanding his frontiers towards the east, profiting from the quarrels between the Mosul *atabegs* and the Artukids, the Turcomans were advancing in western Anatolia, following the valleys of the Menderes and the Gediz. The Emperor Manuel I Comnenus set forth with a great army to drive away the Turks from Anatolia. After clearing western Anatolia of the Turks, he marched towards Konya. He defeated the Seljuk forces in Akshehir, burnt the city, and advanced in the direction of Konya. When Sultan Mas'ūd was informed of the approaching danger, he hastily returned from the east, prepared his army in Aksaray, and encountered the emperor before Konya. The Byzantines had completely devastated the Konya region, killed a great number of people, and even opened some graves. But they were taken by surprise when the Seljuks attacked them. They retreated after being severely beaten, and thus the 1147 campaign had also ended in failure. In spite of this battle, however, the beginning of a new crusade immediately forced the two rulers to reach an agreement in the face of the common danger.

When the *Atabeg* 'Imād al-Dīn Zangī reconquered Urfa (Edessa) in 539/1144, the Second Crusade was organized in Europe under the leadership of the Emperor Conrad III and King Louis VII of France. This was the first time in the history of the Crusades that the rulers themselves took part in the campaign. The German army which was directed by the 'treacherous' guides of the Byzantine Emperor Manuel by wrong roads, suffered surprise attacks by the Turks, and was overwhelmingly defeated near Eskishehir on 28 Jumādā I 542/25 October 1147; some of those who tried to return were destroyed by Greek attacks. As a result of this great disaster, the French king realized the impossibility of passing through Seljuk territory, and tried to follow the route via Ephesus, Denizli and Antalya. But he was only able to reach Antalya after suffering heavy losses through Turkish attacks, and there only those who had money were able to sail to Syria. Those who were left behind suffered from Turkish attacks, Greek pillage, hunger and disease. Their state was so bad that the Turks took pity on them, gave them food and money, and cared for their sick. A Christian chronicler speaks thus of the episode:

Avoiding their co-religionists who had been so cruel to them, they went in safety among the infidels who had compassion upon them, and, as we heard, more than three thousand joined themselves to the Turks when they retired. Oh, kindness more cruel than all treachery! They gave them bread but robbed them of their faith, though it is certain that contented with the services they performed, they compelled no one among them to renounce his religion.[1]

STRUGGLE FOR POWER AND KILIJ ARSLAN II'S VICTORY

After defeating the Byzantine army before Konya, and the armies of the Second Crusade, who threatened the Muslim world, within his boundaries, Sultan Mas'ūd became one of the most powerful rulers of his times. With these victories the period of crisis came to an end for the Anatolian Turks, and an age of stability and progress began. The 'Abbasid caliph sent the Seljuk sultan emblems of sovereignty, such as a robe of honour, a standard, and other gifts, with his blessing. Following these victories, Sultan Mas'ūd defeated the Crusaders in Syria and by his campaigns of 544/1149 and 545/1150, and conquering Mar'ash, Göksun, 'Ayntāb, Raban and Deluk, drove the Franks away from these regions. The *malik* of Sivas, Yaghı-Basan, had, meanwhile, expanded his frontiers towards the Black Sea, and captured Bafra (Pabra). After taking the Danishmendids of Sivas and Malaṭya under his suzerainty, Sultan Mas'ūd entered Cilicia with their support, and in 549/1154 captured several Armenian towns. The planned conquest of the whole of Cilicia was prevented by an outbreak of plague, which made the sultan return immediately. He died in 551/1155. Sultan Mas'ūd who in his long reign had saved the Seljuk state from annihilation by his far-seeing policies and patient effort, also transformed it from a state confined to the environs of Konya into a power dominating Anatolia. Thanks to his just and efficient administration, he even won over some Christians from Byzantium. The policy of construction and the establishment of social services in the Seljuk state also began in his reign.

His son Kılıj Arslan II (551–88/1155–92), who succeeded him on the throne, continued his father's policy, and worked for the political unity

[1] Odo of Deuil, *De Ludovico vii. itinere,* quoted in T. W. Arnold, *The preaching of Islam* (London, 1935), 89.

and the economic and cultural improvement of Anatolia. Kılıj Arslan II, who occupies an exceptional place among the Seljuk sultans, was threatened with hostile alliances in his early years. First he had to fight against his brother Shāhānshāh, the *malik* of Kastamonu and Ankara, and the Danishmendid *malik*, Yaghı-Basan. Profiting from this internal conflict, the Emperor Manuel and the *Atabeg* Nūr al-Dīn Zangī formed an alliance against Kılıj Arslan in 1159. The Armenian prince, Thoros, did not miss this opportunity of attacking the Seljuks either. Faced with so many enemies and alliances, Kılıj Arslan went to Constantinople, the centre of these political manoeuvres. The emperor, in accordance with the Byzantine policy of encouraging the mutual destruction of Turkish rulers, signed a treaty with the Seljuk sultan and provided him with financial aid. After his return from Constantinople, Kılıj Arslan immediately marched out to fight with Yaghı-Basan and defeated him overwhelmingly in 559/1163. He then disposed of his brother and other Danishmendid *emīrs*. Zangī was also forced to return to the sultan the places he had conquered. The Mengüchek *beylik* recognized the domination of the sultan, and thus the Seljuk monarchy extended from the Sakarya to the Euphrates once again.

The Emperor Manuel, who was busy in the Balkans, was disturbed when he realized that Kılıj Arslan had considerably increased his strength by disposing of all his enemies. On the pretext of controlling the Turcoman attacks and conquests in western Anatolia, the emperor organized an army to expel the Turks from Anatolia, and marched towards Konya. He also refused the sultan's offer to renew the treaty, which had lasted for twelve years. Kılıj Arslan therefore led his army past Akshehir, and encountered the Byzantine forces at Myriokephalon, a steep and narrow pass north of Lake Egridir, where in Rabīʿ I 572/September 1176, he dealt them a disastrous blow. Although it would have been possible to capture the emperor and wipe out the Byzantine army, as at Manzikert, for some unknown reason, the sultan accepted the emperor's request for peace, and was content to readjust his frontiers favourably. He even provided the emperor with three Seljuk *emīrs* as escorts, to guard him against the Turcoman attacks on his return journey. With this second great victory after Manzikert, Kılıj Arslan brought an end to the century-old Byzantine illusions of recovering Anatolia from the Turks and treating it as part of the Byzantine empire. The empire which had been on the offensive and advancing since the First Crusade, now returned to a continuous decline and retreat, as in the first period of

Turkish conquests. The importance of this victory, like that of Manzikert, was appreciated in its day, and the poets in Baghdād celebrated it as good tidings. Anatolia had really become a land of the Turks. By the late twelfth century it was already called 'Turkey' in Western sources.

After this victory Kılıj Arslan sent his invading forces as far as the sea in western Anatolia, conquered the regions of Uluborlu, Kütahya and Eskishehir in 578/1182, and besieged Denizli and Antalya. Thanks to these victories, political unity, law and order were established in Anatolia, and a period of economic and cultural progress began. After a long life of struggle, Kılıj Arslan, who felt tired and old, divided his kingdom among his eleven sons, following traditional Turkish policy, and retired in 582/1186 in Konya as the recognized sultan. These *maliks* who reigned independently in the provinces, continued their conquests against the weakened Byzantine empire. The *malik* of Tokat, Süleymān, marched to the Black Sea coast and conquered Samsun, the *malik* of Ankara, Mas'ūd, conquered the regions of Bolu, and the *malik* of Uluborlu, Kay-Khusraw, conquered the valley of the Menderes.

When Frederick I Barbarossa, the German emperor, entered Seljuk territory at the head of the Third Crusade in 1190, old Kılıj Arslan had already lost his power, and was a witness to the rivalry among his sons. There were hostile alliances between Kılıj Arslan and the German emperor, and between the Byzantine emperor and Saladin. When the Third Crusade was organized, as a result of Saladin's capture of Jerusalem and defeat of the Latin kingdom, Frederick obtained from his friend, Kılıj Arslan, permission to pass through Anatolia. But at the Seljuk border, the great German army was first involved with the Turcoman guerrillas, and then in Akshehir with the armies of Malik-Shāh and Mas'ūd, the sons of the sultan. Although Frederick's intention was to reach Syria by going directly through Cilicia, he was forced for reasons of security and supplies to advance towards Konya. The Seljuk *maliks* could not stop the Crusading army. The outskirts of Konya were occupied, the markets were pillaged and destroyed. The sultan who lived in his palace sent an ambassador to the emperor proposing peace, with the excuse that the responsibility and the power were in the hands of his son Malik-Shāh. The emperor answered him that his target was not Anatolia, but Saladin and Jerusalem. So a treaty was signed, and he left Anatolia.

THE GOLDEN AGE OF THE ANATOLIAN SELJUKS

The quarrels between Kılıj Arslan's sons, which began in 584/1188, continued after their father's death in 588/1192, and ended with the occupation of Konya by Süleymān, in 593/1196. More cautious and energetic than his brothers, he had stayed out of their disputes and then, when the time came, he re-established Seljuk unity by either taking them under his power, or disposing of them. He imposed tribute on the Emperor Alexius III, whose men had pillaged Turkish merchants on the Black Sea coast during the internal conflicts. He also defeated the Armenian king, Leo II, who had violated the Turkish border, and drove him out of the territories he had reconquered. When he realized that the Saltukids, who reigned in Erzurum, were in decline, and the Turco-Persian route was threatened by the Georgians, who had advanced as far as Erzurum, the Seljuk sultan marched there in 1201, supported by the Mengücheks and some Artukids. After subjugating the Saltukid state, he hastily marched towards Georgia. But he and his army were surprised by the Georgian-Kipchak army near Sarıkamısh, and had to retreat, leaving a great number of soldiers as prisoners. Although he organized another campaign to conquer Georgia, after recapturing Ankara from his brother Mas'ūd, he died on the way, in 1204, without accomplishing this project.

After Süleymān's death, his brother, Kay-Khusraw I, who had already reigned for a time before Süleymān's accession, regained his throne. He planned his military operations according to an economic and commercial policy. Thanks to the security and peace established during Kılıj Arslan's reign, a flourishing transit-trade was concentrated in Turkey. But the Latin conquest of Constantinople in 1204 threatened the security of the roads which led to the ports on the Black Sea and the Mediterranean. The Comneni, who sought to occupy the Black Sea coast, had blocked the outlets to the ports of Samsun and Sinop, choked Sivas with great numbers of merchants coming from Muslim and Christian countries, and caused much damage. In these circumstances, the Seljuk sultan formed an alliance with Emperor Theodore Lascaris of Nicaea, and opened the outlet to the Black Sea by defeating the Comneni in a campaign in 1206. In 603/1207 he conquered Antalya with the same purpose, provided the Turks with a port for the Mediterranean trade, and arranged for the settlement of Turkish merchants there. He also signed a trade pact with the Venetians. In 606/1209, he punished the

Armenians. When he conquered Denizli and the upper regions of the Menderes, a war with the emperor of Nicaea became inevitable. Although he defeated the Byzantine army near Alashehir (Philadelphia), he was killed by an enemy soldier when the Turkish army was busy capturing booty.

Kay-Kāvūs I (607–16/1211–20) continued his father's policy and conquered Sinop in 611/1214. He invited several merchants from other Turkish towns to settle there, and thus made it a port for transit trade. He also had great walls built around the town for security, and made it the base of his newly built fleet on the Black Sea. He released Alexius, the emperor of Trebizond, whom he had taken prisoner, having first made him accept the ties of vassaldom and tribute. He then expelled from Antalya the king of Cyprus, who had conquered the city during the sultan's disputes with his brother Kay-Qubād for the throne, and in 613/1216 made war on the Armenian king for his violation of the Turkish border. Realizing that he would not be able to stand against the Turkish armies which advanced along the Antalya coastline, the Armenian king was forced to sign a treaty of vassaldom with the conditions that he paid a heavy yearly tribute, recognized the sultan's right to mention on the coinage and in the *khuṭba,* and surrendered his border castles. The sultan also annexed the northern parts of Syria in 1218, profiting from internal conflicts among the Ayyubids. Following the Artukid ruler Maḥmūd, the ruler of Erbil, Muẓaffar al-Dīn Gök-Böri also recognized his sovereignty. Kay-Kāvūs, who is buried in the great hospital he had built in Sivas, gave considerable importance to construction and cultural activities besides his military and political victories.

The reign of 'Alā' al-Dīn Kay-Qubād I (616–34/1220–37) was the most prosperous and the most glorious period of Seljuk rule in Anatolia. At a time when Asia was thrown into turmoil by the Mongol conquest, this powerful and far-sighted sultan set out to counter a probable Mongol danger by fortifying towns like Konya, Kayseri and Sivas with walls and fortresses. He rebuilt and enlarged the fortress of Kalonoros on the Mediterranean coast, which he had captured, renamed it 'Alā'iyya after himself, and made it his winter capital. He also strengthened Seljuk naval power by having a dockyard built there. His expedition to Sughdak (Crimea) in 622/1225 with his Black Sea fleet gives an idea of Seljuk naval power. While he was involved in this overseas operation, he also sent armies to Lesser Armenia from the east, the north and the coast of Antalya. The Armenian national reaction against the aristocrats, because of their tendency to be latinized, enabled Hethoum, the lord of Lampron and a friend of the Seljuks, to be declared king. The Armenian kingdom was reduced still further, and became a vassal-state. The Turcomans who settled in the newly conquered Ichel region formed the basis of the Karaman *beylik* which was to be founded there later.

When Jalāl al-Dīn Mengübirdi Khwārazm-Shāh, in the course of his struggle against the Mongols, appeared on the eastern Anatolian border, and took the *emīrs* of that region under his authority, the centre of political activity moved eastwards. Meanwhile Sultan Kay-Qubād, by defeating the Ayyubids and the Artukids, captured the fortresses of Ḥiṣn Manṣūr (Adıyaman), Kahta and Chemishgezek. In 625/1228 he subjugated the *beylik* of Mengüchek. At that time, the Comneni of Trebizond, confident of the Khwārazm-Shāh's support, revolted against the Seljuks, and attacked the ports of Samsun and Sinop. Kay-Qubād sent his Black Sea forces from the coast and conquered the region as far as Unye. Apart from these forces, the Erzinjan army too advanced through Machka and the city of Trebizond was besieged. When the city was being violently attacked, heavy rains and floods caused the Seljuk army to retreat, and a Seljuk prince was taken prisoner by the Greeks as he was passing through the forests. In spite of this, the Greeks were forced to renew the treaty of vassaldom, providing for an annual tribute and military aid.

Kay-Qubād, who more than any other contemporary ruler saw and prepared for the Mongol threat, realized the importance of an alliance with Jalāl al-Dīn Khwārazm-Shāh. He reminded him that they were both of the same religion and people, and, pointing out that the fate of the Muslim world, under threat of invasion, depended on their policy and action, he recommended that an agreement should be reached with the invaders at all costs. But the Khwārazm-Shāh, a great soldier and a poor politician, himself constituted a more urgent danger for the Seljuks than that of the Mongols. Finally a violent battle took place between the two sultans at Yassıchimen, between Erzinjan and Sivas, on 28 Ramaḍān 627/10 August 1230. The Khwārazm-Shāh suffered a bitter defeat from which he was never able to recover. Sultan Kay-Qubād also removed his cousin, the *malik* of Erzurum, who was an ally of Jalāl al-Dīn. From Erzurum, he sent his army to Georgia, captured a number of fortresses, and subjugated the Georgian queen. He then drove away the Ayyubids from Akhlāṭ and the environs of Lake Van. He had all the fortresses in the east rebuilt and repaired, with the help of lime-kilns opened by his orders. While he was taking these precautions against the Mongols, he signed a peace treaty with the Great Khan Ögedei Khan by sending an ambassador. He was treated as befitted his high reputation, equalled by no ruler among his contemporaries, and saved his country from invasion and depredations by the Mongols. The Ayyubids of Syria and the Artukids of Diyār Bakr recognized his sovereignty. In Kay-Qubād's reign, Seljuk Anatolia reached its highest peak, not only politically, but economically as well. The sultan set out on a great scheme of construction. Apart from reconstructing towns and fortresses, he built the towns of Qubādābād on the shore of Lake Beyshehir, and Kayqubādiyya near Kayseri. The mosques, *medreses,* caravanserais, bridges and hospitals built in his time still preserve their magnificence and beauty. It was also a glorious period for sciences and arts. Because of these qualities Kay-Qubād became a legendary ruler among the Anatolian Turks, and for a long period was remembered as Kay-Qubād the Great.

THE MONGOL INVASION AND THE DECLINE OF THE RŪM SULTANATE

The most important factor in the decline of the Anatolian Seljuks was Kay-Qubād's early death in 634/1237, and the absence of a powerful sultan among his successors. His son and successor, Kay-Khusraw II, was a worthless character who was the cause of the first crisis. Behind him there was even a more sinister statesman called Sa'd al-Dīn Köpek, who had helped him to gain the throne, and had complete control over him. He used his influence over the sultan against rival statesmen, and by so doing reduced the Seljuk state to a headless body. Nevertheless, the vigour and the power of Seljuk Anatolia concealed signs of decline, and there were even important victories such as those of Diyār Bakr and Tarsus, while the Greek emperor of Trebizond, the Armenian king of Cilicia, and the Ayyubids of Aleppo remained Kay-Khusraw's vassals. But the Baba Isḥāq rebellion showed that the Seljuk state, while retaining its outward appearance of strength, was rotten within.

The Mongol conquest caused the migration of a Turcoman population to Anatolia similar to that of the first Seljuk conquest. A Turcoman shaykh, Baba Isḥāq or Baba Resūl, claiming to be a prophet, announced the coming of a new age, gathered the economically distressed Turcomans around himself, and called on them to rebel against Kay-Khusraw's corrupt administration. The rebellious Turcomans in Mar'ash, Kahta, and Adıyaman organized themselves, and defeated the Seljuk forces in Elbistan and Malaṭya. From there they marched on Sivas, and, after pillaging it, turned towards Amasya. Before the Turcomans could join their shaykh, Baba Isḥāq, at his retreat, the Seljuks had killed him. But the Turcomans, who believed that Baba Isḥāq was holy and could not be killed by a mortal, followed the defeated Seljuk army towards Konya with their women and children, increasing in number. Frightened by them, the weak sultan could not remain in Konya, and fled to Qubādābād. The Erzurum army arrived as reinforcement, and the Turcomans were suppressed with difficulty on the plain of Malya near Kirshehir in 638/1240. Baba Isḥāq, who acted more like an old Turkish shaman than a Muslim shaykh, had a great spiritual power; this penetrated even to the Seljuk soldiery, and contributed to their defeat. The fact that even the Christian Frankish mercenaries in the Seljuk army made crosses on their foreheads before fighting his followers is significant of his spiritual power.

When the weakness of the Seljuk state was exposed as a result of this rebellion, the Mongol invasion began. In 639/1242, as a first attempt, the Mongols captured and destroyed Erzurum, where they had encountered considerable resistance. In 640/1243 with an army of 30,000 under Bayju Noyon's command they undertook the conquest of Anatolia. The Seljuks, reinforced by the forces of their vassals met the Mongols with a great army of 80,000 under the sultan's own command. When the Seljuk vanguard was scattered by the Mongols at Kösedagh, fifty miles east of Sivas (6 Muḥarram 641/26 June 1243), the Seljuks, who were no longer ruled by the able statesmen of earlier periods, fled in panic with their foolish and frightened sultan among them. This time the sultan went as far as Antalya. The Mongols reached Sivas, and from there went to Kayseri. This town was taken by assault in spite of resistance, pillaged and destroyed. On the Mongols' return, two Turkish ambassadors followed them to their winter quarters in Mughān, where they were able to persuade Baju to make peace on terms of a yearly tribute, by telling him that Anatolia had numerous fortresses and soldiers.

The defeat of Kösedagh is the beginning of a period of decline and disaster in the history of the Anatolian Seljuks. After Kay-Khusraw II's death, the rivalry and the intrigues of ambitious statesmen, in the name of three young princes, prepared the ground for Mongol interventions and military occupations, as well as demands for tribute. Mu'īn al-Dīn Süleymān Pervāne came to an agreement with the Mongols, and, eliminating other princes and statesmen, took control of affairs in the names of Kılıj Arslan IV and Kay-Khusraw III. After 659/1261 he managed to achieve a period of relative peace and stability by his skilful handling of relations with the Mongols. Nevertheless, the Anatolian Turks chafed under the domination of the pagan Mongols, and sought for means of overthrowing it. As a first step, Baybars, the Mamluk sultan of Egypt, whose predecessor, Quṭuz, had defeated the Mongols at 'Ayn Jālūt in 658/1260, was invited to Anatolia. He came in 675/1276 to Kayseri, where he was raised to the throne with due ceremony, according to Seljuk traditions. But anxiety that Baybars would not be able to stay in Anatolia, and fear of the Mongols, prevented a fruitful co-operation between him and the Seljuk statesmen. The Mamluk sultan left after a short stay.

After this episode, the *Īl-Khān* Abāqā, the Mongol ruler of Persia, entered Anatolia, killed a great number of people and executed Mu'īn al-Dīn Süleymān (676/1277). Although the Seljuk dynasty lasted until 708/1308, after Süleymān's death the actual administration of the country was transferred to the Mongol governors and generals, and the Seljuk administration and army were demolished. The unemployed soldiers and civil servants became a source of anarchy. The people were oppressed by the heavy taxes imposed upon them by the Mongols, and a period of poverty and revolt began in Anatolia. In spite of the Mongol domination and the loss of political and military power, there was no serious crisis and change in social, economic and cultural life until Mu'īn al-Dīn Süleymān's death. International trade continued to operate; and there was hardly any decrease in agricultural and industrial production or its import and export. The monuments that were built in the period 641-76/1243-77 also show that construction and other activities for the improvement of communal life continued as before, but after Mu'īn al-Dīn Süleymān and with the Mongol administration the period of decline began. For this reason, some sources talk of the 'Pervāne Age' of peace and stability. Nevertheless, the age of Kay-Qubād was always remembered as a happy period, and the time of the Kösedagh defeat was considered the beginning of all the disasters and called the 'Year of Baju'. The rebellions of the Mongol governors also contributed to the increasing oppression and poverty in Anatolia. In this critical period the governorship of

Timurtash Noyon proved to be relatively just and peaceful, and for this reason he was called the *mahdī*. With his rebellion and flight to Egypt in 728/1328 the disorders began once more.

THE FORMATION OF THE *BEYLIKS* AND THE TURKIFICATION OF THE FRONTIER REGIONS

As the Seljuk state crumbled under Mongol pressure, a new period of vitality and turkification began with the appearance and independence of Turcoman frontier princes (*beys*). The Turcomans, fleeing from the Mongol terror, entered Anatolia in great numbers as at the time of the first conquest; this new migration increased the density of the nomad population and the pressure against Byzantine territory. They soon began to spread, and set out on new conquests. It was impossible for the crumbling Byzantine empire, which was in ruins, to stem this torrent of Turcomans flowing from Turkistān before the Mongols by way of Āẕarbāyjān to all parts of Anatolia. Items of information, which tell us of how the Turks settled in Byzantine territory as emigrants in agreement with the Orthodox priests, are significant in exposing the spiritual decline of the Byzantines. The settlement and the spreading of the Turcomans on the Black Sea coast and in Cilicia followed the same process.

The Seljuk state, under the overlordship of the Īl-Khāns dominated central Anatolia and the plains, but the Turcomans were all-powerful on the frontiers and the mountains. Rebels and pretenders among the Seljuk princes, and statesmen in adversity, took refuge with these Turcomans. One such prince, Kılıj Arslan, rebelled against Sultan Mas'ūd II (682–98/1283–98) with the support of the Turcomans and gave much trouble to the Seljuk state. A great number of religious leaders, shaykhs and Turcoman *babas* (Ṣūfī teachers) who fled before the Mongols from Turkistān, Persia and Āẕarbāyjān, took refuge on the frontiers and converted the half-shamanistic Turcomans to Islam. By so doing they reinforced Islam, and established the ideal of the Holy War for the faith in the border territory. For this reason, the Turcoman conquests were called 'wars for the faith' (sing., *ghazā*) and the Turcoman beys 'frontier warriors for the faith' (*uj ghāzīs*). This was why these marches were full of dervishes and convents.

While the Seljuk state was coming to an end in central Anatolia, independent Turcoman principalities were being formed on the frontiers. These principalities, which were modelled on the institutions of the Seljuk state and the traditions of the nomadic Turks generally recognized the sovereignty of the Seljuk sultans and the Īl-Khān suzerains, and their *emīrs* received from them such emblems of power as a robe of honour, a standard, a diploma and the title of *ghāzī*. But in reality they were independent: they rebelled against the Seljuk state, and co-operated very often with the sultan of Egypt, from whom they received emblems of sovereignty. The oldest and most important of these principalities was the Karamanlı *beylik*. The Karamanlıs not only conquered Armenian lands in Cilicia, but also fought against Mongol domination with the support and encouragement of the Mamluk Sultan Baybars. Their ruler, Meḥmed Bey, marched on Konya in 659/1261 and 675/1276, finally capturing it. Meḥmed Bey proclaimed a member of the Seljuk dynasty, whom the Seljuk chroniclers contemptuously called 'the Miser', as sultan. During his occupation he also established Turkish as the official language instead of Persian, for the first time in Anatolia. However, the Karamanlıs were then defeated by the Seljuk army, and retreated to Karaman. But after the fall of the Īl-Khān dynasty in 736/1335, they settled in Konya, and, as the most powerful of the Anatolian principalities, claimed to be heirs of the Seljuks.

The Germiyan state, which came second in importance, and was formed in Kütahya in 682/1283, became the nucleus of the Aydın and Sarukhan principalities, which were formed in western Anatolia. In these principalities, in accordance with the old Turkish traditions of nomadic feudalism, sovereignty was divided among the members of the royal family. The Aydın princes played a very important historical role by capturing the islands with their fleet, and landing in Greece and the Balkans. They occupy an important place in Turkish naval history. They also encouraged foreign trade by making treaties with Italian merchants in the beginning of the eighth/fourteenth century. Towards the end of the seventh/thirteenth century, the houses of Eshrefoghlu in Beyshehir, Ḥamīd in Uluborlu and Antalya, and Menteshe in Mughla turkified these areas. Antalya was taken in battle from the house of Ḥamīd in 762/1361 by the king of Cyprus, and recaptured in 777/1373 by Teke Bey. When, on the fall of the Īl-Khān dynasty, the Ertene and later Qāḍī Burhān al-Dīn principalities were formed in central Anatolia, they shared the domination of that area with the Karamanlıs.

When the Turcoman principalities occupied and turkified areas which had not been already under Seljuk rule, they made a considerable contribution to Turkish culture because, owing to their nomadic origin, they were unaffected by Persian culture. The Turkish language, which was considered fit for literary composition only towards the end of Seljuk rule, was greatly improved by the work of authorship and translation which they sponsored. The Jandaroghlu principality, formed in Kastamonu, showed considerable effort in this field. The capitals of these principalities were embellished with monuments and similar buildings. In the middle of this century the house of Dulgadır (Dhu'l-Qadr) in Elbistan and Mar'ash, and the house of Ramażān in Adana and Chukurova (Cilicia) also formed principalities. As the Turcoman colonies, established in Cilicia since the beginning of the sixth/twelfth century, were absorbed by the Armenian kingdom of Cilicia, the Seljuks, the Karamanlıs, and, especially, the Mamluks, the settlement of the Turcomans in these areas increased. All these Turcoman tribes, who were originally nomads, were transformed into settled dwellers in a short period of time. The Kara-Koyunlu and the Ak-Koyunlu tribes, who came to eastern Anatolia as a result of the Mongol conquest, formed states which preserved their nomadic characteristics for much longer than the others.

Thus, in the century which followed the fall of the Īl-Khāns, Anatolia was divided among these principalities. The only area that was not occupied by the Turks was the eastern Black Sea, with Trebizond as its centre. Although the Turcomans began to descend on these coasts by crossing over the Black Sea mountains, this region was in fact conquered and colonized by the Oghuz tribe called Chepni, who followed the coast from Samsun. The local Christian tribe of Chan (Tzane) eventually disappeared, and in the coastal regions small principalities were formed. The Turcomans reached Giresun in 702/1302. The Ottoman principality, initially the most modest in Anatolia, developed rapidly, thanks to certain moral factors and geographical conditions. Later it created a political unity by gradually annexing the Anatolian principalities and turned into one of the greatest empires in history. Although the division of Anatolia among the principalities provoked ambitions in Europe for new crusades, the Hundred Years War and the strengthening of the Ottomans prevented the materialization of such projects.

THE SELJUK STATE AND THE PEOPLE

The Anatolian Seljuks and principalities, like the shamanistic Kök-Türks (552–744), the Kara-Khanids (932–1212), and the Great Seljuks before them, considered the state as the common property of the royal family.

Political unity was therefore generally divided, and the death of a ruler frequently caused a dynastic struggle. Only the Ottoman state, endowed from its inception with a centralized authority, prevented such political divisions among the members of its royal family. Nevertheless, a development towards centralization can also be observed under the Anatolian Seljuks after Kılıj Arslan II. The practice of this policy outside the members of the royal family as early as the origins of the state is also significant. The Great Seljuks had given fiefs (sing., *iqṭāʿ*) as big as provinces to their great *emīrs*, who enjoyed political and administrative autonomy in them, and sometimes formed new states with their own names on the coinage and in the *khuṭba*. In Anatolia, however, a fief-system on this scale and of this order never existed. The military chiefs (sing., *su-bashı*) who headed the provincial and local armies in Anatolia were not the legal sovereigns of the soldiers who held small fiefs and of the places that belonged to them, but merely their commanders. For this reason, the fiefs never caused political division in Anatolia, but served as the basis of the Ottoman *timar*-system. The Anatolian Seljuks had a central army of 12,000 soldiers, consisting of bought Turks or captured Christians, who were trained at special schools in the capital and other cities. The Ottoman Janissary corps was modelled on this Seljuk institution. Besides these, there was another detachment of Frankish, Georgian and other Christian mercenaries also quartered in the capital. But the actual military and land administration was carried out by the force of 100,000 Turkish fief-holders, who were supported by the taxes collected from the local peasants.

As early as Süleymān I, the Seljuks distributed the lands which had belonged to the Byzantine aristocrats, or of which the owners were lost, among the landless peasants and serfs, thereby giving them land and freedom. However, in accordance with ancient nomadic practice and the Islamic law of conquest, the sultans abolished private ownership of land (apart from fruit-gardens), by declaring Turkish Anatolia state property (*mīrī*), and left the peasants as large a portion of land as they could work. Thanks to this state system, which was the basis of the Seljuk and the Ottoman agricultural and land policy, the settlement of the local and migrant population became much easier, agricultural production was safeguarded, and the turkification of Anatolia became possible. This system under the control of military administrators contributed to the establishment of a strong and harmonious social order, and prevented the formation of a landed aristocracy on the one hand and a servile peasantry on the other. This social order lasted until the middle of the nineteenth century without basic change.

The Turkish conquest, the counter-attacks of the Byzantines and the Crusaders, and internal conflicts, caused a decrease in the Turkish and the indigenous population, the evacuation of several places, and a fall in production and revenue. Since the majority of Turks still remained nomads during the first century of settlement, and were only gradually sedentarized, the Seljuk state was in great need of indigenous peasants. Hence the Turkish rulers not only protected the Christian agriculturalists, but also deported the local peasantry of the lands they invaded into their own country. Sultan Mas'ūd, Kılıj Arslan II, *Malik* Meḥmed the Danishmendid, Yaghı-Basan and the Artukids undertook the deportation and settlement of as many as from 10,000 to 70,000 people for this purpose. The deportation which Kay-Khusraw I undertook in 592/1196 in the Menderes region gives a fair idea of these deportations. He divided a great crowd of people into groups of 5,000 according to their countries and families, had their names written in a book, and made them settle in the environs of Akshehir by giving them villages, houses, farming tools, seed and fields. He also exempted them from taxation for five years. When other Christians heard of their prosperity, they sought to move under Seljuk administration, and thus escape from Byzantine oppression.

Christian authors who had described the Turks during the years of the first conquest as terrifying plunderers, subsequently began to sing the praises of the Seljuk sultans to a remarkable degree; this was a natural consequence of their just and efficient administration, as well as their compassionate protection of their Christian subjects. The great religious tolerance of the Seljuks, and the freedom enjoyed by the Christians, made the latter more loyal to the Seljuks, and increased their hatred for Byzantium. In a letter which Kılıj Arslan II wrote to his friend, the Syrian patriarch of Malaṭya, he told him that thanks to his prayers, he had won victories over the Byzantines. The Georgian princess had her own priest and chapel in the Seljuk palace. The sultans also held debates and discussions, in which scholars of different creeds took part. These are only a few examples which illustrate the degree of religious freedom and tolerance. The Turks of Anatolia established a harmonious life among the different races and religions; in fact, the Muslim Turks and the local Christians not only shared a common life and culture but even made pilgrimages to the same holy places. The great mystics of universal perception like Jalāl al-Dīn Rūmī and Yūnus Emre were the outcome of such a social climate. The great mystic Muḥyī al-Dīn b. al-ʿArabī also came to Anatolia, and settled in Konya, in order to enjoy intellectual liberty. Disciples who originally belonged to different religions and sects were united and uplifted around Jalāl al-Dīn Rūmī and his successors. When Malaṭya was left without a government during the Mongol invasion, the Muslim and Christian communities were united under the administration of the Syrian patriarch with an oath of loyalty.

The Mongol invasion impaired the harmony between the Muslims and the Christians. The Turkish tendency to support the Egyptian sultans caused the pagan Mongols to treat the Christians more favourably, and this caused several incidents provoked by the Armenians. Such incidents, however, were suppressed before they could get out of control. The conquests had destructive effects during the formation of the *beyliks*, but the establishment of even the smallest political organization enabled the continuation of an administration in harmony with the general structure. It is also significant that the tradition of sumptuary and other discrimination against Christians and Jews in the Muslim countries was not applied in Seljuk Anatolia. This policy explains the existence of an important Christian population there. According to various documents the density of the Christian population in Anatolia of which we have information increased from west to east, in the opposite direction to the Turkish migration. The strong turkification of central Anatolia, apart from the Konya and Kayseri regions, can be explained by historical and geographical reasons. There exist certain documents and Turkish village names which show this ethnic situation. In the eighth/fourteenth century under the *beyliks*, the western and northern parts of Anatolia were more thoroughly turkified than the eastern and even the central parts. This almost complete transformation in a short time was one of the results of the Mongol invasion.

Although the Turks had accepted Islam a century before they arrived in Anatolia, their conversion, because of their nomadic way of life, was still very superficial, and under the veneer of Islam their old shamanistic traditions and beliefs survived. Baba Isḥāq, Barak Baba, Sarı-Saltuk and other Turcoman *babas* were the continuation of the ancient Turkish shamans, rather than Muslim shaykhs. Therefore shamanism deeply influenced Muslim Turkish religious orders and sects by becoming a part of their religious ceremonies. Dancing and music were used to stimulate religious ecstasy, and could not be eliminated, in spite of the censorious endeavours of Muslim scholars. The Seljuk rulers often invited theologians, jurists, physicians, artists and poets from the older Muslim lands, and built schools, *medreses,* hospitals and religious institutions for the development and progress of Islamic culture. When Kılıj Arslan II built the city of Aksaray as a base for his military operations, he invited scholars, artists and tradesmen from Āẕarbāyjān, and made them settle in the *medreses,* caravanserais, and markets he had built around his palace. The Mongol invasion caused a great number of scholars and artists to emigrate to Anatolia, where they contributed to the development of Islamic culture. In Seljuk Turkey, the official and literary language was Persian, the language of religion and scholarship was Arabic and the everyday language of the people was Turkish. The tradition of Turkish Islamic literature and the written language which had its beginnings in Central Asia did not reach Anatolia, but the written language, which began for didactic reasons, made possible the birth of a new Turkish literature in the seventh/thirteenth century and its development during the period of the *beyliks*. Nevertheless, the Baṭṭāl Ghāzī and Danishmend Ghāzī epics, the Oghuznāme and the Dede Korkut stories survived among the *ghāzīs* and nomads as examples of an oral tradition of Turkish literature since the twelfth century.

THE ECONOMIC AND CULTURAL RISE OF SELJUK TURKEY

The economic and social decline of Byzantine Anatolia was due to the Muslim-Byzantine conflict and the diversion of transit trade, resulting from Arab domination of the Mediterranean Sea. The absence in the Byzantine period of monuments and remains comparable to those of the Hellenistic, Roman and Seljuk periods can be viewed as a proof of this decline. According to some Arabic geographical works, eastern Anatolia, which was within the boundaries of Islamic civilization, was an exception to this rule, as were the Mediterranean port of Antalya and the Black Sea port of Trebizond, since they traded with Muslim merchants in the fourth/tenth century, and showed signs of commercial activity. Until the seventh/thirteenth century, central Anatolia which developed under the Seljuk administration, was more backward in its social life than eastern Anatolia. One of the reasons why the Seljuk sultans fought campaigns in the east was this higher degree of civilization. This also explains why the Christians in the east, especially the

Syrians, were so much more advanced than the Byzantines in central Anatolia. After the Arab Muslim conquest, the Arabs had achieved a synthesis of Islamic civilization through their contacts with the Christians of the Near East; such a synthesis was not possible in the Seljuk territories, because by that time Islamic civilization already existed in an advanced stage, and also because the Turks lacked similar local opportunities in their new country. Therefore Seljuk civilization is an extension of Islamic Turkish culture to this region, rather than a synthesis with Anatolian elements. Although there were many Greek painters in Anatolia, the fact that one can trace obvious Central Asian Uigur influences on the wall paintings in Konya and Qubādābād is significant. Nevertheless, besides the many cultural influences of the Turks upon the local Armenians, Greeks, and Georgians, native and even Latin influence can also be traced in Anatolian Turkish culture.

The opening of Anatolia to transit-trade between Muslim and Christian peoples, and its transformation into an advanced and wealthy country, was one of the happy results of the Seljuk conquest. In fact, as soon as Anatolia became a part of the Muslim world and the obstacles which hindered its trade were removed, a period of economic development began. But the Turkish, Byzantine and Crusader conquests, which lasted for a century, caused a serious social and economic decline in Anatolia until 572/1176. With Kılıj Arslan II's victory in that year, a second decisive date in the history of Seljuk and Byzantine relations, the external security and political unity of Anatolia were established, and important transit-routes of world trade were concentrated in that region. A revolution which took place in the Mediterranean had an important part in this change. The transfer of sea-power there from the Muslims to the Europeans after the fifth/eleventh century, the increase of trade with the East accompanying the Crusades, and the economic and social development of Europe which followed, helped the development of important caravan routes in Anatolia. The sultans who had any foresight used their military power to protect the routes and the ports, while they carried out a sound economic and commercial policy. The essential points of this policy were to secure the routes to the Black Sea and Mediterranean ports and the caravan routes, to provide comfortable resting places, to make trade agreements with the republics of Italy and the kings of Cyprus, and to apply a reasonable customs tariff to encourage trade. The sultans even established a sort of state insurance by paying indemnities from the treasury to merchants whose goods suffered damage by the attacks of pirates or brigands. Thanks to the Seljuks, commercial methods and institutions, such as cheques, certain methods of lending money on interest, and bank transactions were developed and carried to medieval Europe.

The organization devised by the Seljuk state for the safety and the comfort of the caravans was also amazingly efficient. The state, in fact, protected caravans which carried valuable goods by appointing security forces under the command of a caravan leader and a guide. Caravanserais were built at the halting-places of these caravans. These were built by sultans and *vezīrs,* were endowed by *waqf,* and maintained to provide every need of the traveller. The travellers could stay in these caravanserais with their horses or camels for three days without any charge, and the meals also were free. In keeping with Seljuk Turkish traditions, the foundation-deeds lay down that the same food should be served to all, Muslims or Christians, rich or poor, free or slave, and that all be treated equally. In the larger caravanserais the sick could have treatment as well. With their fortress-like towers and iron gates, the caravanserais were fortified asylums for traders' goods. An idea of the strength of these caravanserais is given by an incident at the beginning of the eighth/fourteenth century, when a Mongol commander failed to capture a Turkish leader, after besieging the Kay-Qubād caravanserai near Aksaray with 20,000 men for two months.

The development of international trade increased agricultural and industrial production. Mines were opened, and minerals exported to Europe. The wool of Angora goats was sent to England and France for the manufacture of cloth and hats as early as the seventh/thirteenth century and manufactured goods and carpets were exported to other countries. The population of such centres as Konya, Kayseri, Sivas and Erzurum was over 100,000. In these towns, and in the ports of Antalya and Sinop, there were Italian, French and Jewish trading quarters and consulates as well as inns and churches. The Anatolian *beyliks*, which inherited Seljuk traditions, preserved these trading customs as well. These *beyliks*, however, could not mint gold coins, and had to use Seljuk and Venetian ones, imposing a ban on the export of currency. The mosques, *medreses,* hospitals, caravanserais, and mausoleums, are surviving examples that illustrate the economic and social progress of the Seljuks. Not only the travellers, but also the sick, the poor and the dervishes were looked after by hospitals, soup-kitchens (sing., *'imāret*) and convents, free of charge. Ottoman architecture,

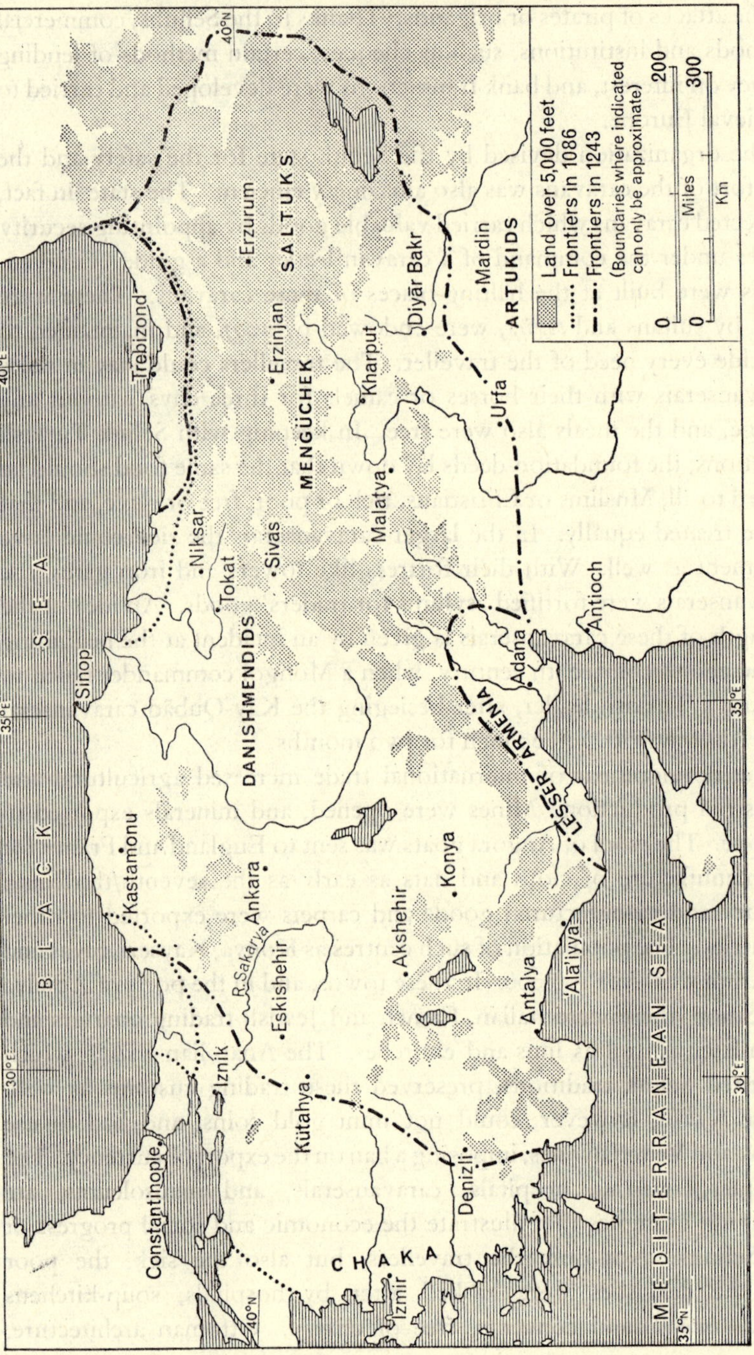

Map 5(*a*). The Seljuk sultanate of Rūm.

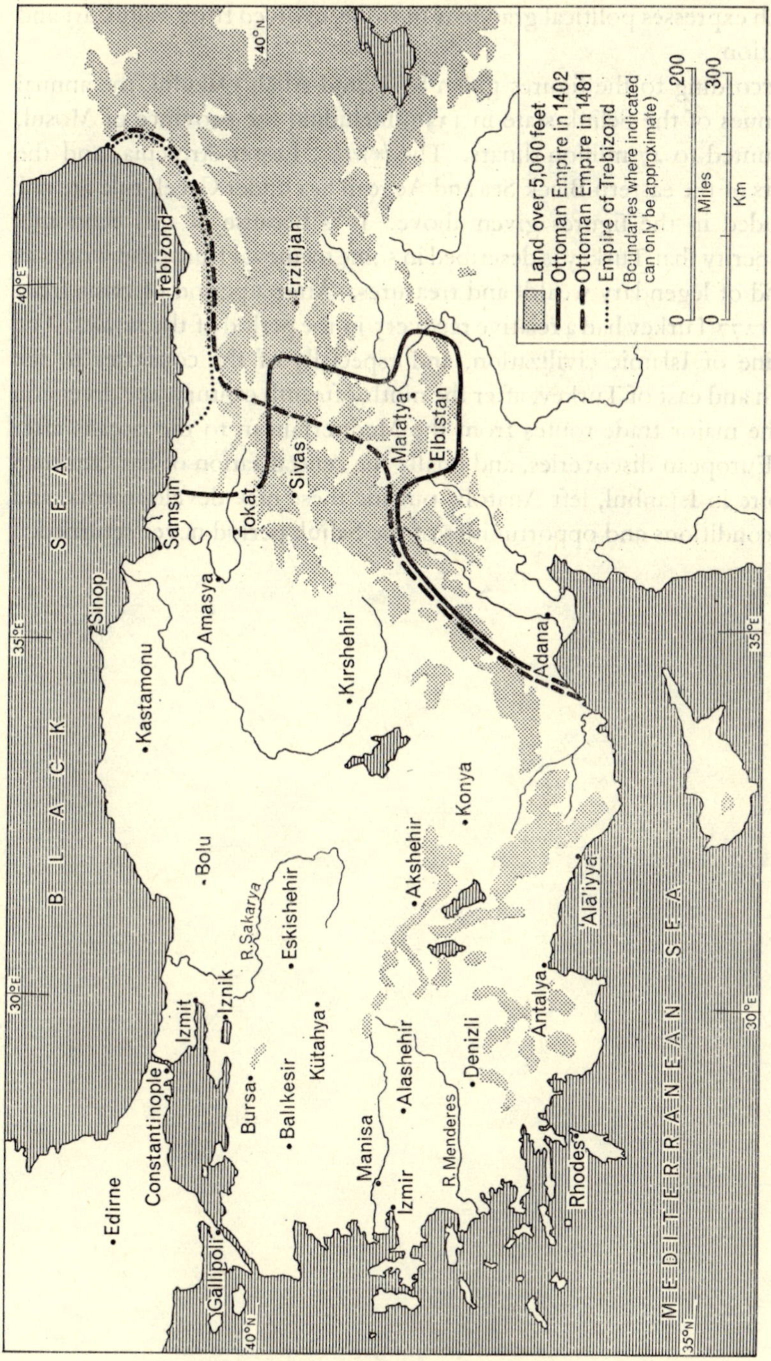

Map 5(*b*). Post-Seljuk Anatolia.

which expresses political grandeur in stone, evolved from Seljuk art and tradition.

According to the figures given by Ḥamd Allāh Qazvīnī, the annual revenues of the Seljuk state in 1336, including the province of Mosul, amounted to 27 million dinars. The *beyliks*, Lesser Armenia, and the coasts of the eastern Black Sea and Aegean Sea under Greek rule are not included in the figures given above. It is because of this economic prosperity that Turkey is described in some medieval European works as a land of legendary wealth and treasures. After a period of crisis from 676/1277 Turkey had a relative recovery in the period of the *beyliks*. The decline of Islamic civilization, and especially of the countries to the south and east of Turkey, after the ninth/fifteenth century, the diversion of the major trade-routes from the Mediterranean to the oceans after the European discoveries, and finally the centralization of the Ottoman empire in Istanbul, left Anatolia outside these new developments, and the conditions and opportunities of the Seljuk period never returned.

CHAPTER 4

THE EMERGENCE OF THE OTTOMANS

In the second half of the seventh/thirteenth century, as the Seljuk state fell apart, a number of principalities (*beyliks*) of a new kind came into being in the western marches of Anatolia. They were in territory conquered as a result of holy wars (sing., *ghazā*) waged against Byzantium, and hence are known as *ghāzī* states. The Ottoman principality was one of these. It was destined within a century to unite Anatolia and the Balkans under its sovereignty, and to develop into an Islamic empire. Let us now examine as a whole the formation of these *ghāzī* principalities. The emergence of the Ottoman state can be understood only in the context of the general history of the marches.

THE EMERGENCE OF TURCOMAN BORDER PRINCIPALITIES IN WESTERN ANATOLIA

When the state of the Anatolian Seljuks developed into a fully formed Islamic sultanate, three areas came to be designated as marches *par excellence,* and attracted settlements of Muslim *ghāzīs*. In the south, facing Cilicia (Chukurova) the 'realm of the Lord of the Coasts' was centred round 'Alā'iyya and Antalya and directed against Lesser Armenia and the kingdom of Cyprus. In the north, on the borders of the Byzantine empire of Trebizond and along the shores of the Black Sea, the Muslim marches consisted of two parts, the eastern, centred round Simere, Samsun and Bafra, and the western centred round Kastamonu and Sinop. Finally, the western marches, whose principal cities were Kastamonu, Karaḥiṣār-i Devle (Afyonkarahisar), Kütahya and Denizli lay along the Byzantine frontier from the area of Kastamonu to the gulf of Makri in the south.

It appears that in each of these three areas of the marches the Seljuk state was represented by a governor-general known as commander (*emīr*) of the marches. These powerful *emīrs* who represented the central authority, generally kept their positions in their families as a hereditary dignity. The post of commander of the western marches on the Byzantine frontier came to be the most important of all. This position was given in 659/1261 to Nuṣrat al-Dīn Ḥasan and Tāj al-Dīn Ḥusayn, the sons of the powerful Seljuk *vezīr* Fakhr al-Dīn 'Alī. We know that this emirate took in the whole area between Kütahya, Beyshehir and Akshehir. Its capital was the impregnable fortress of Karaḥiṣār. The area of the marches formed the basis of the power of Fakhr al-Dīn ʿAlī. The main strength of the marches lay in the Turcoman tribes, governed by their own hereditary leaders, or beys. It should be noted, however, that these tribes were loose social units which could dissolve and reform around leading *ghāzīs* in the marches. They were then usually named after their new leaders, e.g. Aydınlı, Sarukhanlı and ʿO̱smanlı, i.e. Ottoman. These beys of the marches were linked to the *emīr* of the marches largely by bonds of personal loyalty. They exercised independent authority over their own groups. The marches were a frontier area where nomads driven there forcibly by the Seljuk state, as well as refugees from Mongol conquests and oppression, came together in search of a new life. This mountain region which lay between the plateau of central Anatolia and the coastal plains provided abundant summer pastures, and a large proportion of its population was made up of semi-nomadic Turcomans. At the same time highly developed urban forms of Seljuk civilization had also taken root in such border towns as Denizli, Kütahya, Karaḥiṣār, Eskishehir and Kastamonu. These urban centres were destined to influence profoundly the future development of the border principalities. Seljuk chroniclers, who stood for the interests of the Mongol-Seljuk central authority, tended to describe the population of the marches as robber rebels ready to mutiny at a moment's notice.

The Turcomans of the western marches were seen to play an important part in determining the political development of Anatolia at the time of the struggle between Kılıj Arslan IV, who was supported by the Mongols, and Kay-Kāvūs II (643–59/1246–61) who tried to base himself on the western provinces and marches. Kay-Kāvūs was finally forced to seek refuge in Byzantium in 659/1261. The Mongol and Seljuk troops led by Muʿīn al-Dīn Pervāne came to the frontier and pacified the Turcomans. Nevertheless, we know that a fairly numerous group of semi-nomadic Turcomans joined Kay-Kāvūs in Byzantine territory, and were later settled in the Dobruja. At roughly the same time one Menteshe Bey, a coastal bey who was probably a vassal of Kay-Kāvūs, left the southern coastal marches and led a *ghazā* raid against Byzantine possessions in Caria. As the result of these sea raids, Menteshe Bey succeeded in establishing himself first of all in the Carian seaports (659/1261 to 667/1269). It appears that he then co-operated with a numerous group of Turcoman nomads, migrating between summer pastures in the mountains of Denizli and winter pastures on the coast. After organizing these Turcomans, Menteshe Bey extended his authority over the whole of Caria. Then in 677/1278 he advanced in the direction of the valley of the Büyük Menderes, and captured the cities of Priene, Miletus and Magedon. In 681/1282 he advanced further to capture Tralles (Aydın) and Nyssa. Menteshe Bey's conquests were continued by his son-in-law Sasa Bey. Turkish conquests in western Anatolia had by that time assumed the nature of a general advance.

We have already referred to the importance of the area of Denizli and Kütahya in the western marches. Here the most advanced position was occupied by the semi-nomadic Germiyan Turks, who were subject to the 'Alīshīr family in the region of Kütahya-Sandıklı. Karīm al-Dīn 'Alīshīr, who belonged to an old-established family of *emīrs,* had been a supporter of Kay-Kāvūs II, and when the latter fled to Byzantium he was executed by the Mongols. The descendants of 'Alīshīr and the Germiyan Turks were then under the sway of the dynasty of Fakhr al-Dīn 'Alī. In 676/1277 when great disorders broke out throughout Anatolia, they fought bravely on the side of Fakhr al-Dīn 'Alī and of the Seljuk Sultan Kay-Khusraw III and captured the rebel Jimri. Fakhr al-Dīn then suppressed the rebellion of the chief *emīr* of the marches in the area of Denizli. He also pacified the Turcomans who had mutinied round Karaḥiṣār and Sandıklı. Fakhr al-Dīn's two sons were killed in the battle against the rebel Jimri. The 'Alīshīr dynasty which supported Fakhr al-Dīn then became a force to be reckoned with in the marches.

When, however, the Mongols appointed Sultan Mas'ūd II to the Seljuk throne, the successors of 'Alīshīr turned against Fakhr al-Dīn and the central government. It appears that important adherents of the old régime who had sought refuge in the marches incited the Turcomans to rebel. Not only those who had been threatened by the change of sultan but also people dissatisfied with the taxation and land policies of the Mongols fled to the marches. In the summer of 685/1286 the Germiyan Turks raided the province of Gargorum lying between the marches and Konya. Mongol and Seljuk forces had to wage an intense struggle against them until 688/1289. The house of 'Alīshīr joined forces with two other border dynasties, the Karamanlıs and the Eshrefoghlus. The struggle ended with the house of 'Alīshīr winning the position in the marches formerly held by the house of Fakhr al-Dīn. An inscription in Ankara by Ya'qūb Bey I, the son of 'Alīshīr, shows that he held sway over the city while also recognizing the authority of the Seljuk sultan. Under Ya'qūb Bey (d. after 720/1320), who can be considered as the real founder of the Germiyan principality, the descendants of 'Alīshīr turned their forces and their energy against Byzantine territory where they could act independently. They captured Kula and closed in on Alashehir (Philadelphia). The commanders (sing., *su-bashı*) whom Ya'qūb Bey sent to the valleys of the Menderes and of the Gediz founded their own principality: Meḥmed Bey, the son of Aydın, the principality of the house of Aydın, Sarukhan Bey, the principality of the house of Sarukhan, and in the north, in Mysia, Qalam Bey and his son Karası Bey, the principality of Karası. Thus new conquests were made in Byzantine territory outside the province of the marches, and principalities of a new type were founded. The Ottoman principality was one of these. True, these principalities were, legally speaking, considered to be part of the marches and to come under the *emīrs* of the marches, the Seljuk sultans and the Mongol Īl-Khāns in Tabrīz. In reality, however, the *ghāzī* beys felt themselves independent in the Byzantine territories which they had conquered. The formation of independent states by forces in the marches and, later, the emergence of one such state, which turned back from its area of new conquest to win dominion over the old Seljuk part of Anatolia were among the most important developments of the history of the Near East in the seventh/thirteenth and eighth/fourteenth centuries.

THE EMERGENCE OF THE OTTOMAN FRONTIER PRINCIPALITY

The marches from the Byzantine frontier along the River Sakarya to Kastamonu were subject to the *emīr* of Kastamonu. About 690/1291 Kastamonu was ruled by Muẓaffar al-Dīn Yavlak Arslan, a descendant of the famous Seljuk *Emīr* Ḥusām al-Dīn Choban. Yavlak Arslan held the title of captain-general of the marches. A contemporary source, Pachymeres, attributes the emergence of 'Os̱mān Ghāzī to a struggle with the dynasty of 'Amurios', *emīrs* of Kastamonu. When the sons of Kay-Kāvus II returned to Anatolia from the Crimea, one of them, Mas'ūd, obtained the Seljuk throne from the Mongol, Arghūn Khān. At his orders his brother Rukn al-Dīn Kılıj Arslan settled in the marches, probably near Akshehir. When after the death of Arghūn Khān and the election of Gaykhātū to the khanate (23 Rajab 690/22 July 1291) a struggle for the throne broke out among the Mongols of Persia, a state of anarchy developed in Anatolia. The frontier Turcomans rebelled.

Kılıj Arslan rebelled against his brother Mas'ūd. When Gaykhātū arrived in Anatolia in Dhu'l-Qa'da 690/November 1291, Kılıj Arslan went to the march of Kastamonu and gathered the Turcomans round him. He killed the *emīr* of the marches, Muẓaffar al-Dīn Yavlak Arslan, who had been a supporter of Mas'ūd. Sultan Mas'ūd who was sent to the area by Gaykhātū, was at first defeated but was later victorious thanks to the Mongol forces at his disposal (Dhu'l-Ḥijja 690/December 1291). Kılıj Arslan escaped, but was later killed when caught in a raid by Yavlak Arslan's son, 'Alī. 'Alī, who after the events of 690/1291 renounced his allegiance to the Seljuks and their Mongol overlords, attacked Byzantine territory, and conquered the land stretching as far as the River Sakarya. He even raided the far bank of the river. Later, however, he established peaceful relations with the Byzantines. 'Os̱mān Ghāzī's area lay to the south of him, on the far bank of the middle stretch of the River Sakarya around Sögüd. Pachymeres states clearly that when 'Alī broke off the struggle 'Os̱mān took over the leadership of the raids and started waging violent *ghazā* warfare on Byzantine territory. The *ghāzīs* started gathering under his banner. Pachymeres says that they came from Paphlagonia, in other words from the territory subject to the *emīr* of Kastamonu.

By 700/1301 'Os̱mān had advanced far enough to press in close on the old Byzantine capital of Nicaea (Iznik). Old Ottoman traditions on his origin and on his activities before that date, show that he had come under the pressure of the Germiyan dynasty and was thus forced to work in the most forward part of the marches. It was this circumstance which made for his future success and for that of the principality which he founded. According to the same traditions, 'Os̱mān's early activity did not amount to a general and ceaseless struggle against the Byzantines. At first he tried to get on with the more powerful of the Byzantine lords (*tekfurs*) in his area. He appeared in the light of a bey of a semi-nomadic group of Turcomans in conflict with the *tekfurs* who controlled their summer and winter pastures.[1] Old sources, which are legendary in character, attribute 'Os̱mān's decision to come forward as a *ghāzī* to the influence of Shaykh Ede Bali. In fact, however, the factors which

[1] On 'Os̱mān's tribal origin and his membership of the Kayi tribe of the Oghuz Turks, see M. F. Köprülü, 'Osmanlı imparatorluğunun etnik menşei meseleleri', in *Belleten*, 28, 219–303, who defends against P. Wittek the view that 'Os̱mān was the leader of a small clan of the Kayı. According to Köprülü, this tribal nucleus played a negligible part in the formation of a state which did not have a tribal character even at its inception; on this point Köprülü is in agreement with Wittek and Giese.

impelled 'Os̠mān to become a leader of *ghāzīs* were the same factors as motivated the whole activity in the marches of western Anatolia, in other words the pressure of population and the need for expansion resulting from the movement of immigration from central Anatolia, the decay of the Byzantine frontier-defence system, and religious and social discontent in the Byzantine frontier areas, as well as the desire of Anatolian Turks to escape from Mongol oppression and to start a new life in new territory.

'Os̠mān had become master of an area stretching from Eskishehir to the plains of Iznik and Brusa (Bursa), and had organized a fairly powerful principality. When he started threatening Iznik, anxiety was for the first time felt in the Byzantine capital on his score. It was then that the Byzantine empire began counting him among the most important beys of the marches alongside the houses of 'Alīshīr, Aydın and Menteshe. In 701/1301 the Byzantine emperor despatched against 'Os̠mān a force of 2,000 men under the command of the *Hetaereiarch* Muzalon charged with the task of relieving Iznik. When 'Os̠mān ambushed this force and destroyed it at Baphaeon, the local population was panic-stricken and started to leave, seeking shelter in the castle of Nicomedia (Izmit). In another direction 'Os̠mān's forward raiders advanced as far as the approaches of Bursa. In Ottoman tradition this victory is known as the victory won near Yalakova over the forces of the emperor during the siege of Iznik. It was at this time that 'Os̠mān is said to have been recognized by the Seljuk sultan as a bey, in other words as a person wielding political authority. After 701/1301 'Os̠mān's fame is reported to have spread to distant Muslim countries, and his territory was filled with wave upon wave of immigrant Turkish households.

The importance attached by the Byzantine empire to the Ottoman threat is shown by the fact that, in order to stop 'Os̠mān, the emperor tried to conclude an alliance with Ghāzān Khān, and, after the latter's death, with Öljeitü Khān and to bring the Mongol army into play. Nevertheless, around the end of the century the conquests in western Anatolia of the house of Germiyan and its commanders, and of Sasa, the son-in-law of Menteshe, seemed to pose the greater threat. In 677/1278 and 695/1296 the empire tried to reconquer lost territory here by sending two armies, but both attempts proved unsuccessful. The expedition of mercenary Alan and Catalan troops were also fruitless (701/1302 and 703/1304). Ephesus (Seljuk) fell immediately after the withdrawal of the

Catalans. Meḥmed Bey, son of Aydın, captured Birgi (Pyrgion) in 708/1308, made it his capital and, by extending his power as far as Smyrna (Izmir), became the most powerful prince in western Anatolia. Sarukhan Bey captured Manisa (Magnesia) in 713/1313, made it the centre of his principality and became an independent ruler. Further to the north, in Mysia, Karası Bey captured Balıkesir (Palaeocastron) and, having resettled it, made it his capital. This principality expanded, probably after 728/1328, to the shores of the sea of Marmora, of the Hellespont and of the gulf of Adrammytion (Edremid). To the east lay 'Os̱mān's territory. He too made extensive new conquests after 1301, occupied the environs of Iznik and Bursa, and blockaded these powerful fortresses by means of towers which were built nearby. He thus tried to starve them out.

When the Mongol governor Timurtash Noyon, who had forcibly tried to exact obedience from the princes of the marches, had to seek refuge with the Mamluks in 728/1328, after having been proclaimed a rebel, the authority of the Īl-Kāhns in the Anatolian marches became weaker than ever before. The tax-register for the year 1349 still shows Karaman, the principality of Ḥamīd, Denizli, Aydın, Germiyan, the Ottoman principality, Gerdebolu, Kastamonu, Eghridir and Sinop as lying within the borders of the Mongol state, grouped under the general name of marches, but these princes of the marches had long ago become independent rulers, paying only nominal tribute, and minting coins in their own names.

THE CULTURE OF THE MARCHES

The principalities of the marches had a distinct way of life, which could be described as a frontier culture, and this distinguished them clearly from the hinterland. This culture was dominated by the Islamic conception of Holy War or *ghazā*. By God's command the *ghazā* had to be fought against the infidels' dominions, *dār al-ḥarb* (the abode of war), ceaselessly and relentlessly until they submitted. According to the *Sharī'a* the property of the infidels, captured in these raids, could be legally kept as booty, their country could be destroyed, and the population taken into captivity or killed. The actions of the *ghāzīs* were regulated by the *Sharī'a* to which they paid heed. Ceaseless warfare led to the formation of groups commanded by *ghāzī* leaders specially blessed by shaykhs. The *ghāzī* groups were often named after their leaders.

Successful leaders naturally attracted the greatest number of *ghāzīs*. In the Seljuk marches which were dominated by Turcoman nomads, these leaders were also often chiefs of tribal clans. But, as we have seen, many of them had been commanders under the Seljuk sultans. Usually these *ghāzī* beys paid no taxes to the central government, or they sent only nominal taxes as a token of loyalty.

Life in the marches was dangerous, and required great personal initiative. At the other side of the border there was a similar Christian frontier organization, moved by the same spirit, the Byzantine *akritai*. Ethnically, frontier society was very mixed. It included highly mobile nomads, refugees from central authority, heterodox elements and adventurers. In contrast with the highly developed conservative civilization of the hinterland, with its theology, palace literature, and the *Sharī'a,* the marches had a mystical and eclectic popular culture, which had not yet frozen into a final form. They sheltered heterodox sects, bred a mystical and an epic literature and obeyed customary or tribal law. Their ethos was chivalrous and romantic.

References to the life of 'Os̱mān Ghāzī in old Ottoman traditions strongly reflect this way of life. It should not be forgotten, however, that there are considerable distortions of reality in these legends. According to Oruj, the Ottomans were

> *Ghāzīs* and champions striving in the way of truth and the path of Allāh, gathering the fruits of *ghazā* and expending them in the way of Allāh, choosing truth, striving for religion, lacking pride in the world, following the way of the *Sharī'a,* taking revenge on polytheists, friends of strangers, blazing forth the way of Islam from the East to the West.[1]

In 1354 they told Gregory Palamas that the constant expansion westwards of Muslim power was a predestined event reflecting the will of God.[2] They considered themselves as the sword of God, and this view was widespread not only among themselves but also among the Byzantines. Later on, Luther was to view the Ottomans in the same light. In old Ottoman traditions people described as *alplar* (heroes), *alp-erenler,* and *akhiler* were among the closest companions of 'Os̱mān. 'Os̱mān became a *ghāzī,* it was said, as a result of the preaching of Shaykh Ede Bali, who was probably a member of the *akhī* confraternity and who, in accordance with the *akhī* custom tied a sword to 'Os̱mān's waist. As

[1] Oruj, *Tavārīkh-i Āl-i 'Os̱mān,* ed. F. Babinger (Hanover, 1925), 3.
[2] G. Arnakis, 'Gregory Palamas among the Turks', in *Speculum,* XXVI, 110.

for the *alplar,* they followed the heroic tradition of Central Asian Turks. In the marches, the *alplar* cloaked themselves in the Islamic *ghazā* tradition and became known as *alp-erenler*. According to a contemporary source there were seven conditions for becoming an *alp-eren*: courage, strength of arm, endeavour, a good horse, a special dress, a bow and arrows, a good sword, a lance and an appropriate companion. Köprülü believes that the traditions and customs of Central Asian Turks survived strongly among the semi-nomadic Turcomans of the Anatolian marches. Wittek, on the other hand, thinks that it was rather the Islamic traditions relating to the Byzantine frontier districts, developed under the caliphate, that were dominant.[1] It is really a question of degree to determine the strength of each of the two traditions in forming the common way of life in the marches.

Between 730/1330 and 746/1345 the most brilliant *ghazā* exploits in the marches were achieved by Umur Bey of the house of Aydın. Umur Bey extended the *ghazā* to naval engagements. To counter his raids in the Aegean, Christian states agreed on a crusade against him and signed a preliminary agreement on 14 Dhu'l-Ḥijja 732/6 September 1332. They formed a fleet of twenty galleys. In 734/1334 many Turkish ships were sunk in the Aegean, the fleet of Yakhshi Bey, lord of Karası, being destroyed in the gulf of Edremid. On 19 Jumādā II 745/28 October 1344, the castle in the port of Izmir was raided and captured by the Christian forces. Umur was killed in an attempt to recapture it (Ṣafar 749/May 1348). The new bey of Aydın, Khiḍr, seeing the fate of his brother, gave up the policy of *ghazā,* preferring the advantages deriving from trade. Acting through the papacy he made peace with the Christian states concerned and granted them full privileges, allowing them to trade freely in his dominions (20 Jumādā I 749/17 August 1348). He stated in this document that he had put an end to his war with the Christians, that he would protect them in the future, would not alter customs-dues and would allow consuls of the Knights of Rhodes, of Venice, and of Cyprus to establish themselves on his land, and would permit their ships to make use of his ports.

Writing *c.* 730/1330 al-'Umarī describes the beys of Karası, Sarukhan, Menteshe and Aydın as maritime *ghāzīs,* but he distinguishes Umur Bey as one waging ceaseless Holy War (*jihād*).[2] When these principalities were

[1] P. Wittek, *The rise of the Ottoman Empire* (London, 1938), 17–19.
[2] Al-'Umarī, *Masālik al-abṣār*, ed. Fr. Taeschner (Leipzig, 1929), 30–47.

fought to a standstill by the Christian League in the Aegean, they lost their function as bases for the *ghazā*, and, like the Knights of Rhodes, they came to prefer the advantages of trade. Once this choice was made, the classical way of life and the institutions of Islamic society of the hinterland began to predominate. The leadership of the *ghazā* then passed to the Ottomans, who occupied the front line of the marches and crossed into the Balkans, where they established themselves.

The *ghāzī* beys of the marches demonstrated the original spirit of unity of the marches through common action in some of their raids and by helping each other. Cantacuzenus says that a bey embarking on a *ghazā* expedition would willingly accept in his troop *ghāzīs* coming from neighbouring principalities.[1] Nevertheless, there were also frequent dynastic wars in these principalities. In accordance with old Turkish tradition, a bey divided his country among his sons. He then ruled from the centre over his semi-dependent sons. There were frequent internal struggles between brothers. In the Ottoman dominions, which were faced with greater dangers and greater efforts to destroy them, unity was better preserved.

In western Anatolia after the *ghāzī* beys had settled in the rich plains, and conquered international commercial ports, their countries developed commercially and culturally, and assumed the character of little sultanates which had adopted the higher forms of Islamic civilization. This is demonstrated by the accounts of al-'Umarī and Ibn Baṭṭūṭa in 730/1330 and 733/1333. Ibn Baṭṭūṭa admires the beautiful markets, palaces and mosques in these cities. He says that Denizli with its seven mosques and beautiful markets is 'one of the most attractive and immense cities'. Balıkesir, the chief city of Karası, is 'a fine and populous city with pleasant bazaars' and, finally, Bursa is 'a great important city with fine bazaars and wide streets'.[2] In western Anatolia, Ayasolug (Altoluogo, Ephesus) and Balat (Miletus) were two important centres of the Levant trade. In the middle of the eighth/fourteenth century there were Venetian consuls in both cities, and wealthy Christian merchants had settled there. In Ayasolug, the city built on the hill by the Turks was the main commercial centre. Merchants from all over the world came there. Italians bought the products of Anatolia: cotton, rice, wheat, saffron, wax, wool, hemp,

[1] P. Lemerle, *L'émirat d'Aydın, Byzance et l'Occident. Recherches sur la geste d'Umur Pacha* (Paris, 1957), 212–13.

[2] H. A. R. Gibb (tr.), *The travels of Ibn Baṭṭūṭa*, II (Cambridge, 1961), 425, 449–50.

raisins, alum, and valonia as well as slaves. Valuable cotton textiles woven in Denizli and precious silks woven in Balıkesir could also be bought by Western merchants, who sold in exchange valuable woollen cloth, which was used in the *īl-khān*'s palace under the name *saqirlāt*. Other imports were tin and lead. In order to facilitate this expanding trade the Turcoman beys minted in Balat, Ayasolug and Manisa silver coins known as *gigliati*, with Latin inscriptions, modelled on Neapolitan coins.

Ibn Baṭṭūṭa mentions the pages dressed in silks whom he saw at Birgi in the palace of the Aydın prince. He stresses the importance and prestige of the Muslim jurists in the courts of the beys. The first *vezīrs* were undoubtedly chosen from among the jurists invited from the great urban centres of the interior. This was also the case with the first Ottoman *vezīrs* and with the jurists who organized the Ottoman state. Orkhān Bey opened a *medrese* in Iznik in 731/1331, and converted to a *medrese* the monastery inside the castle of Bursa. The complex of buildings, including a mosque, an alms-house, bath and a caravanserai, which Orkhān Bey built in Bursa remains to this day at the centre of the city's life.

The most salient characteristic of the culture which developed in these Turcoman principalities, was the survival of essentially Turkish cultural traditions within the context of Islamic culture. Most significantly, the Turkish language had a predominant position as a language both of the state and of literature. We know that, at the order of these Turcoman princes, classical Persian and Arabic works were translated into Turkish. Creative literary activity began in the second half of the eighth/fourteenth century with writers such as Sheykhoghlu Muṣṭafā and Aḥmedī. In these principalities, deeds of endowment (sing., *waqfiyya*) were drawn up not only in Arabic and Persian but also in Turkish. As for the works of architecture which came into being under the beys in western Anatolia, the two most important ones are the Great Mosque in Birgi built in 712/1312 and the mosque of Orkhān, built in Bursa in 741/1340. In the second half of the century there were such other great works of architecture as the Great Mosque in Manisa, the mosque of 'Īsā Bey in Ayasolug (777/1375), the *medrese* of Aḥmed Ghāzī in Pechin (777/1375) and the Green Mosque in Iznik (781/1379). These demonstrate a refined artistic taste. In decoration these buildings are simpler than the monuments of Seljuk architecture, while their plans also show novel features.

EXPANSION IN THE BALKANS AND ANATOLIA UNDER ORKHĀN AND MURĀD

By capturing in quick succession Byzantine fortresses such as Bursa, Iznik and Izmid, which had long been blockaded, Orkhān Ghāzī, the son and successor of 'Os̲mān, became pre-eminent among the beys of the marches. Bursa fell on 2 Jumādā I 726/6 April 1326. In 729/1329 the effort made by the Emperor Andronicus III to relieve Iznik was defeated, and the town surrendered on 21 Jumādā I 731/2 March 1331. Andronicus having failed to relieve Izmid, that city too fell in 738/1337.

By annexing the principality of Karası by 746/1345, the Ottomans became masters of the area between the gulf of Edremid and Kapı-daghı (Cyzicus), and found themselves facing Europe. The Karası *ghāzīs* entered the service of Orkhān, and encouraged his energetic son, Süleymān, appointed by his father bey of the important march of Karası, to extend his conquests into the Balkans (Rumeli, whence the English term Rumelia). Umur Bey, who was at that time engaged in the Aegean Sea with the Crusaders, had an ally in John Cantacuzenus, to whom he recommended Orkhān. In 747/1346 Orkhān married Theodora, daughter of Cantacuzenus, became his faithful ally, and won the opportunity of intervening in Byzantine affairs as well as in operations in Thrace. At this time the command of the marches was given, in accordance with the old Turco-Mongol tradition, to Orkhān's eldest son, Süleymān, who then moved to Adrianople (Edirne) in Thrace in order to help Cantacuzenus. On his way he occupied the castle of Tzympe (Jinbi) on the isthmus of Gallipoli (Gelibolu) and refused to evacuate this bridge-head in spite of all the efforts and pressing requests of Cantacuzenus. By concluding an agreement with the Genoese in 755/1354 Orkhān obtained valuable allies for his operations in the area of the Hellespont. Süleymān strengthened his position by moving a stream of *ghāzīs* over the Straits and capturing the castle of Hexamilion (Eksamil) which dominated the isthmus of Gallipoli. The great fortress of Gallipoli was thus isolated from Thrace. The embattled front facing Gallipoli was immediately constituted under the command of Ya'qūb Eje and Ghāzī Fāżil who thus formed a new march. Another was formed on the left flank, under the command of Ḥājjī Ilbegi and Evrenuz (Evrenos) in order to extend the conquests to the north. Süleymān himself operated in the middle sector. In the night of 7 Ṣafar 755/2 March 1354, a violent earthquake brought down the walls of Gallipoli and of other fortresses around it. These were immediately occupied and re-fortified by the *ghāzīs*. This event, which allowed the Ottomans to establish a permanent foothold in Europe and opened limitless possibilities before the *ghāzīs*, caused great concern and excitement among the Byzantines and in the Western Christian world. The Venetian ambassador (*bailo*) wrote in Sha'bān 755/August 1354 that Constantinople was ready to accept the protection of a powerful Christian state. Cantacuzenus, who was deemed responsible for this turn of events, had to renounce the throne. In Europe people began to say that a crusade had to be organized, this time not against the Aydın dynasty in Izmir but against the Ottomans. Gallipoli became a base for the *ghāzīs*.

When Süleymān died unexpectedly in an accident in 758/1357 his brother Murād accompanied by his tutor was sent to the command of the marches. In 760/1359 he launched a great offensive against Edirne, which surrendered in 762/1361. Rumours spread in Italy that Constantinople was about to fall. Under papal leadership a stimulus was given to exchanges between the king of Hungary, the Byzantine emperor and the Italian states with a view to organizing a crusade. By a bull dated 25 December 1366 the pope proclaimed a crusade to expel the Turks from the Balkans. The only ruler to respond was the duke of Savoy, Amadeus II, who led his fleet to Gallipoli and recaptured it from the Ottomans (767/1366). The following year he handed over the castle to the Byzantines. This, however, did not check the Ottoman advance.

Murād I (763–91/1362–89) had now succeeded Orkhān, and threatened both the Byzantine empire and the Serbian. When the journey of the Byzantine Emperor John V Palaeologus to Italy to meet the pope and mobilize aid failed to produce results, and when the last joint operation of the Serbian princes in Macedonia was defeated on the Maritza (battle of Chirmen 15 Rabī' I 773/26 September 1371), the emperor and the rulers of the Balkans acknowledged Ottoman suzerainty, one after the other. As early as 773/1372 or 774/1373 John V realized that no hope was left, and agreed to accept the suzerainty of Murād I, taking part in his Anatolian expeditions as an Ottoman vassal. Later, his son Andronicus IV obtained the protection of the Ottomans, thanks to which he succeeded to the Byzantine throne (778/1376). Then he returned Gallipoli to the Ottomans (781/1379).

In brief, Murād had succeeded by 782/1380 in creating in Anatolia and Rumelia an embryo empire made up of vassal principalities. Relations with these were at first so regulated that in exchange for aid or formal alliances the Ottomans subjected local princes to a number of obligations which eventually turned them into Ottoman vassals. When this process was complete, the Ottomans forced these princes and beys to send their sons to the Ottoman court as hostages, to pay tribute, and to participate in Ottoman expeditions with forces commanded by these princes in person or by their sons. At the same time these vassal states remained under the constant pressure of the beys of the marches, lest they should escape from Ottoman dominion. The moment that they renounced their subject status, their territories were considered *dār al-ḥarb,* i.e. a field of battle which attracted the terrifying onslaughts of the *akınjı* raiders (see below, pp. 283 ff). Under Murād I, Ottoman occupation of roads and centres of population in the Balkans followed three main directions: in the centre, the valley of the Maritza, which the Ottomans followed, reaching the foothills of the Balkan range as early as 767/1366 and then going on to conquer Sofia *c.* 787/1385 and Nish in 788/1386; on the right the valley of the Tunja, and on the left, the southern march, commanded by Evrenuz, where Serez (Serrae) was occupied on 21 Rajab 785/19 September 1383, an event which was followed by the beginning of the siege of Salonica. This second largest city in the Byzantine dominions surrendered in Ramaḍān 789/September 1387. Divisions and rivalries in the Balkans and attempts by Balkan states to ally themselves to the Ottomans and win their protection, facilitated these advances. Thus in 766–7/1365–6 the Bulgarian King Shishman, threatened from the north by an invasion of Hungarians and of the prince of Wallachia, and from the Black Sea by the fleet of Amadeus of Savoy's Crusaders, had sought safety in becoming an ally of the Ottomans. It appears that he accepted Turkish help, as Cantacuzenus had earlier done. Between 767/1366 and 771/1370 there are references in chronicles to Bulgarian-Turkish co-operation and to Turkish units fighting alongside the Bulgarians on the Danube. Let us add that Prince Wladislaw of Wallachia also sought Ottoman help in 775/1373 when he turned his back on the Hungarians.

The reign of Murād I also saw the expansion and consolidation of Ottoman power in Anatolia. In 755/1354 the Ottomans had captured Ankara, which was at that time an important economic and political centre. This marked the start of Ottoman expansion into the former Seljuk-Mongol area—the old Islamic hinterland. It embroiled the Ottomans with the *emīr* of Sivas, and with his neighbours and powerful allies, the house of Karaman. The princes of Karaman were the most powerful of the Turcoman frontier-beys in the south. After a long struggle, they had established themselves firmly in the old Seljuk capital of Konya, whence they considered themselves as heirs to the Seljuks—sovereigns of the sultanate of Rūm and suzerains of the other beys of the marches. The Ottomans, greatly strengthened by the success of their *ghazā* in the Balkans, came up against the house of Karaman with precisely the same claim. Resistance to Ottoman overlordship was crushed in 789/1387, when Murād I marched on Konya and won a pitched battle there.

But while Murād was in Anatolia, there was a revolt in the Balkans by the Serbians, whom the ruler of Bosnia joined. The Bulgarians sided with them. Thereupon an expedition was undertaken against Shishman the Bulgarian king in the first place. In 790/1387 he was eliminated from the fray, and Bulgaria was occupied. The following spring Murād marched down to the plain of Kosova against the Serbs. The victory which the Ottomans won (19 Jumādā II 791/15 June 1389) showed that they were destined to stay in the Balkans as the ruling power. Murād was mortally wounded on the battlefield and was immediately succeeded by his son Bāyezīd, called *Yıldırım*, 'the Thunderbolt'. To avoid a civil war Bāyezīd's brother was executed.

BĀYEZĪD I AND THE CLASH WITH TĪMŪR

As soon as news was received of the death of Murād, the beys of Anatolia revolted once again. Thereupon Bāyezīd immediately crossed into Anatolia with prestige of the great victory won at Kosova. Within a year he occupied and annexed to the empire what remained of the *ghāzī* principalities of western Anatolia, i.e. the principalities of Aydın, Sarukhan and Menteshe and the remnants of those of Ḥamīd and Germiyan. He then marched on the prince of Karaman, and forced him to sue for peace (793/1391). He crushed the bey of Kastamonu, and added his territories to the empire. However, in the area of Amasya, further to the east, he was faced with a dangerous rival in the person of the sultan of Sivas, Qāḍī Burhān al-Dīn. In the meantime the Wallachians, acting under Hungarian protection, established themselves on the south bank of the Danube in Silistre (Silistria) and in the Dobruja, while the Byzantines reoccupied Salonica. Once again Bāyezīd crossed over to the Balkans (795/1393) and annexed the Dobruja; Tirnova, Shishman's capital, was occupied on 7 Ramaḍān 795/17 July 1393. He summoned all the vassal princes of Rumelia to attend on him. His object was to underline his rights as suzerain and to punish the Palaeologi who were gravitating towards Venice. However, the princes succeeded in evading the summons. Bāyezīd then reoccupied Salonica (19 Jumādā II 796/21 April 1394) and sent his *akınjı* raiders into the Morea. Having done this, he appeared before the walls of Constantinople and blockaded the city in the hope of forcing it to surrender through the exercise of unrelenting pressure. He then made an expedition into Hungary in order to intimidate the Hungarians and subdue the Wallachians. The army, which he commanded in person, devastated southern Hungary and then entered Wallachia, where he had a fierce battle with a Wallachian army at Argeshe. On his way back, Bāyezīd crossed the Danube at Nicopolis, and had Shishman arrested and executed. This marked the extinction of the Bulgarian kingdom. These operations led to the formation of a crusading army made up of groups of knights from all over western Europe under the command of King Sigismund of Hungary. The Crusaders came as far as Nicopolis, while the Venetian navy stood guard over the Hellespont. Bāyezīd was at that time near Constantinople. He immediately marched off, and encountered the Crusaders outside Nicopolis, which they were besieging. The Crusaders were completely routed (21 Dhu'l-Ḥijja 798/25 September 1396). This victory won the sultan great fame as a *ghāzī* throughout the Muslim world. Returning to Anatolia, with this victory behind him, Bāyezīd occupied Konya the following year and destroyed the state of Karaman (beginning of 800/autumn of 1397). The following year he also put an end to the state of Qāḍī Burhān al-Dīn around Sivas, and, entering the territory of the Mamluks in the upper valley of the Euphrates, occupied several cities including Malaṭya and Elbistan. Thus Bāyezīd was at one and the same time waging war on the most powerful Muslim sultan, the Mamluk ruler, and encroaching on Tīmūr's sphere of influence in eastern Anatolia as far as Erzinjan. His pressure on Constantinople was such that the Emperor Manuel II went himself to Europe (802/1399) in order to plead for a crusade. The sultan of the *ghāzīs* in this way eliminated the petty states of Anatolia and Rumelia and, having founded an empire within a brief spell of time, put it in the forefront of a world-wide struggle for power. Envoys were exchanged between Tīmūr and the king of France. Tīmūr went into action, crushed Bāyezīd's imperial army, which was not yet well integrated, and captured the sultan himself in a battle of Ankara on 27 Dhu'l-Ḥijja 804/28 July 1402.

Bāyezīd, encouraged by his victories and by the forces at his disposal, had tried to transform the empire made up of vassal principalities, which existed under Murād I, into a true empire coming under a centralized administration. He acted with force and determination. He tried to eliminate Hungarian influence from the Balkans. By establishing a fortified naval base at Gallipoli he won control over the Hellespont and challenged Venice at sea. He sought to conquer Constantinople and make it the capital of his empire, joining Anatolia and Rumelia. While challenging the entire Christian world, he sought from the caliph in Egypt the official title of *sulṭān al-Rūm*, as the legitimate heir to the Seljuk possessions in Anatolia. Meanwhile, however, Tīmūr had raised his banner in the East, espousing the cause of the descendants of Chingiz Khān, and seeking recognition of his right to rule over Anatolia and with it over Bāyezīd, whom he considered as simply a bey of the marches. After crushing Bāyezīd at Ankara, Tīmūr revived the Anatolian principalities and placed them under his protection against any further Ottoman encroachments.

The nucleus of the Ottoman dominions was divided among three brothers, Süleymān in Edirne, Meḥmed in Amasya, and ʿĪsā in Bursa. These recognized Tīmūr as their suzerain. Ottoman possessions in Anatolia having now been reduced to the area which they had occupied under Murād I, the centre of gravity of the state moved to Rumelia, Edirne becoming from this date the main Ottoman capital. Even before Tīmūr died in 807/1405, a civil war started among the brothers for possession of the two Ottoman capitals, Edirne and Bursa, and for undivided rule over the empire. This period is known as the interregnum. Finally Meḥmed I triumphed over his rivals and re-established the unity of the Ottoman state in 816/1413. With this end in view Meḥmed adopted a policy of conciliating the beys, princes and local lords, who had reappeared in Anatolia and Rumelia and, above all, of getting on peacefully with the Byzantines. This policy forced him into important concessions. The states in question regained some of their former possessions and won a greater freedom of action in the face of the Ottoman sultan. After the experience of Tīmūr's onslaught, the Ottomans made a point of advancing their policy of conquest and of *ghazā* with greater care, avoiding as far as possible giving rise to crusades in the west and to a fresh intervention in Anatolia, this time by Tīmūr's son, Shāh-Rukh. It was only in the reign of Meḥmed II the Conqueror that the Ottomans launched an offensive policy both in the east and in the west in order to revive the empire of Bāyezīd.

To understand why the Ottomans succeeded in re-establishing the unity of their state, one must remember above all that Bāyezīd had abandoned the traditions of the marches and had introduced the highly developed classical Turkish-Islamic system of central government into the administration of the state. Provincial land and population surveys, fiscal methods developed in the Īl-Khān state in Persia, a central treasury and a bureaucracy which sought from the capital to regulate affairs of the state throughout the provinces, were introduced or strengthened in his reign. The system of control through the sultan's own slaves (sing., *ghulām, kapı-kulu*), which was above all instrumental in establishing the absolute authority of the sultan in the provinces, came to dominate the administration in the time of Bāyezīd I.[1] Military and administrative commanders were chosen largely from among the *ich-oghlans* (slaves educated at the sultan's court), and even the majority of *timar* fiefs in the provinces were granted to the sultan's slaves brought up within the *ghulām* system. The military units made up of the sultan's slaves came to number 7,000 men. These elements helped in the re-establishment of a centrally administered empire, for, as long as there were rival sultans, neither the holders of *timar* fiefs nor members of the *kapı-kulu* slave class could be certain of their positions. The rights and influence which they had acquired could only be guaranteed by a stable centralized administration. It is they who supported first Meḥmed I and then Murād II against his rival, *Düzme* Muṣṭafā. They defended the absolute central authority of a single sultan against the divisive tendencies of the marches.

Furthermore, although weakened in Anatolia after Tīmūr's incursion, the Ottomans maintained their former strength in Rumelia. They were then able to come back to Anatolia from the Balkans and re-establish their supremacy.

THE OTTOMAN RECOVERY

The reign of Murād II (824–55/1421–51) was a time of preparation for the extension of the empire under Meḥmed II the Conqueror. When Murād ascended the throne in Bursa, Edirne and the whole of Rumelia gave allegiance to his uncle Muṣṭafā, known as *Düzme*, 'the Impostor'. Muṣṭafā was also supported by the Byzantines, who hoped to regain Gallipoli. In Anatolia the princes of the Germiyan and Karaman dynasties

[1] Thus *kapı-kulus* were recruited originally from the Sultan's share of prisoners-of-war, and subsequently from a periodical levy (*depshirme*) of Christian boys. Most of the youths entered the Janissary corps.

supported Murād's younger brother, also called Muṣṭafā, who was a governor in Ḥamīd. Like his father, Murād spent the first two years of his reign in dangerous struggles to establish himself on his throne and ensure the unity of his state. The beys of Anatolia did not recognize him. The prince of Karaman occupied Ḥamīd, while the bey of Kastamonu made himself master of the area round Tosya and Qal'ejik. Things had returned once again to the state of affairs which had prevailed in 804/1402. However, Murād II succeeded finally in crushing *Düzme* Muṣṭafā. He besieged the Byzantines in Constantinople as a punishment for the support which they had given to Muṣṭafā (Rajab 825/June 1422). But the beys of Anatolia attacked him and established his younger brother Muṣṭafā as sultan in Iznik. Thereupon Murād, who had been besieging Constantinople for fifty days with guns, crossed into Anatolia. He had Muṣṭafā arrested and executed. He forced the princes of Karaman and Kastamonu into submission, obliging them to return their newly won lands. He annexed the *ghāzī* principalities of western Anatolia, those of Izmir-Aydın, of Menteshe and the Teke branch of the Ḥamīd dynasty. Nevertheless, he followed a policy of conciliation towards the principalities of Jandar and Karaman in so far as they were part of the old Seljuk area of Anatolia which came under the protection of Shāh-Rukh. When the Byzantines who had regained Salonica in 805/1402, ceded the town to Venice in 826/1423 the Ottomans started a war against Venice. This war dragged on for a long time, from 826/1423 to 833/1430, because of the weakness of the Ottoman navy, and passed through some dangerous phases. In the meantime Hungary attempted to establish its supremacy over Wallachia and Serbia. This led to clashes which were ended by the truce signed for three years in 831/1428. The princes of Wallachia, Serbia and Bosnia reaffirmed their allegiance to the sultan. Finally Salonica was occupied in 833/1430.

Although Murād was described as a peace-loving sultan, his court was nevertheless under the influence of people who wished to return to the forceful policy of conquest pursued by Bāyezīd. Their counsels were particularly strong between 837/1434 and 846/1442. In 837/1434 struggle was renewed with Hungary for supremacy in Serbia and Wallachia. Benefiting from the death of King Sigismund in 841/1437 the sultan himself led an army into Hungary (1438). In 843/1439 he occupied and annexed Serbia. The following year the Ottomans made the first attempt to gain from the Hungarians the fortress of Belgrade, which was the gate leading to central Europe. Murād's withdrawal from

Belgrade was a turning point. In 845/1441 and 846/1442 there were large-scale Ottoman raids in Transylvania (Erdel). These were, however, totally crushed by the attacks led by John Hunyadi. These Ottoman defeats raised the hopes of Crusaders in the Christian world. The Hungarians launched a counter-offensive. In another surprise attack Hunyadi captured Nish and Sofia, and pressing on the last Balkan passes, threatened Edirne. Murād II succeeded with difficulty in halting the invading army at the battle of Izladi (Zlatića), on 1 Sha'bān 847/24 November 1443, and thereupon returned suddenly to a pacific and conciliatory policy. He signed a peace with the Hungarians and with the despot of Serbia, George Branković, promising to return Serbia to him and to refrain from crossing the Danube (24 Ṣafar 848/12 June 1444). He then made peace with the prince of Karaman, who had once again gone over to the attack (summer 848/1444). By this agreement Ḥamīd was ceded to Karaman. Thinking that he had thus made peace on all sides, he voluntarily renounced the throne in favour of his son, Meḥmed II (summer 848/1444). The king of Hungary, the Byzantine emperor and the pope saw in this a golden opportunity, and pushed on with their preparations for a crusade. A Hungarian-Wallachian army crossed the Danube. At the same time the Venetian navy held the Hellespont. However, the despot of Serbia, who had been reinstated by the Ottomans, did not join the allies. The army of the crusaders reached the neighbourhood of Varna. Panic broke out in Edirne. In answer to pressing requests and petitions, Murād II came back to command the Ottoman army. Its victory at the pitched battle of Varna (28 Rajab 848/10 November 1444) is one of the vital battles in the history not only of the Balkans and of Byzantium, but also of Europe as a whole. Although Hunyadi later entered the Balkans for a third time, planning to co-operate with the Albanian, Iskender Bey (Scanderbeg); he was again defeated at Kosova (18–21 Sha'bān 852/17–20 October 1448). This proved to be the last effort to free the Balkans and relieve Constantinople.

Among factors which paved the way to the conquest of Constantinople, certain internal developments in the Ottoman state hold an important place. In the first phase of the reign of Meḥmed II, who in 848/1444 was only twelve years old, the sultan was surrounded by a circle of commanders thirsting for war and conquest. This group tried to break the absolute power of the grand *vezīr* Chandarlı Khalīl, who came from the '*ulemā*', and to supplant him. Chandarlı succeeded, however, in retaining the support of the Janissaries, and engineered the return to the throne of Murād II (Ṣafar 850/May 1446). Chandarlı refrained from threatening subject-states, fearing lest this should lead the Ottomans into adventures similar to those of 848/1444. When Murād II died on 1 Muḥarram 855/3 February 1451, Meḥmed II, who was then nineteen years of age, ascended the Ottoman throne for a second time. Power then passed to his governors Shihāb al-Dīn Shāhīn Pasha and Zaganuz Pasha, both of them advocates of further conquests, who had already tried to persuade Meḥmed II to attempt the conquest of Constantinople in 848/1444. The young sultan and his entourage needed a great victory in order to reaffirm their power and their influence against the grand *vezīr*. Preparations were immediately put in hand for the siege of Constantinople.

FACTORS IN THE OTTOMAN CONQUESTS

The Ghāzīs *and the* Akınjıs

The Holy War or *ghazā* was the foundation stone of the Ottoman state. The tradition of the *ghāzīs* of the marches, which lay at its origin, dominated all its history, and constituted the fundamental principle of its policies and its organization. The concept of the *ghazā* stimulated great initiatives and endeavours, and, later, attempts at renewal; it inspired both individuals and society. The Ottomans took in all seriousness the duty of protecting and extending Islam, and even tried to justify their claim to sovereignty over the whole Islamic world, by the argument that they alone were carrying out that duty.

For *ghāzīs* in the marches, it was a religious duty to ravage the countries of the infidels who resisted Islam, and to force them into subjection. The only way of avoiding the onslaughts of the *ghāzīs* was to become subjects of the Islamic state. Non-Muslims could then enjoy the status of *dhimmīs,* living under its protection. Most Christian sources confuse these two stages in the Ottoman conquests. The Ottomans, however, were careful to abide by these rules, and this helped in the expansion of their empire. Faced with the terrifying onslaught of the *ghāzīs,* the population living outside the confines of the empire, in the 'abode of war', often renounced the ineffective protection of Christian states, and sought refuge in subjection to the Ottoman empire. Peasants in open country in particular lost nothing by this change. The institutions and traditions of the marches which existed at the time of 'Os̲mān Ghāzī lived on in Ottoman history, moving, however, to new frontiers. Later *ghāzīs* became known as *akınjıs* (raiders) and the old term *uj* (march) gave place to *serḥadd* (frontier), but the concepts remained unchanged. An investigation into them can give us a clearer picture of the old marches.

From the point of view of organization the *sanjaks* (provinces) of the marches differed considerably from those of the interior. This was particularly true in the eighth/fourteenth and ninth/fifteenth centuries. In Üsküp, for example, the free *sipahi* cavalry was loyal to the person of the bey of the march. These beys of the marches were often descendants of the original frontier leaders and they formed dynasties such as the houses of Evrenuz, Mikhal, Turakhan and Malkoch, which inherited their *sanjaks* and ruled them more or less independently. We have already mentioned that they could at times receive tribute from foreign states. They disposed of vast properties in freehold or in *waqf*. Each of these main leaders, who enjoyed great power and renown in the marches, became a subject of legends, and epic poems were written about their exploits. The troops of these great beys of the marches in the Balkans were known by the names of their leaders as late as the tenth/sixteenth century. The *akınjıs* of the right flank were known as *Mikhallıs,* those of the left flank as *Turakhanlıs*. Seven thousand of the latter were active in the Morea in 966/1559. Under Murād II (824–55/1421–51) the Ottoman sultan began to appoint his personal slaves to commands in the marches, a custom which had existed under the Seljuks.

As for the *ghāzīs* themselves, known now under their new name of *akınjı,* these in the eighth/fourteenth century consisted largely of volunteers (sing., *gönüllü*) who had come from Anatolia, drawn by the prospect of warfare and of booty or by the hope of gaining a fief for themselves. These *akınjıs* were, unlike the old *ghāzīs,* a kind of auxiliary militia. We know also that nomad *yürüks,* and Christian *voynuks* and *martolos* (Greek: *armatolos,* armed irregulars) were enrolled as *akınjıs* for service in the frontier areas, and that they were used for intelligence and other purposes in enemy territory. The *akınjıs* normally set off on an expedition with two horses. The weapons of the *akınjıs,* who constituted a kind of light cavalry, were a sword, a shield, a scimitar, a lance and a mace. The *akınjıs* were formed in units of tens, hundreds and thousands. Their officers were known as *tovija* and were rewarded with fiefs (sing., *timar*). They were commanded by a *sanjak beyi* known as the bey of the *akınjıs*. In the tenth/sixteenth century the duties of the *akınjis* on an expedition were to penetrate into enemy territory ahead of the main army and destroy the enemy's preparations, to carry out raids, to destroy the enemy's sources and routes of supply, to open roads for the Ottoman army, to check bridges and roads which the army had to cross, and to capture prisoners for intelligence purposes. From the end of this century raids became more difficult and, therefore, less frequent in central Europe. From then on Crimean auxiliaries came only when an expedition was in progress and carried out the duties of *akınjıs*. The organization of the *akınjıs* was thus considerably weakened. In 1034/1625 there were only two or three thousand left.

During the early stage of Ottoman history when the Ottoman state could still be considered a frontier principality, the marches played an important part in home politics. Ottoman beys of the marches or members of the ruling house might well have established independent principalities in the Balkans, following the example of the other frontier principalities. However, faced as they were with particularly strong enemies in the Balkans, the Ottoman beys of the marches needed the help which only the central government could provide. What is more, the Ottoman sultans were always personally active on the field of the *ghazā*. Thanks to the *beylerbeyi* organization and the force of the sultan's own retainers or slaves (*kapı-kulus*) the Ottoman sovereigns had the practical means of exerting their authority. Bāyezīd both as a great *ghāzī* himself and thanks to his *kapı-kulu* forces, was fully master of the marches. After his death, when his sons and grandsons struggled for power, the marches once again came to the fore. Contenders who could gain the support of the hereditary beys of the *akınjıs* in the marches could become masters of all Ottoman possessions in the Balkans. They could then ascend the throne in Edirne which had become the main royal residence since 805/1402. Mūsā Chelebi, who had been closely associated with the *akınjıs* in his father's lifetime, utilized their help to defeat his brother Süleymān in the Balkans, and this allowed him to gain the throne (22 Shawwāl 813/17 February 1411). His first action was to appoint to the dignity of *beylerbeyi* the famous bey of the *akınjıs* Mikhal-oghlu. Since the time of Orkhan the function of *beylerbeyi* had been given to the sultan's slaves and this allowed the central government to maintain its authority over the *sipahi* cavalry and the marches in the Balkans. There was always jealousy, open or hidden, between the *beylerbeyis*, who stood for the interests of the central authority, and the beys of the marches. The appointment of Mikhaloghlu meant that the bey of the *akınjıs* was in control of all the military forces in the Balkans. From their side the *akınjıs*, and their officers, the *tovijas*, viewed with jealousy the *sipahis* who had rich *timars* in the interior. Mikhaloghlu and the chief judge (*qāḍī ʿasker*) Shaykh Badr al-Dīn, who was known for his extreme views, granted fiefs in the interior to many *akınjıs* from the Dobruja. Nonetheless, Mūsā continued the tradition of appointing his own slaves to key positions to counteract the influence of the beys of the marches. At the death of Meḥmed I (824/1421), his brother, *Düzme* Muṣṭafā became master of the Balkans and of Edirne, largely through the support of the house of Evrenuz. To outweigh this, Murād released Mikhaloghlu, who had been imprisoned in Tokat after the fall of Mūsā, and with his help succeeded in winning over the beys of the marches and eliminating his rival. Under Murād II the refusal of Turakhan, a powerful bey of the marches, to obey the *beylerbeyi* of Rumeli was one of the factors which led to Murād's abdication. In 1444 a pretender to the throne named Orkhan went from Istanbul to the Dobruja, where he tried to organize a rebellion of the forces in the marches. Meḥmed the Conqueror, as a great *ghāzī* himself, was able to dominate the marches, and attach them to the central government.

Expansion in Byzantine and Balkan territories

When the Ottomans appeared as a dynamic unifying force amidst the anarchy of the Balkans, Byzantine territories and the Balkans were prey not only to political but also to deep social and religious divisions. Civil wars and the absence of a central authority had allowed local lords in the provinces to strengthen their hold over the land and to subject the peasantry to a more or less arbitrary régime. The Byzantine administration struggled hopelessly to free from the grasp of these lords the estates which it wished to see returned to central control. This struggle over land between the central government and local lords was undoubtedly one of the main problems of Balkan history. Serfs tied to the land had to pay the lord a tax on produce as well as render free service in compulsory *corvées*. These services included the provision of firewood and hay, and free labour with oxen two or three days a week. When Ottoman administration was established, there was almost a social revolution through the application of the following principles: first, all agricultural land passed to the overriding ownership of the state, in other words the state established close control over the land. Land which thus passed to the state became known as *mīrī* land. Secondly, all local feudal rights which limited the state's control over the land and the peasants were abolished. Local manorial rights were eliminated. The rights of local lords and, in some cases, of monasteries to exact forced labour from the peasants, and all similar privileges were suppressed. The Ottoman administration was always and everywhere opposed to the *corvée* system. The obligation to transport firewood and hay, and to work manorial estates, was replaced by a tax, known as plough dues (*chift resmi*) amounting to 22 aspers. The commutation of feudal service, which could easily be abused, into an easily payable fixed monetary tax was a major social reform. In addition, it was in principle forbidden to compel the peasants to any service. In brief, the Ottoman régime represented a strong and impartial central administration which extended to the peasants effective protection against feudal lords.

It is true that at the same time the Ottoman invasion deprived the Balkan peoples of their national cultural institutions and of the ruling class which embodied them. The Ottomans incorporated in the *timar* fief-system the local Balkan aristocracy which adhered to them. They left it part of its old lands, which these local nobles continued to hold in the changed capacity of holders of *timars*. In this way they entered the ruling group and came under the close control of the new empire, becoming in time ottomanized. Some of the more important noblemen tried, however, to preserve their position during the Ottoman conquest by relying for help on the Western Catholic world, and eventually fled to the West. Even before the conquest of Constantinople, the Ottomans appeared as protectors of the Church, and considered the Greek Orthodox ecclesiastical organization as part of their administrative system. Greek Orthodox archbishops were granted *timars*. The struggle between Greek Orthodox and Catholics in the Balkans was founded on deep-rooted social causes. It is an historical commonplace that the popular masses, fanatically attached to Greek Orthodoxy in Byzantine territories, preferred the Ottomans to Latin Catholics, and disowned their own ruling class and aristocracy which tried to unite with the Catholics. The ruler of Bosnia complained in 1463 to the pope that the peasants seemed to favour the Ottomans, who treated them well and promised them freedom. In any case, we know that the Balkan peasantry did not support the local feudal lords against the Ottomans, with whom, on the contrary, they sometimes co-operated.

Attempts to describe the conquests made by Anatolian Turks in western Anatolia and the Balkans as a large-scale movement of population have been borne out by recent research in the Ottoman archives. This movement of population not only modified the ethnic composition of the territories in which it occurred, but almost inevitably stimulated further conquests.

Population registers for the provinces (*sanjaks*) of Aydın and of Thrace in the middle of the ninth/fifteenth century show that the overwhelming majority (eighty to ninety per cent) of the population of these areas was already by that time made up of Muslim Turks. It appears therefore that Byzantine sources do not exaggerate when they say that the Turks came to settle in masses. After moving into the Balkans, the Ottomans encouraged immigration into the newly conquered territories where they transferred nomads *en masse*. This old system of transfer of population, known as *sürgün* or 'exile', had already been used on a large scale by the Seljuks. Nomad Turks who were known in the Balkans by the name of *yürük* (yörük), were especially numerous in the districts which lay in the path of the conquering armies and in the marches. *Waqf* deeds and registers of the ninth/fifteenth century show also that there was a wide movement of colonization of western Anatolian peasantry settling in Thrace and the eastern Balkans and founding hundreds of new villages. The newly arrived Muslim Turks did not usually mix with Christian peasants, but settled in their own villages. Villages which kept their old names and where the population was mixed were usually old Byzantine villages converted to Islam. Muslims were also settled in cities which had put up resistance to the Ottomans. These soon became Muslim cities. For example the frontier town of Üsküp (Skopje) which was captured in 793/1391 had by 859/1455 twenty-two Muslim quarters as against only eight Christian ones. But the cities which surrendered remained in most cases Christian. This widespread wave of Turkish emigration to western Anatolia and the Balkans coincided with the conquests of the eighth/fourteenth century. A fresh wave was set off by the conquests of Tīmūr. It appears that emigration slowed down in the second half of the fifteenth century, since we do not see similar concentrations of new settlers in Serbia, Albania and the Morea.

As new conquests were added, the area of the marches moved forward. During the reign of Bāyezīd I (791–806/1389–1403) the march of the Dobruja and Deliorman, centred on Silistria, faced Wallachia (Eflak) and Moldavia (Boghdan); the march of Vidin faced Serbia and Hungary; the march of Üsküp faced Bosnia, Serbia and Albania; and, finally the march of Tırkhala (Trikkala) faced Epirus and the Morea. After the conquest of Serbia and Bosnia, Semendere and Saray-Bosna (Sarajevo) became the centres of the marches facing Hungary. After the conquest of Hungary the marches moved again, this time to the *sanjaks* bordering on Habsburg territory. In Albania, Avlonya (Valona) was the centre of the march facing Italy. The islands of the Aegean, the Morea and the old maritime *ghāzī* principalities of western Anatolia were the marches of the sailor *ghāzīs* of the Mediterranean. These pushed their operations as far as the western Mediterranean, and turned Algeria and Tunisia into a fresh march as a base for expeditions against the Spanish monarchy, which had driven the Muslims from Spain, and against Spanish possessions in Italy. Such is the brief history of the role of the marches in the expansion of the Ottoman empire.

Expansion in Muslim Anatolia

The concepts of the *ghazā* and the marches were applied by the Ottomans not only to conquests of infidel territory, but also to expansion within the confines of the Islamic world. When they annexed the Turcoman principalities of Anatolia, by peaceful means, by threats, or, when necessary, by war, they granted to the former beys, as a general rule, rich *timars* in the Balkans. This often enabled the Ottomans to annex the beys' territories without a struggle. In any case, religion forbade a Muslim, and particularly a *ghāzī,* to use arms on another Muslim (Qur'ān, 4. 90). The reputation of the Ottomans as *ghāzīs* was vulnerable to criticism in the case of wars waged against other Muslims. The Ottomans therefore tried to pass off as licit acts annexations achieved through pressure and threats. The Ottomans argued, for example, that they had acquired through canonically licit ways the lands of the houses of Ḥamīd and Germiyan which were a bone of contention between them and the house of Karaman. The latter refused of course to countenance the acquisition by the Ottomans of centres like Ankara and the land of Ḥamīd, formerly a part of the sultanate of Konya. The struggle between the houses of Karaman and of 'Os̱mān revolved, in the main, round this territory.

As a general rule, whenever they wanted to wage war on Karaman or any other Muslim state, the Ottomans did not neglect to provide themselves with a legal ruling (*fetvā*; Arabic, *fatwā*) from the *'ulemā'* demonstrating that their actions were in accordance with the *Sharī'a* and therefore licit. It was thus argued that it was canonically mandatory to wage war against those who attacked them in the rear while they were engaged in a *ghazā* against the infidels. The house of Karaman and others were thus proclaimed rebels against religion. This view recurs constantly in Ottoman sources. In 848/1444 Murād II obtained from the independent *'ulamā'* of Egypt a *fatwā* proclaiming to the Muslim world and particularly to Tīmūr's successor, Shāh-Rukh, the legality of the expedition against Karaman which he was about to launch. The Ottomans insisted in particular that the house of Karaman collaborated with the Christians, a fact which is confirmed by Western sources.

The second direction of Ottoman expansion in Anatolia followed the Persian silk road. Not content with the capture of Ankara they used that city as well as the city of Bolu as a base for operations aimed ostensibly at protecting the weak *emīrs* of the region of Tokat and Amasya, lying to the east of them, against the pressure of Qāḍī Burhān al-Dīn in Sivas. When Murād I crossed over to the Balkans for an expedition against Serbia in 790/1388, Burhān al-Dīn's commanders argued that a golden opportunity had presented itself for an offensive against the Ottomans. However, the Qāḍī rejected their advice saying that it was tantamount to weakening Islam and strengthening the infidels. Nevertheless, when Murād I was killed on the battlefield of Kosova, as soon as news of it reached Anatolia, Qāḍī Burhān al-Dīn had Mürüvvet Bey capture Kirshehir, while Karaman regained Beyshehir, and the house of Germiyan the territory which it had lost to the Ottomans.

For political reasons the Ottoman sultans attached the greatest importance to safeguarding and strengthening the reputation which they enjoyed as *ghāzīs* in the Muslim world. When they won victories in the *ghazā* in the Balkans they used to send accounts of them (sing., *fetḥ-nāme*) as well as slaves and booty to eastern Muslim potentates. Knights captured by *Yıldırım* Bāyezīd I at his victory over the Crusaders at Nicopolis in 798/1396, and sent to Cairo, Baghdād and Tabrīz were paraded through the streets, and occasioned great demonstrations in favour of the Ottomans. This widespread fame as *ghāzīs* was the source of extensive political advantages to the Ottomans. For example, Tīmūr's entourage long resisted launching an attack on the sultan of the *ghāzīs*. When Tīmūr defeated the Ottoman sultan in 804/1402, he himself felt the need of waging a token *ghazā* by capturing Izmir from the Crusaders. In a letter written some time before 1420 Meḥmed I emphasizes his title as *ghāzī* in order to parry the threats of Shāh-Rukh, and says that he is about to set off on a *ghazā* against the infidels. In a letter sent to Shāh-Rukh justifying his expedition against Karaman, Murād II argues that the latter had impeded the *ghazā* by attacking him from the rear.

In the *fetḥ-nāme* which he sent to the sultan of Egypt after his great victory in Constantinople, Meḥmed the Conqueror concedes to him the duty of 'reviving the obligation of the Pilgrimage', reserving for himself that of being the only king to 'fit out the people waging the holy wars of *ghazā* and *jihād*'.[1] The *ghazā* became so important as a source of political influence and power in the Muslim world that other Muslim kings also tried to gain the title of *ghāzī,* e.g. Tīmūr and Uzun Ḥasan. But none of them could compare in stature with the Ottoman sultans who fought for Islam in ceaseless wars in Europe, the Mediterranean and the Indian Ocean. This is why as the Christian threat grew for the Muslim countries of Asia, the influence and the power of the Ottomans increased proportionately in the Muslim world. The Ottomans did not fail to make the most of this. In Asia as in Europe, the *ghazā* was the main factor in Ottoman expansion.

[1] Feridūn, *Munsha'āt al-salāṭīn* (Istanbul, 1274), I, 236.

PART III

THE CENTRAL ISLAMIC LANDS IN THE OTTOMAN PERIOD

CHAPTER I

THE RISE OF THE OTTOMAN EMPIRE

SULTAN MEḤMED THE CONQUEROR

Imperial expansion

Two independent sources report that Meḥmed II made the following points at the meeting which decided to proceed with the conquest of Constantinople: 'The *ghazā* is our basic duty, as it was in the case of our fathers. Constantinople, situated as it is in the middle of our dominions, protects the enemies of our state and incites them against us. The conquest of this city is, therefore, essential to the future and the safety of the Ottoman state'.[1] These words reaffirmed the policy of conquest pursued by Bāyezīd. They drew attention to cases when the Byzantine empire had given refuge to claimants to the Ottoman throne, thus causing frequent civil wars. They also showed that it was the Byzantine empire which had been the main instigator of crusades. It was also within the bounds of possibility that Constantinople could be surrendered to Western Catholics, as Salonica had been. This would have meant that the Ottoman empire would never be fully integrated. In brief, the conquest of Constantinople was a matter of vital concern to the Ottomans.

The siege of Constantinople lasted for fifty-four days (25 Rabīʿ I–20 Jumādā I 857/6 April–29 May 1453). In the Turkish camp Chandarlı continued to draw attention to the great danger of provoking the Western Christian world, and to advocate a compromise. Zaganuz Pasha argued against this that the Ottomans' adversaries could never unite, and that even if an army were sent from the West, Ottoman forces would prove superior, but that, more probably, the city could be captured before the arrival of assistance from Italy. Success depended on speed. The Venetian navy had already left port. News had come of preparations by the Hungarians. When, therefore, his surrender terms had been rejected by the Byzantine Emperor Constantine XI Palaeologus, Meḥmed II ordered his army on 20 Jumādā I/29 May to deliver a general assault and pillage the city. In any case the sultan could not prevent the pillaging of a city captured against resistance, and we know that he later

[1] H. Inalcık, *Fatih devri üzerinde tedkikler ve vesikalar* (Ankara, 1954), 126.

allowed the return of those Greeks who, after the conquest, paid ransom or who had left the city before the siege. They were granted immunity from taxation for a certain time. The day after the conquest Chandarlı was dismissed and imprisoned. His rival, Zaganuz, was appointed grand *vezīr* in his place.

The conquest of Constantinople turned Meḥmed II overnight into the most celebrated sultan in the Muslim world. He began to see himself in the light of an heir to a world-wide empire. He believed in the absolute character of his power, and wished Istanbul to become the centre of the world in all respects. He devoted thirty years of his reign to the realization of these aims. It was Meḥmed the Conqueror who established the distinctive character and nature of the Ottoman empire.

The ideal of universal empire entertained by Meḥmed the Conqueror was derived from various sources. As far back as the reign of Murād II, a chronicler claimed that as 'Os̱mān Ghāzī had come from the tribe of Kayı, he had been chosen sovereign by the Turkish beys of the marches. He then adds: 'According to the tradition of the Oghuz bequeathed by Gün Khān, as long as the clan of Kayı remains in existence, none other deserves the khanate and sovereignty.' Whatever the historical value of this claim, the Ottoman dynasty made this view its own in order to give a legal title to its dominion over other Turkish princes and, particularly, in order to rebut the claims to overlordship advanced by Tīmūr and his descendants. This is also why the *damgha* or seal of the Kayı clan was used on Ottoman coinage.

At the same time the Ottomans believed strongly in the teaching of Islam on the sources of sovereignty. We have emphasized earlier the great lengths to which Meḥmed the Conqueror himself went to rest his authority on his title of *ghāzī*. But, with the conquest of Constantinople, Meḥmed the Conqueror became heir to a third tradition: in 870/1466 G. Trapezuntios addressed the Conqueror in the following manner: 'No one doubts that you are the Emperor of the Romans. Whoever is legally master of the capital of the Empire is the Emperor and Constantinople is the capital of the Roman Empire.'[1] According to Giacomo de' Languschi, a contemporary of the Conqueror, 'In his [the Conqueror's] view, there should be only one Empire, only one faith and only one sovereign in the whole world. No place was more deserving than Istanbul for the creation of this unity in the world. The Conqueror believed that thanks to this city he could extend his rule over the whole

[1] F. Babinger, *Mehmed II. der Eroberer und seine Zeit* (Munich, 1953), 266.

Christian world.'[1] No doubt Meḥmed II used this tradition as a political weapon and as a point of departure for his conquests. He saw in all three titles, the titles of Khan, *Ghāzī* and Caesar, gates leading to dominion over the whole world. It was for this reason that Meḥmed the Conqueror saw to it that the Greek Orthodox patriarch, the Armenian patriarch and the Jewish chief rabbi all resided in his capital, Istanbul, and ordered the making of a *mappa mundi*. The Conqueror created in his person the prototype of Ottoman sultans combining Turkish, Islamic and Byzantine traditions.

His conquests make it clear that his first aim was to revive the Byzantine empire under his rule. As Kemāl Pasha-zāde says, he sought to leave no one 'among the Byzantine Greeks who could be named king (*tekfur*)'.[2] He thus eliminated the Byzantine empire of Trebizond, the two despots of the Palaeologus dynasty in the Morea, and the Gattilusi family which was related to the Palaeologi. Secondly, he placed the whole Balkan peninsula south of the Danube under his direct rule, removing all local dynasties. Finally, he occupied the ports in southern Crimea (880/1475) and the city of Otranto in southern Italy (885/1480) which used to belong to the Byzantine empire.

The attempt at establishing undivided rule over the Balkans brought Meḥmed the Conqueror into conflict with Hungary across the Danube, and with Venice in Albania, Greece and the Aegean Sea. The papacy tried to lead the whole of Europe on a crusade in support of these two states.

The Conqueror and Venice both tried to avoid war, until it became inevitable in 867/1463. The Conqueror knew that his navy was weak, while Venice had obtained favourable terms for trade under an agreement which it made with the sultan in 858/1454. Freedom of trade was granted to the republic and customs duty at entry and exit was fixed at only two per cent *ad valorem*. Permission was granted to the Venetians to keep a permanent *bailo* in Istanbul to look after their interests. A similar privilege to trade freely was given to the Genoese in the Archipelago and in the Crimea on condition of payment of tribute, i.e. of accepting Ottoman suzerainty. Meḥmed the Conqueror realized the prime importance of trade with the West for his country and for his treasury. In 867/1463, when he broke with the Venetians, he encouraged the Florentines to take charge of trade with Europe.

[1] F. Babinger, 'Mehmed II der Eroberer und Italien', in *Byzantion*, XXI (1951), 140.

[2] Kemāl Pasha-zāde (facsimile edn., TTK, Ankara, 1954), 186, 613.

Between 858/1454 and 867/1463 Meḥmed fought for mastery in the Balkans. In the north, the Serbian principality, revived in 848/1444, formed a gap through which Hungarian influence penetrated to the heart of the Balkans. In the south, the Morea could at any time fall into the hands of the Venetians. Meḥmed led two expeditions into Serbia in 858/1454 and 859/1455, and succeeded in making Serbia more firmly a part of the Ottoman empire. He failed, however, to defeat the Hungarians at Belgrade (860/1456). When Branković, the despot of Serbia, died in 862/1458, Serbia became once again an apple of discord between the Hungarians and the Ottomans. There was a Hungarian party and an Ottoman party in the country. After two further expeditions, in 862/1458 and in 863/1459, the independent existence of the principality was terminated and Serbia was annexed to the Ottoman empire. The Ottomans incorporated the local military class into their own army organization and maintained certain local laws. In the Morea a violent struggle developed between two Palaeologi princes, Demetrius having sought the protection of the Ottomans, while Thomas requested that of Venice. After two expeditions, in 862/1458 and 864/1460, Meḥmed succeeded in occupying the Morea. Nevertheless, the Venetians kept a foothold in the fortresses of Nauplia, Modon and Coron, which were built in inaccessible coastal fastnesses, and could be supplied by sea. When, in 867/1463, local Greeks surrendered the castle of Argos to the Ottomans, the Venetians launched a general offensive. They held the isthmus of Corinth and occupied the peninsula. The Ottomans then declared war on the Venetians. The war lasted from 867/1463 to 884/1479, and brought Meḥmed many problems.

In 867/1463 the Ottoman occupation of Bosnia led to renewed hostilities with Hungary. The Hungarians established themselves in Gajče in northern Bosnia, and acted in alliance with Venice. The allies gave encouragement to Iskender Bey (Scanderbeg), whose rebellion in northern Albania had started in 847/1443. Envoys were exchanged between Venice and Uzun Ḥasan, ruler of the Ak-Koyunlu dynasty, with a view to an alliance. Pope Pius II summoned the crusading armies to Ancona, where he went in person the following year. The allies drew up plans for the partition of the Ottoman empire. The Venetian navy cruised outside the mouth of the Dardanelles. Meḥmed had recourse to extraordinary measures to parry the danger. To cover Istanbul and his naval base at Gallipoli, he built two powerful fortresses facing each other across the Dardanelles, in the winter of

868/1463–4. In Istanbul he had a new shipyard built, and strengthened his navy. He despatched Maḥmūd Pasha at the head of a powerful army into the Morea, which was reoccupied. He himself led two expeditions into Albania in 870/1466 and 871/1467.

The greatest crisis of the war arose in Anatolia on account of the Karaman dynasty. A struggle for succession between members of the dynasty brought Meḥmed into collision with Uzun Ḥasan. In 873/1468 Meḥmed finally annexed the territory of Karaman. Nevertheless, members of the Karaman dynasty continued the struggle at the head of warlike tribes in the Taurus Mountains. In 876/1471 Uzun Ḥasan used his position of ruler of Persia to interfere in central Anatolia, thus following in the footsteps of Tīmūr. He extended his protection to the beys of Anatolia, some of whom had been forced by the Conqueror to leave their lands, and had sought refuge in Persia. In 877/1472 Venice, Cyprus, the Knights of Rhodes and Uzun Ḥasan formed an alliance. Uzun Ḥasan promised to send a force of 30,000 men to the shores of the Mediterranean where they were to be joined by Venetians armed with firearms. In 877/1472 Uzun Ḥasan raided the city of Tokat, which was pillaged and destroyed. The joint army of Karaman and of the Ak-Koyunlu penetrated as far as Akshehir in western Anatolia. Faced with danger on all sides, Meḥmed retaliated by mobilizing his entire army, estimated at 70,000 to 100,000 men, against Uzun Ḥasan. The following year Uzun Ḥasan's forces were completely routed at Bashkent in eastern Anatolia. This victory resolved the greatest crisis which Meḥmed the Conqueror had to face. Uzun Ḥasan made peace, promising to refrain from further incursions into Ottoman territory. In the meantime Gedik Aḥmed Pasha suppressed the resistance of the Taurus tribes and, occupying the coast of the Mediterranean, completed the conquest of Karaman in 879/1474. Between 870/1466 and 875/1470 the Ottomans came up against the Mamluks, who had aided the Karaman dynasty and the Dulgadır (Dhu'l-Qadr) Turcomans further to the east. The struggle for suzerainty over the Dulgadır principality brought these two most powerful states of Islam to the brink of war.

Having thus resolved the problems of Anatolia and extended his rule over the whole country as far as the Euphrates, Meḥmed turned his attention to the war with Venice. He besieged the castle of Scutari in 879/1474 and 883/1478. Ottoman *akıncı* raiders crossed the Isonzo and appeared in sight of Venice. The republic sued for peace. The peace treaty surrendered Scutari, Croia, and the islands of Lemnos and Euboea (Negroponte) to the Ottomans, and provided for the payment of an annual tribute of 10,000 gold pieces. Freedom to trade was, however, restored to Venice.

Meḥmed, having thus forced the strongest naval power in the Mediterranean to make peace, set two further goals to the Ottoman navy: the conquest of Rhodes, considered the gate to the Mediterranean, and the occupation of Italy, which seemed ripe for conquest. In 885/1480 while Mesīḥ Pasha made a landing in Rhodes, Gedik Aḥmed Pasha landed before Otranto. The Knights of St John defeated Mesīḥ Pasha's forces, but Gedik Aḥmed Pasha succeeded in his task, and captured Otranto on 4 Jumādā II 885/11 August 1480. He left a garrison in the city, which thus became an Ottoman bridgehead in Italy. He then returned to Albania, in order to bring together a strong army for further conquests the following year. The pope made preparations to flee to France.

After he had become the undisputed master of the Straits, Meḥmed II succeeded in extending his mastery over the Black Sea. In 858/1454 he forced the Genoese colonies there to pay tribute, and then occupied them one by one. He also exacted tribute from Moldavia (22 Shawwāl 859/5 October 1455). Most important of all, he secured the co-operation of the tribal aristocracy of the Crimea, whom he protected against the Genoese and the Golden Horde. The khanate of the Crimea thus became an Ottoman vassal state in 880/1475.

When Meḥmed the Conqueror died in 886/1481 at the age of forty-nine, the expeditions in Egypt, Italy and the Mediterranean were left unfinished. He had fought the *ghazā* war without a break, to a degree that even a contemporary historian found excessive; as he claimed, he had become, within a space of thirty years, the master of two seas and two continents, and had laid the foundations of Ottoman rule in Anatolia and the Balkans, which were to remain unshaken for four centuries. He also gave their final form to the institutions of the empire and determined the course of its future political development.

The development of a centralized absolutist administration

In order to become an absolute sultan, holding in his hands the authority of the state in its entirety, and ruling the whole empire from his capital, Meḥmed eliminated, or at least transformed, the elements which could have resisted him. At his accession to the throne he suppressed with a heavy hand a revolt of the Janissaries. Many Janissaries were expelled from the corps, and new units were formed from the palace huntsmen. These new formations were known as *Sekban,* and the commander (*agha*) of the Janissaries came to be chosen from among them. The pay of the Janissaries was increased, their weapons were improved and their strength raised from 5,000 to 10,000. Thus reorganized, the Janissaries became the nucleus of the Ottoman army. Thanks to this force, which was always ready for service, and which was immediately subordinate to the sultan, who chose their commanders personally, the sultan could overpower any opponent in the imperial territory or in the marches. The beys of the marches were thus reduced to the level of ordinary beys of *sanjaks*. Janissaries were used to garrison newly conquered castles. They were not subordinate to the local governor or to any local authority, and took their orders direct from the capital. No other force was allowed in the castles which they garrisoned. The Janissaries were also responsible for preventing oppression of non-Muslims by Muslims in the cities outside the castle walls, and for compelling obedience to the orders of the sultan. In brief, the Janissaries represented in the provinces the central authority of the sultan.

Meḥmed viewed his own personal authority in a much wider light than his predecessors had done. He did not frequent the meetings of the Council of State (*Dīvān*), and arranged for affairs to be seen through a Chamber of Petitions, through which important matters were submitted to his decision. Murād II had allowed the grand *vezīr* Chandarlı Khalīl, who belonged to an established family of *vezīrs* and of *'ulemā'*, to decide affairs of state. It was only after the conquest of Constantinople that Meḥmed dared dismiss his aristocratic minister. Thereafter he chose all his ministers, with the exception of Karamanı Meḥmed, from among his personal slaves. The grand *vezīr* became the obedient instrument of the sultan's commands. Meḥmed did not hesitate to order the execution of his most famous *vezīr,* Maḥmūd Pasha. On the other hand, the authority of the grand *vezīr* as his master's steward in all things, was widened. The sultan's old tutor, Mollā Gūrānī, was forced to resign from the office of *qāḍī 'asker* when he made appointments without consulting the grand *vezīr*. Since the time of the autonomous principalities, the *qāḍī 'askers* had always been counted among the sultan's most influential assistants and advisers. As we have seen, *vezīrs* were usually chosen from among them. However, in the reign of Meḥmed, Mollā Gūrānī, when offered the position of *vezīr,* refused the offer on the grounds that this dignity now went to slaves brought up in court. The grand *vezīr* Maḥmūd Pasha also held the post of *beylerbeyi* of Rumelia, which afforded him the control of the greatest force of *timar*-holding *sipahis* in the empire.

Under the Conqueror, not only the grand vezirate, but also a host of other functions went to the sultan's personal slaves. Governors, *timar*-holders, taxation officers and executive officers charged with applying the sultan's regulations and decrees were mostly chosen from among slaves. Under the *Sharīʿa* and state (*ʿurfī*) law, the issue of judicial decisions and the control of the administration were the exclusive privilege of *qāḍīs*. The administration of justice was thus left in the hands of the *ʿulemā*'. The execution of justice, on the other hand, fell to the charge of state officials, in other words, to the sultan's slaves representing their master's executive authority. There were, however, cases of members of the class of *Sharīʿa* officials being transferred to the class of *beys* and of *qāḍīs* being appointed as *beylerbeyis*.

As the absolute steward of the sultan, the grand *vezīr* supervized the work and confirmed the decisions of the *defterdār*, who was in charge of the financial side of the administration, and of the *qāḍī ʿasker* and *qāḍīs*, who were responsible for the administration of justice. These officials were, however, autonomous in their separate departments and directly answerable to the sultan. The grand *vezīr* was not entitled to issue orders directly to the commander of the Janissaries. This prevented him from concentrating in his hands the whole range of state authority. The sultan reserved for himself the last word in these three main areas of state affairs. A fourth area represented the chancery work of the central government and the province of state law. Representatives of these four branches of central government were *ex officio* members of the *Dīvān*. According to the Regulation (*Qānūn*) of Meḥmed the Conqueror, the right to draw up orders and decisions in the sultan's name belonged to the grand *vezīr* in general matters, to the *defterdār* in financial matters, and to the *qāḍī ʿaskers* in matters concerning litigation. Four days a week these officials attended the Council of Petitions and submitted matters to the sultan's decision. Meḥmed inherited this system from his predecessors, but he modified it and added to it, and codified the result in his *Qānūn-nāme*, which established the final form of the institutions of the state. The promulgation of a *qānūn-nāme*, or 'book of laws', which is foreign to Muslim traditions, derives from Turkish state traditions. Muslim Turkish sovereigns never surrendered their absolute authority to promulgate rules for the regulation of their policies and of their administration. In this manner the province of state law kept on expanding by the side of the *Sharī'a*. Until the beginning of the tenth/sixteenth century the Ottomans held that in his capacity of *pādishāh,* the sultan had the absolute right to promulgate state law without the intervention of *Sharī'a* jurists. Meḥmed the Conqueror made use of this right to issue many laws and regulations as the sultan's orders.

The Conqueror's contemporaries report that Meḥmed behaved with great severity in all matters affecting the implementation of laws and regulations and of affairs of state in general. He did not except his own children from the operation of the law. His prestige was such that no one dared object to his actions, in spite of the existence of discontent, and he reacted forcibly to attempts at interference by the '*ulemā*'.

In the Ottoman empire there was no law or rule regulating succession to the throne. To be exact, in accordance with old Turkish tradition, as the ruler derived his authority from God, God should decide who was to be ruler. No legal heir to the throne could therefore be appointed. An attempt by Meḥmed I to nominate a successor proved fruitless. All the sultan's sons were held to have an equal right to the throne. The death of a sultan was inevitably followed by strife among his sons. A striking instance of the danger which this represented for the empire was provided by the struggles among the sons and grandsons of Bāyezīd I. Pretenders who sought refuge with foreign princes were a source of constant danger. An Ottoman prince had fought against Meḥmed on the walls of Constantinople. When Meḥmed succeeded to the throne he had his infant brother strangled. Later, in his *Qānūn-nāme,* Meḥmed the Conqueror stipulated that it was appropriate for a sultan to execute his brothers on his accession to the throne 'for the order of the world' i.e. for the sake of peace in his dominions. An action necessary 'for the order of the world' was in any case canonically licit. He wanted to make no concessions from the principle of the indivisiblity of the state and of sovereignty. These principles were to be tested in the struggles between Jem and Bāyezīd II, and later among the sons of Bāyezīd II and Süleymān I, but the principle of the unity of the Ottoman realm was never sacrificed. However, the same Ottoman opinion which accepted fratricide as necessary for the preservation of order in the ninth/fifteenth century refused to countenance it towards the end of the tenth/sixteenth century. Then, with the help of certain special circumstances, the custom of seniority, viz., that the eldest surviving member of the dynasty was to succeed to the throne, established itself.

Finances, land reform and trade

Meḥmed II's financial and land policies also brought many reforms in their train. In order to be able to extend his empire, he strained to make the fullest possible use of the country's resources. This, however, led to extreme social and political tensions after his death. The Conqueror's measures can be summarized as follows:

Monetary policy. New coins were minted and the old withdrawn from circulation and bought by the mint at five-sixths of their face-value. This measure, which was subsequently used by every sultan on accession, was repeated by Meḥmed II on four occasions, causing great discontent in the country. It meant in effect that the state levied a tax of one-sixth on silver coinage circulating in the empire. To enforce this measure the sultan sent to the provinces executive officials known as 'silver seekers', who searched the houses of merchants and caravanserais, and had the right to confiscate any hidden coins which they found. Meḥmed's policy of changing the standard of silver led to complaints by both local and foreign merchants.

Monopolies. Meḥmed farmed out to private individuals provincial monopolies in essential goods such as salt, soap and candle-wax. The state treasury derived immense benefits from these monopolies, and the sultan's legislation provided for severe penalties for their infringement. A contemporary chronicler protests against these as unprecedented innovations (*bid'at*) in the Ottoman realm.

Confiscation of waqfs *and private property.* A large part of the land held by *waqfs* and private individuals was confiscated by the state and became 'royal land' after 880/1475. This measure led to grave discontent throughout the empire. Much of this land, however, originally belonged to the state and was later transferred by various means to pious foundations or private individuals. Meḥmed ordered the investigation of titles to these lands, and laid down rules for the transfer of land to the state, as in the case of land that went with ruined buildings originally bequeathed as pious foundations. According to a chronicler 20,000 villages or estates held in this way were transferred to the state and then assigned in *timars* to *sipahi* cavalry. This reform was designed to increase the number of *sipahis* for the frequent expeditions. However, numerous people were harmed, and opposition centred round the sultan's son Bāyezīd, governor of Amasya, who was on bad terms with his father. The abolition of many pious foundations harmed mainly the *'ulemā'* and certain old-established Turkish Muslim families. Rich, influential families tried to convert the land which they controlled into *waqf* in the hope that their descendants might derive a sure income from it as trustees. Only a sultan as powerful as the Conqueror was capable of carrying through this reform, but at his death a violent reaction broke out.

The large-scale military and political operations on which the Ottoman empire embarked in the ninth/fifteenth century, were made possible by the development of commercial and economic life in the empire, and by the increase in state revenue which followed. The Ottoman empire tried to put an end to the political dominion and to the privileged economic position of the Franks (Europeans) in the Levant. It abolished the complete immunity from customs dues which the Venetians and Genoese had wrested from the Byzantine empire in its decline. Up to the time of Meḥmed II, customs dues were as low as two per cent. After 865/1460 he raised the tariff to four per cent for *dhimmīs,* and to five per cent to foreigners from non-Muslim lands (*dār al-ḥarb*) who were allowed to trade under treaties of capitulation (sing., *āmān-nāme*). This policy was noisily greeted as a catastrophe by the Frankish merchants who were used to exploiting the Levant trade.[1] In fact, the political order established by the Ottomans produced conditions of safety, provided a link between remote areas and brought about an economic integration of the region as a whole. Istanbul, which developed rapidly in Meḥmed's reign, and cities such as Bursa, Edirne and Gallipoli, which had earlier become centres of international trade, profited from this commercial revival. In trade between provinces, Muslim merchants, as well as non-Muslim Ottoman subjects, such as Greeks, Armenians and Jews, took the place of Italians. Customs-registers show a preponderance of these newcomers. A well-established cotton industry in western Anatolia, the mohair industry in Ankara and Tosya, the silk industry in Istanbul and Bursa were exporters to European markets.

Bursa in the ninth/fifteenth century was also the international entrepôt for Astarābādī (*Staravi*) silks produced in Persia and greatly prized in Europe. It was the goal of annual silk caravans. Bursa was the last stage on the road to the West travelled by Muslim caravans, and was also the entrepôt for Arabian and Indian goods sent through Damascus. Although spices were expensive in Bursa, they were despatched from that city to Wallachia, Moldavia and Lemburg. The

[1] H. Inalcık, 'Bursa and the commerce of the Levant', *JESHO*, III/2 (1960), 131–47.

Florentines considered it more profitable to exchange spices against cloth in Bursa than to buy them with gold in Egypt and Syria. Towards the end of Meḥmed's reign, Maḥmūd Gāwān, the famous *wazīr* of the Bahmanids in India, sent his own agents with merchandise to Bursa, and these Indians then went on to the Balkans. Bursa was also the gateway for the export of European woollens to Eastern countries. Silk merchants took them from Bursa on their return journey to Persia.

Valuable merchandise such as spices, dyes and Indian cloth generally followed the old trade-routes, crossing Anatolia diagonally from Damascus through Adana and Konya. A second way was the sea-route from Egyptian and Syrian ports via Antalya to Bursa. This short and cheap route was used mainly for heavy goods. Logs, planks and iron ore were exported from Anatolia to Egypt by sea from the ports of Antalya and 'Alā'iyya. We know that around 885/1480 Turkish merchants from Bursa, engaged in this trade, formed a company with a capital of half a million aspers. As in Anatolia under the Seljuks, so too in the Ottoman empire in the ninth/fifteenth century, Turkish Muslims were still preeminent in trade and industry and formed an influential class *vis-à-vis* the administration. It was only after the tenth/sixteenth century, when western European trade grew in importance, that *dhimmīs,* such as Armenians, Greeks and Jews, came to dominate trade in the Ottoman empire.

The reconstruction of Istanbul

Among Meḥmed II's main concerns was to make Istanbul one of the world's political and economic centres, to turn it into a populous city, to develop it and adorn it with new buildings. Before the Ottoman conquest, Constantinople had been like a head without a body, and in the last days of the Byzantine empire, it was a poor and largely depopulated city of ruins. After the conquest, Meḥmed tried to repopulate the city, from which its old inhabitants had fled. Until the end of his reign Meḥmed continued to resettle the city through the system of forcible settlement (*sürgün*) and other measures. Greeks, Italians and Jews were brought for settlement to the city from Phocea in western Anatolia, from Argos and elsewhere in the Morea, from the islands of Thasos, Samothrace, Mytilene and Euboea, from Amasra, Trebizond and Kaffa in the Black Sea. Meḥmed encouraged Jews to come from as far away as Germany and Italy. Considerable numbers of Muslim Turks and Christians were forcibly brought from Konya, Aksaray, Bursa and Ereghli in

Anatolia. Prisoners of war were settled in new villages round the city. The Conqueror saw to the repair of roads and bridges leading into Istanbul. In the winter of 859/1455 he ordered the building of the famous covered market known as Büyük Bedesten, 'the Grand Bazaar'. The same year he issued instructions for the repair of aqueducts to ensure adequate water supplies for his capital. He often inspected in person the construction work which he had set afoot. He had his first palace (Eski Saray, 'the Old Palace') built in the centre of the city. Later he found it inconvenient and had another palace built on Seraglio Point, which became known as Yeni Saray, or 'the New Palace'; later the name was changed to Topkapı Sarayı or 'Palace of the Cannon Gate'. This second palace was completed in 868/1464.

As in the case of the development of other Ottoman cities, the institution of *waqfs* (pious foundations) played the primary role in the reconstruction of Istanbul. It was this institution which secured the performance of a variety of public services: the construction and maintenance of public buildings, mosques, premises for trade, lodgings for travellers, fountains, baths, bridges, schools and hospitals. No claim could be further from the truth than the allegation that the Ottoman state had no conception of public service and that it bent all its energies to the exploitation of its subjects. It was considered a religious duty to see to their prosperity.

The Ottoman empire was the most successful Muslim state in developing *waqfs* for this purpose.[1] *Waqfs* were under close official control. Private persons had formerly been allowed to set them up on the strength of a single deed (*waqfiyya*) drawn up by a *qāḍī*. This was later changed and it was made obligatory for *waqfiyyas* to be approved and registered by the central government. At his accession to the throne, each sultan had the *waqfiyyas* checked and then either confirmed them by a diploma (*berāt*) or cancelled them. Pious foundations set up by Christians were subject to the same control. Meḥmed abolished the trusts connected with some monasteries of Trebizond, but confirmed those relating to Mount Athos. In 934/1528 *waqfs* in Anatolia were charged with the upkeep of 45 almshouses for the poor and for travellers, 342 Friday mosques, 1,095 smaller mosques, 110 *medreses*, 626 dervish convents, 154 schools for

[1] In 934/1528 the expenses of pious foundations held in trust and freehold amounted to sixteen per cent of the state revenue: see Ö. L. Barkan, 'H 933-934 Malî Yılına ait bir Bütçe Örneği' in *Iktisat Fakültesi Mecmuası*, (Journal of the Faculty of Economics, Istanbul University), IV, 259.

children, 75 caravanserais, 238 bath-houses and other establishments. In the eighth/fourteenth and ninth/fifteenth centuries, *waqfs* helped numerous Ottoman cities, and not least Istanbul, to become distinctively Muslim Turkish.

BĀYEZĪD II

Reaction and civil war

Meḥmed II's death was followed by a bloody revolt of the Janissaries, a dangerous civil war between two pretenders to the throne, Jem and Bāyezīd, and widespread movement of reaction against the Conqueror's policies.

During the last years of Meḥmed's reign, the conduct of affairs was in the hands of the grand *vezīr*, Karamani Meḥmed Pasha. The grand *vezīr's* land policy, the new taxes which he introduced, his appointment of *'ulemā'* to the *Dīvān* as *vezīrs*, all these factors combined to win him the enmity of old functionaries like Isḥāq Pasha and Gedik Aḥmed Pasha, who had risen from the class of the sultan's slaves. An extensive plot was laid by the opposition as soon as Meḥmed was dead. The opposition found natural allies in the Janissaries and in the Conqueror's son, Bāyezīd, who was at that time governor of Amasya, and was supported by people discontented at Meḥmed's financial measures. Meḥmed's other son, Jem, who was at his father's death governor of Konya, appeared bent on continuing the policy of strict administration and of conquests. Meḥmed had, in any case, favoured him as his successor. Urged on by Isḥāq Pasha, the Janissaries returned to Istanbul from the deceased sultan's camp, murdered the grand *vezīr*, Karamanı Meḥmed Pasha, and plundered shops and other commercial premises. Isḥāq Pasha prevented Jem from reaching the capital, brought Bāyezīd to Istanbul and secured his accession to the throne (21 Rabī' I 886/20 May 1481). The new sultan was made to promise that he would discontinue his father's practice of making frequent issues of new currency, and would return freehold and *waqf* property to its owners. A letter written by an influential adviser recommended the sultan to abandon his father's policies and return to those of his grandfather, Murād II. In the meantime Jem had arrived in Bursa, proclaimed himself sultan, and had coins minted in his name. With the help of Isḥāq Pasha, Bāyezīd persuaded Gedik Aḥmed Pasha to give up his Italian expedition and return from Albania. This great commander, whom the Janissaries worshipped, succeeded in defeating

Jem, and became the real master of the empire. But he overreached himself by openly criticizing Bāyezīd, the sultan's entourage from Amasya, and the hesitant policy he followed. As soon as the danger posed by Jem was overcome by his flight to Rhodes, Gedik Aḥmed Pasha was killed after a banquet (6 Shawwāl 887/18 November 1482). His father-in-law Isḥāq Pasha, was made to withdraw from active life.

Map 6. Ottoman expansion in Europe.

Bāyezīd was now truly master of his throne. For his father's hard policy he substituted a pacific, soft and tolerant approach. He returned much of the property which his father had expropriated and was in consequence praised to the skies as a just ruler. Contemporary writers described him as Bāyezīd the Law-abiding (*Bāyezīd-i 'Adlī*).

Culturally, the reign of Bāyezīd (886–918/1481–1512) also represented a reaction against the trends of the previous reign. Bāyezīd removed the frescoes which his father had commissioned from Italian artists for the walls of his New Palace, and had them sold in the bazaars. He fell under the influence of the '*ulemā*' whom he had brought with him from Amasya. He observed scrupulously the provisions of the *Sharī'a* in order to win popular support and strengthen his power against the claims advanced by Jem. His attachment to a Sunnī policy and to the *Sharī'a* became firmer later on, when Shāh Ismā'īl launched a Shī'ī propaganda campaign in Anatolia. As a further means of strengthening his position after the elimination of Gedik Aḥmed Pasha, Bāyezīd attempted to win new laurels in the *ghazā*. For his field of operations he chose Moldavia, where his father had suffered a reverse. He captured Kili and Akkerman from the prince of Moldavia, Stephen the Great, a protégé of Poland, which was at that time trying to penetrate to the shores of the Black Sea and the Crimea. These two cities were important entrepôts in the Mediterranean trade of northern Europe. Stephen was obliged to accept vassal status in the Ottoman empire in order to safeguard his vital stake in this trade. However, influence and mastery over Moldavia remained the main point at issue in the struggles between Ottomans and Poles. It caused the first great war between the two countries (901–3/1496–8).

The Moldavian expedition earned Bāyezīd the prestige which he needed. Until Jem's death (29 Jumādā I 900/25 February 1495), Bāyezīd's home and foreign policies were governed largely by the fear of his return. Jem, who was in the hands of the Knights of Rhodes, an order under papal jurisdiction, became the subject of protracted negotiation between the papacy and Christian princes, the king of Hungary being chief among them, who wanted to use him in a crusade against the Ottomans. Bāyezīd succeeded, however, in concluding an agreement with the Knights, under which he was to pay them 45,000 gold pieces a year, allegedly to cover Jem's expenses, as long as they held Jem captive. After seven years of internment in France, Jem was removed to Rome (1 Rabī' II 894/4 March 1489) and this important source of revenue passed into the hands of the pope. Although later Charles VIII of France managed by force to gain control of Jem's person, this unfortunate son of Meḥmed the Conqueror died while on his way to Naples. Fear of Jem moved Bāyezīd to conclude agreements with Hungary and Venice, the two states which would have been at the head of a crusade, and this ushered in a period of peace. Bāyezīd established close diplomatic contacts with Italian courts and with the papacy. There was even a *rapprochement* against Charles VIII between Bāyezīd on the one hand, and the pope, Venice and Naples on the other, when the king of France announced that after Italy his objective would be the Ottoman empire (1494). In any case, Bāyezīd needed peace in the West in order to pursue an exhausting war with the Mamluks in the East.

Relations between the Ottomans and the Mamluk Sultanate were already strained. A struggle for control over the Turcoman tribes inhabiting the frontier region was going on. The Mamluk sultan, who kept the caliph as a pensioner at his court, thereby claimed precedence over the Ottoman. The affair of Jem further embittered relations. Sultan Qā'it Bāy received Jem, and later, in 887/1482, encouraged him to undertake operations in central Anatolia jointly with a pretender to the former emirate of Karaman. Hostilities which broke out in 890/1485 developed unfavourably for the Ottomans, but after six major campaigns both sides were sufficiently exhausted to make peace on the basis of the *status quo* (896/1491).

Italian wars and the Ottoman war with Venice

When the danger posed by Jem disappeared, Bāyezīd put in hand an unprecedented naval construction programme. The Ottoman empire was getting ready to make a firm riposte to any crusading adventures. In the course of the Italian wars, the Ottoman state became an essential factor in European diplomacy. Whenever a European state found itself in desperate straits in Italy, it tried, as a last resort, to frighten its enemies by spreading the rumour that it was about to receive help from the Ottomans. In 902/1497 Milan, Ferrara, Mantua and Florence applied to Bāyezīd for help against the Franco-Venetian alliance. They offered him 50,000 ducats a year as payment for an attack against Venice. Conditions in the West thus favoured an Ottoman attempt to clear the last Christian strongpoint in the Balkans. Bāyezīd consented to help. In any case, the Italian campaign, interrupted in 885/1480, continued to preoccupy the minds of some Ottoman commanders. Also, the alliance between Venice and France was causing considerable apprehension to the Ottomans.

The war with Venice (904–8/1499–1502) showed that the Ottoman navy could now meet Venice, hitherto the paramount naval power in the Mediterranean, in equal combat. The Ottoman army, led by the sultan in person, and navy, acting together, captured Lepanto on 21 Muḥarram 905/28 August 1499. The following year French envoys came with threatening messages to Istanbul, hoping to force the Ottomans to make peace. Venice worked hard to organize a crusading alliance. The pope was active in the same field. The Italian rivals of Venice gave, however, further encouragement to Bāyezīd. The sultan promised to assist the king of Naples with 25,000 troops, on condition Otranto was ceded to him. In the campaign in 905/1500 Ottoman land and sea forces wrested from the Venetians the castles of Modon and Coron in the Morea. Venice finally succeeded in persuading Hungary to enter the war. The Hungarians attacked Serbia. The Ottomans feared also lest Poland, Moldavia and Russia should join the alliance against them. In the Mediterranean, Venice received naval assistance from the Spanish, the French, the Knights of Rhodes, the pope and the Portuguese. Faced with this coalition and also with the growing seriousness of the situation in Anatolia, the Ottomans did not attempt to capture the remaining Venetian castles in the Morea, Nauplia and Monemvasia. Bāyezīd's friends in Italy were defeated, first Milan and then, in 906/1501, Naples falling to the French and the Spaniards. Bāyezīd did not dare to cross the sea with his army from Epirus. The French and Venetian navies joined forces in an attack on Mytilene. The following year peace negotiations started in Istanbul. A peace treaty with Venice was signed in Istanbul on 13 Jumādā II 908/14 December 1502; peace with Hungary and the other Christian states was concluded in Budapest on 26 Ramaḍān 908/25 March 1503. The particular importance of this war lay in the fact that it marked the beginning of Ottoman supremacy in the Mediterranean. Secondly, during the first stage of the Italian wars, the Ottomans entered European politics as an important factor of the balance of power.

It is important to note that in 887/1482 the Muslim ruler of Granada sent an ambassador to the Ottoman court asking for the aid of the only *ghāzī* state disposing of naval forces at that time. Handicapped by the affair of Jem, the Ottoman government had to content itself for a long time with expressing its sympathy. Practical assistance was left to Turkish corsairs. When Granada fell to the Spaniards in 898/1492 and the Muslim states of North Africa were threatened with invasion, these corsairs, or more properly speaking, sea-*ghāzīs*, gradually transferred their operations from the eastern to the western Mediterranean. The most famous of them, Kemāl Re'īs, officially entered the Ottoman service in 900/1494. The reforms which he brought about in the Ottoman navy laid the foundation of its future victories. Bāyezīd paid particular attention to his navy. A contemporary historian, Kemāl Pasha-zāde, mentions the Ottoman empire's status as a sea power as one of the causes of its supremacy.

Shāh Ismāʿīl and the Qizilbāsh *danger in Anatolia*

The most important reason which led Bāyezīd to wind up the Venetian war at the earliest opportunity, was the appearance of a serious threat to Ottoman supremacy in Anatolia. The struggle which ensued was in fact a continuation of the struggle for power in central Anatolia which had taken place in the two previous centuries. The Ottoman administration had moved to the Balkans, under the name of *yürüks* (or *yörüks*), i.e. nomads, large numbers of tribesmen who had previously roamed the mountainous marches of Anatolia. The tribesmen who were transferred were split up and settled in widely scattered districts. Nevertheless, large numbers of these Turcoman tribesmen remained in the Taurus mountains from Tekke to Marʿash and either joined forces with pretenders from the Karaman dynasty who had found refuge in Persia, or responded to incitement from Syria or Persia and staged repeated revolts against the Ottomans.

There were important social factors underlying this state of constant discontent. As the Ottoman empire came under a centralized administration, the movements of these tribes were subjected to increasing control. Tribesmen were entered in registers, and had to pay regular taxes. The tribes, which had led an autonomous life under their beys, felt Ottoman rule as an unbearable oppression and tyranny. They tried to evade registration. There are not a few cases of Turcomans attacking Ottoman officials sent to carry out a census among them. Furthermore, as a state based on an agricultural economy and deriving most of its revenue from peasant production, the Ottoman empire tried in its laws to protect agriculture and the settled peasantry, and to restrict the movement of nomadic tribesmen, who were severely punished for the damage they caused, for their raiding expeditions and their attacks. These Turcomans showed at the same time a fanatical attachment to the Ṣūfī orders, which preached a form of Islam adapted to the life and customs of the tribes and to their residual shamanism, against a régime which stood for Sunnī Islam and the *Sharīʿa*. These Turcoman nomads, who were distinguished at the time by their red hats, became known under the general name of *Kızıl Bash*—in its Persianized form *Qizilbāsh*—or Red Heads (see below p. 396).

As early as the first half of the ninth/fifteenth century the *Qizilbāsh* gave their allegiance to the descendants of Shaykh Ṣafī al-Dīn of Ardabīl, who became head of the Zāhidī order, thenceforth known as the Safariyya, in 700/1301. Led by his descendants, such as Shaykh

Junayd and Shaykh Ḥaydar, they fought *ghazā* wars against the Greeks of Trebizond and, later, against the Georgians.

After 906/1501, the Turcoman tribes, led by the Karaman pretender who had rebelled against the Ottomans during the Jem episode, found a focal point in Ṣafī al-Dīn's family. Shaykh Ḥaydar's son, Ismā'īl, became the spiritual and political leader of the *Qizilbāsh,* and as such a dangerous rival to the Ottomans. *Qizilbāsh* envoys spread throughout Anatolia. Furthermore, Ismā'īl, who, like his ancestors, claimed the title of *ghāzī,* was also a rival of the Ottomans in warfare against the infidels. Having inherited the political ambitions of Uzun Ḥasan in Anatolia, Ismā'īl tried to conclude an alliance with Venice, from which he asked for artillery help. In 907/1502 and 913/1507 Ismā'īl made incursions into Ottoman territory. In spite of this challenge, Bāyezīd continued a peaceful policy, although his son Selīm, who was at the time governor of Trebizond, advocated a forcible riposte. In 917/1511 the *Qizilbāsh* rebelled in the country of Tekke in south-western Anatolia. Their leader Shāh-Qulī captured Kütahya and threatened Bursa. The grand *vezīr* 'Alī Pasha set out against him at the head of an army, but was killed in a pitched battle.

The *Qizilbāsh* rebellion was complicated by the fact that the sultan's sons were in violent rivalry with each other. Bāyezīd himself was sick, ageing, and had lost his standing in the army. Selīm succeeded in winning over the Janissaries and, arriving in Istanbul, deposed his father from the throne (7 Ṣafar 918/24 April 1512).

The reign of Bāyezīd II is regarded quite properly as an interval in the history of Ottoman conquests. Nevertheless, it witnessed the appearance of Ottoman naval power in the Mediterranean and saw also a large-scale development of economic and commercial life under conditions of an orderly and trustworthy administration. Important centres, such as Istanbul, Edirne and Bursa, grew rapidly, while public buildings, such as caravanserais, assumed a truly imperial grandeur in their size and artistic quality. Bāyezīd did in fact follow the path of his grandfather, in preference to that of his father, and secured for the Ottoman empire a period of internal development and economic expansion.

SELĪM I

The Persian campaign, annexation of eastern Anatolia

Sultan Selīm, known as *Yavuz* (usually rendered 'the Grim'), who reigned from 918/1512 to 926/1520, was an energetic conqueror like

Yıldırım Bāyezīd I and Meḥmed the Conqueror. Selīm, who ascended the throne in extraordinary circumstances, was also an autocrat who held the empire in an iron grip. For a time he even ruled directly without appointing a grand *vezīr*. In his letter to Sultan Tūmān-Bāy of Egypt, Selīm wrote that he intended to become the ruler of the East and of the West, like Alexander the Great. Selīm's first two years on the throne were spent in the elimination of all members of the Ottoman dynasty who could advance a claim to the throne. Then he entered into peace-negotiations with his European neighbours, and in particular with Hungary, in order to have his hands free in the East. Before embarking on a campaign against Shāh Ismā'īl, Selīm saw to it that the latter's partisans, envoys and agents in Anatolia were hunted out and killed. It is reported that their number amounted to 40,000. Selīm proclaimed his expedition against Ismā'īl as a *ghazā* against heretics who were corrupting Islam. In his reply, Shāh Ismā'īl reminded the sultan that most of the inhabitants of Anatolia had been followers of Ismā'īl's ancestors who had themselves won fame as *ghāzīs,* and asked Selīm to remember the fate of Anatolia under Tīmūr. As Selīm set off on his campaign on 3 Muḥarram 920/28 February 1514, he armed himself with written *fetvās* from the '*ulemā*' and from shaykhs, declaring that it was a religious duty to kill Ismā'īl as a heretic and an infidel. Selīm reached the frontier on 20 Jumādā I/13 July. Ismā'īl tried to lure him on into poor, mountainous country surrounded by deserts, where he hoped to destroy the Ottoman army. The Janissaries who had opposed the campaign from the start, made several attempts at mutiny saying, 'We can see no enemy, so why are we travelling in this desolate country?' Selīm suppressed their discontent with an iron hand. At the same time he sent insulting letters to the shah trying to force him to give battle. The two armies finally met at Chāldirān. Fearing the presence of Ismā'īl's followers in his own army, Selīm ordered an immediate attack (2 Rajab 920/23 August 1514). The Ottoman victory is described in the customary 'despatch of conquest' (*fetḥ-nāme*), which Selīm sent to his son Süleymān. It says that the right wing of the Ottomans was victorious, that the left wing was originally broken, but that the Janissaries and the *kapı-kulu* troops (the sultan's own slaves) saved the position with their guns and rifle-fire. Two weeks later, Selīm made a ceremonial entry into Tabrīz, where the *khuṭba* was read in his name in the mosques. Merchants, artists and notables whom Shāh Ismā'īl had forcibly rounded up in Khurāsān and settled in Tabrīz were now despatched to Istanbul. On his way back, Selīm spent the winter in

Amasya, declaring that he would pursue the war until the final destruction of Ismā'īl. He may have been thinking of conquering and annexing Persia. His army, however, was not willing to make more sacrifices. Thousands of soldiers and animals had died on the way back from Chāldirān.

In the spring of 921/1515 Selīm marched again, not against Persia, but against 'Alā' al-Dawla, prince of the Dulgadır Turcomans. 'Alā' al-Dawla was a vassal of the sultan of Egypt, and had taken up a hostile attitude during Selīm's Eastern campaign. The Dulgadır country was quickly occupied (June 1515). Selīm himself, who had been forced to give up the idea of further campaigning in Persia, hastened back to Istanbul and meted out stern punishment to those who had opposed his projects.

The Ottoman victory at Chāldirān marked a turning-point in the history of Anatolia. Eastern Anatolia was finally annexed to the Empire. Diyār Bakr was occupied in Ramaḍān 921/October 1515, and the remaining eastern Anatolian cities between 921/1515 and 923/1517. Tribes in the area were incorporated into the Ottoman state on favourable conditions. The ruler of Bitlis, Sheref Khān, travelled to Istanbul in Rabī' I 922/March 1516 to kiss the sultan's hand. The annexation of the high plateau of eastern Anatolia had great strategic significance. Anatolia acquired a natural rampart against invasions from the East. Economically, the new conquests were no less important, as through them the Ottomans acquired control of the Tabrīz-Aleppo and Tabrīz-Bursa silk roads. In 934/1528 the revenue of the province of Diyār Bakr amounted to 25 million aspers, or one-eighth of the entire revenue of the Balkans.

In his wars against Persia and the Mamluks, Selīm had recourse to economic as well as to military measures. During the war against Persia, he banned the silk trade, and exiled to the Balkans the Persian silk merchants of Bursa. He hoped in this way to cut the economic lifeline of his enemy, as silk was at that time the main article exported by Persia to the West and, therefore, the main source of the country's silver and gold revenue. Similarly, when he turned against the Mamluks, Selīm tried to stop the trade in Circassian slaves from the Caucasus.

In the eastern Anatolian plateau the Ottomans brought together the numerous Turcoman and Kurdish tribes into 'peoples' (sing., *ulus*), or tribal organizations. The Turcomans became part of the Grey People (*Boz Ulus*), and the Kurds formed the Black People (*Kara Ulus*). The Kurds were mostly Sunnīs of the Shāfi'ī *madhhab*. On the other hand, the

Turcoman tribes being mostly Shīʿī, started migrating to Persia where they formed the main force of the Safavid dynasty. The Turcoman dynasties of the Black Sheep (*Kara-Koyunlu*) and White Sheep (*Ak-Koyunlu*), which had ruled in Persia, originated from this region.

At first the Ottomans left in force the system of taxation which had been codified in the reign of Uzun Ḥasan with respect to the settled peasantry of eastern Anatolia. Between 923/1517 and 947/1540, however, the local population asked for the application of the simpler Ottoman taxation system.

Destruction of the Mamluk Sultanate, occupation of Syria, Egypt and the Ḥijāz

By 920/1514 the Mamluks were faced with the necessity of establishing good relations with the Ottomans in order to parry the threat of Shāh Ismāʿīl on the one hand, and of the Portuguese on the other. Starting from 908/1502 the Portuguese waged a relentless struggle against Arab trade in order to win the monopoly of trade in the Indian Ocean. In 911/1505 the Portuguese occupied the island of Socotra in the gulf of Aden and in 913/1507 they captured Hormuz at the mouth of the Persian Gulf. They penetrated the Red Sea as far as Jedda. In naval resources and firearms the Mamluks were no match for their enemies. With immense efforts they built up a navy in the Red Sea, but this was utterly destroyed by the Portuguese in 915/1509. In these desperate straits the Egyptian Sultan Qānṣawh al-Ghawrī asked the Ottomans for help. The Portuguese on their part offered joint action to the Mamluks' enemy, Shāh Ismāʿīl.

The first convoy bringing Ottoman aid to the Mamluks, consisting of 30 ships carrying timber and 300 guns, was captured by the Knights of Rhodes. The Mamluks were luckier in Shawwāl 916/January 1511 when they received from the Ottomans 400 guns and 40 *ḳanṭārs* (approximately 2 tons) of gunpowder. The Topḳapı Palace archives show that before 918/1512 several Ottoman captains were sent to Egypt to build warships. Egypt also relied on the Ottomans for the supply of timber, tar and iron for shipbuilding. It appears also that Ottoman corsairs from western Anatolia saw service in the Mamluk navy. The Portuguese threat from the rear, which aimed at isolating the Arab lands, naturally moved the rulers to look for help to the Ottoman *ghāzī* sultan. Earlier, when the Ottomans had started their advance in Europe, the threat to Arab lands of a crusade from the Mediterranean had receded. Now, however, the Portuguese were trying to capture Aden, and threatened to occupy Jedda, Mecca and Medina, and exhume the remains of the Prophet. The Ottoman sultan had, like his predecessors, assigned considerable revenues from rich *waqfs* in Anatolia for the upkeep of the holy places in Mecca and Medina. Sultan Selīm tried at the same time to win over the *sharīf* of Mecca. In 922/1516 the descendants of the Prophet in Mecca and Medina despatched a delegation to Selīm, which the Mamluks did not allow to proceed to Istanbul. Selīm made it known that he wanted to liberate the Arabs from Mamluk oppression. In brief, conditions in Arab lands were ripe for the acceptance of Ottoman rule.

Although Shāh Ismā'īl constituted for the Mamluks a danger equal to that of the Portuguese, al-Ghawrī had remained neutral in the war between him and Selīm. He knew, however, that the victor in that war would sooner or later attack Egypt. When, after his victory at Chāldirān, Selīm captured Diyār Bakr and the country of 'Alā' al-Dawla, he infringed the borders of an area which the Mamluks had always claimed for their own. While the Ottoman forces were trying to establish themselves in Diyār Bakr, Selīm did not hesitate to lead his army down the valley of the Euphrates. Seeing that war was inevitable, al-Ghawrī set off for Aleppo at the head of an army, on 15 Rabī' II 922/18 May 1516. Although custom did not require it, he took with him the Caliph al-Mutawakkil. The Mamluks had come to fear a confrontation with the Ottomans, and would doubtless have preferred peace. There was panic in Cairo. In Aleppo the local people turned against the Mamluks. At the beginning of August, Selīm marched on Aleppo. The two armies met at Marj Dābiq (25 Rajab 922/24 August 1516) and the Mamluks were utterly routed. Al-Ghawrī died of a stroke on the field of battle.

The defeat of the Mamluk army was attributed mainly to the treachery of Khā'ir Bey, governor of Aleppo, but also, as at Chāldirān, to the violence of the Ottoman artillery and musket-fire. When the Ottoman army entered Aleppo, the Caliph al-Mutawakkil and three chief judges appeared before the sultan. Selīm treated the caliph with deference, seating him at his side. Later, however, he took measures to prevent the caliph escaping. Khā'ir Bey and some of the Mamluk commanders (*amīrs*) went over to the Ottomans.

On 29 Sha'bān/30 August, Selīm reached Damascus. The Ottoman general, Sinān Pasha, broke the resistance of the governor of Damascus, Jānbardī al-Ghazālī (2 Dhu'l-Ḥijja/27 December), and occupied Palestine as far as Gaza. The Ottomans hesitated, however, before attempting the occupation of Egypt. In a letter to the new master of Egypt, Ṭūmān-

Bāy, Selīm said that the caliph and the *qāḍīs* having sworn allegiance to him, he had now become the rightful ruler of the whole country, but that if Ṭūmān-Bāy minted coins and had the *khuṭba* read in mosques in his name in Egypt beyond Gaza, he would leave him as governor there. Otherwise, Selīm threatened to go to Egypt and destroy the Mamluks. These threats caused panic in Cairo, where Ṭūmān-Bāy had himself proclaimed sultan on 14 Ramaḍān/11 October 1516, thus inviting war. Thereupon Selīm crossed the Sinai Desert and entered Egypt. In Bilbays he issued a proclamation in which he made a distinction between the people of Egypt and the Mamluks, and promised that he would deal kindly with the local inhabitants, including the peasantry. Ṭūmān-Bāy tried to imitate the tactics which the Ottomans employed at Marj Dābiq and prepared a defended position at Raydāniyya on the approaches to Cairo. Raydāniyya was defended with artillery and muskets. However, when battle started, the Ottoman artillery silenced the obsolete Mamluk guns. Selīm outflanked the Mamluks' fortified position, and delivered a successful general assault (29 Dhu'l-Ḥijja/23 January 1517). The following day he sent the Caliph al-Mutawakkil with his troops into Cairo to allay the people's fears. On Friday the *khuṭba* was read in Selīm's name, marking the dissolution of the Mamluk kingdom.

Ṭūmān-Bāy himself escaped from Raydāniyya and organized raids and guerilla warfare, in which he was supported by the population of Cairo. For the first three days the operations undertaken by Ottoman troops in pursuit of the Mamluks gave rise to fears, but also to some resistance among the local population. Violent street fighting took place in Cairo. Finally Ṭūmān-Bāy was captured and executed. After appointing Khā'ir Bey as governor-general (*beylerbeyi*), Selīm left Cairo (23 Sha'bān 923/10 September 1517). He had earlier sent the caliph to Istanbul by sea.

In 930/1524 the Ottoman governor of Egypt, Aḥmed Pasha, proclaimed himself sultan, relying on Mamluk support. His rebellion was put down and the grand *veẓīr* Ibrāhīm Pasha went to Egypt, and settled the administration of that country. Nevertheless, the revival of Egyptian agriculture and the full registration of taxation sources took a long time.

The conquest of Syria and Egypt brought the Ottoman treasury in 934/1528 extra annual revenue amounting to approximately 100 million aspers (at that time 55 aspers were equivalent to one gold piece). The deficit presented by other provinces was thus met from these new sources of revenue.

APPENDIX: THE OTTOMANS AND THE CALIPHATE

According to a tradition which originates in the twelfth/eighteenth century, the 'Abbasid Caliph al-Mutawakkil officially transferred to Sultan Selīm and to his heirs all rights to the caliphate, at a ceremony held in the mosque of Aya Sofya in Istanbul.[1] In fact, however, there is no contemporary record of Selīm receiving or claiming to receive the caliphate from al-Mutawakkil. There were obvious political reasons why Ottoman sultans of the age of decline reformulated and appropriated the classical theory of the caliphate. Thus when Sultan Aḥmed III signed a treaty with the ruler of Persia, Ashraf, in Rabīʿ I 1140/October 1727, he called himself 'Caliph of all Muslims', and subsequently tried to get Nādir Shāh of Persia to recognize the same title. Finally in 1188/1774, the Treaty of Küchük Kaynarja made with Russia, which recognized the independence of the khanate of the Crimea, allowed also the Ottoman sultan to maintain certain rights there in his capacity of 'Caliph of Muslims'.

During their ascendancy, however, the Ottomans looked at the caliphate in a different light. The claim which they made for themselves was that, as foremost among the sovereigns of Islam, they were its protectors. For this reason they claimed to succeed the Prophet and the Patriarchal Caliphs as 'the best of *ghāzīs* and of fighters in the Holy War' (*afḍal al-ghuzāt wa'l-mujāhidīn*).[2]

In Aleppo, Sultan Selīm I assumed the title, formerly held by the Mamluk sultans, of 'Servitor of the Two Holy Sanctuaries' (*Khādim al-Ḥaramayn al-Sharīfayn*); he kept the Caliph al-Mutawakkil at his court, and he had the Prophet's alleged relics sent to Istanbul. In so doing he claimed, as the Mamluk sultans had done before him, to be the most powerful sovereign in the Muslim world and the protector of Islam. In the preambles to their legal edicts (*qānūn-nāmes*) Sultan Selīm and his successors emphasized this title. As for 'caliph' (*khalīfa*), this had been used by the Ottomans as a general title since the time of Murād I, as was the practice of many other Muslim rulers, the title having by then lost its original meaning.

On the other hand, the protection of Mecca, Medina and the Pilgrimage routes conferred a title to pre-eminence in the world of Islam.

[1] M. d'Ohsson, *Tableau général de l'empire ottoman* (Paris, 1787), I, 89; Meḥmed 'Aṭā, *Tārīkh* (Istanbul, A.H. 1291), 92.

[2] Neshrī, *Jihānnümā* (ed. Taeschner), I, 18; also Kemāl Pasha-zāde and Idrīs, all writing at the end of the ninth/fifteenth century.

In the early days, ʿAbd Allāh b. al-Zubayr had claimed pre-eminence over Muʿāwiya, on the grounds that he was the Servant of the Kaʿba and presided over the Pilgrimage. When Shāh-Rukh expressed the desire in Muḥarram 833/October 1429 to have a cover woven for the Kaʿba and a fountain built in Mecca, his wish was rejected by the Mamluk sultan of Egypt on the ground that it was tantamount to a claim to over-lordship. The wish of Sultan Meḥmed the Conqueror to repair the wells and fountains along the Pilgrimage routes met similarly with an unfavourable response. Announcing his victory in Egypt to the Shīrvān-Shāh,[1] Sultan Selīm claimed that the Mamluks had been incapable of protecting the pilgrim route in the Ḥijāz against the depredations of Arab robbers, and that God had entrusted him with the task of bringing order to the laws of Islam and of sending the *maḥmal,* a palanquin symbolizing political authority. On these grounds Selīm claimed the obedience of all the rulers of Islam. He added in his letter that the whole of the Ḥijāz including Mecca and Medina was now subject to him, and warned that he would shortly appear in Persia and conquer it. He demanded that the Shīrvān-Shāh should accept his 'Exalted Caliphate' (*Khilāfet-i ʿUlyā*) and have his name mentioned in the *khuṭba.* Later, in the letter which Süleymān the Magnificent sent on his accession to the *sharīf* of Mecca, he announced that God had brought him to the throne of the Sultanate and the position of the Caliphate.[2] In his reply the *sharīf* of Mecca confirmed that Süleymān had by the will of God come to occupy 'the seat of the Sublime Sultanate and the dignity of the Great Caliphate' (*sarīr al-Salṭana al-ʿUẓmā wa-masnad al-Khilāfa al-Kubrā*) adding 'By conquering the countries of the Franks and of their likes, you are senior to us and to all the sultans of Islam'. These letters are noteworthy for the sultan's claim to the Great Caliphate. In the preface to the *Qānūn-nāme* of Buda,[3] drawn up by Abu'l-Suʿūd Efendi, Sultan Süleymān is described as 'Inheritor of the Great Caliphate...Possessor of the Exalted Imamate, Protector of the Sanctuary of the Two Respected Holy Places' (*Wārith al-Khilāfa al-Kubrā...Ḥāʾiẓ al-Imāma al-ʿUẓmā, Ḥāmī Ḥimā al-Ḥaramayn al-Muḥtaramayn*). It is also noteworthy that the Ottomans claimed to have acquired these titles by the will of God. When the Muslim rulers of India and of Central Asia asked for

[1] Ferīdūn, *Munshaʾāt al-salāṭīn* (Istanbul A.H., 1275), I, 440.

[2] Ferīdūn, *Munshaʾāt,* I, 500–1; cf. the letter sent by the sultan on his accession to the khān of the Crimea, I, 502.

[3] Ö. L. Barkan, *XV ve XVI asırlarda Osmanlı imparatorluğunda ziraî ekonominin hukukî ve malî esasları,* I: *Kanunlar* (Istanbul, 1943), 296.

Süleymān's help against the Portuguese and the Russians, the sultan claimed in his reply that God had granted him the dignity of 'Caliph of the Face of the Earth' and that it was his duty to keep the pilgrim roads open.

This conception of the caliphate was no doubt partly different from that formulated under the 'Abbasids, since for one thing the Ottoman sultan did not come from the tribe of Quraysh. In the reign of Süleymān the Magnificent the question whether it was licit for the Ottoman sultans to use the titles of *imām* and of caliph, in the absence of any lineal descent from Quraysh, was in fact posed.[1] According to Luṭfī Pasha, Süleymān, as the effective ruler of all the Muslim lands from the Habsburg frontier to the Yemen, 'is the *Imām* of the Age in fulfilment of the relevant stipulation relating to the maintenace of the Faith and guardianship of the homeland of al-Islām...He is the *Imām* of the Age without dubiety and he is truly the defender of the *Shar*''. Obedience was due to him as *imām*. The Great Caliphate and Exalted Imamate, as represented by the Ottomans, was a new concept born of historical circumstances. Ottoman sultans considered their *de facto* position as the most powerful rulers and protectors of Islam, to be the result of God's will. This conception was in fact only an extension of the idea of the caliphate which prevailed in the Muslim world in the eighth/fourteenth century, an extension required by fresh historical developments.[2] Thus every Muslim ruler who possessed *de facto* sovereignty and assumed the task of implementing the *Sharī'a* could call himself caliph. The innovation which the Ottomans introduced into this conception was to revive the idea of an Exalted Caliphate applicable to the whole world of Islam. In other words, as they considered it their task to defend the world of Islam against Christian attacks and to protect Mecca, Medina and the Pilgrimage routes, all of which were matters of common Muslim concern, they wished to exercise a predominant influence throughout Islam. In this way the new conception of the caliphate served a policy seeking to establish Ottoman influence and mastery over the world of Islam. The idea was obviously derived from the *ghāzī* tradition. What happened was that after Selīm, the Ottoman state developed the old tradition of a *ghāzī* border-state, and revived the old Islamic caliphate in a new form. The new conception of the caliphate was based on the fulfilment of the tasks of *ghazā* and of the

[1] H. A. R. Gibb, 'Lutfi Pasha on the Ottoman Califate', in *Oriens*, XV (1962), 287–95.

[2] H. A. R. Gibb, 'Some considerations on the Sunni theory of the Caliphate', in *Studies on the civilization of Islam*, ed. Stanford J. Shaw and William R. Polk (Boston, Mass., 1962), 141–50.

defence and protection of Islam. As Luṭfī made it clear, it rested on the power actually exercised by the Ottoman state. In the succeeding age of decadence, the Ottomans changed their standpoint by turning to the theoretical conception of the caliphate developed under the 'Abbasids and enshrined in *fiqh* formularies, in which they hoped to find a source of strength.

In his capacity of caliph representing Sunnī Islam, the Ottoman sultan considered the population ruled by the Persian Safavids as heretics who had to be forced into subjection. Around 1137/1725 the view was accepted that two *imāms* coexisted, the Ottoman sultan and the Indian Mughal emperor, whose separate existence was made possible by the ocean which divided their respective dominions.[1]

[1] Küchük Chelebi-zāde 'Āṣım, *Tārīkh,* 354.

CHAPTER 2

THE HEYDAY AND DECLINE OF THE OTTOMAN EMPIRE

SÜLEYMĀN THE MAGNIFICENT

Süleymān the Magnificent and Charles V

When Süleymān the Magnificent came to the throne on 17 Shawwāl 926/30 September 1520, he, like his ancestors, had to prove himself in the field of *ghazā*. This was the standard way of consolidating the power of a new sultan. Selīm's conquests had enlarged the empire to twice its size and inspired despair in Europe. Selīm had aimed above all at winning a great victory in the West. With this end in view he started building a great shipyard in Istanbul as early as 921/1515. Meḥmed the Conqueror had been checked at Rhodes, the gate to the Mediterranean, and before Belgrade, the gate to central Europe. The pursuit of the *ghazā* in the West depended on the capture of these two fortresses of Christendom. Charles V ascended the Habsburg throne in 925/1519 and soon after, in Rabīʿ II 927/March 1521, the inevitable war broke out between him and the other great Christian ruler, Francis I of France. Europe was thus divided into two camps, and the idea of launching a united European crusade against the Ottomans became impracticable. The Ottomans could not have hoped for a more favourable set of circumstances. It was in these conditions that Süleymān began his reign.

The new sultan succeeded in capturing Belgrade on 26 Ramaḍān 927/30 August 1521, and Rhodes on 1 Ṣafar 929/20 December 1522. No succour came from the West. Three years later, when the king of France was made prisoner by the Habsburg emperor at Pavia in 931/1525, he had recourse to the last remaining way out and asked for the help of the Ottoman sultan. The Ottomans did not let the opportunity slip.

The French ambassador in Istanbul asked the sultan to launch a general offensive by land and sea against the Habsburgs in order to rescue Francis, saying that otherwise France would have to accept the conditions laid down by the emperor, who would then become supreme in the world (Jumādā I 932/February 1526). As a result of the situation prevailing in Italy, Venice too was on the side of the Ottomans in 931/1525. The Ottomans immediately decided to start a campaign. A land and sea assault on Italy to save Francis from the emperor's hands was at first projected. But Ottoman interests required an attack in Hungary. Here too the situation was favourable. A number of magnates led by John Zápolyai were in opposition to the emperor's policy, which was supported by the king of Hungary. The peasants had, moreover, some time earlier revolted against the magnates. The Ottomans succeeded in appearing in the guise of friends both to the magnates and to the peasants. Süleymān invaded Hungary and won a resounding victory at Mohács on 20 Dhu'l-Qa'da 932/28 August 1526. The king of Hungary was killed on the field of battle. The sultan entered Buda on 13 Dhu'l-Ḥijja 932/20 September 1536. Later, however, the Ottomans evacuated the country. When they were gone a number of Hungarian nobles chose Zápolyai as king in opposition to the Habsburgs (4 Ṣafar 933/10 November 1526). Zápolyai was recognized by France and its allies, and joined the anti-Habsburg coalition. Pro-German Hungarians countered this move by holding a diet at Pressburg (Bratislava), and elected to the throne of Hungary the Archduke Ferdinand, brother of Charles V. Ferdinand drove Zápolyai out of Buda in Dhu'l-Ḥijja 934/ September 1527. Ferdinand asked the sultan to recognize him as king of Hungary, offering to pay annual tribute in exchange for this recognition, but his approach was rejected. Since his victory at Mohács the Ottoman sultan considered Hungary to be his to bestow, by right of conquest. He promised the Hungarian crown to Zápolyai, on condition that the latter accepted his suzerainty, and said that he would protect him against Ferdinand (Jumādā I 934/February 1528). In Ottoman eyes at that time Hungary seemed a distant country which was difficult to keep. The Ottomans continued, therefore, with their traditional policy of leaving Hungary under the rule of a vassal king, and contented themselves with annexing Sirem (Szerém). In 934/1528 Francis I made war on Charles V once again, and was soon in difficulties and appealing for the sultan's help. In response to this, Süleymān re-entered Hungary in 935/ 1529. He gave the Hungarian crown to Zápolyai and established him in his capital at Buda on 4 Muḥarram 936/8 September 1529. He then advanced further west against Ferdinand and laid siege to Vienna on 22 Muḥarram 936/26 September 1529. After three weeks the siege was lifted. The sultan then withdrew, leaving a representative in Buda under the protection of a garrison of Janissaries. Zápolyai promised to pay an annual tribute. In the meantime Francis had signed a fairly favourable peace treaty with the emperor (the treaty of Cambrai, 13 August 1529).

Although angered at this, the sultan saw the value of continued co-operation with France, and behaved with understanding. Istanbul then became one of the centres of European politics. In 938/1532 Francis I admitted to the Venetian ambassador that he saw in the Ottoman empire the only force guaranteeing the continued existence of the states of Europe against Charles V.

Francis I followed a personal secret policy of always maintaining the Ottoman connexion, while keeping this secret from the Western Christian world and even from his own subjects. On the other hand, Charles V proclaimed in his propaganda that the king of France was the ally of the Muslims, and, whenever he signed peace with France, he extracted from Francis promises to take part in a crusade. Exaggerated reports of these promises were then communicated to the sultan in Istanbul in order to shake Ottoman confidence in Francis. To counter this, Francis instructed his envoy in Istanbul to explain the true motives of his actions, and to preserve the Ottoman alliance. These explanations succeeded in their purpose. For the Ottomans too the French alliance became an essential part of their Western policy.

From 937/1531 onwards Francis encouraged the sultan to invade southern Italy. In the event of such an invasion he himself hoped to occupy Genoa and Milan. But in 937/1531 Ferdinand attacked Buda once again. The following year the sultan left it to his admiral Khayr al-Dīn Barbarossa to co-operate with the French in the Mediterranean and in Italy, while he himself marched against Austria. He made for Vienna hoping to meet the emperor in a pitched battle. But the emperor did not appear. The sultan took Güns, and after waiting for three weeks, sixty miles from Vienna, he turned back. In the Mediterranean the Turkish fleet was defeated and Andrea Doria captured from the Ottomans the castle of Coron in the Morea. Charles hoped to use this as a trump card in bargaining over Hungary. Deciding that it was essential for him to campaign in the east against Persia, the sultan signed his first truce with Ferdinand in 938/1533, but excluded Charles from it. To continue the war in the Mediterranean Süleymān summoned Barbarossa and gave him the command of all Ottoman naval forces, as governor-general (*beylerbeyi*) of Algiers. Barbarossa was ordered to co-operate closely with the French. The sultan saw an obvious interest in keeping Francis and Zápolyai fighting with the Austrians. He sent Francis the vast sum of 100,000 gold pieces to enable him to form a coalition with England and the German princes against Charles V. After raiding the Italian coast, Barbarossa captured

Tunis in Ṣafar 941/August 1534 and made it his base. Coron was recaptured. Seeing the sultan engaged in the Persian campaign, Francis I tried to sell his alliance at the highest possible price. Negotiations for a formal alliance were started in 937/1532. In 942/1535 Francis sent his ambassador to Istanbul to ask the sultan to launch a general assault against the Habsburgs by land and by sea, and to send to Paris a subsidy of 1,000,000 ducats. At that moment Charles V succeeded in recapturing Tunis from Barbarossa (Muḥarram 942/July 1535). On his return from the Persian expedition, Süleymān put in hand plans for the invasion of Italy. The French were to invade Lombardy, while the Ottoman army was to cross from Albania to Otranto. One of the results of the negotiations with the French was the famous capitulations of Shaʿbān 941/February 1535. It was only in 943/1537 that the sultan was able to turn his attention to Italy by marching to Valona in Albania, but as early as Shawwāl 937/May 1531 the Venetian ambassador was writing to the doge 'Sultan Solyman says "To Rome, to Rome!" and he detests the Emperor and his title of Caesar, he, the Turk, causing himself to be called Caesar'.[1]

Ottoman attempts to capture from the Venetians strongholds along the Adriatic coast and the isle of Corfu in 944/1537 and 945/1538 were in fact a preparation for the invasion of Italy. At the siege of Corfu the Ottomans were reinforced by the French navy. The following year Francis once again made peace with Charles V at Aigues-Mortes in July 1538, promising to take part in a crusade against the Ottomans. Barbarossa succeeded, however, in routing at Prevesa a powerful crusading fleet, which the Venetians had succeeded in bringing together under the command of Doria (28 September 1538). This victory marked the beginning of Ottoman naval supremacy in the Mediterranean which lasted until 979/1571. In the meantime Francis I, having seen that he would not be able to gain Milan from the emperor by peaceful means, returned to his policy of close co-operation with the sultan. As usual the sultan responded favourably. He agreed to make peace with Venice in 947/1540, saying that he did it for Francis's sake. He informed the ambassador sent by Charles V that he would not make peace with the emperor until the latter had given Francis the lands which were his by right. The policy of alliance with the sultan gained France a privileged position in eastern trade and politics as compared with that of other European states.

The death of Zápolyai on 15 Rabīʿ I 947/20 July 1540 brought the

[1] *Calendar of state papers, Venice*, V (London, 1873), doc. 1011.

question of Hungary once again to the forefront of European politics. Ferdinand laid siege to Buda in an attempt to gain control over the whole kingdom of Hungary. Between 948/1541 and 951/1544 the sultan co-operated closely with France. In 1541, as he marched off to Hungary in order to obtain a final decision, he ordered Barbarossa to engage in joint operations with the French in the Mediterranean. In Hungary Süleymān threw back Ferdinand's forces and entered Buda. The central part of the Hungarian kingdom was annexed to the Ottoman empire under the name of the province (*beylerbeyilik*) of Buda. Zápolyai's infant son, John Sigismund, was given the principality of Transylvania. While Süleymān was engaged in Hungary, Charles V sent a large naval force to Algiers in an attempt to destroy Barbarossa. It was utterly defeated, and had to retire (948/1541). In 950/1543 Süleymān led another army into Hungary in order to conquer the remaining strip of Hungarian territory still under the control of Ferdinand. At the same time he put at France's disposition a fleet of 110 galleys, which had been placed under the command of Barbarossa. Barbarossa was joined by a French fleet of fifty ships and laid siege to Nice. The Ottoman navy then wintered in Toulon. The Ottomans came to the conclusion that the French were not making sufficient use of their navy to defeat Charles V. On land, a small force of French artillery joined Süleymān's army in Hungary. Ferdinand lost the castles of Gran and Fehervar and sued for peace. Süleymān too needed peace in the West, as his relations with Persia had worsened once again. In 952/1545 he signed a first truce of one year's duration with Charles V through the intermediary of Francis I, whom he always wanted to impress as a loyal ally. Two years later another truce, this time of five years' duration, was signed with both Ferdinand and Charles in Edirne. Under its provisions, Ferdinand was to pay an annual tribute of 30,000 gold pieces in respect of the Hungarian territory which he held. In the Mediterranean, naval operations against Charles were stopped until 957/1550.

Hostilities with the Habsburgs recommenced in 957/1550 with an attempt by Ferdinand to invade the principality of Transylvania. Ferdinand was thrown back and the Ottomans created a second province (*beylerbeyilik*) centred on Temesvár, leaving the principality of Transylvania to John Sigismund. When Francis I was succeeded by Henry II Ottoman-French military co-operation continued in the Mediterranean. While Henry II was pushing the French frontiers towards the Rhine, the south of France was defended by an Ottoman-French fleet, which even occupied Corsica for France in 960/1553.

After 957/1550 the Ottomans tried to evict the Knights of St John, who had established themselves in Tripoli and Malta, and to conquer these points which dominated the central Mediterranean straits. Tripoli fell to the Turks on 11 Shaʿbān 958/14 August 1551, but the powerful army sent against Malta was completely routed in the summer of 972/1565.

Ottomans and Protestants

At this juncture the king of France put the Ottomans in touch with the Protestant princes who were his allies in Germany. The Ottomans saw the benefits which could accrue to them from a Protestant connexion. In a letter which he sent in 959/1552, Süleymān incited the Protestants against the pope and the emperor and advised them to co-operate with the king of France. He said that he himself was about to embark on a campaign and promised on oath that they would not be harmed when he entered Germany. Ottoman pressure on the Habsburgs between 927/1521 and 962/1555 was an important factor in the consolidation of the forces of the Reformation and in their final recognition.[1] In the sixteenth and seventeenth centuries support and encouragement for Protestants and Calvinists were, like the French alliance, one of the fundamental principles of Ottoman policy. This aimed at keeping Europe divided, weakening the Habsburgs and preventing the launching of a united crusade. Under Ottoman administration Calvinism was propagated freely in Hungary and Transylvania, which became a Calvinist and Unitarian stronghold. Hungarian territory which lay outside the Ottoman frontiers was, on the other hand, dominated by Catholicism. In the seventeenth century the Calvinists in northern Hungary and Transylvania found in the Ottomans their strongest protectors. People began speaking of *Calvino-turcismus*. While Luther described the Ottomans as a plague sent by God to awaken the Christians, another Protestant went so far as to consider them a sign of God's favour.[2] An enemy of Lutheranism, P. Anderbach, compared it with Islam. Melanchthon was directly in touch with the patriarch of Istanbul, who was in effect an official of the sultan.

In a letter to Lutheran princes in the Low Countries and in other lands subject to Spain, the sultan offered military help and saw them as standing

[1] Attention has recently been focused on this subject: see E. Benz, *Wittenberg und Byzanz* (Marburg, 1949); S. A. Fischer-Galati, *Ottoman imperialism and German Protestantism* (Cambridge, Mass., 1959); K. M. Setton, 'Lutheranism and the Turkish peril', in *Balkan Studies*, III/1 (1962), 136–65.

[2] D. M. Vaughan, *Europe and the Turk* (Liverpool, 1954), 143.

close to him, since they did not worship idols, believed in one God and fought against the pope and emperor. In the second half of the sixteenth century it was the Calvinist Huguenots in France who wanted to return to a policy of an Ottoman alliance against Spain. The Ottoman court reacted violently at the news of the Massacre of St Bartholomew, which it saw as the elimination of its partisans.

When Queen Elizabeth I of England became the champion of European resistance against Philip II of Spain, the Ottomans gave a friendly answer to her overtures. Like Francis I before them, the English saw in the Ottomans the only military power capable of keeping the balance of power. The sultan granted capitulations to the English in 1580 as a sign of this *rapprochement*. After this date the English began to take the place formerly occupied by the French in Istanbul. The Ottomans showed an interest also in the struggle waged by Dutch Calvinists against Catholic Spain; they extended their friendship to them and, as a result, granted them, too, capitulations in 1021/1612. In this way the Ottomans not only gave political support to the national monarchies and the Protestants against Habsburg hegemony in Europe, but also, by opening to them the markets of the Levant, extended a large measure of support to their mercantile development. In the first half of the seventeenth century England considered its Levant trade as important as the trade with India. The important part played by the Ottoman empire in the genesis of modern Europe is now increasingly attracting the notice of historians.

Conquests in the East: Tabrīz, Baghdād

Having established themselves in eastern Anatolia, the Ottomans posed a constant threat to Tabrīz and ʿIrāq. Against this, Shāh Ṭahmāsp of Persia continued the policy of his father, Shāh Ismāʿīl, in provoking the *Qizilbāsh* in Anatolia. In 933/1527 there was a revolt led by Qalender Chelebi. Shāh Ṭahmāsp also gave a favourable reception to the envoys sent by Charles V. Relations between the two courts began in 924/1518, and in 935/1529 Charles's envoys were seen at the court of Ṭahmāsp. Finally, the bey of Bitlis, Sheref Khān, revolted against Ottoman suzerainty and placed himself under the protection of the shah. Against this, the shah's governor in Baghdād came to an understanding with the Ottomans. In consequence, war became inevitable by 939/1533. Süleymān's Eastern campaign, which lasted for two years, resulted in the capture and annexation of Tabrīz on 1 Muḥarram 941/13 July

1534, and of Baghdād on 24 Jumādā II 941/31 December 1534. The rulers of Gīlān and Shīrvān, whose wealth derived largely from the silk which they sent through Tabrīz to Bursa and Aleppo, and who were, therefore, economically dependent on the Ottomans, recognized the suzerainty of the sultan. Also, by winning control of the Baṣra–Baghdād–Aleppo road, the Ottomans dominated the second of the trade-routes between India and the Middle East. In 945/1538 the ruler of Baṣra, Rashīd al-Dīn, sent a delegation bearing the keys of his city to the Ottoman sultan. When, however, the Ottoman central administration began to make itself felt, local dynasties and the shaykhs of Arab tribes rebelled. The Ottomans set up in 'Irāq the province (*beylerbeyilik*) of Baghdād and apportioned settled areas as *timars*. They tried to establish security along the Baṣra–Baghdād–Aleppo trade-route by building forts in suitable places to stop the plundering raids of the bedouin, and to organize river transport along the Euphrates. A powerful garrison of 2,000 Janissaries was stationed in the citadel of Baghdād. The trade-route revived under Ottoman administration. The first serious revolt took place in Baṣra in 953/1546, and there was another in 973/1566. The Ottomans then made this area too, subject to a military governor (*beylerbeyi*) in order to strengthen their control.

Struggle against the Portuguese in the Indian Ocean

Immediately after the conquest of Egypt, the Ottomans went into action in order to drive the Portuguese out of the Red Sea. The two Turkish captains, Selmān Re'īs and Ḥüseyn Bey, who had been sent to serve the Mamluks before 919/1513, were still in 922/1516 waging war on the Portuguese in the Red Sea. When they returned, they entered the service of their old masters, who had by now conquered Egypt. A new Ottoman war-fleet, constructed in Suez, sailed to the Yemen and to Aden under the command of Selmān Re'īs. Sawākin had come under Ottoman rule in 926/1520. A memorandum attributed to Selmān Re'īs recommended the permanent stationing of a fleet at Suez in order to keep the Portuguese from the Red Sea, and spoke of the need to keep the trade-route open. The Ottoman fleet foiled a Portuguese attempt to build a fort at Sawākin. An Ottoman force was stationed in the Yemen. The Ottoman fleet sailed into the Indian Ocean and tried to take Aden. In 933/1527 the rajah of Calicut and the sultan of Gujarāt asked for Ottoman help against the Portuguese. In 936/1530 the governor of Egypt, Khādim Süleymān Pasha, brought together in Suez a fleet of eighty ships but did not undertake any action. In 945/1538 when he served his second term as governor of Egypt, he finally sailed on an Indian expedition, and captured Aden on his way. In Gujarāt he besieged, but failed to capture, Diu. On his way back he consolidated Ottoman rule in Aden and the Yemen. The Ottoman governor of Zabīd in the Yemen supported Aḥmad Grāñ against the Christian ruler of Ethiopia who had sided with the Portuguese (948–50/1541–3).

After establishing themselves in Baṣra the Ottomans tried to gain control of the Persian Gulf. They captured Qaṭīf in 957/1550 and Baḥrayn in 961/1554. The Ottoman Red Sea fleet sailed into the Gulf but failed to capture Hormuz at the siege of 960/1552. Another expedition, led by Seyyidī ʿAlī Re'īs in 959/1553, against the Portuguese in the Indian Ocean, was also unsuccessful. In 972/1565 envoys sent by the sultan of Acheh, ʿAlā' al-Dīn, arrived in Istanbul with a request for help against the Portuguese. The Ottomans decided to despatch their Suez fleet, but as a result of a revolt in the Yemen only two ships could be sent with material and gunsmiths. In 974/1567 it was the turn of the rajas of Calicut and of Ceylon to appeal for Ottoman help. Philip II felt considerable concern at the approaches made to the Ottomans by native rulers along the shores of the Indian Ocean. In 993/1585 a fairly large Turkish fleet drove the Portuguese from the coast of East Africa. The ruler of Mombasa accepted Ottoman suzerainty. Before long, however, there was a terrible Negro revolt against the Ottomans (997/1589).

These Ottoman initiatives were not, however, completely fruitless. Recent researches have shown that in the first half of the ninth/sixteenth century pepper was still reaching Antwerp through the Mediterranean. In 961/1554 the Venetians alone bought 6,000 quintals of spice in Alexandria. On several occasions Ottoman activity caused a crisis on the Portuguese spice market. In 991/1583 J. Eldred spoke of ships from Hormuz bringing every month to Baṣra spices, drugs and calico from India. It was only after the Dutch and the English came to dominate the Indian Ocean and the Mediterranean with ships of a new type and new weapons (*c.* 1019/1610), that the Middle East found itself outside the main trade-routes.

Struggle for supremacy in eastern Europe

As soon as the Ottoman army withdrew, the Persians mounted a counter-offensive and recaptured Tabrīz. In 955/1548 Süleymān went on a second Persian expedition and took Tabrīz for a second time. War in the East continued intermittently, until, by the peace of Amasya on 8 Rajab 962/29 May 1555, Tabrīz and Baghdād passed under Ottoman rule.

During this struggle the Ottomans allied themselves against Persia with the Sunnī Shaybanids of Central Asia. In 961/1554 the sultan sent 300 Janissaries and an artillery company to Barak Nawrūz Khān for use against the Safavids. In the reign of Sultan Selīm II, the khans of Samarqand, Bukhārā and, especially, Khwārazm sent letters to the sultan complaining that the shah of Persia and the Muscovites in Astrakhān were stopping pilgrims and merchants. They asked the Ottomans to capture Astrakhān so that the Pilgrimage route could be opened at least through that city.

Until about 936/1530 the Ottoman empire did not see in the grand duchy of Muscovy a source of danger in the north. Before that date the Crimea and the shores of the Black Sea were threatened by the Jagellonian kings of Poland and, until the end of the ninth/fifteenth century, by the khans of the Golden Horde. In order to oppose the alliance of these two forces, the Ottomans supported the weak Crimean khanate and the grand duchy of Muscovy. In consequence, there was a show of friendship for the Russians in 897/1492, and they were allowed to trade freely in Ottoman dominions. When, however, a struggle started between Muscovy and the Crimea over the remnants of the Golden Horde, Astrakhān and Kazan, the Ottomans saw for the first time that the Muscovites were a source of danger to themselves. Ṣāḥib Giray who became khan of Kazan in 929/1523 and of the Crimea in 938/1532, tried to place Kazan under Ottoman protection and, with Ottoman help, to hold the Volga basin against the Muscovites. In 945/1538, as a result of Süleymān's campaign in Moldavia, the Ottomans detached southern Bessarabia from Moldavia and formed the separate *sanjak* of Akkerman. This completed the process of turning the Black Sea into an Ottoman lake. However, on account of their preoccupations with central Europe, and also because they thought that a strengthened Crimean khanate might threaten the Ottoman position in the Black Sea, they did not support Ṣāḥib Giray. Ivan IV (Ivan the Terrible), after assuming the title of tsar in 1547, proceeded to capture Kazan in 959/1552 and Astrakhān between 961/1554 and 963/1556, in spite of Crimean attempts to stop him. He penetrated as far south as the River Terek in the Caucasus, and found allies among the Circassians and the Nogay. In 967/1559 Russian

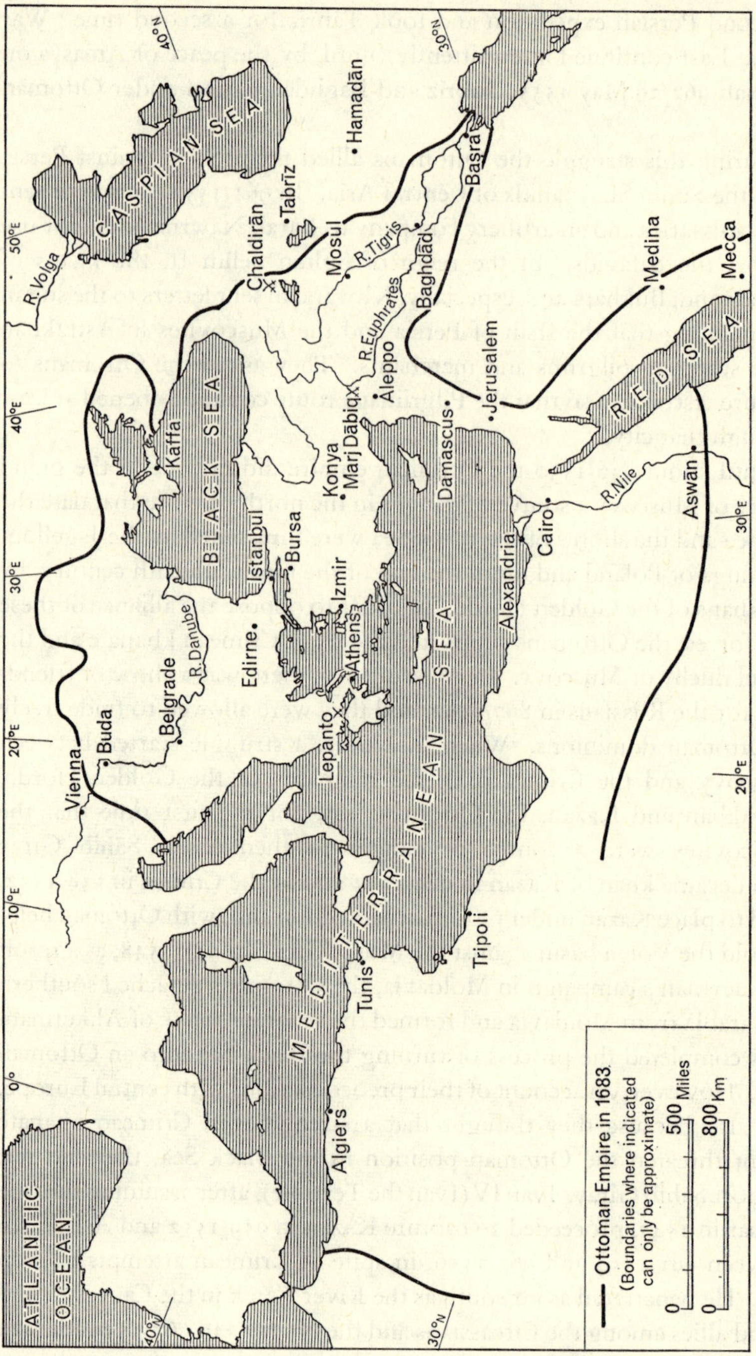

Map 7. The Ottoman empire at its height.

Cossacks raided Azov and the coast of the Crimea for the first time. The prince (*voyvoda*) of Moldavia, Petru Raresh, sought the protection of Moscow against the Ottomans (950/1543). The pope began also to consider the tsar as a possible participant in projected crusades. It was at this time that strong complaints against the Muscovites started coming in from central Asia. In this way the future Russian threat was finally delineated in the middle of the tenth/sixteenth century, and came to the attention of the Ottomans.

As soon as they had made a truce with the Habsburgs in 969/1562, the Ottomans took up the Northern question and projected an expedition to Astrakhān (970/1563), but it was not until 977/1569, after the death of Sultan Süleymān (974/1566), that action was taken. The project is noteworthy for showing the degree of confidence felt by the Ottoman empire in its resources. A canal was to be cut to link the rivers Don and Volga; Astrakhān was to be captured to keep the Russians out of the lower Volga basin; a fleet was to be introduced into the Caspian through the new sea-way, thus encircling Persia and, as a result, the Caucasus was to pass under Ottoman rule. Direct relations were to be established with the khanates of Central Asia and trade was to be revived along the route stretching from Khwārazm through Astrakhān to the Crimea, a route placed securely under Ottoman control. At the same time the rulers of Shīrvān and Gīlān asked for the sultan's help against the Persians. The Ottoman grand *vezīr*, Sokollu Meḥmed Pasha, was thus planning to solve the Persian and Muscovite problem in one stroke. In fact the tsar and Persia hastened to draw together. A Muscovite envoy had already visited the shah's court in 976/1568. The Persians also made ready to move against the Ottomans.

In 977/1569, after considerable preparations, the Ottomans sailed a fleet on the Don, and sent their army to Perevolok, the nearest point between the rivers Don and Volga. Work on the canal was started at the beginning of Rabīʿ I 977/August 1569. Before long the project was seen to be impossible. The fleet was hauled to the Volga. It sailed down to Astrakhān and besieged the fortress, where the Russians put up a fierce resistance. The attempt failed and the Ottomans suffered heavy casualties in the steppes as they withdrew to the Crimea. This failure discouraged further ventures in the north. While the grand *vezīr* Sokollu Meḥmed was determined to continue the northern campaign, his rivals advocated a move against Cyprus. The tsar offered peace, and Sultan Selīm II replied by demanding the opening of the Astrakhān route, the destruction of the fort built in Kabartay and a cessation of hostilities with the Crimeans. The sultan reaffirmed his suzerainty over the Crimean khanate and the Circassian rulers, but made no mention of Kazan and Astrakhān. The tsar seemed to accept these conditions, and even offered an alliance against the monarchs of Europe. Since the sultan was preoccupied with his struggle with the crusading fleet in the Mediterranean, he left it to the khans of the Crimea to fight the Muscovites. In 980/1572 Devlet Giray Khān was encouraged to march on Moscow. Troops were sent to secure the election of Henry of Valois to the throne of Poland against the wishes of the tsar. In the twenty years that followed, while the Ottomans were busy in the Mediterranean and in Persia, the tsar built new forts in northern Caucasus in an attempt to extend his influence over the Cossacks, Nogay and Circassians. In the east, Russian bands armed with firearms extended Russian rule into Siberia. The Siberian khanate was invaded by the Russians in 989/1581. In the course of Ottoman-Persian wars, the Muscovites tried to close to the Ottoman army the road leading from the Crimea to the Caucasus and, by extending their protection to rival khans, succeeded even in threatening the Crimea. Faced with continuing Russian advances, the khan of Bukhārā offered the Ottomans an alliance against Persia and Moscow, and asked once again for the recapture of Astrakhān (Ramaḍān 995/August 1587). The Ottomans were at that time waging a difficult war against Persia.

FAILURE OF THE ATTEMPT AT WORLD SUPREMACY

The Mediterranean front: capture of Cyprus, defeat at Lepanto

In 1559 the treaty of Cateau-Cambrésis ended the great power-struggle in western Europe in Spain's favour. The Ottomans were thus faced with a different set of conditions. The retreat from Malta (973/1566) and Süleymān's last Hungarian campaign (974/1565) showed that on both fronts, the Mediterranean and central Europe, large-scale Ottoman initiatives had stopped. The crisis which then opened with the Ottoman expedition against Cyprus (978/1570) was a turning-point both for Christendom and the Ottoman empire. As they contemplated the capture of Cyprus, the Ottomans considered above all the difficulty of stopping a crusading fleet which they expected to bring assistance from the West. However, the two allies of Venice, Spain and the papacy, were slow in fitting out their fleets, and the Ottoman fleet ferried unhindered a large army from southern Turkey to Cyprus (29 Muḥarram 978/3 July 1570). Nicosia was captured, but the castle of Famagusta resisted for a year until 7 Rabīʿ I 979/1 August 1571. In the same year the Ottoman fleet sailed to the Adriatic in order to intercept the fleet of the Crusaders. At the end of the campaigning season, Ottoman ships withdrew to the gulf of Lepanto. The great crusading fleet, which had been finally brought together under the command of Don John of Austria, attacked the Ottomans in Lepanto on 17 Jumādā I 979/7 October 1571. In the great naval battle which followed, the Ottoman fleet was destroyed. Four hundred and thirty-eight warships took part in the battle, of which 230 were Turkish. Only thirty Turkish ships managed to escape. The casualties given by both sides amounted to 59,000 dead and wounded. Under a triennial treaty of alliance the Christian states were to fit out every year 200 galleys carrying 50,000 troops. When, however, the Christian allies set out for Cyprus the following year, they were surprised to find facing them a new Turkish fleet, and hesitated to renew the assault. In the third year Venice preferred to make peace (3 Dhu'l-Qaʿda 980/7 March 1573). Under the peace-treaty, Venice renounced all its rights in Cyprus and agreed to pay heavy compensation.

The Ottomans reorganized Cyprus in accordance with their standard principles. The Latin Catholics who had formed the ruling class on the island, were eliminated. The Greek Orthodox Church had its old privileges revived, and its property restored to it. Measures were taken to win over the local people and to develop economic and financial resources. The custom whereby the serfs had to work two days a week free for the landowners was abolished. Large numbers of Turkish immigrants, 20,000 according to one calculation, were brought with their cattle and their implements from central Anatolia under the *sürgün* system of compulsory settlement, and settled on empty land in Cyprus.

The co-operation between army and navy in the large-scale operations which led to the conquest of Cyprus, represented the highest point reached by Ottoman military power and ingenuity. On the other hand, the battle of Lepanto witnessed a development which the Ottomans had always feared, in that the Christian states of the Mediterranean succeeded in joining forces and in organizing the crusade in which the Turkish fleet had perished. The Ottomans therefore felt obliged to step more warily in future.

Eastern front: conquest in the Caucasus, counter-offensive of Persia

The Ottomans tried to profit by the internal dissensions which broke out in Persia after the death of Shāh Ṭahmāsp. They entered Persian territory, and the war which followed lasted from 986/1578 to the treaty of Qaṣr-i Shīrīn or Ẕuhāb in 1049/1639. The Persian campaign went through three stages and posed serious threats to the Ottoman empire.

During the first stage, from 986/1578 to the treaty of Istanbul in 998/1590, the Ottomans conquered extensive territories north of the river Kura: Georgia, Shīrvān and Dāghistān. Persian counter-attacks were repelled by Özdemiroghlu 'Os̱mān Pasha, who succeeded in holding the Iron Gates and who was receiving help from the khan of the Crimea by way of the northern steppes (990/1582–991/1583). The Ottomans made themselves a new base by building a powerful fortress in Kars. In 991/1583 they launched another offensive, capturing Erivan in the same year, Tabrīz and Marāgha in 993/1585, and Ganja and Qarābāgh in 996/1588. Further south, Ottoman armies in Baghdād and Mosul went into action in 994/1586 and captured Persian 'Irāq ('Irāq-i 'Ajam). In Central Asia the Shaybanid 'Abd Allāh Khān, who joined the Ottomans' side in 990/1582, invaded Khurāsān and took Herat on 18 Rabī' II 996/17 March 1588. Faced with these conditions, the new shah of Persia, 'Abbās I, who had succeeded to the throne in 995/1587, was forced to sue for peace on the terms demanded by the Ottomans. The Ottomans kept all their conquests, and the shah's brother, Ḥaydar Mīrzā, was sent as a hostage to Istanbul. The treaty provided also that the Sunnīs in Persia were not to be molested.

Ottoman rule did not, however, take root in the newly conquered territories. The local settled population, which spoke Turkish but was Shī'ī by religion, and the tribes which had fled there from Anatolia, remained loyal to the Safavids. Only Shīrvān was Sunnī and favourable to the Ottomans. People in other areas were hostile to them, and fled to the shah's domain. Ottoman administration, with its taxation policy based on the registration of land and population, unaccustomed taxes and the system of *timar*, military fiefs, caused resentment. Local dynasties and tribal chiefs, especially Kurdish and Turcoman nomads who formed the majority of the population in Persian 'Irāq, preferred the largely indirect control of the shah to the new centralized Ottoman administration. They were ready to support the shah at the first opportunity. The

Ottomans were also handicapped by the remoteness of these areas from their main bases in Baghdād, Diyār Bakr and Erzurum. Troops and supplies were moved with difficulty. The grand *vezīr*, Sokollu Meḥmed, was opposed to the whole campaign, believing that the resources of the empire were not adequate to it.

In the second stage of the Persian wars, from 1012/1603 to 1027/1618, ʿAbbās I went over to the offensive, defeated the Shaybanid Özbegs, and formed an army from his personal slaves whom he equipped with firearms. The Persian counter-offensive started in 1012/1603 and, in the same year, Tabrīz was recaptured in Jumādā I/October. An Ottoman army commanded by Jighala-zāde Sinān Pasha was thrown back in 1014/1605. Campaigns against Austria and the *Jelālī* troubles in Anatolia (see below, pp. 347-50) prevented the Ottomans from forming an imperial army against the Persians.

Shāh ʿAbbās had tried since 994/1586 to form an alliance with the European enemies of the Ottomans—the Habsburgs of Austria and Spain. He also endeavoured to re-route through Moscow or the Indian Ocean the Persian silk trade, from which the Ottomans derived much profit. The shah offered to sell England silk worth 3,000,000–4,000,000 gold pieces a year. He built in southern Persia the port of Bandar ʿAbbās which developed rapidly. In the shah's policy of economic and political co-operation with Europe and in his projects of economic warfare, the English Sherley brothers played a prominent part. The Ottomans retaliated by taking strict measures to deprive Persia of valuable metals and copper. A severe currency crisis thereupon developed in Persia. ʿAbbās recaptured Shīrvān, Āẕarbāyjān and Georgia, and offered peace to the Ottomans against payment of two hundred loads of silk a year in respect of these territories. He had earlier monopolized the whole of the Persian silk trade. This peace offer was made in 1019/1610, but it was not until 1027/1618 that the Ottomans felt themselves obliged to make peace on the basis of the treaty of Amasya of 962/1555 and against receipt of only a hundred loads of silk.

During the third stage of the wars, Shāh ʿAbbās recaptured Baghdād, Kirkūk, Mosul and the whole of ʿIrāq (1032/1623). The Ottomans based on Diyār Bakr tried to take Baghdād once again, but these attempts were foiled in Ṣafar 1035/November 1625, and then in 1039/1630. The Ottoman empire was at that time a prey to anarchy. The murder of Sultan ʿOs̱mān II in 1031/1622, the domination of the imperial slaves over the state, and the rebellion started against them in

Erzurum by Abaza Meḥmed Pasha, shook it to its foundations. However, between 1041/1632 and 1045/1635 Sultan Murād IV succeeded through draconian measures in reimposing his authority and then led the army against Persia, capturing Erivan in Ṣafar 1045/July 1635. Baghdād was recaptured after a second campaign on 17 Shaʿbān 1048/24 December 1638. The following year the treaty of Qaṣr-i Shīrīn or Zuhāb finally fixed the border between the two countries (Muḥarram 1049/May 1639). The Ottomans kept Baghdād, Shahrizūr, Van and Kars, but renounced all claim to Āẕarbāyjān.

Central European front: battle of Hachova (1005/1596) *and treaty of Zsitva-Torok* (1015/1606)

In 998/1590 the Persian campaign had resulted in the annexation of the Caucasus and of Āẕarbāyjān to the Ottoman empire after long and exhausting battles. Thereupon the Ottomans turned their attention to the West. There was talk of the need to capture Crete, but the Ottomans feared a Venetian-Spanish alliance as in 979/1571. In Europe the Ottomans were expected to set on foot a Mediterranean expedition against Spain. The Ottoman administration tried to help France to throw off Spanish domination, and, by threatening to put a ban on their trade, forced the citizens of Marseilles to support Henry of Navarre. England was also trying to encourage the Ottomans to send their fleet against Spain. The English envoy in Istanbul tried to sabotage Spanish-Ottoman truce negotiations, while preventing an Ottoman-Austrian war. Istanbul thus became once again a focal point for international politics. Finally the Ottomans decided to give priority to the Hungarian question.

The situation in western Europe appeared highly favourable to them. England and France were keeping Spain busy, while Venice remained neutral. On the other hand Emperor Rudolf II had stopped in 999/1591 sending annual tribute to the Ottomans. To put pressure on him the governor of Bosnia, Ḥasan Pasha, organized large-scale raids in Croatia. These proved a costly failure in which the pasha himself lost his life. When news reached Istanbul, there was much indignation and the *kapı-kulu* army demanded an immediate campaign in the West. The grand *vezīr,* Koja Sinān Pasha, declared war on Austria on 29 Shawwāl 1001/29 July 1593. Towards the end of Dhu'l-Qaʿda/August he led his army against Hungary. With the help of two papal nuncios sent to eastern Europe, Austria succeeded in forming a Christian coalition against the Ottomans. Transylvania, Wallachia, Moldavia and the Cossacks joined the coalition. This second period of warfare in Hungary kept the Ottomans busy for fourteen years along a wide front stretching from the Black Sea to Croatia. The Long War, as it is called, passed through several stages. In 1594 Sinān captured the important city of Raab on the road to Vienna. In the autumn the emperor's allies counter-attacked. The following year Sinān occupied Wallachia and placed it under the rule of a military governor (*beylerbeyi*). On their part the Austrians took the important castle of Esztergom. In Istanbul the army forced Sultan Meḥmed III (1003–12/1595–1603) to take the field in person. The Ottoman army took Erlau (Eghri, Eger) and then met the joint armies of Austria and Transylvania, amounting to 40,000 troops in all and commanded by Emperor Maximilian, in the great pitched battle of Hachova (Mezö-Keresztes). Here the Ottomans won a great victory between 2 and 4 Rabīʿ I 1005/24 to 26 October 1596. However, the Austrians refused to make peace. Hunger, a shortage of money and war exhaustion set in in Istanbul. The Anatolian feudal cavalry, who had fled from Hachova and had been in consequence deprived of their *timars,* revolted in Anatolia. In the following years the Austrians recaptured Raab (1006/1598) and besieged Buda. The war dragged on, with the castles of Esztergom, Kanizsa (Kanija) and Stuhlweissenburg changing hands after a series of sieges. In 1012/1603 the offensive launched by Shāh ʿAbbās in the East placed the Ottomans in an embarrassing position. However, they were helped by the revolt of Transylvanian Protestants, led by Stephen Bocskai, against Austrian rule. The Ottomans granted to Bocskai the title of king of Hungary and placed him under their protection. In 1014/1605 they recaptured Esztergom. In these changed circumstances both sides agreed to make peace. The treaty of Zsitva-Torok provided for the continuation of Ottoman rule in Hungary, where two new Ottoman provinces, those of Eghri and Kanija, were formed. The Ottomans renounced, however, their claims to the portion of the old kingdom of Hungary which had passed to the Habsburgs, and ceased to receive tribute in respect of it. The treaty amounted therefore to a withdrawal. The sultan recognized the Habsburg emperor as his equal, acknowledging his title of Kaiser. This and the fact that the treaty was to last for twenty years, showed that the Ottoman court had abandoned the claims to world supremacy which it had advanced in the time of Süleymān the Magnificent. The war showed to the Ottoman empire both its own weakness and the military power of the Habsburgs. While the war was in progress, the Ottomans had made several peace approaches, from 1003/1595 onwards. Signs of Ottoman decline became obvious.

DECLINE

'It may stand, but never rise again' (Thomas Roe).

Between 1004/1596 and 1019/1610, the Ottoman empire was prey to an internal crisis which threatened its very foundations. The crisis, of which the first signs had already been discerned at the end of Süleymān's reign, became more acute during the exhausting wars which the Ottomans waged between 979/1571 and 1015/1606. True, the crisis was surmounted, but the Ottoman empire which emerged at the end of it was no longer its old self. Ottoman statesmen and writers who sought the causes of this 'change in fortune and deterioration' came to some common conclusions. The critics were agreed on the following points:

Disorder in the Ottoman state was due first of all to the weakening and fragmentation of the authority of the sultan. In earlier times the grand *vezīr* had been the absolute steward of the sultan's will; no one could come between the two. Later, however, orders came to be issued directly from the palace in the sultan's name. Irresponsible persons misused authority for personal gain, took bribes, and sold state offices and revenues. The weakening of the sultans' authority was also a natural consequence of their growing lack of interest in the affairs of state, and, as the central authority grew weaker, disorder developed in the provinces. The *devshirme* system no longer functioned. The admission of peasants (*re'āyā*) into the army was considered as one of the causes of trouble, and Muslim subjects (instead of *devshirme*-slaves) were appointed as court officers. The *sipahi* cavalry no longer existed. *Sipahis* living in their *timars* in the provinces had been the main force of the empire, but from the last years of the tenth/sixteenth century, court favourites and other prominent men, profiting from the weakening of government authority, appropriated *timars*, depriving *sipahi* families of their life-interest in these lands. This led to an increase in the numbers, expense and influence of the *kapı-kulu* standing forces, and weakened the frontier defences of the empire. The peasantry lost the protection of the *sipahi timar*-holders, and drifted from the land, to become irregular troops, or merely bandits, while others fled to the cities, the Balkans, Persia, or the Crimea.

Ottoman writers discoursing on the decline of the empire, couched their observations in accordance with the formulae of oriental statecraft. The classical theory was that the sultan could not be powerful without soldiers, soldiers could not do without money, and the treasury could not have money without the peasants. These last could only be prosperous and pay their taxes if there were justice in the state. The rigidity of these formulae did not, however, prevent accurate historical observations, while the classical theory of statecraft had an advantage in that it made Ottoman thinkers realize the interdependence of the various classes of the population.

Ottoman writers saw the first signs of 'change and corruption' in the reign of Süleymān the Magnificent. But the first real disorders are placed in the reign of Murād III. Writers on the decline attributed it to institutional faults which developed when laws and regulations were disregarded. A modern historian, relying on archive material, can confirm these observations on faults in the state mechanism and institutions. Ottoman writers of the period believed that the situation could be retrieved if only the institutions of the Golden Age, in other words the absolute authority of the sultan in the centre, the system of entrusting important military functions to the sultan's slaves and of keeping a *timar* cavalry, were revitalized.

Reforming statesmen in the eleventh/seventeenth century kept to these views. Naturally, the modern historian will see deeper and more general changes underlying the decline of the empire and will consider the breakdown of institutions as a result of these.

Work done so far on population registers shows that the population of the Ottoman empire increased considerably in the tenth/sixteenth century. It transpires from these registers that this increase in population exceeded the increase in the area of cultivated land. This can be accepted as an underlying cause of social imbalance and disorder. After the conquest of Cyprus the Ottoman government ordered the settlement there of thousands of unemployed, landless Anatolian peasants. This shows that the Ottoman government was not unaware of the consequences of population increase. Registers show the existence of numerous landless young peasants driven by land-hunger to seek a livelihood abroad. These unattached, homeless crowds of peasants were on the increase in the second half of the tenth/sixteenth century. They sought service on the borders, under the names of *gharīb-yighit* (almost 'soldier of fortune') or *gönüllü* (volunteer), in castles as *mustaḥfız* (guards), in the navy as *levend* or *'azab*, and finally in the army, where they were known as *sarıja* and *sekban*. While some served the state, others attached themselves to governors. As a reward for valour, people described as *gharīb-yighit* and *gönüllü* were given pay and, sometimes, *timars*. Such population-pressure of these people had no doubt always been effective in the policy of expansion and conquest pursued by the empire. Already in the reign of Süleymān the Magnificent, records show that large numbers of Muslim Turkish peasants became *timar*-holding cavalrymen. In order to protect the extensive territories won in Āẕarbāyjān after 986/1578, thousands of *gönüllüs* and *gharīb-yighits* had to be attracted to the army by promises of pay and land. However, the expansion of the empire stopped towards the end of the tenth/sixteenth century. In central Europe effective resistance was put up by the Habsburgs, while in the East, Shāh 'Abbās won back all the lands conquered by the Ottomans. As a result thousands of unemployed and unprovided for young men, who had taken part in previous campaigns as *gönüllüs* in the army, or as *levends* and *'azabs* in the navy, and who had been accustomed to the use of arms, flowed back into Anatolia, causing disturbances wherever they went. On the other hand, some of the young, homeless peasants benefited from the free instruction given in *medreses*, and helped to swell the class of jurists and officials. Thousands of *medrese* students (known as *sukhte*, 'burnt up', later corrupted to *softa*) periodically left their schools in Anatolia on alms-collecting expeditions in the surounding villages. Some of these *sukhtes*, whose numbers increased considerably from the middle of the tenth/sixteenth century, formed groups which descended on villages like clouds of locusts. Some were indistinguishable from bandits. The disturbances they caused became a serious danger to the state, particularly after the reign of Selīm II.

A financial crisis developed, when, from about 988/1580, cheap American silver started flooding the empire. As a result currency rapidly depreciated and prices rose. This in turn led to disturbances. All the usual abnormal conditions attending on inflation, such as the adulteration of currency, counterfeiting, speculation, high interest rates and usury, brought incurable ills to Ottoman finances, which were based on a stable coinage, as represented by the silver asper (*akche*), and to economic life in general. Increased prices brought hardship in the first place to fixed income groups, the *sipahi* cavalry, whose livelihood depended on the revenue of *timar* lands, the *kapı-kulus*, who received a fixed pay from the sultan, and the religious classes, who lived on *waqf* revenues. These hardships led to revolts of Janissaries and *sipahis*. *Sipahis* whose *timar* lands were small became too poor to go on expensive campaigns to distant lands. When absence from these campaigns led to the confiscation of their *timars,* they did not delay joining the ranks of rebels and bandits. In these conditions, state officials abused their positions to the detriment of the public, bribery became general, and public morals deteriorated. Officials who were given *timars* forced peasants to pay double the customary dues, and imposed other heavy burdens on them.

Inflation forced the treasury to find new sources of revenue, and to change the system of taxation. In the time of Süleymān, general revenue amounted to 537 million aspers, equivalent to 10 million gold pieces. In 1063/1653 revenue was still 507 million aspers, but this was now worth only 4,200,000 gold pieces. After 1000/1591 the treasury had a growing deficit. Besides the reassessment of some existing taxes, e.g. the capitation tax (*jizye*) on non-Muslims, a new system of taxation was introduced through the impositions known as *'avāriż-i dīvāniyye*. This term had been used in earlier times for services exacted from the people to meet unforeseen military requirements, or for the tax paid in lieu of these services. But towards the end of the tenth/sixteenth century, this became an annual levy, made heavier from year to year. The state also allowed military governors (*beylerbeyis*) to collect from the people a levy (*salma*) to pay provincial irregulars (*sekban*). In another effort to increase revenue, the revenue of *timar* lands was transferred to the state treasury, and the farm of their taxes (*muqāṭa'a, iltizām*) rented to contractors. When the *'avāriż* imposition became a general money-tax on the entire population of the empire, it formed the third main source of revenue, alongside the *'ushr* (tithe) and the *jizye*. These changes, related to the depreciation prevailing at the end of the tenth/sixteenth century, affected profoundly the conditions of life of the Ottoman population.

Ottoman writers rightly insist on the importance of the disappearance of *sipahi* cavalry in the provinces. This resulted in administrative, financial and social changes which shook the Ottoman régime. The real reason why the *sipahis* came to be neglected was that this light cavalry was no match for the heavily armed German fusiliers. The *sipahi* cavalry failed to adapt itself to modern warfare, in respect not only of its equipment, but also of its organization. Its campaigning season was between March and October. Outside these months, the *sipahis* wished to return to their villages to collect the revenue of their *timars,* and to rest their horses. When the asper was devalued, many *sipahis* started avoiding campaigns.

On some occasions, as at the battles of Lepanto in 979/1571 and Eghri in 1004/1596, they withdrew from the Ottoman army before the campaign was over. The government found it necessary, therefore, to raise more soldiers equipped with firearms and drawing regular pay. This meant first an increase in the number of Janissaries. On the other hand, increasing numbers of *sekbans,* armed with firearms, were raised among Anatolian Turks, while the *sipahi* forces were neglected. At the end of the century, they came to be used only for auxiliary duties, such as road-making and fortifications. Other military formations also gradually disappeared. All this meant changes in the classic structure of Ottoman society. One result was the increase in the numbers of the *kapı-kulu* standing forces, many of whom came to be stationed in Anatolia.

The spread of the *kapı-kulus* into Anatolia was caused in the first place by the rebellion of Prince Bāyezīd in 966/1559, when these troops were stationed there for security reasons. The Janissaries and the body-guard cavalrymen of 'the six companies' formed a privileged class in Anatolian towns. They dominated the country, and were held responsible for local security. Some became commanders of the retinues of the local governors, as well as tax-farmers or tax-collectors. They appropriated all the main sources of state revenue and robbed the people. Many local Turks, wishing to profit by the privileges of the *kapı-kulus,* tried to attach themselves to the Janissary corps by devious means.

Even more important was the development whereby the *sekban* irregulars became the main provincial army. The *sekban* became members of governors' retinues, drawing regular pay and armed with muskets. They were to the governors what the *kapı-kulus* were to the sultan. By origin most of them were *levends*. At first their commanders were drawn from *kapı-kulu* officers. These provincial *sekban* troops saw themselves as descending from the *Sekban* division of the Janissaries. There were two classes of *sekbans*: infantry and cavalry. When a campaign was on foot the sultan himself also raised *sekban* formations.

The main characteristic of these troops was that they were armed with muskets, which from about 998/1590 gradually made them the backbone of the Ottoman army. The use of muskets was at that time spreading among the population, in spite of official prohibitions. The importance of the *sekbans* was seen when they formed the nucleus of the paid army of the rebel Prince Bāyezīd. In the eleventh/seventeenth century the *sekbans* were considered the principal force of the empire, alongside the Janissaries. When provincial governors were summoned to a campaign, each one was ordered to bring with him a certain number of *sekbans* in accordance with his revenue. The expenses of maintaining *sekban* musketeers were covered by a levy. When a campaign was in progress, the number of *sekban* companies was considerably increased. Some of these, however, deserted from the war, preferring banditry in Anatolia. *Sekbans* in peacetime received no pay. They then roamed Anatolia under their officers, seeking service with governors as *condottieri* freebooters. Other *sekbans* lived off the people, in which case they were known as *jelālīs*. Sometimes *sekbans* gathered round an energetic leader or a rebel pasha, imposed their own taxes, and exacted tribute from the towns. During this time the *jelālīs* drew their main strength from the *sekban* companies. They were joined by dissatisfied *sipahis,* local vigilantes, and by Turkish and Kurdish nomads. When regular troops left on a campaign, the countryside was given over to these bandits. The troops sent against the *jelālīs* were also drawn largely from among the *sekbans,* so that they often went over to the rebels.

Between 1004/1596 and 1019/1610, as the Ottoman empire was engaged in campaigns against Austria and Persia, *jelālī* bands threw Anatolia into complete anarchy. The *Jelālī* Troubles, as this episode is called, started as Meḥmed III set in hand preparations for the Eghri campaign of 1004/1596. *Jelālīs* were then already in existence, roaming the countryside in small bands. As the campaign was being prepared, the government gave authority to Ḥüsein Pasha and, later, to Kara-Yazıjı ʿAbd al-Ḥalīm to conscript soldiers in central Anatolia. When these two abused their powers, the Ottoman government decided to proceed against them. Thereupon the two press-gang leaders rebelled, and extracted money and provisions from the people to feed the *sekbans* under their commands. Kara-Yazıjı proved a capable commander, and succeeded in uniting dissatisfied elements in Anatolia. This included *sipahis,* since the government had given orders that *sipahis* who had not gone to war should pay compensation in lieu of service, failing which their *timars* would be taken from them. The same would apply to *sipahis* who abandoned the campaign without leave. In all 20,000 *jelālīs* (40,000 according to some sources) gathered round Kara-Yazıjı. From 1006/1598 they formed large groups, which forced Anatolian towns to pay tribute, and made themselves felt in various ways. They dominated the provinces of Sivas and Dulgadır in central Anatolia. When the central government sent against them the *vezīr* Meḥmed Pasha, the *jelālīs* regrouped in south-eastern Anatolia (1007/1599). Kara-

Yazıjı captured the castle of Urfa and made it his centre of resistance. The government tried to win him over by appointing him governor of a *sanjak,* but he refused obedience. Kara-Yazıjı died in 1011/1602. After his death large numbers of *jelālīs* spread over Anatolia. One group led by his brother Deli Ḥasan (Ḥasan the Mad) surrounded Kütahya. The Ottoman government managed to pacify them by appointing Deli Ḥasan provincial governor of Bosnia, and by granting *sanjaks* to some of his followers, while others were enrolled in the imperial cavalry.

The *jelālīs* had no thought of setting up a government of their own. Kara-Yazıjı and his *sekban* irregulars lived off the people, but it seems that they did not indulge in outright robbery and senseless destruction. Nevertheless, the term *jelālī* connoted ruthless plunder and killing. Peasants left their land in panic, seeking refuge in fortified cities. Richer citizens of Anatolia fled to Istanbul, to the Balkans or even to the Crimea. This movement is known in Turkish history as the Great Flight. Several sources confirm that the whole of Anatolia was laid in ruins. As land was left uncultivated, shortages and famine developed. In some places military leaders appropriated abandoned lands which they used for pasture or cultivated as *latifundia.* When the real owners of the land returned, serious clashes inevitably followed.

The *jelālīs* had no well-defined political or social objectives. The *sekbans* had, however, developed a form of group-solidarity. They were in opposition to the *kapı-kulu* troops, who had acquired a predominant position in the provinces. What the *sekbans* in fact wanted was to have a share in the privileges of the *kapı-kulus.* These general characteristics apply to the large-scale rebellions of *sekbans* and *jelālīs,* who sometimes represented a provincial reaction to the domination of central authority by the *kapı-kulus.* At times this reaction was even encouraged by the Ottoman Palace.

The reign of Aḥmed I (1012–26/1603–17) marked the beginning of serious attempts to find a cure for the *Jelālī* Troubles. In 1012/1603 Shah ʿAbbās sought to benefit by the confusion, and launched a new offensive; the suppression of the *jelālīs* (who at this time extended also to the Fertile Crescent) was an indispensable preliminary to effective counter-measures. The grand *vezīr*, Kuyuju Murād Pasha, defeated Jānbulād-oghlu ʿAlī, the ruler of Aleppo, as well as Yūsuf Pasha and Qalender-oghlu, who dominated western Anatolia (1016–17/1607–8). It is said that Jānbulād-oghlu could command 18,000 *sekbans,* 16,000 cavalrymen, and 5,000 *sukhtes.* Qalender-oghlu fled to Shāh ʿAbbās, accompanied by some of his followers. By 1019/1610 the grand *vezīr* had massacred thousands of *jelālīs*. The sultan had a new *Qānūn-nāme* drawn up, to replace that of Süleymān; he also promulgated a number of reforming edicts. Reforms advocated included a reduction of the strength of the *kapı-kulus* and an end to their interference in the administration, allowing the grand *vezīr* full authority to deal with affairs of state, and effective protection of the peasantry. Advocates of reform subsequently tried to have Sultan 'Os̱mān II (1027–31/1618–22) despatched to Anatolia where they wanted him to enforce reforms with the help of provincial troops. However, the *kapı-kulus* revolted and murdered the sultan, who was still young and inexperienced (1031/1622). Thereupon the governor of Erzurum, Abaza Meḥmed Pasha, revolted at the head of his *sekbans*, allegedly to avenge the sultan. Abaza Meḥmed Pasha became master of central and eastern Anatolia, which he dominated for five years, massacring the *kapı-kulus* wherever he went. He was finally forced back into Erzurum, where he capitulated and was bought off with the governorship of Bosnia (1038/1628).

From 1040/1631 onwards Murād IV took forcible steps to reaffirm the authority of the sultan. He carried out reforms at court and in the *ojaks* (companies) of the *kapı-kulus*, among whom discipline was re-established, and he reorganized the *sipahi* cavalry of *timar*-holders. An ordinance was issued for the protection of the peasantry. Nevertheless, in the reign of Ibrāhīm I (1049–58/1640–8) and during the minority of Meḥmed IV (1058–99/1648–87) authority was exercised effectively by the Janissaries and by the sultan's mother. In 1057/1647 Varvar 'Alī Pasha revolted in Sivas, again at the head of *sekbans*. The *jelālī* pashas became a power in the land. One of them, Ibshir Pasha, governor of Sivas and a nephew of Abaza Meḥmed, was given the seal as grand *vezīr*. Ibshir Pasha arrived in Istanbul at the head of his *sekbans*, but before long he too was eliminated by the Janissaries (1064/1654). The *jelālī* pashas, it was seen, were only strong in Anatolia, from which they drew their *sekbans*. The authority of the central government was finally re-established by Köprülü Meḥmed Pasha (grand *vezīr* from 1066/1656 to 1072/1661), who was entrusted with absolute powers at a moment of crisis, when Istanbul lay open to an attack by the Venetian fleet. Forceful measures succeeded in re-establishing discipline among the Janissaries. In the meantime, in Anatolia, Abaza Ḥasan Pasha, who had at his disposal large bands of *sekbans*, joined forces with other provincial governors against the grand *vezīr*. A force of 30,000 men was brought together in the plain of Konya (Shawwāl 1068/July 1658). Köprülü succeeded in dispersing the rebels. Abiding by the advice of reformers, Sultan Meḥmed IV put his undivided trust in Köprülü Meḥmed, and, after him, in his son, Köprülü Fāżil Aḥmed Pasha (grand *vezīr* from 1072/1661 to 1087/1676). From the time of the Köprülüs, the Sublime Porte (*Bāb-ı 'Ālī*), which was the residence of the grand *vezīr*, became the true centre of government. The Köprülü reforms aimed at securing observance of the *Sharī'a* and the *Qānūns*, a reduction in the numbers of the *kapı-kulus*, a reduction also in the burden borne by the central treasury, and the protection of the peasantry by a proper policy of taxation and public order. However, the situation that had prevailed in 1005/1596 reappeared in the war-years which followed the retreat from Vienna. In 1098/1687, at a critical moment in the war, a *jelālī* leader in Anatolia, Yeghen 'Os̲mān Pasha, became with his troops of *sekban* and *sarıja* soldiers, the most powerful personality in the empire. He was appointed commander-in-chief (*serdār*) of the army fighting the Austrians, and acquired a dominating position. To get rid of him the sultan was forced to proclaim a general levy. However, after the assassination of Yeghen 'Os̲mān Pasha, the whole of Anatolia was again given over to the depredations of *jelālī* bands (1099/1688).

Intensification of the war in the Mediterranean and in central Europe; the Cossacks and the Northern Question

The Ottomans lost their supremacy at sea in the eleventh/seventeenth century, and were unable to defend even their own coasts and sea-routes. The Ottoman coasts of the Black Sea were terrorized by Cossacks, who sailed down the Dnieper in their small boats. In 1023/1614 they burned down Sinop, while in 1034/1625 they looted the Istanbul suburb of Yeniköy on the Bosphorus. In 1047/1637 the Cossacks captured Azov, and kept it for five years. The tsar of Muscovy did not yet dare to place the Cossacks under his protection. The Ottomans and the Crimean khan tried to contain the Cossacks by building the castles of Özü and Ghāzī-Kirman, and forming the new province of Özü from the *sanjaks* along the western coast of the Black Sea. The Polish campaign of 'Os̲mān II in 1030/1621 was connected mainly with the Cossack question.

Meanwhile in the Mediterranean, Maltese and Tuscan privateers operated with increased daring. Crete served as their base, and in 1054/1644 when Maltese corsairs captured the ship on which the former chief eunuch was travelling to Egypt, the Ottomans finally made up their minds to attempt the conquest of Crete. Although they took Canea on 24 Jumādā I 1055/18 July 1645, sea-mastery passed quickly to the Venetians, who succeeded in blockading the Straits, Smyrna, Cheshme and the ports of the Morea in 1057/1647, thus stopping the flow of Ottoman reinforcements. The Ottomans on the island found themselves beleaguered. Nevertheless, the Ottoman commander, Deli Ḥüseyn Pasha, succeeded in extending the area under his control, and attempted to win over the local Greeks. Finally, on 18 Shawwāl 1058/6 October 1648, he besieged Candia, the capital. The following year the Ottomans formed a fleet by hiring English and Dutch ships in Istanbul, but it proved powerless against the Venetians. In 1065/1655 an Ottoman official emissary went to England to obtain the help of the English navy. In exchange the Ottomans granted new facilities to English merchants. In 1070/1660 there was even talk of a defensive and offensive alliance between the Ottoman empire and England against the French and the Spaniards. The year 1066/1656 was critical for the Ottomans. An Ottoman fleet attempting to reinforce Crete with troops and supplies was defeated at the mouth of the Straits. The Venetians intensified their blockade after capturing the islands of Tenedos and Lemnos. Istanbul was panic-stricken at the possibility of an attack on the city. It was at this critical juncture that Köprülü Meḥmed was appointed grand *vezīr*. He succeeded, albeit with difficulty, in clearing the Venetians from the Straits and recapturing the two islands (1067/1657). Nonetheless, the Ottomans never regained naval supremacy. The siege of Candia dragged on for twenty-two years, the fortress being finally captured after a violent assault by Köprülü Fāżil Aḥmed Pasha on 1 Jumādā I 1080/27 September 1669. The Cretan campaign witnessed at times Christian alliances reminiscent of a crusade. Venice was at times helped by the Spanish, English and French, as well as by the papacy and by Tuscan and Maltese privateers. The Cretan campaign, with its vast cost in money and casualties, played an important part in the decline of the Ottoman empire.

In the eleventh/seventeenth century the rivalry between the Ottomans and the Habsburgs revolved at first round Transylvania. Later, the Ottomans repeated the attempt, first made by Süleymān, to capture the whole of Hungary. In the end it was the Habsburgs who emerged victorious. During the Thirty Years War the Ottoman-protected principality of Transylvania constituted a Protestant fortress against the Habsburgs. It had been a great political success for the Ottomans to have strengthened Transylvania as a counter-weight to the Habsburgs. However, Transylvanian princes, such as György Rákóczi I (1040–58/1630/48) and György Rákóczi II (1058–70/1648–60), later profited from Ottoman weakness to follow an independent policy. In 1068/1658 Köprülü Meḥmed led a successful campaign in Transylvania, capturing Yanova (Jenö). The province of Varat was formed in this district, and this served to keep Transylvania under control. This change in the *status quo* led to a new war with the Habsburgs. The Ottoman army commanded by Köprülü Fāżil Aḥmed, captured Ujvar on 21 Ṣafar 1074/24 September 1663. This too became the seat of a governor. The following year, however, on 8 Ṣafar 1075/31 August 1664, Fāżil Aḥmed Pasha was defeated at St Gotthard on the Raab. Nevertheless, the latest Ottoman conquests were confirmed by the treaty of Vasvár (1075/1665).

A Hungarian revolt against Habsburg oppression allowed Kara Muṣṭafā Pasha (grand *vezīr* from 1087/1676 to 1094/1683) to resume the offensive. The grand *vezīr* extended Ottoman protection to the Hungarian rebels, while the sultan granted to their leader, Imre Thököly, the title of king of Middle Hungary. In 1092/1681 the Ottomans began to give him armed support against the Habsburgs.

Further north, in an attempt to control the Ukrainian Cossacks, the Ottomans made war first on Poland (with which peace treaties were concluded at Bujash in 1083/1672 and at Zuravno in 1087/1676); then on the tsar of Russia in the campaign of 1089/1678, which was followed by the truce at Bakhchesaray in 1092/1681. Parts of Podolia and of the Ukraine were made subject to the Ottoman empire.

The Ottomans besieged Vienna for a second time between 22 Rajab and 20 Ramaḍān 1094/17 July–12 September 1683. They were beaten by an Austrian-German-Polish army before the city, and retreated in disorder. Thereupon their old enemies joined forces against them in the Holy League, formed in 1684 under the auspices of the pope, by Austria, Poland and Venice, and joined by Russia in 1686. The treaty of Carlowitz which put an end to this long and, for the Ottomans, disastrous war on 24 Rajab 1110/26 January 1699, resolved the Hungarian question in the interest of the Habsburgs, and brought the Austrians to the gates of the Balkans. At the same time Russia established itself firmly in the Ukraine. In 1107/1696 the Russians captured Azov, thus setting foot on the shores of the Black Sea for the first time. The hardships which the great war had brought in its train, the increasing taxation, the first massive revolt of the Porte's Serbian and Albanian-Greek subjects in the Balkans, renewed depredations by the *jelālīs* in Anatolia, and, in general, the impoverishment of the country, threw the empire into a decline from which it was not to recover. Ottoman statesmen now finally accepted the superiority of the 'Franks' and the weakness of their own state. From now on they saw their interests in a policy of peace. In 1114/1703 for the first time, a bureaucrat, Rāmī Meḥmed, was appointed grand *vezīr*. The belief that the state could be revived by a return to the order imposed on it by Süleymān the Magnificent was abandoned, and the Ottomans turned their eyes to the West.

CHAPTER 3

THE LATER OTTOMAN EMPIRE IN RUMELIA AND ANATOLIA

OTTOMAN 'SPLENDID ISOLATION' COMES TO AN END

The treaty of Carlowitz (1110/1699) marks a turning-point in Ottoman history. The Ottoman empire, which had terrified Christendom for over three hundred years, ceased to be an aggressive power. From now on it mainly fought rearguard actions against the overwhelming might of Christian Europe. Yet it survived, its frontiers gradually shrinking, for another two centuries. The reasons for this amazing tenacity were manifold: the rivalry of the great powers, the mutual hostility between the subject peoples of the Balkans and their fear of European domination, the modernization of the empire, and, last but not least, the martial qualities and religious ethos of the Muslim soldier, especially the Turk.

Down to the early decades of the eighteenth century, the Ottomans' chief European foes had been the republic of Venice and the Habsburg empire. The former, now in rapid decline, could no longer maintain its naval supremacy in the eastern Mediterranean. After thirty years of unpopular government in the Morea, whose Greek Orthodox population detested Catholic rule, the Venetians were defeated by Ottoman forces and in the Peace of Passarowitz (1130/1718) had to return the peninsula, their chief gain under the treaty of Carlowitz.

The Habsburg armies, under the brilliant leadership of Prince Eugene, had intervened in the war on the side of Venice to win decisive victories. In the Peace of Passarowitz, however, the Austrians, while not saving Venice from loss of territory, made substantial gains for themselves, forcing the sultan to cede the Bánát of Temesvár, Little Wallachia and Belgrade, the Ottomans' 'House of the Holy War' (*Dār al-Jihād*), with parts of northern Serbia. Twenty years later the Turks fought with greater success and, in the treaty of Belgrade (1152/1739), recovered most of these regions. The favourable peace-terms were largely due to the diplomatic support of France, whose reward was the extended capitulations of 1740. Apart from Bukovina (1189/1775), no further important territory was ceded to Austria in the eighteenth century, and with the Peace of Sistova (1205/1791) a period of over 250 years of hostilities with the Habsburg empire came to a close.

By the middle of the century, the Habsburgs' role as leaders of Europe's fight against the Turks was taken over by the tsars, whose first objective was the mastery of the Black Sea, Russia's back door and the bulwark of the Ottoman capital of Istanbul. In 1107/1696 Peter the Great had secured a first foothold at Azov, but in 1123/1711 had been forced into a commitment to restore it, in order to avert the annihilation of his army at the Pruth. Victorious, but deserted by their Austrian allies in the 1148–52/1735–9 war, the Russians had made few gains in the treaty of Belgrade. During the long peace that ensued, the Turks, unaware of the growth of Russian power, did little to strengthen their forces. Thus, when a new war broke out in 1182/1768, the Russian army was able to inflict heavy defeats on them; a Russian fleet, largely British officered, sailed from the Baltic into the Mediterranean, destroyed the Ottoman navy and stirred up the Greeks in the Morea.

The disastrous peace treaty of Küchük Kaynarja (1188/1774), a milestone in Ottoman-Russian relations, made the Porte recognize the Tatars of the Crimea as politically independent. In religious affairs only did they remain subject to the Ottoman sultan-caliph—the first internationally acknowledged assertion of the sultan's rights over Muslims outside the frontiers of his empire. Russia received parts of the northern shore of the Black Sea, an Ottoman lake hitherto, and secured unhindered commercial navigation in Turkish waters and through the Straits of the Bosporus and Dardanelles. In respect to the Christian religion and churches, the Porte assumed certain obligations upon which the tsars later based their claim to a protectorate over the sultan's Greek Orthodox subjects. Russia's power in the Black Sea area further increased by her annexation, in 1197/1783, of the Crimea, the first Muslim territory to slip from the sultan's suzerainty, and by pushing her frontier westwards to the Dniester (Peace of Jassy, 1206/1792).

With a view to preventing Russian advance into the Caucasus and beyond, and at the same time gaining military laurels and new territory from a weak enemy, the Ottomans took advantage of the anarchy prevailing in Persia after the collapse of Safavid rule in 1134/1722. By solemn *fetvās* the Shīʿī Persians were declared heretics who had to be extirpated, and when the Sunnī Afghan invaders usurped the Persian throne they too were denounced as rebels against the caliphate of the Ottoman sultan. The Turks occupied Georgia and, in accordance with a partition agreement with Russia (1136/1724), large parts of north-western Persia. But as a result of Nādir Shāh's victorious counter-offensives, they had in 1159/1746 to reconfirm the old frontier established under Murād IV.

By the end of the eighteenth century, the Ottomans had to face the bitter fact that they were no longer in a position even to defend themselves single-handed against a major power. They drew the obvious conclusion, to try and integrate themselves more consistently into the complicated mechanism of European diplomacy and, especially, overcome their Islamic scruples against alliance with Christian powers. The first, hesitant steps towards this goal had been made in the course of the eighteenth century. At the peace conferences of Carlowitz, Passarowitz and Belgrade, the Ottomans accepted mediation by representatives of friendly Western powers. Conversely, in 1745 the Porte surprised European diplomats by making the unprecedented, and unsuccessful, offer to serve as mediator between the warring Christian states. It was the growing Russian peril that compelled the Ottoman government to conclude alliances with other enemies of Russia, such as Sweden (1740, 1789) and Prussia (1790). But Bonaparte's invasion of Ottoman Egypt and Palestine (1213–14/1798–9), which temporarily interrupted the traditional friendship with France, led to alliances and military co-operation with Russia and Britain. The Ottomans sensed their dependence on foreign powers even more acutely, when in 1832–3 and again in 1839–40 the very existence of their state was threatened by a Muslim foe, Muḥammad ʿAlī of Egypt, and they were saved only by the intervention of their infidel allies—first the Russians and then the British and others.

THE BREAK-UP OF THE OTTOMAN EMPIRE

During the nineteenth century Russian pressure remained the major factor in Ottoman foreign relations. The tsars' policy wavered between the desire to preserve a feeble, decentralized Ottoman empire under Russian protection, and the wish to partition it by annexing Ottoman territory or creating independent Christian states in the Balkan peninsula. One aim, however, was never lost sight of—the domination of the Black Sea and the Straits. While the expansion of Russia into the Balkans aroused Austrian anxiety, her design on the Straits met with the opposition of Britain and France, who wished to maintain their hegemony in the Mediterranean, secure the route to the East, and preserve the balance of power in Europe. Moreover, both had important economic interests to protect in the Ottoman empire. In the nineteenth century Britain took top place in its external trade. In 1825–52 British exports to Turkey increased eightfold and by the end of that period were almost four times as large as her imports from Turkey. France, who had established a flourishing Levant trade in the eighteenth century, also retained a considerable share in Ottoman commerce. The large amounts of money lent by Britain and France to the Ottoman government, or invested in the empire, further increased their interest in its preservation. Finally, as a counterpoise to Russia's protection of her co-religionists in the empire, France maintained her traditional guardianship over the Catholics, and Britain took upon herself to defend other non-Muslim communities, Protestants, Jews and Druzes.

The stability of the Ottoman empire was further threatened by the fact that its dominions in Europe had an overwhelming non-Turkish and even non-Muslim population, which had never been absorbed or assimilated. Most of the Balkan peoples had not only retained their Christian religion and cultural identity, but also wide internal autonomy. The Christian subjects, organized in their legally recognized *millets*, never identified themselves with the Muslim Ottoman state, in which they ranked as second-class citizens. The ideas of liberty and nationalism engendered by the French Revolution found a fertile ground among these subject peoples, who had begun their westernization much earlier than the Turks, and were encouraged by Christian powers to fight for their national liberation.

In the reign of Maḥmūd II (1808–39), the Ottoman government awoke to this serious internal danger. But for reasons to be discussed below, the measures it took were too late or too half-hearted to turn the Christians into loyal subjects and prevent the successive break-away of Balkan nationalities.

Russia adroitly exploited this situation, and in the first third of the nineteenth century made considerable progress towards her goals. After her annexation of Bessarabia (1812), she intensified her intervention in the affairs of neighbouring Moldavia and Wallachia, and in the treaty of Adrianople (1829) secured the autonomy of these principalities under her tutelage. In the same treaty, confirmed in 1830, a similar status was accorded by the Porte to the Serbs, who in 1804 had launched the first national uprising in the Balkans and had enjoyed generous Russian support. In 1829 the tsar also gained the mouths of the Danube, as well as some key points on or near the east coast of the Black Sea, while his title to Georgia was acknowledged too.

An even graver menace to Ottoman rule in Europe was the Greek revolt of 1821. The Greeks played a major role in Ottoman commerce and shipping and were the predominant religious and cultural factor in the Balkans. The Greek Orthodox patriarchate of Constantinople had been a most important prop of the sultan's domination over his Christian subjects; the Greek aristocracy of the Phanar quarter of Constantinople had held the high government appointments, such as dragomans of the Porte and the Admiralty, and hospodars of Moldavia and Wallachia. Maḥmūd II reacted to the revolt with great determination and violence and, despite Greek naval supremacy, would have succeeded in suppressing it with the help of Muḥammad 'Alī's modern troops, had Britain, France and Russia not intervened at the battle of Navarino (1827). In 1830 the sultan had to submit to their will and, most reluctantly, to acknowledge Greek independence, a severe blow to Ottoman self-respect.

Russian influence in Istanbul reached its climax in 1833, when at the sultan's request a Russian fleet entered the Bosphorus and landed troops to protect his throne against Muḥammad 'Alī. In return, in a secret article of the Treaty of Hünkâr Iskelesi (July 1833), Maḥmūd promised to keep the Dardanelles closed to the warships of all other powers and at the same time—or so some authorities interpreted it—to permit Russian men-of-war to pass through the Bosporus, or even through the Dardanelles into the Mediterranean. Such permission had been granted, though in a more limited form, in the Ottoman-Russian alliances of 1799 and 1805.[1] Alarmed by this Russian advance, Palmerston decided to adopt the policy, first advocated by the younger Pitt, of containing Russia by actively supporting the Ottoman empire. When Muḥammad 'Alī's renewed threat to the empire's existence in 1839 caused another international crisis, Britain succeeded not only in confining the protégé of her French rival to Egypt, but also in annulling Russia's gains of 1833. The Convention of London (1841) re-established the ancient rule that the Straits should be closed to all foreign warships so long as the Ottoman empire was at peace.

As a result of Russia's defeat in the Crimean War, which ostensibly

[1] For the controversy over the interpretation of the relevant articles of these treaties, see J. C. Hurewitz, 'Russia and the Turkish Straits: A Revaluation of the Origins of the Problem', in *World Politics,* XIV, no. 4 (July, 1962), 605–32.

had been caused by her dispute with France over the custody of the Christian Holy Places in Palestine, the tsar's ambitions were further checked. The treaty of Paris (1856) neutralized the Black Sea; except for a limited number of light Ottoman and Russian vessels, no men-of-war were henceforth allowed in those waters. This restriction was denounced by Russia during the Franco-German war, and formally abrogated in 1871. Russia ceded the mouths of the Danube and southern Bessarabia, and a collective guarantee of the powers was substituted for the Russian protectorate over Moldavia and Wallachia. Even more important, from the Ottoman point of view, was the article of the treaty in which the powers formally admitted the Ottoman empire to the Concert of Europe, and guaranteed its independence and territorial integrity. In view of the sultan's promise in the *Khaṭṭ-ı Hümāyūn* mentioned below to improve the conditions of his Christian subjects, the powers even waived the right to interfere in their favour. Thus a fresh lease of life was ensured to the empire, on condition that non-Muslims were given equal rights with Muslims.

As will be seen, however, little progress towards this aim was made, and anti-Christian outrages led to military intervention on the part of the powers at Jedda in 1858, in Lebanon and Damascus in 1860. In the Balkans, Ottoman rule was breaking down. Moldavia and Wallachia were united into the autonomous principality of Roumania (1861), and the Turks had to evacuate their fortresses in Serbia (1867). After the defeat of France in 1871 and the death of the pro-French grand *vezīr* 'Ālī Pasha in the same year, the Ottoman government fell under the sway of the Russian ambassador, Count Ignatiev, who ceaselessly strove to realize the goals of pan-Slavism. In 1875 a serious insurrection broke out in Herzegovina. It was followed in 1876 by a rising in Bulgaria, and the declaration of war on the empire by Serbia and Montenegro. The fierce Turkish counter-measures in Bulgaria aroused a storm of indignation in Britain. Russian armies crossed the Ottoman frontiers, and despite 'O̱smān Pasha's gallant defence of Plevna, occupied Sofia and Adrianople and reached the outskirts of Constantinople. The treaty signed at San Stefano (today Yeşilköy) in March 1878 hopelessly dismembered the remants of Turkey in Europe.

At this stage, Disraeli, even at the risk of war with Russia, intervened to prevent her control of the Balkans and the Straits, as well as her advance through eastern Anatolia in the direction of Mesopotamia. The treaty concluded at the Congress of Berlin (June–July 1878) deprived

Russia of part of the fruits of her victory, and at the same time hastened the dissolution of the Ottoman empire. Batum, Ardahan and Kars were ceded to the tsar, and Serbia, Montenegro and Roumania were granted full independence. Greece was put off with promises; only in 1881 was she to annex Thessaly and part of Epirus. Bulgaria became an autonomous principality; in 1870 its Church had already been given the right to establish a separate national exarchate at Constantinople. But she lost about two-thirds of the territory that had been assigned to her under the Treaty of San Stefano, including her access to the Aegean. Her southern part, Eastern Rumelia, was also restored to the sultan, and was united with Bulgaria only in 1885. The Western powers, despairing of the Ottomans' ability to reform and defend their state and financially hurt by Turkey's defaulting on her debts (1875), gave up their policy of support for the integrity of the empire. Britain secured the right to occupy and administer the island of Cyprus, in return for an engagement to join the sultan in the defence of his Asian dominions against any further Russian encroachment. The French occupation of Tunis and the British occupation of Egypt followed in 1881 and 1882 respectively. With the aim of halting Russian expansion in the Balkans and the union of the southern Slavs, Bosnia-Herzegovina was handed over to Austrian administration, while the *sanjak* of Novi-Bazar, lying between Serbia and Montenegro, was placed under Austrian military occupation. The treaty of Berlin left to the Ottomans about half the territory they had ruled in Europe at the beginning of the century.

At the Congress of Berlin and later, the only great European power that did not seize any part of the disintegrating Ottoman empire was the new German Reich. Bismarck, who played 'honest broker' at the Congress, had taken the view that to Germany the Eastern Question was not worth the bones of a single Pomeranian grenadier, and had encouraged Austria's *Drang nach Osten*. But William II, for economic and strategic reasons alike, displayed great interest in the future of Istanbul and the Ottoman empire in Asia. German military experts, traders and financiers flocked to Turkey; Germany's share in Ottoman commerce rose steeply, and the Deutsche Bank group was granted a concession to build the Baghdād railway, which was to connect Istanbul (and central Europe) with the Persian Gulf.

Despite the easy victory in 1897 of the Ottoman army, reorganized by the German Baron von der Goltz, over the Greeks, the sultan's rule in the Balkans became most precarious. Shortly after the Young Turk

Revolution of 1908, Bulgaria declared her independence, Austria formally annexed Bosnia-Herzegovina, and Crete proclaimed her union with Greece. The final blow fell when the hitherto mutually hostile Balkan nations formed a League, declared war, and in a few weeks routed the Turks completely (1912). As a result, an autonomous Albania was created; Montenegro, Serbia and Roumania enlarged their territories; Greece received the greater part of Epirus, Crete and some Aegean islands; and Macedonia, that 'medley of races and creeds', was divided among Greece, Serbia and Bulgaria. The latter had also taken over most of Thrace, but after a successful Turkish offensive during the Second Balkan War in 1913 had to restore eastern Thrace, including Edirne, to the sultan. The Ottomans retained less than 11,000 square miles, not even a tenth of their European territory under the treaty of Berlin.

The outbreak of the First World War found the Ottoman empire exhausted by war with Italy (1911–12), which had resulted in the loss of Tripolitania and the Dodecanese, and by the two Balkan Wars. The traditional enmity towards Russia, the paramount influence of Germany, and the hope of recovering some of the lost territories and realizing certain pan-Islamic and pan-Turanian dreams, induced the Young Turk leaders to take the fatal decision of concluding a secret alliance with Germany and, late in October 1914, entering the war at her side. The British government's requisition of two battleships under construction for the Turks in England, and the arrival, in August 1914, of the German cruisers *Goeben* and *Breslau,* which joined the Ottoman navy, helped to influence public opinion.

Strongly supported by German officers and war supplies, the Ottoman armies proved their prowess for the last time. The British and Allied forces, which landed on the Gallipoli peninsula in 1915 to strike against Istanbul and open the Black Sea route to Russia, were repulsed, partly due to the inspiring leadership of Muṣṭafā Kemāl Bey, later known as Atatürk. In Mesopotamia and Palestine too, a British advance was halted until 1917. The disintegration of the tsar's empire after the Bolshevik revolution allowed the Turks to reconquer north-east Anatolia, and advance into Transcaucasia and Persia. But the defeat of Germany and Austria-Hungary on the major fronts, the conquest of the western Fertile Crescent by the Allies, and the collapse of Bulgaria, compelled the sultan to sue for an armistice, which was signed on 30 October 1918 at Mudros. The Ottoman empire was finally vanquished.

The death-blow had not been delivered by Russia, the empire's principal foe during the last two centuries, who had twice (in 1829 and 1878) almost attained her historic ambition of planting the Cross on Aya Sofya and succeeding the Turks as custodian of the Straits; in 1915 she had been able to induce Britain and France secretly to agree to her annexing Constantinople and the Straits after Turkey's defeat. By an irony of history, however, the empire was occupied and later partitioned by the Western powers who had supported the Ottomans for many generations, and had served as the main source of inspiration for the social and cultural changes that were to lead to the rise of the new Turkish nation.

THE BEGINNINGS OF WESTERNIZATION

During the eighteenth century the two ruling classes of the Ottoman empire underwent great changes. The 'men of the sword', most of whom used to be the sultan's slaves, born of Christian parents, recruited under the now abandoned *devshirme* system and largely trained in the palace-schools, lost their monopoly of the highest secular offices of state. At the same time the *'ulemā'*, who unlike them could leave their property to their descendants, became a kind of aristocracy. While politically powerful, they grew more and more corrupt morally. The boundless ambition and shameless nepotism of *Shaykh al-Islām*[1] Feyż Allāh Efendi, for example, were one of the main causes of the military rebellion of 1115/1703, which deposed Sultan Muṣṭafā II. The *'ulemā'* now ceased to be the sole educated stratum in Muslim society. Both the 'men of the sword' and the 'men of religion' began to face the rivalry of the rising bureaucrat class.

Most of these 'men of the pen' were the sons of free Muslims, in many cases civil servants. Usually they lacked a thorough *medrese* education, but were trained, from early youth, in government offices. The most gifted among them rose from being simple clerks to high positions in the government, the seat of which had shifted from the palace to the grand *vezīr*'s office, or Sublime Porte (*Bāb-ı 'Ālī*). The grand *vezīr*'s chief secretary (*re'īs ül-küttāb* or *re'īs efendi*) took increasing charge of foreign affairs. With the growing dependence of the empire on friendly powers, the importance of Ottoman diplomats with a basic knowledge of European politics assumed ever greater proportions. It is therefore

[1] *Shaykh al- Islām* was the title of the *muftī* of Istanbul, the head of the Ottoman Muslim establishment.

not surprising that in the eighteenth century many *re'īs efendis* and other high bureaucrats attained the position of grand *vezīr,* including several outstanding personalities.

The members of this new *élite* differed greatly from the uncouth, fanatical and bellicose 'men of the sword' who had served as grand *vezīrs* so often in the past. Many of them were highly educated and cultured men, though as a rule rather incompetent in military affairs. When called upon to lead the army as commanders-in-chief in the field, some of them failed ignominiously. These 'men of the pen' had more in common with the '*ulemā*', but, unlike most of them, they were prone to be influenced by Western ideas, and were therefore destined for a decisive part in the Ottoman reforms of the nineteenth century.

The rise of this new class led to a cultural revival in Istanbul. In the reign of Sultan Aḥmed III (1115–43/1703–30), and especially during the grand vezirate of his son-in-law, Damad Ibrāhīm Pasha (1130–43/1718–30), luxurious pavilions were built and gardens laid out in imitation of Versailles; gifted court poets, headed by the '*ālim* Nedīm, extolled a life of dalliance and worldly pleasure; and a type of Ottoman rococo became the fashion. The first Turkish (and Muslim) printing press, for secular books only, was established in 1727 by a Hungarian renegade, Ibrāhīm Müteferriqa. Hebrew, Armenian and Greek books had already been printed in Constantinople for many years. A committee of '*ulemā*' and learned bureaucrats set up by Ibrāhīm Pasha initiated the translation of various Arabic, Persian and Greek scientific works into Turkish. Aḥmed III and his successor, Maḥmūd I (1143–68/1730–54) also founded several important libraries in the capital.

This period, known as the Age of Tulips (*Lale Devri*) because of the craze for their cultivation, was short-lived. Alarmed by military reform projects, the Janissaries joined forces with other conservative elements who were indignant at the luxury of the court, the new European manners and the loss of military conquests in Persia. They incited the populace, who groaned under high taxation and steeply rising prices, and in 1143/1730 overthrew the sultan and his government.

This rebellion slowed down the process of westernization, but European civilization continued to penetrate through various channels. The many foreign diplomats, merchants, experts and travellers now found easier access to Turkish intellectuals and officials; the Greek and Armenian upper classes increased their contacts with Europe; and the early Ottoman ambassadors to Western capitals in their reports described, not always unfavourably, European life and institutions. The 'iron curtain' between the Ottoman empire and Christian Europe began to lift.

During the eighteenth century it became clear that attempts to renovate the army, the feudal system and the financial and general administration on traditional lines could not arrest the empire's continuous decline. Already at that time, the first, rather tentative measures were in fact taken to recast it according to Western models. With the assistance of European experts, such as Comte de Bonneval and Baron de Tott, the bombardier, artillery and engineer corps were reorganized; new arms (e.g., the bayonet) and new military techniques were adopted, and modern men-of-war built. These reforms, however, failed to stave off disaster in the Russian War of 1182–8/1768–74.

After another defeat by the Russians and Austrians in 1201–6/1787–92, the enlightened Sultan Selīm III (1203–22/1789–1807) decided to launch a more comprehensive series of reforms, primarily in the military sphere. They included the formation of modern army units (*Niẓām-ı Jedīd*), which were armed and drilled on Western lines. Various old-established corps and war industries were also reorganized. The newly founded or reformed military and naval schools of engineering began to produce a Westward-looking class of officers. Relations with the great powers were strengthened by the establishment of the first permanent Ottoman embassies in the major capitals of western and central Europe.

But recruiting for the new army led to a rebellion of Janissaries and '*ulemā*', who in 1807 put an end to Selīm's reign and reforms. In the following year, Bayrakdar Muṣṭafā Pasha, leading a successful *coup*, brought Maḥmūd II to the throne and tried to resume the military innovations. A few months later, however, he perished in a new Janissary insurrection. The dramatic failure of these first westernizing attempts proved that such reforms could not be carried out within the framework of the traditional Ottoman institutions.

THE TANẒĪMĀT

The reforms of the Ottoman body politic were started in earnest by Sultan Maḥmūd II (1808–39), a strong and proud ruler who has rightly been compared with Peter the Great. Their principal aim was to save the empire by modernizing (i.e. westernizing) its decaying institutions. Since the only force recognizing this need was the sultan and his few progressive collaborators, it was considered imperative first of all to establish his absolute and centralist rule. Consequently, Maḥmūd broke the power of the provincial notables (*a'yān*) in Rumelia and of the Anatolian hereditary and virtually independent feudatories (*dere-beyis*), some of whom had set up benevolent and popular administrations. Simultaneously the rebellions of Pasvan-oghlu of Vidin, 'Alī Pasha of Jannina and other governors were put down. Only Muḥammad 'Alī Pasha of Egypt, who had there introduced European reforms earlier, more ruthlessly and much more extensively, succeeded in gaining *de facto* independence.

Later, in 1826, Maḥmūd exterminated the Janissaries, the reactionary and lawless core of the Ottoman army, who had shown their inefficiency as compared with Muḥammad 'Alī's modern troops in the Greek War. Their allies, the Bektashī order of dervishes, were persecuted and many of the Bektashī convents destroyed. Finally, the *'ulemā'*, who could no longer rely on the support of the Janissaries, were either won over or intimidated, and gradually deprived of their functions in the administration, their predominant positions in the judiciary and education, and their lucrative control of the *waqfs*. It should, however, be noted that many prominent *'ulemā'* backed the government for various reasons, even in its westernizing reforms; they thereby deepened the traditional gulf between the *'ulemā'* leaders and the more fanatical *'ulemā'* of lower rank, the *softas* or *medrese*-students, and dervishes, who maintained their reactionary influence over the masses.

With these obstacles out of the way, Maḥmūd II initiated a number of important innovations; under his successors, 'Abd ül-Mejīd (1839–61) and 'Abd ül-'Azīz (1861–76), they were carried on and greatly expanded by several progressive and talented statesmen, such as Muṣṭafā Reshīd Pasha (d. 1858) and his disciples, 'Ālī and Fu'ād Pashas. In these endeavours the reformers were actively supported by Britain (for many years represented in Istanbul by the all-powerful Stratford Canning) and, particularly in 1867–70, by France.

The changes that the powers most insistently urged upon the Ottoman government concerned the status of its Christian subjects. Indeed, Sultan 'Abd ül-Mejīd's charter of 1839, the *Khaṭṭ-ı Sherīf* of Gülkhāne, which is commonly regarded as the starting-point of the reforms called the Tanẓīmāt, guaranteed certain fundamental rights to all Ottoman subjects without distinction of religion. This principle was reaffirmed by the charter of 1856 (*Iṣlāḥāt Fermānı*, known in Europe as *Khaṭṭ-ı*

Hümāyūn), which went even further and assured non-Muslims of religious liberty and equality in the administration of justice, taxation, public employment and military service as well as admission to the civil and military schools.

These promises were made in deference to the demands of the powers, on whose goodwill the Ottoman government had by now become dependent; they did not reflect a growing liberal trend in Muslim public opinion. The religious axiom of the superiority of Islam, and the centuries-old tradition of Muslim domination over the unbelievers, had created an attitude that did not easily lend itself to change. The transformation of the Ottoman empire, spearhead of Islam, into a secular state where non-Muslims were granted complete equality was inconceivable. Even had the Tanẓīmāt leaders sincerely desired such a revolutionary course of action, they would not have been able to carry it out against the fierce opposition or passive resistance of the large majority of the Muslim population. The military victories of the Christian powers, their constant intervention in favour of their co-religionists, and the bloody revolts of the Balkan peoples during the nineteenth century even fanned anti-Christian feeling among the Muslims.

Moreover, the non-Muslim communities too were generally rather reluctant to collaborate with the government in this policy. They were eager for any improvement of their status, but unprepared for the most part to assume the obligations incumbent on fully qualified citizens. A typical case was the newly granted admission of non-Muslims to army service. Not only did it encounter the opposition of the Muslims, who loathed the idea of fighting alongside the unbelievers and obeying the orders of non-Muslim officers; the Christians too were unwilling to forgo the advantages of exemption from military duty and take up arms against other Christians. Lacking a feeling of common Ottoman loyalty and patriotism, they were all the more jealous of their special privileges, which they regarded as the key to their rapid economic and educational progress. Furthermore, the traditional leaders of the non-Muslim communities, the clergy, feared for the loss of their vested interests, since the charter of 1856 expressly called for a strengthening of the lay elements in the administration of the *millets*. By and large, the Christians doubted the sincerity of the Ottoman government, and hoped that with foreign, mainly Russian, aid they would be able to achieve much more: autonomy, and finally independence.

In consequence, the promised emancipation of the non-Muslims took only limited effect. Though Christians and Jews joined the new administrative councils and courts of law, their influence remained restricted. Few non-Muslims were appointed to higher offices. The poll-tax (*jizye*) was abolished, but the military exemption tax took its place for all practical purposes. The administration and judiciary, particularly outside Istanbul, continued to discriminate against non-Muslims, though in fairness it must be pointed out that the Muslim masses also suffered much oppression. Politically and socially the non-Muslims did not attain full equality. In the era of modern nationalism, the integration of the more advanced Christian peoples, supported by the powers, into one Ottoman nation proved to be an impossible undertaking.

In many other fields, however, the Tanẓīmāt achieved better results. Ministries were established and a cabinet was formed on the European model; the executive, judicial and legislative branches of government were gradually separated. The reformers set up a Supreme Council which, after several transformations, split in 1868 into two—a Council of State, charged *inter alia* with the drawing up of new laws, and a High Court of Justice. The provincial administration was also completely reorganized, though overly imitating the French pattern. The governors' rule was somewhat curbed by more independent provincial authorities in charge of military, fiscal and judicial affairs, as well as by the new administrative councils, which included elected, though hardly independent, members. The culmination of this process was the promulgation of the Constitution in 1876.

In accordance with the old Ottoman tradition that the sultan promulgated state law (*qānūn*), the reformers introduced modern criminal, commercial, land, nationality and other laws of Western type, based on the principle of territorial instead of personal validity. But family and inheritance law remained religious, and the new Law of contracts, obligations and civil procedure (*Mejelle*), prepared by a committee under the chairmanship of Aḥmed Jevdet Pasha, was a modern codification of *Sharīʿa* law. To apply the new laws, mixed commercial and criminal tribunals and other non-religious courts were set up. Though fixed salaries were introduced for all government officials, bribery remained an ineradicable evil in Ottoman public life.

Side by side with the traditional schools, new secular institutions of elementary and secondary education were opened; the latter included the famous Imperial *lycée* of Galata Saray with French as the main language of instruction (1868). The new Faculty of Medicine, at first for the army only (1827), and the Military Academy (1834), as well as the vocational schools, teachers' training colleges, schools for civil servants and, in 1870, the short-lived university (*Dār ül-Fünūn*), were all inspired by Western institutions. Prussians such as von Moltke, and other Western advisers and instructors helped to build up a modern regular and reserve army and an up-to-date navy. Following Muḥammad 'Alī's example, cadets, and subsequently civilian students, were sent to Europe in increasing numbers.

In 1831 the first official Turkish newspaper (*Taqvīm-i Veqāyi'*) was published, to be followed by more independent papers. A modern literature, which included translations, plays and novels, began to develop; it was written in a simplified language and deeply influenced by French models. The manners and fashions of the upper classes, as well as the architectural style, as exemplified by Dolmabaghche Palace, grew more and more European.

Surprisingly little, however, was achieved in the field of economic reconstruction. Traditionally, the Turks had left commerce to others, and the Tanẓīmāt leaders, with their administrative, diplomatic and legal training, had a very limited understanding of economic affairs. Primitive methods of cultivation, shortage of manpower, lack of capital, heavy taxation and poor communications prevented agricultural development. For a long time no determined efforts were made to put an end to tax-farming (*iltizām*) and to secularize the vast holdings of the *waqf*. The remnants of the old feudal system were abolished, but under the new laws many tax-farmers on state land became, in fact, landlords and, in consequence, the position of the peasants greatly deteriorated. The potentially rich mineral resources remained largely unexploited. Apart from some new roads and, at a later stage, the first railways, few public works were undertaken.

Many of the traditional crafts, and their guilds, were destroyed by the influx of cheap and modern European products. Attempts to build up new industries largely failed because technical knowledge, capital and entrepreneurs were wanting. The development of the east-west trade routes from Persia via Russia, and through the Suez Canal, diverted part of the important transit trade away from Turkey. Nevertheless, commerce and shipping expanded considerably, but they chiefly remained in the hands of non-Muslim subjects and foreigners. The latter were now granted the right to engage freely in internal trade too and, in 1867, to own real estate. They thus enjoyed the best of both worlds—legal equality with the Ottoman citizens, and continued legal and economic privileges under the capitulations, which long blocked the way to a protectionist policy. Until the later part of the Tanẓīmāt period, customs on foreign goods were much lower than duties imposed on exported local products; they averaged about a quarter of the import duties Turkish goods had to pay in Europe. The Ottoman empire thus became a kind of European colony, which supplied the Western countries with cheap raw material, and offered them a vast market for their industrial products. European capital poured in, and secured highly profitable concessions.

As a result of the outmoded and corrupt system of taxation and the loss of relatively rich European provinces, state revenue became entirely inadequate. At the same time expenditure increased enormously because of the huge bureaucracy, the large army and navy and, most unnecessarily, the sumptuous court. The chronic treasury deficits and the increasingly unfavourable balance of trade led to financial crises, which were aggravated by a disastrous monetary policy—the debasement of the coinage and the issue of paper money. From 1854 the Ottoman government had recourse to large-scale borrowing on increasingly ruinous terms, mainly from French and British sources, and had to pledge a large part of its revenue to pay interest and amortization. This process ended in state bankruptcy (1875) and submission to Western financial control, established in the administration of the Ottoman Public Debt, 1881.

The reforms of the Tanẓīmāt period failed to prevent the dismemberment of the empire, and did not solve its major internal problems. The leaders did not realize, or realized too late, that economic and financial subjection to the powers was no less a threat to political independence than defeat on the battle front. Their reforms did not spring from the people, and were not supported by public opinion; they were imposed from above on a society that was totally unprepared for such a hasty transplantation of alien forms. The introduction of modern secular laws and institutions side by side with traditional ones created a dangerous dualism, and perpetuated serious tensions between the very small westernized *élite* and the conservative majority of the Muslim population, less than two per cent of whom were literate in 1868.[1] But with all their shortcomings and inconsistencies, the Tanẓīmāt laid the foundations for a modern Turkish state and society.

[1] Żiyā Pasha in an article quoted in *Tanẓimat,* I (Istanbul, 1940), 841.

THE STRUGGLE AGAINST DESPOTISM

Perhaps the most important result of the Tanẓīmāt was the formation of a moderately progressive Muslim middle-class intelligentsia, whose membership consisted of civil servants, army officers, writers and a number of '*ulemā*', but very few businessmen. In 1865 some members of this class founded a political movement, later known as the New (or Young) Ottoman Society, which for the first time made use of the press and literature to mould public opinion and criticize the government. Its leaders included several prominent writers and journalists, such as Żiyā Pasha, Nāmıq Kemāl and 'Alī Su'āvī, as well as Muṣṭafā Fāżıl Pasha, a brother of Khedive Ismā'īl of Egypt. Mostly graduates of the modern secular schools and somewhat familiar with European culture and ideas, they developed a kind of Muslim-Ottoman nationalism and attacked the powerful oligarchy of senior bureaucrats and leading '*ulemā*', many of whom belonged to a narrow circle of privileged families. They demanded a restriction of the absolute and arbitrary rule of the sultan, his courtiers and chief ministers, whom they accused of submissiveness to the powers, indiscriminate europeanization and excessive secularism. The main slogan of the Tanẓīmāt had been 'justice' ('*adālet*); theirs were 'liberty' (*ḥürriyet*), and '(love of the) fatherland' (*vaṭan*). While proclaiming the equality of all communities, they nevertheless wished to perserve Muslim, particularly Turkish, supremacy. And though they advocated the adoption of Western material civilization and, to some extent, of European liberal ideas and institutions, they tried to synthesize them with the best in Ottoman tradition and a renascent, idealized Islam, which was no obstacle in their opinion to scientific progress and democratic government.

The articulate Young Ottoman intellectuals were almost continuously engaged in bitter personal quarrels and ideological strife. Most of them lacked political acumen, and several steadfastness of character too, as proved by their willingness to join the hated Establishment whenever the opportunity arose. For a time they had to flee from Istanbul and carry on their propaganda from abroad. In the eventful year 1876, Midḥat Pasha, who had gained renown as progressive governor of the vilayets of the Danube and Baghdād, and had been briefly grand *vezīr* in 1872, realized the Young Ottomans' hopes. In collaboration with more conservative elements he succeeded in deposing Sultan 'Abd ül-'Azīz and a few months later dethroned his mentally deranged successor,

Murād V (1876), also, in favour of 'Abd ül-Ḥamīd II (1876–1909). The new sultan fulfilled his prior pledge to Midḥat (whom he reappointed grand *vezīr*), and on 23 December 1876 promulgated the first Ottoman Constitution (*Qānūn-ı Esāsī*), which instituted a bicameral parliamentary system. As in 1839 and 1856, this new step towards a more liberal régime was taken at a time when the Ottoman government urgently wanted to make a favourable impression on public opinion in Europe and ward off foreign intervention.

The new Chamber of Deputies, in which the religious and national minorities were given ample representation, tried to make good use of its rather limited rights. But the autocratic sultan, who as early as February 1877 had dismissed and banished Midḥat Pasha, prorogued Parliament *sine die* in the following year and practically suspended the Constitution. For thirty years he ruled the empire from his seclusion in Yıldız Palace, with the help of an elaborate system of secret police and informers, a greatly expanded telegraph network, severe censorship and a shrewd exploitation of the religious feelings of his Muslim subjects. Internal unrest, especially among the Armenians, who up to that time had been regarded as 'the loyal community', was cruelly suppressed. The idea of pan-Islam was propagated with great vigour both within the empire and outside it. One of its tangible results was the construction of the religiously and strategically important Ḥijāz railway, financed by contributions from Muslims throughout the world. A number of legal, educational and military reforms were introduced and some material progress was made, mainly with German and other Western assistance.

During this 'Period of Despotism', the place of the defunct Young Ottoman Society was taken by a new revolutionary organization, likewise modelled on the Italian Carbonari. Founded in 1889 by students of military colleges in Istanbul, this organization later took the name of 'Ottoman Committee of Union and Progress' (*'Osmānlı Ittiḥād ve-Teraqqī Jem'īyeti*); its members became commonly known as the Young Turks. It attracted many lower middle-class elements, including Ṣūfī shaykhs, Turkish refugees from Russia, as well as numerous non-Turks—Kurds, Albanians, Arabs and others. When an early plan for a *coup d'état* was discovered in 1896, many of the conspirators were arrested and exiled; some of them joined Young Turk groups in France, Switzerland and Egypt. A number of their leaders, however, deserted, while the rest were deeply split into different schools of thought, such as Prince Ṣabāḥ üd-Dīn's advocates of liberal decentralization, and the majority, more Turkish nationalist in outlook, led by the positivist, Aḥmed Rıżā Bey. Their relationship with the revolutionary organizations of various national minorities, particularly the Armenians, was problematic. This movement of intellectuals remained ineffective until its leadership was taken over by the only efficient social force on the scene, which was to play a major political part in almost every Muslim country in the twentieth century—the nationalist, westernized and secularist officer corps.

The Young Turk headquarters was finally established in the cosmopolitan city of Salonica, capital of turbulent Macedonia, where the Masonic lodges served as a cover for subversive activities. In July 1908, a few weeks after the Reval meeting between King Edward VII and Tsar Nicholas II, which was expected to lead to renewed foreign intervention in Macedonia, the discontented officers of the Third Army Corps stationed in that province suddenly revolted. Almost without bloodshed, they forced Sultan ʿAbd ül-Ḥamīd to restore the Constitution and reconvene Parliament. Following an abortive reactionary rising in 1909, they deposed the sultan, and set up his brother Meḥmed V Reshād (1909–18) as a figure-head. Hailed, particularly in Britain, as liberal and democratic idealists, the Young Turks at first indeed professed, or rather pretended, Ottomanism, i.e. the idea of complete intercommunal equality and co-operation. This ideal, however, was soon abandoned; it completely lost its meaning after the Balkan wars of 1912–13 had reduced the empire to a predominantly Muslim and Asian state, in which the Turks constituted about half the population. The rival ideologies of Islamism and pan-Islamism too were discarded when the Muslim Albanians declared their independence (1912), when the proclamation of the Holy War in 1914 failed to produce the desired effect on the Muslim world, and when finally *Sharīf* Ḥusayn of Mecca rose against the sultan-caliph (1916). This led to the final triumph of Turkish nationalism which, temporarily in its expansionist form of pan-Turanism, had been the principal ideal of the Young Turks from the very first. In those intellectually dynamic years, Turkish nationalism or 'Turkism' was theoretically elaborated by Żiyā Gökalp, who tried to combine it with far-reaching westernization and a drastically reformed Islam.

The almost continuous wars during the Young Turk period served them as pretext for stifling free political life. Parliamentary government became a mockery, and after a *coup* in January 1913 the Young Turks finally established a one-party rule, which soon turned into the military dictatorship of the triumvirate of Enver, Ṭalʿat and Jemāl Pashas. Their harsh policy of turkification gave rise to growing discontent among the non-Turkish nationalities. During the First World War, the Young Turks reacted with the deportation and massacre of the Armenians and the suppression of the Syrian Arab nationalists, both of whom were accused of co-operation with the enemy.

After the outbreak of the war the Young Turk government unilaterally abolished the capitulations. Various economic measures were taken to develop a Turkish commercial and industrial bourgeoisie, but during the war years the tendency towards a state-directed economy increased. While the Tanẓīmāt had to some extent separated state from religion and thereby created two systems of law, judiciary and education, the Young Turks went one step further and attempted to reunite the systems by placing Islamic institutions, such as religious schools and the *Sharīʿa* courts, under secular state control. Consequently, the office of the *shaykh al-Islām,* who in the nineteenth century had become a member of the cabinet, lost much of its power. The social position of Muslim women, many of whom were employed in war work, was improved by the Family Law of 1917, and girls were given wider opportunities for education.

The Young Turks have been generally blamed for setting up an oppressive government and bringing about the final collapse of the Ottoman empire. But there can be no doubt that their rule paved the way to Muṣṭafā Kemāl's nationalist Turkish Republic, its authoritarian and etatist régime, and its radical policy of secularism and westernization.

CHAPTER 4

THE LATER OTTOMAN EMPIRE IN EGYPT AND THE FERTILE CRESCENT

THE OTTOMAN DECLINE IN THE ELEVENTH/SEVENTEENTH CENTURY

The decline of the Ottoman state, which manifested itself in the eleventh/late sixteenth–seventeenth centuries, affected the Arab provinces as well as the older dominions of Anatolia and Rumelia. Some territories were lost to the empire. Baghdād was reoccupied by the Safavids from 1033/1623 to 1048/1638, while in 1045/1635 the Ottomans abandoned their precarious tenure of the Yemen. Even where the form of the sultan's suzerainty was maintained, and the façade of the old provincial administration remained in being, locally based forces were striving for mastery in the provinces, and here and there local despotisms crystallized out of the general anarchy.

The drift to anarchy is well exemplified in the history of Egypt in the early eleventh/seventeenth century which, it may be noted, coincides with the great crisis of the Ottoman empire.[1] A series of military risings against the viceroys (one of whom was murdered by mutinous troops in 1013/1605) culminated in a menacing revolt of the soldiery of the Delta in 1017/1609. The suppression of this revolt (which was described by a chronicler as 'the second conquest of Egypt during the sacred Ottoman government'[2]) did not permanently re-establish the viceregal power. By the middle of the century the beys, who were mostly members of neo-Mamluk households, had emerged as contenders for power with the viceroys and the officers of the garrison-corps.

The formation of local despotisms at this period proceeded furthest in those parts of the empire which were most remote from, or inaccessible to, the central authorities. Thus (as is described in Part VII, chapter 2) the North African provinces of Algiers and Tunis, which had always been virtually autonomous, developed during the eleventh/seventeenth century their own quasi-sovereign institutions, the monarchies of the dey of Algiers and the bey of Tunis. At the other extremity of the Otto-

[1] See above, pp. 342–50.
[2] Muḥammad b. Abi'l-Surūr, *al-Rawḍa al-zahiyya* (Bodleian, MS. Pocock. 80), unfoliated.

man empire, the province of Baṣra passed in 1005/1596–7 into the hands of a local magnate, who established a dynasty, the house of Afrāsiyāb. Perhaps the most interesting of the early local despotisms was that established by the Druze *amīr,* Fakhr al-Dīn II, in Mount Lebanon between 1590 and 1044/1635. The ascendancy which Fakhr al-Dīn obtained over other magnates in Mount Lebanon, as well as the expansionist policy which extended his power, notably to the other highland regions of Ḥawrān, 'Ajlūn and Nābulus, threatened Ottoman control of the Fertile Crescent. In his commercial relations with Christian Europe, his ready acceptance of Western technical knowledge, and his tolerance of religious diversity, Fakhr al-Dīn anticipated attitudes and policies of nineteenth-century rulers in the Middle East.

The autonomy of Fakhr al-Dīn and the Safavid reoccupation of Baghdād were both terminated by Murād IV's vigorous reassertion of the power of the Ottoman sultanate. The Ottoman decline was indeed no steady and automatic process, and it was at least mitigated in the middle decades of the eleventh/seventeenth century by a more active direction of the central government; by Murād IV himself until his death in 1049/1640, and later by the two grand *vezīrs,* Köprülü Meḥmed Pasha, and his son, Fāżil Aḥmed Pasha (1066–87/1656–76). During these years, although local disorder was not eliminated, the tendency to anarchy was held in check. In Egypt, for example, the power of the beys, who had dominated the administration for three decades, suffered a sharp decline after 1072/1662. In 1078/1668, the house of Afrāsiyāb was finally ejected from the province of Baṣra. Although hereditary *amīrs* of Fakhr al-Dīn's family, the Ma'nids, still ruled in Mount Lebanon, they had abandoned the brilliant and dangerous ambitions of their kinsman.

THE LOCAL DESPOTISMS OF THE TWELFTH/EIGHTEENTH CENTURY

The course of the Ottoman decline accelerated during the twelfth/eighteenth century. In Egypt and the Fertile Crescent, factional contests for power reappeared in the great towns, and new local despotisms were established. Like the earlier ones these arose within the traditional Ottoman provincial system, which was ostensibly maintained in being. They originated usually from one or other of three institutions: the provincial governorship, the provincial garrison, or the farm of taxes; but they derived their strength, not from traditional sources of power but from the personal qualities, the private means, and the private military forces of the despots.

The most durable of local despotisms of the first type was inaugurated in Baghdād by the Ottoman governor, Ḥasan Pasha (1116–36/1704–23). A year before he died, the long stability which had existed on the Ottoman-Persian frontier since the time of Murād IV ended with the collapse of the Safavid dynasty. From the coming of the Afghans in 1134/1722 to the death of Nādir Shāh a quarter of a century later, there was almost continuous warfare between the Ottoman sultans and the rulers of Persia. In these circumstances, stable and strong administration in Baghdād was a prime necessity: hence Ḥasan Pasha was succeeded by his able and experienced son, Aḥmad Pasha, who retained the governorship almost uninterruptedly until his own death in 1160/1747. Ḥasan and Aḥmad established a household of Georgian *mamlūks* who provided them with a fighting force and a body of administrative officials. One of the *mamlūk* chiefs succeeded, in 1162/1749, in assuming power in Baghdād, with the unwilling acquiescence of the Ottoman government, and the Mamluk Pashas thus perpetuated until 1247/1831 the local despotism founded by Ḥasan.

In the western Fertile Crescent, Damascus enjoyed a certain pre-eminence as the rendezvous whence the annual Pilgrimage caravan set out for the Holy Cities. The Pilgrimage was a function of commercial as well as religious significance, and its safe conduct was important for the prestige of the sultan. The decline of Ottoman power synchronized in the eleventh/seventeenth and twelfth/eighteenth centuries with a period of unsettlement among the tribes of northern Arabia and the Syrian desert. At the same time, Damascus suffered from the inveterate rivalry of two groups of its garrison forces. These were the conditions which prepared the way for the establishment in Damascus of a local despotism by the ʿAẓm family,[1] who brought a degree of political stability to the city, and provided for the secure convoy of the Pilgrimage. The ʿAẓms were at the height of their power between 1137/1725 and 1170/1757, and governed not only Damascus but also Tripoli and other Syrian provinces. Other members of the family held office even in the early nineteenth century. Yet they failed to establish a true dynasty, and their power was less durable than that of the contemporary governors of Baghdād. Syria, after all, was less remote than the

[1] The form ʿAḍm, which is sometimes found, represents the Syrian colloquial pronunciation. Similarly Ẓāhir al-ʿUmar (see below p. 377) appears as Ḍāhir.

'Irāqī provinces: it was the vital corridor linking Anatolia with the Ḥijāz and Egypt. The 'Aẓms, moreover, unlike Ḥasan and Aḥmad Pashas, did not seize their opportunity to build up a *mamlūk* household as an effective and lasting basis for their exercise of local autonomy.

The geography of the western Fertile Crescent was unfavourable to extensive autonomies, as it had been in the Middle Ages. Aleppo and its vicinity were almost wholly uninvolved in the politics and commerce of southern Syria and were closely linked with Anatolia. Even in the south, the authority of the 'Aẓms was checked by two rival despotisms: that of the Shihāb *amīrs* of Mount Lebanon, and that of Shaykh Ẓāhir al-'Umar in Galilee. The Shihābs, kinsmen of the Ma'nids, had succeeded to the amirate of Lebanon in 1109/1697, and had taken up Fakhr al-Dīn's task of converting a vague paramountcy over the Lebanese magnates into a territorial sovereignty. Factionalism, the jealousy of their great vassals, and the suspicion of their Ottoman overlords, rendered the task difficult, but some successes were achieved.

The lordship of Ẓāhir al-'Umar was very different in origin. In essence it was a mosaic of tax-farms, which was gradually extended westwards across Galilee in the early twelfth/eighteenth century, and was completed by the acquisition of the coastal town of Acre in 1159/1746. Ẓāhir's power rested upon four foundation-stones: a contented peasantry enjoying security and moderate taxation; good relations with European merchants, by which the prosperity of Acre was revived; the help and support of local *dhimmīs*; and an efficient private army of mercenaries. He was thus able to maintain his position against the 'Aẓms and others, so long as no power external to the region intervened in Syrian affairs.

In Egypt the pattern of political history was governed by a complicated factional struggle, and the local despotism which ultimately emerged was the domination of a group, rather than of an individual. The most ancient factions were those of Niṣf Sa'd and Niṣf Ḥarām, which were found both among the urban artisans and the tribes. During the eleventh/seventeenth century, these two indigenous groups became associated with the rival neo-Mamluk households of the Faqāriyya and Qāsimiyya respectively, so that the older names almost disappeared. The neo-Mamluk households were organizationally distinct from the seven corps of the Ottoman garrison, which had a factionalism of their own. The ground of this was the mutual rivalry of the two infantry corps of Janissaries and 'Azebān ('Azabs) but at times of tension, the other five corps tended to ally with the ʿAzebān. The relations between these two sets of factions were neither clear-cut nor stable: in 1123/1711, however, they merged into a general schism within the ruling *élite*, producing a minor civil war.

In the renewed struggle for power in Egypt, which began in the later years of the eleventh/seventeenth century and continued throughout the twelfth/eighteenth, the Ottoman viceroys played, on the whole, an insignificant part. The effective contenders were the senior officers of the seven corps, and the beys, who held high offices as well as military commands outside the regimental cadres. By 1161/1748, the Qāzdughliyya, a household which had been founded about sixty years earlier, and had risen in association with the Faqāriyya, had acquired an unchallengeable ascendancy over all other groups. Its members packed the beylicate, which they dominated until the remains of the neo-Mamluk ascendancy was swept away by Muḥammad ʿAlī Pasha. Meanwhile, a tendency was appearing towards the assumption of a quasi-monarchic role by the leading bey, who was designated *shaykh al-balad*. The instability resulting from the inveterate factionalism among the Qāzdughliyya frustrated this development.

ANTICIPATIONS OF THE NINETEENTH CENTURY

During the last third of the eighteenth century, developments are observable in Egypt and the Fertile Crescent which anticipate some of the major themes in their history during the ensuing hundred years. The first of these is the impact on the region of European military power. Although the Ottomans had been in retreat since the later seventeenth century, the defeats in the field, and the losses of territory, had been in Rumelia and the coastlands of the Black Sea. Behind the Ottoman shield, the political changes in the Arab provinces took place without alien intervention. The European states, so powerful on the Rumelian frontier, were represented in the Arab provinces by the harried merchants and circumspect missionaries who lived under the capricious protection of the local despots. The immunity of these provinces was infringed when, in the Russo-Turkish War of 1182–8/1768–74, a tsarist fleet cruised in the Mediterranean, destroyed its Ottoman opponents, and offered aid and comfort to Shaykh Ẓāhir al-ʿUmar and ʿAlī Bey, the *shaykh al-balad* of Egypt. The piercing of the Ottoman shield was to be still more strikingly demonstrated when Bonaparte occupied Egypt in 1213/1798—an episode which attracted the intervention of Britain, and helped to create the Eastern Question of nineteenth-century diplomacy.

The nineteenth century was also foreshadowed, in the time of 'Alī Bey, by the revival of Egyptian interest in Syria. Since the administrative dismemberment of the former Mamluk Sultanate by Selīm I, the two territories had pursued separate courses. 'Alī Bey, however, the *shaykh al-balad* who came nearest to transforming the ascendancy of the Qāzdughliyya into a personal monarchy, revived, consciously and deliberately, the memory and the policies of the Mamluk sultans. In 1184–5/1770–1 he sent his army against Damascus, in alliance with Ẓāhir al-'Umar, and with Russian connivance. His plans failed, since he could not depend on the continuing support of his Mamluk colleagues. What he tried to accomplish was again undertaken, but with no greater ultimate success, by Bonaparte in 1214/1799. Not until the following century was Muḥammad 'Alī to reforge the links between Syria and Egypt, which had been snapped at the Ottoman conquest.

A third anticipation of later developments was the endeavour of the Ottoman government in this period to break the power of local despots, and reassert the sultan's authority over the territories that they ruled. The activities of 'Alī Bey and Shaykh Ẓāhir during the Russo-Turkish War were particularly alarming. In the schemes for their overthrow, leading parts were played by two disaffected colleagues of 'Alī Bey, his former *mamlūk*, Ibrāhīm Bey Abu'l-Dhahab, and a Bosniak who had entered his service, Aḥmad al-Jazzār. Abu'l-Dhahab, who was in command of the Syrian expedition of 1185/1771, was induced to withdraw from Damascus, and return to Egypt. There he superseded his master (whom he subsequently defeated and killed), and took office as *shaykh al-balad*. He died in 1189/1775, while on a punitive expedition against Shaykh Ẓāhir. Al-Jazzār, who broke with 'Alī Bey in 1182/1768, played a part in operations against Shaykh Ẓāhir. When the latter was overthrown in 1189/1775, al-Jazzār was appointed governor of Sidon, with his residence at Ẓāhir's former capital of Acre. Although the rule of Aḥmad Pasha al-Jazzār, which lasted until his death in 1219/1804, was essentially a local despotism, it was characterized by loyalty to the sultan. This was never more conspicuously displayed than in 1214/1799, when al-Jazzār's steadfastness at the siege of Acre helped to bring about Bonaparte's retreat.

The Ottoman government's dealings with Abu'l-Dhahab and al-Jazzār are perhaps only instances of a traditional policy: the playing-off of one rival against another, the substitution of a loyal subject for one suspected of disaffection. A report ascribed to al-Jazzār, however, indicates a more radical approach to the problem of local autonomy in Egypt, an intention to break the neo-Mamluk ascendancy, and reintegrate the province in the empire. This was attempted in 1200/1786, when an expeditionary force was sent to Egypt under the command of the Ottoman admiral, Jezā'irli Ḥasan Pasha, who, in the previous decade, had played a large part in the suppression of Shaykh Ẓāhir. After initial Ottoman successes against the Mamluk duumvirs, the beys Ibrāhīm and Murād, who dominated Egypt, a deadlock developed with the Ottomans holding the Delta and Cairo, and their opponents inaccessibly established in Upper Egypt. After Ḥasan Pasha had been recalled to Istanbul in 1201/1787, the duumvirs regained power, which they retained until the coming of Bonaparte.

Meanwhile, outside the sphere of Ottoman control, in Najd, an alliance had been established in 1157/1744 between Muḥammad b. Su'ūd, the ruler of a petty amirate, and Muḥammad b. 'Abd al-Wahhāb, an '*ālim* of the strict Ḥanbalī school, who rebuked the errors and laxity of the times, and sought to recall the Muslims to the practices and beliefs of primitive Islam. When Ibn 'Abd al-Wahhāb died in 1792, the house of Su'ūd had established its domination, and the theological principles of the Wahhābiyya, over the whole of central Arabia, while the outposts of Ottoman power in the Ḥijāz and the desert-fringes of the Fertile Crescent were becoming dangerously exposed to the attacks of Su'ūdī tribal warriors.

The Wahhābī movement challenged the Ottoman state at several levels. There was, first, the actual military threat to the provinces adjacent to Su'ūdī-controlled territory. Thus, in 1802 the Wahhābīs captured and pillaged the holy city of Karbalā', a pilgrimage-centre for the Shī'a. Raids into the 'Irāqī provinces continued in the following years. Secondly, the movement raised in a very practical form the question of authority within the Muslim community. Traditionally, the authority of the Ottoman sultan had been accepted by his subjects as sanctioned by God, inasmuch as he was the foremost Muslim ruler and (after 922/1516) the 'Servitor of the Two Holy Sanctuaries'. During the Ottoman decline stress came to be laid on the concept that the Ottoman sultan was the universal caliph of Islam. These juristic structures crumbled under the Wahhābī attacks. Mecca and Medina were occupied in 1803 and 1805, and in 1807 and succeeding years the ruling *amīr,* Su'ūd b. 'Abd al-ʿAzīz, closed the Ḥijāz to the Ottoman Pilgrimage caravan. The third aspect of the Wahhābī challenge was to the whole Ottoman religious establishment, with its hierarchy of *ʿulemā*, and its patronage of the Ṣūfī orders. Two aspects of official Islam seemed particularly reprehensible. The first was the infringement of the sole jurisdiction of the *Sharīʿa,* which was restricted in some matters, and supplemented in others, by custom and the discretionary authority of the sultan embodied in *qānūns*. The second was the acceptance of Ṣūfī beliefs and practices, which fostered an ecstatic mysticism and blurred the distinction between Creator and creature. Wahhabism thus revived old tensions, both within the Islamic community, and in the conscience of individual Muslims.

CENTRALIZATION AND WESTERNIZATION

Bonaparte's invasion of Egypt in 1213/1798 and the French occupation which ensued were an episode of decisive importance. Although British and Ottoman forces expelled the French in 1801, their short period of domination had so shattered the neo-Mamluk ascendancy that the beys were henceforward only one amongst several groups competing for power. In 1805 Muḥammad ʿAlī Pasha, the commander of an Albanian contingent which had served in the operations against the French, established his hold over Cairo, and was appointed viceroy by the sultan. His position was initially precarious, but he succeeded ultimately in acquiring for the viceregal office more extensive and autocratic powers than any of his predecessors had exercised; in retaining his position until he was overcome by senility in 1848, a few months before his death; and in transmitting the viceroyalty by hereditary succession to his descendants. Muḥammad ʿAlī has been called 'the founder of modern Egypt', but he was also the founder of the last and the most successful of the local despotisms.

A second important consequence of Bonaparte's occupation of Egypt was the new importance which that country (as well as the neighbouring Arab territories) acquired in the eyes of European diplomats and strategists. The British reaction to the French occupation was the first of many clashes between the two powers, and their prolonged rivalry in Egypt was only allayed by the *Entente cordiale* of 1904. Thus, Muḥammad ʿAlī formulated his policies and pursued his ambitions within limits which were ultimately set by the great powers of Europe. On two occasions, in his operations against the Greek insurgents in 1827, and his successful opposition to the sultan in 1840, the powers intervened decisively to thwart him.

The Ottoman sultanate was itself a factor affecting the development of Muḥammad 'Alī's autonomy. Under Sultan Maḥmūd II (1808–39) the spasmodic attempts which earlier Ottoman rulers had made to reassert their authority were transformed into a deliberate and sustained policy, having as its object the elimination of local despotisms, and the reintegration of the provinces into a centralized state. As planned, this was a new political structure, not merely a restoration of the old empire. Muḥammad 'Alī was fortunate in that he was able to establish his own autocracy on a firm basis more speedily than was Maḥmūd, and some of his major reforms anticipate similar measures by the sultan. Both Maḥmūd and Muḥammad 'Alī realized the necessity of liquidating internal opposition. The '*ulemā*', who had enjoyed an unusual degree of political power under Bonaparte, and who had contributed to the installation of Muḥammad 'Alī as viceroy in 1805, were cowed into submission in 1809. The tough and tenacious Mamluks were broken by the massacre of their leaders in the Citadel of Cairo in 1811, and subsequent proscription in Upper Egypt. A practical consequence of these developments was the resumption by Muḥammad 'Alī of great tracts of land previously held by '*ulemā*' and Mamluks as religious endowments or tax-farms. In this way, the viceroy and his family became the principal landowners in Egypt, and established their political power on a strong economic foundation.

Like his suzerain, Muḥammad 'Alī Pasha sought to create an efficient, loyal and disciplined army on the Western model, as a safeguard both against internal resistance and external attack. The viceroy's first idea was to follow the course traditional among Muslim rulers, and to create a slave army. But Russian expansion in the Caucasus had dried up the supply of *mamlūks* and, although Muḥammad 'Alī's conquest of Nubia, the Funj sultanate of Sennar, and Kordofan in 1820–1, provided him with thousands of black slaves, their high mortality in Egypt made them unsuitable for his purposes. He therefore took the unprecedented and highly unpopular step of conscripting the Egyptian peasantry, and officered his new army with men of Ottoman or Circassian (*mamlūk*) origin. Thereby he took the first steps towards the creation of an Egyptian army which was to play an important part in the early development of Egyptian nationalism.

Muḥammad 'Alī's determination to secure his position in Egypt was the mainspring of his military reorganization, as of his other reforms.

On the economic side, as well as making the changes in landownership already alluded to, he created a vast system of monopolies, intended to exploit the profits of Egyptian and Sudanese trade. His attempts to produce an industrial revolution in Egypt proved to be premature. Over the years, he gradually evolved a new administrative machine, inspired by Europe in its departmental organization and system of budgeting, and in the process a new terminology was created. To work this machine, and to staff and train his army, an *élite* with some measure of Western education was necessary. So a rudimentary and empirical system of state educational institutions was established, while 'educational missions' of students were sent to study in Europe. The new schools' need of textbooks led to the translation of European works. At first production was haphazard, but from the mid-thirties it was organized under governmental auspices. In these ways Egypt became one of the principal channels by which European culture was communicated to the Near East. The development of Western education as a key to state employment affected adversely the traditional religious education and the status of the *'ulemā'* who purveyed it.

The external activities of Muḥammad 'Alī Pasha were not less important than his reorganization of Egypt. As the agent of the sultan, even before his military innovations, he had been responsible for the campaigns which, between 1811 and 1818, had driven the Wahhābīs out of the Ḥijāz and then broken the power of the house of Su'ūd in Najd itself. As the result of these victories, Muḥammad 'Alī established over the western coastlands of Arabia a dominion which lasted until 1840. The viceroy's new-model army was put at the sultan's disposal also to crush the insurgents in Crete and the Morea between 1822 and 1827, but the intervention of the great powers, and the disastrous naval clash at Navarino, robbed him of the fruits of victory.

After this, conflict developed between Muḥammad 'Alī and Sultan Maḥmūd II. In 1831, the viceroy's troops under the command of his son, Ibrāhīm Pasha, invaded Syria, and went on to penetrate Anatolia, where in December 1832 the grand *vezīr* himself was defeated near Konya. The sultan ceded the Syrian provinces to Muḥammad 'Alī, who ruled them through Ibrāhīm. The new régime found a useful collaborator in the *amīr* of Lebanon, Bashīr II Shihāb. Even with his aid and advice, however, it was not easy to impose upon the insubordinate and particularist inhabitants of Syria the heavy taxation, forced labour and conscription which accompanied Egyptian administration—more just and more tolerant than the old régime though it was. Serious insurrections occurred from 1834 onwards, but it was not these that brought the Egyptian occupation of Syria to an end. An ill-judged attempt by Maḥmūd II to expel Ibrāhīm by force had ended in the total defeat of the Ottoman army at the battle of Nezib (June 1839). When, a few days later, Maḥmūd died, and the Ottoman fleet surrendered to Muḥammad ʿAlī at Alexandria, the empire seemed on the verge of dissolution. But, as in Greece, Muḥammad ʿAlī had been too successful, and the great powers (with the exception of France) intervened against him. Beset by local rebels, and bombarded by British and Austrian warships, Ibrāhīm evacuated Syria in the winter of 1840. Bashīr II, who was closely identified with the Egyptian occupation, and whose own success in establishing an autocracy had won him enemies among the Lebanese magnates, abdicated at the same time. He was not quite the last of the Shihābs to reign, but the ineffective *amīr* who succeeded him was deposed a little over a year later.

Sultan Maḥmūd II, Muḥammad ʿAlī Pasha, and Bashīr II were, each in his different sphere, exponents of government by personal autocracy, which seemed the remedy to the lax administration of the Ottoman empire in its decline. Although Ibrāhīm's government of Syria had not been wholly successful, it had largely destroyed the power of the old privileged groups and factions, and had prepared the way for the reintegration of the western Fertile Crescent in the centralized empire of the Tanẓīmāt. In a very real sense, Muḥammad ʿAlī and Ibrāhīm did Maḥmūd's work for him in Syria.

Lebanon, however, maintained its individuality. After the fall of the Shihāb amirate in 1842, an unsuccessful attempt was made to place the Mountain under direct Ottoman administration. The ensuing years were a period of great political instability. The Lebanese magnates, relieved of Bashīr II's autocracy, reasserted their ascendancy. The Maronites, Lebanese Christians in communion with Rome, were acquiring an equality of status and power with the Druzes, who had traditionally dominated the Mountain. In 1860, antagonisms which had been developing over twenty years flared out, as Druzes and Muslims in Lebanon and Damascus massacred Christians with the connivance of the local Ottoman authorities. Inevitably, the great powers intervened, and secured the promulgation of an Organic Regulation for Lebanon in June 1861. Administered separately from the rest of Ottoman Syria, with safeguards for its constituent religious communities, Lebanon made steady and peaceful progress until the outbreak of the First World War.

The Mamluk Pashas of Baghdād had long enjoyed the kind of autonomy which Muḥammad ʿAlī Pasha acquired in Egypt, and the continued existence of their régime was obnoxious to the centralizing and autocratic policy of Maḥmūd II. Two developments had in some measure strengthened their position. Muḥammad ʿAlī's campaigns against the Wahhābīs had removed a menace with which they themselves had been unable to deal effectively. Then, in 1826, the Janissary corps of Baghdād was dissolved, in accordance with the sultan's orders, but its members were recruited into a new formation, to be trained on the Western model. There was some danger that the Mamluk Pashalic might gain a new vitality, and in 1830 Maḥmūd II set himself to overthrow it. Not until 1831, however, did the sultan's troops enter Baghdād—a city greatly weakened by a recent epidemic of plague—and achieve the deposition of Dāʾūd Pasha, the last of the Mamluk governors. With this success, obtained on the eve of Ibrāhīm Pasha's conquest of Syria, the reintegration of the eastern Fertile Crescent in the empire began.

EGYPT BETWEEN FRANCE AND BRITAIN

The conflict between Britain and France in Egypt at the beginning of the nineteenth century opened over a hundred years of rivalry in the Near East. Although the *Entente cordiale* of 1904 ended the most acute and dangerous tensions between the two powers in the region, traditional animosities persisted, and were to influence developments during and even after the First World War. There was, however, an important difference between French and British interests in the Near East. To the French, the acquisition of influence and power in the countries east and south of the Mediterranean was an end in itself—a tradition which went back ultimately to the time of the Crusades. To the British, on the other hand, these lands were important mainly in so far as they subserved commercial, naval, and imperial interests. Thus, the French, by capturing Algiers in 1830, laid the foundations of an extensive territorial domination, which was ultimately to embrace almost the whole of the Maghrib, and throughout the century assiduously built up their influence with the Maronites of Lebanon. British territorial gains, by contrast, were infinitesimal before 1882: Aden captured by storm in 1839, the Kuria Muria Islands ceded by the sultan of Masqaṭ in 1854. Attempts to win clients among the communities of the region were spasmodic and half-hearted. But the real interests of Britain—the securing of the strategic and commercial routes to the Further East, and the suppression of the slave-trade in the Persian Gulf and Red Sea—were pursued with tenacity and a very high degree of success.

Egypt under Muḥammad ʿAlī and his successors lay at the centre of Anglo-French rivalry in the Near East. The important role played in Muḥammad ʿAlī's schemes of reorganization by French officers and technicians (many of them veterans of the Napoleonic era) began that gallicization of Egyptian culture and institutions which continued under Khedive Ismāʿīl (1863–79), and which has left an enduring mark. The diplomatic patronage of the French was more consistent than that of the British, who were deeply committed to the Ottoman sultans; but Britain, by providing a market for Egyptian agricultural produce, first corn, later cotton, was indispensable to the maintenance of the country's economy. Under Muḥammad ʿAlī, the British inaugurated the Overland Route for the transport of passengers and mails between Alexandria and Suez via Cairo, and under ʿAbbās I (1848–54) and Muḥammad Saʿīd (1854–63) this was rendered more effective with the construction, by British engineers, of the first railway in the Near East.

British control of international communications through Egypt was menaced when, in 1854, Muḥammad Saʿīd granted to Ferdinand de Lesseps a concession for the construction of a maritime canal through the isthmus of Suez. The project was not officially sponsored by the French government, any more than the railways had been by the British, but in both cases national interests and prestige were at stake, and diplomatic pressures were exerted to advance or retard the realization of the engineers' schemes. Over the Suez Canal, successive British governments fought a long delaying action in Cairo and Istanbul, and it was not until 1869 that Khedive Ismāʿīl, with the Empress Eugénie as his guest of honour, formally opened the new waterway.

The reign of Ismāʿīl marks the climax and the catastrophe of the hereditary viceroyalty. In many ways, he was the true successor of Muḥammad ʿAlī. In 1867 he obtained from Sultan ʿAbd ül-ʿAzīz the title of 'khedive' (Perso-Turkish, *khidīv*) which marked his unique status among Ottoman provincial governors.[1] A year earlier, the sultan had issued a firman which established the succession to the viceroyalty by primogeniture in the line of Ismāʿīl. His Armenian minister, Nubar Pasha, succeeded in setting up the Mixed Courts for the adjudication of

[1] The title had, however, been used informally since the time of Muḥammad ʿAlī.

cases between foreigners and subjects of the khedive—the first breach in the great wall of privileges for aliens which had been erected on the foundation of the capitulations. Although wholly an autocrat at heart, Ismāʿīl set up, in 1866, a consultative body, the Assembly of Delegates, chosen by indirect election. In later years this became a sounding-board for the politically conscious members of the richer peasantry and the professional classes. During the American Civil War (1861–5) the agriculture and economics of Egypt took a decisive turn by a vast expansion of cotton-growing, from which the khedive and the peasantry alike profited.

When American cotton again came on the world market, the Egyptian boom suddenly collapsed, creating a problem of peasant indebtedness, as well as menacing the khedive and his government with bankruptcy. The finances of Egypt had recurrently been threatened with insolvency from the time of Muḥammad ʿAlī onwards. Ismāʿīl's indiscriminate and thriftless borrowings from European financiers exacerbated the situation, and by 1876 he was nearly £10 million in debt. The consequence of foreign indebtedness was foreign political control. An international *Caisse de la Dette publique* was set up to provide for the service of the debt, and two controllers, one British and one French, were appointed to supervise revenue and expenditure. Meanwhile the French and British governments were becoming increasingly involved in the situation. Under their auspices an international ministry, with responsibility for the administration of Egypt, was set up in 1878. When, in the following year, Ismāʿīl procured its overthrow, he brought about his own downfall. The sultan, exercising (on Anglo-French initiative) his suzerain power, deposed Ismāʿīl.

In the attempts to control Ismāʿīl, the French and British governments had acted together, and their collaboration was to continue during the early part of the reign of the new khedive, Muḥammad Tawfīq (1874–92). Although the French took the lead at the outset, the British government had acquired a new stake in Egypt by Disraeli's purchase (in 1875) of the khedive's holding of Suez Canal shares. The situation on Tawfīq's accession was confused and menacing. The prestige of the dynasty had collapsed on Ismāʿīl's deposition. A national movement, hostile to the old Turco-Circassian ruling *élite,* and lacking enthusiasm for the khedive, was strong in the army and the Assembly of Delegates. The power of France and Britain to intervene and control was deeply resented. The nationalists, who found a figurehead rather than a leader in Colonel Aḥmad 'Urābī, compelled the khedive step by step to concede their demands. An Anglo-French Joint Note, in January 1882, intended to reinforce the khedive's authority, weakened it further, and strengthened the anti-European tendencies of the nationalists. Throughout the summer the situation deteriorated, until in July a British naval squadron bombarded Alexandria. In September, British forces in the Canal Zone defeated 'Urābī at Tel el Kebir, and brought the khedive back to his capital. The British occupation of Egypt had begun, and, although at first it was intended to be only temporary, it was converted in the ensuing years into a protectorate in all but name. Ironically, the French had ended their collaboration with Britain during the summer of 1882, and so failed to gain a share of the fruits of the occupation.

THE END OF OTTOMAN RULE

In the early years of the twentieth century, the Ottoman position in the Arab lands showed features both of strength and weakness. Egypt and the North African territories had in effect been withdrawn from the sultan's authority, although the form of Ottoman suzerainty was preserved in Tunisia under the French protectorate, and in Egypt under British occupation. In the Fertile Crescent and the Arabian peninsula, on the other hand, Ottoman rule had become more firmly established. The application of the Tanẓīmāt reforms to the provinces of the Fertile Crescent had met with some success. The age of the local despots had passed away, and although factionalism was by no means extinct it found its expression in the new provincial and municipal councils, rather than in the street-riots and conflicts of earlier days. Centralization increased: a uniform system of provincial administration was envisaged in the Law of Vilayets of 1864, which was applied in the Fertile Crescent in the following years,[1] while the development of railways and telegraphs strengthened the hold of the government in Istanbul over the provinces. Since the middle of the nineteenth century, the Ottomans had been struggling to regain the Yemen, lost two hundred years before to the Zaydī *imāms*. Ottoman control of the Ḥijāz was strengthened by the improvement of communications: first, the construction of the Suez Canal, then (in 1908) the opening of the Pilgrim Railway, which directly linked Medina with Damascus. In 1908 also the Ottoman government

[1] Its application in the province of Baghdād was the work of Midḥat Pasha (governor from 1869 to 1872), who later held office in Damascus, after being dismissed from the grand vezirate by 'Abd ül-Ḥamīd II.

made its last effective intervention in the affairs of the Hashimite rulers of Mecca by appointing *Sharīf* Ḥusayn b. ʿAlī as *amīr*.

This appointment was the decision of the Young Turk government, which had ended the autocracy of Sultan ʿAbd ül-Ḥamīd II. The sultan had taken considerable pains to conciliate his Arab subjects. Seeing in them a useful check on the Turks, he recruited an Arab body-guard, and permitted Arab notables (amongst them heads of Ṣūfī orders, influential Syrians and the court *imām* Abu'l-Hudā al-Sayyādī) to acquire considerable influence in his palace. With his downfall, the Arabs lost their privileged position, and encountered the unsympathetic, ottomanizing policy of the Young Turks. The consequence was that Arab nationalism, hitherto the ideology of a few disaffected individuals on the fringe of Ottoman politics, obtained the support of a larger (although still numerically minute) group of Syrian and ʿIrāqī intellectuals and officers, who felt themselves alienated from the new régime.

In spite of this advance of Arab nationalism (which hindsight has tended to magnify) the future prospects of Ottoman rule in the Fertile Crescent and Arabia were by no means unfavourable when the outbreak of the First World War in 1914 introduced a wholly new factor. The entry of the Ottoman empire into the war on the side of the Central Powers confronted the Allies with two problems: one immediate, that of counteracting the prestige of the sultan-caliph among their own Muslim subjects; the other more remote and hypothetical, that of partitioning the Ottoman territories in the event of an Allied victory.

The British, who, as rulers of Egypt and the Sudan, were particularly apprehensive of the danger of a *jihād* proclaimed by the sultan-caliph, entered upon negotiations with *Sharīf* Ḥusayn. As the actual master of the Holy Cities, and a descendant of the Prophet, he could be a valuable counterweight to the Ottoman sultan. Ḥusayn himself was an ambitious dynast, who was anxious to secure himself and his branch of the Hashimite clan in independent possession of the Ḥijāz. Through his sons, he established contact with the Arab nationalists of Syria, and thus was enabled to present himself as the spokesman of a nascent 'Arab nation'. On the British side, the negotiations were handled by Sir Henry McMahon, the British high commissioner in Egypt. The correspondence between the two resulted (on 24 October 1915) in a statement of British intentions in regard to the Fertile Crescent and Arabia. This excluded from discussion the 'districts of Mersina and Alexandretta and portions of Syria lying to the west of the districts of Damascus, Homs,

Hama and Aleppo' (i.e. the *northern* Syrian littoral). It safeguarded existing British treaty-rights with Arab chiefs, and envisaged 'special administrative arrangements' to secure British interests in the vilayets of Baghdād and Baṣra. There was another proviso: the British declaration was limited to those regions 'wherein Great Britain [was] free to act without detriment to the interests of her ally, France'. With these far-reaching limitations, McMahon gave Ḥusayn the assurance that 'Great Britain [was] prepared to recognise and support the independence of the Arabs'. It should be noted, however, that the 'independence' envisaged was very limited, since Britain was to advise the Arabs and 'assist them to establish what may appear to be the most suitable forms of government in the various territories'.

The allusion to French interests was significant. From the outset of the war, the French saw the possibility of establishing their rule in the Levant on the dissolution of the Ottoman empire, and believed that the British government would regard this aim with sympathy. In 1915 the need to clarify projects of partition had become urgent, not only because of the negotiations with Ḥusayn, but also because Russia had put forward a claim to Constantinople and the Straits, and demurred at the French aspirations to control the Christian Holy Places in Palestine. The British, for their part, were anxious to whittle down French claims in Syria, which might instal a European great power on the frontier of Egypt. Discussions were therefore undertaken, which resulted in May 1916 in a statement of intentions, known (from its negotiators) as the Sykes-Picot Agreement. As far as the Fertile Crescent and its hinterland were concerned, its terms were as follows. The northern Syrian littoral, west of the line Damascus-Ḥims-Ḥamāh-Aleppo, was allotted to the French 'to establish such direct or indirect administration or control as [she desires]'. The Baghdād-Baṣra region, and also a small coastal enclave of Palestine containing Haifa and Acre, were similarly allotted to Britain. The rest of Palestine, west of the Jordan and as far south as Gaza, was to be placed under an international administration after consultation with Russia, the other Allies, and Ḥusayn's representatives. Finally, the remainder of the Fertile Crescent and the Syrian Desert was divided into two areas, in which 'an independent Arab state or a confederation of Arab states' would be set up under the protection of France and Britain respectively.

Although the Sykes-Picot Agreement went beyond the McMahon declaration in providing for a French as well as a British sphere of influence in the territory occupied by the 'independent Arab state or confederation', and in proposing an international régime for Palestine, there was no real conflict between the two partition schemes in these matters. Both the French and Ḥusayn were informed of Britain's commitments. The terms of McMahon's letter of 24 October 1915 show that 'independence' promised to the Arabs was to be severely circumscribed by British advice and assistance. The Sykes-Picot Agreement conceded to France a share in these supervisory functions. Palestine, as an area in which France (to say nothing of Russia) had interests, clearly fell under the proviso enunciated in McMahon's letter.

By 1917, then, the British had taken the lead in negotiating with the French and with *Sharīf* Ḥusayn arrangements for the future disposition of the Ottoman Arab territories. These arrangements were secret, and it was clear that the undertakings offered to the Arabs were contingent upon the securing of British and French interests in the region. In other words, down to that date, the future settlement was conceived in terms of classical great power diplomacy. During 1917, however, several developments occurred which altered the situation. The collapse of Russian military resistance removed one of the parties interested in the partition of the Ottoman empire, and rendered obsolete the scheme for an international régime in Palestine. The entry of the United States of America into the war imposed upon the Allies a respectful attention to President Wilson's political ideas. In particular, his advocacy of open diplomacy and national self-determination ran counter to the assumptions on which the British had acted in their dealings with Ḥusayn and the French.

Two events brought into the open the conduct of British policy in regard to the Near East, and made its principles a matter of public controversy. On 2 November 1917, the British government in the Balfour Declaration announced that they '[viewed] with favour the establishment in Palestine of a national home for the Jewish people, and [would] use their best endeavours to facilitate the achievement of this object'. This gesture towards the Zionists was perhaps motivated in the first place by a desire to secure control over Palestine through grateful clients, but its immediate purpose was to conciliate Jewish opinion in Russia and America, and win Zionist support for the Allied war-effort. A month later, the contents of the Sykes-Picot Agreement, which had been communicated by the new Bolshevik government in Russia to the Ottomans, were published in Syria. Thereafter, the compromise of interests embodied in that agreement and in the Ḥusayn-McMahon correspondence could not be maintained. The British, the French, the Hashimites, the Arab nationalists and the Zionists fought confusedly, each for their own interests. In particular, the British, to secure their own position, ostensibly adopted without reservations the Wilsonian doctrine of national self-determination. This was enunciated in a statement made to some Syrian Arab nationalists in June 1918 (the Declaration to the Seven) and in the Anglo-French Declaration published in the following November. These announcements temporarily secured their object, but when, in the months following the end of the war, a political settlement had to be worked out, it soon became clear that neither France nor Britain was prepared fully to implement these later promises, or to abdicate the position won by victory over the Ottomans.

That victory had been won by operations conducted separately in the two arms of the Fertile Crescent. For the western part, Egypt was the indispensable base. In December 1914, its anomalous legal status was ended by the British declaration of a protectorate, while the pro-Ottoman Khedive ʿAbbās II was deposed. An Ottoman attack on the Suez Canal, in February 1915, was repulsed and never repeated, and in the following year the British assumed the offensive. Until November 1917, the Ottoman line held, but Allenby's victory at Gaza enabled him to break through into Palestine. In June 1916, *Sharīf* Ḥusayn had proclaimed a revolt against the sultan. Although the Ottoman garrison at Medina held out until the end of the war, Arab tribal forces, commanded by Ḥusayn's son, Fayṣal, assisted by a handful of British officers, and subsidized by the British government, mopped up resistance in the Ḥijāz, and went on to operate on Allenby's flank in Transjordan. Caught in a great pincer movement, the Ottoman forces were defeated in September 1918 at Darʿa. The Hashimite troops (briefly preceded by a brigade of Australian light horse) entered Damascus on 1 October. At the end of the month, with the signing of the armistice of Mudros, the Ottoman empire withdrew from the war.

Operations in the eastern Fertile Crescent were controlled by the government of India, which had a traditional concern with the Persian Gulf region. There were already important British oil installations at Abadan, and it was in order to protect these that an expeditionary force was despatched in October 1914. Baṣra was occupied in November, and the head of the Gulf secured. In 1915 an advance up the Tigris took place, but an attempt to capture Baghdād failed. This first major offensive ended with the surrender of a British force at Kūt al-ʿAmāra in April 1916. After several months of preparation, the advance was resumed in December, and Baghdād was captured in March 1917. Thus the British obtained control of the region in which they had asserted a special interest in both the Ḥusayn-McMahon correspondence and the Sykes-Picot Agreement. Further north, although Kirkūk was captured in May 1918, it had to be abandoned, while Mosul was not occupied until after the armistice of Mudros.

So ended four centuries of Ottoman rule in the Arab lands. In spite of the long erosion of the empire, its downfall in this region was sudden and, in a sense fortuitous, since it was less the consequence of local developments than of the conflict of great powers in the First World War. The passing of Ottoman power brought neither peace nor unity to the region, and its history in the ensuing decades was to be governed by the relations and rivalries of four principal parties: the British, the French, the local rulers and the nationalists.

CHAPTER 5

SAFAVID PERSIA

Despite recent research, the origins of the Safavid family are still obscure. Such evidence as we have seems to suggest that the family hailed from Kurdistān. What does seem certain is that the Safavids were of native Iranian stock, and spoke Āẕarī, the form of Turkish used in Āẕarbāyjān. Our lack of reliable information derives from the fact that the Safavids, after the establishment of the Safavid state, deliberately falsified the evidence of their own origins. Their fundamental object in claiming a Shīʿī origin was to differentiate themselves from the Ottomans and to enable them to enlist the sympathies of all heterodox elements. To this end they systematically destroyed any evidence which indicated that Shaykh Ṣafī al-Dīn Isḥāq, the founder of the Safavid *ṭarīqa* was not a Shīʿī (he was probably a Sunnī of the Shāfiʿī *madhhab*), and they fabricated evidence to prove that the Safavids were *sayyids,* that is, direct descendants of the Prophet. They constructed a dubious genealogy tracing the descent of the Safavid family from the seventh of the Twelver *Imāms,* Mūsā al-Kāẓim—a genealogy which is seduously followed by the later Safavid sources—and introduced into the text of a hagiological work on the life of Shaykh Ṣafī al-Dīn, a number of anecdotes designed to validate the Safavid claim to be *sayyids.* Viewed dispassionately, the majority of these anecdotes appear ingenuous, not to say naïve.

The first member of the Safavid family of whom we have any historical knowledge is a certain Fīrūz-Shāh, who was a wealthy landowner on the borders of Āẕarbāyjān and Gīlān, in north-west Persia, at the beginning of the fifth/eleventh century. Either he or his son moved to the region of Ardabīl, a town in eastern Āẕarbāyjān situated at an altitude of 5,000 feet on a plateau surrounded by high mountains, and Ardabīl henceforth became the focal point of Safavid activity. Fīrūz-Shāh and his descendants busied themselves with agricultural pursuits, and acquired a reputation for abundant piety and zealous religious observance, to such an extent that numbers of the local population were moved to declare themselves their *murīds* or disciples.

In 650/1252–3 Ṣafī al-Dīn, from whom the Safavid dynasty derived its name, was born.[1] The youthful Ṣafī al-Dīn, we are told, did not mix with other boys, but spent his time in prayer and fasting. He experienced visions. None of the local *pīrs* (spiritual directors) could satisfy his spiritual needs, and at the age of twenty he went to Shīrāz in search of a *pīr* who had been recommended to him. On his arrival there, he found that this *pīr* was dead, and he was advised that the only man in the world who could analyse his mystical state was the head of a local Ṣūfī order, a certain Shaykh Zāhid-i Gīlānī, whom he traced in 675/1276–7, after a protracted search, to a village near the Caspian Sea. At that time, Ṣafī al-Dīn was twenty-five years of age, and Shaykh Zāhid sixty. As the latter grew older, he became increasingly dependent on Ṣafī al-Dīn, who married Shaykh Zāhid's daughter, and gave his own daughter in marriage to Shaykh Zāhid's son. On Shaykh Zāhid's death in 700/1301 at the age of eighty-five, Ṣafī al-Dīn succeeded him as head of the Zāhidiyya, which from then on became known as the Safavid order, or Ṣafaviyya, with its headquarters at Ardabīl.

For the next century and a half, from 700/1301 to 850/1447, the Safavid shaykhs of Ardabīl proceeded with great tenacity of purpose to extend their influence. The significant contribution of Ṣafī al-Dīn to the rise of the Safavids is that he transformed a Ṣūfī order of purely local importance into a religious movement whose influence was felt not only within the borders of Persia, but also in Syria and eastern Anatolia. In these areas the religious propaganda (*da'wa*) of the Safavids won many converts among the Turcoman[2] tribes which later formed the *élite* of the Safavid fighting forces. The most important of these tribes were the Ustājlū, Rūmlū, Shāmlū, Dulgadır (Dhu'l-Qadr), Takkalū, Afshār, and Qājār.

The death of Ṣafī al-Dīn in 735/1334 coincided with the break-up of the Mongol empire of the Īl-Khāns in Persia and the eastern Fertile Crescent. For nearly fifty years there was anarchy in Persia, and then for a further twenty years the successive waves of the Turco-Mongol (Tatar) forces led by Tīmūr swept across the country. During these disturbed times Ṣafī al-Dīn's son and successor, Ṣadr al-Dīn Mūsā, not only managed on the whole to preserve the lands belonging to the Ardabīl sanctuary from the exactions of local officials and military commanders, but also to enrich the sanctuary itself by the construction of the sacred enclosure

[1] The derivation of Safavid from Ṣūfī, a theory derived from contemporary Western accounts, which refer to the Safavid shah as 'the Great Sophy', is erroneous.

[2] Turcoman should not be confused with Turkmān. 'Turcoman' is used as a generic term for the semi-nomadic tribes, of Turkish ethnic origin, which carried on a pastoral existence remote from the towns. 'Turkmān' is the proper name of one such tribe.

of the Safavid family, comprising a mausoleum, a convent, and ancillary buildings. Ṣadr al-Dīn was held in great veneration by many of the Mongol nobility, some of whom declared themselves to be his disciples.

Under Khwāja 'Alī (head of the Safavid order from 794/1391–2 to 830/1427), there was a movement away from the orthodox type of mystical belief and practice, and for the first time Safavid religious propaganda assumed a Shī'ī flavour. The Safavid movement—for such it now was—began to gather momentum, and, under the leadership of Junayd (851–64/1447–60), its frankly revolutionary character became apparent. Junayd, unlike his predecessors, aspired to temporal power as well as spiritual authority. His followers were called on to fight for their beliefs. His political ambitions at once brought him into conflict with the ruling temporal power in Persia—the Kara-Koyunlu, or Black Sheep Turcomans. He was driven into exile, and eventually took refuge in Diyār Bakr at the court of Uzun Ḥasan, the ruler of the Ak-Koyunlu, or White Sheep Turcomans. Logically, the Shī'ī Safavids should have had more in common with the Shī'ī Kara-Koyunlu than with the Sunnī Ak-Koyunlu, but at the time the dominant political power in Persia and the eastern Fertile Crescent was the Kara-Koyunlu state, and the Safavids and the Ak-Koyunlu sank their religious antipathy in a political alliance cemented by Junayd's marriage to Uzun Ḥasan's sister. In 863/1459 Junayd made an abortive attempt to recover Ardabīl. The following year, on his way to attack the Circassians, he was attacked by the ruler of Shīrvān, and killed.

Junayd's son, Ḥaydar, became head of the Safavid order, and maintained the close alliance with the Ak-Koyunlu by marrying Uzun Ḥasan's daughter. Ḥaydar devised the distinctive red Safavid headgear, with twelve gores or folds commemorating the twelve Shī'ī *Imāms*. As a result, Safavid troops were dubbed *Qizilbāsh* (Turkish: *Kızıl Bash,* Red Head), a term later used pejoratively by the Ottomans. In 872/1467 the Ak-Koyunlu overthrew the Kara-Koyunlu empire, and became in their turn the target for Safavid political and military ambitions. The alliance, based on mutual political advantage, collapsed as soon as the Safavids constituted a political threat to the Ak-Koyunlu. In 893/1488, when Ḥaydar, like his father before him, decided to blood his forces by an expedition against the Circassians, and *en route* attempted to avenge his father by attacking the ruler of Shīrvān, the Ak-Koyunlu sent a detachment of troops to the aid of the latter, and these troops constituted the decisive factor in the defeat of the Safavid forces. Ḥaydar himself was killed.

It would not have been surprising if the Safavid revolutionary movement, having suffered for the second time in little over half a century the stunning blow of the death of its leader in battle, had collapsed at this point. That it did not do so, but on the contrary rapidly gathered strength to sweep aside all opposition, is a tribute to the thoroughness and effectiveness with which the Safavid propagandists, radiating from their base at Ardabīl and penetrating deep into the Armenian highlands, Syria and Anatolia, had carried out their work. During the long period of preparation for the Safavid revolution, these propagandists periodically returned to Ardabīl to draw new inspiration from their *murshid* or spiritual director, the head of the order.

Within a short time of the death of Ḥaydar, a large number of Safavid followers had gathered at Ardabīl to congratulate his son ʿAlī on his accession to the leadership of the order, and to urge him to avenge his father and grandfather. Thoroughly alarmed by this demonstration of Safavid power, the Ak-Koyunlu ruler, Yaʿqūb, seized ʿAlī, his two brothers, Ibrāhīm and Ismāʿīl, and their mother, and imprisoned them in Fārs for four and a half years (894–8/1489–93). In 898/1493 the Ak-Koyunlu prince, Rustam, released ʿAlī on condition that the Safavid forces fought for him against his cousin and rival for the throne. After defeating Rustam's cousin, ʿAlī returned to Ardabīl in triumph.

Rustam realized too late that he had released the genie from the bottle. Events moved swiftly. At the end of 899/middle of 1494 Rustam re-arrested ʿAlī and took him to Khoy (Khwuy), but ʿAlī escaped and made for Ardabīl. Rustam knew he had to stop him. 'Should ʿAlī once enter Ardabīl', he said, 'which God forbid!—the deaths of ten thousand Turcomans [i.e., Ak-Koyunlu troops] would be of no avail.' ʿAlī, having a premonition of his coming death, nominated his younger brother Ismāʿīl as his successor, and sent him ahead to Ardabīl in the care of seven picked men. ʿAlī was overtaken by Ak-Koyunlu forces, and killed. For the third time the Safavid revolutionary movement had lost its leader, and its new leader, Ismāʿīl, was only seven years old. Ismāʿīl eluded a house-to-house search instituted by the Ak-Koyunlu in Ardabīl, and escaped to Gīlān, finding sanctuary at Lāhījān. Dynastic feuds prevented the Ak-Koyunlu from invading Gīlān and seizing Ismāʿīl.

In Gīlān, Ismāʿīl and his small band of dedicated Safavid supporters perfected their plans for overthrowing the Ak-Koyunlu empire. For five years (899–905/1494–9), Ismāʿīl maintained close contact with his followers in Āẕarbāyjān, Syria, and Anatolia. At the end of that time, he decided to make his bid for power. In the summer of 905–6/1500, 7,000 of his men assembled at Erzinjan, on the Euphrates, 200 miles west of Erzurum. After settling an old score with the ruler of Shīrvān, Ismā'īl marched on Āẕarbāyjān, and in the spring of 906/1501 he routed an Ak-Koyunlu force of 30,000 men at the battle of Sharūr near Nakhchivān. Although the rest of Persia was not brought under Safavid control for another ten years, this was the decisive battle of the revolution. In the summer of 906–7/1501 Ismā'īl entered Tabrīz, and proclaimed himself Shāh Ismā'īl I the first ruler of the new Safavid dynasty, as yet with authority over Āẕarbāyjān only.

Ismā'īl's first action on his accession, the proclamation of the Shī'ī form of Islam as the religion of the new state, was unquestionably the most significant act of his whole reign. By taking this step, he not only clearly differentiated the new state from the Ottoman empire, the major power in the Islamic world at the time, which otherwise might well have incorporated Persia in its dominions, but imparted to his subjects a sense of unity which permitted the rise of a national state in the modern sense of the term. Ever since the Arab conquest in the first/seventh century, Persia had been a geographical rather than a political entity. Either it had been part of a larger empire, or it had lacked any central governing authority, and had been divided piecemeal among a number of petty dynasties. With the exception of the territory lost during the eighteenth and nineteenth centuries to Russia in the north-west and north-east, and to Afghanistan in the east, the boundaries of Persia today are substantially the same as in the later tenth/sixteenth century, and we may assert, therefore, that the rise of the modern state of Iran dates from the establishment of the Safavid state in 907/1501.

The imposition of Shi'ism on a country which, officially at least, was still predominantly Sunnī, obviously could not be achieved without incurring opposition, or without a measure of persecution of those who refused to conform. Disobedience was punishable by death, and the threat of force was there from the beginning. As far as the ordinary people were concerned, the existence of this threat seems to have been sufficient. The '*ulamā*' were more stubborn. Some were put to death; many more fled to areas where Sunnism still prevailed—to the Timurid court at Herat and, after the conquest of Khurāsān by the Safavids, to the Özbeg capital at Bukhārā. It is extremely difficult to judge how far the ground may have been prepared for the change by the efforts of Safavid propagandists, by such factors as the transfer of large numbers of pro-Shīʿī Turcomans from Āẕarbāyjān to Khurāsān between 823/1420 and 870/1465, and by the activities of heterodox and antinomian groups. It is equally difficult to assess with any certainty to what extent the activities of the other Ṣūfī orders in Persia may have helped the Safavids by the transmission of Shīʿī ideas. In general, however, one can say that heterodox beliefs were, and are, endemic in Persia, and the transition to Shiʿism may not have been as abrupt and revolutionary as would appear at first sight.

Within a period of ten years from the date of his accession at Tabrīz, Ismāʿīl conquered the whole of Persia, and incorporated the eastern Fertile Crescent in the Safavid empire. The main stages in the consolidation of empire were: the defeat of the remaining Ak-Koyunlu forces near Hamadān (908/1503), which gave Ismāʿīl control of central and southern Persia; the subjugation of the Caspian provinces of Māzandarān and Gurgān, and the capture of Yazd (909/1504); the pacification of the western frontier, and the annexation of Diyār Bakr (911–13/1505–7); the capture of Baghdād and the conquest of south-west Persia (914/1508); the subjugation of Shīrvān (915/1509–10); and the conquest of Khurāsān (916/1510), which had been overrun by the Özbegs of Transoxania three years before. Although the head of the Özbeg confederation, Muḥammad Shaybānī Khān, was killed, the Özbeg menace remained, and the Safavids never solved the problem of the defence of the eastern marches against these nomads. Only a year after the conquest of Khurāsān, Ismāʿīl was drawn into an attack on Samarqand through the ambition of the Timurid prince Bābur to recover his Transoxanian dominions. Safavid forces installed Bābur at Samarqand, but as soon as they returned home the Özbegs drove him out, inflicted a crushing defeat on a Safavid army in Ramaḍān 918/November 1512 just east of the Oxus, and swept on into Khurāsān, capturing Herat, Mashhad and Ṭūs. Punitive expeditions despatched by Ismāʿīl restored the position along the eastern frontier, and there was an uneasy truce with the Özbegs for eight years.

Throughout the tenth/sixteenth century the Safavids had to fight on two fronts—against the Özbegs in the east, and against the Ottomans in the west. The outbreak of war with the Ottoman empire occurred in 920/1514. It had been precipitated by a series of acts of provocation committed by the Safavids, but the fundamental reason for the outbreak of war was the establishment of the Safavid state itself. The imposition of a militant form of Shiʿism in Persia constituted a political threat to the Ottoman empire, and this threat was the greater because in eastern Anatolia, within the borders of the Ottoman empire itself, were large numbers of Turcomans who were supporters of the Safavid cause. In 918/1512 Ismāʿīl had made a deliberate attempt to undermine Ottoman authority in this area. The Ottoman Sultan Selīm I considered the danger so real that, before he invaded Persia, he put to death all the adherents of Shiʿism in Anatolia on whom he could lay hands.

On 2 Rajab 920/23 August 1514, the Ottoman and Safavid armies confronted each other at Chāldirān, in north-western Āẕarbāyjān. Ismāʿīl had two commanders who possessed first-hand experience of Ottoman methods of warfare, but he chose to ignore their advice to attack at once before the Ottomans had completed the disposition of their forces. The Ottomans were therefore able to follow their usual practice of stationing their musketeers behind a barrier of gun-carriages which were linked by chains. On the gun-carriages were placed mortars. This formed an insuperable obstacle to any force which, like the Safavid army, was composed almost entirely of cavalry. The Safavid cavalry, led with desperate valour by Ismāʿīl in person, launched charge after charge against the Ottoman guns, but were driven back with heavy casualties. The failure of the Safavids to equip themselves with artillery and hand-guns is one of the puzzling features of the period. The claim of the Sherley brothers, two English gentlemen-adventurers, to have introduced firearms into Persia in the reign of Shāh ʿAbbās the Great (996–1038/1588–1629) has now been proved to be quite without foundation. It is known that at least a hundred years before the time of ʿAbbās, the Ak-Koyunlu possessed a number of cannon, and there is no doubt at all that the Safavids could have developed the use of artillery and hand-guns had they chosen so to do. It has been suggested that the Safavids, like their contemporaries the Mamluks of Egypt and Syria, considered the use of firearms to be unchivalrous and unmanly. Whatever the reasons for Safavid neglect in this regard, it is clear that it was primarily Ottoman superiority in firearms which enabled them to inflict a signal defeat on the Safavids at Chāldirān. Among the Safavid dead were many high-ranking *Qiẕilbāsh* officers. The Ottoman losses were not negligible, particularly on their left, where the Safavids had broken the Ottoman line, and the commander was killed. Selīm occupied Tabrīz, but eight days later, because his officers refused to winter in Persia, he withdrew from the Safavid capital.

In terms of territory, the Safavids escaped with the loss of the province of Diyār Bakr, and of the regions of Marʿash and Elbistan, over which in any event they exercised little more than nominal authority. Of much greater consequence was the psychological effect on Ismāʿīl himself, which had repercussions on his conduct of the affairs of state, on his relations with the *Qizilbāsh,* and on the balance between the Persian and Turcoman elements in the Safavid administration. Chāldirān destroyed Ismāʿīl's faith in his invincibility. To his *Qizilbāsh* Turkish followers, Ismāʿīl was both their temporal ruler and their spiritual director. But he was much more than that. He himself, addressing these often illiterate tribesmen in their own tongue, and using simple language, had fostered the belief that he was the manifestation of God himself. The Safavid state, in its early years, was in a real sense a theocracy. The contemporary accounts of Venetian merchants bear witness to the fanatical devotion of the *Qizilbāsh* to their leader, whom they considered immortal. This belief received a shock at Chāldirān. Ismāʿīl became a recluse, and attempted to drown his sorrows in drunken debauches. Much of his time was devoted to hunting. During the last ten years of his life, he never again led his troops into battle. Ismāʿīl's loss of personal prestige meant a corresponding increase in the powers both of the Turcoman tribal chiefs and of the high-ranking Persian officials in the bureaucracy. As a result, serious internal stresses were set up, and within a year of Ismāʿīl's death on 19 Rajab 930/23 May 1524, civil war had broken out as rival groups of *Qizilbāsh* tribes fought for supremacy, restrained neither by allegiance to the shah as their temporal ruler, nor by reverence for his person as 'the Shadow of God upon Earth'. Once the religious bond between Ismāʿīl and the *Qizilbāsh* had been broken, the authority of the ruler could only be maintained by a strong and effective personality. Ṭahmāsp I, who at the age of ten succeeded his father on the throne of Persia in 930/1524, did not at first have an opportunity to exercise any authority, because the *Qizilbāsh* military aristocracy assumed control of the state.

As already noted, the Safavid state at its inception had a theocratic form of government. There was no formal boundary between the religious and the political aspect of the state. Consequently the highest officer of state, termed *wakīl-i nafs-i nafīs-i humāyūn,* or vicegerent of the shah, represented the ruler in both his religious and his political capacity. He was the shah's *alter ego,* and was responsible for the orderly arrangement of the affairs of religion and the state. The first holder of this office was a high-ranking *Qizilbāsh* officer of the Shāmlū tribe, one of the small group of trusted companions who had been with Ismā'īl in Gīlān and had planned the final stages of the Safavid revolution. Since the *Qizilbāsh* constituted the backbone of the Safavid fighting forces, they considered it proper that the *wakīl* should be drawn from their ranks. They also considered as their prerogative the post of *amīr al-umarā'*, or commander-in-chief of the *Qizilbāsh* tribal forces. To begin with, the same man seems to have held both these high offices. The *qūrchībāshī*, a high-ranking military officer whose function during the early Safavid period is extremely obscure, was also a *Qizilbāsh* chief.

The two remaining principal offices of state were filled by Persians. One was the office of *wazīr*, traditionally in medieval Islamic states the first minister and head of the bureaucracy. In the early Safavid state, the importance of the *wazīr* was greatly reduced by the creation of the office of *wakīl*, and by the intervention of the *amīr al-umarā'* in political affairs. The other was the office of *ṣadr*, who was the head of the religious institution, and whose prime task after the establishment of the Safavid state was to impose doctrinal unity on Persia by the energetic propagation of Twelver Shi'ism—a task which was virtually completed by the death of Ismā'īl I.

Within a short time, friction developed between the Turcoman and the Persian elements in the administration. This friction was aggravated by the lack of any clear definition of the function of the principal officers of state. This confusion of function and overlapping of authority derived in part from the circumstances which attended the rise to power of the Safavids, and in part from the predominantly military character of the early Safavid state. Even the *ṣadr* from time to time took part in military operations. Before the end of Ismā'īl's reign, there are clear signs of a movement away from the theocratic state, and towards a separation of religious and political powers. This was reflected in changes both in the scope and function, and in the relative importance of the principal offices of state. There was a tendency to lay less emphasis on the paramount position of the *wakīl* as the vicegerent of the shah, representing both the temporal and religious authority of the latter, and to regard him rather as the head of the bureaucracy. In time, the title *wakīl* itself fell into disuse. There was a decline in the power of the *ṣadr*. From time to time the *ṣadrs* made abortive attempts to regain some of their former influence in political affairs, but their activities were increasingly restricted to the administration of the *waqfs,* and the exercise of a general supervisory role over the religious institution.

One of the problems which face all leaders of successful revolutions is how best to deal with those who have been responsible for bringing them to power. The qualities which make people devoted members of a fanatical revolutionary movement are precisely those which make it difficult to absorb them into the post-revolutionary administrative system. The Safavid revolution was no exception. Only six years after his accession, Ismāʿīl was so apprehensive of the power of the *Qizilbāsh* tribal chiefs that he dismissed the eminent Turcoman officer who held the post of *wakīl* and replaced him by a Persian. Another Persian succeeded to this office in 915/1509–10. *Qizilbāsh* resentment at being excluded from a post which they regarded as their prerogative led to open friction between them and the *wakīl.* Ismāʿīl also took steps to curb the power of the *amīr al-umarāʾ*. The heavy casualties suffered by the *Qizilbāsh* at Chāldirān weakened their influence to some extent during the last decade of Ismāʿīl's reign, but even so, a *Qizilbāsh* chief governed the important province of Khurāsān from 922–8/1516–22 with an insolent disregard of orders emanating from the shah and the central administration. As the belief of the *Qizilbāsh* in the shah as their spiritual director and the Shadow of God on Earth weakened, they reverted to their former tribal loyalties. Since in practice they no longer held the person of the shah in any special respect, whatever the official myth might be, it is not surprising that the youthful Shāh Ṭahmāsp was unable to exert his authority over them for at least a decade. In 937/1530–1, during one incident in the civil war between rival factions of *Qizilbāsh,* a group of Turcomans even burst into the royal tent, and two arrows struck the shah's crown.

The decade from 930/1524 to 940/1533 may be termed the *Qizilbāsh* interregnum. After an initial period of rule by a triumvirate of *Qizilbāsh* chiefs, drawn from the Rūmlū, Takkalū, and Ustājlū tribes, there was civil war between the Ustājlūs and the rest of the *Qizilbāsh* tribes in 932–3/1526–7; then followed a duumvirate of a Rūmlū and a Takkalū, a period of Takkalū hegemony (933–7/1527–30), and, finally, a period of Shāmlū hegemony (937–40/1530–4). In 940/1533–4 Ṭahmāsp executed Ḥusayn Khān Shāmlū, the head of the Shāmlū tribe and the virtual ruler of the state. As this chief was the guardian of Ṭahmāsp's infant son, Muḥammad Mīrzā, and a cousin of Ṭahmāsp himself, the shah's action had the greater effect. It indicated his intention of ruling from then on in fact as well as in name, and two further actions taken by the shah at this time underlined this resolve. Ṭahmāsp refused to allow another Shāmlū chieftain to take command of the tribe, but placed it under the direct command of his younger brother, Bahrām Mīrzā; and he appointed a Persian to fill the office of *wakīl*. During the ten years of *Qizilbāsh* rule, this office had reverted to their exclusive control. Having thus gained the upper hand, Ṭahmāsp managed to keep it for the next forty years, until in 982/1574 his failing health gave the *Qizilbāsh* another opportunity to defy his authority.

Shāh Ṭahmāsp is something of an enigma. His reign of fifty-two years was longer than that of any other Safavid monarch. Yet his personal character seems to have made little impression on Western observers, and the picture left to us by the Carmelites and others is wholly unfavourable. Great emphasis is laid on his parsimony. It is even alleged that he sent his disused clothing to be sold in the bazaar. He is said to have alternated between extremes of asceticism and intemperance. He was capable of great cruelty. He was given to melancholy, and in his latter years was more or less a recluse. No source, Oriental or Western, credits him with any strength of character, or with any particular skill in the arts either of peace or of war. On the other hand, the fact that he asserted himself as *de facto* shah after ten years of unchallenged *Qizilbāsh* supremacy, postulates moral toughness and flexibility. The mere fact that the Safavid state survived a series of most determined onslaughts by its principal enemies, the Ottomans in the west and the Özbegs in the east, at a time when it was seriously weakened by internal faction, by the defection of large bodies of *Qizilbāsh* troops to the Ottomans, and by the plots of the shah's brothers against the crown, argues that Ṭahmāsp was not devoid either of courage or military ability. Between 930/1524 and 944/1538, for instance, the Özbegs launched five major invasions on Khurāsān. In the west, the Ottoman Sultan Süleymān the Magnificent mounted four full-scale invasions of Āẕarbāyjān. In 940/1533–4, to meet the first of these attacks, delivered by 90,000 men under the grand *vezīr* Ibrāhīm Pasha, Ṭahmāsp could raise only 7,000 men, and the loyalty of many of these was suspect. Further Ottoman invasions followed in 941/1534–5, 955/1548, and 961/1553. Baghdād was entered by the Ottomans in 941/1534. Tabrīz was occupied on several occasions, and, because of its vulnerability to Ottoman attack, Ṭahmāsp transferred the capital to Qazvīn.

It is remarkable not that the Safavid state suffered certain losses of territory to the Ottomans, but that it was not overwhelmed. One explanation may be sought in the fact that the Ottomans in Āẕarbāyjān were operating at the end of a long and vulnerable line of communication. The Kurds in particular were past masters in the art of cutting off straggling units and raiding baggage trains. The severe winters and mountainous terrain of Āẕarbāyjān were allies of the Safavids. But when all due allowance has been made for these factors, it is clear that no small measure of credit must go to Ṭahmāsp for his masterly use of Fabian tactics. Given the internal difficulties with which he was faced, he could wage only a defensive war. He therefore decided on a 'scorched earth' policy. The frontier areas of Āẕarbāyjān were systematically laid waste. The further the Ottomans advanced into Persian territory, the more difficult their position became. There was a shortage of food for the troops, and their pack-animals died by the thousand. Eventually the Ottomans were forced to fall back. As they retreated, they were continually harassed by Safavid regular and irregular forces. The lessons of Chāldirān had been well learnt, and at no time did Ṭahmāsp commit his numerically far inferior forces to a pitched battle. Ismā'īl was a man of great personal bravery, and an inspiring leader. Ṭahmāsp was neither, but he has not been given sufficient credit for the way in which he husbanded his meagre resources, and successfully resisted two such powerful enemies as the Ottomans under their greatest conqueror, Süleymān I, and the Özbegs under one of their greatest leaders, 'Ubayd Allāh Khān. Ṭahmāsp received loyal support from his brother Bahrām Mīrzā who, until his untimely death in 956/1549 at the age of thirty-two, was a fearless, if sometimes impulsive, commander, very much in his father's mould. The treachery of Ṭahmāsp's other two brothers, Sām Mīrzā, governor-general of Khurāsān, who rebelled against the shah and intrigued with the Ottomans in 941–2/1534–6, and Alqāṣ Mīrzā, governor of Shīrvān, who rebelled and joined the third Ottoman invasion of Persia in 955/1548, was a source of great grief to Ṭahmāsp. Ṭahmāsp rendered a great service to the Safavid state by negotiating the peace of Amasya (962/1555), which inaugurated a period of over thirty years of peace with the Ottomans.

The control of the state by the *Qizilbāsh* chiefs between 930/1524 and 940/1533 was naturally reflected in the relative importance of the principal offices of state. The office of *wakīl,* and that of *amīr al-umarā',* to which Ismā'īl had appointed Persians in an effort to curb the power of the *Qizilbāsh,* reverted to the latter. Both offices were often held by the same man. In such cases, the military and political aspect of the *wakīl*'s function was predominant. Indeed, the holding of military command was an essential part of the *wakīl*'s function as originally conceived. There was, however, a lack of differentiation between the various administrative offices at this time; and the term *wakīl* was also used in regard to the official who was the head of the bureaucracy, in other words, the official more properly known as the *wazīr*. This has resulted in considerable confusion in the sources. After 940/1533, when the execution of Ḥusayn Khān Shāmlū ended for the time being the military control of the political institution by the *Qizilbāsh* chiefs, the *amīr al-umarā'*, as an officer of the central administration, disappears from the scene. The title continued to be used by the military governors of important provinces. With the decline of the *amīr al-umarā'*, the importance of the formerly subordinate *qūrchībāshī* increased. From about 945/1538–9 onwards, the sources indicate a steady extension of the authority of the *qūrchībāshī* in both political and military affairs. It is interesting to note that, over a period of forty years (955–95/1548–87), the majority of the officers appointed to the office of *qūrchībāshī* were from the Afshār tribe; moreover, a hereditary tendency became apparent. In appointments to the office of *ṣadr,* the hereditary tendency was even more marked, particularly during the latter part of Ṭahmāsp's reign. The decline in the political and religious power of the *ṣadr,* already noticed during Ismā'īl's lifetime, became more marked during the reign of Ṭahmāsp. After 932/1525–6, the obituary notices in the sources, instead of extolling the zeal of *ṣadrs* in propagating Shi'ism and in rooting out heresy, lay emphasis on their learning and scholarship. During the second half of the reign of Ṭahmāsp, there is hardly any indication of political activity on the part of the *ṣadrs*. Their position as head of the religious institution was already being challenged by powerful theologians known as *mujtahids*. By the time of 'Abbās the Great, the *mujtahids* had become the principal exponents of the Shī'ī orthodoxy achieved through the efforts of the *ṣadrs* of the early Safavid period. In general, during the reign of Ṭahmāsp the administrative system was still undergoing a process of change and evolution.

The reign of Shāh 'Abbās I the Great (996–1038/1588–1629) is rightly considered not only to be the high-point of the Safavid empire, which thereafter began to decline, but also to mark the dividing-line between the early Safavid state, developing slowly and painfully out of its theocratic origins, and seeking, for the most part unsuccessfully, to reconcile these origins with the practical requirements of administering a large empire, and the later Safavid state, reorganized on entirely different lines by Shāh ʿAbbās I. While this may be accepted as a generalization, it must be pointed out that the measures introduced by ʿAbbās were frequently the logical outcome of processes which had begun during the reign of Ṭahmāsp and during the short and disturbed reigns of his successors Ismāʿīl II (984–5/1576–7) and Sulṭān Muḥammad Shāh (985–95/1578–87). For instance, one of ʿAbbās's most far-reaching measures, which transformed the whole structure of the Safavid state, was the creation of the corps of *ghulāms,* or *qullar* ('slaves'). These *ghulāms* were Georgian prisoners, converts from Christianity, and the immediate purpose of the formation of this corps was to enable ʿAbbās to resist the *Qizilbāsh,* who had once again got out of hand and threatened to usurp the authority of the ruler as they had done at the accession of Ṭahmāsp. ʿAbbās instituted a policy of appointing *ghulāms* to provincial governorates, and to high administrative posts in the central government, in place of *Qizilbāsh* chiefs. Within a short time these measures had the effect of radically altering the social and ethnic structure of the administrative system.

The supremacy of the *Qizilbāsh* in the Safavid state, however, was being challenged before the end of the reign of Ṭahmāsp, and it was Ṭahmāsp himself who introduced the new Georgian and Circassian elements who were responsible for this challenge. Hitherto there had been a relatively uncomplicated rivalry for the key positions between the Turkish (Turcoman) elements and the Persian elements, with the shah playing off the one against the other and achieving a fairly satisfactory working relationship. Periodic outbursts of violence indicated the depth of the hostility between the two groups, and, as we have seen, when Ṭahmāsp came to the throne as a minor the balance of power was temporarily upset. Ultimately, Ṭahmāsp managed to restore the balance and to maintain the working relationship for about forty years, but trouble was always only just below the surface, and in 982/1574, when Ṭahmāsp fell sick, there was immediate dissension among the *Qizilbāsh.* The situation in 982/1574, however, was very different from that obtaining fifty years earlier, at the outbreak of the civil war between the *Qizilbāsh* tribes in 932/1526. In 982/1574 it was no longer a struggle to determine which tribe could outstrip its rivals in a state in which the *Qizilbāsh* tribes as a whole enjoyed a dominant and privileged position, but whether the *Qizilbāsh* tribes as a whole could maintain their privileged position against the threat from the new elements in Persian society, the Georgians and Circassians, whose remarkable energy and ability rapidly enabled them to exert an influence in the state out of all proportion to their numbers. This struggle was not decided before Ṭahmāsp's death, or even during the reigns of his successors Ismā'īl II and Sulṭān Muḥammad Shāh.

The majority of the Georgians had been taken captive in the course of the four campaigns fought by Safavid forces in Georgia between 947/1540–1 and 961/1553–4. From each of these expeditions Ṭahmāsp brought back captives, mainly women and children. In the campaign of 961/1553–4, the number of prisoners taken to Persia amounted to 30,000; among them were a number of Georgian nobles. By the end of Ṭahmāsp's reign, the offspring of unions with these Georgian prisoners must have constituted a new and not inconsiderable element in the Safavid state. The influx of Georgian elements was not limited to prisoners. During Ṭahmāsp's reign, a nobleman, closely related to the king of Georgia, who had been sent to the Safavid court as an ambassador, severed his connexion with his native land, and, together with all his retainers, entered Safavid service. He eventually became governor of a province in Shīrvān. In 994/1585–6 another Georgian nobleman was the *lālā*, or guardian, of one of the Safavid princes. The post of *lālā*, like the offices of *wakīl* and *amīr al-umarā'*, had always been considered a *Qizilbāsh* prerogative. These are isolated instances, but, taken in conjunction with the other evidence, they are sufficient to indicate that serious breaches had been made in the *Qizilbāsh* position long before the accession of 'Abbās.

The Georgian and Circassian women taken into the royal harem played a vital part in supporting the efforts of their compatriots to increase their influence in the Safavid state at the expense of the *Qizilbāsh*. These women became an important factor in political affairs. Dynastic quarrels and court intrigues, of a type not previously known in the Safavid state, flourished, as mothers of different nationalities pressed the claims of their respective offspring to the throne. The Safavid leaders Junayd and Ḥaydar had married wives of Ak-Koyunlu Turcoman stock. Ṭahmāsp's own mother was also a Turcoman. On the death of Ismā'īl, the issue of who was to succeed him was never in doubt; the point in dispute was which of the rival *Qizilbāsh* tribes should dominate the young Ṭahmāsp. In 982/1574–5 and subsequent years, the question was rather, which of Ṭahmāsp's sons would succeed him, one born of a Turcoman mother, or one born of a Georgian or a Circassian mother. The *Qizilbāsh* did not at once perceive the true nature of the threat to their position. To begin with, instead of presenting a united front against the Caucasian faction, various groups of *Qizilbāsh* weakened the whole *Qizilbāsh* position by supporting candidates of the Caucasians. In 982/1574–5, for instance, certain *Qizilbāsh* chiefs intrigued in favour of Ṭahmāsp's son Sulaymān, whose mother was the sister of a Circassian chief. By the following year (983/1575–6), the *Qizilbāsh* had split into two opposing factions, one supporting Ṭahmāsp's son Ismā'īl, whose mother was a Turcoman, the other supporting Ṭahmāsp's son Ḥaydar, whose mother was a Georgian slave. Of the nine sons of Ṭahmāsp who reached adolescence, seven were the offspring of Circassian or Georgian mothers. Only two were born of a Turcoman mother: Ismā'īl, who had been imprisoned for twenty years, and whose mind was known to be deranged by his long confinement; and Muḥammad Khudābanda, the eldest son and therefore the rightful heir to the throne, who was at first considered unfit to rule because of his poor eyesight. After the death of Ṭahmāsp on 15 Ṣafar 984/14 May 1576, the Georgian faction, supported by the Ustājlū tribe, made an unsuccessful attempt to place Ḥaydar on the throne. They were defeated by the other *Qizilbāsh* tribes, supported by the Circassian faction and a group of Kurdish troops. Ḥaydar was killed. Next, the Rūmlū tribe and the Circassians attempted to enthrone a prince born of a Circassian slave, but this attempt, too, was frustrated. At this point the *Qizilbāsh,* perhaps impressed by the prowess of the troops led by two Georgians, who were both maternal uncles of Safavid princes, and by a Circassian chief, who was the maternal uncle of Ṭahmāsp's daughter, at last realized that their own best interest lay in unity. 30,000 *Qizilbāsh* assembled and pledged their support to Ismā'īl, who was enthroned at Qazvīn as Ismā'īl II on 27 Jumādā I 984/22 August 1576, at the age of forty.

Ismā'īl II at once confirmed the worst fears of those who realized that his mind had been warped by his experiences. Unexpectedly released from prison and placed on the throne, his sole aim was to prevent himself from being ejected from his new position of power. To this end he began systematically to murder or blind all male members of the Safavid royal house who might conceivably become the centre of a conspiracy against him. Five sons of Ṭahmāsp were put to death, together with four other Safavid princes. Ismā'īl also had put to death large numbers of *Qizilbāsh* officers, not only members of the Ustājlū tribe which had supported his brother Ḥaydar, but also many others whose only fault was that they had held important positions under his father. 'The royal tents,' he said, 'cannot be held up by old ropes.' The *Qizilbāsh* realized that the ruler to whom they had given their support, far from preserving their own privileged position in the state, was in fact undermining it by the execution of so many of their number. The *Qizilbāsh,* who naturally were staunch supporters of the Twelver form of Shi'ism which was the official religion of the Safavid state, also strongly resented Ismā'īl's apparent dislike of Shi'ism. The shah made no open profession of Sunnism, but some of the more fanatical Shī'ī theologians found themselves excluded from court circles, and their books confiscated. The ritual cursing of the Caliphs Abū Bakr, 'Umar and 'Uthmān in the mosques was banned. The *Qizilbāsh* therefore planned to assassinate the shah. Their task was made easier by Ismā'īl's addiction to narcotics. With the connivance of the shah's sister, Parī Khān Khānum, poison was inserted in a mixture of opium and Indian hemp which Ismā'īl and one of his intimate companions consumed. Ismā'īl II was found dead on 13 Ramaḍān 985/24 November 1577.

The *Qizilbāsh* had no alternative but to place on the throne the prince whom they had passed over at the death of Ṭahmāsp on the grounds that his poor eyesight disqualified him from kingship, namely, Muḥammad Khudābanda. All the other sons of Ṭahmāsp had been murdered or blinded by Ismā'īl II, and only an accident had saved Muḥammad Khudābanda and his three sons, Ḥamza, Abū Ṭālib and 'Abbās. 'Abbās owed his life to the governor of Herat, 'Alī Qulī Khān Shāmlū, who had deliberately delayed putting the order into effect. Muḥammad Khudābanda reached Qazvīn on 5 Dhu'l-Ḥijja 985/13 February 1578, nearly three months after the death of Ismā'īl II, and was proclaimed ruler with the style Sulṭān Muḥammad Shāh. He was forty-seven years of age.

Apart from his physical disability, Sulṭān Muḥammad Shāh was 'a man of quiet nature', who did not care much about worldy affairs. For eighteen months, the administration of the state was in the hands of his wife, Mahd-i 'Ulyā, who is described as a jealous, ambitious, quick-tempered, obstinate and vindictive woman. Mahd-i 'Ulyā was the daughter of a former local ruler in Māzandarān, belonging to a dynasty which boasted of its descent from the fourth Shī'ī *Imām,* Zayn al-'Ābidīn. She was hostile to the interests of the *Qizilbāsh,* and promoted the interests of the Persian elements in the administration. The *wazīr,* Mīrzā Salmān, who had been appointed by Ismā'īl II, was confirmed in office by Sulṭān Muḥammad Shāh, and became Mahd-i 'Ulyā's right-hand man. All her actions were directed towards two ends: first, to secure the eventual succession of her favourite son, Ḥamza Mīrzā; second, to revenge herself on Mīr Sulṭān Murād, who had murdered her father and had usurped her family's territory in Māzandarān. To attain her first object, she put to death various persons whom she regarded as obstacles in her path. These included Parī Khān Khānum and her uncle (a Circassian chief), and Ismā'īl's infant son. To prevent 'Abbās, her stepson, from constituting a threat to her plans for Ḥamza, Mahd-i 'Ulyā sent courier after courier to Herat demanding that he be sent to Qazvīn, but the governor, 'Alī Qulī Khān, refused to comply with her orders. To attain her second object, she sent three successive expeditions against Mīrzā Khān, who had succeeded his father, Mīr Sulṭān Murād, as ruler of Māzandarān. Mīrzā Khān resisted all efforts to capture him, and finally gave himself up only on the solemn promise of safe conduct. While on his way to the capital, Qazvīn, with an escort of *Qizilbāsh* chiefs, he was murdered by minions sent by Mahd-i 'Ulyā who, in her determination to be avenged, refused to take cognizance of the promise of safeconduct. The indignation of the *Qizilbāsh* at this action was one of the factors which led them to request the shah to remove Mahd-i 'Ulyā from her position of influence.

The Ottoman Sultan Murād III chose this moment (986/1578) to break the long peace with Persia, and to launch a major invasion under Muṣṭafā Pasha. The Crimean Tatars made common cause with the Ottomans. The Safavids suffered defeat after defeat. A large part of Georgia submitted to the Ottomans. The north-west frontier was stabilized by the prince, Ḥamza Mīrzā, and the *wazīr* Mīrzā Salmān, who captured 'Ādil Giray, the brother of the khan of the Crimea, in Shīrvān, and led him in triumph to Qazvīn. The *Qizilbāsh* found in 'Ādil Giray the pretext for the assassination of Mahd-i 'Ulyā. Accusing her of a criminal liaison with the prisoner, a group of *Qizilbāsh* burst into the harem on Jumādā I 987/26 July 1579 and murdered her. 'Ādil Giray was also killed. The six principal conspirators represented all but one of the leading tribes, and in this way the *Qizilbāsh* hoped to prevent retribution falling on any one tribe.

The death of Mahd-i 'Ulyā did not mean an increase in the authority of the shah, for the *Qizilbāsh* took over control of the state. At Qazvīn, the Turkmān and Takkalū tribes held a dominant position. In Khurāsān, an Ustājlū-Shāmlū coalition led by 'Alī Qulī Khān Shāmlū, the governor of Herat, and Murshid Qulī Khān Ustājlū, the governor of Khwāf and

Bākharz, raised the standard of revolt, and swore allegiance to ʿAbbās, the ten-year old son of Sulṭān Muḥammad Shāh (Rabīʿ I 989/April–May 1581). The rebels made several attempts to extend the area of Khurāsān under their control, and in particular tried unsuccessfully first to persuade by peaceful means and then to overthrow by force their chief opponent in Khurāsān, the Turkmān chief Murtaḍā Qulī Khān Purnāk, the governor of Mashhad.

In Shawwāl 990/November 1582 the royal army appeared in Khurāsān. The Ustājlū leader, Murshid Qulī Khān, declared his allegiance to Ḥamza Mīrzā, and received the royal pardon. The Shāmlū leader was now isolated, and the royal army drove him back to Herat, and laid siege to that city (Rabīʿ II 991/May 1583). The *Qizilbāsh* besieging forces showed no enthusiasm for their task. It is alleged that their chiefs were opposed to the whole idea of the Khurāsān expedition, because they considered that the Ottoman threat was the more urgent. This was only an excuse. In reality this represents a recrudescence of Turcoman-Persian antipathy in its most violent form. More than anything else, the *Qizilbāsh* resented being placed under the command of a Persian, the *wazīr* Mīrzā Salmān. It was over seventy years since a Persian, or, to use the pejorative term favoured by the *Qizilbāsh,* a Tājīk, had held such high military command. The fundamental dichotomy in the Safavid state between Turk and Persian was nevertheless as sharp as ever. Mīrzā Salmān determined to enforce the shah's authority by executing certain *Qizilbāsh* chiefs. Before he could carry out his plan, he was himself seized by a group of Afshār chiefs and put to death. There is a close parallel between this incident and that of 918/1512, when the *Qizilbāsh* defied the authority of the Persian *wakīl.* In the circumstances, all the shāh could do was to conclude a truce with ʿAlī Qulī on the basis of the *status quo ante*. On 15 Shaʿbān 991/3 September 1583, the Shāmlū leader reaffirmed his allegiance to the shāh and to Ḥamza Mīrzā, and in return secured the dismissal of the hostile governor of Mashhad.

After the assassination of the powerful *wazīr* Mīrzā Salmān, the prince Ḥamza Mīrzā, then about nineteen years of age, played an increasing part in state affairs. Though a man of outstanding physical bravery, he was arrogant, impulsive, and hot-tempered. He lacked the maturity of judgment and diplomatic skill which the critical situation required. Moreover, he was a heavy drinker, and, by choosing a number of the younger *Qizilbāsh* officers as his drinking companions, he became embroiled in *Qizilbāsh* faction at Qazvīn. He listened to those who wished to weaken the position of the Turkmān tribe, and he first dismissed from the governorship of Āẕarbāyjān, and then put to death, the Turkmān leader, Amīr Khān. Preoccupied with these internal troubles, Ḥamza was unable to prevent the occupation of Tabrīz by Ottoman forces under ʿOs̱mān Pasha on 27 Ramaḍān 993/22 September 1585. Shortly afterwards, the Turkmāns and their allies, the Takkalūs, seized control of Qazvīn and swore allegiance to Ḥamza's brother, Ṭahmāsp. Ḥamza succeeded in dispersing the rebels and recovering his brother. The following year, while campaigning against the Ottomans in the Qarābāgh region, Ḥamza was assassinated in mysterious circumstances (24 Dhu'l-Ḥijja 994/6 December 1586).

In a dramatic turn of events, Murshid Qulī Khān Ustājlū, who had already demonstrated his ability to trim his sails to the prevailing wind, seized control of Mashhad, and, in the ensuing clash with ʿAlī Qulī Khān Shāmlū (12 Rajab 993/10 July 1585), gained possession of the latter's trump card, namely, the young prince ʿAbbās, then about fourteen years of age. The Ustājlū chief pressed his advantage. He sent an envoy to Qazvīn to sound the *Qizilbāsh* chiefs at the capital, where there had been an abortive attempt to place yet another of the shah's sons, Abū Ṭālib, on the throne. The chiefs promised support, but hesitated to commit themselves irrevocably. In Muḥarram 996/ December 1587 a huge force of Özbegs under ʿAbd Allāh Khān poured across the frontier into Khurāsān and laid siege to Herat. This invasion decided Murshid Qulī Khān to risk a march on Qazvīn. If he remained in Khurāsān, he might well be overwhelmed by the Özbegs. When he reached Qazvīn, a public demonstration in favour of ʿAbbās decided the wavering *Qizilbāsh* chiefs. On 10 Dhu'l-Qaʿda 996/1 October 1588, Sulṭān Muḥammad Shāh, a pathetic figure in the grip of forces beyond his control, handed over the insignia of kingship to his son, who was crowned Shāh ʿAbbās I. The latter was seventeen years old. Murshid Qulī Khān, who had placed him on the throne, was the most powerful man in the kingdom, and received the title of *wakīl* of the supreme *dīwān*.

Thus ended the second and final period of *Qizilbāsh* domination of the Safavid state. The first period had lasted from 930/1524 to 940/1533, when Shāh Ṭahmāsp was too young to impose any effective control. The second period, also roughly a decade in duration, lasted from the assassination of Mahd-i ʿUlyā to the abdication of Sulṭān Muḥammad Shāh in favour of ʿAbbās (987–96/1579–88). Sulṭān Muḥammad Shāh, suffering from the eye affliction which eventually made him nearly blind,

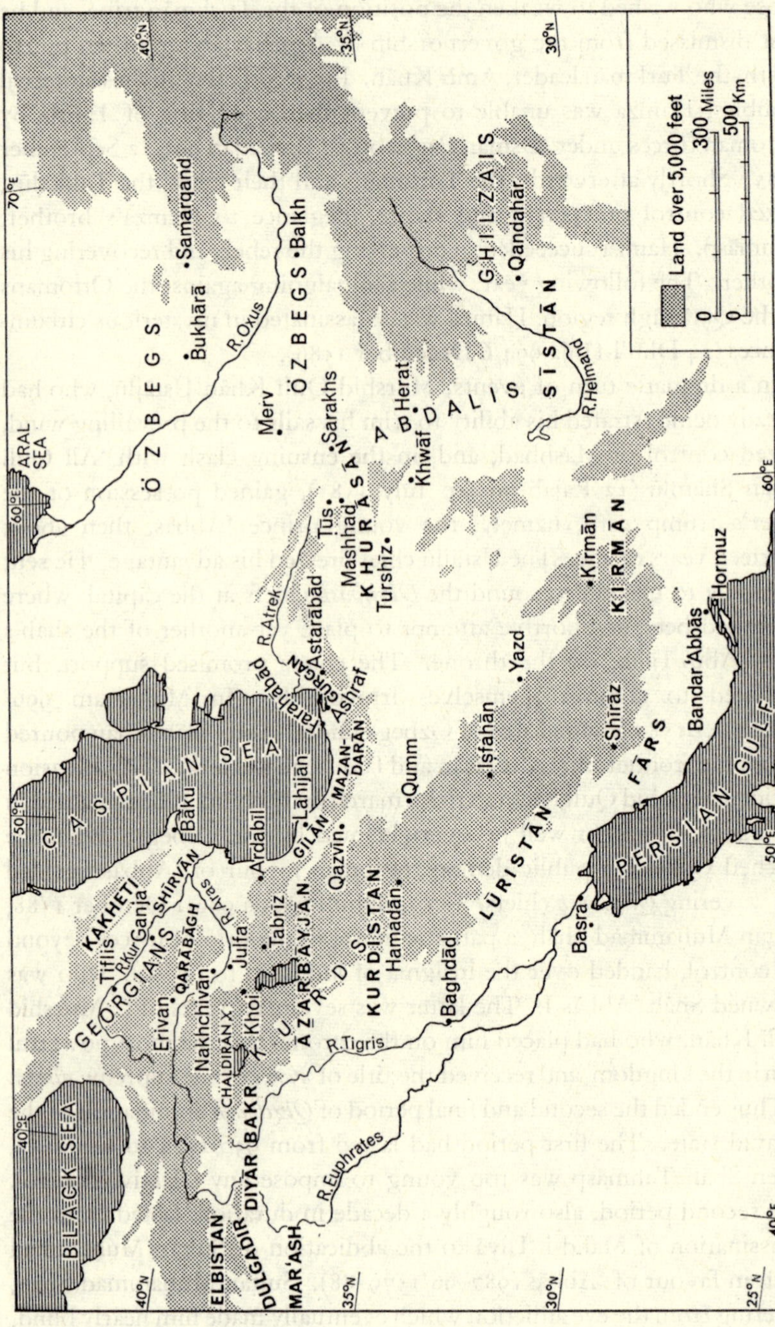

Map 8. Safavid Persia.

and temperamentally unsuited to rule, was unable, even with the aid of his son Ḥamza, to keep the *Qizilbāsh* under control. The result in each case was the same. The Safavid state, torn by *Qizilbāsh* faction, was at the mercy of its traditional enemies, the Ottomans and the Özbegs. The citadel at Tabrīz had been in the hands of an Ottoman garrison since 993/1585, despite efforts to dislodge it. At Herat, ʿAlī Qulī Khān Shāmlū, after a heroic defence lasting nine months, was treacherously put to death when the Özbegs finally stormed the city in Rabīʿ I 997/February 1589. His old rival, Murshid Qulī Khān Ustājlū, had deliberately delayed the departure of a relief force from Qazvīn. The Özbegs advanced to lay siege to Mashhad and Sarakhs. ʿAbbās realized the impossibility of fighting on two fronts with the forces at his disposal, and in order to free his hands in the east he signed in 998/1589–90 a peace treaty which ceded large areas of Persian territory to the Ottomans. The regions of Āẕarbāyjān, Qarābāgh, Ganja, Qarājadāgh, together with Georgia and parts of Luristān and Kurdistān, were to remain in Ottoman hands. Never before had the Ottomans made such inroads into Safavid territory. The acceptance of such a humiliating peace is an indication of the weakness of ʿAbbās's position at his accession.

ʿAbbās realized that he must lose no time in bringing the *Qizilbāsh* to heel. Any punitive measures, however, would limit his ability to take the field against Persia's external foes, because the *Qizilbāsh* troops were still the backbone of the Safavid army. He therefore at once formed the cavalry corps of *ghulāms* already referred to, drawn from the ranks of Georgian, Armenian and Circassian prisoners, or their descendants. Many of these prisoners had been brought to Persia during the reign of Shāh Ṭahmāsp. They were converts to Islam. This new corps, which was eventually brought up to a strength of 10,000 men by new recruitment, was paid direct from the royal treasury. The *ghulāms* thus owed their allegiance first and foremost to the person of the shah, and not to any tribal leader. The decision to pay this corps from the royal treasury immediately raised the problem of how the shah was to acquire the necessary funds. Hitherto, most of the Safavid empire had been held by the *Qizilbāsh* chiefs, who as provincial governors consumed the greater part of the revenue of their provinces. In return, they were obliged to maintain a stated number of troops at the disposal of the ruler, and to be ready to take the field in answer to his call. If these provincial governors also held a post in the central administration, as was frequently the case, they would remain at court and sub-assign the government of their province. These *Qizilbāsh* governors remitted to the central government only a small proportion of the taxes which they levied, and even then, these monies were not under the direct control of the ruler, but were administered by a special ministry of state lands (*dīwān-i mamālik*). The revenue needed by the shah for the expenses of the royal household was derived from crown lands, known as *khāṣṣa,* the revenue from which was levied by the shah's comptrollers or intendants, and remitted to the royal treasury. Since 'Abbās I increased the number of troops paid directly by himself, he must have also increased the extent of the crown lands at the expense of the state lands. This process was accelerated under his successors, and ultimately crown lands were extended to a degree which was detrimental to the health of the state. For whereas it was in the interests of a provincial governor to maintain his province in a flourishing condition and thereby to increase the amount of revenue which he enjoyed, the comptrollers who collected the revenue in the *khāṣṣa* provinces were interested only in remitting the maximum amount of money to the royal treasury in order to satisfy the shah. This necessarily led to extortion and abuses of all kinds. The people were oppressed by officials who had no interest in the prosperity of the area from which they were collecting taxes.

'Abbās was quickly put to the test. His *wakīl,* Murshid Qulī Khān Ustājlū, was forewarned of a plot against his life in which members of nearly all the *Qizilbāsh* tribes were involved. The *wakīl* fled to the court, pursued by the conspirators, who urged 'Abbās to dismiss him and set up a council of *amīrs,* similar to that which existed during the reign of Sulṭān Muḥammad Shah, to govern the state. Had 'Abbās shown any sign of weakness, he would have condemned himself to a subordinate role of the sort endured by his father. But he reacted with characteristic determination. He executed the ringleaders of the conspiracy, and, invoking the aid of 'all who loved the shah' among the *Qizilbāsh,* he hunted down and put to death all those he suspected of complicity in the plot. A few escaped to Baghdād and took refuge with the Ottomans. The *Qizilbāsh* were given no time to recover. On 10 Ramaḍān 997/23 July 1589 'Abbās arranged the assassination of the too-powerful *wakīl,* Murshid Qulī Khān, and executed the leader of the Turkmān tribe who had proclaimed his brother Ṭahmāsp shah at Qazvīn in 993/1585. These summary displays of royal authority caused some detachments of *Qizilbāsh* to desert in fear of their lives. In 999/1590, 'Abbās's sense of insecurity led him to blind his unfortunate father and brothers, all of whom had been kept under close guard since his accession.

Despite all his efforts, 'Abbās was unable to restore order and build up his forces quickly enough to prevent the further deterioration of the position in eastern Persia. Mashhad in Khurāsān had fallen to the Özbegs, and the province of Sīstān had been overrun. Qandahār, which had been in Safavid hands since 943/1537, was lost to the Mughal empire in 999/1590–1. By 1000/1592 the eastern frontier of Persia was roughly where it had been a hundred years previously, at the accession of Ismā'īl I. 'Abbās took an army to Khurāsān, but achieved nothing permanent because he still hesitated to commit his forces to a pitched battle. He continued to take disciplinary measures against the *Qizilbāsh* chiefs. Those who had been slow in joining the royal camp, or who had not sent their proper quota of troops, were dismissed from their governorships, which they could only regain on payment of a heavy fine. 'Abbās could never rid himself of his distrust of the *Qizilbāsh* which had been engendered by the events of his boyhood. A *Qizilbāsh* chief, even if he had served the shah loyally, was liable to be executed without warning if the shah considered he had become too powerful. In 1007/1598, for instance, 'Abbās executed Farhād Khān Qaramānlū, who, after years of hard and skilful fighting, had pacified the provinces of Gīlān and Māzandarān, which were annexed to the Safavid empire in 1006/1597.

The death of the formidable Özbeg leader 'Abd Allāh II in 1006/early 1598, and of his son the following year, gave 'Abbās his chance in the east. The Özbegs were engaged in dynastic struggles and the control of Transoxania ultimately passed to the Astrakhān khanate. The transfer of the capital from Qazvīn to Iṣfahān in 1006/1597–8 indicates 'Abbās's confidence that the eastern frontier would ultimately be made secure. In Muḥarram 1007/August 1598 'Abbās completely defeated the Özbeg army and liberated Herat. By a series of alliances with the local Özbeg chiefs who held the frontier areas such as Merv and Balkh, 'Abbās sought to achieve a lasting pacification of the eastern frontier. Although these chiefs occasionally departed from their allegiance, 'Abbās's measures were sufficiently successful to enable him to suspend operations in the east in 1011/1602–3, and to turn his attention to the arch-enemy in the west, the Ottomans. In 1014/1605–6 'Abbās inflicted a decisive defeat on the Ottomans near Tabrīz, and reoccupied Nakhchivān and Erivan, Ganja and Tiflis. The Ottomans evacuated all forts south of the Aras river. By Rabīʿ II 1016/July 1607 the last Ottoman soldier had been cleared from Persian territory as recognized by the peace of Amasya in 962/1555. Further desultory fighting on the north-west frontier was temporarily terminated by the peace of Sarāb in 1027/1618.

For the first ten years of his reign, until he defeated the Özbegs in 1007/1598–9, ʿAbbās was essentially conducting a holding operation on all fronts. By 1003/1595, however, the policy which ʿAbbās had introduced on his accession, of training *ghulāms* to counterbalance the influence of the *Qizilbāsh*, had begun to bear fruit, and ʿAbbās was able to appoint to the governorship of the important province of Fārs a Georgian named Allāhvardī Khān, who held the office of *qullar-āqāsī*, or commander of the *ghulāms*. Allāhvardī Khān had already proved his devotion to the shāh by being a party to the assassination of the *wakīl* Murshid Qulī Khān in 996/1589. For his services on that occasion, he was rewarded with the title of *sulṭān* and a small governorate near Iṣfahān. By his new appointment, he became the first *ghulām* to attain equality of rank with the *Qizilbāsh* chiefs, and to have an equal voice with them in council. Implicit obedience to the shah, rather than membership of one of the *Qizilbāsh* tribes, was henceforth to be the criterion for royal favour. The number of *ghulāms* appointed to such posts steadily increased, until they filled some twenty per cent of the high administrative posts. Allāhvardī Khān became the commander-in-chief of the Persian armed forces in 1007/1598, entrusted with the reorganization of the army along the lines suggested by Sir Robert Sherley, who had just arrived at the shah's court with his brother, Anthony, and a group of some twenty-five soldiers of fortune. As already mentioned, the Sherleys' claim to have introduced the Persians to artillery and hand-guns is entirely without foundation, but the advice of the Sherleys and their companions, particularly in the problems of training the new units and of casting cannon, was much appreciated by the shah, who appointed Sir Robert 'Master General against the Turks'. In addition to the corps of *ghulāms*, now increased in strength to 10,000, three new regiments were formed: a personal body-guard for the shah, numbering 3,000, also composed of *ghulāms*; a regiment of musketeers, 12,000 strong, recruited mainly from the Persian peasantry; and a regiment of artillery, with 12,000 men and 500 guns. ʿAbbās thus had a standing army of about 37,000 men paid directly from the royal treasury, and owing allegiance only to him. The aversion of the Persians to the use of firearms, referred to earlier, was still strong. They particularly disliked artillery, because it hampered the free movement of their cavalry. In 1011/1602, in an action against the Özbegs near Balkh, the Safavids abandoned 300 of their new guns without having brought them into action. In general, the Safavids made good use of artillery in siege warfare, but never made any effective use of it in the field. 'Abbās II (1052–77/1642–66) even went so far as to abolish the corps of artillery, and it was not reformed until the reign of Shāh Sulṭān Ḥusayn (1105–35/1694–1722).

The revolution in the social structure of the Safavid state effected by 'Abbās I was naturally reflected in the principal offices of state. The title *wakīl,* representing the outmoded concept of the vicegerent of a theocratic ruler, fell into disuse. The use of this title by Murshid Qulī Khān Ustājlū during the early years of 'Abbās's reign was an attempt to revert to the original concept of the *wakīl.* When 'Abbās demonstrated that he did not intend to be subordinate to the *Qizilbāsh* chiefs, it was logical that he should allow this title to lapse. The principal spokesman of the *Qizilbāsh* in the highest counsels of state was now the *qūrchībāshī,* the commander of the *qūrchīs,* the name by which the old *Qizilbāsh* tribal cavalry was henceforth most frequently known. The title *amīr al-umarā',* by which the commander-in-chief of the *Qizilbāsh* troops was formerly known, occurs only rarely. The head of the bureaucracy, the spokesman for the Persian elements, and in fact the most powerful official in the state, continued to be known as *wazīr,* or by one of two new and more grandiose titles, *i'timād al-dawla* or *ṣadr-i a'ẓam*—the latter being identical with the title of the Ottoman grand *vezīr.* It should not be confused with the *ṣadr,* whose decline and eventual eclipse reflects the growing secularization of the Safavid state from the time of 'Abbās I onwards. The commanders of two of the new regiments, the *qullar-āqāsī* and the *tufangchī-āqāsī,* respectively in command of the *ghulāms* and the musketeers, ranked among the five principal officers of state, and the new Georgian, Armenian and Circassian elements in the state were thus represented at the highest level. The remaining official, the *ishīk-āqāsī-bāshī,* or major-domo, was usually a *Qizilbāsh* chief. 'Abbās made quite certain that he would have an adequate reservoir of Caucasians from whom *ghulāms* could be recruited in whatever numbers were needed to offset the influence of the *Qizilbāsh.* In 1013/1604, 20,000 Armenians were enrolled in the *ghulāms*; in 1025/1616, 130,000 Georgians were taken prisoner. Under the guise of military necessity, 'Abbās transferred large bodies of people from one area to another: in 1023/1614, 15,000

Georgian families were moved from Kakheti to Māzandarān; and 3,000 Armenian families were taken from Julfā in Āẕarbāyjān and settled in a suburb of Iṣfahān. Further, 'Abbās tried to weaken the tribal bonds which were the source of *Qizilbāsh* strength, by transferring groups from one tribe to a district belonging to another.

During the reign of 'Abbās I, there was an increase of diplomatic and commercial activity in Persia. The Dutch, the Portuguese and the English fought fiercely for commercial supremacy in the Persian Gulf. In 1031/1622 'Abbās was able to turn this rivalry to his advantage when he invoked the aid of the English to expel the Portuguese from the island of Hormuz. Spain, Portugal and England sent ambassadors to the Persian court. The French sent an ambassador, who was arrested by the Ottomans at Istanbul and forced to return to France. The envoy of Philip III of Spain made three visits to Iṣfahān between 1017/1608 and 1029/1618. The first accredited ambassador from England arrived at the Persian capital in Sha'bān–Ramaḍān 1036/May 1627, but his mission was a failure. Christian religious orders, such as the Carmelite, Augustinian, and Capuchin friars, were given permission to found convents at Iṣfahān and, after its recapture from the Ottomans in 1033/1623, at Baghdād.

To sum up, 'Abbās's reign was one of solid achievement. Coming to the throne at a critical time, he established the Safavid state on a new basis by a series of far-reaching measures. Although these measures contained within them the seeds of future decay, the measure of the achievement of 'Abbās is that the Safavid empire continued to go forward for another century under the momentum which he imparted to it, despite the fact that for the greater part of this period it was in the hands of inept rulers. 'Abbās made his capital, Iṣfahān, one of the beautiful cities of the world. Although Safavid architecture is in general not noted for its originality, 'Abbās I, in the Masjid-i Shāh (begun in 1020/1611) and the Masjid-i Shaykh Luṭf Allāh (begun in 1012/1603), was responsible for two of the undoubted masterpieces of Persian architecture. The energy which 'Abbās expended on public works is demonstrated by the fact that at his death there were in Iṣfahān alone 162 mosques, 48 colleges, 1,802 caravanserais, and 273 baths. Outside Iṣfahān, 'Abbās's principal architectural work was the reconstruction of the shrine of the *Imām* 'Alī al-Riḍā at Mashhad. He made generous benefactions to this shrine and to that of the Safavid family at Ardabīl. Unlike the Sasanids and the Achaemenids, the Safavid monarchs did not seek to impress posterity by the construction of grandiose palaces. Shāh 'Abbās's residences at Iṣfahān were on a modest scale. 'Abbās himself much preferred his country retreats on the shores of the Caspian, Ashraf and Faraḥābād, which he built about 1021/1612–13, and where during the latter part of his reign he regularly spent the winter. Faraḥābād in particular became virtually a second capital. To give access to these winter residences 'Abbās constructed his famous causeway along the marshy Caspian littoral. For this purpose he had blocks of stone and marble brought from Baku. Faraḥābād was sacked by the Cossacks in 1078/1668; Ashraf was devastated successively by Turcomans, Afghans and Zands, and the main palace was destroyed by fire in the time of Nādir Shāh.

During the Safavid period as a whole there was a remarkable flowering of the arts, and the reign of 'Abbās marks its high point. Although Safavid metalwork cannot equal the production of the Seljuk and early Mongol period, in book painting and the illumination of manuscripts, in ceramics, in textiles, and in carpets and rugs, the Persian genius found its highest expression during the Safavid period. The sumptuous apparel and elaborate pavilions with rich hangings excited the admiration of travellers who visited the Persian court, and a taste for Persian luxury articles arose in Renaissance Europe and in Russia. The skilful use of complicated weaves, the combination of brilliant colours in varigated designs, and an apparently unfailing inventiveness in the use of arabesque and floral ornament, enabled the Persians to produce textiles of a unique richness and variety. The extension of royal patronage to the weavers raised carpet-weaving from the level of a cottage industry to the status of a fine art, and the renaissance of Persian pottery culminated in the reign of 'Abbās I. Only, perhaps, in painting must pride of place be given to the productions of the reign of Ṭahmāsp. In 928/1522 Shāh Ismā'īl brought the famous Timurid painter Bihzād from Herāt to Tabrīz, and made him director of the royal library. His successors who worked for Shāh Ṭahmāsp at Tabrīz formed a brilliant school, and some of the finest Persian manuscript illustrations date from this period.

Shāh 'Abbās the Great does not suffer by comparison with the other great rulers of the age—Elizabeth I, Charles V, Süleymān the Magnificent and the Mughal Emperor Akbar. In personal courage he recalls his great-grandfather Ismā'īl I. What he achieved, he achieved by unremitting labour in the interests of the state. Not only did he personally direct and supervise the administration of the Safavid empire, but he kept in close touch with the common people by frequenting the markets and the tea-houses, concerned to learn of and root out corruption and oppression wherever it might be found. His zeal for justice was one of his great qualities. It is the more tragic, therefore, that his youth, spent in an atmosphere of treachery and insecurity, should have made him ruthless when there was a real or fancied threat to his own person or position. His harsh treatment of *Qizilbāsh* chiefs has already been mentioned. Historians have found it difficult to excuse his treatment of his own sons. ʿAbbās seems to have been haunted by the memory of the way in which he had overthrown his own father, and constantly to have feared that one of his own sons would treat him in the same way. This fear caused him to lend too ready an ear to informers. The extraordinary lengths to which he went to segregate his sons from political and military leaders are well attested. To begin with, ʿAbbās followed the traditional Safavid administrative pattern by appointing his sons to provincial governorates, and sending them to these in the charge of *Qizilbāsh* chiefs. Thus, his eldest son Muḥammad Bāqir, also known as Ṣafī, was made governor of Khurāsān when ʿAbbās marched westward to seize the throne from his father, and a year or so later his second son, Ḥasan, was appointed governor of Mashhad. But the revolt of the *Qizilbāsh* chief who was Ḥasan's guardian seems to have marked the turning-point in ʿAbbās's relationship with his sons. Henceforth their only companions were the court eunuchs and their tutors. It became a capital crime to display undue friendship towards the princes. They left the capital only to accompany the shah on his campaigns; ʿAbbās feared that, if they remained in the capital during his absence, they might become the centre of a plot against him. In fairness to ʿAbbās, it must be admitted that these fears were not without foundation. The *Qizilbāsh* revolt in favour of Ḥasan was followed in 1023/1614–5 by an alleged conspiracy to kill the shāh involving Muḥammad Bāqir and certain Circassian elements at court. Whatever the truth was on this occasion, the execution of those Circassians on whom suspicion had fallen led the Circassian chiefs to come out openly in support of Muḥammad Bāqir, and ʿAbbās, now thoroughly alarmed, had his son assassinated in Muḥarram 1024/February 1615. It is fairly certain that Muḥammad Bāqir was the innocent victim of Circassian intrigue, and ʿAbbās was filled with remorse at his action. Unhappily these events increased ʿAbbās's fears, and created in him a morbid fear of assassination. In 1030/1621 ʿAbbās fell ill. His third son, Muḥammad, also known as Khudābanda after his grandfather, prematurely celebrated his death, and openly solicited support among the *Qizilbāsh*. On his recovery, 'Abbās ordered him to be blinded. As his second son, Ḥasan, and his fourth son, Ismā'īl, had already died from natural causes, 'Abbās had only one son eligible to succeed him, his fifth son, Imām Qulī Mīrzā, and he, too, was blinded in 1036/1626–7. Two years later, on 24 Jumādā I 1038/19 January 1629, Shāh 'Abbās died, at the age of fifty-eight, having reigned for over forty years.

As Shāh 'Abbās had no son able to succeed him, his grandson Sām Mīrzā, was proclaimed ruler under the title of Shāh Ṣafī on 23 Jumādā II, 1038/17 February 1629. Ṣafī's reign marks the beginning of Safavid decline. It has already been pointed out that the formation by 'Abbās I of a standing army of *ghulāms* necessarily meant the expansion of crown lands at the expense of the 'state' provinces ruled by *Qizilbāsh* governors, in order to provide the royal treasury with sufficient funds to pay these new regiments. Ṣafī's *wazīr*, Sārū Taqī, represented to him that, as the Safavid state was now relatively secure from its external enemies, to allow the greater part of Safavid territory to remain under *Qizilbāsh* government, contributing virtually nothing to the treasury, was unnecessarily to deprive the central government of revenue. The shah agreed, and the rich province of Fārs which, by reason of its distance from the frontiers of Persia, was not immediately threatened by foreign invasion, was brought under the direct control of the shah, and was administered on his behalf by an overseer. Every increase in the extent of crown lands at the expense of 'state' lands meant a corresponding decrease in the strength of the *Qizilbāsh* forces.

This policy was carried to such lengths by Shāh 'Abbās II (1052–77/1642–66) that the provinces of Qazvīn, Gīlān, Māzandarān, Yazd, Kirmān, Khurāsān and Āẕarbāyjān were all brought under the direct administration of the crown except in time of war, when governors were reappointed. The evil effects of this policy have already been stressed. Sound, if somewhat wasteful, administration was replaced by oppressive government which impaired the prosperity of the provinces. The country was weakened militarily, partly because the reduction in *Qizilbāsh* strength was not made good by a corresponding increase in the size of the *ghulām* forces, and partly because in practice the *ghulāms* did not possess the fighting qualities of the old *Qizilbāsh* troops. In most respects, however, Shāh 'Abbās II stood head and shoulders above all the later Safavid monarchs. He was a strong, capable, and energetic ruler, and during his lifetime the various conflicting forces in the Safavid state were kept in check. In 1057/1648 he recovered Qandahār from the Mughals, who had seized the city from Shāh Ṣafī some ten years earlier. In his passion for justice, and his unremitting concern for the welfare of the common people, he most resembled his great-grandfather, 'Abbās the Great. After his death, the process of decline not only resumed, but accelerated.

The second important factor contributing to Safavid decline was the degeneration of the dynasty through the confinement of the royal princes in the harem. In the time of Ismā'īl I and Ṭahmāsp I, it was the custom for the heir-apparent to be appointed to the government of the important province of Khurāsān. He was placed in the care of a *lālā* or guardian, a high-ranking *Qizilbāsh* chief, who carried on the actual business of government, and was also responsible for the training and welfare of his charge. The young prince thus received from an early age an education and training which fitted him to succeed to the throne in due course. His brothers were usually appointed to other important governorates, similarly in the charge of *lālās*. Of course this system had its dangers. The *lālās* might encourage their wards to rebel against the shah. But this danger was infinitely to be preferred to the dangers of keeping the princes in the harem, subject to the debilitating influence of harem life, and a prey to the intrigues and rivalries of the women of the harem and the court eunuchs. In place of a possible, but by no means inevitable, provincial revolt in favour of one of the princes during the lifetime of the shah, there was the virtual certainty of a struggle over the succession as the mothers of rival princes, and the court eunuchs, strove to place their own candidate on the throne. By the time of Shāh Sulaymān (1077–1105/1666–94), the eunuchs had usurped the authority of the shah. Sulaymān was an alcoholic. The contemporary observer, Sir John Chardin, comments on the shah's astonishing ability to hold his liquor; no Swiss or German, he asserts, could compete with him. The shah was also a recluse. He is said to have remained in the harem for seven years without once emerging. His successor, Shāh Sulṭān Ḥusayn, was of a pious and kindly disposition, and was nicknamed 'Mullā Ḥusayn'. A probably apocryphal, but nevertheless significant, story alleges that Shāh Sulaymān did not nominate an heir, but said in effect to his officers of state, if they wanted peace and quiet, they should choose his son Ḥusayn, but if they wanted a powerful ruler and expanding empire, they should elect his son 'Abbās. The court eunuchs elected Ḥusayn because they hoped to establish their ascendancy over such a mild and pliant monarch. Their hopes were fulfilled. Shāh Sulṭān Ḥusayn (1105–35/1694–1722) soon abandoned his austere way of life, and, like his father, took to drink and debauchery. He became so uxorious that the size and magnificence of his harem was a serious drain on the exchequer. Like his father Sulaymān, he had no interest in state affairs, and the court and the harem had little difficulty in bending the shah to their will. The religious classes, led by the *mujtahid* Muḥammad Bāqir al-Majlisī, strove in vain to counteract their influence. Occasionally the forces of religion achieved a temporary success, as when 60,000 bottles of wine from the royal cellars were brought out and publicly smashed.

There was increasing corruption and inefficiency in provincial government. Insecurity on the roads, always a sign of the breakdown of the central administration, was widespread. The very officials responsible for the security of travellers were often those who looted them. The army was neglected, and the military weakness of the country was thrown into sharp relief in 1110/1698–9, when a band of Balūchī tribesmen raided Kirmān, nearly reached Yazd, and threatened Bandar ʻAbbās. Shāh Sulṭān Ḥusayn turned to the Georgian Prince Giorgi XI, ruler of Kartli, who happened to be at the Persian court, for help in repelling these marauders. Giorgi was appointed governor of Kirmān in 1110/1699, and held this post until 1115/1704. The Balūchīs were defeated. This episode suggests first, that the shah felt that the Georgians were the only people on whose loyalty he could rely; second, that there was no commander, either among the *Qizilbāsh* or the *ghulām* forces, capable of dealing with the crisis. Georgian influence at the Persian capital was at its height at this time. Giorgi's brother, Leon, and his nephew, Kay Khusraw, both held important posts in Iṣfahān. In 1117/1706 the shah left the capital and visited the two important Shīʻī shrines in Persia, that of Fāṭima the daughter of the seventh *Imām,* at Qumm, and that of her brother, the *Imām* ʻAlī al-Riḍā, at Mashhad. He took with him the harem, a retinue of courtiers, and an escort of 60,000. He was away for nearly a year, and the cost of this expedition not only drained the exchequer still further, but placed an intolerable burden of additional taxation on the provinces through which the shah passed. During the shah's absence from the capital, a revolt broke out in favour of his brother ʻAbbās. This was suppressed by a force of Georgian troops under Kay Khusraw.

In 1120/1709 the weakness of the eastern frontier was further demonstrated when the Ghalzay Afghans under Mīr Vays seized Qandahār and assassinated Giorgi XI. Qandahār had been in Safavid hands since 1058/1648. Kay Khusraw, despatched from Iṣfahān, was unable to restore the situation. One reason for this was that Kay Khusraw, though he had nominally accepted Islam, was like so many Georgian renegades, still a Christian at heart, and he did not command the full support of the *Qizilbāsh* detachments in his army. Mīr Vays ruled at Qandahār until his death in 1127/1715, and the following year his son Maḥmūd assumed the leadership of the Ghalzay Afghans. On the northern sector of the eastern frontier, the Abdālī Afghans rebelled at Herat, laid siege to Mashhad, and defeated three successive *Qizilbāsh* forces sent against them. The shah was so alarmed by the situation that he transferred his capital from Iṣfahān to Qazvīn, ostensibly to organize a new force against the Afghans. He remained at Qazvīn for three years, from winter 1131/1718–19 to spring 1133/1721, but nothing was done. Maḥmūd of the Ghalzay Afghans achieved what the shah could not, the subjection of the Abdālīs, and thereby substantially increased his own power. Shāh Sulṭān Ḥusayn recognized him as governor of Qandahār, and gave him the title of Ḥusayn Qulī ('the slave of Ḥusayn') Khān. The irony of this title was doubtless not lost on the shah when Maḥmūd occupied Kirmān for nine months in 1131–2/1719 and, encouraged by the lack of opposition, launched a more serious attack in the autumn of 1133–4/1721. At Iṣfahān, there were divided counsels. Some advised the defence of the city, on the grounds that the Safavid troops available were no match for the Afghans in the open field. The only seasoned troops at hand were the tribal levies of the governor of Luristān, and a *ghulām* detachment under the Georgian prince, Rustam. There was a hasty levy of untrained peasants and merchants in the Iṣfahān area. This scratch force, whose chances of success were vitiated even at this critical moment by dissension among its commanders, was routed by Maḥmūd at Gulnābād, about eighteen miles east of Iṣfahān, on 30 Jumādā I 1134/8 March 1722.

In the capital, the irresolute shah was in the hands of a traitorous pro-Afghan faction, but even so, Maḥmūd's force was too weak to allow him to follow up his victory by storming the city, and the most he could achieve was the gradual extension of a cordon around it. Early in June, the troops of the governor of Luristān reached a point some forty miles north-west of the capital, and demanded the abdication of the shah in favour of his more energetic brother, 'Abbās. The shah refused.

The conspirators kept under close guard in the harem the shah's two elder sons, who had shown signs of courage and resolution, but the third son, Ṭahmāsp, who was weak and ineffectual like his father, was passed through the Afghan lines on the night of 3–4 Ramaḍān/7–8 June. Even Ṭahmāsp might by his mere presence have constituted a rallying-point for loyalist troops, had he joined forces with the governor of Luristān. Instead, however, he went to Qazvīn, and remained inactive. From Sha'bān–Ramaḍān/June onwards, the people of Iṣfahān were subject to severe famine. They consumed cats, dogs, mice, and even human flesh. The streets were piled high with rotting corpses. On 1 Muḥarram 1135/12 October 1722 Shāh Sulṭān Ḥusayn surrendered unconditionally, after six months of siege. At least 80,000 people had died from starvation and disease, more than four times the number who fell in battle. Iṣfahān never recovered from its ordeal, and its population today, about 650,000, is perhaps one-half of its population in Safavid times. On 14 Muḥarram/25 October Maḥmūd entered Iṣfahān, and assumed the crown of Persia. For over fifty years, during the reigns of Shāh Sulaymān and Shāh Sulṭān Ḥusayn, the social, political and moral foundations of the Safavid state had been steadily undermined, and, at the last, the once-imposing edifice collapsed with ridiculous ease before a blow administered by a handful of Afghan tribesmen.

The Afghans, though the nominal rulers of Persia, never succeeded in making themselves masters of the whole country. For fourteen years, representatives of the Safavid house maintained a shadowy existence in various parts of northern Persia. On 30 Muḥarram 1135/10 November 1722, the ex-shah's son Ṭahmāsp proclaimed himself Shāh Ṭahmāsp II at Qazvīn. When the Afghans marched on Qazvīn, he fled to Tabrīz. A rising of the townspeople of Qazvīn on 1 Rabī' I 1135/8 January 1723 drove the Afghans out of the city, and at Iṣfahān, Maḥmūd, fearing a similar rising, slaughtered many high-ranking Persian officials and nobles, together with about 3,000 *Qizilbāsh* guards. This panic-stricken action clearly demonstrates the precarious nature of the hold of the Afghans on Persia, but the modicum of leadership necessary to dislodge them did not exist. Shīrāz held out against them for nine months, and Yazd repulsed them with heavy losses. In Rabī' I–Jumādā I 1137/February 1725 Maḥmūd, alarmed still further by reports that Ṣafī, another of the ex-shah's sons, had escaped from Iṣfahān, ordered a general massacre of all members of the Safavid royal house with the exception of the ex-shah and two young princes. At least eighteen persons perished.

Two months later Maḥmūd, who had shown increasing signs of madness, was overthrown by his cousin, Ashraf, who was proclaimed shah on 29 Dhu'l-Ḥijja 1137/26 April 1725.

The territory under Ashraf's control comprised central and southern Persia, the province of Sīstān, and the western part of Khurāsān. Ashraf inaugurated his reign first, by putting to death Maḥmūd's guards, together with those officials and courtiers who had been Maḥmūd's intimates and might conspire against himself; secondly, by executing those officers who had placed him on the throne; thirdly, by blinding his own brother. In the autumn of 1139/1726 the Ottomans, who had been at peace with Persia since the treaty of Ẕuhāb in 1049/1639, resumed their invasions of Persia. This time, their avowed object was to reinstate the legitimate ruler of Persia. Ashraf retaliated by executing the ex-shah, Sulṭān Ḥusayn. When the two armies met near Hamadān on 14 Rabīʿ I 1188/20 November 1726, Ashraf disrupted the Ottoman army by emphasizing their common adherence to Sunnī Islam, and by calling on them to unite against their common foe, the heretically Shīʿī Safavids. So successful was his propaganda that some 20,000 Kurdish troops in the Ottoman army deserted to the Afghans, and the majority of the Ottoman army refused to attack. In Ṣafar–Rabīʿ I 1140/October 1727 Ashraf negotiated peace, and recognized the whole of western and north-western Persia as Ottoman territory.

The *soi-disant* Ṭahmāsp II, after a period in Māzandarān, had established himself at Astarābād in north-eastern Persia, where the powerful Qājār tribe gave him their support. In 1138/1726 he was joined by Nādir Khān Afshār, who gradually gained an ascendancy over Ṭahmāsp, and eliminated rival chieftains whose ambitions clashed with his own. After hard fighting against Abdālī Afghans in the Herat region (1139–41/1727–9) in a series of campaigns designed to protect his rear when he advanced south, Nādir marched on Iṣfahān. Ashraf decided to anticipate a possible pro-Safavid rising in the capital by the method used by his predecessor, namely, the massacre of large numbers of theologians and members of the nobility. The Afghan army was routed in a battle thirty-five miles north-west of Iṣfahān, and Nādir, entering the city on 24 Rabīʿ II 1142/16 November 1729, summoned Ṭahmāsp to ascend the throne, which had been in the hands of Afghan usurpers for seven years. In December, Nādir defeated Ashraf near Shīrāz. The Afghan leader fled, and the Afghan interlude was at an end. Nādir, however, had no intention of allowing a restoration of the Safavid dynasty on a permanent basis. He had professed his allegiance to the Safavid cause solely to enlist the support of pro-Safavid elements. In Rabīʿ I 1145/August 1732 Nādir deposed Ṭahmāsp II in favour of the latter's son ʿAbbās, who was crowned as ʿAbbās III. ʿAbbās III was only an infant, and Nādir was the real ruler of the country. On 24 Shawwāl 1148/8 March 1736 Nādir had himself crowned as Nādir Shāh, and the Safavid dynasty, which since 1135/1722 had existed in name only, now ceased to exist even in name.

CHAPTER 6

PERSIA: THE BREAKDOWN OF SOCIETY

The seeds of the decline of the Safavid empire are already to be seen after the death of Shāh 'Abbās I, and when the Afghan invasion finally brought about its fall in 1135/1722 a period of disorder followed. Trade was interrupted and a general decline in civic and cultural life took place. This was not a new experience for Persia: earlier empires had disintegrated before the inroads of nomadic or semi-nomadic invaders. On this occasion, however, the invader did not succeed in establishing an empire as had, for example, the Seljuks, the Mongols and the Timurids.

Ṭahmāsp, the son of Shāh Sulṭān Ḥusayn, the last Safavid ruler, who was besieged by the Afghans in Iṣfahān, sought the assistance severally of Peter the Great and the Ottoman sultan. The former captured Darband and Baku and concluded in 1723 a treaty with Ṭahmāsp, who ceded to Russia all the Persian possessions on the Caspian Sea on condition Peter expelled the Afghans and put him (Ṭahmāsp) on the Persian throne. In 1724, however, anticipating the disintegration of the Persian kingdom, the Russians and the Ottomans made an abortive treaty for the partition of Persia. In 1140/1727 the Ottomans forced Ashraf, who in 1137/1725 had succeeded Maḥmūd, the first Afghan ruler of Persia, to cede to them those provinces which they had occupied in return for an agreement to acknowledge him as shah.

In 1142/1729–30 Nādir Shāh, whose original name was Nādir Qulī, and who belonged to the Afshār tribe, one of the main Turcoman tribes upon which Safavid power had originally rested, expelled the Afghans. He became the *de facto* ruler of Persia but did not assume the crown until 1148/1736. Nādir's reign was not a reintegration of the Safavid empire: if a parallel is to be sought it is to be found rather with the empires of Maḥmūd of Ghazna and Tīmūr; and like them Nādir is chiefly remembered for his Indian exploits.

After expelling the Afghans, Nādir recovered the provinces taken from Persia by the Ottomans and the Russians. Russia restored Lāhījān, Gīlān, and the Persian provinces up to the River Aras by the treaty of Rasht in 1144/1732; and Baku and Ganja by the treaty of Ganja in 1147/1735. Treaties delimiting the frontier were signed with the Ottomans in 1146/1733 and 1159/1746; in 1160/1747 part of 'Irāq and Āẕarbāyjān was ceded. Nādir Shāh invaded India in 1151/1739 and reached Delhi; in the following year he invaded Sind, and in 1153/1740 Bukhārā and Khīva. In 1154/1741–2 he undertook a campaign against the Lesganis of Dāghistān. Thereafter until 1158/1745 he was largely occupied in putting down internal rebellions, and in campaigns against the Ottomans.

There was a tendency during the reign of Nādir Shāh towards a more direct administration and a strengthening of the central government, but no effective measures were taken to develop the resources of the country. The cost of his numerous military expeditions was heavy and much of the countryside was adversely affected by repeated levies and over-taxation.

In the religious field there was an attempt to heal the breach between Sunnī and Shī'ī Islam by the institution of a fifth *madhhab,* the Ja'farī *madhhab*. The purpose of this seems to have been political, Nādir hoping thereby to establish his claim to the leadership of the Islamic world against the Ottoman sultan and the Mughal emperor. The attempt failed. Shi'ism had become firmly established as the religion of the majority in most of the provinces of Persia under the Safavids; and the new rite which Nādir attempted to introduce had no widespread appeal and did not take root.

On Nādir's asassination in 1160/1747 his kingdom disintegrated. Aḥmad Shāh Abdālī took Herat and Qandahār; Karīm Khān Zand, after struggles with the Bakhtiyārī leader 'Alī Mardān Khān, and Muḥammad Ḥasan Qājār, established himself as a ruler of Lār, Fārs, 'Irāq-i 'Ajam, Āẕarbāyjān and Māzandarān; only Khurāsān remained to Nādir's grandson. Karīm Khān (1163–93/1750–79) established some degree of order and security in those parts of Persia over which he ruled and enjoyed a reputation for good government. He did not assume the title of shah, claiming to rule as the deputy (*wakīl*) of the Safavids, although there does not appear to have been, in fact, any movement in favour of a Safavid revival.

On the death of Karīm Khān, southern Persia became the scene of widespread disorders, Āqā Muḥammad b. Muḥammad Ḥasan Qājār escaped from Shīrāz, where he had been held captive, and went to Gurgān, then the home of the Qājārs. They, like the Afshārs, were one of the Turcoman tribes which had supported the Safavid revolution. Shāh 'Abbās had settled a branch of them in Shāhījahān on the Özbeg frontier, and another in Astarābād on the Turcoman frontier.

Āqā Muḥammad Khān, having assembled his followers, made himself master of Gurgān, Māzandarān, and Gīlān by 1204/1789; he then extended his authority to Tabrīz, Hamadān, Tehran and Iṣfahān, and in due course defeated Luṭf 'Alī Khān, the son of Karīm Khān, outside Shīrāz. He took Kirmān in 1208/1794 and captured Luṭf 'Alī near Bam.

Although Āqā Muḥammad Khān had by now defeated his main rival, eastern and north-eastern Persia were fragmented among a number of local rulers, and the Özbegs under Jānī Beg held Bukhārā. Leaving for the moment the eastern provinces, Āqā Muḥammad Khān turned his attention to the restoration of Persian power in the north-west. Tehran became the new capital. There were various reasons for this, apart from the fact that new dynasties tended to choose new capitals. It was within easy reach of Gurgān whence the Qājārs drew their main support, and of Sulṭāniyya, with its extensive spring pastures, where troops could be assembled and despatched to the north-west or north-east, the two most vulnerable areas. It was also in a central position in the northern provinces, which were the most fertile and the most heavily populated provinces of the empire.

After the fall of the Safavids, Georgia was disputed between the Ottomans, Persia and Russia. In 1762, after the disorders on the death of Nādir, east and west Georgia became united under Heraclius (Erekle) II. Between 1762–83 the Georgian kingdom became increasingly orientated towards Russia, and in 1783 Heraclius made an agreement with the Empress Catherine II, placing himself under Russian protection and renouncing all dependence on Persia or any other power. In 1795, Āqā Muḥammad reached Ardabīl with the intention of reducing Georgia to the status it had held under the Safavids. Heraclius refused the demand that he should return to his position as a tributary of Persia. Āqā Muḥammad, who had already come into conflict with Russia when he had expelled a Russian settlement from Ashraf in 1195/1781, thereupon invaded Georgia and sacked Tiflis (1209/1795). In the following year he was crowned shah.

Āqā Muḥammad Khān then marched eastwards to reimpose Persian control over Khurāsān, still nominally under the Afshārs. Mashhad was taken without fighting in 1210/1796. Meanwhile, a Russian force marched against Persia in retaliation for the sack of Tiflis, but on the death of Catherine in 1796 it withdrew. Āqā Muḥammad, who had returned to Tehran from Khurāsān in Rabī' I 1211/September 1796, set out in the spring of the following year on a campaign against Russia. He crossed the Aras and took Shusha. While in camp he was murdered by two slaves who, although under sentence of death for some misdemeanour, had been left free. His nephew, Bābā Khān, who at the time of his uncle's death was governor of Fārs, succeeded under the name of Fatḥ 'Alī Shāh (1797–1834). Various attempts at rebellion were put down without difficulty.

With the Qājārs (1794–1925) Persia entered upon a new period of her history. During their reign Persia was transformed from a medieval Islamic monarchy, with an administration following the traditional pattern which had prevailed in the eastern provinces of the former 'Abbasid caliphate, into a constitutional monarchy having the outward forms of a representative parliamentary government. The crucial factor bringing about this change was the contact which developed between Persia and western Europe and Russia in the nineteenth century.

The state over which Fatḥ 'Alī Shāh reigned had much in common with the earlier kingdoms of the Seljuks, the Īl-Khāns, the Timurids and the Safavids; and some of the problems to which the Qājārs had to seek a solution were not dissimilar to those faced by the preceding dynasties. Externally the Qājārs, like the Safavids, were forced to undertake repeated expeditions to defend their frontiers against the Ottoman Turks on the one hand and the Özbegs and Turcomans on the other. Internally there was the problem of the integration of the tribal element into the state; and as centralization increased and the administration expanded, so the problem of paying the officials of the state became more acute. But in addition to the problems which had been to a greater or lesser extent faced by earlier dynasties, the Qājārs were subject also to new external pressures, which enormously complicated their other problems.

In the early nineteenth century Russia pressed down through the Caucasus threatening Persia with the loss of Āẕarbāyjān, one of her most valuable provinces, and sought to establish a position which would enable her to dominate Tehran; and in the second half of the century Russia also bore down upon Persia from Central Asia, threatening Gurgān and Khurāsān. Because the Russian advance was thought to threaten British possessions in India, Britain joined with Russia in rivalry to gain influence at the Persian court.

There are indications that the balance between the tribal and settled elements of the population—always precarious—was changing during the period of Safavid decline and in the ensuing period, and that there was an increase in the numbers and influence of the tribal groups. The leading members of society in the early years of Qājār rule were the great tribal leaders as, indeed, had been the case in the early Safavid period. Under Nādir Shāh favour had been shown to the Sunnī tribes, the Turcomans and the Afghans. Under the Qājārs, other than the Qājārs themselves, the most powerful groups were the Bakhtiyārīs, the Kurds, the Afshārs, the Qārā Guzlūs, the Qashqā'īs and the Arabs of Fārs; the Turcomans were important and numerous, but only very imperfectly under Qājār rule. The power of the tribal leaders derived from the military forces which they were able to assemble, and which they were bound to provide when called upon to do so by the shah. Although the heads of the great tribes were appointed by the shah, he usually had no alternative but to appoint to these offices the natural leaders. In general, the central government was unable to administer the tribal areas directly.

The provinces were under governors, who were chosen for the most part from among the tribal leaders. Gradually, as the power of the latter, other than the Qājārs, declined, the provinces were largely governed by Qājār princes. In 1799 a son of Fatḥ 'Alī, 'Abbās Mīrzā, was made heir to the throne (*valī 'ahd*) and given the governorship of Āẕarbāyjān; while four other sons were appointed governors of Kirmānshāh, Fārs, Khurāsān and Māzandarān respectively. Several other princes, who were too young to exercise the functions of government themselves, were in due course appointed to other provinces and sent to their governments with *wazīrs,* who carried on the administration for them, much as had the *atabegs* for their wards in Seljuk times. In the case of the prince who himself carried on the government, the function of the *wazīr* attached to him was, as in Safavid times, in some measure to watch over his actions on behalf of the central government. The provincial governors were not the paid servants of the state. All they were required to do was to remit to the central government a definite sum by way of provincial revenue annually together with a New Year present, and to provide troops when called upon by the shah to do so. Their exercise of the power delegated to them in their government was absolute.

The tax assessment was prepared by the office of the *mustawfī* in the capital and sent to the province. The taxes were of two kinds, ordinary or fixed, and extraordinary. The most important of the former was the land-tax. In most provinces it was from five to twenty per cent of the produce after the deduction of seed and certain other expenses, varying according to the method of irrigation. It was paid partly in cash and partly in kind. Often the landowners farmed the tax to prevent the interference of government officials. Different rates prevailed for rich, intensively cultivated land round the towns and for gardens. Other fixed taxes were the cattle-tax paid by nomads and taxes levied on real estate in the towns and duties on merchandise. Revenue from fines amounted to a considerable sum. Among the extraordinary taxes, New Year presents formed an important category. These, with presents of an *ad hoc* nature, given for example on appointment to office, and public requisitions for special purposes, were considerable. The provincial governors were entitled to collect over and above the ordinary and extraordinary taxes the cost of the expenses of the provincial administration. Taxes were frequently in arrears and their collection often necessitated military expeditions. Fatḥ ʿAlī, at the time of his death, was on his way to collect arrears of revenue from Ḥusayn ʿAlī Mīrzā, the governor of Fārs.

Had the central government been strong, and had there been solidarity between the members of the Qājār family, the system might have worked. Neither condition was achieved; and ambitious princes were encouraged to use the provincial resources at their disposal to rebel. Further, in the absence of financial control, the existence of the provincial courts imposed an added burden on the local population. Fatḥ ʿAlī, although he established his succession to the throne with little difficulty, had to contend with various rebellions by relatives and others. His death was followed by struggles between rival claimants to the throne; and on the death of his successor, Muḥammad Shāh, in 1848 there were widespread disorders. It was the custom of the shah to declare one of his sons *walī ʿahd*; and by convention the mother of the prince thus chosen was also a Qājār. But the declaration of the *walī ʿahd* was often the occasion for bitter rivalry; Fatḥ ʿAlī, indeed, delayed after the death of ʿAbbās Mīrzā (1833) in declaring Muḥammad Mīrzā (ʿAbbās's son) *walī ʿahd,* because he feared that this would give rise to civil war.

The nature of the military forces of the Qājārs did not contribute to stability. As in earlier times, the army was largely formed by provincial contingents and irregular cavalry and infantry, with a small body of regular troops. There was no clear dividing line between the provincial governor, the tribal leader, the landowner, and the military commander. This facilitated rebellion and made the control of the shah almost always precarious. Āqā Muḥammad Khān's total forces probably did not exceed 70–80,000 men and his revenues were so small that he could not maintain them for more than six or seven months of the year. Their principal arms were bows and arrows, clubs, lances, swords and daggers. The cavalry wore coats of mail and some used small shields. Fire-arms consisted of long muskets, mostly matchlocks. Artillery was seldom employed. Under Fatḥ 'Alī there was a considerable expansion in the numbers of the army. In the early years of the nineteenth century the royal body-guard was composed of some 3–4,000 men and the standing army of some 12,000 men, mostly recruited from the Qājār tribe and Māzandarān. The most numerous provincial contingents came from Āẕarbāyjān and 'Irāq-i 'Ajam. Pay was often in arrears; and the fact that there was no proper provision for the pay of the troops was one of the factors which contributed to the seasonal nature of campaigns: the troops could not be maintained throughout the year. During campaigns they were expected to live on the country.

Although originally tribal leaders, like their predecessors the Safavids and the Afshārs, the Qājārs once having taken possession of the throne, became like them absolute monarchs. They took over the concept of the ruler as 'the Shadow of God upon Earth'[1] and the pomp and circumstance of the royal court rapidly increased. Although the Qājārs did not claim to be descendants of the 'Alid *Imāms,* as had the Safavids, they sought to impress their subjects with the high and almost sacred character of their power. Nevertheless, the shah was in theory accessible to the lowest of his subjects. At the same time, in spite of the pomp observed on official occasions, the background of the steppe was not far away: and much of the time of the ruler was spent in camp and on expeditions, the government, in such cases, being carried on in the camp.

The civil administration was based on the pattern of that of the Safavid empire, the origins of which are to be found in much earlier times. All officials were the shah's deputies. He was the sole executive. Officials had no real responsibility. They were elevated and degraded at his pleasure. Under Āqā Muḥammad the administration was comparatively simple. There were two chief officials under the *wazīr,* the muster-master (*lashkarnivīs*) and the *mustawfī*, who was the head of the financial administration. His *wazīr,* Ḥājjī Ibrāhīm, had served the Zands before

[1] See further A. K. S. Lambton, 'Quis custodiet custodes? Some reflections on the Persian theory of government', in *Studia Islamica,* V (1956), 125–48; VI (1956), 125–46.

the Qājārs. During the reign of Fatḥ 'Alī the administration was expanded. The chief minister was known as the *ṣadr-i a'ẓam*. After him the three most important officials were the *mustawfī al-mamālik*, the *wazīr-i lashkar*, and the *munshī al-mamālik*. The first had under him *mustawfīs* for each province or group of provinces, whose duty it was to prepare the revenue assessment of the province or provinces under their charge, pass the accounts of the province, and verify and sanction drafts on the provincial revenue; the second was the chief muster-master, or minister of war, though his functions were mainly administrative and bureaucratic; he was not concerned with policy. The third was a kind of chief secretary. There were a host of other officials belonging to the court and to the central and local administration. Some officials, especially local officials, were paid by dues; the high officials of the state, however, were mainly paid by drafts on the revenue.

The members of the bureaucracy at the beginning of the period held an inferior position in society to the tribal leaders and the landowning classes, who regarded them with slight contempt. They were often men of education and polish; and through them and their class the tradition of administration had been handed down over the centuries. Unlike the tribal leaders, they seldom practised martial exercises. As the administration became more complicated, the status of the higher ranks of the bureaucracy rose relative to the rest of society; and the distinction between the tribal and landowning classes on the one hand and the bureaucracy on the other became less sharp. Many members of the bureaucracy became large landowners themselves.

The high offices of state usually went to the great families, first among whom was the Qājār, and after them the foremost tribal families, and families who drew their power from their landed estates. Nepotism was marked; and a strong hereditary tendency, especially in the office of *mustawfī* (because of the skill and training required for this office), was to be seen. It was not, however, impossible, though it was difficult, for an able man irrespective of birth to obtain high office, and thus wealth. The perquisites of office were great; but so also were its dangers. A fall from favour was often followed by mulcting, exile, and sometimes death. Power which was measured by wealth gave security and so there was a general tendency to seek to accumulate wealth. This was expended by its holders to defend their interests; they also used it to enable them to live on a grand scale, both because open-handedness and hospitality were among the prized virtues of society, and because in this way they could attract clients, which meant an increase of power. Moreover, because of the fundamental insecurity of society, there was a tendency for the weak to attach themselves to some patron. The obligation to protect a dependant was generally acknowledged; and since an insult to a dependant was regarded as tantamount to an insult to his protector, attachment to the train of a powerful man was a way of achieving some degree of security.

Customary law was administered in the capital by the shah, and in the provinces by the provincial governor. Cases concerning the conduct of ministers or high officials, corruption or treason were judged by the shah in person. Local offences in the towns and bazaars came under the *dārūgha,* who was a kind of police officer. Matters of personal law were referred to the *qāḍī's* court.

Besides the tribal leaders, the landowners and high military and civil officials, there were two other groups which played an important role in society: the religious classes and the merchants. The most important religious dignitaries were the *mujtahids,* whose studies and eminence were such as to permit them to give decisions in religious matters. They enjoyed a position of respect and in some measure provided a sanctuary for the oppressed. Appeals through a *mujtahid* to the shah or a provincial governor seldom went unheard. There was a head of the local religious establishment (*shaykh al-Islām*) and a leader of congregational prayer (*imām jum'a*) in the large cities; they were nominated by the shah, and like the *qāḍīs* and many of the *'ulamā',* received stipends from the shah, which limited their independence. There was a strong hereditary tendency in the religious offices and also some movement from the religious classes into the bureaucracy.

The merchants, in the absence of banks, played an important part in the provision and transmission of funds. They provided the liquid funds without which the ruling classes could not have lived as they did. The two were often in actual partnership. A provincial governor sometimes had to find a merchant to guarantee his remission of the provincial revenue to the central government. By marriage alliances, the acquisition of land and government service, the large merchants sometimes managed to become assimilated to the ruling classes. The bazaar merchants tended to be closely allied to the religious classes and it was a familiar phenomenon for the bazaar, often at the instigation of the *'ulamā',* to close in protest at some action of the government.

The cities, on the whole, tended to be isolated from each other; and each to have its own particular ethos. Such contact as existed was mainly through the religious and merchant classes, who, together with the bureaucracy and the educated classes in general, felt themselves to belong to a common civilization expressed in terms of Perso-Islamic culture. But, although this gave a certain underlying unity and stability to society, it would be an exaggeration to claim that these various classes consciously or actively directed or controlled political events.

There was often a strong corporate sense among the craft guilds in the large cities and sometimes among the inhabitants of the different quarters. Factional strife was common. In some cities such as Iṣfahān, Yazd and Shīrāz there were from time to time popular outbreaks against the extortion and oppression of the governors. But they were seldom sustained or organized.

Lastly there was the majority of the population formed by the peasants whose function was to pay taxes and to provide recruits for the army, and who had little or no influence on the course of political events. Their only remedy in the event of exploitation was flight or emigration.

The general tendency of Islamic political and religious thought on the whole made for conservatism. Intellectual effort was directed to an ever more perfect restatement of the familiar. This is clearly to be seen in politics, art, and literature. The whole movement of reform and change which had begun in western Europe and led to great technological advances was alien to the concepts and traditions of thought and government which prevailed in nineteenth-century Persia.

The rule of the shah was absolute. There was, however, no sound financial and military basis to his power: the weaknesses of the kingdom were manifold. The position of the ruling classes was fundamentally insecure: the power they exercised was either delegated by the shah and could thus be revoked at will and without cause, or was usurped. In general, the exercise of power by a minister was regarded with jealousy both by the shah and by other members of the ruling classes. Intrigue and insecurity prevailed on all sides. The balance between order and disorder was precarious. Rumours of wars, a defeat suffered in war by the government, or the death of the shah at once created uncertainty and fear in the big cities, and in the countryside any weakening of the government was likely to be followed by raiding by tribal groups and an interruption of travel and commerce.

It was partly these weaknesses which led to Persia's great dependence on Britain and Russia in the new circumstances of the nineteenth century when, because of her proximity to Georgia on the one hand and India on the other, she was drawn into the Eastern Question, and her relations with Europe assumed an importance and character different from her relations with her Asian neighbours.

Persia was separated from the Ottoman empire and Afghanistan by religious differences: she was Shīʿī and they were Sunnī, which prevented any *rapprochement* or common front. The issues between them were seen largely in terms of Shīʿī-Sunnī strife. The war with the Ottomans was not renewed on the scale of Safavid times but there were frequent frontier wars and skirmishes accompanied by bitter sectarian hostility. The aims of both sides were, however, limited, and there was no real fear of a complete conquest or domination of the one by the other. The territory in dispute was frontier territory, notably Kurdistān, which had never been fully integrated into either empire. The memory of Safavid rule over Herat, and the brief period when Nādir Shāh had regained possession of that city, remained, and led to several attempts to re-establish Persian rule. Perso-Turkish and Perso-Afghan relations were in due course also subordinated to Persia's relations with Russia and Great Britain. The intrusion of these two powers was accompanied by new techniques, new ideas, and an overwhelming power. It provoked religious hostility and eventually nationalism, which relations with the Ottomans had done only on the limited basis of Shīʿī-Sunnī strife.

British interest in Persia was dictated by her Indian commitments, and the policy she adopted towards Persia was directed to countering the actual and potential threats to India, which she believed to come at different times from Afghanistan, Napoleonic France and Russia. Her commercial interests played a minor role. In the years following the fall of the Safavids, trade with Persia, as stated above, declined. By the close of the eighteenth century, trade between the Persian Gulf and India was once more increasing, but had not regained its former importance. About 1830, the Trebizond-Tabrīz route was opened, and by 1836 there had been some increase in trade, but it was still comparatively unimportant and there was difficulty in obtaining a suitable return in Persian goods. During the second half of the nineteenth century the volume of trade grew, and there was some investment by private companies in Persia, but trade considerations on the whole remained subordinate to political ones.

The basic assumption on which British policy rested was that it was in

Britain's interest, in the light of the defence of India, to preserve an independent Persia. The policy which Britain adopted in Persia to defend her Indian interests varied with the circumstances of the time, but the aim in all cases was the same. Wellington, in a letter to Canning dated 21 November 1826, written when Persia was at war with Russia, wrote, 'We have a real interest in the preservation of the independence and integrity of the Persian monarchy.'[1] Rather less than a hundred years later Sir Arthur Hardinge in 1905 wrote that the maintenance of the integrity and independence of Persia was the main object of British diplomacy in Tehran.[2] Broadly speaking, therefore, British policy was directed to strengthening the government of Persia, and favourable to internal reform, since it was hoped that this would contribute to the maintenance of Persian independence.

Russia was interested in Persia as a possible route to India and the Persian Gulf, and as an area in which, or from which, she could put pressure on Britain. She had no interest in a strong and independent Persia. Consequently she opposed Persian reform. The Russian threat to Persian independence in the nineteenth and early twentieth centuries was persistent.

Militarily, the Russian and British positions in Persia were not comparable and the dilemma facing Britain was to avoid on the one hand a policy which would provoke a collision with Russia in circumstances which would inevitably be unfavourable and which would, therefore, hasten the coming of Persia under Russian domination, and, on the other, inaction which would almost certainly lead to Persia's complete submission to Russia. British statesmen did not want a common frontier with Russia and did not, therefore, want to exercise a protectorate, veiled or otherwise, in Persia; and, beginning in the reign of Fatḥ 'Alī Shāh, there were repeated efforts by Britain to achieve an agreement with Russia on the preservation of the independence and integrity of Persia.

Both Russia and Britain, because of Persian maladministration, internal disorders, and financial weakness, intervened in Persian internal affairs, though their motives were different. Neither could contemplate with equanimity the prospect of civil war in Persia: Britain could not afford to see the *walī 'ahd* or another Persian prince riding down to Tehran supported by Russian troops and the establishment of a puppet government,

[1] Quoted by J. W. Kaye, in *Life and Correspondence of Major-General Sir John Malcolm, G.C.B.* (London, 1856), ii, 453.

[2] *British Documents on the Origins of the War* 1898–1914, iv, 375.

since it was believed that this would have meant the establishment of Russia on the frontiers of India; while Russia, though prepared to go to all lengths short of war to bring Persia under her control, also could not afford civil war for fear that this might lead to a British occupation of southern Persia which would block her eventual advance to the Indian Ocean.

British and Russian policy towards Persia was thus dictated, not by Persian considerations, but by their relations with each other; and the effect of their presence was to create a division between those who looked to Russia and those who looked to Britain. It also engendered feelings of resentment and humiliation in the Persian people. By hastening the breakdown of the traditional institutions of society, and by contributing to the spread of westernization, it ultimately led to the constitutional revolution of 1905–6, as a result of which Persia adopted, at least formally, parliamentary government. This was not an evolutionary process, but rather a break with the past.

In spite of the difference in the policy of the two powers towards Persia—a difference which many Persian statesmen recognized—Persia nevertheless felt herself threatened by both. Although she feared the military advance of Russia, she also feared the extension of British dominion over southern Persia by means of trade, if not by force of arms. The various occasions when discussions took place for the cession of Kharg (Karrack) or some other island in the Persian Gulf, lent colour to the suspicions of British intentions. Britain had in fact no wish to occupy southern Persia, but the threat to do so was her ultimate sanction against both Persia and Russia; and this was the main reason why Persia feared and resented British influence. The fact that on two occasions in the nineteenth century a military expedition was despatched to the Gulf to counter a Persian attack on Herat gave point to Persian fears. British policy towards Afghanistan, where Persia had irredentist designs, also brought Persia and Britain into conflict.

During the early years of the nineteenth century, Persia was courted by both France and Britain; and Fatḥ ʿAlī Shāh hoped to recover Persian territories lost to Russia by means of an alliance with one or other of them. France for her part used Persia at different periods as a means of embarrassing Russia and furthering her plans against England, while the latter hoped by an alliance with Persia to raise up a barrier to the advance of France towards India. The result of these policies were the Anglo-Persian treaty of 1801 (which was never ratified) and the short-lived

Franco-Persian treaty of Finkenstein signed in 1807. Both Fatḥ 'Alī Shāh and 'Abbās Mīrzā recognized the imperative need for modern weapons and methods to enable Persia to resist the Russian advance through Georgia and the Caucasus. It was partly this which made them turn to Britain and France. Attempts at modernization were, therefore, made in the first instance in the military field in response to external pressure.

Some knowledge of European tactics was brought to the Persian army by Russian deserters and renegades, who took refuge in Persia; but the first reorganization of the Persian army was attempted by Frenchmen who came to 'Abbās Mīrzā's camp bringing letters from Napoleon, and by the Gardane mission which reached Persia in 1807 as a result of the treaty of Finkenstein. Their stay was brief and did not achieve lasting results. They were followed by British officers who came to Persia as a result of the treaties signed in 1809, 1812 and 1814. Their sojourn also was for the most part short and their influence on the military organization transitory. Various freelance officers, Frenchmen, Italians, Russians and others, found their way to Persia from about 1814 onwards and were to be found in the armies of 'Abbās Mīrzā and other Qājār princes. Among the earliest Persian students who came to Europe were two Persian youths sent to England in 1815 to learn military engineering and surgery respectively. Military reform, however, in the absence of administrative and financial reform proved abortive; but it was the need for military reform which first aroused interest in European civilization and stimulated enquiry into modern scientific knowledge.

Hostilities with Russia in the Caucasus, which had been intermittent from about 1805, were resumed in 1811; and from this time onwards the Perso-Russian wars and their results dominated the reign of Fatḥ 'Alī Shāh. In February 1812 the Persian army defeated the Russians at Qarābāgh. Russian forces were reinforced, crossed the Aras river, and defeated the Persians at Aslāndūz (31 October/1 November). Hostilities continued intermittently for nearly a year. On 24 September 1813 a preliminary treaty was signed at Gulistān, by which Persia ceded to Russia the provinces of Georgia, Darband, Baku, Shīrvān, Shakī, Ganja, Qarābāgh, Mughān and part of Tālish, and agreed thenceforth not to maintain a navy on the Caspian Sea. Russia agreed to aid 'Abbās Mīrzā, the *walī 'ahd,* to secure his succession to the Persian throne.

The Russian victories, together with the fact that 'Abbās Mīrzā might one day owe the crown of Persia to Russian assistance, and the need for courting Russian favour with a view to the adjustment of the frontier, contributed to the establishment of Russian influence at Tabrīz. The Persians, although they had experienced the power of Russian arms, were not yet fully convinced of the impossibility of defeating Russia. Although disappointed in the lack of support received from Britain in the Russian war and the British government's wish to limit its interests in Persia, the Persian government was seized of the importance of its connexion with the courts of St James and St Petersburg and sought to use their mutual jealousy and fear to strengthen its own position. Fatḥ 'Alī himself showed an astonishing confidence in, and attachment to, the British connexion, as well as tenacity in resisting Russian demands.

The Russian war had, however, considerably depleted the resources of the government and the defeat suffered by Persian arms at the hands of the Russians had an adverse effect on internal security. A number of disorders broke out; and an Afghan fomented a rebellion in Khurāsān in 1813. This was put down and Herat taken, but it was not held. There were also repeated disorders on the Turkish frontier but war did not actually break out until 1821. It lasted until 1823 when it was concluded by the treaty of Erzurum.

Neither Russia nor Persia had intended the treaty of Gulistān to be permanent. The lack of precision in its wording over the demarcation of the frontier gave rise to repeated disputes. It was largely tribal territory, the inhabitants of which were accustomed to move freely across the ill-defined frontiers. By nature they were little disposed to submit to a central authority, and the maladministration and extortion of both the Russian and the Persian authorities heightened their reluctance. Eventually the governor-general of Georgia occupied Gokcheh, the principal disputed district, in 1825 with a military force. The war was resumed on 2 August 1826.

Persia gained considerable initial success, recovering most of the territories ceded by the treaty of Gulistān. The Russian forces were then reinforced and inflicted a series of severe defeats on the Persian army. Abortive negotiations for peace took place. The war was resumed in the spring of 1827. The Russians advanced rapidly. By October the situation of the Persian army was desperate. Tabrīz fell and various discontented leaders in Āẕarbāyjān went over to the Russians. Negotiations for peace began in November and a treaty was signed on 21 February 1828 at Turkomānchāy. By it Erivan and Nakhchivān were ceded to Russia and the cessions of territory made earlier by the treaty of

Gulistān were confirmed. The shah agreed to pay an indemnity of 30 million silver roubles. Russia received the exclusive right to appoint consuls wherever the good of commerce required. The tsar engaged to recognize 'Abbās Mīrzā as *walī 'ahd,* and to consider him as the legitimate sovereign of Persia from the moment of his accession to the throne.

By a commercial treaty concluded on the same date it was laid down that Russian traders should enjoy in Persia all the privileges accorded to the subjects of the most favoured nation; goods passing from one country to the other were to be subject to a sole duty of five per cent. Extra-territorial privileges were granted to Russian subjects, which were in due course claimed by other foreign states for their nationals also. This agreement set the pattern for Persia's foreign trade, though it was not until the second half of the century that Russia dominated Persian trade. It also regulated the position of foreign merchants, and because of the protection which their diplomatic missions were able to give them, placed them on the whole in a favourable position *vis-à-vis* Persian merchants.

The treaty of Turkomānchāy marked a major change in Persia's position towards Russia, and also in the position of Britain and Russia in Persia. Militarily Russia was unassailable. Under the treaty of 1814 Britain was bound to come to Persia's aid if she was attacked by a European power. Aid had not in fact been provided in 1826–7 on the alleged grounds that Persia had been the aggressor (though the documents do not bear this out), and after the war this obligation was cancelled. These circumstances suggested to Persia that Britain had disinterested herself in the fate of Persia, and when Persian appeals for the substitution of some guarantee or declaration of support for Persia's independence were not complied with, Persia fell increasingly under Russian influence.

Fatḥ 'Alī Shāh had no wish to place himself in this position. But his resources had been wasted by the Russian wars, campaigns against the repeated inroads of the Özbegs and Turcomans, and internal rebellions. He could not rely on the support of the mass of the people, who, exposed to the arbitrary exactions of the government and its subordinate authorities, regarded the threat of foreign invasions with indifference. They could, it is true, be stirred, as they were when the religious leaders called for a *jihād,* and forced Fatḥ 'Alī Shāh to reopen the Russian war in 1826, and again when they were roused against the Russian envoy

Grebayedov, who had come to Tehran in 1828 to clear up various differences arising out of the execution of the treaty of Turkomānchāy and was killed in a sudden ebullition of popular frenzy in 1829. But these outbreaks were fleeting; and without substantial measures of military and administrative reform, which pre-supposed a thorough-going reform of the tax administration, there was no possibility of the Persian government gaining sustained and popular support, which would have enabled it to resist Russian encroachments. But reform was contrary to the whole outlook of society and the traditions of government. Further, the growing avarice of Fatḥ ʿAlī Shāh made him increasingly reluctant to expend those resources which remained to him on putting his army in better shape.

ʿAbbās Mīrzā, too, had no wish to give up his independence, but the instability of his temperament prevented him adopting an effective policy to counter Russian influence, and above all the article in the treaty of Turkomānchāy guaranteeing his accession to the throne made him susceptible to Russian pressure. And as long as the indemnity due to Russia under the treaty was not fully paid Russia had a ready means of exerting pressure. In the prevailing uncertainty the ruling classes began to turn increasingly to Russia, some out of ambition and in the hope of furthering their own particular schemes, and others as an insurance.

The treasury was almost empty; and the army in a state of disorganization. The authority of the central government was disputed in the south and in Khurāsān; and local rebellions had broken out in Yazd and Kirmān. These were put down by ʿAbbās Mīrzā in 1830–1. After his return to Tehran he set out for Khurāsān in November 1831 with the avowed intention of restoring the authority of the shah up to the Oxus. Having taken Khābūshān and Sarakhs, he asked Fatḥ ʿAlī Shāh for reinforcements to attack Herat, then under Kāmrān Mīrzā, the son of Maḥmūd Shāh. Fatḥ ʿAlī agreed, but ordered ʿAbbās Mīrzā to return to Tehran and to leave his son, Muḥammad Mīrzā, in command of the Herat force. In 1833 ʿAbbās Mīrzā again set out for Herat but died *en route* at Mashhad. Muḥammad Mīrzā thereupon raised the siege of Herat and returned to Tehran. He was given his father's governments and military commands and set off for Āẕarbāyjān. The Persian expedition against Herat aroused alarm in India. In an effort to regain influence at the Persian court, a supply of arms and a detachment of officers were sent from India. This attempt to reorganize the Persian army was even less successful than the first attempt, and the officers were withdrawn in 1836.

The death of 'Abbās Mīrzā led to an important exchange of notes between the British and Russian governments which illustrates the weakness of Persia's position and the anxiety of Britain to prevent the outbreak of civil war and to secure agreement with Russia for the preservation of Persian independence. Fatḥ 'Alī Shāh feared that a declaration of Muḥammad Mīrzā as his successor would be the sign for civil war between his sons and other claimants to the throne. Āẕarbāyjān had suffered from maladministration during the preceding four years and the treasury was empty; the pay of the army was four years in arrears; the Bakhtiyārīs in the south were in open rebellion; the Mamassanīs were plundering Fārs; and the governor of Kirmānshāh was threatening to seize Sulaymāniyya, which was likely to lead to war with Turkey. Russia, meanwhile, declared her readiness to acknowledge Muḥammad Mīrzā, and made peremptory demands for the payment of the sum still due by way of indemnity, threatening to occupy Gīlān if payment were delayed. On 20 June 1834 Muḥammad Mīrzā was nominated *walī 'ahd*. An exchange of notes then took place between the British and Russian governments expressing their mutual desire to act together over the matter of the succession of Muḥammad Mīrzā and in the maintenance not only of the internal tranquillity of Persia but also of her independence and integrity.[1]

Fatḥ 'Alī Shāh died on 23 October 1834. The succession of Muḥammad Mīrzā was immediately disputed by various Qājār princes, notably Ḥusayn 'Alī Mīrzā, governor of Fārs. Muḥammad Mīrzā was in Tabrīz without the means of marching to the capital to assert his claim to the throne. His troops were almost in a state of mutiny for want of food, clothing and pay. The Russians offered troops, officers and stores to any amount required to put him on the throne. The British envoy meanwhile acted with vigour and came forward with the means to induce the troops to march; and on 10 November the army set out for the capital. On 16 November Muḥammad Mīrzā left Tabrīz accompanied by the British and Russian envoys (who, since Fatḥ 'Alī had entrusted the conduct of his foreign relations to 'Abbās Mīrzā in 1810, normally resided at the court of the *walī 'ahd*). Tehran was taken in

[1] The British government extracted a reiteration of this agreement with regard to Persian independence from the Russian government in 1838, 1865, 1873, 1874, and 1888; but it is questionable whether the Russians ever felt these pledges binding (see R. L. Greaves, *Persia and the defence of India*, 1884–1892 (London, 1959), 102).

December and an expedition sent to the south, which defeated the attempt of Ḥusayn ʻAlī Mīrzā to seize the throne. The danger of the disintegration of the Persian monarchy was thus averted, but its weakness had been clearly revealed.

The early years of the reign of Muḥammad Shāh (1834–48) were marked by the growing weight of the Russian presence and a fear of Russia. There were renewed efforts by Britain to recover her position at the Persian court, but there was also a reluctance to give any specific undertaking to preserve Persian independence. This made Persia alarmed and suspicious, although there was at the same time another and conflicting trend, namely the belief that Britain's interests were so closely bound up with the existence of Persia as a barrier to India that Britain would in the last instance support Persia at whatever cost. The general effect was to lessen the urgency felt by the Persian government to strengthen its own resources by internal reform, or to resist Russian influence.

By 1835 Russia was showing a growing interest in the eastern shores of the Caspian Sea. The Persian government also, convinced at last that it could not recover the territories lost in the Russian wars, began to look again to the east. Muḥammad Shāh, in spite of the disorganization of his army, the almost complete paralysis of the financial administration and the troubles prevailing in the kingdom—the Balūchīs were raiding Kirmān, the Turcomans were making inroads into Khurāsān, the Kurds were committing disorders in Āẕarbāyjān, and disturbances had occurred in Iṣfahān in the autumn of 1835—determined to march to the east, put down the Turcomans, and resume operations against Herat; and in this he was encouraged by the Russian envoy.

It was, in fact, essential for Persia to assert her control over the Turcomans: if she failed to do so Russia would sooner or later take over effective control of the Turcoman steppe, as she later did. With regard to Herat there were Persian grievances: various undertakings given by the ruler of Herat, during the reign of Fatḥ ʻAlī Shāh, had not been fulfilled, and provocation had been offered by raiding-parties, who had captured Persian subjects and sold them into slavery.

Britain, because of growing Russian ascendancy over Persia, had meanwhile begun to reconsider her policy towards Afghanistan in relation to Persia and the defence of India. Accordingly she warned Persia that any schemes for extended conquest in Afghanistan would be looked upon with great dissatisfaction. A Persian attack on Herat eventually led to the withdrawal of the British mission in 1837 and the despatch of a small expedition to Kharg island, which forced the Persian army to retire from Herat.

Internal conditions were adversely affected by the Herat expedition, as they had been in the Russian wars. In 1839 there were renewed outbreaks of disorder in Iṣfahān and disturbances in Shīrāz, Kirmānshāh, Qumm and other towns. The levy of troops in Āẕarbāyjān was also proving difficult and the financial situation was critical. There were an enormous number of government bills in the hands of the people which had not been paid. Army pay was, as usual, in arrears. Provincial revenues failed to come in. Bribery was widespread, and the purchase of offices was growing. Turco-Persian relations had also deteriorated. News of British reverses in Afghanistan in 1841, however, temporarily excited Persian hopes of renewed operations against Herat. These proved short-lived, partly because Persian appeals to Russia on this occasion received no response—there had been as a result of events in Europe an improvement in Anglo-Russian relations—and the British mission returned in October 1841.

Internal conditions continued to be disturbed; and because of the part played by Britain and Russia together in securing the accession of Muḥammad Mīrzā, the tendency to blame the powers (and in particular Britain) for the woes of the country, which was to bedevil Persian political life for many years to come, first became noticeable. By this time a new weakness was attacking the Persian state: the dichotomy between the north and the south. The fact that Āẕarbāyjān was normally the seat of the *walī ʿahd* and that when Muḥammad Shāh came to Tehran he was accompanied by a large number of Āẕarbāyjānī Turks, had already created a division between the Turkish and Persian elements of the population. This was now reinforced by Anglo-Russian rivalry, and by the fact that it had become clear that the north must be predominantly the sphere of Russian influence and the south of British. There was also a recurrent fear on the part of the Persian government that some Persian prince in exile—of whom, from the time of the accession of Muḥammad Shāh onwards, there were several—might return with the support of one or other of the powers and foment insurrection, or even set up a state in the north or the south, dominated by Russia or Britain respectively.

The position of the north and the south was not by any means equal. The most productive provinces were in the north, where was also the heaviest concentration of population; and Tabrīz had by this time become the first commercial city of Persia. In the north Russia could bring military pressure to bear at any moment. Also the fear that the inhabitants might seek refuge in Russia acted in some measure as a restraint on the government in the northern provinces. Southern Persia, on the other hand, had not fully recovered from the ruin and decay brought by the disorders between the fall of the Safavids and the rise of the Qājārs, and was subject to perennial disorders and misgovernment.

Persia's sensitiveness to intervention by the great powers was shown by the unfounded attribution of the revolt of Āqā Khān Maḥallātī in Kirmān to British intervention. He achieved considerable success in the spring of 1842 but was eventually defeated and retired to India. This episode, however, continued to trouble Anglo-Persian relations throughout the latter years of Muḥammad Shāh's reign.

The position of Persia *vis-à-vis* Russia and Britain is also illustrated by the question of protection, which, bound up with the question of asylum (*bast*), became a major cause of dispute during the reign of Muḥammad Shāh. Originally the two issues were independent. In the nineteenth century, because of the venality of the administration of justice, asylum was increasingly used to protest against injustice or supposed injustice. The frequency with which recourse was had to asylum from about the middle of the century onwards was a measure of the breakdown which was taking place, partly as the result of the intrusion of European influence, and partly because of the increasing weight of the despotism arising from the improved techniques of government which were not accompanied by any system of checks and controls. Asylum was almost the only refuge against the arbitrary exercise of power by the government. Muḥammad Shāh in 1843 sought, without success, to limit or abolish the practice of sanctuary. The usual places in which sanctuary was taken were mosques and shrines, the houses of religious dignitaries, and the royal stables. By 1850 a struggle had developed between the religious classes and the government relative to the right of asylum, and in 1858 Nāṣir al-Dīn Shāh tried to abolish the practice. This attempt also failed.

With the establishment of foreign missions in Persia, a new aspect was given to asylum, which was also sought in their premises, and thus became associated with protection. It was not normally granted to common malefactors, but only to political figures who had fallen into disfavour and whose lives were in danger. Such a practice was detrimental to the independence of the Persian government; but experience had shown that the individual could place little reliance on a safe conduct granted him by his own government, and so, because of the weight of the British and Russian presence, the tendency grew to seek the protection of one or other mission, or both. British officials sought to limit its use, but were not entirely successful; and with the growing weakness of the Persian government *vis-à-vis* the two powers, the venality of the administration and increasing Russian intervention, there were numerous bitter exchanges over the exercise of protection.

One of the most notorious cases was that of Bahman Mīrzā, a fairly popular and successful governor of Āẕarbāyjān, who, having fallen foul of the first minister, Ḥājjī Mīrzā Āqāsī (who dominated Muḥammad Shāh in the latter years of his reign, and whose exercise of power was alleged to be extremely venal), took sanctuary in the Russian mission in March 1848, and was subsequently given asylum in Russia. This event caused a great sensation in Persia and apprehension lest Bahman Mīrzā should, with Russian support, disturb the tranquillity of Āẕarbāyjān; or lest future disorders might give Russia an excuse for interference, and even lead her to seize the province to convert it into an independent principality ruled by Bahman Mīrzā under her protection.

By 1844 the practice of selling government offices had become more widespread. This was a sign of the complete financial breakdown of the state, comparable to that which had prevailed in Buyid times prior to the emergence of the land-assignment (*iqṭā'*) as the dominant political and economic institution of the state; but on this occasion the new system which was eventually to emerge was a centralized government based on the model of western Europe. The governors had to reimburse themselves for the outlay they had made to gain their governments by impositions upon the local population, and with as little delay as possible since they were never sure of retaining their appointments. Deputations would come to the court, and the governor would sometimes be sacrificed to appease their complaints. Another would then be found who would buy his office in the same way, and the only advantage to the local people would be if they obtained a more merciful and lenient governor. Salaries were largely paid by assignments on the revenue, and the assignees, like the governors, and for the same reasons, were bent on obtaining as much as they could in the shortest possible time. By 1846 scarcely any provincial revenue was reaching Tehran. Payments by the government were made almost entirely in the form of bills, which were issued for an amount far in excess of the revenue. Consequently their value was nominal.

Various chiefs in Māzandarān were disaffected. Āṣaf al-Dawla, the governor of Khurāsān, had been dismissed and gone into exile in Turkey; his son, Sālār al-Dawla, who had remained in the province, was in open rebellion. Evidence of a rather different kind of unrest was provided by the disorders committed by the followers of Sayyid ʿAlī Muḥammad, who was known as the Bāb, in different parts of Persia in 1848. He had declared himself in 1844 to be the long-awaited *mahdī*. Originally he was a disciple of Sayyid Kāẓim of Rasht, the leader of the Shaykhīs, an extreme Shīʿī sect, who held the doctrine that there must exist at all times an intermediary between the twelfth *Imām* and his followers. The prototype of this intermediary was to be found in the four successive *bābs,* or gates, through whom the twelfth *Imām,* during the period of his minor occultation, held communication with his partisans. The Bābīs, like the Ismāʿīlīs, looked for the establishment of the kingdom of God upon earth, and like them had messianic and esoteric tendencies. The movement was regarded by the religious class with horror, and by the government as a threat to stability. The Bāb was arrested in 1847 and held in confinement.

Muḥammad Shāh died on 4 September 1848. Nāṣir al-Dīn, the *walī ʿahd,* who had become governor of Āẕarbāyjān after the fall of Bahman Mīrzā, had no money in his treasury to enable him to march on Tehran to establish his claim to the throne. The merchant community having been persuaded to make the necessary funds available, he arrived in Tehran on 20 October. Although he succeeded to the throne without actual fighting, the situation was far from promising. The treasury was empty, and revolts had broken out in Iṣfahān, Kirmān and Khurāsān. There were also serious risings by the Bābīs. The first was in Māzandarān and lasted from December 1848 to July 1849. It was followed by a second in Zanjān (May–December 1850), and a third in Nayrīz, during which the Bāb was brought out of prison and publicly executed.

During the long reign of Nāṣir al-Dīn (1848–96) new trends began to emerge and new influences to be felt. The first attempt at change was again made in the military field. Nāṣir al-Dīn's first minister, Mīrzā Taqī Khān, entitled the Amīr Niẓām, who had been *waẓīr* of Āẕarbāyjān since 1843, began to reorganize the army. He had been to Russia with the mission in 1830, which was sent to apologize for the murder of Grebayedov, and as Persian representative on the Turco-Persian frontier commission during the reign of Muḥammad Shāh had seen the introduction of the Tanẓīmāt in the Ottoman empire. Existing battalions were brought up to strength and new battalions were formed. The number of troops permanently stationed in Tehran and Tabrīz was increased. A major change was made in the manner of recruitment. Each town or village was required (unless exempted for some reason) to provide as part of its tax quota a number of soldiers, or in some cases a sum equivalent to the wages of so many soldiers. The task of the provincial governor and the local landowner was merely to expedite their despatch to the capital or the provincial capital. Military service thus became a charge on the land and not upon the holder of the land; and the army was no longer composed mainly of contingents furnished by the local governors and landowners, whose loyalty was to their own commanders and not to the state. In practice, however, the main change in the first instance was that the burden upon the peasantry was further increased by constant demands for recruits.

In 1851 a new college was opened, the *Dār al-Funūn,* the purpose of which was to provide officers for the new army and officials for the new bureaucracy. Instructors were obtained from Europe. The college was, as it turned out, not of great use to the army since few of its pupils obtained employment in the army, but it played an important part in the general enlightenment, turning out hundreds of young men who had become possessed of some training in military and other modern sciences.

The Amīr Niẓām, who succeeded for a brief period in concentrating great power in his own hands, made vigorous efforts to abolish some of the abuses in the financial administration. Pensions and salaries were in some cases withdrawn, in others reduced. This led to great dissatisfaction among the upper and religious classes, especially in Āẕarbāyjān. The small allowances which had been given to the *mullās* and *sayyids* in the villages were also withdrawn. This too led to discontent.

The war against rebels in Khurāsān and the raiding of the caravan-routes in the south was meanwhile seriously affecting trade, and there were numerous bankruptcies among the mercantile community in Āẕarbāyjān in 1850. Crop-failures in three successive years in parts of the province further aggravated the situation and there was a large exodus from Urūmiyya to Tiflis. The Shaqāqī Kurds were in open rebellion, and had not paid taxes for two years.

The concentration of power in the hands of the Amīr Niẓām and his efforts at financial reform gave rise to much opposition and eventually the shah lent his support to the intrigues against his minister, who was dismissed and murdered in 1851. The energies of his successor, Mīrzā Āqā Khān Nūrī, were largely occupied in defeating the machinations of numerous rivals and in a contest with the shah for the sole exercise of power.

Efforts at financial reform having proved abortive, misgovernment continued, and, as disorders in the provinces spread, the unpopularity of the government grew. One of the factors contributing to this was the practice of transacting government business through the agency of officials known as *muḥaṣṣils*. This was not new, but the extent to which *muḥaṣṣils* were being used was almost reminiscent of the government of the Īl-Khāns before the reforms of Ghāzān. They were sent on every conceivable occasion for the execution of government orders, for the collection of taxes, the summoning of recruits, the recovery of debts and the collection of fines. Their functions were often exercised with the utmost brutality and their extortions were heavy. There was no security of life or property, and the peasants in particular were subjected to grinding tyranny.

The Bābīs, after the suppression of the revolts at the beginning of the reign of Nāṣir al-Dīn, had been quiet for a period, but in 1852 three of them made an attempt on the life of the shah. The severity with which the movement was put down after this appears to have destroyed its militancy, so that it subsequently existed mainly as a religious movement. It was subject to schism within its own ranks: in 1863 Mīrzā Ḥusayn 'Alī Bahā' Allāh declared himself to be the new leader manifested by God, and his followers came to be known as Bahā'īs. They rapidly outnumbered the Bābīs.

All hope had meanwhile not been given up of reincorporating Herat into the Persian dominions. After the death of its *de facto* ruler in 1851, an expedition was sent nominally to reduce the Turcomans, but in reality with the intention of occupying Herat. In October 1852, in spite of warnings by the British envoy that the British government could not be indifferent to a Persian occupation of Herat, Persian forces occupied the city. In January 1853, however, an engagement was signed by the Persian government to abstain from interference in the affairs of Herat and the Persian forces withdrew.

Shortly afterwards the Persian government undertook at the invitation of Russia to prepare military expeditions at Tabrīz and Kirmānshāh to move against the Ottomans. These expeditions came to nothing, and when Britain declared war on Russia in 1854, there was a brief revival in Persia of the hope that Britain would turn to Persia and help her to regain the territories lost to Russia, and that an Anglo-Persian force would be thrown into the Caucasus to co-operate with Shāmil in Dāghistān. No overtures were in fact made to Persia, and she remained neutral. Britain's alliance with the Ottoman empire did little to improve her relations with Persia. The fact that Britain was strengthening her relations with Afghanistan, Persia's other Sunnī neighbour, and the signature of the treaty of Peshawar on 30 March 1855 with Dost Muḥammad Khān also rankled with Persia, both because of the intention to strengthen Persia's eastern neighbour, and the mistrust which it indicated of Persian policy.

There had been various differences with Britain since the resumption of relations in 1841, and a certain coolness and misunderstanding. This, coupled with the internecine strife which prevailed in Afghanistan, and the opinion held by some Persian officials that the population of India would rise against the British if a Persian army appeared at Jalālābād, encouraged the Persian government to suppose that the time was ripe to reincorporate Herat into Persian dominions. The disputes with Britain culminated in 1856, and when Nāṣir al-Dīn Shāh ordered the governor of Khurāsān to march on Herat and occupy it, Britain declared war on Persia. A force was despatched to southern Persia. After a brief campaign, a treaty of peace was signed in Paris on 4 March 1857.

The war had been unpopular: compulsory levies had been made on the towns to provide for the expenses of the army, and in some cases resisted. Appeals by the *mujtahids* for a *jihād* for the most part went unheard. Serious disorders took place in Tabrīz in 1857, and there were threats by the people that they would emigrate to Russia and return with Bahman Mīrzā at their head. Trade was interrupted; prices rose; the roads were infested with robbers; and disorders were of almost daily occurrence in Tabrīz and some of the other big towns.

Perhaps the most important result of the war was to strengthen the opinion, which was beginning to gain ground in some circles, that the main reason for the superior power of western European nations was their form of government. There had been by this time a great increase in contact with Europe through diplomacy, trade, travel and education, and for the first time thought began to be given not merely to the reform of abuses but to a reform of the actual system of government.

Malkam Khān Nāẓim al-Dawla, a Persian Armenian educated in Paris, who later became Persian minister in London, drew attention in an essay written probably between 1858 and 1860, to the internal woes of Persia, the possible threat of encroachments by St Petersburg and Calcutta, and the technical advances being made in Europe, and urged administrative reform. In 1858 Nāṣir al-Dīn decided to abolish the post of *ṣadr-i aʿẓam,* or first minister, and to appoint a cabinet or council of ministers, each of whom would be directly responsible to him. They were not, however, given responsibility, collective or individual. Often, public business was transacted by the shah over their heads. In 1859 there was an abortive attempt to set up a council of state.

Some years later Persia was brought into direct telegraphic communication with Europe, as a link in the line connecting England with India. The first convention was signed in 1862. The opening of telegraphic communication profoundly affected internal conditions and marked an important step forward in the centralization of the government. On the one hand it enabled the government to make its control more effective in the provinces by a quicker transmission of news and orders, and on the other it brought the population into closer contact with the centre, thereby reducing the power of the local governors.

In 1871 there were further changes: a council of state composed of sixteen members was set up to carry on the affairs of government. In December of that year Mīrzā Ḥusayn Khān Mushīr al-Dawla, who had been appointed minister of war in September, was made *ṣadr-i aʿẓam,* the office being filled once more after some thirteen years. He began a thoroughgoing reform of the administration; and in the spring a military council was instituted. The council of state was reorganized; and a number of ministries were set up under the presidency of the *ṣadr-i aʿẓam,* in December 1872. This council was probably modelled on the imperial council of Russia. It was a purely consultative body, convened sometimes to advise the shah beforehand, or more commonly to discuss the fulfilment of his orders already delivered. The shah continued to be the sole executive.

At the close of the Crimean War, foiled of her schemes in the Near East, Russia turned her attention to Central Asia. By 1863 she had subjugated the Kirghiz steppe. Tashkent fell in 1865, Khojand (Khojent) in 1866, and Bukhārā soon afterwards. In June 1866 it was announced that a secret understanding existed between Persia and Russia, by which the Russian government promised the shah that if he would not intrigue against Russia, she would do her utmost when she acquired the Jaxartes and Oxus valleys to enable him to obtain Herat. But when Russia landed troops at Krasnovodsk in 1869 with the intention of crossing the desert to Khīva, Persian anxiety was aroused. From Krasnovodsk the Russian forces began to exercise authority over all the country to the north of the Atrek, confining Persian jurisdiction to the south of the river. In 1873 they established a military post at Chikishlar near the mouth of the Atrek; and from then onwards they claimed the course of the Atrek to be the frontier.

It had by now become clear to Nāṣir al-Dīn and his minister, Mīrzā Ḥusayn Khān, that it was from Russia that the fundamental threat to independence came, and that Persia could not resist the Russian advance unaided. On the other hand they did not wish to become the clients of Britain; and so they began to consider the possibility of interesting the great powers in the economic development of Persia, in the hope that they would, if they had a stake in the country, be interested in the maintenance of its independence. The difficulty was that at this time none of the great powers except Russia and Britain were interested in Persia. It was these considerations which led to the grant of a concession to a British subject, Baron Reuter, in 1872. It was extremely far-reaching, providing *inter alia* for railway and road construction, irrigation works and the establishment of a national bank. The Russians were furious. When the shah went to Europe the following year he found that there was much criticism of the concession, and on his return to Persia he cancelled it, under heavy pressure from the Russian government.

The fact that Nāṣir al-Dīn was able to visit Europe in 1873 was a measure of the progress which had been achieved in the preceding years in establishing the control of the central government. Another important step in this respect was the organization of the Cossack Brigade. As a result of the shah's second visit to Europe in 1878 an Austrian and a Russian mission came to Persia to reorganize the cavalry. The Austrians left in 1881 but the Russian officers remained and raised the formation which came to be known as the Cossack Brigade. The first regiment was formed in 1879 and a second in 1880. Both were officered by Russians on short-term commissions. The arms and munitions of the brigade were supplied by the Russian government and the head of the brigade was under the orders of the Russian war office. The Cossack Brigade, which was the only efficient and reliable force in Persia, had a major role in maintaining the rule of the central government; it was later to play an important part in furthering Russian designs in Persia.

The efforts to strengthen the internal and external position of the Persian government by the introduction of changes to the forms of government, however, proved no more successful than the efforts at military reform during and after the Russian wars in the early years of the century. And the reasons were similar. The efficiency with which the orders of the government were executed was increased, but there was no change in the spirit of government, no transfer of responsibility and no involvement of the population in general in the affairs of the country. Discontent was not allayed.

The later years of Nāṣir al-Dīn's reign were marked by increasing Russian pressure, matched by British efforts to persuade the Persian government to open up the country to trade, and to attack the corruption which was eating into the kingdom, in order to arrest the Russian advance. But these efforts were largely unavailing because Nāṣir al-Dīn was becoming increasingly frightened of Russia, and more susceptible to Russian coercion.

In 1879, as a result of the Second Afghan War, Britain began negotiations with the shah concerning the possibility of Persia acquiring Herat and Sīstān. For different reasons neither side pushed the negotiations, and they were suspended by the shah in 1880. In 1882 Russian encroachments to the east of the Caspian Sea, however, caused alarm in Persia, and when the Panjdeh crisis occurred in 1885, Nāṣir al-Dīn asked Britain for a formal guarantee of protection against Russian aggression. The British government was not prepared to give this—there was no way in which British help could reach Persia—and so it merely urged Nāṣir al-Dīn to improve the quality of his administration, and to establish better communications between the Persian Gulf and the north.

Russian intimidation continued, and in 1887 a secret agreement was signed by which the shah pledged himself not to give orders or permission for the construction of railways or waterways to foreign companies before consulting the Russian emperor. When in the following year a new British minister, Sir Henry Drummond Wolff, was sent to Persia, his instructions were to endeavour to preserve Persian integrity and to develop Persian resources. In pursuing these aims he sought to obtain Russian co-operation, both in the promotion of commerce and the encouragement of better government, hoping thereby to transform

Persia into a stable buffer state. Russia, however, had no interest in such a policy and continued her intimidation.

At the beginning of 1888 the shah again negotiated with Britain for a definite pledge to resist Russia if she seized Persian territory; and in reply received an assurance of a general nature. The Russo-Persian secret agreement had not yet become public, and the advantage of railways, which would enable the Persian government to have recourse to external support in resisting attacks or pressure from the north, was again urged upon the shah.

On 22 May 1888, as a result of promptings by Wolff, Nāṣir al-Dīn issued a decree giving security of life and property to all Persian subjects unless publicly condemned by a competent tribunal; the effect of this on the lives of the people was negligible. Wolff next turned his attention to the opening of the Kārūn river to navigation, a project which had first been promoted in 1874. On 30 October 1888 Nāṣir al-Dīn issued a circular opening it to vessels of all nations. This news was received in Russia with fury. Throughout the negotiations the shah bargained for an assurance against Russian aggression from Britain, and received a written promise that earnest representations would be made in St Petersburg if Russia infringed Persia's sovereign rights.

Early in the following year, Baron Reuter was given permission to found a state bank, to be called the Imperial Bank of Persia, as compensation for the cancellation of his earlier concession. This, too, was opposed by Russia, but Reuter's claims were upheld by the *ṣadr-i aʿẓam,* Amīn al-Sulṭān, partly because he saw the Reuter concession as a means of liberating Persia from the dictation of Russia. By March 1889, however, the shah had submitted once more to Russian pressure, and agreed to a delay of five years on all railway construction; and on 12 November 1889, as a result of further Russian threats, a Perso-Russian railway agreement was signed by which the Persian government agreed to an embargo for ten years on all railway construction. These negotiations mark a critical stage in Persia's relations with Russia and Britain. On the one hand they showed that Russia would not only not cooperate in the development of Persia but would oppose any attempt to open up the country; and on the other that Nāṣir al-Dīn was not to be persuaded by Britain to take steps to defend his own position by developing the country.

Dissatisfaction inside Persia was meanwhile growing. In March 1890 a monopoly for the sale and export of tobacco and control over its production was acquired by a British subject. This became the occasion for the open expression of discontent on a wide scale. Russian hostility to the tobacco *régie* had been declared at the outset; and the opposition to the *régie* which rapidly developed was in the first instance instigated by Russia. Led by the religious classes and the merchants, it was rapidly transformed into a movement of protest against internal corruption and misgovernment on the one hand and foreign influence on the other. The motives of the religious classes, who became the leaders of the movement, were probably mixed. Some took part in the movement, because they were opposed to any attempt to open up the country, lest this should lead to a decline in their own influence over the people; others feared that Persia was falling under the influence of non-Muslims as had Egypt and India, and that the tobacco *régie* and the presence of Europeans working in it would lead to a weakening of Islam in Persia. The *mullās* in their protests against the *régie* and Muslims abroad, notably Jamāl al-Dīn al-Afghānī, made much of the alleged danger to Islam; and it was probably largely the call to rally to the defence of Islam which moved the people to support the movement of protest. The merchants opposed the *régie* partly because they feared that their activities and profits would be curtailed.

The shah began to feel himself threatened on two sides: on the one hand by Russia who threatened intervention and on the other—and for the first time—by an internal popular movement. Disturbances spread in many of the major cities. A *fatwā* was issued in the name of the chief *mujtahid* declaring that the use of tobacco was tantamount to war against the *Imām* of the Age. Smoking was abandoned in the capital and largely in the provinces also. The bazaars closed and opposition to the government grew. In December 1891, frightened by the extent of the popular movement and the possibility of Russian intervention if civil war broke out, the shah abolished the monopoly. The agitation died down immediately; but it had shown that the government could be forced by popular protest to alter its course. The payment of compensation to the concessionaires led to negotiations for a loan, an agreement for which was signed with the Imperial Bank of Persia on 14 May 1892, and secured on the receipts of the customs of the Persian Gulf.

Certain changes were meanwhile taking place in Persian society. Increased contact with Europe had begun to give rise to feelings of nationalism, although this was at first expressed in terms of Islam. The timidity of Nāṣir al-Dīn towards Russia and the intimidation of him by

Russia were also contributory factors in the changing situation. Fear of Russia was not new: but Fatḥ ʿAlī had steadfastly resisted Russian pressure; while Muḥammad Shāh and his minister, Ḥājjī Mīrzā Āqāsī, had also on various occasions shown themselves unwilling to submit. Neither had been publicly compromised by negotiations for the sale of Persian resources to foreigners, or by foreign travel. Their support for Islam and respect for the religious classes were not questioned by the population at large. This was not so with Nāṣir al-Dīn: in the early years of his reign there had been vigorous attempts to reduce the power of the religious classes. The changes in the forms of government and the increase in centralization during his reign were not accompanied by any change in the conception of power. All power was still wholly arbitrary. No potential centre of opposition could be tolerated, and so the religious classes were attacked; partly it is true, because some of them were obscurantist and opposed to change, but mainly because they were by tradition a refuge for the oppressed. Gradually the opinion spread that Persia was being threatened by foreigners, that the government was conniving at this, and that the country's weakness was due to the government's neglect of the *Sharīʿa*. Consequently the discontent against the government came to be expressed, not in terms of unorthodoxy as it had been in the past, but in terms of Islam, since the government was no longer regarded as Islamic, or as justified (even though unrighteous), because it preserved order and defended the frontiers of the country.

With the increased centralization and the growth in the strength of the regular army, although the tribal leaders and big landowners were still powerful and exercised locally many of the functions of government, they no longer dominated society in the capital as they had done at the beginning of the century. They were not greatly affected by the question of foreign monopolies or foreign intervention: in the north the Russians from time to time supported them against the central government; in the south, as long as they prevented disorder in the areas which they controlled, foreign concessionaires were prepared to treat with them. It is not without interest, in view of the dichotomy between north and south, that when eventually the constitution was attacked by Muḥammad ʿAlī Shāh in 1908–9, the tribes in Āẕarbāyjān, broadly, favoured the despotism, while the Bakhtiyārī supported the constitutional movement.

The bureaucracy continued to be drawn from much the same classes as before. It continued to serve the shah, and, because of the fundamental insecurity of its position, continued to show little initiative. Amīn al-Sulṭān, like Mīrzā Taqī Khān and Mushīr al-Dawla, attempted a policy of reform, but when his policy proved inconvenient to the shah, he was sacrificed; and at the end of his life he became a tool of the Russians, as had Ḥājjī Mīrzā Āqāsī. All ministers merely held office at the whim of the shah, and were subject to dismissal and disgrace at his caprice. It was this, above all, that made Persian ministers and politicians turn to one or other of the great powers for support; though such support, if granted, merely served to perpetuate the situation they wished to avoid.

The merchants, because of the establishment of banks, were now less important in financing the government than they had been. Both they and the artisans and craftsmen, because of their alliance with the religious classes and because of foreign competition, were also becoming increasingly opposed to the government on the grounds that it was selling the country to foreigners.

There was meanwhile emerging in very general terms a demand for liberal reform, owing to a belief that the secret of Western superiority and progress, and the source of the greater material ease and security of life and property which prevailed in western Europe were to be sought in democracy. The propriety of the exercise by the shah of unfettered power was questioned; shame and disgust were felt at the corruption of the official classes; and also distress at the obscurantism and hypocrisy of the religious classes. And so gradually there came to be tentatively expressed a demand for equality before the law and a share in the government, or rather a demand to be consulted in the affairs of the country. This demand was not clearly formulated or accompanied by a definite programme. There was still no conception, except among a small minority, of a government which was not based on religion, or of two societies, one religious and the other temporal.

Although these intellectuals, for want of a better name, who tentatively put forward this demand for liberal reform were drawn from almost all classes, their background was largely that of the ruling classes. Some, such as Malkam Khān, had served the state in important positions; some of them had travelled or studied abroad; many of them belonged to the religious classes and had been influenced by modernist trends, which had reached them through contact with Muslims abroad or with their writings; and some were merchants who had come into contact with modern thought through their commercial activities, especially in Istanbul, Calcutta and Baku. It was perhaps because they were drawn from a wide and varied background, and because the central body of them came from the religious classes, that they were later able, for a brief period from 1905 to 1909, to carry with them the middle and lower classes with their intuitive clinging to Shi'ism. Many of the religious classes were obscurantist, and they often made common cause with the official classes in exploiting the people, and in so far as they received stipends from the state, their independence was limited. But in spite of these factors, the religious classes enjoyed more respect than any others, and since their leaders acted as a shield for the people from the exactions of the government, it was to them that the people looked for protection and guidance; and the intuitive clinging of the people to Shi'ism made it almost inevitable that the *mullās* should be their natural leaders.[1] Although the new movement became nationalist, its basis was thus still religious feeling. Its leaders demanded reform not revolution, and were in effect carrying out the old Muslim duty of enjoining that which is good and forbidding that which is evil. What they demanded was freedom from tyranny: their protest was against the arbitrary actions of the government, and the freedom they envisaged was seen strictly within the limits set by Islam and did not involve a revolutionary concept.

During the later years of Nāṣir al-Dīn's reign conditions further deteriorated: the government barely functioned, the administration of justice was a mockery; and the pay of the army and officials in general was in arrears. The shah, caring for nothing but money and sensuality, neglected affairs of state, which fell into the hands of corrupt officials. Public offices were put up to auction and extortion reached downwards through successive levels until eventually the poor paid the bill.

On 1 May 1896 Nāṣir al-Dīn was assassinated by a follower of Sayyid Jamāl al-Dīn al-Afghānī. He was succeeded by his son, Muẓaffar al-Dīn, whose reign was weaker than that of any of his predecessors. Although a rapid deterioration took place in Persia's external position, it was paradoxically partly the rival ambitions of Russia and Britain which saved the state from dissolution. Russian encroachments became more open and other governments and nationalities, attracted by a desire to share in the probable spoil, began to appear on the scene. Financial difficulties occurred almost immediately. There had been a large increase in the copper coinage during the last three or four years of Nāṣir al-Dīn's

[1] See further A. K. S. Lambton, 'Persian Political Societies 1906–11', in *St Antony's Papers, No. 16, Middle Eastern Affairs, No. 3* (London, 1963), 41–89.

reign; this had caused much distress among the poorer classes and paralysed small trade. The withdrawal of the excess of copper coinage, which was ordered after Muẓaffar al-Dīn's accession, was not accomplished until about 1899 and then only at considerable loss to the government. Attempts made by Nāṣir al-Mulk, who was appointed minister of finance in February 1898, to reorganize the finances had meanwhile met with resistance from officials, and proved abortive.

For a variety of reasons, some connected with internal conditions and others with the state of international affairs, Russian economic penetration increased at the turn of the century. An important instrument in bringing this about was the Russian Loan and Discount Bank founded in 1897, when the State Bank of St Petersburg advanced funds to buy up a bank set up by Lazar Poliakov under the concession granted some years earlier after the Imperial Bank of Persia was established.

In 1897 the Persian government had negotiated unsuccessfully in Europe for a loan, and negotiation for a British loan in the following year had also been abortive. In March 1899 the customs, upon which it was hoped to secure a foreign loan, were reorganized. Belgian officials were placed in charge of the customs at Kirmānshāh and in Āẕarbāyjān. They succeeded in increasing the customs revenue and their control was extended in the following year to the whole customs administration. On 30 January 1900 a loan from Russia was secured on the customs receipts, excepting those of Fārs and the Gulf ports, a promise having been obtained by the British from the Persian government in October 1879 that the customs in southern Persia would not be placed under foreign supervision or control. Among the conditions for the loan were the stipulations that Persia might not borrow from foreign powers without consulting Russia, and that the loan contracted from the Imperial Bank of Persia in 1892 should be paid off. Further, the Persian government agreed in December 1899 during the negotiations to prolong the railway agreement for another ten years.

Muẓaffar al-Dīn visited Europe in 1900 and 1902. The cost of these visits was met by the Russian loan of 1900 and a second loan was contracted in 1902. The conditions of the latter were more onerous than of the first. It was laid down that future loans could only be contracted from Russia. A concession for the construction of a road from Julfa to Tehran was also obtained, early concessions for road construction in the north having been held by Lazar Poliakov. In 1903 a Russo-Persian customs treaty, negotiated in 1901–2, became effective. Under its terms the five per cent *ad valorem* duty established by the treaty of Turkomānchāy was replaced by specific imposts. As a result of the new tariff Russian trade with Persia greatly increased and British trade was adversely affected. The Russian hold on Persia was thus further tightened, though it was temporarily slightly eased by Russian defeats in the Russo-Japanese war.

Towards the end of Nāṣir al-Dīn's reign a number of secret or semi-secret societies, formed by those who supported the movement for liberal reform, began to meet in Tehran and in some of the provincial cities. Their discussions were mainly confined to the desirability of the liberation of the people from the yoke of tyranny and the benefits which accrued from freedom, justice and education. An important part was played in the enlightenment of their members by Persian papers published abroad—there was no press in Persia at this time. Among those which exercised great influence were the *Ḥabl al-matīn,* first published in Calcutta in 1893, *Akhtar,* a weekly founded in Constantinople in 1875, and *Qānūn,* edited by Malkam Khān and first published in London in 1890. Arabic and French newspapers were also avidly read. After the assassination of Nāṣir al-Dīn the members of these societies advocated reform more openly and their membership spread especially among the middle ranks of the '*ulamā*'. They still regarded their main function to be the awakening of the people to the evils of despotism and the benefits of freedom, and with this in mind they encouraged their members to found schools in which the new learning would be taught; and this some of them did.

By 1903 discontent against the government, which had been increased by the loans of 1900 and 1902 and the subservience of the *ṣadr-i a'ẓam* to Russia, had become more open. In the following year a general sense of urgency, and a belief that the Persian people were faced by a choice between freedom and independence on the one hand and a continuation of the despotism and enslavement to foreigners on the other, caused various groups, which had hitherto acted independently, to meet together. They agreed to work for the establishment of a code of laws, the rule of justice, and the overthrow of tyranny. Their main purpose, however, was still the dissemination of information. In February 1905 another group, mainly drawn from the religious classes, was set up. Its main concern was to restrain corruption and curtail foreign intervention in Persian affairs. Its members were convinced that the despotism and tyranny of the government on the one hand and the possibility of intervention by Britain and Russia on the other constituted a threat to Islam; they also believed that the ills of the country could only be cured by education. Like the movement of opposition to the tobacco *régie,* these various groups and societies also became both nationalist and Islamic. They played an important part in preparing the people for modernization, canalizing the growing discontent, and bringing the disaffected elements together.

Discontent came to a head in April 1905 when the shah was on the point of leaving for his third visit to Europe. A group of merchants took refuge in Shāh 'Abd al-'Aẓīm, a shrine outside Tehran. The immediate cause was their dissatisfaction with the customs administration and its Belgian director, M. Naus. A promise was given that the latter would be dismissed on the shah's return, and the merchants dispersed. In May 1905 one of the secret societies circulated an open address to the *ṣadr-i 'aẓam* calling his attention to the decay and disorder in the country, protesting at the lack of security and corruption of officials, and demanding *inter alia* a code of justice and the setting up of a ministry of justice, administrative, military, and tax reforms, a cleaning up of the customs administration, the foundation of technical schools and factories, a proper exploitation of the mineral resources of the country, and a limitation on the powers of ministers, ministries, and *mullās* according to the *Sharī'a.* Various acts of tyranny and extortion by the government and its officials meanwhile fanned the discontent, producing a state of sullen resentment among the people at large and tension in the capital. Finally, a large number of *mullās,* merchants, and members of the craft guilds took refuge in Shāh 'Abd al-'Aẓīm. Their demands included the dismissal of M. Naus and the governor of Tehran, and the setting up of a ministry of justice.

In January 1906 the shah gave orders for the establishment of a ministry of justice (*'adālat-khāna-i dawlatī*) for the purpose of executing the decrees of the *Sharī'a* throughout Persia, so that all the subjects of the country should be equal before the law. This temporarily satisfied those who had taken asylum, and they returned to the city. But no steps were taken to implement the promises given. Public opinion became increasingly stirred by denunciations of the despotism by the *mullās,* and when an attempt was made to expel one of the leading preachers from the city, riots ensued. A large concourse of the religious classes, merchants, artisans and others took refuge in Qumm. The bazaars closed in Tehran, and in July large numbers of merchants and members of the craft guilds took refuge in the British legation. They demanded the dismissal of the *ṣadr-i aʿẓam*, the promulgation of a code of laws, and the recall of the religious leaders from Qumm. The shah finally yielded to their demands and on 5 August 1906 issued an imperial rescript setting up a National Consultative Assembly.

Thus the movement for change, which had begun in the early years of the nineteenth century among the ruling classes in response to external pressure, and became during the second half of the century a dual movement for reform against internal corruption and resistance to foreign encroachment, was finally transformed, by the intransigence of the government, into a nationalist and Islamic movement demanding constitutional reform. Once more the state, which had so often appeared to be on the point of dissolution, was saved—but this time by a popular movement demanding a law which was equated with the *Sharīʿa,* and calling for a government which was believed to be Islamic. In fact, the success of the popular movement marked the final breakdown of the traditional forms of government it thought it was restoring, and marked the opening of a new system which was ultimately virtually to transform society.

CHAPTER 7

CENTRAL ASIA FROM THE SIXTEENTH CENTURY TO THE RUSSIAN CONQUESTS

THE CHANGING SITUATION OF CENTRAL ASIA

After the formation of the three great Islamic empires of the Ottomans, the Safavids and the Mughals, the situation of Central Asia in the following centuries was determined. After the death of Muḥammad Shaybānī in 916/1510 and the expulsion of Bābur from Transoxania and Samarqand in 918/1512, it was clearly impossible for the Turks of Central Asia to subjugate the Persian plateau again as they had done in previous centuries. In spite of prolonged molestation by the Turcomans —comparable with that of Poland and Lithuania by the Crimean Tatars in the same centuries—the Safavids were able to hold out and to make Persia into an independent state with its own unique character.

The border area consequently created between Persia and Central Asia on the Oxus and to the south became not only a political frontier but also in equal degree a religious frontier. Transoxania and the greater part of the eastern Persian settlement area—approximately what is now Afghanistan and Tājīkistān—remained Sunnī; Persia became Shī'ī. Even though there was no complete barrier against the spread of Persian culture into Central Asia in the following centuries, the difference of faith obstructed its diffusion. Persian culture, moulded by native Sunnī forces in India just as much as in Transoxania, in general developed independently and without direct connexions with the culture of the Persian plateau. It was no longer feasible simply to take over works of literature, still less of theology, from thence and to make them a model for local productions. Even though the Persian classical models continued to have an influence in this area, the vital exchange with continuing developments was in any case interrupted. There is certainly justification for seeing this as largely responsible for the subsequent marked decline of the Persian language in Transoxania, which allowed Turkish, henceforward so to speak the 'Sunnī language', to become the idiom of western Central Asia apart from the mountains of Tājīkistān. This shift of language and the weakening of links with Persian culture brought the development of the country down, very gradually, from the high level that had been ensured by the common cultural development of the Middle Ages.

Until the Turks were converted to Islam, which they began to be around 349/960, the north-east frontier of its expansion area had lain in the neighbourhood of Samarqand, in Farghānā, and in the Afghan mountain country. The conversion of the Turks of Transoxania had not really opened its path to Central Asia, while the Kara-Khitay and the Mongols adhered to other religions. The Muslim Turks between the fourth/tenth and seventh/thirteenth centuries themselves had focused their attention almost entirely on Persia and the Near East, and spread out in that direction. It did not occur to them to advance their settlement area, and with it their faith, further eastwards into Central Asia.

It was not until the seventh/thirteenth century, when Islam prevailed among the Chaghatay Mongols, and found a not entirely amiable champion in the person of Tīmūr, that Mughulistān, including the Tarim basin, was progressively penetrated by the doctrine of the Qur'ān. Some of the local rulers regarded themselves as its champions against their eastern neighbours. Thus from the eighth/fourteenth century onwards large stretches of Central Asia were won over to Islam; at that time it also gained an increasing number of adherents in China. The only effective barrier against Islam was the conversion of the tribes in Mongolia to Lamaist Buddhism: they went over to it decisively at the close of the tenth/sixteenth century. Until then the Turkish peoples and tribes of Central Asia had been, almost without exception, united under the sign of the Qur'ān.

Thus, whilst Transoxania had been cut off from its old connexions in the south since the early tenth/sixteenth century, the situation in the east had not yet been stabilized. There was for the time being no cause for fear of attack by non-Islamic peoples; the continuous extension of Islam made a Holy War (*jihād*) unnecessary there for the time being. The sources indeed tell us almost nothing about this highly significant change in the structure of Central Asia in the tenth/sixteenth century; even the political history of the time is inadequately presented in them.

About this period, an opponent was emerging in the north-west whose importance was far beyond that of Chingiz Khān or Tīmūr—namely Russia. At just this time the tsar was putting out his first feelers towards Persia, to find out whether the Safavids could be made his allies against Bukhārā and also against the Ottoman Turks. The Central Asian peoples, prevented from developing outwards by their powerful neighbours, no longer had the strength to create a great empire, or the inward mental concentration necessary for outstanding cultural achievements. The following centuries were therefore a period of decline and decay.

Central Asia was thus isolated from the early tenth/sixteenth century. States that came into existence in this area could have no supra-regional importance unless they could be extended towards Persia, and thereby brought large parts of the central Islamic countries under their control, as did the Seljuks, the Khwārazm-Shāhs, the Īl-Khāns and Tīmūr. But the Shaybanids, in spite of all their political power in the tenth/sixteenth century, were unable to make any incursion into the core of the Islamic heartlands, and therefore led an existence on the margin of world history. From the threshold of modern times Central Asian history becomes provincial history. This justifies us in giving no more than a rapid sketch of the following centuries.

KHĪVA, SIBIR AND THE ÖZBEGS

The repelling of Safavid interference in Transoxania in 916–18/1510–12 left the country very much disunited. After 918/1512 a scion of the Shaybanid house, Ilbars, came to power in Khwārazm, henceforward more frequently called by the name of its capital, Khīva; the old name eventually disappeared. Ilbars made it an outpost of the Sunnī faith against the Shī'a and also a base for incursions into neighbouring Persian areas. His descendants held out against all attempts (for example by the Kalmuks) to subdue them in the tenth/sixteenth and eleventh/seventeenth centuries, and the country continued to exist for centuries as an independent state.

The extreme north-west of this area, the khanate of Sibir (Siberia), also kept its independence after Kuchum, a scion of a collateral line, had superseded the ruling khan there after prolonged struggles (1563–9). From 1579 onwards he was engaged in warfare with the Russians, who were advancing across the Urals; he was driven back in 1581, but in 1584 he was able to gain a victory over the Cossack leader, Yermak, who fled and was drowned. He did not, however, stop the Russian advance. A Russian settlement was established in 1586 in Tümen and another in 1587 in Tobolsk. Kuchum was defeated on the Ob in 1598 and had to flee to the Nogays, where he was murdered two years later. His son Ishim Khān, in spite of collaboration with the Kalmuks, had no further success. The conquest of the khanate of Sibir by the Russians was the starting-point for their domination as far as the Pacific and also deep into Central Asia. This also had the effect that traffic between eastern Europe and eastern Asia moved over to Siberia in the next centuries and went through Russian territory; there was a considerable decline in the economic importance of Turkistān.

The other areas of Central Asia (apart from Khīva and the eastern approaches of the Urals), and above all the Özbeg settlement area, were united once more when the Shaybanid ʻAbd Allāh II succeeded, from 958/1551 onwards, in warding off his enemies by a vigorous defence of his main possessions along the Zarafshān. The most dangerous of his attackers was the Özbeg, Nawrūz Aḥmad Khān (959–63/1551–6). From then on ʻAbd Allāh steadily increased his sphere of influence, even though his reign was not free from insurrections. In 964/1557 he conquered Bukhārā, which he made his capital, then between 981/1573 and 991/1583 he took Balkh, Samarqand, Tashkent and Farghānā. ʻAbd Allāh assumed the title of khan in 991/1583, after the death of his feeble-minded father, Iskandar, whom he had proclaimed ruler of the Özbegs in 968/1561, though he never actually reigned. As khan, ʻAbd Allāh continued to show consideration for the Islamic religious organization, to which he made generous gifts. The strongly centralist policy directed against the influence of the Özbeg chiefs was unchanged, even though they were allowed to retain their rich fiefs. Henceforward the administration and the coinage were reorganized; public buildings and the like were erected, often by purchased slaves. At the same time there was a series of military campaigns. These put him in possession of Kulāb, Badakshān (where a branch of the Timurid line had held out), and Gīlān. On the other hand he was only able to devastate Khīva and also Mashhad and the Tarim basin, without being able to hold on to them. The Persian Shāh ʻAbbās the Great expelled the Özbegs again from their conquests in Khurāsān (Herat and Astarābād) in 1007/1598. ʻAbd Allāh II tried to outmanoeuvre ʻAbbās, the greatest adversary of his closing years, by means of an alliance with Sultan Murād III and Akbar, with whom he exchanged ambassadors in 1585. His tactics were similar to those of ʻAbbās himself, who kept up contact with the Habsburgs in the hope of correlating the fight against the Ottomans in the west (Hungary) with that in the east, along the Zagros mountains and in Āẕarbāyjān.

Round about 1000/1590 a renewed unification of Central Asia under the strong personality of ʻAbd Allāh II seemed within reach. Then the Özbeg ruler quarrelled with his only son, to whom he had made over Balkh in 990/1582 and who was now trying to become actual ruler—just as his father had done with Iskandar Khān. This involved father and son in a lengthy feud that allowed the Kazakhs to reach the very gates of Tashkent and Samarqand, and dragged on until 'Abd Allāh II died in 1006/1598 while on a punitive campaign against the intruders. His son proved an ineffective successor; he was removed after a few months. 'Abd Allāh's state fell asunder, and his descendants disappeared.

Thus the last attempt at unification in Transoxania foundered just at the moment when the Safavid empire was at its zenith under Shāh 'Abbās the Great. North-east Persia suffered in the next centuries from continual raids by Turkish nomads, but these were in fact no more than pinpricks. The Persian plateau was now spared any serious attacks from the usual source of trouble in the north-east. The two dangerous thrusts made almost simultaneously against Persia in the first half of the eighteenth century, the Afghan invasion and Peter the Great's attempt to seize Gīlān, came from other directions.

THE TARIM BASIN UNDER THE LAST CHINGIZIDS AND JUNGAR SUPREMACY

Before continuing our consideration of the fate of Transoxania, we turn our attention to the south-east, to the last offshoot of the state of Mughulistān. In the eastern half of this state the Chaghatay dynasty established itself from the beginning of the sixteenth century. Two brothers, Manṣūr and Sa'īd Khān, had succeeded in breaking the power of the dominant Dūghlāt family. The two brothers now shared the territory in such a way that Sa'īd came into possession of their domains in the south-western part of the Tarim basin. Manṣūr ruled over Semirech'ye, Yulduz and the Turfān oasis. In mutual quiet and amity they succeeded in keeping off the Shaybanids and giving the country a long period of peace. The brothers were convinced Muslims and were rooted in an urban culture. They drove back the influence of nomadic elements and opened the way into the Tarim basin for the culture of Samarqand and Bukhārā, which had now gathered strength again. Here in the Tarim basin eastern Turkish (Chaghatay) had probably completely superseded the Indo-Germanic speech of earlier centuries, even though Muḥammad Ḥaydar Mīrzā Dūghlāt (*c.* 905–58/1500–51) wrote his well-known historical work *Tārīkh-i Rashīdī* in Persian. There was no traceable Chinese influence in this area in the tenth/sixteenth century.

The two brother-princes also shared their military tasks. Manṣūr turned his attention to the east, where it was still a question of fighting for the spread of Islam. In 919/1513 the oasis of Qomul (Ha-mi), which even earlier on had been the goal of Muslim rulers in this area, put itself under his sovereignty. In 923/1517 Manṣūr chose this place as his capital and made it his base for further attacks on China. At various times he advanced as far as Tun-huang, Su-chou and Kan-chou (in Kan-su); thus Chinese chronicles mention him as well as native ones. Even if it was not granted to the people of eastern Turkistān to get these territories permanently under their rule, nevertheless the spread of Islam in just these western provinces of China may well have been furthered by numerous conversions that occurred at this period.

At the same time Sa'īd Khān invaded the province of Ladakh, which was in those days united with Tibet. The historian Ḥaydar Mīrzā, whom we have previously mentioned, was commander there in 937/1531; this indicates that there were still friendly relations at that time between the khān and the powerful Dūghlāt clan. However, this state of affairs did not last—one might say, unfortunately for the country. 'Abd al-Rashīd, who succeeded his father Sa'īd Khān in Kashgar in 939/1533, strove for greater independence and was no longer satisfied with the existing balance of power. Ḥaydar therefore fled from his service and established himself in Kashmir in 948/1541.

This opened the way for a development that was to lead to an entirely new situation. The two Chaghatay brothers and their descendants were tied down by military factors in the south and the east, and this gave the Kazakhs free play to spread out in northern Mughulistān. The Ili and Kunges valleys passed into the possession of the Kazakhs. 'Abd al-Rashīd found himself restricted to Kashgar, which was inaccessible to the Kazakhs, it being impossible for them to get over the Tien-Shan range.

Secondly, there were new forces at work in the country itself, and their influence grew steadily after the death of Sa'īd Khān. Here, as everywhere in the Islamic countries, the reputed descendants of the Prophet and his Companions were held in high respect. They were especially revered in an orthodox Islamic area like the Tarim basin, where the high morale of the march-warriors (*ghāzīs*) still existed. The descendants of Muḥammad, together with those of the other Patriarchal Caliphs, formed clans, the leading members of which were called *Khōjas*.

These clans split into two parties, the Ak-Taghlık ('of the White Mountain') and the Kara-Taghlık ('of the Black Mountain'), with their centres of power at Kashgar and Yarkand respectively. Their importance was increased by the discord among the sons of Manṣūr (d. 952/1545); the period of peaceful development in the Tarim basin was once again at an end. According to Chinese sources, Shāh-Khān (952–c. 978/1545–c. 1570) and Muḥammad were at enmity with one another. With the help of the Oirats Muḥammad was able to seize part of the Qomul oasis. After 978/1570 he was fighting against a third brother. There is no clear information about the details of this development, for even Chinese sources are silent after the cessation of the threat from Qomul. We are only told of envoys sent by a Turkish khan from Turfān in 1654 and 1657, after the victory of the Manchu dynasty in 1644.

In the west of the country ʿAbd al-Rashīd had died in Kashgar in 1565 or 1570. His son ʿAbd al-Karīm (or ʿAbd al-Laṭīf) came to power soon after, and reigned until after 1593; he assigned Yarkand to his brother Muḥammad as an appanage. He was evidently still ruling there in 1603 when the Portuguese Jesuit missionary, Benedict Goës, travelled across the country. The granting of this appanage certainly averted an open quarrel within the dynasty, but it also accelerated the break-up of the country, and helped to make the Khōja families its real lords. Consequently the Tarim basin, with its oasis-type individual settlements, steadily disintegrated again into city-states of the kind that had characterized it during the struggles of the Chinese and the Hiung-nu about the beginning of the Christian era, and that subsequently became famous as stations on the Silk Road. Not only Yarkand and Kashgar but also Ak-Su and Khotan became the centres of such Khōja clans. At the same time the Ak-Taghlık group kept up connexions with the Kazakhs. The latter were at that time split into three hordes, the Great or Older, the Middle, and the Little or Younger Horde; they were settled north of the Aral and Caspian Seas and up to the rivers Irtysh and Tobol; they had meanwhile subjugated the Ili valley. The Kara-Taghlık on the other hand relied on the Kirghiz on the southern slopes of the Tien-Shan range.

Alongside them, the khans descended from Chaghatay were tolerated as they had no real power. When Khān Ismāʿīl tried to alter this state of affairs by an attempt to overthrow the Ak-Taghlık, the latter called in the Mongol tribe of the Jungars. Thus in 1089/1678 the Ak-Taghlık defeated Khān Ismāʿīl and at the same time the Kara-Taghlık of Yarkand. The leader of the Ak-Taghlık now established himself as khan in his rivals' former centre. Thereby the last descendant of Chaghatay (and consequently of Chingiz Khān) was eliminated from Muslim eastern

Turkistān. At that time, however, there were still descendants of Chingiz ruling in Bukhārā and—in the Giray branch—in the Crimea. Now the period of the 'holy state' of the Khōjas began for the Tarim basin.

The holiness of this state was by no means impaired by its exposure to the entirely un-Islamic influence of the Buddhist-Lamaist Jungars. In connexion with the upheaval of 1089/1678, the Jungars had advanced into the neighbourhood of Kashgar, where they had arbitrarily set up members of the two rival Khōja groups as khans of the Tarim basin. From this area the ruler of the Jungars, the Lamaist Galdan (1671–97), with the moral support of the Tibetān Dalai Lama, attacked and occupied Semirech'ye, and also the oases of Turfān and Qomul, hitherto ruled by descendants of Chaghatay, who were now superseded. From 1688 onwards Galdan tried to encroach on the territories of other Mongol tribes, but was prevented from doing so by the intervention of the Chinese emperor. The Jungar leader eventually found himself driven to suicide.

Galdan's successor, his nephew Tsewang Rabdan (1697–1727), fought the Kazakhs in the north, and in 1723 won Tashkent and the town of Turkistān (Yasi) from them; he also fought the Chinese around Qomul and Turfān (1715–24) until he had occupied both oases. Tsewang Rabdan, who had as his military adviser a captured Swedish sergeant from the army of Charles XII, was able to maintain his supremacy over the Tarim basin unimpaired. His son and successor, Galdang Tsereng (1727–45), eventually divided the basin into four independent states, namely Kashgar, Ak-Su, Yarkand and Khotan. He was able to extend his influence westwards over the Kazakhs, but in 1732 he lost certain other, more northern, parts of his state to the Chinese. After the death of Galdang Tsereng there was an insurrection among the inhabitants of the Tarim basin. The division into four city-states was abolished; and, in consequence of internal quarrels among the Jungars, in 1753–4 and finally 1757, the Turks living there were able to shake off Jungar supremacy. This was, however, an empty victory, for after the subjection of the Jungars in Jungaria in 1755–8, the Chinese advanced with a strong army against the former Jungarian possession, the Tarim basin, which had in fact on various occasions already been subject to the Chinese in earlier centuries. In 1757-9 after bitter and fluctuating battles they conquered the country, and it was now transformed into the 'New Marches' (Sin-Kiang) of the Manchu empire.

The collapse of the last nomad empire in Central Asia had the effect that the Kirghiz and the Kazakhs, hitherto oppressed by the Jungars, and forced out into the oases, became active again. They regained possession respectively of Semirech'ye and of the northern part of the Tien-Shan range. The leading Kazakh groups of the Great Horde and Middle Horde turned towards the Chinese empire and paid tribute to it down to the middle of the nineteenth century, in order to ensure thereby the exchange of their horses and cattle for Chinese silk. This trade went on for decades to the mutual satisfaction of both parties. Chinese trading-stations were set up at several points in the Kazakh settlement area; Kazakh trading caravans penetrated Outer Mongolia and the Tarim basin. Ultimately, as Russian influence also spread more and more from Orenburg (founded 1735), the two Kazakh hordes finally submitted themselves around 1845. Their Chinese trade was now at an end.

COMMON FEATURES IN THE DEVELOPMENT OF INNER ASIA FROM 1600 ONWARDS

Between the sixteenth and nineteenth centuries, Transoxania and western Turkistān had no common political history, and we are forced to make a separate study of each of the various states that came into being. None the less, we must not forget the many common features that they possessed, and we shall also have to mention numerous mutual contacts between them.

There were some common traits that transcended political frontiers. There was, for instance, the strict Sunnī orthodoxy which all the inhabitants acknowledged, Turks and Tājīks, settled peoples as well as nomads, peasants and courtiers, administrative officials and the rulers. It gave Central Asia its characteristic stamp down to the present time and, as we have seen, it differentiated the cultural development of this country from that of Persia (which was now Shī'ī) more clearly than before. Even if one takes into account that the following centuries were not particularly fertile in new religious ideas, or in the development of any theology adapted to the changing circumstances of the times, none the less Sunnī orthodoxy gave the population a firm support that enabled it to regain its tranquillity and re-discover its own personality after the many horrors it had experienced between the thirteenth and sixteenth centuries. The charitable activities constantly practised by Islam, not only in *medreses* and mosques but also by means of organized institutions like the Ṣūfī convents with their feeding of the poor and their educational work among young artisans and the like, also did much to make the material conditions of life more peaceful.

A religious spirit pervaded all public life, every class and tribe. One can therefore understand the practically unshakeable position of the '*ulemā*' and *fuqahā*', and the Ṣūfī orders, the strongest of which were the Naqshbandiyya and Kubrāwiyya. For a ruler who relied on them and collaborated with them they were a very powerful support; they were, moreover, in close contact with the population as *qāḍīs* and their assistants, as administrators of various kinds and as *imāms* among the nomads. Attempts to curb the power or restrict the influence of the '*ulemā*' were always dangerous, even on occasions when there was undeniably some element of justification for them. Several khans came to grief through endeavours of this kind. Such events reverberate in the writings of the historians, who took up a correct Sunnī attitude, and delivered their judgments on leading personalities from that standpoint—as indeed they were compelled to do, by reason of the contemporary social structure.

Theology was completely integrated into the general Sunnī tradition and a supervisory body under a *re'īs* (comparable with the *ṣadr* in Shī'ī Persia) took care that correct doctrine was taught in these countries. Historical writing, having to depict a changing age, could not restrict itself to the repetition—or at best the reorganization—of what already existed. New states of affairs and new developments made reinterpretation necessary, however much the philosophical basis remained unchanged. Admittedly the historiography of this period has not yet been investigated in all its details; the student is here largely dependent on a number of Russian learned works which very often cannot be checked against their sources. In historical writing the decisive religious opposition to Persia made itself felt to the extent that contemporary Persian chronicles could no longer simply be considered as authoritative. Historical accounts written by natives of Central Asia stressed the spiritual opposition to Persia; the compulsion to view and judge historical events from their own standpoint caused a large increase in the number of these writings.

In these centuries the mental life of Central Asia was homogeneous. This was in accordance with sound Islamic tradition, for during the whole of the Middle Ages there had been free intercourse between artists and scholars and also merchants, to a much greater extent than in the West. This phenomenon now repeated itself on a smaller scale on the other side of the Oxus. The inclusion of the whole of Persia in the Shīʿī orbit caused many Sunnī scholars, and also many poets, to go to Transoxania in order to preserve their faith. In particular, personalities who had lived in Herat at the court of Ḥusayn Baykara fled northwards and continued the Persian Sunnī tradition of Herat among the Özbegs. The tenth/sixteenth and eleventh/seventeenth centuries were still rich in important figures who tried their hand at the traditional forms of the *ghazal* and the *qaṣīda* in praise of the ruler. Any writer who did not accommodate himself to the framework of convention naturally could not reckon on gifts from the ruler. In the twelfth/eighteenth century the Indo-Persian poet Bēdil from ʿĀẓimābād in north-western India (1054–1133/1644–1721) was much admired for his sceptical philosophy of life; he had imitators even in the nineteenth century. This is, by the way, an interesting cross-connexion between two areas of Sunnī Persian culture, leaping over a homeland that had turned Shīʿī.

The Persian literature of this period has not yet been definitely investigated, and we are also ill-informed about the details of works in the indigenous Turkish language—including various epics—such as were written especially at the court of Khokand. One of the Turcoman poets of this period is Makhdūm Qulī (*c.* 1735–80), who lived for a long time in Khīva; his poems have become popular and there have been various editions of them in recent years. Besides these original works there was also a not inconsiderable literature of translations from Persian into Turkish, for example of legends and also of historians such as Mīrkhwānd. The nineteenth century brought further stagnation: writing seemed restricted to mere imitations. Musical productions (songs, poetic declamations and instrumental music) were bound by tradition in the same degree as literature. They enjoyed great popularity with this people of music-lovers.

Considering the general state of development in Central Asia, it is not surprising that the school-system, intended mainly for boys, had hardly risen above the level of the Islamic Middle Ages. In the primary schools (sing., *mekteb*) children from six to fifteen years of age learned to read by rote from Arabic or Persian religious works, chiefly the Qur'ān, which they understood hardly or not at all. The teaching was often done by the *imāms* of neighbouring mosques, who were paid by the parents. Corporal punishment was frequent. Similar *mektebs* also existed in limited numbers among nomads; among the Kazakhs there were relatively many Tatar teachers employed in this work.

Above the *mektebs*—as was the case everywhere in the Islamic orbit—there were the *medreses,* mostly dependent on *waqfs,* and serving as theological colleges. These naturally had to impart a thorough knowledge of Arabic, but as far as teachers were available they also taught the fundamental operations of arithmetic. *Medreses* were almost entirely confined to the settled Özbegs and Tājīks. The pupil stayed at them for eight years—not infrequently even for fifteen or twenty years. He generally concluded his studies without any formal examination, but received from a respected *khōja* a diploma attesting his fitness to teach. The *medreses* also produced the judges and their assistants, also *imāms* and future administrative officials—the last especially in Bukhārā. Educational institutions of this kind in Khīva, together with Bukhārā, had an especially high reputation. Students came to them even from India and Kashmir, from Russia and eastern Turkistān. Tradition has it that the total number of theological students round about 1790 was approximately 30,000.

The spatial situation of the states of Central Asia was also an important factor in the shaping of their common destiny. While the population of Transoxania became ever more settled, and at the same time the urban population of the Tarim basin found peace again and recovered its former self-confident attitude of mind, the whole borderland extending northwards and eastwards from the areas settled by Persians and Afghans passed entirely into the Islamic cultural sphere of a settled urban and rural population. The nomadic element, however, survived and continued to play a significant—and at times very important—role even in the nineteenth century, above all in Khokand. The nomads were none the less felt to be a disturbing element in the three khanates and their settling down was encouraged and welcomed, especially in Khīva. The khans also evolved methods of keeping order among the Turcomans, as well as the Kazakhs and Kirghiz pushing in from the north, by maintaining an intermediate class of tribal chiefs: the tribes were usually allowed to keep these after they had been subjected to a khan. There were indeed repeated insurrections, but they could usually be put down quickly. They were largely caused by internal discord among the nomads themselves and by the splitting up of their tribes. Khokand was the only area in which the nomads were for a time in political control.

As a natural consequence of this development the khanates of Central Asia became a bulwark against the advances of nomads like the Kazakhs and Kirghiz, or of Mongol tribes like the Jungars; the first thrusts from the latter had in fact been parried by the Kazakhs and Kirghiz themselves. Although the khanates lost certain northern districts, they warded off a nomad inundation to the best of their ability, and thus also unintentionally defended the Persian settled area. Anyone who wanted to invade this would first have had to get control of the khanates on the Oxus and the Jaxartes. The Turcomans indeed remained a serious nuisance to neighbouring Persia and also at times to Khīva and Bukhārā, but they were no longer a danger to the independence of Persia, especially at the period when the Safavid state was firmly established.

To appreciate fully the situation of the Central Asian khanates it is necessary to understand that the nomad peoples living in the north, the Kirghiz and the Kazakhs (in tsarist Russia known as Kara-Kirghiz and Kirghiz respectively) had in the sixteenth century generally kept their hold on Semirech'ye but had not, either then or in the seventeenth century, consolidated into any settled political order. Since 1533 the Kazakhs had been under increasing pressure from the Oirats, who were advancing south-westwards. Around 1570 the Oirats ruled the area between the Ili valley and upper Yenisei. Time and time again they put the Kazakhs in a desperate situation. It was understandable that the unrest among the northern nomads also made itself felt between the Oxus (Amu Darya) and the Jaxartes (Syr Darya) and to a certain extent influenced the dismembering of this region into individual states which occurred around 1600.

According to one hypothesis, the Kirghiz pushed forward from the Yenisei in the sixteenth century, occupied the northern part of what is now the Soviet Republic of Kirghizia and were able to defend it against the Kazakhs and the inhabitants of Mughulistān. In 1586—possibly once more under pressure from the Oirats—they tried to invade the Tarim basin and to advance towards Farghānā. The Kara-Kalpaks first appear under that name in the sixteenth century. Around 1590 they were living on the lower Jaxartes. Prior to this they had evidently shared a nomadic life with the Nogais. By warding off the northern nomads the Central Asian khanates protected the Persian plateau, and by standing their ground they also safeguarded the traditional social organization of their own countries. This assigned the leading position to the ruling family but did not allow it to assert complete autocracy. The reason was that the leading clans and their *biys* (*begs*, beys) supplied the officers for the troops—who were almost always numerous—and consequently their influence, as well as that of the religious hierarchy, could hardly ever be completely eliminated. An energetic and autocratically inclined ruler had to take both factors into account. The fall of many a ruler was brought about by an attempt to eliminate one or the other of them.

Until the Russian conquest, the structure of this aristocracy of tribal princes and religious leaders was patriarchal. The peasants were personally free—there were also freedmen among them—and could rely on the landowners for aid in times of famine or in other distress. In such cases they received cattle, which they only had to restore to the donors if the latter were themselves in distress. If they were not in a position to do so, they might become slaves by reason of their indebtedness; but even then, although bound to the soil, they were not completely without rights. Road-building, as well as the constant and careful maintenance of irrigation and the construction of new canals, forced at least all the settled inhabitants to work in close co-operation under the supervision of the *mīrāb* or *ak-sakal* ('whitebeard'), to enter into agreements for the apportionment of water, and to share the financial burdens of irrigation-works. When the shortage of land was aggravated by an increase in the population, state-land or the private property of the ruler was made available to enlarge the private property of the landowners and also the small farmers. Further, the founding of *waqfs* offered security against confiscation by the state, and at the same time the possibility of stabilizing conditions of tenure and assuring permanent provision for their administrators.

The land-tax (at that time called *māl vajihāt,* as in Safavid Persia) levied on farmland was widely paid in kind, though payment in money became increasingly frequent; for this there was a legally fixed rate of ten per cent, but often considerably higher rates (up to about twenty per cent) were deducted. No further details are known. Besides the land-tax there were also a number of other taxes, some of them inherited from older times, the nature of which is not always known, as well as turnover and property taxes on trade, commercial goods and cattle (*zakāt*)—officially two and a half per cent, but often more. In addition taxes were levied on caravan traffic and horticultural establishments. At irregular intervals the khan claimed special contributions for himself or for the needs of the army.

The collecting of taxes was often done by means of tax-farms; this always meant additional contributions by those concerned. The tax-gatherer usually required a sheep as his own bonus, and demanded certain 'presents' for the ruler. Besides these taxes there was the performance of *corvées*, for example in the constructions of roads and canals. There was also conscription for military service, which took a heavy toll of human lives in the frequent wars of the khanates among themselves, or against the nomads and Persia, and kept many country lads away from the soil for lengthy periods.

Great quantities of land accumulated not only in the hands of the dynasty but also in those of the *biys* (among the northern Kirghiz also called *manap*), of influential individuals and of the religious classes, together with the *medreses* and the Ṣūfī convents. Their property might also consist of craft-establishments, caravanserai stud-farms or other profitable enterprises. The mutual interest in safeguarding landed property was one of the reasons for the generally very close co-operation between these two leading groups of the population. The amount of ploughed and grazing land owned by them was not infrequently increased by the ruler through assignments (*soyurghāl, tiyūl*) granted to influential families, or by the creation of new *waqfs*. Ground thus acquired could be sold, in practice even if not in theory, especially when it was free from taxes.

The cultivation of such extensive estates was effected by using tenant-farmers (who had to hand over up to half the harvest) and also slaves, i.e. prisoners taken in the khanates' frequent battles with one another and with their neighbours. A slave-market existed in Bukhārā and was usually well supplied. In the nineteenth century the question of redeeming or liberating slaves frequently played a part in negotiations between the khanates and Persia or Russia. Persia, which was politically weak, was at that time usually refused any request for their liberation, simply because the slaves were indispensable for agriculture.

Besides agriculture and cattle-breeding as the nomads' main sources of income, industry and commerce were the economic backbone of the Central Asian states. Industry was carried on chiefly in the fields of lustre craftsmanship, miniature painting (in the style of Bihzād), silk production and metal-working. Gold for this purpose came largely from Persia and Russia; silver came from China by way of Farghānā. Manufacture of utility articles (such as pottery and the casting of cannon) was, however, still on a very primitive level. On the whole the craftsman's skill was steadily declining; remarkable nineteenth-century lustre decorations on mosques and *medreses* are found only in Khīva. It was only in the art of carpet-making that the ancient skill—even though subjected to tasteless variations—endured beyond the nineteenth century and the Russian annexation. In this field the Özbeg workshops have kept a leading position beside those of Persia, Afghanistan and Turkey, and they too have had a decisive influence on European and American taste. On the technological side there was the system of irrigation that has been regarded as a model and has become familiar, at any rate throughout the Soviet Union, under the name of the 'Farghānā method'.

Central Asian trade with its old far-reaching connexions was largely in the hands of the Sarts in Bukhārā and Samarqand: these were linguistically turkicized merchants, mostly of Persian descent, though some part of them were of Soghdian origin. Merv and Tashkent (the latter increasingly from 1790 onwards) were also important as great trading cities. The exchange of goods continued in considerable volume during the eleventh/seventeenth and twelfth/eighteenth centuries, and included traffic with Russia. It was conducted from Kazan by way of the intermediate stations of Ufa and Bashkiria as before, and later also from Orenburg and Astrakhān with Mangıshlak as an intermediate station. Other countries available to Transoxania for trade, by way of Farghānā, were the Tarim basin, Persia, and to a limited extent India. Russian merchants had as yet no direct access to India, although a Russian envoy was received by the Awrangzēb in 1696.

The Central Asian khanates thus supplied the northern steppes and also Russia with the products of their native crafts and their weaving industry. In exchange for cottons and silks, Persian lambskins, carpets and occasionally also precious stones, Central Asia (and thereby also the more southerly countries) received cloth, satin, furs, hides, silver (also from China), falcons and wooden utility goods (pins, nails, dishes and also clubs). In addition it received metal goods, axes and firearms; these were intended for the court and often came as part of an exchange of presents. It has been suggested that the renewed minting of gold coins, for the first time since the Mongol period, may have been due to the importation of gold from Europe by way of Orenburg. The Tarim basin, and in transit also China and India, supplied mainly tea, porcelain goods and silver. However, the discovery of the sea-route to East Asia rendered the Silk Road increasingly superfluous, so that the volume of trade was not significantly greater than in the Middle Ages and in any case did not share in the universal upswing of this period.

BUKHĀRĀ

In Bukhārā, the heartland of its dominion, the Shaybanid dynasty did not perish completely; it continued at any rate in the female line. In 1007/1599 Bāqī Muḥammad, son of a Shaybanid princess (a sister of ʿAbd Allāh II) and a Prince Jān from the dynasty of Astrakhān, succeeded in taking possession of his maternal grandfather's heritage in Transoxania. However, in the process parts of it—especially Tashkent and the town of Turkistān (Yası)—were lost to the Kazakhs, and thereby remained shut off from Islamic urban civilization for a considerable period. After the death of ʿAbd Allāh II in 1006/1598 Khurāsān finally came back to the Safavids. The members of the dynasty founded by Bāqī Muḥammad were called Janids after his father, or else Ashtarkhanids (from the Tatar name for Astrakhān) after their place of origin. For a long time this dynasty possessed the Balkh area south of the Oxus, and the heir to the throne (rarely the khan himself) resided there. Renewed extension of Bukharan power in a north-westerly direction had only temporary success, countered as it was by the Kazakhs thrusting in to the south. In the course of this struggle Khān Imām Qulī (1020–53/1611–43) advanced as far as the mouth of the Jaxartes and for a time occupied Tashkent, where he caused a gruesome massacre. After the death of his energetic second successor ʿAbd al-ʿAzīz (1055–91/1645–80) a period of general disintegration set in, beginning with an insurrection in the Zarafshān valley. Around 1121/1710 the Farghānā valley broke away from Bukharan domination and formed the state of Khokand. The importance of Bukhārā and its dynasty for the cultivation of Sunnī orthodoxy, elegant literature and the writing of history has already been indicated. Many of the details of this period, especially with regard to political events, have not yet been investigated. The constant struggle between the khans (for whose reigns we sometimes have no dates) and the influential Özbeg clans in the country ruled out any far-reaching external political ventures and led to a weakening of the central authority. The chiefs of the noble clans were becoming more and more independent—a development that calls to mind the increasing importance of the *dere-beyis* in Anatolia at the end of the eighteenth and the beginning of the nineteenth century. Nevertheless, and in spite of a deterioration of the coinage in 1709, agriculture (aided by new irrigation works) and trade developed favourably; Bukhārā became the most important entrepôt for foodstuffs in all Central Asia.

Bukharan merchants owned establishments in the Tarim basin and far over towards Siberia; there they worked hand in hand with Tatar merchants.

The establishment of an extremely powerful régime in Persia by the Sunnī Nādir Shāh caused the Janid ruler, Abu'l-Fayż (1123–60/1711–47), to lose the area around Balkh. The many wars, internal disturbances and famines of this period led to a new migration to Farghānā. After these troubles the Janids were increasingly under the influence of a dynasty of major-domos (*ataliks*), the Mangits. The Mangit dynasty superseded the Janids with Murād Ma'ṣūm Shāh (1199–1215/1785–1800), who married a princess from the former line. Its first representative, Muḥammad Raḥīm Bey (d. 1171/1758), had styled himself khan in 1167/1753, whereas later members of his house bore the title of *emīr*. The social structure of the country and the distribution of land were preserved under the new dynasty. The influence of the religious classes increased rather than diminished; pupils streamed into the *medreses* from far and wide.

However, fraternal wars with the other khanates continued. Khān Ḥaydar (1800–26), who murdered many of his relatives at the beginning of his reign, and by these barbarous means prevented internal feuds, was able to ward off an attack from Khīva in 1804, and afterwards fought a long and obstinate battle against the khanate of Khokand. He then found himself in a really critical situation when an insurrection of the Özbeg Kitay-Kipchaks between Samarqand and Bukhārā, brought about by the weight of taxation and forced enlistment, came on top of an advance by the Khīva troops up to the very gates of Bukhārā in 1821. This insurrection went on until 1825 and was put down after complicated fighting. A second attempted insurrection, and a rising in Samarqand itself in the following year, were also unsuccessful.

Ḥaydar had died in the meantime. He had squandered the state treasure, not only in his military ventures but also in great expenditure on the harem. His successor, Naṣr Allāh (1826–60), made his way to power by murder, as Ḥaydar had done before him; he is described by contemporary travellers as a cruel tyrant, aided and abetted by accomplices of a similar kind and mostly of obscure origin. He strengthened the army and developed the artillery; he waged wars against his neighbours, including Khokand, against which he made various thrusts from 1839 onwards without any ultimate success. From 1842 to 1846 he was at war with Khīva. He fought the town of Shahr-i Sabz throughout his life;

it was conquered only in the year of his death. The constant battles exhausted the country's strength. Various parts of it—not only Shahr-i Sabz, but also what is now Afghan Turkistān, and also Balkh (which belonged to Bukhārā from 1826 onwards)—were practically independent of the central government. Merv passed temporarily into Afghan hands, and in 1849 Afghanistan finally took over Balkh. Afghanistan now asserted itself with increasing vigour as a middle power and caused the Central Asian khanates to sink more and more into the background.

The British and the Russians were watching this kingdom; they now also turned their attention more and more to the Central Asian khanates, and sent their representatives to the court of the ruler of Bukhārā. Naṣr Allāh's son and successor, Muẓaffar al-Dīn (1860–85), however, did not allow the by no means disinterested attitude of his powerful neighbours to prevent him from continuing the internecine wars against the other rulers. He fought Khokand until 1866, made an abortive attack on Tashkent in 1865 and, while all this was going on, soon lost Shahr-i Sabz again.

From the middle of the nineteenth century the Russian empire, though not actually an immediate neighbour of the khanate of Bukhārā, was none the less nearly adjacent to it on the north. Travellers at the beginning of the nineteenth century estimated the population of the khanate at two and a half to three millions, one half of them being farmers and the other half cattle-breeders; the town of Bukhārā had about 70,000 inhabitants (three-quarters of them Persian-speaking) and Samarqand had about 30,000. The khanate extended to Afghan Turkistān, Ḥiṣār (in what is now Tājīkistān) as far as the western entry of the Farghānā basin—where there was repeated fighting with Khokand for possession of Ura-Tübe and even Khojand (Khojent)—and finally as far as the town of Turkistān. It lost Merv to Khīva around 1825.

Bukhārā, exposed to progressive Russian advances from the north and repeatedly defeated, had to recognize a Russian protectorate in July 1868 and to relinquish a large part of its territory, including Samarqand, which had already been occupied by General K. P. Kaufman (von Kauffmann) on 14 March 1868. The *emīr* was, however, able, with Russian support, to get some compensation in the south of his country. The Russian domination allowed the country to retain its internal administration and its religious life; it was deprived of its freedom of action only in matters of foreign policy.

KHOKAND

During the many struggles and disorders of the closing years of the seventeenth century the region around Khokand, with the Farghānā basin as its heartland, had already become increasingly independent of Bukhārā. The basin of the middle Jaxartes was protected by mountains: it was therefore less affected by the Jungars than the other territories in the north and west, and it became a place of refuge for the hard-pressed. Many of these brought a wealth of experience with them, and the racial composition of Farghānā was fundamentally altered by this immigration. As early as the ninth/fifteenth century Turks and Sarts (i.e. Persians, Tājīks) had shared the region in such a manner that the latter were settled in the area around Margelan and Sokha and the former mainly in Andijān. Özbegs appeared at the beginning of the sixteenth century, and Kirghiz at its end. During the eighteenth century these races slowly but steadily took over the slopes of the Alai range and subsequently the mountain chains situated in the east and north-east of the country. Finally the Kipchaks had gained importance; linguistically they belonged to the Özbegs, but their social structure was more closely related to that of the Kirghiz. In addition to these fragments of various races, the eighteenth century also saw the arrival of Sarts from Samarqand and Bukhārā, Özbegs from the areas that had suffered from the Jungars, and also parts of the Kara-Kalpaks and other Turkish tribes. Eventually Turkish and 'Arab' fugitives moved in from the Tarim basin, when this was conquered by the Chinese after 1759.

It was apparent that most of these immigrants had no ties with the khanate of Bukhārā, and they accepted without demur the political severance of the Farghānā valley under Shāh-Rukh (d. 1135/1722–3), a descendant of Abu'l-Khayr the Shaybanid. The dynasty that had thus come to power proved itself energetic, encouraged the extension of the towns, supported agriculture (especially the breeding of silkworms) by means of improvement and irrigation, and kept an eye on the ever-important transit trade, especially with eastern Turkistān. However, even though the influence of the Khōja families was gradually diminished, the power of the ruling house was for a long time severely restricted by the smallness of the state. After the subjection of eastern Turkistān by China in 1759, Khokand, shaken by various internal disorders, had to recognize Chinese suzerainty—at any rate nominally. Besides Khokand, there were also several other small states. In these there was clear evidence of the fact that the various elements of the Farghānā valley population had as yet by no means fused with one another. It was only in the nineteenth century that a gradual *rapprochement* occurred, even between Özbegs and Tājīks. However, other tribes like the nomad Kipchaks preserved their organization during the nineteenth century—thus making it certain that they would have important influence—and avoided any contact with the Özbegs, although these were linguistically closely related to them. Khojand and the mountain valleys south-west of Khokand remained in the hands of the Persians, inhabited mainly by Tājīk highlanders.

The political unification of the Farghānā valley under the khan of Khokand was thus an achievement of the nineteenth century. It began after 'Ālim Khān (1799–1809; according to Nalivkin, 1808–16) had gained the victory over several antagonists. By supporting Ura-Tübe and Jizak (at the south-west end of the Farghānā valley) against Bukhārā, he started the state's rise to power, and also prepared the way for the gradual decline of Bukhārā. In contrast to Khokand, and also to Khīva, the khanate of Bukhārā almost always suffered losses of territory in the nineteenth century.

The *biys* of Khokand, however, watched the rise of their khan with a certain amount of dissatisfaction. They were indeed well aware that an increase in his power would lessen their own influence. Hence they repeatedly refused to co-operate in the ruler's military ventures, and he was forced to recruit a new body of troops consisting of Tājīks. When he had succeeded in doing this, the chiefs of the individual clans were in a less important position, and did not need the same consideration as before. Thus 'Ālim Khān could now set out to seek further conquests, in the first place to the north, where in 1808 Tashkent with some 70,000 inhabitants fell into his hands; it was an important centre for trading traffic, especially in the direction of Orenburg. Hitherto the town had been under the *de facto* control of a Khōja aristocracy, but nominally it had belonged to Bukhārā. The Kazakhs of this area wanted to avoid acknowledging a superior authority and attempted an insurrection, but 'Ālim Khān was able to suppress it in the bitter winter of 1808–9. However, he was murdered in 1809 (or 1816); according to the historians 'in consequence of his cruelty and tyranny', but perhaps in reality because the Özbegs were jealous of his Tājīk army.

His brother and successor 'Umar (1809 [or 1816]–1822), who assumed the title of *amīr al-mu'minīn* ('commander of the faithful', the ancient title of the caliphs) is, however, highly praised by the historians. He held fast to traditional forces, the religious classes and the leaders of the dominant clans, and at the same time encouraged literature—which, however, could be nothing more than court poetry. The khan himself wrote some poetic works.

Renewed battles for Ura-Tübe and Jizak were indecisive, in spite of support from Shahr-i Sabz, and Bukhārā took possession of Samarqand itself; meanwhile, in the spring of 1814, there was the successful capture of the town of Turkistān and its environs, which had nominally belonged to Bukhārā but in reality had been independent under a Kazakh sultan. Now the Kazakh chieftains as far away as Semirech'ye also subjected themselves to the khan of Khokand. He allowed them to retain internal self-government under his supremacy, but from 1817 onwards sought to buttress his somewhat insecure position by establishing a number of strongholds. Around them there soon arose market settlements with mosques and *medreses*. From these bases it was possible in 1821 to suppress an insurrection by the Kazakhs to the north of Tashkent.

'Umar's son and successor, Muḥammad 'Alī (in shortened form, Madalī) inherited the throne in 1822 at the age of twelve; in 1831 he added to his father's conquests the southern highlands, where the Tājīk population lived in patriarchal conditions as mountain-shepherds or gold-washers; the menfolk had often gone down into the Farghānā valley in the summer as seasonal workers. A number of native Tājīk princes were allowed to retain their positions. The growing tyranny of the ruler, who was noticeably devoting himself more and more to wine and the harem, and dissipating the strength of his country in fruitless attacks on the practically independent frontier fortresses of Jizak and Ura-Tübe, had the effect that in 1839 the population led by the '*ulemā*' called upon the Bukharans for aid. They took Khojand and forced Madalī to acknowledge their supremacy. In a second advance they took Khokand itself in April 1842, and the much-hated khan was torn to pieces.

In the next year the Bukharan occupation troops were successfully expelled with the help of Kirghiz and Kazakhs, and both Khojand and Tashkent were retaken. However, Khokand did not regain internal peace, for now nomad elements—not only the Kirghiz but also especially the Kipchaks—got the upper hand over the war-weakened noble families. They deposed the new khan (who came from the old dynasty) and in 1845 transferred the actual control of Khokand to their own leader, Muslimān Qul. In consequence the arable land—in any case barely adequate—was transformed into pastures that were common property of the nomad tribes. Farmers were required to pay for irrigation, and the nomads forced the natives to give up local girls as wives for members of the tribe without the customary payment of bride-money for them. All this, together with another fruitless attack on Ura-Tübe, led in October 1851 to the expulsion of the nomads, the removal of their leader and the distribution of their pasture lands among the settled inhabitants. But Khān Khudāyār, who had only just gained effective power, was unable to hold out against his brother, Mallā Beg, and was deposed by him in 1858. Consequently the Kipchaks were again predominant, and former pasture-lands were returned to them; this caused renewed and violent quarrels between the settled inhabitants and the nomads. All this happened during the approach of the Russians, who took Ak-Mesjid in 1853, and turned it into the fortress of Perovsk (named after the victorious general), and soon also had control of Tokmak and, for a time, of Pishpek.

There had been various disorders in recent years which it had been possible to suppress with the aid of the fortresses established in the large towns. The struggle with Bukhārā for Ura-Tübe had at any rate been indecisive. However, when Mallā Beg called his army together in the spring of 1862 for a campaign against the Russians (with infantry, cavalry and artillery he had some 40,000 men), his troops refused obedience, and in March of that year he met a violent death in his own capital.

That was the end. In the same year, and again in 1865, the Bukharans occupied Khokand; they forced the ceding of Tashkent, which was, however, conquered in June 1865 by the Russians under General Chernyayev after two days of sanguinary street-fighting. In 1866 Khān Sayyid Sulṭān lost the stronghold of Khojand, and thereby found himself restricted to the Farghānā basin; however, by the treaty of 1868 the Russians allowed the country to retain its independence. It was only in 1875, when Khān Khudāyār (who had returned to the throne in 1871) was driven out by an insurrection, that the Russians intervened, and forced his son, Nāṣir al-Dīn, to renounce his sovereignty. Unlike Khīva and Bukhārā, the country was now directly incorporated into the Russian empire. Farghānā had already made a great deal of economic progress in its last years of independence. Its irrigation system, carefully organized for hundreds of years, was expanded in the nineteenth century by the construction of a series of new canals. Allocation of water was under state control; among the nomads it was administered by the elders of the tribes. A fixed sum had to be paid for the provision of water. This certainly bore heavily on some people, and meant that others got no water at all, or at best only an irregular supply; but it was the only way of securing the funds needed to maintain and reconstruct the canals, in so far as the inhabitants themselves were not personally called upon to do the work. As long as the course of development was normal—that is, before the disasters that set in from 1842 onwards—the nomads tended to become sedentaries. Arable land increased, though not to an adequate extent. In consequence of the dense population of the Farghānā basin and the relatively large size of the towns (Khokand had about 8,000 houses, with 360 mosques and twelve *medreses* and also caravanserais and bath-houses), market-gardening took on great importance. Moreover, as long as the well-established administration continued to function on a basis of patriarchal conditions, assuring a leading position for the religious classes as well as the heads of the clans, the pre-conditions for favourable economic developments existed.

KHĪVA

As we have seen already, the area south of the Aral Sea, the khanate of Khīva, had in the long run been able to escape incorporation into the Shaybanid state; it was therefore not directly and adversely affected by the collapse of that state in 1006–7/1598–9, but rather freed from the burden of pressure upon it. Khīva was now powerful enough to ward off a whole series of Kazakh attacks on it between 1022/1613 and 1042/1632, moreover at a time when the capital was transferred from Urgench to Khīva because of the drying up of the arm of the Oxus on which Urgench lay (*c.* 1024/1615). Renewed Kazakh attacks in 1058/1648 and 1063/1652–3 were repelled by Abu'l-Ghāzī Bahādur Khān (1054–74/1644–63), a prince who deserves mention for his informative *Shajarat al-Atrāk,* written in Chaghatay Turkish. The work is one of the most important sources for the history of his own khanate. In 1073/1662 he succeeded in advancing into the vicinity of Bukhārā. His son and successor Anusha (1074–99/1663–87) was also able to keep his neighbours at bay and, in command of Özbeg and Turcoman forces, to do them considerable damage. Khurāsān, without any reliable protector after the death of Shāh 'Abbās the Great, also had to suffer much from him.

Subsequently Khīva never rose to anything more than local importance. From the end of the eleventh/seventeenth century the khans—there were nine of them in the years between 1687 and 1716—became ever more powerless. Alongside them the Kungrat family gained steadily increasing influence, and was able to save the country from direct intervention by giving nominal recognition to Nādir Shāh between 1153/1740 and 1160/1747. An expedition against the country sent by Peter the Great had failed to reach its goal because of the severity of the climate and severe casualties. Around 1184/1770 even the Turcoman nomads could not penetrate into the country. The Kungrat prince, Muḥammad Amīn (d. 1204/1790) was, as *inak* ('captain of the army'), the virtual head of the state, but the family did not assume the title of khan until 1804.

In cultural matters Khīva was far inferior to Bukhārā. The many defensive wars against the nomads had raised the military class to a much more important role than that of the scholars and civil administrators. The servicing of the canals was neglected, and at that time a great deal of former arable land reverted to steppe.

The shortage of land may therefore have been one of the reasons for the expansionist policy pursued by Khīva from the beginning of the nineteenth century onwards. Until then the khanate had included only a small area in the delta at the mouth of the Oxus. On the real estuary to the north, the Aral Sea area with its capital of Kungrad and a predominantly Kara-Kalpak farming and fishing population, had been able to preserve its independence ever since the seventeenth century. It was not incorporated into Khīva until 1811; Bukhārā had then refused to give it help.

Even in the khanate of Khīva, the basic population consisted of Özbegs together with the so-called Sarts, the latter being descendants of the old Khwarazmians who had been gradually turkicized, probably over a long period from the thirteenth or fourteenth century. These were mainly merchants living in the towns; they were especially numerous in the district of Hazārasp on the lower Oxus. Parts of the neighbouring Kazakh population, and especially the Turcoman nomads, had close relations with Khīva, and were tied to it by the mutual exchange of their products; this trading had the effect that the Turcomans increasingly became cultivators instead of cattle-breeders. The influence of Turcoman *mullās* trained in Khīva made itself felt among them, especially within the leading Yomut tribe.

These factors certainly made it easier for Khān Muḥammad Raḥīm of Khīva to find numerous helpers when, after his accession to the throne in 1806, he undertook a systematic extension of his sphere of influence. He took over Aral in 1811 and several Kara-Kalpak tribes, then from 1812 onwards the area settled by Kazakhs up to the mouth of the Jaxartes, then the Tekke Turcomans up to the borders of Khurāsān, and finally he took Merv in 1822 in the course of a war with Bukhārā. New Merv was founded in the neighbourhood of Merv in 1824. The frequent campaigns strengthened the influence of the military class; the khan was compelled to reward the leaders of these campaigns—and also his collaborators in general, among them many religious dignitaries—with large tracts of land that he had taken from various noble clans. This brought about the formation of a number of estates of considerable size, whereas the normal agricultural structure of Khīva was characterized by fairly small holdings of land. Muḥammad Raḥīm died in 1825: for some time thereafter the internal situation in the khanate was tense. The Kara-Kalpaks rebelled in 1827 and in 1855–6; so also did the Kazakhs in 1842, the inhabitants of Merv in 1827, 1842 and 1854, and Turcomans and Kara-Kalpaks engaged in a stubborn struggle led by Sayyid Muḥammad in 1856–64. Even though it was possible in the end to subdue all these rebellions, which were largely provoked by the pressure of taxation, charges on landed property (for the construction of canals) and oppressive recruitment for military service, none the less they noticeably impaired the internal strength of the small state. In 1819 its population was estimated at about 300,000 persons; the capital had at that time about 3,000 houses, and in 1842 it was said to have 4,000 inhabitants.

It has been alleged that the failure of these rebellions was due not only to internal discords among the insurgents but also to the absence of any aid from the outside on the part of Persia, Afghanistan or Bukhārā. After the middle of the nineteenth century this situation gradually changed. When battles raged in the Kungrad area in 1858–9 the Russians intervened; their attitude towards Khīva had stiffened considerably in the preceding years. Mangishlak fell into their hands in 1834, and by 1842 they had established the stronghold of Raimsk (presumably so named after Raḥīm; also called Aral'sk) on the lower Jaxartes. From 1869 onwards Krasnovodsk on the eastern coast of the Caspian gained ever-increasing importance. Russian slaves were handed back, in spite of the failure of an expedition sent by the tsar in

1839–40, while similar negotiations with Persia in 1851 were deliberately allowed to come to nothing. British diplomatic missions failed to establish any close relations with the khanate.

In spite of this threatening situation the petty Central Asian states failed to unite in any common defence against the Russians. Khīva was still repeatedly at war with Khokand until 1873; also, quarrels with the Yomut Turcomans never ceased throughout this period. Meanwhile, Bukhārā came under the sway of Russia in 1868; the tsar's position in the east and the north *vis-à-vis* Khīva (which was enfeebled by wars, rebellions and frequent changes of ruler) became ever more menacing. It was no surprise that the khanate was only able to use delaying tactics against a Russian attack thrusting in simultaneously from the west, north-west and east, and consequently, after a brief period of fighting, had to surrender to General K. P. Kaufman on 2 June 1873. The dynasty indeed retained its sovereignty, but the khan was not allowed to have dealings with other states, or even with other khanates, and was obliged to have Russian assent to any treaties he made.

In the same year the Turcoman hinterland of Krasnovodsk came under Russian dominion as far as the borders of Khīva and over to the river Atrek. As was to be expected, the nomadic Tekke Turcomans further eastwards, isolated and without support from Persia, were also unable to hold out for any length of time against the Russians who were attacking them from 1879 onwards. After a glorious defence lasting for forty days, their main fortress, Gök-Tepe, fell into the hands of General Skobelev on 24 February (new style) 1881.

The khanate of Khīva was now encircled in every direction by Russian territory, which for all practical purposes included the khanate of Bukhārā. Even though the Kungrat dynasty remained formally on the throne until 1920, the last remnants of independent political power had been taken away from Khīva in 1873. Finally, on 31 January 1884 the inhabitants of the northern Murghāb valley as far as Merv found themselves obliged to submit to the Russians. After an Afghan intervention on the river Khushk in 1895, the areas of Tash-Köprü and Panjdeh (both lying further to the south) came under Russian sovereignty. With this the Russians arrived at the frontier that has remained definitive down to the present day.

APPENDIX
THE GOLDEN HORDE AND ITS SUCCESSORS

Jochi (*c.* 1176–1227), the eldest son of Chingiz Khān, had been granted the most westerly part of the area dominated by the Mongols as his appanage. At his death this area was divided among his sons. The eldest, Orda, took the most easterly part (including most of what is now Kazakhstān and parts of western Siberia) where his subject clans became known as the 'White', or, occasionally, the 'Blue Horde'. Another son, Shiban, arabicized as Shaybān, held a fief to the north of this area, east and south-east of the Urals, around the headwaters of the Irtysh, Ishim and Tobol rivers, from which later emerged the khanate of Sibir. But in the immediate future the most important inheritance was that of the second son, Batu (d. 1255), who was given the most westerly part of Jochi's appanage, in the region of the Emba and Ural rivers. Batu thus became the logical leader of the new western campaign, which was launched in 1236, and which brought under Mongol control the steppe-land to the north of the Black Sea, established Mongol dominion over the Slavic states to the north, ravaged eastern Europe and led to the formation of the political unit known to the Russians, and so to Europe, as the Golden Horde.

Batu's campaign spread fear and horror throughout Europe. The rapidity of the movements of the Mongol troops and their strange appearance contributed to the enduring legend that they represented the imposition of a novel and alien rule. In fact this is a distortion of the truth. The steppes to the north of the Black Sea and their extension into Hungary had, from the earliest times, been under the domination of successive waves of nomadic peoples, most commonly of Turkish origin. Such were the Pechenegs, the Khazars and the Kipchaks (also called Comans or Polovtsians). These Turkish peoples had raided into, and traded with, the surrounding Slavic states. Fundamentally the Mongols were no more than a more powerful and efficient edition of these previous Turkish peoples. Nor, indeed, were they mainly Mongols. The greater part of the clans which constituted Batu's fief were Turks. Although his original army was stiffened by Mongol troops drawn from other fiefs, probably no more than one-third of the 100,000 to 150,000 troops at his disposal were Mongols. Many of these Mongols were later withdrawn and in their place Batu gathered up the Kipchak clans like a snowball as he moved. The Golden Horde developed as a basically Turkish unit with a Mongol aristocracy.

After his withdrawal from eastern Europe in 1241 Batu established his winter headquarters at (Old) Saray, about sixty-five miles north of modern Astrakhān. In summer he moved northwards up the banks of the Volga. Other subject groups of Tatar clans (as they came to be called) moved in parallel in other areas of the steppe. The Golden Horde was in being.

Since the Horde was primarily a dominion over men and not over territory, it is difficult to describe its boundaries with precision. In the east they faded into the territories of the White Horde; in the south-east Khwārazm, on the lower Oxus, an area valuable both for trade and as a recruiting ground for administrators, was the subject of disputes both with the Īl-Khāns and the Chagatays of Central Asia, although usually held by the Horde. In the south the Black Sea and the Caucasus range formed a natural frontier and Derbend usually marked the limit of the power of the Horde. In the west the line of the Carpathians, the Transylvanian Alps and the Balkan mountains demarcated the limits of regular Tatar authority. In the north the boundary followed the geographical division between the steppe zone and the northern forest area. The Russian states of the forest area were outside the Horde but paid tribute to it.

The Russian states provided one of the principal sources of revenue for the Horde. Authority over them was exercised in various ways. In the south-west, around Kiev, the princes were removed and the Horde assumed the administration. More usually the prince was left in charge and controlled by the granting or withholding of patents of authority and by frequent summons to attend the khan in the Horde. Such visits not uncommonly led to the death of the prince. Behind these forms of control lay the ultimate deterrent of a Tatar raid, such as that which destroyed Tver in 1327. But at least while the Horde was strong, during its first hundred years of life, the Russian princes, such as the wily Alexander Nevsky (d. 1263) of Novgorod, and the princes of Moscow, were ready to collaborate. So too was the Russian church, treated with especial favour by the Tatars, and certain groups of merchants, who exploited the new trade-routes which had been opened by the Mongol conquests. After 1360, with the breakdown of the central authority of the Horde, the bonds of Tatar authority rapidly loosened, first in western Russia, where the power of the Lithuanian dukes supplanted that of the Horde, and then in eastern Russia, where the lead was taken by the princes of Moscow.

The mailed fist was always conspicuous in Tatar dealings with their Russian vassals. With their other European vassals, the Genoese, and later the Venetian merchants in the Crimea, it was more frequently the velvet glove. The Russian had to pay or suffer; they could not defect. The Italians, however, would go elsewhere if ill-treated. Their trading establishments, centred on Kaffa, provided the pump which accelerated both the profitable east–west trade which passed through the territories of the Horde, and also the interchange of the products of the Horde with those of western Europe, relations between the great Tatar nobles of the Crimea and the Italian merchants were characterized by a continuous, delicate struggle for the lion's share of these commercial profits, until Tīmūr, insensitive to the nuances of this contest, and seeing only Christians defying Muslims, brutally tore the Italians from the Crimean coast.

The Italian merchants also performed an important function in the foreign relations of the Horde. They were one of the agencies through which a steady supply of Tatar slaves from the Kipchak steppes was sold to the Mamluk rulers of Egypt to become *mamlūks* themselves. This profitable trade was one of the two main reasons for the alliance with Egypt which was an enduring feature of the Horde's external policy. The other reason was the common hostility of both powers to the Īl-Khāns of Persia. The endemic struggle between the two great Mongol powers in the west has never been satisfactorily explained. It has been attributed to the reflexion of struggles for power in Mongolia, and to the earlier conversion of the rulers of the Horde to Islam, although, despite the acceptance of Islam by Berke Khān (655–65/1257–67), Islam was not really established in the Horde until after the accession of Özbeg Khān (712–41/1313–40). Most probably it originated in disputes over authority in Transcaucasia and Āẕarbāyjān. Its effect was to produce continual unprofitable wars, the drain of resources, and injury to trade.

The importance of the part played by trade in the economic life of the Horde has already been indicated. Historians have always stressed the significance of the position of the Horde at the centre of great international trade-routes, linking China, the Baltic and the Mediterranean.

It seems clear that a valuable revenue was derived from this trade, and that it provided some of the impetus towards the growth of urban life. But the glamour of this trade has, perhaps, led to an underestimate of the importance of local trade. The Horde was a great producer of animal products, of immense importance in the medieval world, and a great consumer of grain and manufactured goods. This situation led to the growth of centres of exchange such as Saray, the winter capital of the Horde, which developed industries for processing animal products and for producing metal goods. There is evidence that substantial amounts of capital were employed in these industries and something like an artisan group makes a short-lived appearance. Still, the basis of the economy of the Horde remained nomadic stock-breeding, although around the towns there was market-gardening and, in the Crimea, cash-crops were grown for export.

In its political structure the Horde was not an independent state. It was part of the Mongol empire and its rulers owed homage to the great khan. As late as the reign of Özbeg Khān there is evidence that this was still given. But for all practical purposes the khan of the Horde was an independent ruler from the accession of Berke Khān. The title 'khan' was normally used, although after 710/1310 'sultan' was quite common. At the end of the eighth/fourteenth century, Tokhtamısh, like one previous ruler, actually employed the title '*khaqan*'. The khan was nominally supreme, subject only to the *Yasa* (i.e. the Law of Chingiz Khān) and later the *Sharīʿa*. In practice, however, his power depended upon the extent of his control over the great vassals, known as *emīrs,* both members of the house of Chingiz and chiefs of lower origin but increasing power. Within their own fiefs the great vassals were virtually independent. Some, especially those with access to the wealth of the Crimea, such as Nogay (d. 699/1299), Mamay, and Edigü (d. 822/1419), wielded power which at times overshadowed that of the khan. Although they were usually kept under control by strong rulers like Batu, Berke, Tokhtu (689–712/1290–1312) and Özbeg Khān, yet, after the death of the last, power passed into the hands of the *emīrs,* who manipulated puppet khans for their own ends. The process was temporarily suspended when a new ruler with outside support, Tokhtamısh (d. *c.* 802/1399), ruler of the White Horde, defeated Mamay at the battle of the Kalka in 783/1381. But Tokhtamısh's own conflict with Tīmūr led to the great attacks by the Turks of Central Asia in 792/1390 and 797/1395 which severely injured the economic life of the

Horde and permanently loosened the bonds of political allegiance which held its vassals in check. After the death of Edigü in 822/1419 the Horde rapidly and finally disintegrated.

The collapse of the Horde led to a situation not unlike that which had prevailed before 633/1236. Throughout the steppelands north of the Black and Caspian Seas roamed large numbers of semi-independent Turkish nomads, under their clan chiefs. In certain favoured areas settled agricultural and commercial life continued, and these areas became the centres of political units which formed rallying points for the steppe-dwellers, and which continued to claim the same rights as the Horde. The most important of these were the khanates of Kazan, Astrakhān and the Crimea, all of which emerge in the latter part of the first half of the ninth/fifteenth century.

The khanate of Kazan is traditionally supposed to have been founded by one Ulugh Muḥammad (d. 849/1445–6) in 841/1437, although it seems likely that it may have led an independent existence for some time before that date. It was located on the bend of the middle Volga at the confluence with the Kama, an important grain-producing area, at the junction of the forest and steppe zones, with good communications with surrounding areas. This area had, long before the Mongol invasions, been the centre of the prosperous Bulghar state. The population was Finno-Ugrian, overlaid by Turkish immigrants who formed the military aristocracy. The unassimilated non-Tatar, non-Muslim element in the population was a feature which the Russians were able to exploit in their attempts to control Kazan. This was important because the levying of tribute from Russia, and the organization of raids into the Slavic area, were an important part of the life of the khanate. But the ability of the Kazan khans to enforce their claims on Moscow was limited by the weakness of their own position as they balanced uneasily between the rival claims of their great nobles, the steppe Tatars, the khanates of Astrakhān and the Crimea, Russia and the Ottoman empire, which, from the late ninth/fifteenth century onwards, sought to achieve a predominant influence in the state. However, the khans were still able to launch most destructive attacks on Russian territory, such as that of 927/1521, under Ṣāḥib Giray Khān, who declared himself an Ottoman vassal in 929/1523. Russian influence aimed first at trying to maintain a pro-Russian khan. When this failed, an attempt was made to weaken the khanate by detaching the unassimilated elements. When this too was unsuccessful Tsar Ivan the Terrible decided to annex Kazan. The town fell on 10 Shawwāl 959/2 October 1552, although another five years of bitter struggle was required before the provinces were finally subdued. The importance of Kazan, however, was not ended. Although Russia entirely remodelled the political structure of the khanate, Islam was not attacked and the Tatars of Kazan came to play a very important part in the subsequent relations of Russia with the Muslim peoples to the south.

The khanate of Astrakhān was at the mouth of the Volga. After the break-up of the Horde two organizations emerged in the area of the lower Volga. One, called the Great Horde, which is usually taken to be the rump of the Horde itself, retained some links with Saray and nomadized in the area between the Caspian and the Don. The Great Horde was finally broken up by the Crimean Tatars in about 908/1502, and the allegiance of its clans nominally passed to the second organization, which had grown up around Astrakhān, and is usually supposed to have been founded in 871/1466 by Qāsim, grandson of a ruler of the Golden Horde. Astrakhān had some importance as a commercial centre, and several wealthy merchants settled there. Their wealth, indeed, became the bait which attracted the attention of the neighbouring Nogay and Circassian tribes who frequently interfered in the life of the khanate. Like Kazan, the Astrakhān khanate fought on various sides in the confused political struggles of the ninth/fifteenth century, and supplied mercenary troops at times to the rulers of Poland and Russia. But, as with Kazan, Ottoman influence prevailed in the second quarter of the sixteenth century to help to produce a united Tatar front against Russia. The fall of the Kazan shield, however, found the khanate too weak to stand against Russian influence, which in 962/1554 established a puppet khan before final annexation took place in 964/1556.

The most important of the successor states of the Horde was the Crimean khanate. Its origins are obscure. It seems likely that the Crimea enjoyed a substantial independence from the end of the fourteenth century under the family of Ḥājjī Giray (d. 871/1466) who is usually taken to be the founder. In its early years the khanate seems to have acted in co-operation with the Lithuanian dukes of Poland, but after the Ottoman annexation of Kaffa in 880/1475, which enabled the Ottomans to exercise a stranglehold over the economy of the Crimea, the khans became their vassals. None the less, the internal autonomy of the Crimea, the way in which it made Ottoman policy serve the pursuance of its traditional policies of raiding to the north, and the very influential position of its Giray rulers, warrants regarding the khanate as a separate, if subordinate, state.

At first the capital of the khanate was still in the steppeland outside the Crimea, but at the end of the ninth/fifteenth century it was moved to Baghche-Saray (Simferopol). In the course of the tenth/sixteenth century there developed a tendency for the Tatars to settle in the Crimea, and the khanate entered upon a period of prosperity. Industries were established, usually in Christian hands; a flourishing horticultural industry grew up to supply the expanding towns; and commerce was carried on through Kaffa and other ports. An organized bureaucracy emerged to serve the needs of the state. A degree of sophisticated political, economic and social life was developed which was unknown in any other Tatar state. But this was only in the Crimea itself. Among the Nogays of the northern steppes, over whom the Crimean khans exercised authority, the traditional forms of nomadic life prevailed. The Crimean khans also laid claim to power over the Circassians, the Kabardans and occasionally even the Dāghistānīs of the south-eastern Caucasus, while they possessed appanages within the Ottoman empire in Rumelia.

The khans had little power as khans. Their revenue was slight, and their authority limited not only by the Ottomans, who exercised the right of deposition more frequently in the eleventh/seventeenth and twelfth/eighteenth centuries, but also by the existence of the great Tatar noble families of the Crimea, such as those of the Shīrīns and the Manṣūrs, who ruled their hereditary independent fiefs. The greatest of the Crimean khans drew their strength from their reputations as war-leaders.

For, despite the appearance of settled government in the Crimea, the khanate, like other Tatar successor states, remained a state organized for, and dependent upon, war. The earlier sporadic raids into Polish and Russian territory became massive expeditions such as that of 978/1570 which burned Moscow. The Crimean Tatars also formed an essential part of the Ottoman armies in south-eastern Europe, operating as light cavalry, scouting and ravaging the countryside around the path of the main force. The khans were able, if adequately subsidized, to put a force of 150,000 to 200,000 in the field.

These continual raids into the exposed southern border territories of Russia forced the tsarist government to organize counter-measures. After two centuries of conflict, Russia finally established herself on the Black Sea and at the treaty of Küchük Kaynarja in 1188/1774 forced the Ottoman government to recognize the independence of the Crimea.

When this means of controlling the khanate failed it was annexed by Russia in 1197/1783.

The annexation of the Crimea was accompanied by profound changes. Its economy had already been ruined by the removal of the Christian population. Now, although given certain privileges, the Tatars found themselves unable to accept their new, depressed position. The formerly free Tatar peasantry, newly converted to being Russian state peasants, began to follow the nobility into exile. Possibly as much as one-half of the population emigrated to the Ottoman lands in the years which followed annexation. The Giray khans reappeared in Ottoman service for a time as khans of Bujak (southern Bessarabia). The place of the emigrants was taken by Russian peasants, and the Tatars became a minority. The Nogays were removed, first to the Kuban, and subsequently to the steppes to the north of the Sea of Azov and the east of the Volga, where they were eventually converted from nomadism to settled farming under the enlightened government of the *émigré* Duc de Richelieu.

Two other Tatar states deserve to be mentioned in conclusion, although not actually successor states to the Horde. The khanate of Kasimov was established at Gorodetz on the river Oka in the mid-fifteenth century to guard the southern frontier of the Russian lands, and survived for over two centuries as a Russian puppet Tatar state. The khanate of Sibir grew out of the fiefs of other branches of the Jochid family as an amalgam of Tatar nomads and the Finno-Ugrian peoples of western Siberia. The ruler Kuchum Khān (*c.* 971–1007/1563–98) resisted the famous expedition of the Cossack Yermak in 1579–84 but was ultimately unable to withstand Russian pressure. Russia gradually established full control over the area, which became a springboard for the Russian drive to the Pacific. In more than one sense Russia might be regarded as the last of the successor states of the Horde.

CHAPTER 8

TSARIST RUSSIA AND THE MUSLIMS OF CENTRAL ASIA

THE RUSSIAN ADVANCE INTO THE KAZAKH STEPPES

The Kazakhs originated as tribal groups which broke away from the hegemony of the Shaybanid, Abu'l-Khayr Khān, in about 870/1465–6, and fled to the Chu river in the Semirech'ye region, where they were protected by the khan of Mughulistān, Esen Bogha. After the death of Abu'l-Khayr in 873/1468, their nomadic area spread westwards, and they were joined by other Turkish groups. They wandered along the Chu and Talas rivers during the conquests of Muḥammad Shaybānī Khān (d. 916/1510), and gained control of the region between the Issıq Köl and the Ural river. This vast area was divided into three parts, to provide suitable grounds for three nomadic groups. The nomads of the Yedi-Su (Semirech'ye) region were called the Greater Horde, those between the Irtysh and the Jaxartes the Middle Horde, those further west the Lesser Horde. The Kipchak, Naiman and Kungrat tribes, which subsequently played an important part in the history of Khīva, Bukhārā and Khokand, were all members of the Middle Horde. The Kazakh tribes, who were somewhat superficially islamized, sometimes united under a strong khan, but separated again after his death.

Relations between the Kazakh khans and chiefs and the Russians start soon after Ivan the Terrible occupied Kazan khanate (959/1552) and the banks of the Volga. The cities of Tümen, Tobol'sk, Tara and Tomsk, which the Russians founded after they occupied western Siberia, were places on the route of trade with the Kazakhs. The city of Tobol'sk had a special importance in this respect. The caravans coming from the Kazakh province passed through here. The city of Yayitsk on the Ural river, founded in 1620, became a centre of trade with the Kazakhs, besides being a fortress on the Russian border.

During the reign of Peter the Great, the Russians planned to enter eastern Turkistān by going up the Irtysh river. Peter the Great wanted to take over the 'gold mines' in eastern Turkistān around Yarkand. For this purpose, a relatively large military force under Buchholtz's command

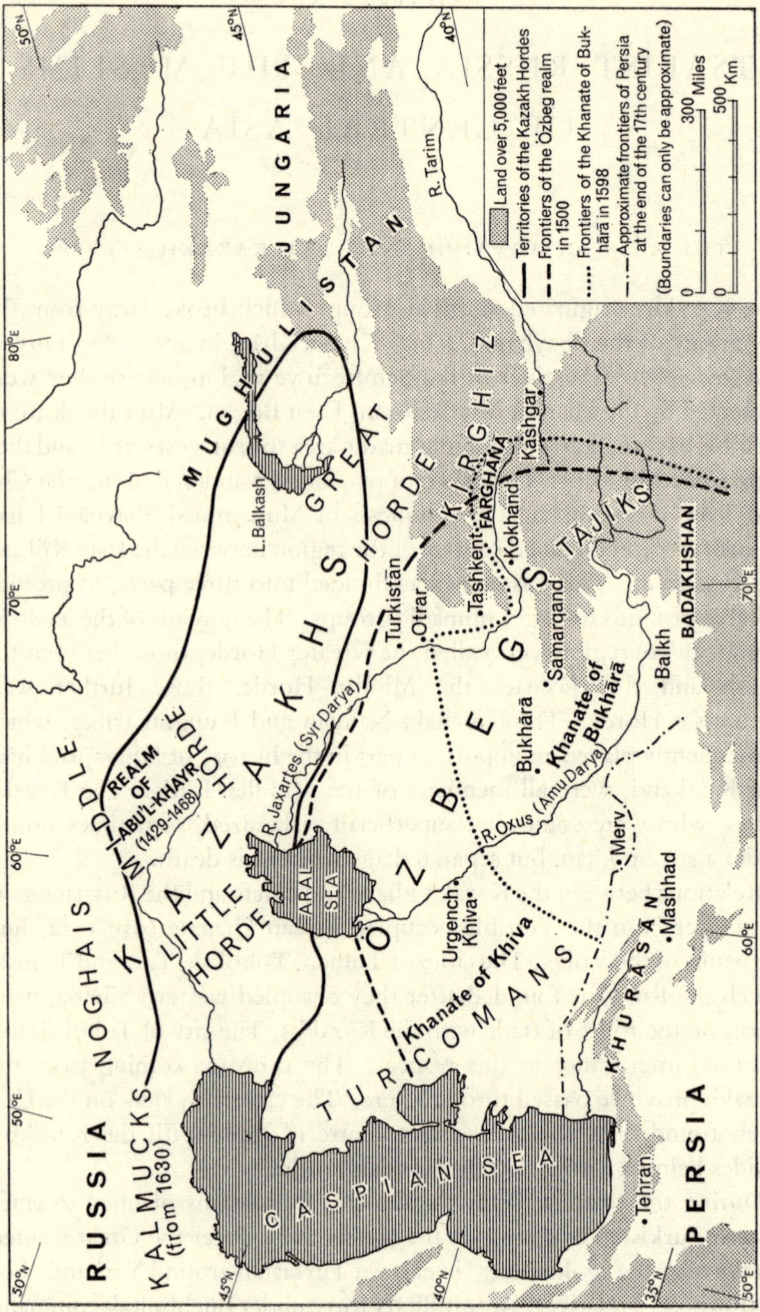

Map 9(*a*). Central Asia: sixteenth to eighteenth century.

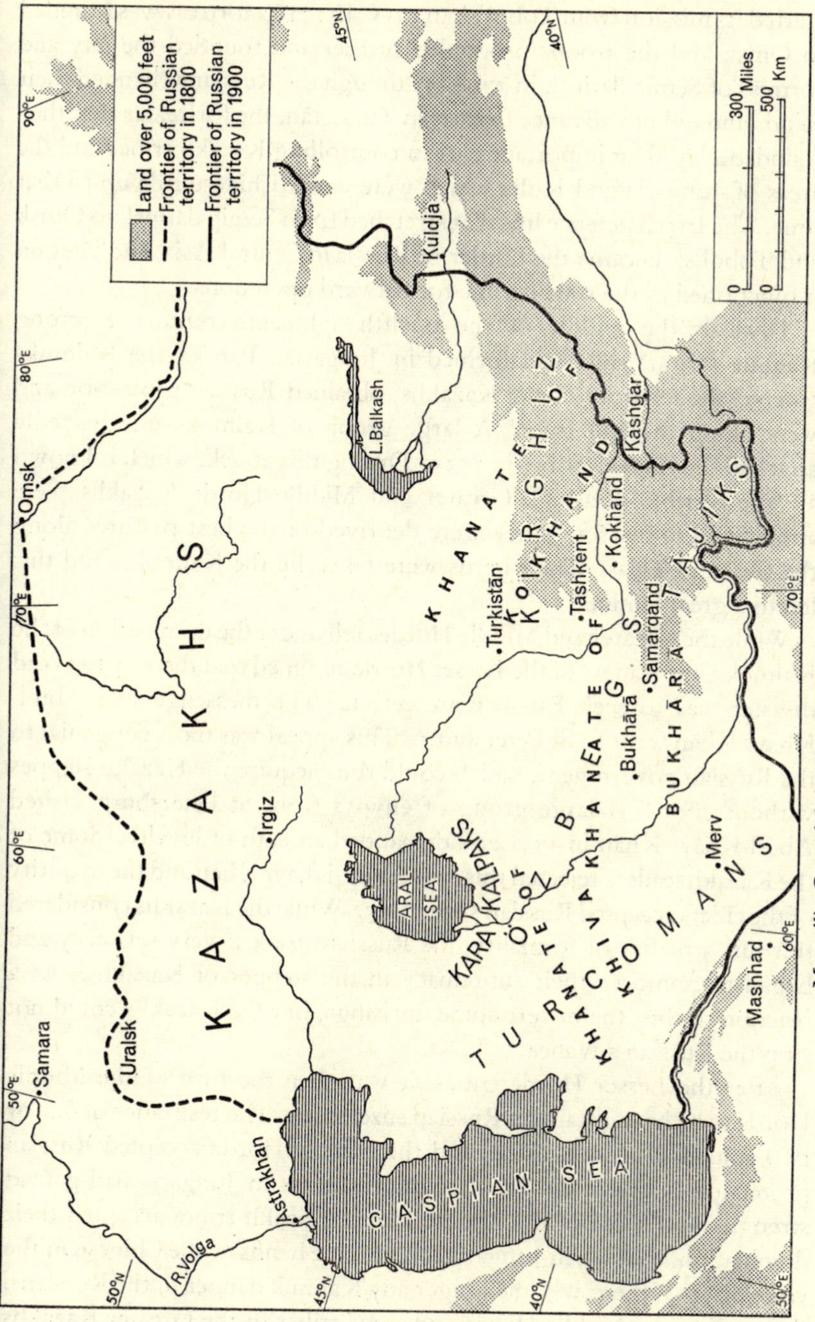

Map 9(*b*). Central Asia: Russian conquests in the nineteenth century.

started its mission from Tobol'sk in 1715. In 1716 a fortress was founded in Omsk and the troops proceeded further and founded the city and fortress of Semipalatinsk in 1718. Although the Russians changed their minds and did not advance to eastern Turkistān, the fortresses that they founded played an important part in controlling Kazakh tribes and the areas of Jungaria and Kulja which were under Chinese rule up to that time. The Irtysh defence line that stretched from Semipalatinsk to Omsk and Tobol'sk became the border of Russia in Central Asia, and later on it functioned as the starting line for forward operations.

Towards the middle of the twelfth/eighteenth century a strong Kalmuk (Oirat) state had formed in Jungaria. Part of the Kalmuks entered the territory of the Kazakhs, obtained Russian protection and went along the Idil river. A large group of Kalmuks unexpectedly attacked the Kazakh tribes in 1723. During this attack, which is known as 'the terrible disaster', Greater and Middle Horde Kazakhs were annihilated in masses. They were deprived of the best pastures along the Chu and Talas. Their herds were taken by the Kalmuks, and this led to a great famine.

While the Greater and Middle Hordes fell under the domination of the Kalmuks, the leaders of the Lesser Horde assumed that the way to avoid disaster was to seek Russian protection. The messengers of Abu'l-Khayr Khān went to St Petersburg. This appeal was most congenial to the Russian government, which could thus acquire the Kazakh steppes without effort. A large group of envoys from St Petersburg visited Abu'l-Khayr Khān in 1731 and demanded an oath of loyalty. Some of the Kazakh leaders rejected this, but Abu'l-Khayr Khān and the majority of the chiefs accepted Russian suzerainty. While the Kazakhs considered this just a matter of formality, the Russians took it very seriously and began to reinforce their supremacy in the steppes of Kazakhs. As a reaction to this, there were some uprisings, but the Kazakhs could not stop the Russian advance.

After the Lesser Horde tribes, it was then the turn of the Middle Horde to be brought under Russian suzerainty. The resistance of one or two sultans was suppressed, and the Middle Horde accepted Russian protection in 1740. By this time the Kalmuks in Jungaria had gained strength, and some of the Middle Horde Kazakh tribes accepted their domination. But when Jungaria fell into the hands of the Chinese in the years 1753–5, there was no longer any Kalmuk danger to the Russians. As a result, the Middle Horde and some tribes of the Greater Kazakhs were brought under Russian rule. From then on, Russian 'protection' over the Kazakhs gradually took the form of oppression.

When Abu'l-Khayr Khān accepted Russian protection, he had assumed that no harm would come to the property of the Kazakhs. But this was not so. The Russian Cossacks living along the Ural river attacked the Lesser Horde Kazakhs and carried away their herds and even the men themselves. Apart from this, the Russian government interfered in the internal affairs of the Lesser Horde. They adopted the policy of appointing heads of tribes who would be loyal to them. But this policy created reaction, and increased the antagonism of the Kazakhs towards the Russians. Indeed, when the Bashkir Turks launched an uprising in 1755 many of the Kazakhs fought with them against the Russians.

A good example of the antagonism towards the Russians is the struggle of Sırım Batır, who belonged to the Lesser Horde. This struggle, which took place between 1774 and 1797, seemed to be directed against the khan of the Horde, but was actually against Russian oppression. Sırım Batır fought for nearly twenty-five years in order to save the Kazakh tribes. He intended to join the Kazakh tribes with Bukhārā, Khīva and the Turcomans in order to make a joint front against the Russians, but it was not possible for the Turkish Islamic groups to reach agreement with each other.

After Sırım Batır's withdrawal from the scene, Russian pressure on the Kazakhs gradually increased. Their khans were no longer elected by the tribal leaders, but appointed by the Russian government. When the khan of the Middle Horde died in 1819, the Russians did not appoint a successor. In 1822 the Russian government abolished the khanate of the Middle Horde by decree. In 1824 the khan of the Lesser Horde was dismissed, and this territory was also attached to Russia. The Middle Horde was divided into three regions and a 'sultan' was appointed to each region by the Russian government.

In this way, by the 1840s the whole of the Kazakh country was taken under Russian rule, and the borders of Russia had reached Turkistān. The Russian defence lines, fortresses and patrol stations controlled a vast area stretching from Semipalatinsk to the Ural river. Suitable conditions for an attack on the khanates of Khīva, Bukhārā and Khokand had been created. However, Russian pressure on the Kazakh tribes sometimes caused reactions, and there were some large uprisings. The most important of these was the one directed by Kine-Sarı in the years

1837–47. But none of these risings was successful. The Russians suppressed them all very easily with their superior forces and modern weapons. It was impossible for the nomadic Kazakhs alone to resist the tsarist forces. Now it was the turn of the khanates of Bukhārā, Khīva and Khokand.

THE RUSSIAN ANNEXATION OF CENTRAL ASIA (TURKISTĀN)

After the fall of the Kazan khanate in 959/1552 it was certain that Russia would expand towards the east and the south until she met resistance. The acquisition of Siberia had been a matter of invasion. As mentioned above, the Kazakh steppes were also easily taken. The rapidly developing industry and capitalism in Russia in the middle of the nineteenth century would certainly have tried to find new fields of activity. The activities developed in the form of imperialism with the purpose of obtaining the cotton of Turkistān and also of reaching as far as India. Therefore Russian expansion was in the direction of Turkistān, and from here on the Russian borders expanded by the end of the nineteenth century all the way to the foothills of the Himalayas without meeting any resistance. In this way, ancient centres of Islamic civilization, Bukhārā, Samarqand and Khīva, the region formerly known as Khwārazm, could not resist the Russian forces from the north, and had to submit.

Diplomatic and commercial relations between Russia and Central Asia developed in the sixteenth and seventeenth centuries. The cotton and silk products of Turkistān and especially Persian lamb were much favoured in Russia for a long time. Western European products entered Bukhārā via Russia, and the products of India and Afghanistan were sent to Russia via Turkistān. There were two main trade-routes that connected Russia and Central Asia at the end of the eighteenth century. The oldest one reached the Caspian Sea via the Volga and then Khīva and Bukhārā via Mangıshlak. The second route made a connexion with Orenburg via Tashkent and the Jaxartes. There was also another route that reached Tashkent via Semipalatinsk and Kızılyar (Petropavlovsk), passing through the Kazakh steppes. Tashkent thus became a commercial centre of increasing importance.

Russian trade with Turkistān developed rapidly at the beginning of the nineteenth century. Between 1801 and 1820 Russian trade with the khanates of Turkistān rose from one million to four million roubles. Within the same period the exports of Turkistān to Russia rose from two million to six million roubles. The increase in trade dominated the development of relations between Russia and the khanates. The most important market for the products of Turkistān was the famous fair of the Russians on the Volga (at the modern Gor'kiy, formerly known as Nizhniy Novgorod). Merchants from all over Turkistān, especially from Bukhārā, came here and brought large amounts of cotton goods and Persian lamb with them. Turkistān cotton was particularly important for the Russians. As the textile industry in Russia developed, the desire of Russian capitalist circles to acquire Turkistān became stronger. However, the Russian government was busy with other problems, and therefore postponed attention to the occupation of Turkistān.

Between the years 1830 and 1840 British trade in Central Asia suddenly developed in competition with the Russians. The Russian government was suspicious of British activities, and began sending commissions to study the situation of the Central Asian khanates. These commissions gathered detailed information about Khīva and especially Bukhārā. Furthermore, they also determined the routes and places which had military significance. The Russians moved towards Central Asia in 1847 by building the fortress of Raimsk (Aral'sk) at the estuary of the Jaxartes.

The appointment of General Perovskiy as the governor of Samara and Orenburg in 1851 was quite significant. He was in favour of immediate military action. Indeed, a year later Russian operations along the Jaxartes to the south started and they founded a patrol station at Ghazālī (Kazalinsk). In 1852, they attacked Ak-Mesjid, a castle built by the Khokand khanate. The commander of the fortress, Ya'qūb Bey (later known as Badevlet Ya'qūb Bey, the ruler of Kashgar) fought fiercely against the Russians, and caused them to suffer large casualties. But it was impossible to oppose the Russian guns, and Ak-Mesjid was occupied in 1853. After this the way to Tashkent was open. It was now obvious that the Russians were determined to occupy Central Asia, and indeed plans for the invasion of Central Asia were discussed and concluded at a meeting attended by Tsar Nicholas I in person.

However, the outbreak of the Crimean War in 1853 deferred the realization of these plans, while the Russian defeat in that war immediately reduced their prestige in Turkistān. Some Ottoman Turkish agents who were sent to Khīva and Bukhārā, made an appeal to the people of Turkistān to unite, and probably also promised military aid, which was discussed by an envoy from Khīva who was in Istanbul for some time. The British also sent agents to Bukhārā and Khīva, and tried unsuccessfully to win over their rulers. As far as is known, neither military equipment nor a military commission came to Khīva or Bukhārā from the Ottomans. Even though the Russians were defeated in the Crimea, nothing happened in Central Asia to weaken their position there.

After the Treaty of Paris (1856) the Russian government took up the problem of Turkistān again. First of all, immediate measures were to be taken to stop British activities in the Central Asian khanates and to develop Russian trade. A commission headed by Colonel Ignat'yev was sent to Khīva and Bukhārā in 1858. Ignat'yev's mission ended in complete failure in Khīva. The Russians were given a cool reception, and they could not obtain the trade concessions they desired. However, Naṣr Allāh, the *emīr* of Bukhārā, received Ignat'yev's commission warmly, since he was inclined towards the Russians, and he gave them some commercial privileges. In spite of this, the Russians could not get what they had hoped for. On the other hand, they identified the military roads and places of strategic importance. It is possible that this was the primary object of Ignat'yev's mission.

Internal problems connected with the emancipation of the serfs by Alexander II delayed operations directed towards Turkistān, as did the war with Shaykh Shāmil in the Caucasus, which ended in 1864. On the other hand, it has been suggested that the American Civil War also pressed the Russians to invade Central Asia, since all imports of cotton from America had stopped, and Russian factories could only obtain their cotton from Turkistān. Hence, if the Russians occupied Turkistān, they could get cotton more abundantly and cheaply, and Russian industrialists may have encouraged the government in its invasion schemes. It was obvious that the Central Asian khanates could be easily occupied. It was not probable that the British would stop this Russian venture. In the light of these considerations the Russian government decided at the end of 1864 on occupation.

The Russian foreign minister, Gorchakov, sent a memorandum to the ambassadors in St Petersburg on 21 November 1864, announcing that the Russian government was going to take measures to provide security and civilization for the people who lived in the areas of Central Asia under Russian rule. He added that these measures did not mean an indefinite expansion, and the Russians would not go further than

Chimkent, just beyond Tashkent. This note was intended to pacify the British, and to reassure them that Russia had no claims on India. According to these explanations, the first Russian target was to establish a defence line from the Ili to the Jaxartes. A young general, Chernyayev, had been commissioned for this task. Actually the Russian military operation had started before Gorchakov's note.

General Chernyayev occupied Chimkent city by a sudden attack in September 1864. He wanted to do the same at Tashkent, but his army was driven back. However, a year later, in the summer of 1865, a military force of 1,950 men and twelve guns under Chernyayev's command attacked the city. Tashkent, with a population of 80,000, belonged to the Khokand khanate. There were about 30,000 soldiers and sixty-three guns in the city; but the soldiers had neither discipline, able commanders, nor modern weapons, and Tashkent was occupied in June 1865. The Russians had hardly any casualties. The event had great repercussions throughout Turkistān, and predetermined the end of the three khanates in Central Asia.

However, the *emīr* of Bukhārā, Naṣr Allāh (1826–60), wanted to stop the Russian advance and even retake Tashkent with his improvized army. The forces of Bukhārā suffered a great defeat in May 1866. However, the main blow of the Russians was directed towards the Khokand khanate. In May 1866 the cities of Khojand and then Ura-Tübe were taken by the Russians. The entire area acquired in these campaigns was annexed to Russia, and a governorate-general of Turkistān was established in 1867. General K. P. Kaufman (von Kauffmann), who was of German origin, was appointed governor-general. The area was divided into two parts: Syr-Dar'ya province, with Tashkent as its capital, and Semirech'ye province. General Kaufman was given great authority. He could declare war, make treaties and take all kinds of administrative action. During his governor-generalship (1867–82) he played a great part in the establishment of Russian rule and administration in Turkistān.

General Kaufman's main purpose was to render the Bukhārā khanate harmless in regard to Russia. The annexation of the khanate was not actually in view. The Russians would be content to have places of strategic importance under their rule. A military operation started in 1868 with this purpose. On 1 May, Samarqand was taken by the Russians without any resistance. The impotence of Muẓaffar al-Dīn, the *emīr* of Bukhārā, against the Russians aroused great indignation among his people. 'Abd al-Malik, the *emīr*'s son, declared a *jihād* against the

Russians, and his men occupied the city of Samarqand. But the Russian garrison retreated into the inner fortress, and resisted the large numbers of local people. Finally General Kaufman's relieving forces overwhelmed Malik's men.

Further resistance was impossible for Bukhārā, and Muẓaffar al-Dīn signed a treaty with General Kaufman, according to which Khojand, Ura-Tübe, Jizak and Samarqand with their surroundings were given to the Russians. The whole of this area was annexed to the governorate-general of Turkistān. Apart from this, the *emīr* was to pay a war-indemnity of 500,000 roubles, recognize full freedom of action for Russian merchants in Bukhārā, and ban the slave-trade. Five years later, in 1873, a peace treaty was signed between Russia and Bukhārā. With this treaty Bukhārā accepted Russian protection. It was left autonomous in internal affairs, but the Russians were given many financial privileges. The *emīr* was forbidden to establish relations with foreign countries. In this way, the Bukhārā khanate finally lost its independence.

However, the resistance against the Russians was not completely broken. The *emīr* of Shahr-i Sabz and certain other princes rebelled against the *Emīr* Muẓaffar al-Dīn, and declared ʿAbd al-Malik to be khan. But the struggle did not last long. The Russian forces came to the support of the *emīr*, and annexed the provinces where the uprisings had taken place to the Bukhārā khanate, and thus Muẓaffar al-Dīn's position was restored. The Russian policy was to flatter the *emīrs* of Bukhārā, and in return the *emīrs* were to be completely loyal to the tsar.

The Russian advance was not made only in western Turkistān. In 1870 there was an uprising against the Chinese near Kulja, in Jungaria. The local people who lived here were Muslim Dungens, Kazakhs, Kirghizes, and Turks from eastern Turkistān. Some time before this, Yaʿqūb Bey (who had fiercely defended the fortress at Ak-Mesjid in 1853) had founded a state of his own in the territory of eastern Turkistān, with Kashgar as his capital. Yaʿqūb Bey made contact with the British and Ottoman governments and accepted the protection of Sultan ʿAbd ül-ʿAzīz, and even had coins minted in his honour. An Ottoman military commission had come to Kashgar to train Yaʿqūb Bey's army, and a certain amount of weapons was received from the British. The Russians were suspicious of this. They decided to occupy Kulja and started their operations in 1871. The Kulja region was under Russian rule for ten years. When the Chinese reoccupied Kashgar in 1881 the Russians deserted Kulja, and the border with China was left as before.

After the Bukhārā khanate had been taken under Russian protection, it was merely a matter of time for the Khīva khanate to end in the same way. Indeed, a military force of considerable strength under General Kaufman entered the Khīva khanate from five different positions in the summer of 1873. The people of Khīva wanted to resist but they were not able to continue. The khan of Khīva, Muḥammad Raḥīm, accepted all the conditions imposed by General Kaufman, and signed a treaty in 1873. According to this treaty, the Khīva khanate maintained its internal autonomy and became a protected state. The Russians held financial and military control, and Khīva was not to have relations with foreign countries. In this way, the Khīva khanate also lost its independence.

It was now the Khokand khanate's turn. At this period Khokand was ruled by Khān Khudāyār, who was disliked by everybody because of his failings. The Kipchaks were especially resentful of his oppression. When in 1875 the Kipchaks made an uprising, Khān Khudāyār escaped from Khokand, and his son Nāṣir al-Dīn was brought to the throne. The Russians were believed to be involved in the unrest, and a *jihād* was declared against them. The uprising spread not only to Farghānā, but also to the area under Russian rule. The Russians intervened with organized forces against Khokand, which in a short time was badly defeated. The city of Khokand was occupied, and the khanate was officially abolished. All its territory was annexed to Russia in 1876.

In this way, the Russians occupied all Turkistān in the decade following the fall of Tashkent. The main reason for the Russian success was that the khanates did not have the means to protect themselves. It was impossible to resist the Russian army with improvized forces and inefficient weapons. The five or six million Turks in Central Asia, especially the people of Bukhārā, had remained untrained as warriors. On the other hand, Turcomans, who were fewer in numbers but able in fighting, were brought under control with considerable difficulty.

The Russian province of Transcaspia lay to the east of the Caspian Sea, with Krasnovodsk as its capital. In 1877 the Russians started a military operation to bring the Tekke Turcomans under control, using Turcoman plundering at Mangıshlak as an excuse. A military force of 11,000 men and 107 guns started an operation from Krasnovodsk in 1880 under the command of General Skobelev, who had proved himself in the liquidation of the Khokand khanate. The Russian army marched against the fortified positions of the Tekke Turcomans at Gök-Tepe, which was attacked on 15 January 1881. The Turcomans put up a fierce resistance, but were defeated, and their leader Tikma Serdār surrendered. The total Russian casualties were 398, and the resistance of the Tekke Turcomans and the war of Gök-Tepe became an epic in Turkistān.

Naturally this local resistance could not stop the Russian advance. All the Turcoman tribes submitted. The city of Merv fell in 1884 and the Russians reached the borders of Afghanistan. The Afghan forces, which had some British officers, and the Russians fought in March 1885, and the Afghan forces were drawn back. When, in 1888, an Anglo-Russian Boundary Commission completed the demarcation of the border between Afghanistan and Russia, the Russian advance in Central Asia came to an end.

From time to time the British had opposed the occupation of Central Asia by the Russians. They never liked the Russian advance towards India, and they wanted to stop the Russian occupation of the Khīva, Bukhārā and Khokand khanates. They sent British agents to encourage the local people to resist, but no other serious steps were taken. It is not clear that British diplomacy had any success in the khanates. As a matter of fact, the attitude and behaviour of the British in India were known in Bukhārā, and made a bad impression. Little reliance was placed by the *emīr* of Bukhārā on the messages sent to him by the governor-general of India. On the other hand, the Russians were very tactful in their contacts with the people of Turkistān, and they did much to win the local people. The *emīr* of Bukhārā was highly praised in the messages sent by the Russian authorities, who thus had a psychological advantage over the British.

After the demarcation of the boundary between Afghanistan and Russia, the Russians fortified and garrisoned Kushka, near the border. Some time later, this place was connected to the Krasnovodsk–Samarqand railroad. In 1907 a convention was signed between Britain and Russia which contained a formula for the satisfaction of both parties.

THE KHANATES OF BUKHĀRĀ AND KHĪVA UNDER RUSSIAN RULE

After the treaties that were signed between the Russians and the *emīr* of Bukhārā, Muẓaffar al-Dīn, in 1862 and 1873, the khanate was left as a Russian protectorate. It was completely independent in its internal affairs, and the old organization was not changed. However, when the construction of a railroad from Krasnovodsk to Samarqand and Tashkent was begun, the Russians were not slow to acquire the territory of the khanate. Russian towns were built along the railroad, and Russian guards were placed at the Afghanistan-Bukhārā border. Before long, Russian soldiers were placed in cities which belonged to Bukhārā. The Russians even attempted for a time to forbid the *emīr* to mint money. All the coins minted in the *emīr*'s name were under the control of the Russian Bank, and the Russians took control of economic life. On the other hand, they did not interfere in religious affairs, or the schools and *medreses*. In the opinion of the Russians, these institutions were the best means of letting Bukhārā rot from inside. Their policy was fundamentally opposed to permitting any progress to enter Bukhārā or the Islamic community in Central Asia.

In the reign of 'Abd al-Aḥad (1885–1910), who succeeded his father, Muẓaffar al-Dīn, Bukhārā became a complete satellite of Russia. 'Abd al-Aḥad was most loyal to Tsars Alexander III and Nicholas II, and he did nothing to arouse suspicion. In reward, he was given the rank of adjutant-general, and was furnished with 2,000 old-fashioned rifles and some guns to equip the army of Bukhārā. However, *Emīr* 'Abd al-Aḥad was not altogether indifferent to new ideas and movements. His toleration of a few *uṣūl-u jedīd* ('new method') schools is proof of this. He was very economical, but contributed an important part of the cost of the mosque in St Petersburg, as well as a considerable amount of money for the construction of the Ḥijāz railway.

Sayyid 'Ālim, who succeeded his father in 1910, showed full loyalty to the Russians. In spite of his Russian education, he was very reactionary. The *Emīr* Sayyid 'Ālim was not behind his father and grandfather in increasing his personal wealth. All the cotton factories were in his hands, and the cotton-growers had to sell their produce to him at a low price. The *emīr* sold this cotton to the Russians, and made a big profit. He completely monopolized the most important commercial product of Bukhārā, Persian lamb. There was corruption in the internal administration. In this way, those in power in Bukhārā were preparing their own downfall. In 1915 the Russian government had practically decided to abolish the Bukhārā and Khīva khanates, and take them under direct rule, but because of the First World War this could not be carried out.

The Khīva khanate was in an even worse situation than Bukhārā. Contact between the Russian government and the *emīr* of Bukhārā was made through the Foreign Ministry, but the Khīva khanate was under the local Russian administration of Turkistān. The khan of Khīva, Muḥammad Raḥīm, was most loyal to the tsar. His son, Isfandiyār

Khān, took his place in 1910. Both Muḥammad Raḥīm and Isfandiyār were progressive rulers; moreover, Isfandiyār Khān knew Russian, and he followed both Russian and Muslim publications. He was well-informed about the facts of the world. Isfandiyār Khān made some efforts to open *uṣūl-u jedīd* schools in Khīva, and invited some well-known teachers from Kazan. There was not much change in the internal administration of the khanate, but there was some progress in the cultural field. Isfandiyār Khān was unnecessarily involved in a dispute with the Turcomans, and was killed in 1918. After his death there was unrest in Khīva, and finally 'Young Khivans', who were supported by the Bolshevik forces in Russia, took possession of Khīva and started to sovietize it.

CENTRAL ASIA UNDER TSARIST RULE

Between the years 1865 and 1886, the Russians acquired an area of two million square kilometres. The administration of this territory (which had a population of seven to eight millions, ninety per cent of whom were Turkish Muslims) faced the Russians with some new problems.

There was a great difference between the occupation of Central Asia and previous Russian acquisitions. Since the Volga and Ural regions were adjacent to Russia, it had been quite easy to colonize and administer them. Western Siberia was taken by the Cossacks under Yermak. Central and eastern Siberia were occupied by Russian hunters, pioneers and Cossacks. Only then was the Russian state administration established in these areas. The steppes of the Turkish Kazakhs were annexed to Russia by their own request, and geographical conditions there were not attractive to Russian colonists. But the occupation of Central Asia was the result of state military action.

The administration of Central Asia was therefore attached to the Russian Ministry of War, which appointed a governor-general to rule the area. New administrative regions were established as the conquest advanced. At the beginning, the Russians treated the people of the occupied area very kindly. The traditions, law and the law courts of the people were left just as they were. Some time later, they started the implementation of some principles of Russian policy. One of these was the change in the way of electing the *ak-sakals*, that is, the village headmen. Before the Russian invasion, the *ak-sakals* were chosen by the people of the village according to their merits and without a limited term of office. But afterwards they were elected for a term of three years, and had to be approved by the administrative authorities. In this way, the village administration was put under Russian control.

On the other hand, the Russians did not interfere with the way of life, religion or the language of the people. The *Sharī'a* was retained. According to the opinion of Kaufman, Islam represented a decaying culture: it was destroying itself, and interference with it was unnecessary. However, in the views of the local people, this Russian policy was considered a virtue. As a result of another Russian policy, the local people were freed from military obligations. Although the Russians tried to present this as a privilege, their reason was to avoid the possibility of armed resistance.

The people under Russian rule had very little contact with the Russians. Even in the cities the Russians lived in their own districts. But the seizure of the most fertile land, the constant arrival of Russian immigrants, the imposition of new taxes and obligations, the railway which crossed the country from one end to the other, were all obvious signs of Russian sovereignty. The aim of Russian policy was to supply cotton to the Russian factories, and find room for the migration of Russian peasants into Central Asia.

The export of cotton from Turkistān to Russia in 1900 was five million *poods* (1 *pood* is equal to 16·38 kilograms), and by 1915 it rose to 18·5 million *poods*. The cultivation of cotton in Turkistān increased and became compulsory in many instances. Meanwhile the cultivation of wheat declined at the same rate, as the Russians wanted to make the people of Turkistān dependent on Russian wheat. While the export of wheat from Russia to Turkistān was 33,000 tons in 1908, it rose to 227,000 tons in 1912, and 354,000 tons in 1916. Without these exports, the people of Turkistān would have starved. The urban population was especially dependant on Russian wheat.

The settlement of Russian and Ukrainian peasants in Central Asia was one of the most important aims of Russian colonialism. Russian Cossacks had already been settled in the Semirech'ye area since 1855. Attempts were made to seize the land of the Kazakhs and Kirghiz for this purpose. The seizure of land increased progressively and between the years 1880 and 1900, 11,610,000 *dessiatinas* (1 *dessiatina* is equal to 1·09 hectares) of land were distributed to the Russian Cossacks. By 1917, the total area of land acquired in this way was more than 30 million *dessiatinas*, and the number of Russian immigrants reached 1·5 million. They were concentrated especially in the cities. There were cities like Vernyi (now Alma-Ata) which were populated exclusively by Russians, and also some new cities were constructed for the Russians besides the old ones. Tashkent is a classical example of this. According to the statistics of 1910, the population of Tashkent was 201,000, and of these 55,000 were Russians. The Russian section with all its European appearance of broad streets, squares, parks and buildings was entirely different from the typical oriental city of the local people, where the streets were narrow, the houses of mud bricks and insanitary.

It was in the interests of the Russians to propagate their culture in Central Asia in order to win sympathizers for the new administration. The Russian administrators considered this matter as early as 1873, and some principles were determined then. The conversion of the people in the khanates of Bukhārā, Khīva and Khokand to Orthodox Christianity (as had been done in Kazan), could not be considered at all. Indoctrination in Russian culture would be possible first of all by teaching the Russian language. It was decided to open schools for the Özbegs, Sarts and Kazakhs, where the teaching would be in Russian, and the graduates of these schools would proceed to Russian higher grade schools. Experiments of this kind had been made with the Kazakhs in the province of Semirech'ye with some positive results. Russo-native schools, which were opened with great expectations on the part of the Russian administrators, did not achieve what was expected of them. Very few of the local people sent their children to these schools, because they were afraid that the children would be converted. Still, there were some who went to these schools, and even some who received a higher education. The few Kazakh and Özbeg lawyers were from among them.

The people of Turkistān never really took to the Russian administration, but they showed submission because they were obliged to. The continuation of risings against the Russians was a clear expression of this dissatisfaction. One of these risings was headed by Dukchi Ishan of Andijān in 1898, who even sent, unsuccessfully, to Istanbul to ask for aid. This was followed by another rising in 1916. During the First World War, the Russians increased the pressure on the local people; they had levied great amounts of money in various ways, and introduced new obligations. Although the men of Turkistān were exempt from military service, those between the ages of nineteen and forty-three were ordered by an edict of 1916 to be conscripted for labour duties. This decision by the Russian government created great resentment and shortly afterwards the rising began.

The first to rise were the Kirghiz, immediately followed by the Kazakhs and the Özbegs, and the movement became widespread. The Kipchak and Naiman tribes were the leaders. The tribes in revolt formed an organization and chose as their leader 'Abd al-Ghaffār Khān of the Kipchaks. The area of Lake Issyk-kul, and especially around Jizak, was the stronghold of the uprising. The movement spread from Farghānā to Talas, and from there to Samarqand. Its participants were determined to annihilate everything Russian. The houses of the Russian colonists were burned, their property and herds were taken away, and they themselves were killed. 4,725 Russians were killed (2,222 from among the immigrants), 2,683 Russians were reported lost, and 9,000 houses were destroyed.

The Russian suppression of this rising was just as violent. A large military force was brought to Turkistān, withdrawing reinforcements of considerable importance which would have gone to the German front. It is reported that the number of people killed in Semirech'ye alone was 205,000, while 300,000 people took refuge in Chinese territory. Of those captured, 168,000 men and women are said to have been sentenced to death.

The governor-general Kuropatkin ordered all Kirghiz living in the area of Lake Issyk-kul, and along the Chu and Naryn rivers to be banished, but before this order was carried out the revolution of February 1917 took place. In spite of the revolution, the fight between the Kirghiz, Kazakhs and Russians went on. Many of the Kazakhs did not submit to the Russians, and went on fighting. On the other hand, the Russian soldiers who were sent to Turkistān to suppress the rising became the support of the Bolshevik revolution, and played an important part in the Bolsheviks' victory and their control of Tashkent in 1918.

The conscripts whose levy had caused the rising of 1916 did not reach the front and were not used for labour duties. They must have returned home following the February Revolution and the consequent dissolution of the Russian army.

THE LIFE OF THE PEOPLE IN TURKISTĀN UNDER TSARIST RULE

After the Russian occupation, there was no fundamental difference in the lives of the people who lived in the territory annexed to Russia or who lived under the Bukhārā khanate. However, in cities where Russians were numerous, they undoubtedly influenced the local people.

Educated Russians considered themselves to be the representatives of European civilization, and therefore thought themselves superior to the Özbegs, Sarts, Kazakhs and Kirghiz. On the other hand, the Russians were considered as usurpers by the local people, and could not possibly win their sympathy. In the views of the conservatives, they were above all enemies of religion. The '*ulemā*' and other religious leaders were especially antagonistic towards the Russians. Some groups, however, especially the merchants, were happy with the Russian rule to some degree, since there were more opportunities for profit-making. Those who learned Russian, or were educated in Russian schools, got along better with the Russians, but the number of such people was very small.

This general antagonism of the people of Turkistān towards the Russians gave birth to nationalist feelings, which did not previously consciously exist. Formerly the dominant bond in Central Asia was membership of a social class or tribe. The suppression of the Özbegs, Kazakhs, Kirghiz, Turcomans and the citizens of Bukhārā and Khīva by the Russians resulted in the *rapprochement* of the various Turkish Muslim groups, and created a national awareness. This development was partly due to a common culture and tradition. But the most effective movement in this field was the *uṣūl-u jedīd* ('new method') which was started by Ismā'īl Gasprali (Gasprinskiy) of the Crimea. Ismā'īl Gasprali was influential even in Turkistān with the newspaper *Terjumān,* which he began to publish in Baghche-Saray in 1883. Kazan Tatar teachers, whom the *uṣūl-u jedīd* movement influenced most, were also active in the cities of Turkistān. Many Kazan Tatar families had moved to Turkistān after the Russian invasion, and the schools with new methods which they started became models for the people. It is certain that these Tatar schools were even more effective than the Russians in regard to spreading Western civilization.

Of those who started the *uṣūl-u jedīd* movement in Turkistān, the Kazakh Ibray (Ibrāhīm) Altınsarın, who was educated in a Russian school, is one of the most important. He continued his activities as late as 1883. But the person who provided the greatest service in this field is Münevver Kari, who was a religious student from Tashkent, and later on a teacher. In 1901 Münevver Kari opened an *uṣūl-u jedīd* school in Tashkent, which continued for quite a long time in spite of pressure from the Russians and conservative Muslim scholars, and played a great role in the awakening of the people of Turkistān. As a result of his activities, the number of *uṣūl-u jedīd* schools reached twelve in Tashkent, five in

Bukhārā, two in Samarqand, seventeen in the province of Semirech'ye, and thirteen in the Khokand area in 1913. This movement was concentrated especially in Tashkent, Bukhārā and Andijān. The survival of *uṣūl-u jedīd* in places like Bukhārā, where religious reaction was dominant, was due to the assistance or tolerance of some influential people: 'Abd al-Aḥad, the *emīr* of Bukhārā and his minister of justice supported the *uṣūl-u jedīd* to some extent, but the movement did not become a public one in Bukhārā and other parts of Turkistān as it had in Kazan, Persian Āẕarbāyjān or the Crimea.

The Russian revolution of 1905 had little significance in Turkistān, producing only a demonstration of Russian workers in Tashkent, and no reaction among the local people. They had lost their right to vote after the second State Duma (1907), and were excluded from the political life of Russia. Only afterwards did the Russian political parties in Turkistān establish local relations, but the number of Özbegs and Kazakhs who joined the Russian parties could not be more than three or four.

The *Kazak* newspaper, first published in 1913 by Kazakh intellectuals, reported the political movements and economic problems of the time. It pointed to the economic and political rights of the Kazakhs, and implicitly demanded an end to Russian exploitation. The *Alash Orda* party which was founded some time before, and which had a completely nationalist nature, indicated that by then political activities had started among the Kazakh Turks, but such movements were just at the beginning and far from producing any serious results.

The influence of the Committee of Union and Progress (Young Turks) which came to power after the revolution of 1908 in the Ottoman empire, also had a great influence on the young people of Turkistān. There had long been a Bukhārā convent (*tekke*) in Istanbul, and many of the people who came to Istanbul from Turkistān used to stay there. Apart from the pilgrims who came and went, the number of students who came to Istanbul for their education was on the increase. In 1910 the *Terbiye-i aṭfāl* society ('society for the education of children') which was secretly founded in Bukhārā, decided to send students to study in Istanbul, and collected donations for this purpose. Fifteen students were sent to Istanbul in 1911, and the number reached thirty in 1912.

'Abd al-Raḥmān Fiṭrat, Muqīm al-Dīn and 'Os̱mān Khōja, who were well-known poets and writers among the Özbegs in Istanbul, met with the Young Turk leaders, and received information especially on the purposes and activities of the party. Fiṭrat the poet wrote two pamphlets criticizing the situation in Bukhārā, and had them published in Istanbul. The young people of Bukhārā who came to Istanbul for their education observed the new movements, and many of the intellectuals who had new ideas and were later known as 'Young Bukharans' were the products of Istanbul. A society for the propagation of education in Bukhārā was also founded in Istanbul.

At the beginning, these societies were only engaged in educational problems, but they were soon involved in politics. The national problems which developed among the Kazakhs of Āẕarbāyjān, Kazan and the Turkish Kazakhs were soon to develop in Bukhārā and other parts of Turkistān as well.

When the revolution of February 1917 started, the rising of 1916 had not been fully suppressed. There was still some fighting going on in the mountainous areas. But the Russians were in control of the situation, and were punishing the participants in the revolt. The news about the revolution reached Turkistān quite slowly, and the governor-general, Kuropatkin, did not want to announce it publicly 'until the situation became clear'. But since the news had leaked out by way of the telegraph officials, it was obvious that it could not be kept secret any longer. Finally, Kuropatkin announced on 12 March that the tsarist régime in Russia had been abolished and a republic had been founded. After this, the Russian political parties in Tashkent began to emerge. On 17 March, a Workers' and Soldiers' Soviet was founded, following the example of Petrograd and other cities. Soon, this organization began controlling the administration. Bolshevik propaganda came to dominate the Soviet, which gradually moved leftwards. The railway workers in Tashkent, and the Russian soldiers sent to suppress the 1916 revolt, were especially supporters of the Bolsheviks. The strength of the leftist group was shown in the great demonstration held in Tashkent on 12 September 1917. Kerensky's Provisional Government was completely helpless, as in all other parts of Russia. The local people were rather indifferent to the entire process. In these circumstances the October (Bolshevik) revolution occurred.

Following the 1917 revolution some movements began among the Muslims of Turkistān. Since there no longer was any censorship, newspapers and journals began publishing articles in the spirit of the revolution and on the subject of freedom. Following the Russians, the Muslim people also began holding meetings and congresses, such as the first All-Muslim Congress held in April 1917 in Tashkent, where much was said about freedom and reforms. It was decided that Russia should become a federated republic, and Turkistān should be given autonomy. Problems concerning religion and land were discussed, and some decisions were reached, among which, the cessation of Russian immigration was given special importance. Naturally, all these decisions were theoretical, since there was neither the personnel nor the means for their implementation.

At this time the Kazakhs and Özbegs in various cities were holding congresses, and taking decisions on matters concerning themselves. The largest of these was the first All-Russian Muslim Congress held in Moscow from 1 to 11 May 1917, with nearly 800 delegates. At this congress, which was arranged through the efforts and finance of the Kazan Tatars, religious and cultural problems were discussed, rather than political matters. The only organization of the Muslims of Russia up to this time was the Religious Council in Ufa, and this fact played an important part.

One of the problems which was discussed at length was the administration of the Muslims of Russia. There were two schools of thought on this matter. One of them, composed of Kazan Tatars and northern Caucasians, were content with national and cultural autonomy. The other school, mainly representatives from Āẕarbāyjān and a majority of Bashkirs, proposed territorial autonomy on a federal basis. The latter view was finally accepted by 446 votes against 271. The people of Turkistān were also in favour of a federation. But there were no means of implementing the decisions taken at the Congress. The Muslims of Turkistān were without any military power. The Turkish Islamic community of over 10 million people in Central Asia had none of the prerequisites to decide their future for themselves, and therefore it was impossible to make use of this great opportunity.

PART IV

THE CENTRAL ISLAMIC LANDS IN RECENT TIMES

CHAPTER I

MODERN TURKEY

(A) POLITICAL DEVELOPMENTS: 1918–50

The War of Liberation and the downfall of the old régime

The Mudros armistice signed on 30 October 1918, by the government of Aḥmed ʿIzzet Pasha appointed by the sultan for this task, marked the defeat of the Ottoman empire in the First World War. The war was fought valiantly on several fronts, but many officers and intellectuals with a new outlook on life and government realized that the war had proved the bankruptcy of Ottoman political and military philosophy, and threatened the independent existence of the Turks.

Defeat appeared inevitable as early as 1917, and compelled many officers and intellectuals to reckon with its consequences. The multinational Ottoman state could not be revived, whereas the unifying idea of a Turkish national state was barely emerging. The Allies had already agreed to divide the empire. On 13 November 1918, Allied troops landed in Istanbul and established a military administration. In the spring of 1919, the French advanced into the regions of ʿAynṭāb (later Gaziantep), Marʿash and Adana, the Italians landed in Antalya, and the British in Samsun and the Dardanelles. The sultan in Istanbul, Meḥmed VI Vaḥīd al-Dīn, acquiesced in the occupation.

Soon he was busy persecuting the remaining Union and Progress leaders, after the main ones, Ṭalʿat, Enver and Jemāl Pashas, had fled abroad. The sultan's governments, headed alternatively by Tevfīq and Damad Ferīd Pashas, gradually became preoccupied mainly with defending the sultanate. The leading groups associated with the court and the Istanbul press appeared to have reconciled themselves with the idea of occupation. A series of political parties established in Istanbul after the armistice was concerned mainly with the policy to be followed towards the Allies.

Many Turks had looked at the beginning upon the Allied occupation as a temporary measure necessitated by the armistice. The fallacy of this soon became evident, when on 15 May 1919, the Greeks landed in Izmir under the protection of Allied warships, and began to advance into the interior with the clear intention of annexing western Anatolia to a greater Greece. The indignation was unanimous even among those who had settled for Allied occupation in the hope that at least their life, faith and property would be respected.

Muṣṭafā Kemāl landed in Samsun in northern Anatolia on 19 May 1919, amid these circumstances. His official duty as army inspector was to supervize the disarming of troops as demanded by the armistice. But Kemāl's actual goal was to organize national resistance to occupation as decided in Istanbul after months of fruitless efforts, and to stir the sultan's government into action. Shortly after arriving in Anatolia, Muṣṭafā Kemāl established contacts with military commanders and eventually with the associations for the defence of rights.

These associations began to be established as resistance groups by local leaders in Thrace and Anatolia towards the end of 1918. They were middle-class organizations. The town notables, *'ulemā'*, landlords and merchants established the associations as means of self-defence and independence, and also for the preservation of the traditional way of life. In many instances members of the Union and Progress party, dissolved in 1918, were instrumental in providing leadership. Ṭal'at Pasha, among other unionist leaders, is supposed to have urged his followers to organize passive resistance in Thrace. With the signing of the armistice a good many reserve officers, former teachers in towns or petty officials, returned home, and eventually assumed leading positions in the associations along with traditionally minded leaders. The former decided to publish newspapers, to establish branches in smaller localities and to contact army units. However, some associations remained conservative in character, local and regional in scope, as revealed later by their opposition to Muṣṭafā Kemāl's national goals.

The activities of Muṣṭafā Kemāl in Anatolia created suspicion in Istanbul and consequently his appointment was terminated. He then resigned from the army in July 1919. His success as a civilian depended on his ability to mobilize support for the movement without antagonizing further the Istanbul government. The sultan-caliph as the legitimate head of the state and community still commanded profound loyalty among the population, and even among Kemāl's close supporters.

The resistance movement began to acquire momentum with the congresses of defence associations held in Erzurum, from 23 July to 7 August 1919, and Sivas, from 4 to 11 September 1919, which formulated the *Millī Mīs̱āq,* or National Pact. The Pact expressed the decision to maintain national independence and integrity, eventually through a government elected by a National Congress, if the Istanbul government failed to fulfil its duties. Loyalty to the sultan-caliph was, however, stressed, while the blame for his actions was placed on his ministers. The two congresses appeared in fact as popular assemblies, whereas the Pact, although couched in traditional language, seemed an expression of national will.

Thus, the movement of national liberation, although initially directed only against the foreign invader, began to shape itself also as a revolution against the established authority at home. Muṣṭafā Kemāl's point of departure, that is to say the idea of national sovereignty, was modern in essence, and could not be reconciled with the sultanate's traditions or interests. Unavoidably the difference between the two came into the open.

The sultan, still formally assured of the loyalty of his subjects and commanders, decided on the insistence of nationalists in Anatolia to hold elections in the autumn of 1919, and eventually convened a parliament in Istanbul on 20 January 1920. The deputies represented chiefly the nationalist viewpoint, and helped to strengthen Muṣṭafā Kemāl's position in Istanbul. The British in Istanbul, faced with growingly aggressive deputies and popular unrest, finally arrested the nationalists and sent them to Malta, causing the legislature to prorogue itself indefinitely on 18 March 1920. Next day, Muṣṭafā Kemāl called for the election of an assembly with extraordinary powers to meet in Ankara. This town of about 20,000 people was already the seat of Kemāl's Representative Committee.

The Grand National Assembly was opened by Muṣṭafā Kemāl on 23 April 1920, two days after he had solemnly prayed for the well-being of the sultan-caliph and issued a circular to this effect to province administrators. The same day the United States recognized the Armenian government formed in eastern Anatolia. The Grand National Assembly stressed the need for a government, and defined itself as the paramount representative of the national will. The break with Istanbul was complete, despite the nationalists' vows of loyalty to the sultan-caliph.

The latter had already issued early in April a *fetvā* from the *shaykh al-Islām*, authorizing the killing of nationalists as a religious duty. He eventually organized special units for this purpose, and condemned to death *in absentia* Muṣṭafā Kemāl and other leaders. The nationalists countered this by securing *fetvās* from Anatolian *muftīs*, by declaring null all treaties, agreements and conventions signed by Istanbul after 16 March 1920, and by defining disloyalty to the National Assembly as treason. A few days later the Assembly passed the Law against Treason and established the 'Independence Courts', which were repeatedly reactivated, and finally abolished in 1949. These efforts seemed to have had limited response since a series of anti-nationalist local revolts broke out. Some of these were put down by troops under the command of nationalist commanders and others by the irregulars of the Circassian Ethem, whose support of the nationalists was followed by his desertion to the Greeks.

The sultan-caliph had used his religious powers to stamp out the nationalist movement, and thus sanctioned indirectly the foreign occupation of Turkey in violation of his basic religious obligation to defend the community against outside invaders. The sultan's position was clarified and further weakened by the treaty of Sèvres, signed on 10 August 1920. This treaty reduced the Ottoman empire to the Istanbul area and northern Anatolia, and gave the remaining territories to the Allies. The Sèvres treaty caused the final break with Istanbul, the loss of hopes of agreement with the West, and led to a search for support from anywhere, including the Soviet Union. Buoyed by the rising nationalist sentiment in Anatolia, the Grand National Assembly began to levy troops and supplies. The first major military victory was won against the Armenians who evacuated Kars and then signed the treaty of Gümrü on 3 December 1920. The eastern front had been strengthened politically by friendly relations with the Soviets, which began in the summer of 1920, and eventually led to the treaty of Moscow on 16 March 1921. The nationalists began to be recognized abroad as a force to reckon with, especially after the heavy defeat inflicted upon the Greeks in August 1921. The victory, coming after continuous Greek advances freed Ankara from the danger of occupation and earned Muṣṭafā Kemāl the title of *Ghāzī*, a fighter in a religious war.

On the south-eastern front the French advance was checked in 1920. Finally, a treaty signed in 1921 established the southern border. The Italians also left Anatolia. The greatest battle in the interior took place within the Grand National Assembly, which assumed control of government, and gradually extended its authority in the countryside. The study of the social structure of various groups in the Assembly and of their ideologies ranging from Islam to socialism are essential for understanding the nature of modern Turkey. Landlords, conservative religious leaders, nationalist *muftis,* patriotic notables, modern-minded officers and intellectuals were represented in the Assembly.[1] These formed the middle classes in the Ottoman empire, and although separated by differences of philosophy and attitudes, they united against the foreign occupation, and through it against the upper order represented by the throne and the high bureaucracy.

The war had started for defence and unavoidably became a social front. It turned out to be also a populist movement, particularly since the idea of national sovereignty at its base was broad enough to lend itself to diverse interpretations. The intellectual group advocated economic and social measures beneficial to the population, as well as a legislature based on a kind of professional representation. The government programme of 13 September 1920 paid lip-service to the caliph, but in the second article described the sole purpose of the Turkish Grand National Assembly as being the delivery of people from the oppression of capitalism and imperialism. It promised to 'eradicate the misery of the people and accept as basic principle the achievement of happiness and welfare' through adequate measures in matters of land, education, justice, finance and all other social fields as rendered necessary by the modern age and the people's true needs. The government vowed to draw its political and social principles from the nation's heart, and enforce them according to its needs and tendencies. The socialist group in the Assembly, a series of newspapers and organizations with Marxist leanings, and the Islamic communists formed the extreme wing of the populists. The bitter animosity towards the West caused by the Sèvres treaty directed all the hopes to the East which became 'a ray of hope... to produce welfare and independence for the country'. The representatives of rural groups had a different concept of populism. They attacked primarily the ruling groups in the administration and described them as the cause of all evil, despite their vain efforts to reform the country by imitating Europe. Some of the proponents of social ideas—always respectful to religion—were encouraged by the growing friendship with the Soviets, but chiefly by the backwardness at home. Muṣṭafā Kemāl, although leaning towards the social-minded group of intellectuals, and often using their terminology, did not commit himself totally to them,

[1] For information on the social background of nationalist officers, see Dankwart A. Rustow, 'The Army and the founding of the Turkish Republic', in *World Politics* (July 1959), 513–52.

and least of all to communism, as is implied at times. He was preoccupied primarily with the form and the functions of government institutions and envisaged populism in terms of power, authority, sovereignty and administration. He wanted to establish first a modern political structure, and used the existing ideologies to the extent they suited this purpose.

The struggle between conservatives and modernists concerning the political régime eventually forced the social problems into a secondary position. The Constitutional Act passed by the Assembly on 20 January 1921 did not reflect the social issues. It recognized the principle of national sovereignty and assembled all powers, including the execution of the *Sharīʿa,* in the National Assembly. Thus the Assembly with its conception of unity of powers became *de facto* absolute ruler of Turkey.

The ideological struggle reshaping itself as modernism versus traditionalism within the Assembly was brought to a conclusion by the final defeat of the Greeks in 1922. The armistice of Mudanya signed on 11 October 1922, recognized in the main the territories demanded by the nationalists, and put an end to the foreign occupation. The forthcoming negotiations for a peace treaty precipitated a final clash between Ankara and Istanbul. Both were invited to send delegates to Lausanne. The sultan was offered therefore a unique opportunity to regain his power and prestige, to the eventual detriment of the nationalist modernists who were in power in Ankara. The National Assembly, prodded by Muṣṭafā Kemāl, deprived him of this chance by abolishing the sultanate on 1 November 1922, and by declaring, significantly enough, that the sultan's authority had ended on 16 March 1920. The separation of the offices of sultan and caliph was, according to Muṣṭafā Kemāl, closer to the spirit of early Islam, when the caliph had authority over lay *amīrs*. He described the sons of ʿOs̱mān as having seized the sovereignty and sultanate of the Turkish nation, who had now taken the sovereignty into their own hands. The Lausanne treaty, concluded on 24 July 1923 after prolonged sessions, accepted the basic claim of Turkey, offered the Greeks a generous settlement and opened a new era of friendlier relations with the West. Henceforth Muṣṭafā Kemāl and the National Assembly were the masters of Turkey's destiny.

The establishment of the republic and the reforms

The second major phase of modern Turkish history began after the national elections of 1923. The elections, in addition to unseating the deputies opposed to Muṣṭafā Kemāl, and to his modernist goals, now easily discernible, sanctioned also the transformation of the defence associations into a political party. The People's party, later the People's Republican party, established in 1923, became Muṣṭafā Kemāl's instrument for power and reform and also the ladder through which new groups from the lower bureaucratic-intellectual order ascended to power and fortune.

The new Assembly opened on 11 August 1923, ratified the Lausanne treaty, and later in October, made Ankara the capital of Turkey. On 29 October the Assembly accepted an amendment to the Constitutional Act of 1921 to make Turkey a republic. Muṣṭafā Kemāl was elected president and ʿIṣmet Pasha (İsmet İnönü) became the first republican prime minister. The establishment of a republican régime was the logical consequence of the idea of national sovereignty and national statehood. It marked at the same time the beginning of a new ideological orientation. The nationalism dominant in the War of Liberation was the outgrowth of populist ideas and religious loyalties, and in this form it was instrumental in defining the territorial limits of Turkey. The nationalism emerging after the establishment of the republic aimed at reshaping the state and its institutions according to a secular modern model inspired by the West. The names 'Turks' and 'Turkey' mentioned frequently by leaders appear henceforth in a national context, whereas in the past they had chiefly a religious connotation. Consequently the universalist idea of pan-Islamism and pan-Turanism, both of which had played such important roles in the Union and Progress era, were rejected.

But a modern national state and a Turkish nation could not be established as long as the traditional theocratic foundations remained intact and their symbol, the caliph, maintained his position. The latter, still supported by a large group of loyal followers, could have easily regained his traditional powers and rendered meaningless the idea of a modern republic. The issue, therefore, appeared in need of speedy solution, if the progress achieved so far was to be preserved. Consequently, after a preliminary preparation, the caliphate was abolished on 3 March 1924, and the incumbent ʿAbd ül-Mejīd sent into exile. Knowingly, Turkey renounced a position of influence in the Muslim world, despite insistent demands from Islamic leaders for the preservation of the caliphate. The abolition of the caliphate was followed by the closure of the Ministry of *Sharīʿat* and of the religious courts, and by the unification of the educational system. The judicial functions were reserved to independent courts, and education placed under the sole responsibility of the Ministry of Education. The traditional institutions which had governed society and government for centuries were liquidated, and the way was open to a new mode of life.

The caliphate, in addition to its political position, was also the culminating point of the social hierarchy which had controlled the masses for centuries. The economic and social changes occurring in the past had created new forces and forms of economic and social relations which, contained within the framework of religion, could not follow the natural course dictated by causes at their birth. The abolition of the caliphate, therefore, threatened to liberate these forces, to challenge the authority of the religious leaders and undermine their social and economic status. Already many of the old '*ulemā*' families had become landowners, merchants or craftsmen combining conviction with interest, and thus preserving their position in society.

The Constitution of 20 April 1924 had legalized the new order, but still preserved Islam as the state religion. The National Assembly was defined as the legal repository of all powers. This unicameral legislature elected the president, who in turn nominated the prime minister. The cabinet was responsible to the Assembly, which alone could decide its own dissolution. The entire organization, however, was controlled by the Republican party headed by Muṣṭafā Kemāl. The government structure reflected its revolutionary background, and left no doubt as to where authority stood.

The reaction to reform and the power group emerging in the Republican party came out in 1924, in the form of a Progressive Republican party established by former associates of Kemāl. The party's outward intention was to oppose authoritarianism and promote democracy and liberalism, whereas loyalty to the caliphate was its inner cause. A few months later in 1925, Shaykh Sa'īd launched his revolt to restore the caliphate and establish an independent Kurdistān. The government responded swiftly by bringing back 'Iṣmet Pasha as premier —he had been replaced by Fetḥī Bey (Fethi Okyar)—and by passing a Law for the Maintenance of Order. The revolt was quelled, and the Progressive party abolished. The law marked the beginning of a series of new reforms to liquidate the vestiges of the old régime. It also sealed the Republican party's full ascendancy to power.

Secularism so far was implemented in the government, whereas society at large preserved its traditional way of life and customs, rooted directly in Islam. It seemed that a total modern change could be achieved only by reshaping the institutions, manners and attitudes which perpetuated the hold of traditionalism over the masses. The suppression of the dervish orders and convents, dress reform (the abolition of the fez and the discouragement of the veil), the introduction of the solar calendar, and the emancipation of women between 1925 and 1935, were part of the attempt at cultural modernization. The adoption of the Civil Code of Switzerland in 1926, and of penal and commercial codes from other European countries, though connected with secularism, were also prompted by the need for a more systematic economic life and proper protection for the new régime of private property and middle classes, which had sought legal protection since the nineteenth century. The abolition of social titles, the introduction of the Roman alphabet and the prohibition of the Arabic script (1928), the recital of the call to prayer in Turkish, and the establishment of history and language institutes, were reforms with cultural, but mostly nationalistic purposes.

The surname law of 1935, after which Muṣṭafā Kemāl took the name of Atatürk (father—Turk), ended the confusion created by the use of first names. It unwittingly gave at the same time legal recognition to the family names of the surviving old aristocracy of Anatolia, as well as to the new rising middle classes. The surnames were to become distinguishing social marks. The reforms did not hinder the practice of Islam although the ecclesiastical schools and other religious activities lost official support. In 1928 the reference to Islam in the Constitution was dropped. Nevertheless, on occasions the press and the public showed great reaction to any apostasy from Islam. It seemed that Turkey had a secular government set to rule a society fully dedicated to Islam.

The reforms, although more profound in their symbolic meaning and orientation towards the future than usually credited nowadays, dealt largely with the form of society and were enforced through state authority. The nationalist and secular aspects of modernization gained in importance to the detriment of truly social issues. Moreover, prompted by changes of social structure, nationalism became the ideology of the new power-groups, and deprived populism of its social democratic content. Society, according to the new official view, was composed not of classes but of individuals divided into occupational groups. The state was the only institution entitled to total allegiance, thus differing little in this aspect from its Ottoman predecessor.

While achieving some of the political objectives sought by the intelligentsia since the turn of the century politically and ideologically Turkey had reached an impasse by 1930. The revolutionary régime had injected society with a few revitalizing reforms, and hoped that it could move forward by self-generated dynamism. The Liberal party experiment of 1930 came out of this search for return to 'normalcy'. It was in part prompted by Muṣṭafā Kemāl's desire to check the increasing power and relative stagnation in the Republican party through an opposition, and also bring in a measure of self-rule. The atmosphere seemed suitable, since the Law for the Maintenance of Order was abolished, and a small Kurdish revolt easily put down. The Liberal party was established by Fethi Okyar at Kemāl's own suggestion. It received unexpected popular support. It was dissolved in November 1930, largely on the insistence of the Republican party hierarchy, who eventually convinced Muṣṭafā Kemāl to give up his neutral position with exaggerated reports of impending religious reaction. It is highly significant that government officials, often acting under the orders of local Republican party leaders, often created difficulties for Fethi. In the end Muṣṭafā Kemāl personally had to intervene, and assure him freedom of movement. The dissatisfaction in the countryside, as discovered later by Muṣṭafā Kemāl during a three months' trip, was caused by economic stagnation and the usurpation of lucrative positions by party members. The first effort to establish democracy produced no visible results, except for giving a chance to the opposition in the countryside to organize itself and wait for another propitious moment, which finally came in 1946.

Foreign relations, economic policy, social and ideological development

The failure of the democratic experiment, the world economic crisis of 1929, which affected Turkey's agricultural exports, coupled with the rise of totalitarian systems in the West, produced its effects in Turkey. Theoretically the entire movement of reform and modernization since 1839 appeared directed against autocracy, and came to idealize the Western democratic, parliamentary order as the ultimate goal. Practical considerations, on the other hand, pleaded in favour of strong measures and quick results, and incidentally appealed to long traditions of authority. Turkey more than any country, owing to its geographical position, social structure and political traditions, has often oscillated between East and West in the course of modernization. This became more evident after the revolution of 1917 in Russia, and the emergence there of a modern socialist régime. The influence of the Soviet Union was strong during political alienation from the West, or during the failure of the Western system and institutions to provide satisfaction or results. As long as the West maintained its vitality, the influence of measures inspired by the Soviets—and these are numerous—remained local. Thus, the new *rapprochement* with the Soviets which began in 1929 (despite previous Russian propaganda against Kemāl who had been described as a fascist) was caused partly by fear of Italy's expansionist aims (notwithstanding a treaty of mutual neutrality signed with Mussolini in 1928) but mostly by the economic crisis in the West. The exchange of visits between the statesmen of the two countries and the intensification of trade led to a loan agreement for the development of the textile industry.

A new authoritarian trend was evident in ideology and government organization. The ideology of the republic, already defined in the Republican party convention of 1927, was expanded and clarified in 1931, and incorporated in the party programme, and then in the Constitution in 1937. The six principles (republicanism, populism, nationalism, etatism, secularism and reformism), represented by six arrows on party publications, thus aimed at encompassing all Turkey's problems. Of these principles, etatism was to receive considerable attention in the next decade, and even to force nationalism and secularism to follow its authoritarian and partly materialistic philosophy.

The Republican party increased its influence in the government and by 1935, it became identified with the state and nation. The corporative ideas of the Italian system, owing to their convenient rejection of class differences and idealization of the state were borrowed along with the Soviet methods of party organization; Recep Peker became the party's secretary-general. He was an ultra-conservative in social matters, a nationalist and a bitter enemy of the Ottoman dynasty. His philosophy, which was widespread in the party, was expressed in his university courses. The Republican party claimed that the republic was a *party* state, and that people were to address party organizations to have their needs met. Populism and national sovereignty had all but lost their initial meaning. The people were not forgotten though. The forceful reforms, according to the memoirs of one member, were to continue, for 'the motto that reforms are for people despite the people was an unchanged law.... Those who achieve social and political changes in the social structure are the leaders who do it for the people by opposing the people.'[1]

These internal political developments were accompanied by an active foreign policy under the resourceful minister, Rüştü Aras, from 1925 to 1938. The basic principle was expressed by Atatürk as 'peace at home and abroad'. It was a policy marked by flexibility and freedom of initiative, facilitated in part by lack of international political blocs which might have forced Turkey to commit herself to one side. Moreover, as the first Muslim country to modernize and victoriously to oppose the West, she enjoyed prestige and popularity both in the Orient and the Occident.

Relations with the West improved after the treaty of Lausanne, but the award of Mosul to Iraq was followed by a treaty of friendship with the Soviets in 1925. The settlement of oil-rights with Britain for a pittance straightened the balance in favour of the West. Relations with Greece improved greatly after the signing of a treaty of neutrality, arbitration and conciliation in 1930, and enabled the two countries to adopt a common policy in the Balkans. The conferences which began in 1930 led to the Balkan Pact of 1934 with Greece, Roumania and Yugoslavia, and assured Turkey both peace and trade with these former Ottoman territories. Italy's renewed threat of expansion in the early 1930s brought Turkey closer to France and Britain, and caused a partial deterioration of the relations with the Soviets, already marred by the latter's support of communist activities in Turkey. The Montreux convention signed in 1937, which permitted Turkey to militarize the Straits, while preserving freedom of passage, was made possible by the fears caused by German and Italian dreams of expansion.

The Sa'dābād Pact of 1937 with Afghanistan, Iraq and Iran, although of limited consequence, guaranteed peace in the East and maintained Turkish influence in the region. Thus by 1937 Turkey had established friendly relations with all her neighbours, and this enabled her to carry out her own internal policy. However, the annexation of Hatay (Alexandretta) in 1939, after a series of diplomatic moves and agreements with France, the mandatory power, opened a still unhealed rift with the Syrians.

The Turkish leaders, who all came from the lower echelons of the ruling class and were heirs to Ottoman elitist views, had a keen understanding of the art of ruling. But the brilliancy shown in military and

[1] Avni Doğan, *Kurtuluş, kuruluş ve sonrası* (Istanbul, 1964), 222.

administrative fields was not matched in economic matters. In the first they had a philosophy and a tradition, in the second neither. Hence they adopted a pragmatic approach to economic policy, which, deprived of sound theoretical foundations, often fluctuated according to the personal views of its enforcers.

The importance of economics as the foundation of a modern state, already recognized by the Union and Progress party in 1911, was fully endorsed in the republic as indicated by the Economic Congress of Izmir held in February 1923. The subsequent economic policy developed without the support of a native middle class and against the sad memories of the capitulations, abolished in the Lausanne treaty. The Turkish leaders did not reject the idea of private enterprise, although at no time, except between 1950 and 1952, was there a policy geared to its requirements. Economic liberalism as well as etatism were judged primarily in terms of authority, state interests, historical and political traditions, rather than as questions of production and distribution, involving people and interests. The goal at the beginning was to stimulate economic activity by providing capital for local industries, and opening up, and eventually taking over, some foreign enterprises in mining and transportation. The Work, Industry and Mining Banks became the cornerstone of Turkish economic policy, but without achieving spectacular results.

The place of the Greeks (most of whom departed in the exchange of population in 1924) and Armenians, who controlled the manufacturing and commercial enterprises in towns, could not be taken overnight by the incoming Balkan Turks, mostly from rural areas. The resulting economic stagnation was made worse by the world economic crisis of 1929, and was a new blow to private enterprise. At this time Turkey received a Soviet loan of eight million dollars for industrial development, to be followed later by similar loans from the Western states.

The five-year plans of 1934 and of 1939, partly shaped according to the Russian model, were limited in scope, and had few of the organizational features of modern planning projects. Nevertheless, they promoted state investment. But the outbreak of war in 1939 resulted in an increase of defence expenditure, and forced a drastic reduction of economic investment. Some basic industries for consumer goods, such as textiles, paper, glass, ceramics, chemicals and a steel mill, were already established. The national income in 1938, according to rather unreliable figures (the first statistics were compiled in 1927), was one-third above the figure for 1927.[1] Nowadays those who consider the material results of etatism tend to hail it, whereas those who look at the production costs and poor management are inclined to play down its achievements. Agriculture, the backbone of the economy, was neglected and often exploited, ending eventually in lowering the peasantry's living standards.

Students of the Turkish economy, misled by leaders' statements and changing policies, claim that the country had no clearly defined economic ideology. Actually, etatism was the basic ideology, if etatism is to be taken out of its economic context and considered in the broader spectrum of tradition, history, political authority and *élite* rule. The government wanted to modernize the economy of Turkey by solving the problems of production and industrialization within the framework of state authority. It wanted to use free enterprise as a lever at its own discretion to spur Turkey's economic vitality. There was no question of transferring political power, or sharing it with the representatives of productive forces: capitalists or workers. Hence etatism became necessary. It is, therefore, understandable that pure capitalism and socialism were equally condemned.

There was a notable attempt at framing an economic-political ideology, which represented chiefly the viewpoint of the state and the groups in it. The review *Kadro*, published originally with government support, tried to combine and use socialist and corporative ideas to create a modern apparatus of production, free of exploitation and controlled by a nationalist state which would impart justice to all. There was no question of growth from below, or even interest in cultivating the creative forces of the masses. The latter were to be used in attaining the goals established by the *élite* cadre of the state.

The Turkish rulers faced the fundamental problem encountered by all emerging modern systems, namely the establishment of a new pattern of relations between state and individual. But, without a basic constitutional foundation such as that provided in the past by Islam, the state, still immersed in its own ruling habits, was searching for new arguments to justify, legitimize and perpetuate its traditional supremacy.

The idea of preserving the existing traditional social structure as distinct from the power-structure, although irreconcilable with modernistic aims, appeared essential for maintaining the primacy of the state. The rejection of social classes, political parties, the class-struggle, and trade unions resulted partly from the need to foster unity, but mostly

[1] *First five year development plan 1963–1967* (Ankara, 1963), 8.

from the logical necessity of the etatist ideology and its conservative social philosophy. Consequently the trade union movement was banned and labour relations strictly regulated through a Labour Law of 1936, modelled on the Italian counterpart. The supporting socio-political basis of the etatism was nationalism, which, in line with internal developments, changed from a humanist philosophy into an arch-conservative rightist ideology.

A series of measures intended to spread the nationalist republican secularism of the new régime to the masses unavoidably reflected the conservative ideas of this etatism. The People's Houses, established in 1931–2, aimed at providing a general education for the masses in the Western spirit, but also at indoctrinating them politically. By 1950, 478 People's Houses and 4,322 People's Rooms (founded in villages after 1940) had been established. The activities of the Houses included language and literature, fine arts, drama, sports, social assistance, adult education, library and publications, village welfare, museums and cultural exhibitions. In the end their political role, as the cultural outlets of the Republican party, prevailed, and undermined their efficiency. There were other consequences of this etatist elitist ideology. The peasants, hailed earlier as the true masters of the country, were soon forgotten and left to lead their traditional life attached to family and kin. It is no exaggeration to say that after a good beginning in 1925 little changed in the villagers' life, except for the worse treatment received from the tax-collector and the village police. There was, however, in 1938 a renewed interest in agriculture as expressed by Atatürk to 'make the fifteenth anniversary of the Republic the beginning of a systematic and planned agriculture and village development'. But the first Village and Agricultural Development Congress did not produce much.

A new power-group was at the helm, working through the Republican party. The ruling circles consisted of men with a military, bureaucratic background, who had been associated with the establishment of the republic and its reforms. The populist and religious-minded groups in the first National Assembly had long been left out. The lower ranks of the constantly expanding bureaucracy were made up of graduates of *lycées* and universities with a smattering of general culture and limited professional training, but holding tight to a diploma which was considered sufficient to assure them a career. The offspring of the former Ottoman families, if not totally compromised by association with the sultanate, easily acquired high positions in the administrative apparatus, notably in the Ministry of Foreign Affairs, by virtue of their education, refinement and knowledge of foreign languages, as well as family connexions.

In the countryside, the notables, the old *a'yān* and *'ulemā'* families, after a brief period of hesitation came to terms with the new régime, once their social status and property rights appeared assured. Next to this group there rose the craftsmen, small merchants and local intellectuals who had provided the leadership in the War of Liberation. These became the new middle class, some based on inherited properties or those acquired from the departing minorities (a special law granted to these people the right to purchase property at very low prices), or through association with the state enterprises. They often acted as the distributors of state products, the representatives of monopolies and of commercial enterprises in buying the peasant's products and selling him manufactured items. Thus, there emerged new political and economic groups, who, out of interest if not conviction, supported the new régime, the national state and its modernistic aims, and, unwittingly perhaps, shaped their own lives accordingly.

The educational process was determined in good measure by the social development and its political undertones. The rate of illiteracy in 1927–8 was ninety per cent, and in 1935–6, it fell to eighty per cent, and has remained about sixty per cent since 1950. The *lycées,* as might be expected, expanded forty-one times between 1927 and 1960. University enrolment grew at about the same rate. But as late as 1960, the total number of village children in elementary schools was 1,455,254 out of a total of 2,372,778 village children of school age, as against 823,947 from a total of 945,624 town children. The relatively slow development of education was caused by a variety of physical difficulties; the small size of villages, the cost of schools and training. A more important cause, however, was the lack of a sound educational philosophy, which in turn resulted from a failure to develop an adequate populist social philosophy. Education at upper levels became a yardstick of social status, and consequently some conservatives expressed doubts about the wisdom of spreading primary education. Some even proposed to train an aristocratic *élite* of technicians and administrators in the West, and entrust the modernization of Turkey to them. Education placed emphasis on instruction, theoretical knowledge and far less on doing, creating and participating. The schools did not visualize the intellectual refinement of the human being as the ultimate goal but contented themselves merely with preparing good citizens for the state. The only major and genuinely Turkish experiment in mass education, the Village Institute programme, was altered just when it began to produce results.

The relative stagnation which seized Turkey in the mid-1930s could be considered as the symptoms which accompany the closing of one period and herald the beginning of another. The generation which won the War of Liberation and created the first reforms had reached the end of its creativity. Their ideals and philosophy were inspired by the political and intellectual objectives of the Young Turk era: to create a national Turkish state and give to it a modern political form. Despite their limited background, the early reformers' achievement is monumental indeed. They started to modernize a society shaped by political and social traditions rooted in Islam, and amidst most adverse internal and external circumstances. They created a new state, and through it undermined permanently—often without desiring it—the belief in the permanence of social organization, and the sanctity of customs, *mores* and authority. The leaders' greatest achievement was the establishment of a modern political structure, the national state, supported by an institutional basis easily adaptable to modern functions. These were results obtained through a policy of appraising the phenomenon of power without the religious bias.

The man behind this achievement, Atatürk, died on 10 November 1938. He was a strong man, a ruler by the virtue of his training, but not a dictator. He detested the title and continuously stressed his allegiance to national sovereignty. Atatürk was a soldier-ruler and as such had a keen understanding of the virtues and defects of his people. Unlike the Ottoman ruling class, he used his insight for the people's own good. In so doing, he did not beg for popularity, but ordered, punished and rewarded with the habit of a soldier used to obedience. But beneath the determined appearance there was a man, the orphan who was raised in the healthy, human atmosphere of the village, and then the small Balkan town of Salonica. He preserved a freshness and spontaneity towards life even after he became the most powerful man in Turkey. Some of the reforms, particularly the cultural ones, are in fact a direct expression of his own view of life.

Atatürk's coffin was deposited in 1953 in his monumental tomb overlooking Ankara, now a city of about 700,000 people. Every year on the anniversary of his death, the officials deliver their speeches, the youth swear eternal observance of his reforms. In the afternoon throngs of common men travel miles by foot from the city and surrounding villages to pay their respects to the man who opened the way to their happiness. Theirs is a simple and moving testimony to a popular love which permanently guarantees the existence of Atatürk's modern Turkey.

Turkey during the Second World War

After Atatürk's death, İsmet İnönü (b. 1884) became president. He had been replaced by Celâl Bayar (b. 1883) as premier in 1937, in circumstances that still remain obscure. A few months later in 1939, Celâl Bayar's place was taken by Refik Saydam. A military man by training and highly respected by the army, Inönü's basic philosophy differed from Bayar's. Inönü was the opposite of Atatürk. A man devoted to his family, cautious and a skilful politician, he idealized law and order, the primacy of government authority, and the stability of the established régime. Bayar was a banker and economist with a rather authoritarian nature, with many friends among civilians and business groups, but only a limited following among the military and the intelligentsia.

The Republican party convention of 1938 made Inönü permanent chairman. A second convention assembled the following year created an Independent Group to simulate an opposition in the Assembly, and, while tightening centralization, decided to release the party leaders from administrative positions. It also declared that many party members did not know much about Kemalist ideology and stressed the need to formulate and disseminate it. The administration was eventually filled by men of lesser stature, who represented the new groups emerging in the 1930s; these were firmly dedicated to the republic but had a limited cultural and social horizon.

Foreign relations rather than internal policies became the dominant theme of this period. The first major question concerned the future of Hatay (Alexandretta). The treaty with the French in 1921, confirmed by the Lausanne treaty of 1923, recognized the special status of the Turks in Hatay. Eventually, in 1936, the League of Nations proposed autonomy for Hatay, but France supported by Great Britain accepted a joint Franco-Turkish administration in order to secure a military alliance with Turkey. The Hatay assembly, chosen by elections which gave a slight majority to the Turks, applied for incorporation, and by July 1939, the territory became part of Turkey. On 19 October 1939, Turkey signed a treaty of alliance and mutual defence with France and Great Britain, largely to insure herself against possible Soviet designs as evidenced by the latter's demands for a revision of the Montreux convention. The Soviets had indeed signed a secret agreement with Nazi Germany and secured the promise of bases on the Straits, territory and a sphere of influence in the north. The collapse of France in 1940, the German conquest of the Balkans and advance deep into Soviet territory in 1941, created repercussions in Turkey. The mistrust of Russia manifested itself in the form of growing pro-German feeling among some intellectuals and military groups. Nationalist thought began to acquire racialist undertones, and a few extremist circles encouraged by German agents spread Nazi and fascist ideas.

Germany began to exercise pressure on Turkey to join the Axis powers, or at least to permit the passage of troops to support the pro-Nazi Iraqi rebels who had taken control of government. Turkey resisted threats and promises, and gave time to Great Britain to re-establish control in Iraq. The Germans, however, secured a treaty of friendship and trade in 1941, but without neutralizing the Turkish-French-British alliance. In 1943 it was the turn of the British to press Turkey to enter the war against Germany, but without success, since the Allies could not meet Turkey's demand for arms. Eventually Turkey suspended the shipment of goods to Germany, and then broke off diplomatic relations on 2 August 1944. Finally on 23 February 1945 Turkey declared war on the Axis powers and thus qualified to attend the San Francisco conference. Thus Turkish policy during the war remained consistent with the basic idea of peaceful coexistence, preservation of independence and refusal of territorial aggrandizement—even later, when Greece acquired the strategic Dodecanese islands from Italy at the peace conference.

The war did not cost Turkey loss of men or territory but did impose heavy economic hardships. The National Defence Law, which gave the government absolute powers to control the economy, paralysed the market. The requirements of troops, mobilized at the beginning of the war and kept in readiness until the late 1940s, created a shortage of basic consumer goods. The shortage was aggravated by the sale abroad of raw materials and agricultural products. The peasants were forced through the Land Products Office to deliver pre-established quotas of wheat at a price fixed by the government below that of the free market. In many instances the delivery was secured by force, and villagers often sold their belongings to meet the quota. The black market which flourished from the beginning of the war permitted profiteers to accumulate fortunes overnight. Imported goods, and even home-produced items, such as flour and bread, came on the black market. The substantial amount of foreign currency accumulated from exports was spent after 1946 on a variety of imports and household goods purchased mainly by urban groups with the money hoarded during the war.

The wartime inflation and shortages caused hardship among the lower urban classes, but less among the salaried groups, which were assisted with food and clothing. Faced with growing economic difficulties and defence expenditure, the government finally rammed through the Assembly in 1942 the *varlık vergisi,* a sort of capital tax. The premier, Şükrü Saracoğlu, presented it as a measure of social justice and national self survival aimed at those enriched by the war, but as it turned out, chiefly at the minority groups. The law was enforced drastically at the beginning, causing the bankruptcy of small artisans and businesses. It was abolished in 1944, after having damaged the prestige of Turkey abroad, shaken profoundly the confidence of the business community, harmed the economy by causing a flight of capital, and added to the speculative fever on the market.

The increase in the volume of demand, the shortage of imports and the rapid accumulation of capital in private hands during the war combined to stimulate the growth of an entrepreneurial class, composed predominantly of commercial and manufacturing groups, as well as of contractors who supplied the army and the market with food and a variety of home-made items to replace foreign imports. The number of industrial workers in private enterprises grew during the war to about 300,000 people. Thus the war produced the conditions for a new type of social and economic balance by forcing the growth of the private sector to match and eventually surpass in size the state sector. This rise of private enterprise which afforded possibilities for quick profits created in turn a materialistic social and economic outlook.

The war also provided a convenient excuse to intensify the restrictions on freedom of assembly, press and thought through the Law of Associations passed in 1938. The reforms were also enforced thoroughly wherever possible, although there was more emphasis on their formal observance than on their spirit. The implementation of secularism became dogmatic, as did the language reform. Religious practices, never forbidden by law or by the government, continued, but without a supporting theological basis, intellectual speculation and thought. There was a deterioration of spiritual values, which, cut off from Islam, could not be connected with a new secular, philosophical source. Nevertheless, for lack of other sufficiently strong cohesive social force, religion still continued to be the criterion for determining Turkishness. Intrinsically Islam as a faith regressed, as shown by the growth of various religious orders and superstitious beliefs among villagers. The peasant had regarded his religion as a normative moral order, in fact the only major force which regulated relations in the village and formed the basis of his ethical code. For all practical purposes the republic offered him laws, regulations, authority, but nothing to nurture his inner life. The intellectual had books, libraries, universities and a variety of other sources to meet his spiritual and moral needs, and to replace in part his dependence on religion. He had also a positivist view to explain the universal order. The peasant had none of these. He remained opposed to secular reforms, lest his life end in chaos.

The middle classes too began to look upon Islam as a moral force which could be used to regulate the new economic relations, and contain the materialistic urges of the masses. The problem as usual appeared as a moral crisis. Where the intellectual wanted to use state power to preserve social morality (later expressed as socialism), the middle class sought salvation in religion, partly because of tradition (the craftsmen and small businessmen remained deeply attached to Islam), and partly because of mistrust of the state. The family, already a cherished institution, became further idealized, for the intellectual and the new middle-class groups alike found in its customs and philosophy the habitual climate of Islam, which many had rejected formally but sought subconsciously for the sake of their own psychological security.

The establishment of democracy

The end of the Second World War found Turkey exhausted physically and morally at the hands of a rightist bureaucratic order closely resembling a dictatorship. The president was the National Leader and the Republican party his instrument of power. But the war had discredited the one-party systems, the rightist dictatorships, and naturally weakened Turkey's moral position, which seemed to be aggravated by her failure to join actively the Allies in the war. Internal tensions at home and conditions abroad necessitated a profound change. The signs of change were evident in 1944, when the racialists and pan-Turanists were tried for subversive activities. The San Francisco conference, attended by a large Turkish delegation, pointed towards a democratic world-order.

President İnönü's declaration of 19 May 1945, promising a democratic régime at home, raised further hopes of an imminent change.

The government appeared prepared to tolerate some kind of opposition when a land reform bill was submitted to the Assembly on 14 May 1945. The reform, the first of its kind, was opposed from the start by a group of landowning deputies and representatives of some commercial groups in the countryside. These, headed by Adnan Menderes, the spokesman for the Agricultural Committee, criticized the expropriation clauses as threatening to destroy middle-sized farms. The debates in the Assembly eventually touched upon a wide range of political issues in an effort to demonstrate that the one-party system and the ever-expanding government authority violated the Constitution and democracy in general. The government reaction to criticism was relatively mild.

The Land Law was passed after creating a profound social and political rift in the Republican party, and encouraging the formation of opposition groups in the countryside. In fact, through its widespread social and economic implications and political effects, it could be rightly considered the turning-point in Turkey's internal life. The Land Law, incidentally, was hardly enforced, and eventually amended in 1950, to render it meaningless. By 1954, a total of 1,551,206 hectares of land, mostly owned by the state, had been distributed to about 100,000 families, leaving at least ten times more peasants in need of land. The main difficulty arose of course from the fact that Turkey had not sufficient cultivable land for all, even if landholdings were brought down to the minimum size.

The political régime began to be liberalized in the summer of 1945, when the first opposition party, the National Resurgence party, with a programme of moral rejuvenation, was established by a rich contractor, Nuri Demirağ. Turkey was about to give a unique example of conversion from a semi-dictatorial system to a democracy. This decision, if considered in the light of the élitist, authoritarian background of Turkish governments appears as a true revolution. The people were free to cast off the rule of a selected few, and to learn to govern themselves by establishing through voluntary action and agreement a government representative of society.

The main opposition party was formed on 7 January 1946, after the press, through its leftist and liberal journals *Tan* and *Vatan,* had prepared the ground by subjecting the Republican party to bitter censure. The founders of the Democratic party were Celâl Bayar, Adnan Menderes, Refik Koraltan and Fuat Köprülü, all of whom had belonged formerly to the Republican party, and supported its policies. The ruling Republicans encouraged, and, according to unverified reports, even supported the establishment of the Democratic party, presumably in the hope of using it as a democratic façade. After a short period of indecision, the people began to join the Democratic party, and swelled its membership to one million within six months. Peasants, workers, the lower middle classes and other dissatisfied groups supported the party, and in fact forced its leaders to take seriously their opposition to the government.

Meanwhile, the government liberalized the press and the Law of Association, and introduced the system of direct voting. The president's title of National Leader was dropped. The first national elections were held in 1946, in an atmosphere rendered tense by the Republicans' tampering with the election results. The Democratic Party, nevertheless, elected sixty-four deputies who found in the Assembly the most effective propaganda rostrum. The Republicans, faced by increasingly hostile crowds angered by the election frauds, brought Recep Peker to the premiership.

This internal development started from the hope that Turkey might be able to preserve a balanced position between all the war-time Allies. Consequently political liberalization was extended also to the leftists, who responded by issuing publications, and establishing their own organizations. The Soviets, however, forced Turkey out of this would-be neutral position. In March 1945 they denounced the 1925 treaty of friendship, and, on the basis of the Potsdam agreements, demanded on 8 August 1946 the revision of the Montreux convention to limit control of the Straits to the Black Sea countries. They asked for bases on the Straits, and even territory in the north. Turkey rejected all demands and remained on the military alert until 12 March 1947, when President Truman issued his promise of aid (the 'Truman Doctrine') to countries threatened by communism.

Thus, menaced from the north, Turkey was forced to consolidate her internal front by suspending in 1946 several leftist publications, trade unions, and two political parties. The right-wing elements in both the Republican and Democratic parties, encouraged by the fears caused by the Soviet Union, eventually attacked the Village Institutes, the People's Houses, as well as several university intellectuals as being leftist in character. The reaction which started in Turkey in 1947, contrary to the generally held opinion, was not religious but social and political, and was triggered by the turn of events in foreign policy. The religious reaction started initially as a corollary to the reaction against communism.

Meanwhile, the struggle between the Republican and Democratic parties reached breaking point. The impasse was solved by İnönü's declaration of 12 July 1947, which accepted the opposition on an equal basis with the governing party, offered it legal protection, and assured the country that the government would change according to the people's wish. The declaration of 12 July is the basic document recognizing the multi-party system in Turkey.

The Republican party in turn attempted to adapt itself to the requirements of democratic life by amending its by-laws and programme in a convention assembled late in 1947. For the first time the convention paid close attention to the opinion of its rural representatives, whose close knowledge of people at large was considered essential in achieving victory at the polls. The convention recommended a series of liberalizing measures in education, secularism and land reform, the main purpose of which was to counteract the Democrats' similar promises and secure votes. The liberal policy followed by the Republican government after 1948, which included the introduction of religious education in 1949, and the acceptance of an election law in 1950, are to be found in the recommendations of this convention.

Meanwhile a small group, representing the liberal, individualistic, and also the unruly elements in the Democratic party, broke away in 1948, and formed the National party. Marshal Fevzi Çakmak joined the party after becoming disillusioned with the Democrats, but even his prestige did not win it popularity. This indicated that Turkish politics are bound not only to personalities but also issues. The party has remained a small regional organization. The two major parties did not differ drastically in programmes and leadership, but did present striking dissimilarities in organization and mentality. The Democratic party had at the beginning a very broad popular basis. It was dominated by the lower-level organizations, unlike the Republicans whose power was concentrated at the top. The Democrats represented the lower classes and some business groups. The Republicans were supported by intellectual bureaucratic groups and the richer upper circles of the etatist enterprises. The first defended liberalism and the latter etatism; although the terms had little in common with their Western meanings.

They represented essentially currents of thought born from historical conditions specific to Turkey and the Islamic world in general—the struggle of the popular masses against the ruling order at the top. But underneath the traditional influences there was also a crucial modern issue. The Democratic party promised to be an aggregate of interests with potentialities of broad representation, whereas the Republican party remained committed to an ideology with narrowing effects which alienated many groups. This was the most important facet of the Democrats' liberalism.

The multi-party struggle after 1946 might not have changed the rulers' mentality, but it did provide a unique type of social and political education for the peasants, workers and lower groups of businessmen. Truly voluntary associations, freedom of discussion and thought, criticism of government and other types of activities encountered in a democratic society, notwithstanding the abuses coming from novelty and inexperience, appeared after 1946. The individual gradually emerged and began to demand his share in electing the government that would rule him. For the first time in the entire history of Islam, the individual's political role and his secular rights against the government were accepted, and permitted to take institutional forms. The elections held on 14 May 1950, brought the Democratic party to power. Celâl Bayar became president and Adnan Menderes prime minister.

(B) TURKISH NATIONALISM

General remarks

The history of nationalism in Turkey is intimately associated with the evolution of state ideology from Islamic universalism to multi-national Ottomanism, and finally to one-nation Turkism and patriotism. Nationalism in the Ottoman empire did not start as a movement of liberation but was adopted by the state as a means to rally the population around a common concept and thus maintain its territorial integrity. The ideas of nation, language and fatherland did not follow one uniform line of development but varied constantly according to changing internal and external conditions. Islamic traditional influences supplied the emotional stamina of Turkish nationalism, long provided for some sense of unity, and only recently began to be replaced by objective local influences.

Turkish nationalism appears as a series of successive movements, differing in their ideological foundations and goals, and often conflicting with each other. For instance, the pan-Islamic universalist concepts developed under ʿAbd ül-Ḥamīd (1876–1909) were adjusted to the pan-Turanian ideas of the Young Turks (1908–18) and finally discarded in the War of Liberation (1919–22) and the Republic (from 1923) for a limited concept of Turkish nationalism.

Islamic universalism, which was a special kind of nationalism, if nationalism is to be taken as loyalty to a set of ideas, is only implicitly touched upon in this article. The main attention is devoted to Ottoman and Turkish nationalism. These two movements were genetically related to each other, and appeared as an integral whole. But their differences were greater than their similarities, chiefly because the political framework, namely the type of state in which each developed, had a different structure and different goals. The aim of both movements was to create a nation. But the Ottoman state could hardly hope to give the community of its people the feeling that they belonged together, shared a common heritage and had a common destiny. This state could create a nationality, as it did in fact, but not a nation in the modern sense of the word. The existence of the Ottoman state was inherently dependent on maintaining its multi-national polyglot population under the supremacy of a ruling *élite,* whose political thought derived from universalist Islamic concepts of state and government.

Turkish nationalism proper developed primarily within the framework of a national state. It was a secular movement, which aimed at creating a nation with an identity of its own, based on the specific cultural characteristics of the Turks. Territorially, it was confined to the well-defined areas in which Turks were an overwhelming majority. Socially, it represented the populist democratic aspiration of the lower middle classes. Politically, it was based on the idea of national sovereignty.

Taking the narrow view, one may well say that nationalism in its modern sense can develop only in a national state. Modern nationalism entails emphasis on local and national characteristics, and, therefore, conflicts with Islamic universal concepts of social and political organization. Although Islam survived several challenges of localism and nationalism in the past, it seems that now the odds are in favour of nationalism.

Nationalism in the Ottoman empire

Ottoman nationalism was born in the nineteenth century as a reaction to the struggles of Christian minorities, who strove to establish independent national states according to the liberal ideas of the French Revolution. The Ottomans were also inspired by Western nationalism, primarily as it affected the internal administration of the state. But they purposely ignored its ideological content, for its acceptance would have amounted to a recognition of the minorities' viewpoint, as well as of a secularist, particularist philosophy of government. The terms 'nation' (*millet*) and 'fatherland' (*vaṭan*) used by Ottoman nationalists did not coincide. 'Fatherland' was the territory under Ottoman rule, whereas the *millet* encompassed in essence only the Muslim subjects.

The Christian groups were treated as different *millets*. The legal equality and common Ottoman citizenship, given to all subjects after 1839 and 1856, aimed at creating some bases for national unity. These attempts were unsuccessful, primarily because they were not supported by cultural or linguistic bases for a real unity and nationhood. The idea of a 'fatherland', as framed by Ottoman nationalists, could appeal emotionally to Muslim, but not to Christian, subjects. The Ottoman nationalists sought to identify the territory with Islam, and impose its defence on the citzen as a religious duty. This approach was something new indeed. The Muslim Turk certainly had a natural attachment to his village and his town. He would defend his village, but would not show the same readiness to die for far-flung territories without relating his sacrifice to something deeper in him. The zeal to preserve the integrity of these territories could be aroused only by appealing to those feelings, images and symbols associated with their original acquisition. It is in this sense that Ottoman nationalism had to identify the defence of territory with the defence of Islam. This was relatively easy among the unsophisticated Turks, who for centuries had fought for Islam, and had become so identified with it as to forget their own national identity.[1] Mīzānjı Murād Bey could write towards the end of the nineteenth century that the government and the peasant came to agree that war with the

[1] It is true that the nomads and villagers spoke vernacular Turkish, and quite often they knew, as their folklore reveals, that they were not Arabs or Kurds. However, no political significance was attached to these differences. Nevertheless the Turkish nomads and villagers, even though identified with the state's Islamic goals (the state was actually thought to be the sultan) seem to have developed also a sense of hostility towards the administration, as revealed by references in the folklore of the nineteenth century.

West was a matter of life and death, that it would continue without mercy and truce, and that all this was the consequences of the Crusades, which had taken now a modern form.

The intelligentsia, however, closely concerned with the fate of the state, needed a more sophisticated interpretation of nation and nationalism to tie their own emotional and traditional attachments with their modern yearnings.

Nāmıq Kemāl's play *Vaṭan yahut Silistre* (1873) is indeed the fundamental work which defined the fatherland and the Ottomans' duties towards it. It has exercised a continuous and powerful influence on all nationalists until our own days. The setting of the play, significantly enough, is Silistria, a frontier fortress on the Danube. The hero is an ex-officer, Islām Bey, and the entire theme exalts sacrifice for the fatherland.[1] The *vaṭan* (fatherland) for Nāmıq Kemāl was 'a celestial body...leaning with the head on one continent, the body on the other and the legs stretched on the third'. The nation (*millet*) was a notion inspired by his mystical mentor, the poet Leskofchalı Ghālib, who had no dealings with contemporary political problems but used it in a religious context. The greatest 'virtue was to sacrifice one's body made of the fatherland's earth for the fatherland's glory'. No Ottoman should hesitate to die for his fatherland, established through courage and sacrifice, for there was no reason to be born without being ready to die for the fatherland. There is in this play a song sung by volunteers going to war. It epitomizes Nāmıq Kemāl's idea of loyalty to the fatherland:

> 'Our purpose and thought is the fatherland's future. . . .
> We are Ottomans, the bloody shroud is our dowry.
> We seek martyrdom (*shehādet*) in battle.
> We are Ottomans, we give life and receive glory.
> The greatness of our ancestors is world renown.
> Don't think that one's nature changes,
> This is just the same blood.
> Let the cannon boom and spread flames.
> Let the Heavens open the door to dead brothers.
> What did we find in this world to avoid death?'

Nāmıq Kemāl's romantic interpretation of history, his mystical exaltation of heroism and Islamic idealism, had profound influence in

[1] In Turkish, *anavatan* (motherland) is commonly used for fatherland. It implies a more intimate association with the territory than *vaṭan*.

defining the approach to history writing, as is clearly evident in the textbooks written for secondary schools in the second half of the nineteenth century.[1] Important to note is the fact that the political meaning attached to Islam was something new and modern. This was one of the first developments to pave the way for the eventual rise of a true power state, a national state, utterly incompatible with the Islamic concept of a moral universal state. Nāmıq Kemāl occasionally used the word Turk as being synonymous with Muslim, as clearly indicated by his introduction to his novel *Jezmi,* or *Evrāq-ı perīshān,* written as answer to Michaud's *Histoire des Croisades*.

The rise of Ottoman nationalism was accompanied by a linguistic movement, which has been often described as the real beginning of Turkish nationalism. Indeed, the Young Ottomans, Ibrāhīm Shināsī, Żiyā Pasha, Nāmıq Kemāl and 'Alī Su'avī, wrote of the need to simplify the official language by eliminating some of the cumbersome expressions, as well as Arabic and Persian words for which there was a Turkish equivalent. These were journalists and writers seeking for means to reach a greater number of people. A simplified Turkish language could facilitate communication with larger audiences and help generalize the new political ideas developed by the intelligentsia.[2] They were aware of the need for a new literature, new symbols and topics, and needed a language to express them. It is in this context that they sought to make the Turkish language a more efficient means of communication, without giving to it a definitely nationalist meaning.

There is, however, some evidence to indicate that the discussion on language differences (court language versus that of lower urban groups) expressed also a sort of resentment against the growing elitist bureaucracy. 'Alī Su'āvī, who referred clearly to Turks and their own language, implied that the Ottoman rulers were separated from their subjects, and that the Turks were one, but the most important, of the many national groups under Ottoman rule. Aḥmed Midḥat Efendi also could write in the first issue of his review *Dagharjık* (1871) that 'our nation has lost its mother tongue, the Turkish, [elsewhere he says the language brought from Turkistān] and had to learn in its place a language which we cannot call other than Ottoman.... This language is not Arabic nor Persian nor

[1] On historical writing in this period, see Ercüment Kuran, 'Ottoman historiography of the Tanzimat Period', in Bernard Lewis and P. M. Holt (eds.), *Historians of the Middle East* (London, 1962), 422–9.

[2] See Kemal H. Karpat article in Robert Ward and D. A. Rustow (eds.), *Political modernization in Japan and Turkey* (Princeton, 1964).

Turkish, but had become the language of a minority...who subjected the majority and left it without a language.'[1]

The scholarly evidence to support the claim for an independent Turkish language, as well as a history of the Turks apart from Islam, came from some Western writers such as Léon Cahun, Arminius Vambéry, Arthur Lumley Davids, and converts like Muṣṭafā Jelāl al-Dīn Pasha. These works provided the inspiration for Fu'ād and Jevdet Pashas to write their grammar, *Qavā'id-i 'Os̱mānīye,* in 1851. These were followed later by other grammars and dictionaries. It is through these historical-linguistic writings that the intelligentsia discovered the rich pre-Islamic history of Turkic peoples in Central Asia. Now they began to think of a Turkish existence outside Islam, although the Turks' association with Islam was so intimate and so strong as to create insurmountable difficulties in accepting emotionally any other existence.[2]

The linguistic awakening, as well as Ottoman nationalism as a whole, was affected by nationalist thought among the Tatars and Turks of the Crimea, the Caucasus and Kazan. Their leaders published a series of newspapers and reviews in the second half of the nineteenth century with the purpose of educating their people and imbuing in them a sense of nationality as defence against the tsarist government's pan-Slavic drive. Some of these publications entered the Ottoman empire, but awakened little interest at the beginning. The emphasis of folk-culture, language, and local character held little appeal for the Ottoman leaders raised in the universalism of Islam. But when the outside Turkish nationalism adopted some broader aspirations, such as pan-Turanism, the bulk of Ottoman intellectuals became interested in it. Yūsuf Akchuraoghlu, in his essay *Üch ṭarz-i siyāset* ('Three kinds of policy') dismissed Ottomanism and Islamism, and suggested Turkism—a national policy based on the Turkish race—as the basis for the state. Akchuraoghlu's view on race came from German sources, and was rather alien to the Turks' own cultural understanding of race. But it had a touch of universalism, and in the following decade racialism acquired power as a basis for both pan-Turanism and later pan-Turkism in Russia and the Ottoman empire.

[1] Aḥmed Midḥat (1844–1912) was an Islamist, but more in the moral than the political sense. A man of modest origin, he disagreed with Nāmıq Kemāl, who expressed basically the views of the bureaucratic intelligentsia.

[2] Yet these efforts to give life to the Turkish language were partially offset by a return to an obscure language laden with Arabic and Persian constructions, in the literary school known as *Edebīyat-i jedīde* (New Literature) at the end of the nineteenth century.

In tsarist Russia, nationalism stemmed from the Turkic minority's desire for survival, and operated in a natural environment conducive to national consciousness. But in the Ottoman empire it was the Muslims (Turks) who held government power and were accused of oppressing the Christian minorities. Pan-Turanism here became predominantly a principle of foreign policy, and a welcome substitute for the fading dream of pan-Islamism. Eventually pan-Turanism lost its vigour in Russia, whereas in the Ottoman empire it gained additional momentum and was instrumental in the decision of the Committee of Union and Progress government in 1914 to enter the war on the side of Germany, in the hope of gaining territories in the Balkans and Russia.

The early Ottoman nationalists were not concerned with the positive objective elements which made up a nation, but searched for an ideology capable of assuring the state's survival. This attitude was preserved in the understanding of pan-Turanism since scant attention was paid to the actual life, culture or welfare of the individuals living in the 'country of Tūrān'. What mattered was the state, not the individual.

Jamāl al-Dīn al-Afghānī's stay in Istanbul at the end of the nineteenth century, and his Islamic propaganda, particularly his ideas that 'the unity between men is dependent on unity of language and religion', seem to have impressed some intellectuals. It is in this sense that language and religion together gradually began to be regarded by intellectuals as forming the basis of nationalism, and relegated the earlier idea of common nationality (Ottomanism) to a secondary role. And since the language was Turkish it is obvious that this was to give the Turks a dominant ruling position in the state. Meḥmed Emīn Yurdakul (1869–1944) in his *Türkche shi'rler* ('Turkish Poems', 1897), written in simple Turkish (he said, at the urging of al-Afghānī), declared for the first time his pride in being a Turk and extolled the greatness of his faith and race. Thus language, faith, and race for him were indeed the necessary foundations to form a nation. Meḥmed Emīn's nationalism was humanist and democratic in essence, for it was born from a direct observation of his social and human environment. Yet, its Islamic content could hardly appeal to Christian minorities, or in fact to the Ottoman government, which could not accept openly Turkism without undermining its hold over other national groups.

Nationalism in the Young Turk era

Until the advent of the Young Turks to power in 1908, nationalism had developed as a movement with three interconnected ideologies:

Islamism supported by conservatives, Ottomanism by the bureaucracy and Turkism by the younger generation. All three ideologies attached varying importance to Islam. The conservatives and Ottomanists backed by ʿAbd ül-Ḥamīd, viewed it as the basic principle of state, whereas the Turkists regarded it as an element to go into the making of a nation. But none had fully clarified the vital relation between the nation and the state. The Ottoman state, still a multinational structure, was deeply entrenched in its own traditional philosophy of government whereas the nation proper did not yet exist. The situation persisted after 1908. The Young Turks while out of power could afford to promise liberal measures to any dissatisfied group. But once in power they became identified with the state and its political philosophy. Ṭalʿat Pasha, the premier, stated in his memoirs that to meet the demands of Christian minorities for independence would have resulted in the liquidation of the six-hundred-year-old Ottoman empire, built by ancestors through endless sacrifice.

The government of the Young Turks tried to maintain intact the territory of the empire while engaging in an active policy of turcification of Muslim groups, such as Albanians and Arabs. But this policy, which was utterly unsuccessful, was in fact the effort of the ruling group to identify the government with a national group, even before developing some concept of national culture, or nation in the modern sense of the word. In the economic field, the Young Turks made massive efforts to give Turks a place in the economy, particularly in trade and industry, where Armenians and Greeks were in almost absolute control.

The government's view of nationalism was not necessarily accepted by all the nationalists and Turkists. The difference in approach between the government and intellectuals is well dramatized by the fact that Enver Pasha, one of the ruling trio, refused to accept Meḥmed Emīn as an Istanbul representative to the Union and Progress convention, since Emīn defended Turkish nationalism, whereas the government was committed to Ottoman nationalism under the guise of Turkism. This was an expansionist nationalism which soon, as mentioned before, became identified with pan-Turanism.

Yet the Young Turk period witnessed the rise of the first organized nationalist movements among the intellectuals. The *Türk Derneği* ('Turkish Society') was established in 1908, by leading nationalists such as Meḥmed Emīn and Yūsuf Akchuraoghlu, as well as Ottoman non-Muslims, with the purpose of studying the past and present achievements of Turks in all fields of endeavour. It was a sort of scholarly organization at the beginning, and published a review *Türk Derneği* which later became *Türk Yurdu* ('Turkish Homeland'). The latter has appeared intermittently up to the present and has usually expressed conservative nationalist views. The *Türk Ojakları* ('Turkish Hearths') established in 1912, aimed at popularizing the ideas of nationalism, and at raising the cultural level through education, lectures, practical courses on language, literature and drama, as well as welfare activities. The review *Gench Kalemler* ('Young Pens') published in Salonica in 1911, used simple Turkish, and chose its topics from the country's life, to give to literature a national and more natural orientation.

Turkish nationalism since 1908 was profoundly affected by Żiyā Gökalp (1875–1924). Differing from other nationalists who were trying to develop new concepts, Gökalp relied on accepted cultural and social values, and organizational understanding, and used them to shape a traditionalist conservative brand of nationalism. He defined the nation (*millet*) as the last stage of organization of human society. *Kavim* (Arabic *qawm*, kinship group) and *ümmet* (Arabic *umma,* community) were the first two. He developed a theory of internal cohesion in the nation by combining the family attachments prevailing in the kinship groups and the feeling of brotherhood in the Muslim community.

Gökalp spoke of the language, political form and culture of the nation as being Turkish, but he failed to indicate how these outward modern forms would change the Islamic conservative traditionalist content which, he thought, constituted the essence of the nation. Gökalp looked upon the nation as a collectivity, a term borrowed from Durkheim, and assigned to it absolute supremacy over the individual who could not have a life or identity outside his community.

These were the characteristics of the traditional Muslim *umma,* which Gökalp redefined by using modern terminology and ended by producing the blue-print for a Turkish *umma* as a modern nation. For Gökalp, political and cultural goals had the same power, and in fact appeared as identified with moral and ethical issues, and formed the essence of nationalist feelings. Consequently, his nationalism was all-embracing, had a mystical touch, offered emotional nourishment, and could easily serve as a substitute for religion, as in fact it did. Moreover, Gökalp, owing to his own background, had a mystical view of human problems, a tendency towards exaltation and myths, as symbolized by his ideal of Tūrān and *Kızıl Elma* ('Red Apple'). Tūrān, the country to include all the territories in which Turks lived, was a myth which became the ideal of pan-Turanism. *Kızıl Elma,* a term appearing frequently in nationalist literature, was a legendary mythical country towards which the Turks converged.

Gökalp was not fond of the Ottoman ruling group, primarily because he regarded them as an alien group who had perverted the basic Islamic foundations of the empire. Eventually he sided with the Union and Progress party, and worked diligently to unite around one common concept of nationalism all the feuding nationalist groups of his time, the Islamists, Westernists, and Turkists. But instead of fusing their ideas into a new concept, Gökalp put them side by side: Islam supplied the essence of the nation, Westernism its outward appearance and Turkism its name and ideals. Later, when the dismemberment of the Ottoman empire appeared inevitable, Gökalp placed emphasis on Turkism and secularism without altering fundamentally his communal view of the nation.[1]

In conclusion it may be said that the ideas about nation and state between 1908 and 1918 stemmed from political and cultural sources which did not coincide with each other. The state was disintegrating, while the nation was about to emerge. The intellectuals seemed to agree that the Turkish nation was to have its own language, its own culture (primarily based on Islamic values) and its own history. Some stressed the Central Asian heritage, others the Seljuk and Ottoman history, that is to say the Islamic period.[2] No definite agreement on territory was reached.

Nationalism in the republic

The fate of nationalism in Turkey was determined by actual events more than theory. The Balkan War of 1913, and then the First World War, resulted in the liquidation of Ottoman territories in the Balkans and the Middle East. This development destroyed the sustaining foundations of Ottomanism. Pan-Islamism was affected too. The loss of the Arab territories after 1916 seemed to have left among Turks no lasting wounds or haunting memories similar to those resulting from the

[1] As recently as 1963, a nationalist director of a high school in Kayseri claimed that he belonged to the Turkish nation, Islamic *Ümmet* and contemporary civilization.

[2] Some Islamists in the Young Turk era went so far as to say that the Ottoman empire, and in fact the contemporary Turks and their state, could not have survived without Islam, and that religion was so much part of them that neither the nation nor the state could afford to eliminate them.

liquidation of the Rumelian territories. The first were mere transfers from one Islamic rule to another, the second formed the essence, the political *raison d'être* of the Ottoman empire. But the fact that the Arab irregulars attacked and murdered the Ottoman soldiers, who in their innocence thought they were defending the abode of Islam against infidels, destroyed not only the pan-Islamic ideal, but the very idea of the brotherhood of Islam.

One may cite various incidents to prove that the Arabs were discriminated against and maltreated by the Ottoman government, although probably no more than other Islamic groups. But this hardly detracts from the fact that the Ottoman state and the Turkish population were fully identified with Islam, and had exhausted their human and national resources in maintaining the territorial integrity of lands under Islamic rule. If one reads the poems of the Islamic poet Meḥmed 'Ākif glorifying the deeds of Turkish soldiers in the First World War, and then vehemently rejecting the idea of Turkish nationalism, one can better appreciate how recent and strong was the Turks' identification with Islam.[1] The *shehīd* (martyr) fallen in the battle with the infidel was, according to popular beliefs, to be rewarded with a place in heaven, but where would the martyr go who found death at the hands of another Muslim? The real daybreak for Turkish nationalism began indeed somewhere in the sandy dunes of Arabia, where the idea of a universal Islamic empire was born, and where finally it was proved false. The war destroyed also the pan-Turanian dreams of expanding into the Turkic lands of Russia, first because this was militarily impracticable; and secondly, because the new Soviet régime was the first to recognize and develop friendly relations with the nationalist government of Muṣṭafā Kemāl.

Thus, by the end of the First World War in 1918, the universalist influences which nourished Ottoman nationalism had lost their bases. The only remaining thing was a piece of territory in the arid Anatolian hinterland inhabited primarily by Turks, whereas the rich coastal lands were occupied by the enemy. The sultan was in Istanbul, a virtual

[1] Meḥmed 'Ākif wrote the Turkish national anthem. After the First World War he went to live in Egypt, and finally returned and died in Turkey. In his poem 'Unknown Soldier', he wrote:

'Martyr son of a martyr
Do not ask me for a tomb;
With arms open for you
Is waiting the Prophet.'

Compare this with Nāmıq Kemāl's play to see a continuity of thought. Today both men are still venerated as true nationalists.

prisoner of the Allies, and unable to exercise a direct influence on the movement of independence in Anatolia.

The War of Liberation, which began in 1919 under the leadership of Muṣṭafā Kemāl (later Atatürk), had genuine modern nationalist characteristics from the very beginning. It was the Turks' own war to save a piece of territory and create a fatherland. (The first proclamations urging the population to join the war spoke cautiously mainly about saving the caliph and Islam.) The National Pact, defining the purposes of the movement appealed to Ottoman Muslims united in religion, race and aim, but no longer addressed them as a group charged with a universal mission, but as a nation called to defend its own territory. Furthermore, terms such as 'national will', 'national sovereignty', frequently used by nationalists, stemmed from a modern understanding of state and nation as indicated by Muṣṭafā Kemāl's speech of 1 March 1922. 'The people of Turkey' he declared 'form a social body united in race, religion and culture, bound to each other by mutual respect and feeling of sacrifice, common interest and destiny.'[1] In the same speech he described the peasants as the country's true masters. Later, in another speech justifying the abolition of the sultanate (1922), Muṣṭafā Kemāl declared that the Turkish nation, after having founded the states of Chingiz, the Seljuks and the Ottomans, 'had decided this time to create a state directly under its own name and in accordance with his own attributes'.[2] Eventually he rejected pan-Turanism and pan-Islamism. The above passages indicate that much of the essence of nationalist ideas prevailing during the Young Turk period had been absorbed by republican leaders. But these ideas were interpreted and adapted to the requirements of a nation living in a well-defined territory.

It must be stated also that the occupation of Turkey by foreign powers, and the subsequent strong anti-imperialist ideas, developed during the War of Liberation, added a new political dimension and dynamism to Turkish nationalism. In the past nationalism had appeared as a device adopted to save the empire. It was passive and lacked driving motivations. In the War of Liberation, it turned into a dynamic ideal with a definite goal; the creation of a state and nation for Turks alone, and eventually it led to the adoption of a republican régime and national statehood (1923). Thus, the state emerged before the nation. The young officers, intellectuals, and, to a lesser extent, the civil servants, took the main part in creating the national state. The same groups also

[1] *Atatürk'ün söylev ve demeçleri* (Istanbul, 1945), 215. [2] *Ibid.*, 269–70.

undertook the difficult task of creating a nation by following at the beginning, for lack of anything better, Gökalp's blue-prints.[1] But there were individuals associated directly with the state, and ultimately it was the state philosophy that prevailed and was forced on the nation.

The immediate problem was to find common bonds to provide internal unity and cohesion. The departure of minorities (the last group being the Greeks, exchanged in 1924 for the Turkish population living in Greece), had left the Turks in an overwhelming majority. They were somewhat aware of the new political form of the state, but not quite sure yet as to what constituted their cultural identity. The Turkish language, even though described officially as a distinctive national characteristic, struck little emotional response. It was still Islam which commanded loyalty, and created internal unity. Of necessity, the state made full use of it, despite the secularism, which meanwhile had become a state principle. The practical criterion for Turkishness was not language or nationality, but religion, as indicated by the hesitation to encourage the immigration of Turkish-speaking Christian Gagavuz of Bessarabia (then part of Rumania), or to oppose the departure of Turkish-speaking Christian Karamanlis. The same is seen in the readiness to accept Greek-speaking Muslim Cretans, or the Slavic-speaking Muslim Bosnians and Pomaks of the Balkans. Much of this affinity towards the Balkan Muslims was engendered by past common allegiance to the Ottoman empire. In government posts, marriage, and everyday relations, the line of demarcation was still religion. It would have been inconceivable at this early stage for Turkish nationalism like Arab nationalism to have Christian spokesmen. It must be pointed out, however, that Islam was no longer a goal, but merely a convenient force to be used for building a national state.

The existing concepts of state and nation did not quite coincide until the early thirties. The *Türk Ojakları*, echoing their old pan-Turanian ideas, still defended the view that the nation was based on culture and race. The idea of finding objective elements for nationhood in the very territory of Turkey and the life of Turkish people emerged in 1931–2, in the People's Houses. These establishments replacing the *Ojakları* were charged with the development of a national Turkish culture, i.e. they were to give a new cultural identity to Turks, by studying the folklore, people, and towns; and by creating a new literature built around the love

[1] Ẓiyā Gökalp's views on *ümmet* was the basic reason for his temporary eclipse during the heyday of secularism (1928–45).

of country, people and life. The Houses were to disseminate also the nationalist, and secularist ideals of the Republic.

Just about this time, Muṣṭafā Kemāl launched the theory that Central Asia, the original home of the Turks, was the cradle of civilization, that Turkish was the mother of all languages, and that Turks had carried them to the world, including today's Turkey. The purpose of those theories was to give to Turks a sense of national pride, lessen their inhibition towards the Western world, and cut off their attachments to Islamic and Ottoman traditions. Subsequent archaeological and anthropological studies tried to prove that Anatolia was part of Western civilization, and that it had been the homeland of Turks for millennia. However, the idea of a Turkish civilization in Central Asia, besides adding new arguments to pan-Turanism, created also a romantic yearning for some remote lands and nostalgia for the past, and pushed aside the preoccupation with present conditions. All the conquerors from Central Asia became national heroes. Their deeds were cited as national achievements. Race once more proved to be a convenient link to tie together the Turks of Central Asia and Anatolia. Books, plays and articles, written on the subject, were so subjective in approach as to overshadow, and in fact pervert, the objective view of culture adopted in the People's Houses. The Ministry of Education became, and to a large extent remains, the centre of this kind of nationalism.

Meanwhile, the history of the Ottoman empire was ignored. The remains of Turkish civilization in the Balkans were utterly neglected, even when the local governments, Greek, Bulgarian, Yugoslav, Rumanian, destroyed mosques, bridges, baths and entire Turkish towns and villages. As usual, the West was untroubled by such sacrilege, since Muslim Turks were the victims. History was rewritten and reinterpreted with a view to glorifying the Turkish pre-Islamic past, in the same manner, often with the same arguments and words, as the Arabs glorify their own past now. Meanwhile, nationalism, which had been defined as one of the principles of Turkish revolution in the Republican party programme, was incorporated into the Constitution in 1937, and became one of the six principles of the Turkish state.

In the late thirties, the search for national culture had deviated from its objective goals. A new nationalist intelligentsia, mostly sons of notables from arch-conservative Anatolian towns and small bureaucrats, came into existence. Many teaching positions and government posts, as well as the leadership of student organizations, fell into their hands.

Their nationalism was akin to chauvinism—fanaticism and opposition to any kind of social thought and inquiry. This is also the period when secularism was harshly implemented and religious practices were even frowned upon. Nationalism became indeed a type of religious passion, and the nation a political myth.

In due time, between 1939 and 1944, nationalism deviated towards racialism, as pan-Turanic hopes were awakened by the German advance into the Soviet Union. Reviews such as *Gökbörü, Çınaraltı, Orhun,* to name just a few, are good samples of the nationalist trend of the time. The strengthening of one-party rule, the identification of the state with the nation, the rise of totalitarian régimes and the war in Europe, were some of the outside causes for this extremist course taken by nationalism. In reality this extremist nationalism was a social and psychological crisis caused by the breakdown of ancient concepts of organization and loyalty. Indeed a series of reforms in language, the legal system and the economy, undertaken by the state, had undermined the old system and caused a crisis of identity. Peyami Safa's confused nationalist writings of the period clearly indicate the extent of this crisis, as well as the attempts to fit old loyalties and concepts into a new fold. On the other hand, influential publications, such as *Varlık,* under the direction of Yaşar Nabi, found enough courage to withstand the lure of extremism and defend the initial objective, patriotic goals of Turkish nationalism.

It must be pointed out, however, that the influx of a variety of religious and conservative ideas into Turkish nationalism between 1933 and 1945, helped to identify various groups in the countryside with the nation and state. The population began to think of itself as being Turkish, and although it was still loyal to Islam as a faith, its thoughts and aspirations were confined to the territorial boundaries of Turkey. Islamists, racialists, socialists and pan-Turanists, although still dedicated to universal goals, were in reality thinking as nationals of the Turkish state.

Physically there was now a Turkish national state and one nation (culturally it still needed definition) and this was the major achievement of nationalism. Probably the greatest differences between the Turks and the Arabs in their present struggle for political modernization lies in the success of the first and the failure of the second to achieve stable national statehood.

CHAPTER 2

THE ARAB LANDS

(A) POLITICAL DEVELOPMENTS: 1918–48

The Arab lands of the Near East which were part of the Ottoman empire for nearly four hundred years, fell under Allied military occupation by the end of 1918. Great Britain and France had in their hands the destiny of the twin historic capitals of the once mighty Muslim empire: Damascus of Umayyad fame, and Baghdād of ʿAbbasid grandeur. And, for the first time since the Crusades, Jerusalem and, indeed, the whole of Palestine were occupied by a Christian power. The Arab nationalist leaders' joy at the liberation of their lands from what they called the Turkish yoke, soon turned to disillusionment, righteous anger and even hostility when the truth became widely known, i.e. the existence of certain agreements and correspondence, whereby the former Arab provinces of the Ottoman empire—Iraq, Syria, Lebanon and Palestine—were to be divided between the British and French governments. Iraq and Palestine (with Transjordan) were to be under direct British military rule. France was to be installed in Syria and Lebanon. An Arab government was, however, established in Damascus early in October 1918. The story of this government, the establishment of which was due to unexpected circumstances, and the special case of Lebanon which clung to its own independence—special because of its religious and social background and because of its cultural and economic ties with the West—deserve to be related briefly. On 1 October 1918, the Arab forces of Fayṣal entered Damascus. On 5 October, Fayṣal announced the establishment in Syria of an Arab constitutional government fully and absolutely independent, in the name of 'our lord, Sultan Ḥusayn'. The British government was prepared to recognize an Arab administration under Fayṣal as representative of his father, King Ḥusayn, in territory east of the Jordan river, from ʿAqaba to Maʿān and Damascus inclusive. However, he would have to get in touch with the British and French governments regarding the affairs of the Arab administration through two liaison officers, one British and the other French. He had also to remember that the territory under his administration—until a short time ago part of the Ottoman empire—was now only 'occupied enemy territory' in the absence of a peace settlement with Turkey. Meanwhile Fayṣal's government would receive a financial subsidy of £150,000 a month.

It may be of interest to note that Lawrence's romantic association with the Arab revolt came to an end in Syria at the end of the first meeting which took place between *Amīr* Fayṣal, General Allenby and Lawrence himself on 3 October at the Victoria Hotel in Damascus. Lawrence told Allenby that he would not be able to work with a French liaison officer, and asked for leave. Leave was granted, and he left Damascus for Cairo the next day.

Lebanon was occupied by British and French forces on 8 October after having lived for a week under an 'Arab Hashemite Government' established 'illegally' by a small Arab force which had been sent by Fayṣal from Damascus to hoist the Arab flag in the name of the king of the Ḥijāz. A few days later, the French military governor of Lebanon, Colonel de Piépape, in a warm and friendly speech, announced that he was now reinstating in office the Lebanese Administrative Council, and restoring the independence of Lebanon under the protection of the French Republic. Thus, when the armistice with Turkey was signed on 30 October 1918, either the Union Jack or the Tricolour was flying in all the Arab towns and cities which became later the capitals of the independent Arab countries of the Fertile Crescent. It is true that the Arabs were jubilant because their countries had been liberated from the horrors of war, but they could not help being filled with misgivings and suspicion about the future of their lands. On the one hand, there were the war-time pledges and commitments of the Allies and the Principles of President Wilson: 'government by the consent of the governed...and for the benefit of the populations concerned', and 'self-determination... an imperative principle of action which statesmen will henceforth ignore at their peril...'[1] On the other hand, they were face to face with a military and political West which occupied their lands. Hence, what guarantee was there that they were going to achieve their hopes and aspirations for political independence and national sovereignty? Meanwhile, another element of anxiety had been added to the Arab leaders' fears for the future, although its real significance and incalculable results could not, at the time, be fully grasped or envisaged. This was the Balfour Declaration made in a letter to Lord Rothschild on 2 November

[1] From President Wilson's addresses to the Senate on 22 January 1917 and to Congress on 11 February 1918.

1917, and stating that the British government viewed with favour 'the establishment in Palestine of a national home for the Jewish people...' Doubt of the sincerity and suspicion of the intentions of the Allies became unavoidable.

The *Amīr* Fayṣal was at the time the only recognized Arab leader with whom the Allies were dealing. His engaging personality, his dignified demeanour, his reasonableness and understanding of Western diplomacy, gained for him the respect and admiration of those who came to know him. He stood firmly for the Arab nationalist aims of political independence and the ideal of uniting the Arabs eventually into one nation. In a memorandum which he submitted to the Peace Conference in Paris on 1 January 1919, he wrote, 'I came to Europe on behalf of my father and the Arabs of Asia... They expect the Powers to think of them as one potential people, jealous of their language and liberty, and ask that no steps be taken inconsistent with the prospect of an eventual union of these areas under one sovereign government.'[1] On 29 January, he submitted another memorandum to the Peace Conference in which he wrote:

> As representative of my father who, by request of Britain and France, led the Arab rebellion against the Turks, I have come to ask that the Arabic-speaking peoples of Asia, from the line Alexandretta–Diarbekr southward to the Indian Ocean, be recognized as independent sovereign peoples under the guarantee of the League of Nations... I base my request on the principles enunciated by President Wilson (attached), and am confident that the Powers will attach more importance to the bodies and souls of the Arabic-speaking peoples than to their own material interest.[2]

1919 was a year of long and bitter controversies between Great Britain and France over the Syrian Question, particularly over the Arab government of Fayṣal in Damascus. Clemenceau maintained firmly that the setting up of this government by the British was untenable, and inconsistent with the Sykes-Picot Agreement. Lloyd George appeared to give his full support to Fayṣal and to an independent Arab government in Syria. But he had to give way, finally, to Clemenceau's uncompromising attitude, and the year ended with Fayṣal in Paris trying to reach some understanding with the French government.

In January 1920, when Fayṣal returned to Damascus from Paris, after a stay of nearly four months, he was a tired and worried man. He was

[1] D. H. Miller, *My diary at the Conference of Paris*, 1918–1919 (New York, 1924), IV, 297–9.
[2] Miller, *My diary*, IV, 300.

suspected by his own people, warned by his father not to compromise the independence of Syria, and harassed by deputation after deputation who came to see him and urge immediate action. The Iraqi leaders had their grievances against Great Britain who had occupied Iraq; the Syrians were against the French and also the British, whom they blamed for having abandoned them to France; the Palestinians, after the Balfour Declaration, accused Britain of having 'sold' Palestine to the Zionists, and some Lebanese were distressed by France's direct and full intervention in all their affairs. In view of the deteriorating situation in Syria and the failure of Fayṣal's policy of moderation, the General Syrian Congress 'representing the Syrian Arab nation', drew up a historic resolution on 7 March 1920, proclaiming the full independence of a united Syria, i.e. Syria with its 'natural boundaries', including Palestine (thus rejecting the claim of the Zionists for a National Home for the Jews) and Lebanon with the understanding that the latter would have its autonomy within its pre-war frontiers provided it did not accept any foreign influence in its affairs. The Congress also asked for 'the full independence of Iraq' and its eventual political and economic union with Syria. The following day, 8 March, Fayṣal was proclaimed, in Damascus, king of the 'United Kingdom of Syria' while his brother the *Amīr* 'Abd Allāh was proclaimed king of an independent Iraq. As 'Abd Allāh was at that time about a thousand miles away in the Ḥijāz, and Iraq was in British occupation, his proclamation as king of Iraq could not be taken seriously. Fayṣal's kingship was repudiated by the British government, and ignored by King Ḥusayn, who felt that it was contrary to the original aim of the Arab revolt, and a blow to Arab unity. The French government was greatly irritated, and protested to the British. The Lebanese took matters into their own hands—with the knowledge and support of the French authorities—to maintain their freedom, and protect their sovereignty. The Lebanese delegation in Paris had already protested to the prime minister, Millerand, against the *Amīr* Fayṣal proclaiming himself king over Lebanon, and the Maronite Patriarch Hoyek (Ilyās al-Ḥuwayyik) had received, on 17 March 1920, renewed assurances that the interests of Lebanon would be safeguarded by France. Consequently, on Monday, 22 March, in the midst of an imposing ceremony, the first Lebanese flag was unfurled on the Government House at Ba'abdā and the independence of Lebanon was thus proclaimed.

Events were now moving fast, and it was more than ever necessary for Great Britain and France to work out their own final plans for the

Arab lands of the Near East. Hence it was that the Allied Supreme Council met at San Remo, and on 25 April the assignment of mandates for Mesopotamia (Iraq), Palestine, Syria and Lebanon took place. These were the 'A' mandates, and the mandatories chosen by the principal Allied powers were Great Britain for Mesopotamia and Palestine, France for Syria and Lebanon. Cynics have considered the mandate system a substitute for the old imperialism. Actually, the idealism on which the Covenant of the League of Nations was based could not admit the principle of annexation by the victorious powers of any new country arising from the break-up of the states they had defeated. But, in the words of General Smuts's memorandum on the League of Nations, 'The peoples left behind by the decomposition of Russia, Austria and Turkey are mostly untrained politically; many of them are either incapable of or deficient in power of self-government; they are mostly destitute, and will require much nursing towards economic and political independence.'[1] This nursing towards independence was expressed in mild and conciliatory language in article 22 of the Covenant of the League of Nations which stated,

> Certain communities formerly belonging to the Turkish Empire have reached a stage of development where their existence as independent nations can be provisionally recognized, subject to the rendering of administrative advice and assistance by a Mandatory until such time as they are able to stand alone. The wishes of these communities must be a principal consideration in the selection of the Mandatory...[2]

Nevertheless, the plain facts were that the 'power vacuum' created by the destruction of the Ottoman empire was filled by the combined presence of Great Britain and France in the form of mandatory governments, and that the Arab provinces fell under the tutelage of those two powers. If this was not virtual annexation, it certainly was Western domination. This foreign control was, however, sugar-coated by the steps which it took to establish local Arab governments in the mandated territories. Unfortunately the first experiment in establishing an Arab government came to a violent and bitter end. Twenty-one months and twenty-two days after Fayṣal's triumphal entry into Damascus, his Arab government in Syria was brought to an end. On 25 July 1920, Damascus was occupied by an imposing French force, and Fayṣal had to abandon

[1] D. Lloyd George, *The truth about the peace treaties* (London, 1938), I, 622.
[2] *Ibid.* I, 549.

the city. He finally left Syria for Haifa, on his way to England, on 1 August 1920. France had, at last, obtained her Syrian share of the Sykes-Picot Agreement, though not without being obliged to resort to force.

The events in Syria had a profound effect on Iraq. Ever since 1918, when virtually the whole of Mesopotamia was under British military occupation, there had been opposition and resistance to British rule in Baghdād and in various parts of the country. Iraqi nationalists and religious leaders rebelled in April 1920; the rebellion became an insurrection, in July of the same year. Its suppression towards the end of 1920 was costly in men and materials, and embittered the relations between the nationalists and the occupying authorities.

The occupation of Syria by General Gouraud's troops and the Iraqi revolt marked the end of an era in the relations of the Arab lands of the Near East with Great Britain and France. The events which led to the downfall of Fayṣal in particularly humiliating circumstances convinced the Arab nationalist leaders that, for the success of their nationalist aspirations, an armed conflict between the Arabs and the West would, in the long run, become inevitable.

The situation of Egypt was different from that of the Arab territories of the Fertile Crescent. No sooner had Turkey entered the war against the Allies in November 1914 than Egypt was declared a British protectorate. The proclamation of this protectorate created many problems and much discontent among Egyptian nationalists, who considered it the extinction of Egypt's autonomy. No solution short of independence could satisfy them.

Egyptian nationalism at the end of the First World War, like Lebanese nationalism, was stronger than the ties of Arabism with the rest of the Arab lands. It is of much interest to note that, when the Arab revolt started in 1916, the Egyptian leaders had neither the interest nor the time to get involved in it. Nūrī al-Sa'īd, who was then in Cairo, went to confer with the distinguished Egyptian nationalist, Sa'd Zaghlūl, before proceeding to Mecca to join the revolt. Zaghlūl's observations were to the effect that the Arab lands in those days did not form any political or sovereign entity which might perish if the revolt failed. They did not constitute an independent state, the very existence of which was in jeopardy, as was the case with the Ottoman empire. Those who worked for the future of the Arabs and who struggled for their independence and national sovereignty were pioneers and might even become martyrs. But as far as he, Zaghlūl, was concerned, he was too busy working for the independence of Egypt. All that he could do was to wish the *Sharīf* Ḥusayn and the Arabs every success in their 'noble endeavours'.

Two days after the war came to an end, i.e. on 13 November 1918, Zaghlūl had an interview with Sir Reginald Wingate, the British high commissioner in Egypt, and 'demanded complete autonomy for Egypt, as an ancient and capable race with a glorious past—far more capable of conducting a well-ordered government than the Arabs, Syrians and Mesopotamians to whom self-determination had so recently been promised'.[1] On the same day, the Egyptian prime minister, Rushdī Pasha, made it clear to Wingate that it was very necessary that he with 'Adlī Pasha Yegen, the minister of Education, and a deputation (*Wafd*) representing the Egyptian nationalists, headed by Zaghlūl should be invited to London to discuss the Egyptian question. The British Foreign Office replied on 27 November that 'no Nationalists should be allowed to leave Egypt'. In the days that followed, political tension and agitation began to mount ominously, and by 1920 the nationalists had intensified their demands for 'complete independence' for Egypt.

Thus, as far as Egypt was concerned, the year 1918 came to an end with Great Britain in full control of the country. But dark clouds were gathering on the horizon ready for the violent storm which burst during the next three years in the form of strikes, demonstrations and a widespread insurrection.

Turning to Arabia, where the Arab revolt had started in 1916, we find that here, by 1920, the tide of events had gone against King Ḥusayn. He had, finally, become so inflexible and uncompromising that British support for him had dwindled greatly. When he was proclaimed 'king of the Arabs', on 30 October 1916, the Allies refused to recognize him as such, and finally accepted the title of king of the Ḥijāz. In 1919 he came into conflict with 'Abd al-'Azīz b. Su'ūd, the recognized Wahhābī leader from the House of Su'ūd. In the summer of 1924, a serious attack by the Wahhābīs on the Ḥijāz led to the abdication of King Ḥusayn on 5 October, in favour of his son 'Alī. On 11 March 1924, King Ḥusayn had been proclaimed caliph while on a visit to 'Ammān in Transjordan. It may well be that this event hastened the Wahhābī attacks on him. The king withdrew to Jedda then proceeded to 'Aqaba and, later, in July 1925, left for Cyprus on board a British destroyer. The Wahhābīs renewed their attacks and occupied Jedda, Medina and Yanbu'. 'Alī abdicated and went into exile to Baghdād, where he died in 1934. Three

[1] Ronald Wingate, *Wingate of the Sudan* (London, 1955), 229.

years earlier, in 1931, King Ḥusayn had passed away in 'Ammān at the age of seventy-five. He was the last descendant of the Prophet to become grand *sharīf* of Mecca, and the first illustrious Arab victim of the exigencies of power politics after the First World War. He did not know the rules of Western diplomacy, and was militarily and financially weak. He played for very high stakes, and lost. But whatever may be said of King Ḥusayn, of his shortcomings and limitations, he had, in most testing circumstances, the courage of his convictions and a clear conscience. He did not compromise and did not falter, but remained, to the end, loyal to his principles of the Arab revolt and to his ideal of Arab unity.

Although King Ḥusayn was not destined to rule Arabia, no foreign power dominated that country at the end of the war. Eventually, central Arabia became an independent kingdom under King 'Abd al-'Azīz b. Su'ūd, originally the ruler of Najd. In the coastal regions, however, the British government had direct or indirect control, through treaty relations, over no less than twenty rulers of various principalities and shaykhdoms—from Kuwayt, at the tip of the Persian Gulf, to Aden Colony and Protectorate, and the island of Perim at the southern entrance of the Red Sea, passing by the island of Baḥrayn, Qaṭar, the Trucial Coast (known originally as the Pirate Coast), and the sultanate of Masqaṭ and 'Umān. In certain cases, British relations with some of the rulers in this area were of long standing, such as with Masqaṭ, whose treaty of alliance with Great Britain started in 1798. Various other agreements dated from 1820, 1835, 1839 (when Aden was occupied), and thereafter. Thus, a ring of British protection and advice given by resident British advisers encircled almost the whole of eastern and southern Arabia.

While speaking about Arabia, perhaps one other Arab country should be mentioned here; a country which remained outside the political and social influence of the Western Allies. This was the Yemen. It had preserved its own independence and its own way of life. Although it remained loyal to the Ottomans during the First World War, and was attacked from 'Asīr to the north by Idrīsī invaders with the support of the British in Aden, and although the latter were in turn attacked by the Turkish troops in the Yemen, the country, on the whole, was very little affected by the war. When the Ottoman empire was defeated and lost the war, the Yemen became independent and continued to be ruled by the Rassid dynasty of the Zaydī *imāms*. The extreme religious conservatism of the Yemenis, their intrepid valour as fighters and soldiers, as well as the inhospitable deserts, and the formidable mountain fastness of the Yemen, kept this country well protected from foreign invaders and foreign ideas until the last few years.

In the light of the foregoing events, the years 1918–20 seem to have been crucial in the modern history of the Arabs. They ushered in the first phase of Arab struggle with the West for political independence. Arab nationalism reached its formative age, became more militant, more anti-Western and anti-imperialist. It lived almost exclusively on deep-seated suspicion, resentment and hostility towards Anglo-French domination in Arab lands, and towards the establishment of the Jewish National Home in Palestine.

Meanwhile, the mandatory powers were, on their part, trying to show as much goodwill as was possible and compatible with their own national interests. On 1 September 1920, General Gouraud, the French high commissioner, proclaimed the birth of the state of Greater Lebanon with Beirut as its capital. The *Amīr* Fayṣal, who had been forced out of Syria, was proclaimed king of Iraq on 23 August 1921. However, on 24 July 1922, the Council of the League of Nations approved the mandate system for Syria, Lebanon, and Palestine with Transjordan.

During the period between the two World Wars, Great Britain, and, to a lesser degree, France, tried to regulate their relations with the countries under their tutelage by means of various treaties, which slowly granted larger measures of self-government, and which helped in laying the foundations of indigenous governments in those countries. Thus, in the British-dominated areas, Egypt was the first country to become formally independent and sovereign by a British declaration on 21 February 1922 terminating the British protectorate, subject to a number of conditions which secured certain rights and responsibilities for the British in Egypt. This was followed by the promulgation of a constitution on 19 April 1923 which made Egypt a constitutional, hereditary monarchy under King Fu'ād I. Negotiations continued for several more years until a new Anglo-Egyptian treaty was signed in 1936. Though in this treaty Britain retained, among other rights she had stipulated in the 1922 declaration, that of protecting British lines of communication through Egypt, and that of defending the country, it was on the whole more palatable to the Egyptians.

During the following years, the British government signed with Iraq a number of treaties for close alliance and collaboration. On 10 July 1924, an Iraqi Constituent Assembly enacted a constitution for the kingdom of Iraq in which the latter was declared 'a sovereign State, independent and free'. Iraq was the first of the mandated Arab countries to become formally independent by being admitted to the League of Nations on 3 October 1932, as a result of the support and recommendation of the British government. Syria and Lebanon under the French mandate developed a republican parliamentary form of government. Constitutions were promulgated in both countries—in Lebanon on 23 May 1926, and in Syria on 14 May 1930.

Nevertheless, nationalist leaders in the vast majority of Arabs opposed the mandates from the start. To them the mandates were simply foreign domination with the ultimate objective of keeping the Arabs divided and deprived of genuine and untramelled independence. Consequently, in spite of all the treaties signed and the independence conferred, the resentment of the nationalists increased in a climate of mutual suspicion and distrust, and they never abandoned their common aim: to eliminate completely Anglo-French domination and attain unconditional independence. Strikes, demonstrations and agitation followed, in which schoolboys and politically minded university students took a prominent part. It must be said that during this period the educated and uneducated youth of the Arab countries, with their enthusiasm and idealism, became a fertile soil for political exploitation and, at times, perhaps without realizing it, the tools of unscrupulous extremists and agitators.

Perhaps the most violent insurrection was the one which broke out in Jabal al-Durūz in Syria in July 1925, and led to serious fighting in which several thousand French troops took part. Soon afterwards, disaffection and unrest grew also in Damascus, and disorders spread to other towns. The French authorities took energetic and drastic military measures to check the rebellion and to prevent a general conflagration. For three days, certain quarters of Damascus were shelled and bombed. Unfortunately, much bloodshed and destruction occurred. It was only in June 1927 that armed rebellion was finally brought to an end.

In addition to Arab nationalism, which was becoming almost daily a more potent force, against the mandatories, there was another force, equally if not more potent. This was Islam. It is idle and superficial thinking to ignore or to minimize the influence of Islam in politics in the Arab lands of the Near East, where Islam is the religion of the great majority of their inhabitants. At the beginning of the twentieth century of the Christian era, Islam was getting into its fourteenth century. The

Arab Muslims were the heirs of a culture and a civilization which were deeply rooted in Islam. Islam had glorified the Arabs, not only by its moral power, but also by its conquests and military triumphs, and had also awakened Arab national consciousness. The Muslim leaders, and with them the vast majority of the Muslim Arabs, felt that Western domination was not only humiliating to their splendid and glorious past, but that its secular and materialistic culture was a threat to the sacred religious principles embodied in Islam. Hence, the Arab struggle against Great Britain and France was also a revolt against the cultural imperialism of the West.

Another factor which tarnished the prestige of the West, and greatly encouraged the Arabs in their opposition to the mandatory powers, was the spread of communism, and the rise of Hitler and Mussolini in Europe. Nazi Germany and Fascist Italy, by their military defiance of the West, became very popular in the Near East, and their ideologies caught the imagination of the nationalists. Between the two World Wars, the Western powers were bullied, vilified and challenged by the new dictators in Europe. Following the Arabic proverb, 'The enemy of my enemy is my friend', the Arab nationalists felt a secret joy that the political superiority of the West, long admitted and grudgingly admired, that its military power, long held in awe and terror, seemed neither respected nor feared by the European dictators. The spectacle of Chamberlain, prime minister of an empire on which the sun never set, going with nothing more than an umbrella on pilgrimage to Munich to appease an ex-corporal thundering ruin to that empire, of Daladier, prime minister of a haughty France which had fought, bled and won, with her Allies, the First World War, trotting sheepishly on that same journey, was considered a humiliating sign of the decline of the imperialist powers. Why could the Arabs not defy the West? Its armour was full of holes.

Needless to say that the Arabs, at this time, received much encouragement from this new revolutionary Europe, Communist and non-Communist alike. Communism began to take root in Arab lands after 1928. It presented itself as the liberator of the Muslim world from Western imperialism and the rule of the bourgeoisie in general. Indeed ten years earlier, in 1918, the Union for the Liberation of the East had been organized in Moscow. Was it not the Soviet government that had revealed to the world for the first time, in 1917, the existence of the secret arrangements made by the Allies during the war, particularly the Sykes-

Picot Agreement, for the partitioning of the Arab lands among themselves? These documents were made public by orders of Trotsky, as commissar for foreign affairs. Their full text was published by *Izvestia* and *Pravda* in their issues of 23 November 1917; and the *Manchester Guardian* was the first paper in Great Britain to produce summaries of these documents in its issues of 26 and 28 November 1917. The Turks also learned through the Bolsheviks about the Sykes-Picot Agreement, and they gave it the widest possible publicity in the Arab countries.

The resentment of the nationalists increased all this time, and led to more unrest and agitation in 1936, in Iraq, Syria, Lebanon, and Palestine. General Bakr Ṣidqī, supported by young nationalist army officers, carried out a successful military *coup d'état* in Baghdād on 29 October 1936. The military dictatorship he established came to an end within ten months, but the army's interference in the government continued in the years that followed. The French government entered into prolonged negotiations first with a Syrian and then with a Lebanese delegation for the purpose of 'turning a new page' of peace and friendship between France and the Arab nationalists. The result was a Franco-Syrian treaty and a Franco-Lebanese treaty. The first was initialled in September and the second in November 1936, both were to last for twenty-five years. There were certain difficult and complicated conditions to be fulfilled before these treaties were to enter into force. Syria and Lebanon were first to be admitted to the League of Nations and, of course, the French, Syrian and Lebanese parliaments had to ratify the treaties; finally, after a period of transition which was to last three years, Syria and Lebanon were to emerge as fully independent states. Hopes ran high for a little while. However, the next blow to nationalist aspirations was the loss of the district of Alexandretta which, after Franco-Turkish negotiations, became autonomous as Hatay in 1937, with the consent of the Council of the League of Nations, and in 1939 was integrated in Turkey. Moreover, after waiting for two years, the French government, under various national and international tensions, and especially with the gathering of menacing war clouds in Europe, was still hesitating to ratify these treaties.

Great Britain's troubles in Palestine were not any less than France's tribulations in Syria. The enormous increase of Jewish immigration into Palestine between 1933 and 1936 intensified Arab resistance and opposition to the Balfour Declaration, and led to disorders, strikes, bloodshed, and finally open rebellion from 1936 to 1939. Soon after the outbreak of serious disturbances on 19 April 1936, a Royal Commission of enquiry was appointed on 7 August 'to ascertain the underlying causes of the disturbances which broke out in Palestine...and whether, upon a proper construction of the terms of the Mandate, either the Arabs or the Jews have any legitimate grievances...' On 22 June 1937, the commissioners submitted their report, with the conclusion that partition was 'the only method we are able to propose for dealing with the root of the trouble' on the basis that 'half a loaf is better than no bread'. They added in a last paragraph:

> Nor is it only the British people, nor only the nations which conferred the Mandate or approved it, who are troubled by what has happened and is happening in Palestine. Numberless men and women all over the world would feel a sense of deep relief if somehow an end could be put to strife and bloodshed in a thrice hallowed land.[1]

But the Woodhead Commission, which was sent out to Palestine in 1938, found it impossible to recommend a workable scheme of partition. The White Paper of 1939 was one more attempt made by the British government to solve the Palestine problem. The gist of the White Paper was a proposal of self-government for an Arab-Jewish Palestinian state at the end of ten years. But neither the Zionists nor the Arabs were satisfied: the former demanded a higher quota of Jewish immigrants and no restriction on the sale of Arab lands to Jews, while the latter demanded a stop to all Jewish immigration and all Jewish land purchase. The White Paper was condemned by the Zionists, and rejected by the Arabs. A major clash between Zionism and Arab nationalism in Palestine was avoided only by the great convulsion which burst upon the world in September 1939.

On the eve of the Second World War, Egypt was a constitutional monarchy. By the convention of Montreux in 1937 the capitulations had been abolished, and in the same year, Egypt had been admitted to the League of Nations. Iraq was also a constitutional monarchy and a member of the League. And finally, there was the Sa'udi Arabian kingdom. Thus, here were three Arab kingdoms and three Arab kings: Fārūq I in Egypt, Fayṣal II in Iraq (with the *Amīr* 'Abd al-Ilāh as regent) and 'Abd al-'Azīz b. Su'ūd in Sa'udi Arabia. To all appearances they had achieved national sovereignty. Syria and Lebanon too had achieved a certain measure of independence through their democratic institutions and parliamentary form of government.

[1] Palestine Royal Commission, *Report* (Cmd. 5479) (London, 1937), 380–97.

However, complete political independence was still far from being a reality. Moreover, after twenty-one years, Arab unity was further from realization than ever before. Cynics and realists pointed out that there was more Arab unity under the 'yoke' of the Ottoman empire, which the Arabs had thrown away in order to gain their freedom and independence. During the four hundred years of Ottoman rule, an Arab could travel from one end of the Near East to the other without having to stop at any political frontiers. Only the physical obstacles of geography—deserts and mountains mainly—could hinder or retard his movements.

When the Second World War began in September 1939, the Syrians, the Lebanese and the Iraqis had had twenty-one years of experience of either British or French administration; the Egyptians, by then, had known British rule directly or indirectly for fifty-seven years. These were years of trial and tribulation for all concerned. It is true that this period of foreign rule imposed upon the Arabs by military conquest and victory was unpopular, but it is untrue to say that there was no co-operation whatsoever with the representatives of Great Britain and France in this region. There were those who by education, temperament and political inclination, admired the Western institutions of democracy, Western culture, and Western ways of life. They were a minority, but some of them were influential and helpful to the mandatory powers. At the same time, the struggle for political independence consolidated regional and territorial nationalism in the mandated territories. Thus, while the ideal of Arab unity was maintained, a strong attachment developed in every newly born country to the preservation of its independence.

It would also be unjust to ignore the benefits that the mandates bestowed, and to lay the blame for all disillusionments, frustrations and, at times, even bloodshed, at the door of the 'Allied and Victorious Powers'. It is, of course, undeniable that these powers had their national interests to safeguard, and their political prestige to maintain, that their minds were still engrossed in the patterns of international politics which had characterized the European diplomacy of the eighteenth and nineteenth centuries. But there is no evidence that the Allies were devoid of good intentions, that they desired to create political, economic and social evils to retard the progress of the inhabitants in their mandated territories. They believed that their victory in the Near East had insured 'the complete and final emancipation of all those peoples so long oppressed by the Turks'. They equally believed that, being themselves highly civilized states, their guidance and tutelage would be necessary to make it possible for those people to progress from a medieval to a modern society. France believed in her *mission civilisatrice,* and Great Britain in the superiority of her system of 'order and good government'. An unbiased student of the mandate period must admit that much progress took place in Arab lands during that time. There were great improvements in the systems of communication and transport. Telephone and telegraph lines were multiplied. Cars and aeroplanes immensely reduced travelling-time between the Arab countries. Large numbers of roads were newly built, widened or asphalted. New schools and hospitals were opened. In the economic field, trade with foreign countries expanded, and new industries sprang up. The basis of a modern administration, and of a system of public finance and taxation, was laid; the judicial system was reorganized, civil courts with modern codes of law were introduced, and security services established law and order throughout the land. Above all, democratic institutions were established for the growth of self-government based on principles of individual liberty and individual equality before the law without distinction as to race, language or religion.

However, what was important to the extreme nationalists was the fact that foreign domination was still over their lands, and that Arab leaders had no direct authority in their own countries. It seemed as if they were still where they were almost a quarter of a century earlier.

But the extraordinary events which took place during and after the Second World War did not keep the Arabs in the same place. The Arab lands found themselves directly involved in the war after the collapse of France in 1940. In June 1940 the French authorities in the Levant threw their weight on the side of the Vichy government in France, with the result that British and Gaullist Free French forces, operating from Palestine, attacked and defeated the Vichy forces in Syria and Lebanon in July 1941.

Another theatre of war, for a short time, was Iraq. Following Rashīd 'Ālī al-Gaylānī's rebellion in 1941, supported by the army and by German arms and aircraft, British and Indian troops defeated the Iraqi army. Rashīd 'Ālī and his ministers left the country. Once more Iraq returned to the fold, under the premiership of Nūrī Pasha al-Sa'īd.

In Syria and Lebanon, General Catroux was appointed by General de Gaulle, chief of the Free French, as delegate-general of Free France in the Levant. On 8 June 1941, the day on which Free French troops and

Imperial forces entered Syria and Lebanon, General Catroux said in a declaration on behalf of General de Gaulle that he was putting an end to the mandatory régime, and proclaiming the Syrians and the Lebanese to be free and independent. On the same day, in another declaration, the British ambassador in Cairo, Sir Miles Lampson, said, 'I am authorised by His Majesty's Government in the United Kingdom to declare that they support and associate themselves with the assurance of independence given by General Catroux on behalf of General de Gaulle to Syria and the Lebanon.'[1]

Having checked the establishment of a German bridge-head in Syria, Lebanon and Iraq, the Allies won another victory over the Axis, this time on Egyptian soil, when the Afrika Corps, commanded by Field-Marshal Rommel, was finally and decisively defeated by the Eighth Army under General Montgomery at al-'Alamayn on 2 November 1942. A few days later, the Anglo-American Expeditionary Force landed in North Africa under General Eisenhower, and put an end to any Axis threat to Africa and the Near East.

But the Allies had not ended their long-standing problem of giving full independence to the areas still under their control. Nationalist fronts were being consolidated in Syria, Lebanon and Egypt. In Lebanon, where Christian, Muslim and Druze communities had lived side by side for centuries, it was more necessary than ever before that good relations should exist among them, so that they might be able to stand by themselves in a free and independent state. Consequently, the National Pact was born in September 1943. This pact was not a written, signed and sealed contract. It was a 'gentleman's agreement' between the Christian and Muslim leaders to live in a united and independent Lebanon without allowing any outside influences, whether from the West or from the East, to interfere with that unity and independence. The pact became one of the corner-stones of Lebanese political independence and territorial integrity.

Soon elections were held in Lebanon for a Chamber of Deputies, and on 21 September Bishāra al-Khūrī was elected president of the republic. He, in turn, appointed as prime minister Riyāḍ al-Ṣulḥ of a well-known Sunnī family. Elections were also held in Syria during the same year and Shukrī al-Quwatlī became president of the republic. Both governments wanted now to delete from their constitutions those articles

[1] *Syria No. 1 (1945): Statements of policy...in respect of Syria and the Lebanon,* 8 *June–9 September 1941* (Cmd. 6600) (London, 1945).

conceding attributes of sovereignty to the mandatory. A Free French Committee of National Liberation sitting in Algiers under the presidency of General de Gaulle refused to recognize the validity of any unilateral amendment of the Lebanese constitution. When the Lebanese parliament went ahead with the constitutional amendments, Jean Helleu, the French delegate-general in the Levant states, had the president of the republic and most members of his cabinet arrested at 4.00 a.m. on 11 November 1943. Strikes, demonstrations and riots in Beirut and other Lebanese towns were followed by a British ultimatum to General Catroux, supported by the United States government. The president and Lebanese ministers were set free on 22 November—a day which continues to be celebrated as Independence Day.

Further tensions in Lebanon, and two serious crises which developed in Syria in 1944 and 1945, led the nationalists to press more vehemently their demand for complete independence, until finally the withdrawal of all foreign troops and the end of foreign occupation took place in Syria on 17 April 1946, and in Lebanon on 31 December of the same year. It was also during 1946, on 22 March, that independence was granted to Transjordan. Two months later, the *Amīr* ʿAbd Allāh was proclaimed king, and two years later the Hashimite Kingdom of Jordan was born.

With the tide of the Second World War receding from the Arab lands, the tide of Western domination had also ebbed. Two World Wars and over a quarter of a century of Arab-Western relations had produced numerous and painful lessons for anyone who wanted to learn. One thing was very clear indeed: Arab nationalism and Arab unity could no longer be ignored. Hence it was that less than two months before the end of the war, on 22 March 1945, the Arab League was born. The Arab League not only confirmed and respected the independence and sovereignty of its member states but it also laid down the foundations of an Arab federation, in which the Arabs could develop and strengthen to the utmost their political, economic and cultural ties without interfering in one another's system of government. The precursor of the Arab League was Anthony Eden's statement in the Mansion House on 29 May 1941, in which he said,

> The Arab world has made great strides since the settlement reached at the end of the last War, and many Arab thinkers desire for the Arab peoples a greater degree of unity than they now enjoy. In reaching out towards this unity they hope for our support. No such appeal from our friends should go unanswered. It seems to me both natural and right that the cultural and

economic ties between the Arab countries, and the political ties too, should be strengthened. His Majesty's Government for their part will give their full support to any scheme that commands general approval.[1]

Between the end of the Second World War and the present day, five new factors have produced the greatest impact on the internal conditions of the Arab countries and their external relations with the West: Arab oil production, the birth of Israel, the entry of the United States and of the U.S.S.R. into the political and economic arena of the Near East, and the Egyptian revolution of 1952. No event, whether minor or major, which has happened in any corner of the Arab lands since 1945 can be divorced from the direct or indirect influence of either one, or a combination, of these factors.

Much has been written, and numerous statistics compiled, on the oil reserves and oil industry of the Arab countries. The ever-expanding oil operations of American oil companies in the Arabian peninsula since 1933 has resulted in the discovery of new oil-fields, the building of new refineries, and the laying of pipelines from the Persian Gulf to the Mediterranean. Oil revenues have brought fabulous wealth to the governments of Sa'udi Arabia, Kuwayt and Iraq, and have provided them with a golden opportunity, unprecedented in their history, to develop their resources, raise the standard of living of their peoples and give financial aid, in the form of loans, to other Arab countries with no oil income. At the same time, the oil of the Arab lands is a great source of income to the foreign oil companies, and is of major importance to the economy and industrial life of western Europe. The safeguarding of these oil interests thus became interwoven with Western politics in the Near East.

The Arab leaders were determined, however, to put an end after the Second World War to all forms of Western domination. They would deal with the West only on equal terms. Hence the Arab reaction during this period was violent; first, though unsuccessfully, against the Zionists in Palestine in the war of 1948 on the termination of the British mandate on 15 May; secondly, in a series of political assassinations and military upheavals, overthrowing the previously established Arab governments and Arab dynasties, which were considered to be either pro-Western or old-fashioned and reactionary. The immediate consequences of the Arab-Zionist war were the consolidation of the state of Israel which was proclaimed in May 1948, and recognized immediately by the U.S.A. and

[1] G. Kirk, *The Middle East in the War* (2nd edn.) (London, 1953), 334.

the U.S.S.R.; the presence of over a million Palestinian refugees in the neighbouring Arab countries—more than half of them in Jordan; and intense bitterness and lack of confidence in Arab-Western relations.

(B) ARAB NATIONALISM

The first obstacle to the understanding of Arab 'nationalism' by a non-Arab and a non-Muslim is that of language. There is no word, no expression in the English language that could convey the exact meaning and, particularly, the exact concept of *al-'urūba, al-umma al-'arabiyya* and *al-qawmiyya al-'arabiyya* loosely translated in English as 'Arabism', the 'Arab nation' and 'Arab nationalism', respectively. Indeed, the term 'Arab' has a much wider meaning today than it had at the beginning of the twentieth century. A 'pure' Arab was then considered to be a bedouin or nomad of Arabia. He was traditionally and popularly associated with the Arab symbols of a *kūfiyya* and an *'iqāl* for his headwear, a loose flowing gown, a curved dagger, a black tent, a camel, occasionally a palm-tree, and he was always surrounded by an interminable desert of sand dunes. Today, the word 'Arab' has a much more inclusive significance, and applies to all the Arabic-speaking (and generally Muslim) inhabitants of the Middle East, whether riding on a camel and living in a tent, or owning a chauffeur-driven car and living in an air-conditioned and centrally-heated villa in one of the capitals of the Arab countries.

In addition to the language obstacle, there is a further difficulty which lies in the fact that many writers on 'Arab nationalism' are either Westerners with their own Western concept of nationalism, or are from among the non-Muslim Near Eastern intelligentsia, with a western education and a western secular view of nationalism. The latter have tried to draw their own image of 'Arab nationalism' either out of ignorance or wishful thinking. They find it more convenient and comfortable to live in a make-believe world of their own, than to face the reality of the Muslim world, on the margin of which they themselves happen to be. Hence, all the confusion and ambiguity in the use of such terms in English as 'Arabism', the 'Arab nation' and 'Arab nationalism', leading to much misunderstanding and misinterpretation of their original Arabic meaning.

Arabism—the nearest equivalent to *al-'urūba*—signifying the sum total of the ethnic, linguistic, social and cultural characteristics which distinguish an Arab from a non-Arab, is as old as the Arabs. It certainly existed before the birth of Islam in the Arabian peninsula, because there were Arabs before there was Islam. As to the concept of *al-umma al-'arabiyya,* i.e. of an Arab 'nation', embodying the religious, social and political unity of the Arabic-speaking peoples, this concept is inseparable from the rise of Islam and the islamization of the Arabs. *Al-'urūba* was, naturally, the bedrock upon which the notion of *al-umma* was built.

There remains the modern idea of *al-qawmiyya al-'arabiyya,* generally rendered in English as 'Arab nationalism'. Actually, the word 'nationalism' is not equivalent to the Arabic *al-qawmiyya*; indeed, the latter, derived from *qawm,* is a newcomer to Arabic political terminology. The Arabic word *qawm* refers to 'a number of people' specially to 'a number of men', particularly those men who have achieved 'great and important things'. The Qur'ān speaks of *qawm Nūḥ,* 'the people of Noah', and of *qawm Mūsā,* 'the people of Moses', and the word is similarly used in other passages. Before the twentieth century, the word *qawm* had no political or patriotic connotation, but as used during the last two decades, it has come to denote all the Arabic-speaking or Arab peoples, disregarding, in principle, the geographical and political boundary lines which separate the Arab states. Thus, the term *al-qawmiyya al-'arabiyya* stands, today, not only for Arab 'nationalism' but also for Arab unity, and should not be confused with the idea of patriotism (*al-waṭaniyya*), i.e. the love of one's fatherland or place of habitation.

What, then, is the origin of Arab nationalism and what evolutionary process has it followed? To begin with, Arab nationalism is inconceivable without Arabism. When the Arabs embraced Islam in the seventh century of the Christian era, they became even more conscious of their Arabism. Indeed, Islam itself, although a universal religion which addresses itself to all mankind, was revealed by an Arab Prophet, in the Arabic language, in Arabia. We read in the Qur'ān: 'A Messenger has now come to you from among yourselves.' It was the Muslim Arabs of Arabia whom the Prophet glorified in these words: 'Ye are the best *umma* that hath been raised up unto mankind.' There was no place in the universal, all-embracing Faith of Islam for kinship and tribal ties existing among the Arabs in pagan days, or for any colour-bars and geographical boundaries separating its adherents. As far as the Arabs were concerned, they were to be united into one great community, which was the *umma* of Islam. 'Verily, you are of one *umma* and I your Lord: Therefore, worship me', and 'Verily, the believers are brethren'. Thus, Islam gave the Arabs a special consciousness of their identity and a sense of pride and superiority in their '*urūba*. Consequently, in the case of the Arabs who became Muslims, Islam and the Arabic language became the two prime movers of their national unity and political sovereignty. The birth of modern Arab nationalism, or *al-qawmiyya al-ʿarabiyya,* is, however, a very recent event. It is closely associated with the decline and fall of the Ottoman empire, and with Arab aspirations to political independence and unity.

The Turks and the Muslim Arabs lived side by side for four hundred years in a non-national Ottoman empire as members of one great Muslim community, united by their Faith and their allegiance to a Muslim sovereign who was sultan and caliph at the same time. But, towards the end of the nineteenth century and the beginning of the twentieth, the reign of Sultan ʿAbd ül-Ḥamīd II and, subsequently, the government of the Young Turks, led to increased discontent and rebelliousness in the Arab provinces of the Ottoman empire. The rule of ʿAbd ül-Ḥamīd was disastrous for the survival of his multi-racial and multi-national empire. Despotism, corruption, injustice, and an army of spies intensified the disaffection of the Turks and the Arabs alike towards Turkish misgovernment. Forced at the beginning of his reign into accepting Midḥat Pasha's reforms, and particularly his Constitution of 1876, ʿAbd ül-Ḥamīd acted for a while as a constitutional monarch. The first Ottoman Parliament met on 18 March 1877. But on 14 February 1878, the Parliament was dissolved *sine die* and the constitution suspended by the sultan's command. As for the deputies, the more enlightened and outspoken in their criticism were ordered to leave Constantinople. Among them were a number of prominent Arab representatives.

ʿAbd ül-Ḥamīd's next attempt to win over his discontented subjects was through the ingenious device of pan-Islam. The dream of uniting the Muslim world and rebuilding the Muslim empire had been very close to the hearts of many Muslim leaders. The sultan was persuaded by some of his very close associates to utilize his position as caliph and as the champion of Islam for politically strengthening and preserving his throne. He was led to believe that if he put himself at the head of the Muslims as the protector of those who were living under Christian governments, particularly under Britain and France in Asia and Africa, the Sunnī Muslims, Arabs and non-Arabs, would rally round the Ottoman caliphate and give it their full allegiance. The Ḥijāz Railway which was built with monetary contributions from Muslims throughout the world, was not only of great strategic value for the quick transport of troops to troublesome areas in Arabia, but it was, undoubtedly, a demonstration of the pan-Islamic policy of ʻAbd ül-Ḥamīd. Nevertheless, this policy did not affect the Arab and Turkish demands for reforms, as the internal situation continued to deteriorate with alarming speed.

Meanwhile, ʻAbd ül-Ḥamīd's iron hand and oppressive measures led to the rise of secret revolutionary societies with the object of overthrowing his régime and restoring Midḥat Pasha's Constitution of 1876. The secret societies were driven underground, or beyond the boundaries of the empire, particularly to Geneva, Paris, London, Brussels, and (after the British occupation of Egypt in 1882) to Cairo. Many of their members belonged to the main body of the Young Turks and to the latter's Committee of Union and Progress. The anti-Hamidian journals, pamphlets and leaflets which were printed in Europe and clandestinely introduced into the Ottoman empire, greatly frightened the sultan. During this time, no conscious Arab national movement had yet developed in the Arabic-speaking provinces of the empire to replace the loyalty of the vast majority of the Muslims to the sultanate and the caliphate. Most of the reformers were apostles of pan-Islam. The best known among them, Jamāl al-Dīn al-Afghānī, Shaykh Muḥammad ʻAbduh, ʻAbd al-Raḥmān al-Kawākibī and Muḥammad Rashīd Riḍā, sought to cleanse and to strengthen the Ottoman empire by a return to the purity of Islam and Muslim institutions, for the defence of the Muslim peoples against the encroachments of the West. But, here and there, during the second half of the nineteenth century, principally in Damascus, Beirut and Cairo, there were small groups of Arab patriots who preached *ḥubb al-waṭan*—love of one's birthplace. Buṭrus al-Bustānī in Beirut, Shaykh Rifāʻa Rāfiʻ al-Ṭahṭāwī, ʻUrābī Pasha and Muṣṭafā Kāmil in Egypt—to mention only a few well-known names—were among these early patriots; but their patriotic movements did not seek the secularization of the Muslim institutions of the Ottoman empire, or the unification of the Arab countries against the Turks. Indeed, Egyptian patriotism was, after 1882, more anti-British than anti-Turk.

During the latter part of the nineteenth century, and particularly in the vilayets of Damascus and Beirut, the anti-Turkish struggle emphasized Arabism and Arab unity rather than local patriotism. Hence Arab nationalism became a secret and revolutionary movement. Actually there is a remarkable indication of the possible existence of a nationalist sentiment for Arab independence, at an earlier date. On 31 July 1858, the British consul-general, I. H. Skene, reported from Aleppo on 'the hatred felt by the Arab population of this part of Syria for Turkish troops and officials in general...', and he concludes with the extraordinary remark that 'it would also appear that the Mussulman population of Northern Syria harbours hopes of a separation from the Ottoman Empire and the formation of a new Arabian State under the sovereignty of the Shereefs of Mecca...'[1] But most of the Arab nationalist activities were born after 1878, particularly after the Russo-Turkish war and the dissolution of the Ottoman Parliament. The despatches of the British and French consuls from Beirut and Damascus to their respective embassies in Constantinople contain several reports on the growth of Arab national sentiment against Turkish despotism and misgovernment.

The French consul, Delaporte, wrote from Beirut on 9 October 1879 about the possible existence of an Arab conspiracy with ramifications in Aleppo, Mosul, Baghdād, Mecca and Medina, and the intention of forming an Arab kingdom ('un royaume arabe') at the head of which there would be an Arab ruler. The consul was not in a position to confirm this rumour but he added that the Ottoman empire was in such a state of disorganization and anarchy that the realization of such a scheme was neither improbable nor impossible.[2] About a year later, on 28 June 1880, the British acting consul-general in Beirut, John Dickson, considered it important enough to inform by telegraph the British ambassador, G. T. Goschen, in Constantinople, that 'revolutionary placards' had appeared in that town. The telegram was followed by his despatch of 3 July 1880,[3] in which he wrote that such placards had recently appeared several times in Beirut, 'calling upon the people to revolt against the Turks', and he enclosed two placards—an original and a copy. The despatch contains various theories as to the origin of these placards, one of them being that they may have emanated from a 'secret society'. Indeed there was a revolutionary society in Beirut, and its existence was one of the best kept secrets of the time. Many of its members belonged to the young Christian *élite* of Lebanon, some of whom had studied at the Syrian Protestant College (now the American University of Beirut). The last surviving member of that *élite*, the late Fāris Nimr Pasha (who was for many years the owner and editor of the well-known Egyptian newspaper, *al-Muqaṭṭam*) told the writer that this society was responsible for

[1] F.O. 78/1389—Turkey—Despatch No. 33 of 7 August 1858, enclosing copy of Skene's despatch No. 20 of 31 July 1858.

[2] France, Ministry of Foreign Affairs—Turkey—vol. 22, 1879, Despatch No. 19.

[3] F.O. 195/1306—Turkey—1880, vol. II, Despatch No. 47.

issuing the anonymous placards and that many of them were in his handwriting, including the one enclosed in the above-mentioned despatch.

More placards continued to appear towards the end of 1880 in Syria where 'a certain amount of discontent manifests itself amongst a class of persons connected probably with some secret society'.[1] Even in far-away Baghdād, revolutionary leaflets apparently printed in London appeared, entreating the Arabs and 'the Christians of Syria' to unite and emancipate the 'Arab *umma*' from its enslavement by the Turks.[2]

These anti-Turkish sentiments soon received a powerful stimulus from the revolt of ʿUrābī Pasha in Egypt, and the subsequent British occupation of that country in 1882. ʿUrābī was regarded as a champion of Islam and of Arabism. On 14 July 1882, the vice-consul, John Dickson, wrote from Damascus to the Earl of Dufferin, British ambassador in Constantinople[3]: '...There is no doubt, however, that among a few persons, especially Moslems, there has been a tendency to adopt the ideas of the National Party in Egypt[4]...It is certain that the object of the Authorities in Syria is to crush out, at once, any patriotic sentiments that might exist amongst the people...' About two months later, on 23 September, John Dickson reported again from Damascus that ʿUrābī Pasha 'has always had on his side the sympathies of the whole Mussulman sect and by some has been even looked upon as a prophet almost equal to Mohamet...'[5] On that same day, the British consul in Jerusalem, N. T. Moore, stated in a despatch to the Earl of Dufferin that 'it is quite certain that the native Moslems profoundly sympathised with Arabi both as a Mohamedan...and more especially, as the champion of the Arab Mussulman race, upon whose success they based possibilities affecting the future of their race other than the mere repelling of the invasion of Egypt.'[6]

Two years later, the rebellion of the Mahdi in the Sudan stirred up, again, not only anti-British but also anti-Turkish feelings. On 19 April 1884, John Dickson's despatch to the Earl of Dufferin contained the following statement:

With regard to the state of feeling amongst the Mussulman population in consequence of recent affairs in Egypt and the British expedition to Eastern

[1] F.O. 195/1368—Turkey—1881, vol. II, Despatch No. 1 of Beyrout, 3 January 1881.
[2] F.O. 196/1370—Turkey—1881, vol. I, Despatch No. 21 of Baghdad, 20 May 1881.
[3] F.O. 195/1412—Turkey—1882, Despatch No. 3.
[4] A reference, undoubtedly, to *al-Ḥizb al-waṭanī* formed by a group of Egyptians in 1879.
[5] F.O. 195/1412—Turkey—Despatch No. 10. [6] *Ibid.*, Despatch No. 7.

Soudan, I have the honour to report that, as far as I am able to gather, from my own observations and from inquiries I have made of persons generally well informed, there has been almost entire sympathy with the Mahdi ... and it is undoubtedly a fact that the Mahdi has been considered by the Arab race in Syria as not only the champion of the Mohammedan religion but as an opponent of the Turkish Government ...[1]

But these early rumblings against Turkish misgovernment should not be interpreted as widespread and organized attempts on the part of the Muslim Arabs to break away from the Ottoman empire and establish an independent Arab state based on Arab nationalist aspirations. Dickson ended his despatch of 3 July 1880 by saying that the placards had produced 'very little effect' on the minds of the people. 'However,' he added, 'they may be taken as an indication of the times, and that the Moslem as well as the Christian has at last begun to raise his cry against Turkish misrule.' Thus, it is an error to consider any Arab who came out openly against the Ottoman sultan and the Turkish government to have been an Arab nationalist. It is equally wrong to conclude that an Arab who wanted to preserve the Ottoman sultanate and caliphate was not a nationalist.

When the Young Turks came to power in 1908, they promised equality to all Ottoman subjects, without distinction of religion or race. But they soon realized that the political ideals of the non-Turkish nationalities —Arabs, Armenians, Greeks and Slavs—were not compatible with a centralized Ottoman state. They even fell back, for a time, on the pan-Islam of Sultan 'Abd ül-Ḥamīd. This policy, also, was doomed to failure: it was too visionary and unpractical. Moreover, many Turks and Arabs doubted the religious sincerity of the Young Turk Committee of Union and Progress. The only alternative for the Young Turks was to rely on the Turkish element in what remained of their empire, to stir the Turks to a national regeneration, and to seek the eventual unification of all Turkish-speaking peoples, to fulfill their new ideal of pan-Turan.

As a result of the turcification programme of the Young Turks based on Turkish nationalism, the Arabs' pride in their race, religion and language spurred them to assert their Arabism. Moreover, the increasing impact of Western education and Western political ideas of independence and nationalism, coming mainly from French and British sources, and the revival of interest in the study of the Arabic language and literature, particularly in Lebanon, led the Arab leaders to carry their objective of

[1] F.O. 195/1480—Turkey—Despatch No. 16.

independence a great step forward. Thus, it was the national and racial policies of the Young Turks which, eventually, intensified the Arabs' desire for political independence and national unity. A number of Arab secret societies and political parties were formed to defend the Arab cause, to protect Arab rights, and, finally, to obtain complete autonomy for the Arab provinces of the Ottoman empire. Well-known among these organizations were *al-Muntadā al-Adabī* ('The Literary Club'), *al-'Ahd* ('The Covenant'), *al-Fatāt* ('The Young Arab Society') and *Ḥizb al-Lāmarkaziyya* ('The Decentralization Party'). But it can safely be asserted that until the eve of the First World War (and with the exception of the Maronites of Mount Lebanon, the Wahhābīs and, in general, the Arab tribes of Arabia), the majority of the Muslim Arab leaders had no intention of destroying the Ottoman empire, 'the only powerful Islamic Empire that remained'. Their aims and aspirations were expressed in the resolutions passed by the First Arab Congress (*al-Mu'tamar al-'Arabī al-Awwal*) which was held in Paris under the auspices of *al-Fatāt* and *Ḥizb al-Lāmarkaziyya,* from 18 to 23 June 1913. They were summed up in the following words of Iskandar 'Ammūn, the vice-president of the Decentralization Party:

The Arab *umma* does not want to separate itself from the Ottoman Empire... All that it desires is to replace the present form of government by one more compatible with the needs of all the diverse elements which compose that Empire, in such wise that the inhabitants of any province (vilayet) will have the final word in the internal administration of their own affairs... We desire an Ottoman government, neither Turkish nor Arab, a government in which all the Ottomans have equal rights and equal obligations, so that no party or group may deprive any other party or group of any of its rights, or usurp them for reasons of either race or religion, be it Arab, Turk, Armenian, Kurd, Muslim, Christian, Jew or Druze.[1]

When the Ottoman empire entered the First World War in 1914, many of the Arab leaders, after much hesitation, found it imperative for the Arabs to think in terms of complete separation from that empire and the establishment of their independence. The despotic policy of Jemāl Pasha, commander-in-chief of the Fourth Army in Syria, during the war, widened still further the gap between the Arabs and the Turks. Finally, the promises of the Allies to liberate the Arabs from the Turks and help them to determine their own future, encouraged the Arab Revolt which started in Mecca on 10 June 1916, under the leadership of the *Sharīf* Ḥusayn.

[1] See *al-Lujnat al-'Ulyā li-Ḥizb al-Lāmarkaziyya, Al-Mu'tamar al-'Arabī al-Awwal* (Cairo, 1913), 103–4; 132–4.

The Sykes-Picot Agreement of 16 May 1916 and the mandate system which was approved by the Allied Supreme Council on 20 April 1920 for the former Arab provinces of the Ottoman empire, ushered in the next stage of the evolution of Arab nationalism between the two World Wars. The presence of the mandatory powers as foreign rulers and imperialists intensified the struggle for political independence, and consolidated Arab opposition to the West. In particular, the successful Turkish revolution led by Muṣṭafā Kemāl Pasha (Atatürk) and his establishment of a modern Turkish state, had a profound influence on Arab nationalist leaders.

The Arab struggle for independence continued during the Second World War. By the end of that war, all the Arab countries of the Near East had obtained their political independence and sovereignty. But at the same time, regional nationalism in the various Arab states was inevitably accentuated and consolidated with a distinctness and particularism of its own. Although in the Arab lands which were preponderantly Muslim, religion and the Arabic language remained, potentially, the most important factors of unity, various divisive forces based on social, economic and individualistic factors, dynastic rivalries and the struggle for power made the Arab states cling jealously to their political boundaries and separate political existences. Indeed, a new Arab state was created recently and recognized by all the other Arab countries: Kuwayt became a fully independent state in June 1961.

Nevertheless, the ideal of Arab unity, based on *al-qawmiyya al-ʿarabiyya* and on the oneness of the Arab *umma* continued to be the major goal of the new leaders of Arab nationalism during the second half of the twentieth century. From a small *élite* of literary men, students and middle-class intellectuals, often working in secret and with little following, the new nationalist leadership had now moved to a much larger group of the military, professional and proletarian classes—soldiers, lawyers, doctors, teachers, journalists, government officials and an increasingly vast number of students, backed and supported by the masses.

It is worth noting that several projects for Arab unification had already been put forward by a number of Arab leaders. When the Arab Revolt of 1916 started, the *Sharīf* Ḥusayn envisaged the establishment of an all-embracing sovereign Arab kingdom arising out of the dissolution of the Ottoman Empire. In a memorandum submitted to the Peace Conference on 1 January 1919, the *Amīr* Fayṣal wrote:

> The country from a line Alexandretta–Persia southward to the Indian Ocean is inhabited by 'Arabs'—by which we mean people of closely related Semitic stocks, all speaking the one language, Arabic... The aim of the Arab nationalist movements...is to unite the Arabs eventually into one nation...We believe that our ideal of Arab unity in Asia is justified beyond needs of argument...[1]

In an eleventh-hour attempt to foil the Sykes-Picot Agreement and reject the claim of the Zionists to a National Home in Palestine, the General Syrian Congress in Damascus proclaimed Fayṣal, on 8 March 1920, as king of the 'United Kingdom of Syria', i.e. of Syria, Lebanon and Palestine. About four months later, the French occupied Syria, and Fayṣal was forced to move out of Damascus. After 1921, with Fayṣal as king of Iraq and his brother, 'Abd Allāh as *amīr* of Transjordan, Baghdād and 'Ammān became the two focal centres of Arab unification. Two major schemes embodying the concept of Arab unity were submitted to the British government; one in 1941 by the *Amīr* 'Abd Allāh, and the other in 1943 by Nūrī Pasha al-Sa'īd. The *amīr* pressed with untiring zeal for the establishment of a Great Syrian state, which was to include Syria, Lebanon, Palestine and Transjordan.[2] Nūrī Pasha, at the request of Richard Casey (subsequently Lord Casey), British minister of state for Middle East affairs, worked out a Fertile Crescent plan which advocated the union of Syria, Lebanon and Transjordan, while recognizing the 'special position' of the Maronites of Lebanon.[3] The Fertile Crescent countries were to be joined immediately by Iraq, and to form an Arab League. Both projects, viewed in the light of the circumstances of the day, were very unpractical and failed to be realized.

For some time, it was believed that the Arab League formed in 1945 was a major step towards the establishment of a federation of the Arab countries. But soon after 1952, Egypt moved, full steam ahead, into the sphere of Arab nationalism and Arab unity. On 1 February 1958, the birth of the United Arab Republic, formed by the union of Egypt and Syria, was proclaimed in Cairo. This was followed, almost immediately, on 14 February, by a union between the kingdoms of Iraq and Jordan. This latter union was soon brought to an end by the Iraqi *coup d'état* of 14 July 1958, and Syria severed its ties with Egypt in September 1961.

[1] David Hunter Miller, *My Diary at the Conference of Paris,* 1918–1919, IV (New York, 1924), 297.

[2] See Government of Transjordan, *The Jordan White Book on Greater Syria* ('Ammān, 1947), 19–23.

[3] General Nūrī al-Sa'īd, *Arab Independence and Unity* (Baghdad Government Press, 1943), 11–12.

But Egypt (which retained the name of the United Arab Republic) remained the rallying point of Arab unification.

The Arab nationalists believe today that it is through Arab unity that Arab independence can best be defended, and an Arab victory over Israel and imperialism can best be ensured. One of the major aims of the Arab unity movement is to gain more military, political and economic power to defend the territorial integrity, and preserve the political sovereignty, of the Arab lands. Hence, *al-qawmiyya al-ʿarabiyya* becomes a protective armour, an instrument of resistance to the West, the major weapon in the Arab struggle against the imperialists, and a movement of emancipation from the political, social and religious evils of the past.

Meanwhile, the tensions, the conflicts, and the pressures, both internal and external, in the struggle for unification and for the leadership of the Arab world, have led to several military, political and economic upheavals since the end of the Second World War, overthrowing several régimes and dynasties. As a result, revolution and socialism have become closely associated with *al-qawmiyya al-ʿarabiyya* and its new motto of 'Unity, Freedom and Socialism'.

The unity of the Arabs in the past was part of a larger Muslim spiritual unity, and led to the establishment of a theocratic Muslim empire. It was Islam that gave the Arabs their spiritual and political unity and their place in history. Will the final stage in the evolution of *al-qawmiyya al-ʿarabiyya* be Arab unity on the principles of arabism and secularism, or on the basis of the universalism of Islam which commands the final loyalty of every Muslim, or will there be yet a third alternative? If the Muslim Arabs separate their culture from its Islamic moorings, will they not run the risk of abandoning the most valuable contents of their past history? Secular nationalism demands the supreme loyalty of the citizen to the national god of his country. If the evolution of Arab nationalism in the independent Arab Muslim countries should follow the Western pattern and become rooted, finally, in the political and economic organization of a nation-state, it can only do so at the expense of Islam. Islam will then become a private matter, left to the conscience of any individual who may continue to believe in it, but it will inevitably lose its supreme authority. On the other hand, to what extent could religion—in this case, Islam—remain one of the fundamental pillars of a purely nationalistic and materialistic state? Only time, education and enlightened leadership may be able to work out a happy compromise between Arab nationalism and Islam.

CHAPTER 3

MODERN PERSIA

(A) POLITICAL DEVELOPMENTS: 1906–47

On 30 December 1906, the Qājār monarch Muẓaffar al-Dīn Shāh signed the fundamental law (*qānūn-i asāsī*). By his signature of this instrument, the shah in theory converted Persia from a traditional Islamic society to a constitutional monarchy. The fundamental law provided for the establishment of a National Consultative Assembly (*Majlis-i shawrā-yi Millī*), which actually met for the first time on 7 October 1906, prior to the signature of the fundamental law by the shah, and of an upper house or Senate, which was not called into being until 1950. The instrument of the constitution was completed by the ratification by Muḥammad ʿAlī Shāh, on 7 October 1907, of the supplementary fundamental law. This dealt with the rights of the Persian people and of the members of the National Consultative Assembly, and defined the powers of the crown, ministers, judicial tribunals and the army. The real dividing-line between traditional Persia and modern Iran, however, is not 1906, but 1921 when Riżā Khān (later Riżā Shāh Pahlavī) came to power by a *coup d'état*. The promulgation of the constitution was, of course, an important step forward, but for a variety of reasons it did not fulfil the hopes of the constitutionalists, and did not lead immediately to the remodelling of Persian political, economic and social life along Western lines. The measures introduced by Riżā Shāh, on the other hand, represented a definite break with the traditional past. It was he who launched Persia into the twentieth century.

The bloodless victory over absolutism proved an illusion. In reality, the struggle between the new National Consultative Assembly and the shah had barely begun. On 8 January 1907, just over a week after he had signed the fundamental law, Muẓaffar al-Dīn Shāh died, and was succeeded by his son Muḥammad ʿAlī Shāh. Although the latter had countersigned the constitution, and had sworn a solemn oath not to subvert it, he at once set out to do so by every means possible, including a plot to assassinate the leaders of the Constitutionalist party at Tabrīz. For its part, the *Majlis*, as the National Consultative Assembly was popularly known, hastened to pass legislation designed to curtail the power of the throne; to restrict, by means of sumptuary laws, the extravagant spending and huge allowances of the royal family; and to prevent the negotiation by the shah or his supporters of further foreign loans. The assassination on 31 August 1907 of the prime minister, Amīn al-Sulṭān (Atābeg-i A'ẓam), who, in defiance of the law, was trying to win support in the *Majlis* for a new Russian loan, temporarily had a sobering effect on the more extreme reactionaries, and the *Majlis* took advantage of the favourable climate of opinion to persuade the shah to sign the supplementary fundamental law.

The assassination of the prime minister coincided with the publication, on the same day, of the Anglo-Russian convention of 1907. By the terms of this convention, Persia was divided into a British and a Russian sphere of influence, separated by a neutral zone. The convention was inspired by a mutual fear of resurgent German militarism: it was designed to demarcate each party's sphere of influence in Persia in order to avoid the possibility of armed conflict in that area, and to leave the signatories free to give their full attention to events in Europe. The Persians saw the convention as an instrument which would reduce their country to semi-colonial status. The publication of the convention had three immediate consequences: first, Britain at one stroke lost the goodwill which it had acquired by its support of the Constitutionalists in 1905–6; secondly, Persia began to regard Germany, a strong power with no previous history of interference in Persian affairs, as a possible bulwark against Anglo-Russian pressure; thirdly, the Russians were given a free hand in their sphere of influence. They interpreted 'sphere of influence' as 'protectorate', and saw in the convention an opportunity to tighten their grip on northern Persia with relatively little danger of provoking British retaliation.

Meanwhile the relations between the shah and his supporters on the one hand, and the *Majlis* and the Constitutionalists, or nationalists as they were more commonly termed, on the other hand, had again worsened. In December 1907 Muḥammad 'Alī attempted to overthrow the constitution by a *coup d'état,* his instrument being the Persian Cossack Brigade, formed in 1879 by Nāṣir al-Dīn Shāh as a royal body-guard. The nationalist *anjumans,* or political societies, successfully rallied to the defence of the parliament building in Tehran. A temporary reconciliation between the shah and the *Majlis* was followed by a rapid deterioration of their relations, and on 2 June 1908 both the Russian and the British diplomatic representatives in Tehran threatened direct intervention if the shah were deposed. Heartened by this support, the shah became even more intransigent. On 11 June he placed the capital under martial law, and on 23 June the Cossack Brigade surrounded the *Majlis* and opened fire on it with artillery. Many nationalist leaders were killed or executed on the spot, others were arrested later. Colonel Liakhov, the commander of the Cossack Brigade, governed Tehran as a military dictator for a year. The *mujtahids* denounced the tyranny of the shah, and urged the people to resist, but the existence of a state of martial law made opposition in the capital impossible. Thus ended what the Persians call the 'First Constitutional Period', which extended from the granting of the constitution on 5 August 1906 to the forcible closure of the *Majlis* by Muḥammad 'Alī Shāh on 23 June 1908.

In the provinces, various forces rallied to the defence of constitutional government in Persia. At Tabrīz, nationalist forces resisted troops who blockaded the city. The blockade of Tabrīz was raised under Russian pressure to allow foodstuffs in, and Russian forces occupied the city on 29 April 1909. At Iṣfahān, the Bakhtiyārī tribe had meanwhile risen in support of the nationalist movement, and a third nationalist force assembled at Rasht in Gīlān. The two nationalist columns from Iṣfahān and Rasht respectively marched on Tehran, which they occupied on 13 July. Muḥammad 'Alī, refusing to meet their minimum demands, which included the evacuation of all foreign (i.e. Russian) troops, and the restoration in full of constitutional government, abdicated on 16 July 1909 and went into exile. An *ad hoc* meeting of members of the former *Majlis* and *mujtahids* formally declared Muḥammad 'Alī deposed, and named his eleven-year-old son, Aḥmad, as the new ruler of Persia.

This action inaugurated the 'Second Constitutional Period', which extended from 16 July 1909 to 24 December 1911. If constitutional government was difficult between 1906 and 1908, it was virtually impossible between 1909 and 1911. Dominating the whole political scene was what Shuster justly termed 'the open hostility of Russia, and the scarcely less injurious timidity of England'.[1] The entente between Germany and Russia signalled by the Potsdam Agreement (November 1910) enabled Russia to pursue a more blatantly aggressive policy in regard to Persia. Even without external pressures, however, it is doubtful how far the nationalists would have been successful in restoring orderly and stable government during this period, because serious dissension within the nationalist ranks had led to the appearance of several mutually hostile factions.

[1] W. Morgan Shuster, *The strangling of Persia* (London and Leipzig, 1912), 43

On 19 July 1911, the ex-shah Muḥammad ʿAlī was landed by the Russians in northern Persia, in the hope that he would be able to overthrow the constitution for a second time. After suffering several defeats at the hands of the nationalist forces, the ex-shah fled, and took refuge on a Russian vessel on the Caspian. It became clear that Russian support of Muḥammad ʿAlī had been merely an excuse for strengthening Russian control of northern Persia. On 29 November 1911, the Russians presented an ultimatum to the Persian government, demanding *inter alia* the dismissal of the American treasurer-general Morgan Shuster. Faced with the presence on Persian soil of over 12,000 Russian troops, and by the imminent occupation of the capital by a Russian detachment, the government capitulated on 23 December. The following day the *Majlis* was closed, and the 'Second Constitutional Period' was at an end.

Between 1911 and the outbreak of the First World War in 1914, no restraint was placed upon the activities of the Russians in northern Persia, and they continued to violate with impunity both the spirit and the letter of the 1907 convention. The Russian forces seized and executed nationalist leaders at Rasht, Tabrīz and Enzelī (now Bandar Pahlavī). In March 1912, they gratuitously bombarded the shrine of the *Imām* Riżā (ʿAlī al-Riḍā) at Mashhad, one of the holiest of Shīʿī sanctuaries. A helpless Persian government was forced to grant concessions in respect to fisheries, railways, and mineral resources, and was saddled with still further debts. The Swedish-led gendarmerie alone prevented the complete breakdown of the civil administration and a lapse into anarchy.

During the First World War, Persian territory became a battlefield for Turkish, Russian and British forces. An imperial firman dated 1 November 1914 stated that Persia's official policy was one of neutrality. Simultaneously with the advance of Turkish forces into Āẕarbāyjān, the Germans launched a major diplomatic offensive designed to turn to profit the fund of pro-German sentiment which was the legacy of the 1907 convention. They hoped to win over the cabinet and the *Majlis* to the cause of the Central Powers, and they achieved a marked degree of success in this aim. On 16 November 1915 the German minister in Tehran, von Reuss, led to Qumm a rump parliament in which all the four principal groups in the *Majlis* were represented. This rump eventually established itself at Kirmānshāh, and called itself the 'national government' (*ḥukūmat-i millī*). The success of the German *putsch* was to a large extent nullified by the fact that the British and Russians managed to persuade the shah to remain in the capital. At the same time, German agents such as Wassmuss and Zugmayer were active in southern Persia, with the object of exploiting inter-tribal feuds and disrupting the operations of the Anglo-Persian Oil Company in south-west Persia. Since the decision in 1913 to convert the ships of the Royal Navy from coal to oil fuel, Persian oil had become vitally important to the British war effort. To protect the oil installations and prevent sabotage of the pipeline, the British raised a body of levies known as the South Persia Rifles, and established the East Persia Cordon in an attempt to prevent German agents from reaching Afghanistan. In order to deny German agents freedom of action in the 'neutral' zone, Britain, by agreement with Russia, added most of this zone to its own sphere of influence. In return, the Russians demanded full liberty of action in their sphere of influence.

Persia emerged from the war in a state of administrative and financial chaos. Famine prevailed; there was a complete breakdown of the authority of the central government, and the treasury was empty. The Anglo-Persian treaty of 1919 was designed to remedy this situation. Lord Curzon saw this treaty as a means of preserving Persia as an independent state, under the guidance of British financial and military advisers. The Persians viewed it as a thinly veiled attempt to make Persia a British protectorate; the *Majlis* refused to ratify the treaty, and Sayyid Żiyā al-Dīn Ṭabāṭabā'ī's government repudiated it in 1921.

The Bolshevik Revolution of 1917 at first promised to inaugurate a new era in the relations between Persia and Russia. These hopes were embodied in the Soviet-Persian treaty of 26 February 1921, which renounced the imperialist policies of the former tsarist régime. As a corollary, it annulled all treaties concluded with that régime, and cancelled (with the important exception of the fisheries concession) all concessions granted to it. To the traditional tsarist weapons of open aggression and economic pressure was now added the characteristic Communist weapon of subversion from within. Persia was seen by Marxist theorists as the key to the Communist liberation of the East. As K. M. Troianovsky put it: 'Owing to Persia's special geopolitical position, and because of the significance of its liberation for the East, it must be conquered politically first of all. This precious key to revolutions in the East must be in our hands; at all costs Persia must be ours.'[1]

[1] Quoted in X. J. Eudin and R. C. North, *Soviet Russia and the East 1920-1927* (Stanford, California, 1957), 92.

At the Second Congress of Muslim Communists, held in Moscow in 1919, two main lines of policy were agreed upon: first to form local Communist parties throughout Asia as branches of the Comintern; secondly, to support local nationalist movements as a means of overthrowing Western imperialism in Asia. Persia was considered to be the Asian country most ripe for the application of these policies.

In regard to the formation of a Persian Communist party, the Soviet government had ready to hand a useful nucleus in the '*Adālat* ('Justice') party, which had been formed in 1916 among the Persian oil-workers at Baku, and which claimed a membership of 16,000. The '*Adālat* leaders proceeded to establish local Communist party committees at Tabrīz, Tehran, and in the Caspian provinces. In regard to the use of local nationalist movements as a means of promoting their revolutionary goals, the Bolsheviks again had an instrument ready to hand, in the form of the Jangalī movement in Gīlān. On 18 May 1920 Soviet forces under the command of Raskolnikov landed at Enzelī, and on 4 June the Autonomous Soviet Socialist Republic of Gīlān was officially founded. This was the first such organization to be set up outside Soviet territory. At the same time, the name of the '*Adālat* party was officially changed to 'the Communist Party of Persia' (*Ḥizb-i Kumūnīst-i Īrān*). In October 1921 the Soviet government withdrew its troops from Persia, and the authority of the central government was restored in Gīlān. The reasons for the withdrawal of Soviet support were: first, the fourth *Majlis* delayed ratification of the Soviet-Persian treaty pending the withdrawal of Soviet troops; secondly, the Bolsheviks had become to some extent disenchanted with the Jangalīs; thirdly, by 1921 there had been a significant shift away from the dogma formulated by Lenin at the Second Congress of the Comintern in 1920, namely, that it was possible for the primarily agrarian countries of Asia to proceed directly to the phase of Communist revolution, by-passing the stage of bourgeois capitalism postulated by Marxist theory as a prerequisite of revolution. The Gīlān experiment had led some Soviet theorists to declare that revolution in Persia would have to be postponed pending that country's completion of the phase of bourgeois development. In other words, direct revolutionary methods would be temporarily abandoned in favour of more conventional diplomacy.

At the beginning of 1921, Persia seemed weaker than at any time in the nineteenth century. Foreign troops, both Russian and British, were still on Persian soil. The government was virtually without troops, and unable to maintain internal law and order. As the Persian minister for foreign affairs put it: 'Iran was...in a state of anarchy, with bands of brigands infesting the country, destroying commerce and endangering the lives of its citizens.'[1] On 20 February 1921, Rižā Khān overthrew the government by a *coup d'état* and assumed the titles of commander-in-chief of the armed forces and minister of war. The previous year, he had become the first Persian to be appointed to the command of the Cossack Brigade, which had been raised to the strength of a division in 1916.

Rižā Khān's first thought was to abolish the monarchy and establish a republic, with himself as president. There seemed to be 'a general feeling of disillusionment among the people in regard to the monarchical principle which was caused by the character and behaviour of the last three rulers of the Qajar line'.[2] The '*ulamā*', with the spectre of secularized Turkey before them, reacted strongly against the idea of a republic, and in 1924 Rižā Khān performed a *volte-face* on this issue. A republic, he declared, was contrary to the tenets of Islam; he was willing to retain the monarchy if he were made shah.

Between 1921 and 1925 Rižā Khān proceeded steadily along the path to supreme power in Persia, or Iran, as it was henceforth to be known. His principal means to this end were unification and control of the army; restoration of the authority of the central government in the provinces; the temporary appeasement of the '*ulamā*'; domination of successive cabinets; and manipulation of the *Majlis*. After forcing into exile his partner in the 1921 *coup,* the prime minister, Sayyid Żiyā al-Dīn Ṭabāṭabā'ī, Rižā Khān caused the resignation of four prime ministers and six cabinets between 1921 and 1923. On 28 October 1923, Aḥmad Shāh finally capitulated and appointed Rižā Khān prime minister. By this time, Rižā Khān had sufficient control of the *Majlis* to risk a head-on clash with the shah, and on 31 October 1925 he obtained approval in the *Majlis* of a bill terminating the Qājār dynasty, and entrusting to himself the provisional government, pending a decision on the nature of the permanent government of Iran. Among the handful of deputies who voted against this bill was Dr Muṣaddiq (see below). On 12 December 1925 a Constituent Assembly (*Majlis-i Mu'assisān*) voted 257–3 to vest the monarchy in Rižā Khān, and in the spring of 1926 he was crowned as the first ruler of the new Pahlavī dynasty, with the style Rižā Shāh Pahlavī.

[1] Naṣr Allāh Sayfpūr Fāṭimī, *Diplomatic history of Persia, 1917–1923* (New York, 1952), 83.
[2] L. Lockhart, 'The constitutional laws of Persia', in *The Middle East Journal*, Autumn 1959, 383.

Riżā Shāh's most significant characteristic was his intense patriotism, accompanied by a not unjustified, but nevertheless at times pathological, suspicion of the motives of foreigners. His principal aims were to rid Iran of foreign political influence, and to lessen its economic dependence on foreign countries, especially the U.S.S.R. It may be argued that his domestic policies were largely subordinated to these cardinal aims of his foreign policy. He wanted Iran to be taken seriously as a modern nation; he wanted to get away from the picture of a country where the only forms of transport were the horse, the donkey and the camel, and where the women appeared in public only if heavily veiled.

Shortly after the 1921 *coup d'état* Riżā Khān was attracted by the idea of enlisting the support of a distant and disinterested power, both to offset British and Russian influence, and also to aid in the reconstruction of the economy. In 1921, the United States was an obvious choice as a third power. Iran's previous experience with Americans had been a happy one; Morgan Shuster had been both vigorous and popular until foreign pressure terminated his work in 1911. President Wilson appeared to be the champion of the small nations; the United States had denounced the 1919 Anglo-Persian agreement, and had disapproved of Britain's refusal (on the grounds that Iran was a non-combatant) to allow Persian representatives to appear at the 1919 Paris Peace Conference. Finally, the American 'open-door' economic policy suited Iran, which wished to prevent its economy being tied exclusively to Britain and Russia. It was decided to invite an American financial adviser for a second time and on 14 August 1922 Dr Arthur C. Millspaugh was appointed. He was voted wide powers by the *Majlis* and given the title of administrator-general of the finances. He was to have 'general charge of the financial administration and the preparation of the government budget', and 'effective control over the personnel of the financial administration, over expenditures, and over the creation of financial obligations'.[1] The exercise of these wide powers brought Millspaugh into conflict with Riżā Shāh, who first demanded a reduction of his powers, and then, in 1927, terminated his contract.

In 1925, Riżā Shāh set the seal on his creation of a new, unified standing army from the motley units of provincial and tribal levies, palace guards, the Cossack Brigade, gendarmerie, and South Persia Rifles which he had inherited, by introducing a conscription law which provided for a twenty-five-year term of service—two years of active duty

[1] A. C. Millspaugh, *The American task in Persia* (New York and London, 1925), 20-1.

followed by twenty-three years on various types of reserve. Backed by this new army, Riżā Shāh felt strong enough to challenge those forces in the traditional social order, which were likely to oppose his programme of westernization and modernization, namely, the landowning classes and religious classes, the merchants, and the tribes. The vested interests of each of these were likely to be affected in a different way: as the shah arrogated more power to himself, the prestige and influence of the landowners would wane; the power of the religious classes would be drastically curtailed by the secularization of the legal system and of education; the extension of state control in industry and commerce would restrict the free enterprise of the individual merchant; and the shah's determination to make the writ of the central government effective in the tribal areas, and his policy of forcible settlement of the tribes, would strike at the base of tribal life.

The most hated symbol of western domination was the system of capitulations, or extra-territorial privileges granted to foreign nationals resident in Iran. The most controversial of these privileges was that which accorded foreign residents exemption from the jurisdiction of Iranian courts. This right had been demanded by foreign powers because of the maladministration of justice and the corruption of the courts, and because of the conflict of jurisdiction between the religious courts (*maḥākim-i shar‘*) and those which tried cases on the basis of customary law (*maḥākim-i ‘urf*). Riżā Shāh, realizing that the establishment of a modern legal system along Western lines was a prerequisite of the abolition of the capitulations, charged the minister of justice with the preparation of new legal codes. In 1926 the draft penal code, and in 1928 the draft civil code, were completed. These were subject to repeated amendment, and the definitive versions did not appear until 1940 and 1939 respectively. On 10 May 1928 the capitulations were declared to be abolished, and new non-capitulatory treaties were signed with Britain, France, Belgium, Austria, Czechoslovakia, the Netherlands, Italy and Sweden. The U.S.S.R., as part of its policy of repudiating all agreements made by the tsarist régime, had already concluded such a treaty on 1 October 1927.

The abolition of the capitulations represented a major victory for Riżā Shāh in his struggle to restore Iranian sovereignty and national self-respect, but his reform of the legal system was also a severe blow to the power of the religious classes. The religious courts were progressively stripped of their functions, as whole categories of law were transferred to the jurisdiction of the civil courts, and, when a secular law degree was laid down as the minimum requirement for judicial office, the majority of the religious classes were automatically disqualified. Indeed, the shortage of properly qualified persons was for a number of years a serious obstacle to the implementation of judicial reform.

The second area which Riżā Shāh considered to be in urgent need of modernization and reform was the educational system. In general, elementary education was still carried on in *maktabs*—schools in which children of all ages from seven upwards were taught by a religious teacher (*ākhūnd* or *mullā*). The curriculum of the *maktab* was confined to reading and writing, calligraphy, the study of the Qur'ān and Arabic grammar, the Shīʿī catechism, a little poetry, and book-keeping. Great emphasis was placed on rote-learning. Parents paid whatever fees they could afford. Secondary education was conducted mainly on a private, tutorial basis, and the principal institutions of higher learning were the *madrasas* at such places as Qumm and Iṣfahān.

It is true that a *Dār al-Funūn,* or polytechnic school, had been established in Tehran in 1851, and that from about 1861 onwards some of its students had gone to Europe for further studies. This school was intended to train officers for the army and officials and administrators for the bureaucracy; although its establishment had important political implications, it did not materially affect the overall educational picture. The same is true of the School of Political Science, founded in Tehran in 1901, from which students entered the Ministry of Foreign Affairs and other government departments. It is also true that, between 1898 and 1921, attempts were made to establish a number of state schools, and in 1910 a Ministry of Education, *Waqfs* and Fine Arts was set up. Its name betrays its close association with the religious institution; and, because of the opposition of the religious classes, many of its regulations regarding the recognition of schools, the training of teachers, the standardization of textbooks, and the regularization of examinations, remained a dead letter. Perhaps the most important educational development prior to the accession of Riżā Shāh was the establishment of a large number of foreign missionary schools. Some of these, such as the American Presbyterian Mission School in Tehran, and the Church Missionary Society's Stuart Memorial College in Iṣfahān, assumed national importance, and many of the leading figures of Riżā Shāh's period received their education at these schools.

Soon after the 1921 *coup d'état,* a comprehensive, compulsory system of state education was introduced, with a westernized curriculum covering six years of primary and six of secondary education. For the first time, girls' schools were established. Gradually all foreign schools were brought under the control of the Ministry of Education, and finally closed in 1940. In 1928 the *Majlis* voted to send a hundred students annually to Europe and America for their higher education. In 1934 a law was passed which led to a rapid growth of teachers' training colleges, and the following year the university of Tehran was founded, initially with five faculties: arts, science, medicine, law and engineering. In 1936 Riżā Shāh launched a programme of adult education, designed to combat illiteracy and to give training in good citizenship. Classes were held in secondary schools, six days a week, in the evenings. The response was astonishing. Nearly 10,000 adults received certificates of literacy in the first year, and in 1940 over 150,000 people, from many walks of life, were enrolled. Students of school age were also accepted in these classes if they were obliged to work during the day.

The net result of Riżā Shāh's educational reforms was to effect a drastic break with Islamic tradition, and to cause a major upheaval in the social order. Taken in conjunction with his reform of the legal system, they permanently reduced the power of the religious classes. No previous ruler had questioned the authority of the *Sharī'a,* and all previous attempts to restrict the power of the *'ulamā'* had been made within the Islamic framework of society.

The third important component in Riżā Shāh's programme of westernization and modernization was the development of commerce and industry. In this aspect of his programme, as in many others, domestic interest and foreign policy objectives were closely linked. The incompetent financial administration and the extravagance of the later Qājār monarchs had left Iran economically weak, and had enabled foreign concessionaires to obtain control of important sectors of the economy. Further, the U.S.S.R. in particular was pursuing a policy of economic colonialism designed to keep Iran in a state of permanent dependence on Soviet trade. In the absence of any industry of its own, Iran was obliged to sell its raw materials to the U.S.S.R. and buy them back in the form of manufactured articles, or to exchange them for industrial goods. The Soviet practice of channelling commerce entirely through state trading organizations and state economic agencies enabled these to trade on terms with which the individual Iranian merchant could not compete. Russia was a natural outlet for the produce of the Caspian provinces:

fruit, rice, livestock, fish and hides. Between 1921 and 1927, when trade between Iran and the U.S.S.R. was not regulated by any commercial treaty, the Soviet policy of low tariffs on Iranian exports encouraged the Caspian merchants to think only in terms of the Russian market. In order to exert powerful economic and political pressure on the Iranian government, therefore, the U.S.S.R. had merely to place an embargo on Iranian imports, as it did in 1926. But the U.S.S.R. brought economic pressure to bear in a variety of other ways also. Embryonic Iranian industrial enterprises were bankrupted by Soviet undercutting and dumping. The Soviet government from time to time refused to provide foreign exchange, or suddenly withdrew transit privileges for Iranian exports across Russian territory, a practice which left the Iranian merchants with stocks of unsaleable goods.

Riżā Shāh realized that this state of affairs could not be changed overnight, but he was determined to make his country economically less dependent on the U.S.S.R. A series of *ad hoc* trade agreements with the Soviet government were concluded in 1927, 1931 and 1935; the terms were generally unfavourable to Iran, and the best that can be said for these agreements is that to some extent they regularized trade relations between the two countries. Despite the existence of these agreements, the Soviet state trading organizations continued to apply economic pressure by the methods mentioned above, and it was not until the volume of Iranian trade with Germany increased that any relief was felt.

The U.S.S.R. retained about one-third of Iran's total foreign trade until 1938–9. In 1938, when the trade agreement with the U.S.S.R. expired, Iran demanded, and failed to get, better terms from the Soviet government. Iranian trade with Germany had by that time increased to the point at which Riżā Shāh for the first time felt able to move from the defensive to the offensive in his negotiations with Russia. Ordering a virtual cessation of trade with Russia, he stepped up trade with Germany dramatically. Between 1938 and 1941, Russia's share of Iran's exports fell from thirty-four per cent to just over one per cent, while Germany's rose from twenty per cent to forty-two per cent; over the same period, Iran's imports from Russia fell to 0·04 per cent, while those from Germany increased to forty-seven per cent. On 25 March 1940 Iran signed a commerce and navigation treaty with the U.S.S.R. which was the most comprehensive commercial agreement as yet concluded between the two countries.

Meanwhile Riżā Shāh took urgent and effective measures to develop

Iranian industry in order to reduce dependence on imported manufactures and heavy goods. At the same time he took two other steps which demonstrated his determination to be master in his own house: first, he dismissed the efficient but unpopular Belgian officials who controlled the customs, and, secondly, he established a National Bank (*Bānk-i Millī*), and transferred to it the sole right to issue banknotes, a privilege previously held by the Imperial Bank of Persia (later the Imperial Bank of Iran), a British concession.

A prerequisite of the development of industry in Iran was the improvement of communications, and Riżā Shāh's most striking achievement under this head was the construction of the Trans-Iranian railway. Begun in 1927, and completed in 1938, the railway ran 850 miles from Bandar Shāhpūr on the Persian Gulf to Bandar Shāh on the Caspian. The construction of this railway was a magnificent engineering feat: at one point on the northern section the altitude drops 4,500 feet in twenty miles. It was paid for by means of a tax on tea and sugar, without recourse to a single foreign loan. The actual construction was begun by an American-German syndicate, and completed by Scandinavian contractors. The Czech firm of Skoda was active in the construction of new highways, bridges and other public works.

The industrial plant and factories installed by Riżā Shāh were mainly in the nature of light industry. One of his principal concerns was to reduce Iran's dependence on Russian textiles, and in this area he achieved a large measure of success. Textile factories were established at Iṣfahān, Kirmān and Tehran, and in Māzandarān, and the value of imported Russian cotton piece goods dropped rapidly from 21 million roubles in 1930 to 8½ million in 1932. In the case of sugar, another basic Iranian need, eight new factories increased production twelvefold between 1932 and 1940. Large quantities of cement were needed for construction projects and public works, including the imposing new government buildings being built in Tehran, and cement factories were built to satisfy this need. Other factories built by Riżā Shāh included tea-drying and packing plants, a fruit-drying and packing plant (dried fruit is still one of Iran's most valuable exports), a tobacco factory, meat and fish canneries, a paper-manufacturing plant; vegetable oil refineries, bakeries, rice-cleaning plants, factories for the production of soap, glass, matches and cigarettes; and breweries, wineries and distilleries. Plans for an iron and steel plant proved abortive. In the absence of any domestic steel production, Iran continued to be entirely dependent on imports for machinery, automobiles and vehicles of all kinds, locomotives and rolling stock, and both industrial and domestic appliances. German and, after the German conquest of Czechoslovakia, Czech firms supplied a large part of the machinery and industrial equipment which Iran needed; the German firm of Siemens, for instance, had a monopoly in telephone equipment and electrical installations.

Many of the new factories were owned by the state, and were under the jurisdiction of the Department of Industry and Mines, itself a branch of the Ministry of National Economy. In some cases, these state-owned factories had a monopoly of the production of a particular commodity; it was the fact that the production of tea and sugar, for instance, was a government monopoly, that enabled the government so effectively to impose the tax which paid for the Trans-Iranian railway. Riżā Shāh, however, had another, and even more important, object in creating these state monopolies, namely, to enable Iran to meet the Soviet state monopolies, if not on equal, at least on their own terms, and also to prevent their dealing with private merchants. In 1929 the Soviet government tightened its control of foreign trade still further by the establishment of a central Soviet organization for trade with the East, and, as a result of this, Iranian merchants were debarred from free trade in the Russian market. In 1931 Iran retaliated with its own state trading monopolies, which probably afforded as great a measure of relief as was possible in the circumstances.

Iran's most important industry was and is the oil industry. Oil was first struck at Masjid-i Sulaymān, in Khūzistān, in 1908; the Anglo-Persian Oil Company was formed in 1909, taking over the concessionary rights granted to William Knox D'Arcy in 1901; and the great refinery on the island of Abadan, at the head of the Persian Gulf, was completed in 1915. The first major dispute between the Iranian government and the company occurred in 1915, when the company, declaring that the government was responsible for the maintenance of law and order in Khūzistān, claimed £500,000 for the loss it sustained when the pipeline from the oilfields to the refinery was cut by tribes roused by the German agent, Wassmuss. The government made various counter-claims: they complained, *inter alia,* that the Anglo-Persian Oil Company had sold oil to the British Admiralty at less than the market price.

After the accession of Riżā Shāh, further conflict between the government and the company was inevitable. The existence on Iranian soil of a foreign oil company, particularly one in which a foreign government held a controlling interest, may have been an affront to Riżā Shāh's nationalist instincts. Moreover, the Iranian government was not satisfied with its share of the profits, in view of the rapidly increasing scale of the company's activities; it alleged that its share of the revenue was unfairly reduced by such devices as the omission of the profits of the Anglo-Persian Oil Company's subsidiary companies; that the process of introducing Iranians into responsible positions within the company was proceeding far too slowly; and, finally, that the concession itself was far too extensive. The fact that the company by 1931 gave employment to over 20,000 Iranians; that the conditions of work it offered far exceeded any contractual obligations; and that it provided housing, medical services and educational facilities on a generous scale counted for little in the eyes of the nationalists. All they saw was a company, controlled by a foreign government, in which Iranians held none of the high executive or managerial positions. This emotional, and therefore irrational, viewpoint did not undergo any fundamental change during the twenty years which preceded the final oil crisis and the nationalization in 1951 of the Anglo-Iranian Oil Company—the name by which the company was known from 1935 onwards.

Riżā Shāh's political realism, which had stood him in good stead in his dealings with the Russians, again served him well when he determined to extract from the Anglo-Persian Oil Company terms which were more favourable to Iran. After discussions between the Iranian government and the company between 1929 and 1931 had failed to yield any result, Riżā Shāh, on 27 November 1932, cancelled the concession, but left the door open to negotiations. As a result of direct negotiations between the company and the Iranian government, a new contract was signed in 1933; this extended the duration of the concession until 1993, but drastically reduced its area.

Another aspect of Riżā Shāh's skilful diplomacy was his unremitting efforts to improve relations with Iran's neighbours, Iraq, Turkey and Afghanistan. With all three countries, Iran had long-standing boundary disputes which were a constant source of friction. The dispute with Iraq over the boundary in the Shaṭṭ al-'Arab, and that with Afghanistan over the regulation of the waters of the Helmand river, were perhaps the thorniest problems. Relations with Turkey, despite the centuries-old Ottoman-Persian conflict, were more readily placed on a friendly basis, because Riżā Shāh was an ardent admirer of the Kemalist régime. The culmination of more than fifteen years of diplomatic activity was the signature of the Saʿdābād Pact on 8 July 1937. This was a non-aggression pact between Iran, Iraq, Turkey, and Afghanistan; the treaty called for the establishment of a permanent council and secretariat. Largely as a result of the support of its fellow treaty-members, Iran was elected to a seat on the Council of the League of Nations in September 1937. The Saʿdābād Pact represented a complete reversal of Iran's foreign policy from the sixteenth to the nineteenth centuries. There is no doubt that Riżā Shāh's primary object was to free Iran's hands in its dealings with Great Britain and the U.S.S.R., but it must be admitted also that, in pursuing a policy of regional friendship and co-operation, and the settlement of boundary disputes by arbitration, Riżā Shāh was ahead of contemporary Middle Eastern political thinking. The Saʿdābād Pact was the first regional treaty of friendship in the Middle East.

Riżā Shāh's most positive achievements—the establishment of internal order, the restoration of government control in the provinces and the crushing of separatist movements, and the emancipation of Iran from foreign political and economic domination—were accomplished only at the cost of the curtailment of individual liberties and the suspension of certain constitutional rights. With the increasing concentration of power in the hands of the shah, he became progressively less tolerant of criticism. Newspapers which opposed his policies were suppressed; the *Majlis* existed only to give approval to legislation which he initiated. When the largely Communist-organized trade unions caused widespread labour strikes which threatened the shah's programme of industrial development, he not only outlawed the Communist party but abolished the trade unions as well (1931). Other political parties gradually faded from the scene as Riżā Shāh demonstrated his uncompromising hostility towards criticism of his policies. Riżā Shāh, essentially a man of action, was naturally impatient with politicians, who, he considered, had had their chance between 1906 and 1921 to rebuild Iran. They had failed, and he was not going to allow them to obstruct him.

In agricultural and tribal matters, Riżā Shāh was less successful. Such progress as was made in agriculture during his reign was confined to forest conservation, the establishment of a veterinary college and an agricultural college, and research stations which conducted experiments to improve seed strains and the quality of farm stock; and the development of new crops, such as tobacco and tea. He failed to bring about any fundamental change in the system of land tenure or to integrate the tribal element into society. He failed not only because of the harsh and sometimes treacherous methods he employed to subdue the tribes, but also because his policy of forcible resettlement was impractical as well as inhumane. He was blinded to other considerations by the fact that the tribes constituted a threat to internal security, and that as long as they were allowed to flout the authority of the central government they could avoid such ordinary civic responsibilities as the payment of taxes. He felt, too, that the transhumant pattern of life of the tribes, the most important groups of which migrated in the spring from the lowlands near the Persian Gulf to the mountain valleys of the Zagros, and returned in the autumn, was anachronistic, and did not conform to the picture of a modern, progressive Iran which he wished to project abroad. In the hot, waterless lands of Khūzistān which were amongst the areas allotted to some of the tribes under the resettlement project, men and beasts died in large numbers.

Something has already been said about the growth of German influence. Already before the advent of the Nazis to power, the Weimar Republic had done much to regain the lost influence of imperial Germany in Iran. As early as 1920, commercial relations were restored when firms resumed their import-export business in Tehran, and the important part played by German companies in supplying the machinery and equipment demanded by Riżā Shāh's industrial development programme has already been noted. Before long, German capital was at work, or German technical assistance was being provided, in almost every branch of Iranian industry other than oil. German firms participated in the building of the northern section of the Trans-Iranian railway, and the first airline to operate an external route from Tehran was Lufthansa, which in 1937 inaugurated its Berlin-Baghdād-Tehran route.

After 1933, the Germans rapidly extended not only their economic control of Iran, but also energetically fostered cultural relations of all kinds. In 1934 the Deutsche Orient Verein was founded, and the Deutsch-Persische Gesellschaft issued publications and arranged lecture-tours. From 1933 onwards, the curricula of German universities began to indicate a marked interest in the Orient. In 1936, the Nazi minister Dr Schacht visited Iran, and assured the Iranians that Hitler considered them to be pure Aryans; as proof of this, Iranians were specifically exempted from the provisions of the Nuremburg race laws. The *rapprochement* between Germany and Russia in November 1940 caused Riżā Shāh some uneasiness, but he still believed that Germany had no imperialist designs in the Middle East.

By 1941, Germany had organized in Iran an effective fifth column and espionage system. The abortive pro-German coup by Rashīd 'Ālī in Iraq in May 1941 was a portent of what might be expected in Iran, where Rashīd 'Ālī took refuge. The invasion of Russia by Germany in June 1941 transformed the German espionage system in Iran from a potential to an actual threat to Britain and Russia, and introduced a note of extreme urgency into the situation. As in the First World War, the Iranian oilfields were vital. Britain could not afford to have them sabotaged. Britain was also extremely anxious to open up a supply-route through Iran in order to pass munitions and war material of all kinds to the Russians, then fighting desperately to check the German advance across southern Russia. The only other available route, the Arctic route round the north of Scandinavia, was fraught with extreme climatic difficulties, and was also within range of German submarines and aircraft. The Russians also saw the German fifth column as a threat to their security. With Vladivostok threatened by the Japanese, and Murmansk icebound for part of the year, they were even more anxious than the British to open a supply-route through Iran. A vital link in this supply-route was the Trans-Iranian railway, which German agents were in a position to sabotage as long as their espionage network remained intact.

Accordingly, on 19 July and 16 August 1941, the U.S.S.R. and Britain addressed notes to Rižā Shāh, demanding the expulsion of a large number of Germans as a matter of urgency. There is no evidence that Rižā Shāh ever intended to take effective action to comply with the Allied demands, and on 25 August 1941 British and Russian forces invaded Iran simultaneously. Only in the Abadan area did the Iranian army make a determined stand, and within forty-eight hours all resistance had ceased. When Rižā Shāh procrastinated over the expulsion of German diplomats and the internment of German citizens resident in Iran, British and Russian troops marched on Tehran. Leading German intelligence agents, however, had already escaped; and it was not until August 1943 that the main body of German agents and their Iranian collaborators was rounded up. One group continued to operate in Fārs until the spring of 1944.

Rižā Shāh abdicated in September 1941, and was succeeded by his son, Muḥammad Rižā Pahlavī. In the Tripartite Treaty of Alliance (29 January 1942) the Allies promised to withdraw their troops not later than six months after the end of all hostilities with the Axis powers. This undertaking was reinforced by the statement issued at the Tehran conference (1 December 1943) by Churchill, Roosevelt and Stalin. This statement recognized the assistance rendered to the Allies by Iran, promised economic aid, reaffirmed Iran's independence, territorial integrity and sovereignty, and reiterated the adherence by the Allies to the principles of the Atlantic Charter. Nevertheless, government during the war years was fraught with difficulties. Normal economic life was impossible, and the large sums of money expended in Iran by the Allies caused inflation. In political life, there was sudden freedom, with the removal of the strong hand which had ruled Iran for twenty years. Political parties proliferated, and anti-liberal forces, both of the extreme right and the extreme left, made their reappearance. The Shī'ī *'ulamā'* sought to regain some of the power of which they had been deprived by Riżā Shāh. After the Persian Communist party had been banned by Riżā Shāh it had been kept in being by a small group of activists living in exile, particularly in Germany. The new leaders of the party tended to be Western-educated Iranians who had learnt their Marxism in Europe, rather than the old-style professionals trained in Russia. Typical of these expatriates was Dr Taqī Irānī, a Berlin-educated physicist from Āẕarbāyjān, who returned to Iran about 1935 and began to gather together a small group of supporters. In 1937 he and some fifty of his associates were arrested on charges of violating the 1931 anti-Communist act, and were imprisoned. Dr Irānī died in prison in 1940, but his supporters were released in 1941 under the general amnesty for political prisoners, and formed the nucleus of the Tūdeh party which was founded in January 1942.

Paradoxically, Riżā Shāh had aided the cause of Communism in Iran by bringing into being some of those ingredients for a successful revolution which had been lacking in the early days of Communist activity in Iran, namely, a middle class, an intelligentsia, and a labour force. This enabled the Tūdeh party to have a broader basis of membership than the former Persian Communist party. It described itself as a 'mass[1] organization based on a union of workers, peasants, artisans and intellectual democrats'. Initially, it was careful to disguise its Communist affiliations. After the German reverses at al-'Alamayn and Stalingrad in 1942, many pro-German intellectuals joined it. In 1943 the Freedom Front, backed by a formidable section of the press, was formed, and the Tūdeh got eight members elected to the fourteenth *Majlis*. The

[1] The word *tūdeh* means 'mass'.

Tūdeh party worked actively to revive the trade unions. Its first party congress in 1944 was attended by 168 delegates claiming to represent a total membership of 25,000. At this congress, the central committee successfully overrode the protests of those who considered that participation in democratic elections was a betrayal of Communist principles.

When, in 1941, relations with Germany came to an abrupt end, the Iranians turned again to the United States as the third power which would protect them from Anglo-Russian pressure. In 1942, Dr Millspaugh was appointed a second time, with the title of director-general of the finances, and was empowered by the *Majlis* to engage sixty American experts. The measures he recommended to restore the health of the Iranian economy—income tax, price controls, cuts in government spending—aroused great opposition. Further, like Shuster in 1911, Millspaugh was hampered by the obstructiveness of Russian officials in northern Iran, who prevented Iranian government officials from carrying out their duties. In 1945, Millspaugh's attempt to secure the dismissal of the director of the national bank raised a storm of protest, and Millspaugh resigned.

In 1942, American influence in Iran was reinforced by the creation of the Persian Gulf Command. Some 30,000 American troops were engaged in facilitating the flow of supplies to the U.S.S.R., and to that end they rebuilt and modernized harbours on the Persian Gulf and in the Shaṭṭ al-'Arab, constructed roads and airports, and improved the Trans-Iranian railway from the Gulf to Tehran. Between 1942 and 1944, some 150,000 vehicles and 3,500 aircraft were delivered to the Red Army. American military missions to the Iranian government had more success than their financial one; in particular the Ridley military mission (1942), and the mission appointed to reorganize the gendarmerie, headed by Schwarzkopf, former chief of the New Jersey State Police, achieved a large measure of success. As American influence gradually replaced that of Britain in Iran, the United States ceased to have any function as a third power; moreover, in so far as the United States took Britain's place in the dialogue with Russia in Iran, it incurred the opprobrium formerly reserved for Great Britain. Until the end of the Second World War, American policy in Iran was characterized by a reluctance to take a long-term view, by a desire to avoid foreign commitments. In 1947, however, the United States extended the Truman Doctrine to include Iran as well as Turkey and Greece, and thus made a definite commitment to preserve Iran's independence.

Whereas the British considered the presence of Allied troops in Iran to be a temporary expedient, the Russians used the opportunity to exert pressure on the Iranian government for political purposes, to foster separatist movements in the areas occupied by the Red Army, and to assist the Tūdeh party in its efforts to prepare for Communist revolution in Iran. The north of the country, the zone in which Russian troops were stationed, was virtually cut off from the rest of the country. This policy was in line with the secret protocol to the Four Power Pact (13 November 1940), between the U.S.S.R. and the Axis powers, which had stated: 'The Soviet Union declares that its territorial aspirations centre south of the national territory of the Soviet Union in the direction of the Indian Ocean.'

As the war progressed, it became increasingly difficult for the Tūdeh to maintain its fiction of non-alignment with the Comintern. The most dramatic illustration of the fact that the aims and policies of the Tūdeh party and those of the Soviet government were identical occurred in 1944, when the latter launched a major diplomatic offensive for an oil concession in northern Iran. The Tūdeh party at once adopted as a principal point in its programme the concept of 'positive equilibrium', that is, the granting to the Soviet Union of an oil concession analogous to that held in the south by the Anglo-Iranian Oil Company. At the end of October, Dr Muṣaddiq made a speech in the *Majlis* in the course of which he advocated a policy of 'negative equilibrium'; the implications of such a policy, namely that the existing concession of the Anglo-Iranian Oil Company should be cancelled, were not fully realized at the time. On 2 December 1944, Dr Muṣaddiq tabled a bill in the *Majlis* under double urgency procedure which made it a punishable offence for any member of the government even to enter into negotiations for the granting of an oil concession without the prior approval of the *Majlis*, and further specified that no oil concessions of any kind would be granted while foreign troops were in the country. The passage of this bill isolated the Tūdeh party, which alone supported the Soviet demand.

The Soviet Union reacted in two ways to this check: first, the Tūdeh party stepped up its subversive activities in Tehran and the provinces; secondly, the Soviet government, playing on the susceptibilities of minorities, engineered two separate revolts, in Āẕarbāyjān and Kurdistān. In Āẕarbāyjān, the Democrat party formed by the veteran Communist leader Ja'far Pīshavarī (who as Mīr Ja'far had been secretary to the Communist '*Adālat* group in Baku in 1918) seized power by a *coup d'état* on 4 November 1945. On 8 November an Iranian detachment despatched to deal with the insurrection was stopped near Qazvīn by Red Army troops. Pīshavarī demanded complete provincial autonomy, and on 13 December 1945 the establishment of the autonomous republic of Āẕarbāyjān was proclaimed. The programme of the Democratic party included the introduction of Āẕarī Turkish into the schools and its use as the official language, the nationalization of the banks, and the distribution of land to the peasants. Two military units were formed: the *Qizilbāsh* (a word obviously calculated to have emotional overtones in Āẕarbāyjān, the birthplace of the Safavids), or regulars; and the *Fedāīler*, or irregulars. The Kurdish revolt occurred on 15 December 1945, and in January 1946 Qāżī Muḥammad was elected president of the Kurdish People's Republic.

On 19 January 1946, Iran, on the grounds that Soviet interference in Iranian internal affairs had created a situation which might constitute a threat to international peace, requested the secretary-general of the United Nations to bring the matter before the Security Council. This was done. The Council referred the matter to direct negotiations between Iran and the Soviet Union. The new Iranian prime minister, Qavām al-Salṭana, spent two months in Moscow, negotiating with Stalin and Molotov. All Allied troops were, under article 5 of the 1942 Tripartite Treaty of Alliance, to be withdrawn from Iranian soil by 2 March 1946. Britain and the United States honoured the agreement, but the Soviet Union, far from withdrawing its troops, had moved in fresh ones. In April, Qavām al-Salṭana returned to Tehran, having finally reached an understanding with the Soviet government. Iran promised to grant the U.S.S.R. an oil concession, and to reach a peaceful solution with the Āẕarbāyjān Democrats having due regard to their legitimate grievances; in return, Soviet troops were to be withdrawn within six weeks if no unforeseen circumstances occurred.

Qavām al-Salṭana gave the impression that he intended to carry out his side of the bargain. The most outspoken anti-Soviet politicians and journalists were muzzled. Sayyid Żiyā al-Dīn Ṭabāṭabā'ī, who had returned from exile in 1943 and whose National Will (*Irāda-yi Millī*) party was the only party apart from the Tūdeh which possessed a definite programme and effective organization, was arrested, and the party disintegrated. May Day 1946 was celebrated by some half million Tūdeh party members. Qavām al-Salṭana still continued to give evidence of his good intentions. In June, he reached agreement with the Āẕarbāyjān Democrats by means of conceding all essential points: the Āẕarbāyjān *Majlis* was to continue in being, but was to be termed a 'provincial council'—a type of body sanctioned by the constitution but never, except in the very early days of the constitution, set up; the Āẕarbāyjān minister of the interior was to be called the governor-general; Persian was again to be taught in the high schools, but Āẕarī Turkish was to remain the official language. In August, Qavām al-Salṭana reshuffled his cabinet, and included three members of the Tūdeh party—a clever tactical move which both further placated the Russians and alienated the extremist elements in the Tūdeh party from the party leadership; the radicals were outraged by the readiness of the Tūdeh central committee to co-operate with the bourgeoisie in order to obtain power by constitutional means. At this time, the Tūdeh party was still confident that it would win the elections to the fifteenth *Majlis*—the fourteenth *Majlis* had come to the end of its term in March 1946.

Behind the scenes, Qavām al-Salṭana was planning his counterstroke. In June 1946, he formed the Democrat party of Iran. In September, there occurred a rebellion in the south by a coalition of Bakhtiyārī and Qashqā'ī tribes. The rebels demanded similar status to Āẕarbāyjān and Kurdistān if these two provinces were granted provincial autonomy, and the expulsion from the cabinet of the three Tūdeh ministers. Qavām al-Salṭana acquiesced. In November, he suddenly arrested in Tehran a number of Tūdeh leaders, and ordered the Iranian army to march into Āẕarbāyjān to supervise the elections. After only token resistance, the Āẕarbāyjān satellite régime collapsed in mid-December. Ja'far Pīshavarī escaped to the Soviet Union, and was later reported to have been killed in a road accident near Baku. Shortly afterwards, the Iranian army overthrew the rebel régime in Kurdistān, and Qāżī Muḥammad and his brother were hanged.

With the authority of the central government restored in these two provinces, the way was open for the elections to begin. In July 1947, Qavām al-Salṭana's Democrat party was returned with a substantial majority; the group led by Dr Muṣaddiq secured some twenty-five seats. In October, Qavām al-Salṭana kept his promise to the Soviet Union to the extent of submitting to the *Majlis* a bill proposing the granting of an oil concession to the U.S.S.R. The bill was rejected by 102 votes to 2, the two Communist deputies voting for the bill.

(B) PERSIAN NATIONALISM

Nationalism in Persia has meant different things at different times, and has also been interpreted differently by different groups of people at one and the same time. Of recent years, for instance, it has been possible for such disparate groups, with such widely divergent aims and ideologies, as the shah and his supporters, Dr Muṣaddiq and the National Front, and the Communist Tūdeh party, each to claim to be promoting the cause of nationalism, and each to brand the others as traitors and enemies of the Persian people. In order to see how this has come about, it will be necessary to trace the origins and development of the concept of nationalism in Persia.

It is axiomatic that foreign rule, or foreign political and economic pressure, is the principal means of fostering nationalist sentiments. It is logical, therefore, to look for the emergence of such sentiments in Persia from the beginning of the nineteenth century, when the great powers began to exert political and economic pressure, and Britain and Russia entered upon one hundred and fifty years of rivalry for dominance.

Āqā Muḥammad Khān, whose coronation in 1210/1796 inaugurated the one hundred and thirty-year dominion of the Qājār dynasty, had, by his campaigns in Georgia, given the Russians a pretext to resume their expansion southwards. The blows fell in quick succession: in 1800, under the guise of coming to the assistance of the Georgians, Russia annexed their country; by the Treaty of Gulistān (1813), Iran lost all her rich Caucasian provinces; by the Treaty of Turkomānchāy (1828), Persia ceded still further territory, and the imposition of the capitulatory system represented an infringement of its rights as a sovereign and independent nation. In the east, the creation of Afghanistan, and the occupation of Transcaspia by the Russians during the second half of the nineteenth century, reduced the province of Khurāsān to half its former size. In addition, the incompetence and extravagance of the Qājār monarchs led them to burden Persia with foreign debts, and to place much of the country's economic resources in the hands of foreign concessionaires.

Given that in the nineteenth century Persia was still a traditional Islamic state, it was to be expected that social protest against the Qājār administration would be expressed in the traditional way, that is, through the medium of a religious movement of a revolutionary and heretical nature. The revolts which began in 1848, following the manifestation of the Bāb in 1840 as the 'gate' between man and the Hidden *Imām* (the *Imām* of the Age, i.e. the twelfth *Imām*), and hence between man and God, were in the long tradition of messianic ultra-Shī'ī heresies and, significantly, of pre-Islamic Iranian socio-religious revolts such as that of Mazdak. Although certain 'proto-nationalist' tendencies have been noted in Babism, for instance, its rejection of the existing Islamic culture, and revival of certain pre-Islamic Zoroastrian beliefs and practices, it was not a nationalist movement in the generally accepted sense. It is possible, however, that the minority branch of the Bābīs known as the Azalīs, who remained faithful to the Bāb's appointed successor, may have transmitted in political terms, to the Iranian intellectuals of the Constitutional movement, ideas which were originally expressed in religious terms, and may in this way have contributed to the development of a nationalist ideology.

The first genuinely nationalist movement arose in the last quarter of the nineteenth century. In 1892 the Shī'ī *mujtahids* and '*ulamā*' had led the people to a signal victory by forcing Nāṣir al-Dīn to rescind the 1890 Tobacco Concession granted to a British company. This was the first concerted expression of popular opinion, and it contained one of the essential ingredients of nationalism, hatred of the foreigner. Since the shah was considered to have bartered away the national birthright to foreign concessionaires, he became one of the principal targets for nationalist attack. Here were the seeds of a second basic ingredient of nationalism, the desire to vest sovereignty in the people rather than in a despotic ruler. The reformer and pan-Islamist Sayyid Jamāl al-Dīn al-Afghānī, whose personal feud with Nāṣir al-Dīn Shāh had moved him to support the demonstration against the Tobacco *régie*, followed this up by circulating throughout Persia literature which demanded the deposition of the shah, and called on the '*ulamā*' to take the lead in freeing the country from the tyranny and corruption of the governing classes, and in preventing foreigners from extending their control of the economy. In the spring of 1896 one of his supporters assassinated Nāṣir al-Dīn Shāh. Here was a demonstration of a third characteristic of nationalist movements, the capacity for conspiracy, violence and murder.

The new ruler, Muẓaffar al-Dīn Shāh, was weak and indolent. He made no attempt to introduce reforms, or to check his personal extravagance. His constant need for money enabled the Russians to tighten their grip on the Persian economy, and behind their economic pressure lay, as usual, the threat of military aggression. Popular discontent increased after the appointment of 'Ayn al-Dawla as prime minister in 1904. 'Ayn al-Dawla was held responsible for the increasing power and arrogance of the Belgian customs officials. Corruption and nepotism, not only in the central administration but also in provincial government, had reached proportions which wrung a protest even from those well accustomed to such practices.

In 1905 matters came to a head when a group of merchants, and members of the religious classes, using the traditional method of *bast*, or sanctuary, made certain specific demands of the shah: the dismissal of the prime minister, and the establishment of an *'adālat-khāna*, or house of justice. On this occasion, there was no talk of a constitution. The demand for a constitution was first heard the following year, when the nationalists (or Constitutionalists; the two terms were used indifferently), frustrated by the failure of the shah to carry out his promises, and provoked by further acts of oppression by 'Ayn al-Dawla, again took *bast*, this time in the grounds of the British legation in Tehran. Muẓaffar al-Dīn Shāh acceded to their demands; a National Assembly was convened in October 1906, and on 30 December the shah signed the fundamental law (*qānūn-i asāsī*) which, together with the supplementary fundamental law of October 1907, is the instrument of the Persian constitution.

The events of the ensuing years, described in the preceding section, engendered in the nationalists a hatred of Britain and Russia, progressively blinded the nationalists to political realities, caused them to make serious errors of policy, and led to the emergence of the characteristic syndrome that every happening in Persia, no matter how trivial, is directly attributable to the machinations of a foreign power. This belief, by paralysing independent thought and action, has done more to hamper political development than have the direct interventions of foreign powers.

The nationalists' lack of success cannot be attributed solely to foreign pressure, harmful though that was. The monarchy, the traditional unifying force, had been discredited, but nationalism had not proved an effective substitute. There was no real unity of aim among the different groups which made up the nationalist movement, and some of the groups had no clear idea of what constitutional government entailed. As a result, at an early stage serious rifts began to appear in the nationalist ranks. The most important elements were the religious classes, the *mujtahids* and *mullās*, and the members of the lower middle-class craft and artisan guilds. Members of both these groups were to be found in the nationalist societies (*anjumanhā-yi millī*), which came into being in the second half of the nineteenth century and were active both in Persia and in the Shīʿī centres in ʿIrāq. As Professor Lambton has pointed out, these societies 'had little resemblance to the political parties of the West. Their affinity was rather with the secret societies characteristic of the extreme religious sects of medieval Islam.'[1] Both the religious classes and the guilds were inspired more by a hatred of social injustice and autocratic oppression, and resentment of foreign interference in the internal affairs of Iran, than by any desire for or understanding of constitutional government. Neither group wished to take any steps incompatible with the religious law of Islam. In short, the two principal groups supporting the nationalist movement were not Western-inspired, and had their roots in traditional Islam. The Western-educated intellectuals, whose exposure to Western political ideas had given impetus to the nationalist movement, were not well represented in the first *Majlis*. Their goals of westernization and modernization could not be achieved without detriment to the traditional position of religiously oriented groups and, as their influence grew, so the gap between them and the religious classes widened. Finally, the tribes were doubtful allies of the nationalists. Some, more through hope of reaping financial gain and political power than from any lofty political ideals, had rallied to the defence of the constitution, but many others continued to give their primary loyalty to the shah. A major weakness of the nationalist government was its inability to curb the lawlessness of the tribes, and its failure to maintain internal security led to further intervention by Britain and Russia.

As stated above, on the outbreak of the First World War Iran declared a policy of 'strict neutrality'. It soon became clear that strict neutrality meant only non-alignment with the Entente powers, for the strenuous efforts of the German minister in Tehran, von Reuss, to win the nationalists over to the side of the Central Powers, were attended by a large measure of success. A considerable number of *Majlis* deputies, moved less, perhaps, by the sight of the German diplomat von Kardoff weeping for the Shīʿī martyrs during the Muḥarram celebrations, than by a desire for revenge on Britain and Russia, sank their differences in their enthusiasm for the Central Powers. The German *putsch* ultimately failed. From the beginning of 1916 until the end of the war, the policy of the Persian government on the whole favoured the Entente, although some nationalists continued to desire an unattainable neutralism.

[1] A. K. S. Lambton, 'Secret societies and the Persian Revolution of 1905–6', in *St Antony's Papers, Number 4; Middle Eastern Affairs, Number One* (London, 1958), 49.

Two branches of the mainstream of Persian nationalism deserve brief mention at this point. The first is the Jangalī movement, so called because it had its headquarters in the forest-country (Persian, *jangal*) of Gīlān. Its leader, Mīrzā Kūchik Khān, a member of the Moderate (*I'tidālī*) Group of the nationalist movement and a one-time pan-Islamist, gradually gained control of Gīlān during the First World War with the help of arms from Germany and Turkey. He stood for the overthrow of the monarchy and the abrogation of 'unjust' agreements between Persia and foreign powers. His view of society was characterized by a desire to return to a rather nebulous 'Islamic democratic order'. In 1920 the Jangalī movement was taken over by the Bolsheviks, and the Soviet Autonomous Republic of Gīlān was declared, to be overthrown by Riżā Khān in October 1921. The second local nationalist movement was that led by Shaykh Muḥammad Khiyābānī in Āẕarbāyjān. Khiyābānī's National Democrats, initially aided by the Germans, did not join forces with the Gīlān Bolsheviks, and the revolt was soon suppressed by the government (1920).

The whole question of the relations between indigenous, predominantly bourgeois, nationalist movements and international Communism, has exercised Marxist dialecticians for half a century. In 1921, seeking to rationalize the failure of the first experiment in revolutionary Communism outside the Soviet Union, some Marxist theorists saw the incompatibility between Asian nationalist movements, which were essentially xenophobic, and Communism, which advocated an international class-struggle. At the Baku Congress of the Peoples of the East in 1920, the chairman, Zinoviev, cautioned against narrow-minded nationalism, and at the Third Comintern Congress in 1921, delegates were warned that their first duty was the promotion of world propaganda against nationalism. At the Sixth Comintern Congress in 1928, a relentless struggle against bourgeois nationalist movements was advocated, but at the Seventh Comintern Congress in 1935, the Soviet leaders, alarmed by the growing threat of Nazism, performed a complete *volte-face,* and advocated an alliance with bourgeois nationalist movements in the common struggle against imperialism. A great deal of the Soviet leaders' perplexity derived from their disconcerting experience in Gīlān, where the peasants rallied to the support of the *'ulamā'* when the latter were exposed to ridicule by the Communists. Eventually, the Communists evolved a rule-of-thumb: nationalist movements were 'progressive' as long as they were concerned with the struggle against feudalism and imperialism; they became 'retrogressive' if they impeded the advance to socialist revolution. Even so, this formula could not always be applied with precision to specific cases.

In 1921, Riżā Khān seized power by a *coup d'état* and presented Persian Communists and nationalists alike with a teasing problem: could Riżā Khān (from 1925 Riżā Shāh) be considered a nationalist? He satisfied many of the criteria: about his patriotism there was no doubt—his every utterance was redolent of the most intense love of his country; he had an equally intense dislike of foreigners—at least of those whom he suspected of having designs on Iran's independence; in overthrowing the established order by force, he had the tacit approval of the majority of Iranians, and could therefore be said to be giving expression to popular nationalist sentiment; finally, and most importantly, he reached many of the objectives, and carried through many of the reforms, which successive nationalist governments between 1906 and 1925 had aimed at but had, for whatever reason, failed to achieve. These governments had failed to maintain law and order; had neglected to reorganize and modernize the armed forces; had made only limited progress in administrative and judicial reform, and virtually none in educational reform; and had entirely failed to restrict foreign influence in Persia's political and economic affairs. Why then did the nationalists choose to oppose Riżā Shāh so implacably, and even to deny that he deserved to be called a nationalist?

Basically, the nationalists, and particularly the intellectuals among them, opposed Riżā Shāh because they considered that his assumption of power represented a setback to constitutional government. In the short term they were right. Riżā Shāh was able to carry out his reforms only because he increasingly concentrated power in his own hands. He wanted to get things done quickly, and so he brooked no obstruction from the *Majlis,* which existed solely to approve his legislation, and tolerated no criticism in the press. His reorganized and greatly expanded army, on which he relied not only to maintain internal security, but also to supervise the effective implementation of his reforms, came to be hated by the nationalists as a symbol of oppression and the restriction of individual liberty. An uneducated man, and a man of action, Riżā Shāh did not disguise his contempt for what he considered to be the inadequacies of more literate and articulate, but vacillating and disunited, reformers. Unlike Atatürk, he had no ideology which the intellectuals might have accepted as a salve to their wounded pride, and which might have reconciled them to the loss of their intellectual freedom and constitutional rights. What the intellectuals failed to realize was, that nationalism and political liberties do not necessarily go together.

The rejection of the Pahlavī dynasty by the intelligentsia produced a fundamentally unhealthy and potentially dangerous situation in the Iranian body politic. The more intransigent the stand adopted by the nationalist intelligentsia, the sterner the measures needed to preserve the régime, and these measures in turn made it necessary for the intelligentsia to adopt an ever more revolutionary attitude. During Riżā Shāh's reign, the decision of the intelligentsia to oppose the régime led them into all sorts of absurdities. Thus when for a brief period it seemed that Riżā Shāh might establish a republic in Iran they opposed this movement. Similarly they opposed his efforts towards secularization and social and economic reform, although in theory they were in favour of secularization and reform. The same romantic unrealism, typical of extreme nationalists everywhere, has led the intelligentsia, during the reign of the present shah, to support Muṣaddiq, to rebuff every overture made to them by the shah, and finally to allow themselves to be manoeuvred into the absurd position of opposing the shah's six-point reform programme. During both reigns, it led them to support the Iranian Communist party and thus, paradoxically, to help to undermine the very independence of Iran as a sovereign nation, the preservation of which was supposedly their primary concern.

In an attempt to rationalize their hostility towards Riżā Shāh, the intelligentsia affected to consider him to be a British appointee. Although this view had not the slightest basis in fact, it was eminently satisfactory as a myth. If Riżā Shāh owed his rise to power to the British, clearly he was subject to the influence of foreign masters, and consequently could not be regarded as a nationalist. The nationalism of the intelligentsia prevented them from appreciating the positive achievements of Riżā Shāh. The nationalism of Riżā Shāh blinded him to the danger of choosing Germany, from 1927 onwards, as a 'third power' to offset British and Russian influence in Iran.

The abdication of Riżā Shāh in 1941 meant the end of a decade and a half of strong centralized government directed by a despot. The new shah, Muḥammad Riżā Pahlavī, had been brought up in a more liberal school than his father, and believed that a constitutional monarchy was the form of government most conducive to national unity and progress.

In this more liberal atmosphere, the *Majlis* returned to life, and political parties flourished. Newspapers appeared overnight and disappeared just as suddenly. The religious classes won back some of the ground which they had lost under Riżā Shāh. There was, however, no political stability. Ministries rose and fell, and once again excessive individualism militated against the formation of political parties with any real strength and cohesion. There were two exceptions, the Tūdeh party, formed in 1942, and the *Vaṭan* ('Fatherland'), later *Irāda-yi Millī* ('National Will') party, formed in 1943. The former was the old Persian Communist party under new management. Though its affiliation with the Comintern was only thinly disguised, many of the intelligentsia professed to regard it as a genuine reform party. Once it became evident that Germany might not, after all, win the war, many nationalists who had supported Germany during the First World War, hastened to declare themselves 'anti-Fascists', and joined the Tūdeh party. The *Irāda-yi Millī* party was a coalition of right-wing elements led by the old nationalist hero and co-organizer of the 1921 *coup d'état,* Sayyid Żiyā al-Dīn Ṭabāṭabā'ī. The cohesion and discipline of the Tūdeh party made it infinitely the more effective of the two.

In 1944 the nationalists found a new leader in Dr Muḥammad Muṣaddiq, now aged sixty-five, who because of his opposition to the policies of Riżā Shāh had lived in retreat during the latter's reign. The two driving forces behind Muṣaddiq were xenophobia, unrestrained by practical considerations or political realities, and hatred of the Pahlavī régime. In October 1944, in his famous 'negative equilibrium' speech, Muṣaddiq put forward the view that no oil concessions should be granted while foreign troops were on Iranian soil. In 1949 he formed the National Front, a widely based popular movement which embraced bourgeois nationalists, non-Tūdeh leftist intelligentsia, landowners, tribal leaders, members of the religious classes (including the fanatical groups of the extreme right) and bazaar merchants. Each of these disparate groups had its own reasons for fearing a recurrence of royal dictatorship.

One marked difference between the nationalism of Riżā Shāh and that of Muṣaddiq is that, whereas the former sought impartially to eliminate all foreign influence from Iran, the latter directed his whole attack against Britain. This was partly because Muṣaddiq had accepted Communist support (whereas Riżā Shāh had banned the Communist party in 1931), and partly because the only target selected for attack—the Anglo-

Iranian Oil Company—was a British one. A fundamental weakness in the National Front position was that, having achieved its goal of oil nationalization, it was devoid of further ideas, and made no attempt to introduce any social and economic reforms. In representing Britain as the sole source of all Iranian ills, Muṣaddiq was merely demonstrating once again his complete lack of political realism.

Why have the Nationalists always been ready to direct more virulent abuse at Britain than at Russia? There are three main reasons: first, they were bitterly disillusioned with Britain, the mother of parliamentary democracy, which in 1905–6 supported the Constitutionalists, but in 1907 signed the Anglo-Russian convention, regarded by the nationalists as an act of betrayal, and in 1919 negotiated with the Persian government the Anglo-Persian agreement, regarded by the nationalists as a stratagem to establish a British protectorate in Iran. Secondly, the romantic unrealism inherent in nationalism made it impossible for the intelligentsia to make a rational appraisal of political realities at any given stage. Thirdly, fear of reprisals usually prevented the nationalists from going too far in their attacks on Russia. They were not inhibited in the same way in their attacks on Britain, because every nationalist in his heart knew that no action he took was likely to cause the British to behave in the way the Russians behaved in 1909–16, 1920–1 and 1941–6.

CHAPTER 4

ISLAM IN THE SOVIET UNION

The Tsarist Russian Empire had the third largest Muslim population in the world, being surpassed only by the British empire, especially India, and the Ottoman empire. After the Orthodox Church, the Muslims were the largest religious group in Russia, with a population of between 15 and 18 millions. This Muslim population was found in all parts of Russia: the Volga-Ural region, Siberia, Central Asia (Turkistān), the Crimea, and the Caucasus. In the main cities of European Russia there had always been large groups of Muslims, especially Kazan Tatars, who, like the people of Āẕarbāyjān were advanced materially and culturally, and were to some extent westernized. The Religious Council of the Muslims of Russia in Ufa[1] had been established in 1788 by an edict of Catherine II. The head of this organization, which was attached to the Ministry of the Interior, was a *muftī* appointed by the Russian government. There also was a board of *qāḍīs*. The Kazakh Turks eventually passed under the control of the Religious Council in Ufa in religious and cultural matters. After the Russian occupation and annexation of Turkistān (1865–84), the *muftī* of Ufa wanted to subject the Muslims in Central Asia to his administration, but the Russian government did not approve of this, and no central religious organization was founded following the annexation of the Crimea, Āẕarbāyjān and the northern Caucasus. So, by the time of the Revolution in 1917 the only organization of the Muslims, which was officially recognized and had its expenses paid by the government, was the Religious Council in Ufa. Therefore this institution was of particular importance, and as soon as the Revolution started the possibilities of developing the organization were considered. The *muftī* 'Aṭā' Allāh Bayazitov (known for his absolute loyalty to the government), appointed by the tsar's administration, was removed from his post, and at the first All-Russian Muslim Congress which met in Moscow on 1 May 1917, 'Ālimjān Bārūdī was chosen as *muftī* of the Muslims in European Russia, Siberia and Kazakhstān.

The problems which most concerned the Muslims for some time were

[1] Since Ufa was in the province of Orenburg, the council was also known as the Orenburg Spiritual Council.

religious and civil rather than political. Under Russian rule they, mainly the Kazan Tatars and Bashkirs, had been subject to open or concealed pressure, and therefore the preservation of religion and of the national existence had become identical. For this reason, when the Revolution of 1917 began, the Muslims sought the means of obtaining the full religious freedom which they considered paramount. This large population of diverse origins took the same stand at least in matters of religion and culture. It was certain that this mass of people, if organized, would have an important political potential. Furthermore, the presence of the Muslims in large numbers in the frontier regions such as Turkistān, Caucasia and the Crimea was also significant. The Muslims would expect much from the Revolution, so the political organizations which could serve their purposes would easily draw them to their side. The Bolshevik party started to attract attention with its policy of making use of the Muslims.

After the October 1917 Revolution, Lenin and other Bolshevik leaders gave a special emphasis to the Islamic world. In the first place, the propagation and the reinforcement of the fundamentals gained by the Revolution could only be achieved with the backing of large masses. It was necessary to win the support of the people who had been 'oppressed' under tsarist rule, the most important of whom were the Muslims. Since, moreover, the military ability of the Kazan Tatars, Bashkirs and northern Caucasians had long been known, the Bolsheviks would profit greatly if they could gain their support. On the other hand, outside Russia there were more than two hundred million Muslims under imperialist, and especially British, rule. The Soviet leaders could create a completely new situation by assuming the role of protector of these oppressed people. According to the Bolsheviks, the importance of Islam was not as a religion, but as a description of the oppressed people of the East who had this name. They believed in the possibilities of using the Islamic world for the purposes of Bolshevism.

As soon as the Bolsheviks came to power, they started working towards winning the Muslims both inside and outside Russia. A declaration addressed to the Muslims of Russia and the eastern countries, and signed by Lenin and Stalin (the commissar of nationalities), was issued in December 1917. It contains the following appeal:

Muslims of Russia, Tatars of the Volga and the Crimea, Kirgiz and Sarts of Siberia and Turkestan, Chechens and mountain Cossacks! All you, whose mosques and shrines have been destroyed, whose faith and customs have been violated by the Tsars and oppressors of Russia! Henceforward your beliefs and customs, your national and cultural institutions, are declared free and inviolable! Build your national life freely and without hindrance. It is your right. Know that your rights, like those of all the peoples of Russia, will be protected by the might of the Revolution, by the councils of workers, soldiers, peasants, deputies![1]

Following this, the Muslims of the eastern countries (especially, that is, the Muslims of India) were asked to support the October Revolution. This declaration produced great repercussions. The majority of the Muslims in Russia, especially the intellectuals, believed in the religious and national freedom promised by the Bolsheviks, and started to support the Soviet régime. During the Civil War, a great number of Tatars and Bashkirs served (some of them voluntarily, but a great many as conscripts) in the Red Army. There were many Muslim soldiers, especially on the eastern front in the Fifth Red Army, and they played an important part in the defeat of Kolchak. Bashkir and Tatar soldiers played an important role on either front as well, for instance, in the suppression of the Kronstadt revolt of 1921, and Muslim troops were extremely useful in the battles against Denikin. However, it was soon realized that the promises made in the declaration of December 1917 had no validity. The national institutions and traditions of the Muslims, and especially Islam, were persecuted. But now the October Revolution had succeeded everywhere and, just as in tsarist Russia, the Muslim population in the Soviet area was left in the hands of the Russian administration.

Since Lenin and Stalin were Marxists and atheists, they of course would not protect the Islamic religion or any other. They had clearly declared that religion was the opium of the people and harmful to them, and that it could not be reconciled with a materialistic approach. Soon after the Soviet régime was established, religion was completely separated from the state, and no help of any kind could be expected from the state for religious institutions. The protection of the oppressed Muslim people was purely political, and had nothing to do with religion itself. Because the oppressed Muslims did not know the doctrines of the Bolshevik leaders, they regarded them as the friends and patrons of Islam.

One of the largest claims of the Bolsheviks after they came to power was that they would find a solution to the problem of nationalities. Every nation would be given the right to choose its own way of life and

[1] Quoted from G. Wheeler, *The modern history of Soviet Central Asia* (London, 1964), 188. The complete text is given in J. C. Hurewitz, *Diplomacy in the Near and Middle East* (Princeton, 1956), II, 27-28.

its own administration, and even be permitted to break away from Russia if it wished. The Tatars of Kazan had tried to organize their national life before the October Revolution. The three congresses that met in Kazan (the religious, military and General Assembly) came together and declared national and cultural autonomy on 22 July 1917. In November, a National Assembly had met in Ufa, prepared a constitution for the application of autonomy, and established national institutions—namely, a Department of Religious Affairs, with the *muftī* 'Ālimjān Bārūdī at its head, a Department of Education and a Department of Finance. These three departments formed the National Administration which was headed by Ṣadrī Maqṣūdī. In the meetings of the National Assembly it was also proposed to establish a republic with the name of the Idil[1]-Ural States, and a committee was chosen to work on this matter. This committee defined the borders and the institutions of a state of seven or eight million people in the Idil-Ural territory where the Kazan Tatars and Bashkirs lived in large numbers. The final decision on this matter was left to the National Assembly which was to meet in March 1918.

However, after the October Revolution, and especially after the establishment of the Soviet régime in the cities of Kazan and Ufa, these activities came to an end. The nationalist movement of the Tatars in Kazan was stopped by the Bolsheviks on 28 March 1918, and the national organization dissolved. On 12 April 1918, the National Administration in Ufa was dissolved by the Red Tatar troops, and only the Department of Religious Affairs was left, on condition that it would not engage in politics. This action of the Soviets was absolutely contrary to their declaration of December 1917.

Among the Muslim leaders the illusion persisted that the dissolution of the national institutions might be the arbitrary actions of native communist extremists, unknown to the central authorities, that is the leaders in the Kremlin. A committee composed of Ṣadrī Maqṣūdī, the head of the National Administration in Ufa, 'Ālimjān Bārūdī the *muftī*, and Kurbangali, the head of the Education Department, came to Moscow early in May 1918 to meet the high Soviet authorities. They presented a long memorandum to the head of the Soviet Executive Committee. Their purpose was to avoid interference with the national institutions of the nine million Muslim people, Tatars and Bashkirs who had united according to the principles of national and cultural

[1] Idil is the Tatar name for the Volga.

autonomy declared in Kazan, and who were represented by the National Assembly and the National Administration at Ufa. The memorandum stated that these national activities had no relation with politics; that religion was of great importance to the Muslims. It added that the separation of religion and state by the Soviet government had caused the prohibition of religious teaching in Muslim schools and that the confiscation of the properties belonging to the *waqfs* was considered to be unjust. These activities would have an unfavourable effect on the Muslim people; therefore, the representatives of the National Administration asked the Soviet leaders to show some tolerance to the Muslims in religious and national matters. They are also said to have reported their demands to the Ottoman ambassador in Moscow, and to have expected some support.

The appeal to the Soviet authorities brought no positive results. In the Muslim territories where the Soviet régime was already established, the national organizations were to be readjusted according to Bolshevik principles, as nationalist in form, but socialist in essence. In this system, religion was not going to be given a high position.

Following the declaration of December 1917, the Commissariat of Nationalities, an important organ of the Soviet government, directed by Stalin, established the Central Commissariat for Muslim Affairs, to establish the Soviet régime and propagate the Communist ideology among the Muslim people. Mullā Nūr Vakhitov, a Kazan Tatar, who soon became a Bolshevik, was put at the head of this organization. The other two members who also soon became Reds were 'Ālimjān Ibrahimov, a well-known Kazan Tatar writer, and Sherīf Manatov of the Bashkirs. This Commissariat of the Muslims started to establish Muslim Communist parties in the cities of the Idil-Ural region. Also through this Commissariat the Bolshevik leaders, mainly Stalin, tried to find some practical means for the solution of the nationalities problem. The first experiment in this matter was made on the Tatars and Bashkirs.

It has already been mentioned that the National Administration wanted to found the Idil-Ural States. The Tatar Communists now wanted to carry out this same project, but with the methods of the Soviet régime. After negotiations in the Kremlin, Stalin and Lenin approved of this project, and on 24 March 1918, it was announced that a Tatar-Bashkir Soviet Republic was to be founded. However, this project was not realized, mainly because a Muslim republic with a large population so close to Kazakhstān and Turkistān seemed dangerous. The Czech revolt of May 1918, and the Civil War which followed it, also hindered the realization of the project, which moreover was resisted by some Bashkir leaders, who did not wish to submit themselves to the domination of the Tatars.

After the Civil War, local republics began to be founded. The Bashkir Autonomous Soviet Republic, established in 1920, was the first of these experiments. In June 1920 the Tatar Autonomous Soviet Republic was founded, and it was followed by other republics at various dates in the areas where Turkish and Muslim peoples lived. These were patterned on the Soviet Russian Republic, and the same constitution and organization was accepted for all of them. No place was given to the Islamic religion. There was some toleration for the Islamic institutions of the Central Asian republics (such as the *Sharīʿa* and the *medreses*) but this was temporary. However, since the people of the Tatar, Bashkir, Kazakh and other Central Asian republics still belonged to Islam, these countries were regarded as Muslim. The Soviet government unwillingly accepted this situation and felt the necessity of a reconciliation with the religious beliefs of some twenty million people who lived in those lands. This can be explained both as a result of domestic considerations and also (probably more so) as a requirement of foreign policy.

According to the records of the Religious Council in Ufa, there were 7,800 communities attached to the office of the *muftī,* and the number of mosques and schools was 8,000, including some secondary schools and seminaries in the cities. None of these institutions was given any support by the Russian government; they were run with the money collected among the Kazan Tatars. They were open to the Bashkirs, Kazakhs and people of Turkistān, as well as to the Kazan Tatars. They played a great part in the enlightenment of the Turkish-Muslim people; and the rate of literacy in the Kazan province was as high as fifty per cent before 1917. A number of daily papers and periodicals were published in Kazan, and there were extensive publishing activities. *Shūrā,* published in Orenburg, was one of the best journals in the Islamic world as well as in Russia. In Āẕarbāyjān, Baku, the Crimea and Siberia, campaigns for the propagation of religious and secular education were vigorously pursued in a number of cities, and teachers' training schools both for men and women had extensive activities. As a result of relations with Turkey and Egypt, the new movements in these countries had repercussions among the Muslims in Russia. The religious books published before 1917 included serious studies on Islamic religion, and important works on

Islamic philosophy were also being written. The Muslims in Russia were on the road towards a real awakening.

After the October Revolution all activities of this sort were suddenly stopped. Beginning early in 1918, *medreses* were closed down, and the '*ulemā*' were eventually prosecuted for one reason or another. After the state was secularized, religious lessons in the schools were stopped, but this was done gradually, and religious teaching continued in many places under the Soviet régime.

The parts of Russia where the Muslims lived had been most damaged by the Civil War. The revolt which the Czechs started in May 1918 spread towards Siberia along the Volga. The fiercest fights between the Whites and the Reds took place in Muslim areas. During these battles, many Muslims, especially from the higher classes and the '*ulemā*', were killed, and part of the people emigrated. The year following the foundation of the Soviet Tatar Republic, there was a great famine (1921–2). The total number of people who died of hunger or who emigrated from the Kazan province for this reason exceeded half a million. The majority went to Turkistān. In these circumstances, the establishment of the Soviet system in the Tatar Republic proceeded slowly, and the Soviet government showed tolerance in some national and religious affairs.

In order to win the sympathy of the Muslim peoples, the Twelfth Congress of the Russian Communist Party in 1923 decided that the struggle should be fought against religion without using force but with propaganda. It was thought that the centre of the propaganda and fight against religion would be the village schools. While decisions of this kind were being made, the publication of works which introduced the methods of fighting religion was also started. Among the first works published in this field was one by Mīr Sayyid Sultangaliyev (Sulṭān 'Alīoghlu), one of Stalin's assistants. Publications of this kind started to provoke popular reaction rather than support.

The organizations of the Russian Muslims had applied to the Soviet government to hold a congress for the discussion of problems concerning themselves, and this was finally permitted. Some considerations in foreign policy, especially the desire to resume the policy of inciting the Muslims in India against the British, were an important factor in this matter.

A congress was held at Ufa on 15 June 1923, with the participation of 350 delegates from various parts of Russia. Among the important items for discussion were the organization and operation of the Department of Religious Affairs (i.e. the former Religious Council), and the recognition of 'Abd ül-Mejīd, who had been made caliph on 18 November 1922 by the Turkish Grand National Assembly. It was decided to send a telegram of gratitude and congratulations to Muṣṭafā Kemāl Pasha through the Soviet commissar of Foreign Affairs. The telegram mentioned Sultan Meḥmed VI Vaḥīd al-Dīn's treachery and the cruelties of the Entente powers. Muṣṭafā Kemāl was thanked for making 'Abd ül-Mejīd caliph, and the action of the Turkish Grand National Assembly was praised. News about this telegram appeared in *Izvestia*, the official paper of the Soviet government. After the Congress was over, delegates paid a visit to the Turkish ambassador, to express orally what was in the telegram. All these moves were of course made with the knowledge and direction of the Soviet government, and demonstrated that it attached a special importance to the Muslims, both inside and outside the country.

According to a decision taken by the Central Committee of the Russian Communist Party on 2 November 1923, Muslim children who had completed their fourteenth year could study Islam. This decision brought great happiness to the Muslim people. Lists of people who remained loyal to religion were immediately prepared in all districts, and arrangements were made for teaching in the mosques. But this decision of the central authorities was counteracted by the native Communist extremists. For instance, only one day in a week was appointed for religious lessons, or difficulties were put in the way of the teachers. Nevertheless the Department of Religious Affairs organized the teaching of religion, and children over fourteen years of age in the villages and towns were regularly given lessons on the fundamentals of religion, and on ritual and prayers. The teaching of religion to the children below the age of fourteen was forbidden by Soviet laws, and those who violated these laws were liable to three years penal labour in work-camps, but in spite of all these threats, there is no doubt that children learned their religion in their families. As a result, Islam did not disintegrate during the Soviet régime. The Islamic customs were kept as before, and the boys were still circumcized. The aid given to the mosques and *mullās* was an expression of the intensity of popular religious feelings. At that time, the economic conditions of the Kazan Tatars and other Muslims were rapidly improving as a result of the New Economic Policy of Soviet Russia, so people could afford financial aid to religious organizations and men of religion.

After 1923 the Department of Religious Affairs in Ufa had relatively convenient working conditions. When 'Ālimjān Bārūdī died on 6 December 1921, Rižā al-Dīn Fakhr al-Dīn was elected in his place. He was one of the most distinguished Russian Muslims, as a scholar, an historian and a writer. Among the *qāḍis* there were able persons, such as Keshshāf al-Dīn Terjümānī and Żiyā al-Dīn Kemālī, and also a woman *qāḍī*. The organization and functions of the Department of Religious Affairs had been determined in the Moscow Congress of 1917, but had to be readjusted according to Soviet conditions.

A new statute was accepted in the Congress that met in Ufa in June 1923, and was sent for approval to the Commissariat of the Interior to which the Department of Religious Affairs was attached. On 30 November 1923, it was approved by the Commissariat. According to new regulations, the Muslims in the republics of Tatarstān, Bashkiria, Kazakhstān, Ukraine, and the autonomous territories of Chuvash, Votyakh and Kalmukh, the cities in inner Russia (that is Moscow and Leningrad), and Muslims of other cities, as well as those in Siberia were to be subjected to the religious administration in Ufa. Thus eight to ten million Muslims were brought under the *muftī* of Ufa. In other areas, such as the Crimea, northern Caucasia (Dāghistān), Āẕarbāyjān and Turkistān, there were local organizations and establishments. As a matter of formality, the decision taken at the centre had to be registered by the local authorities in different republics in order to be put into practice. Tatarstān was the first to act in this matter. Their decision was registered by the Commissariat of the Interior of the Tatar Republic on 1 February 1924. Bashkiria registered on 5 July 1924. Kazakhstān raised some problems in this respect. It is possible that the Kazakh Communists or others did not wish the Kazakhs to be subject to the Tatars even in respect to religion. In order to convince the Kazakhs, Keshshāf al-Dīn Terjümānī was sent to Orenburg and the decision was finally registered on 2 January 1925.

According to the new statute, the local administration of the communities, that is, the boards of trustees in the villages and cities were the first step on the ladder of the religious organization. The head of the board was the *imām,* and the members were the muezzin and a few others chosen from the public. Above the boards stood the *muḥtesibs,* and at the very top was the *muftī,* the head of the Department of Religious Affairs. There was a board of *qāḍīs* attached to the *muftī*. The religious administration was connected to the Commissariat of the Interior, as in tsarist times.

The religious administration supervised the activities of the *muḥtesibs,* the local administrations, the *mullās* and the muezzins, the construction and repair of mosques, and the teaching of religion. Under Soviet law, religious institutions and men of religion had a special status. The mosques were subject to certain taxes. As second-class citizens, *mullās* and muezzins were deprived of many rights. They could not participate in elections; they could not even obtain coupons for bread rations, since they were considered to be a parasitic group. The children of the *mullās* and muezzins were deprived of the right to education. Therefore thousands of *mullās* and muezzins resigned from their posts in order to obtain education for their children. In spite of this, thousands of men of religion went on carrying out their duties, sometimes openly and sometimes secretly, and as a result they faced hardships and persecution. The people supported them as much as they could, and made sacrifices when needed.

The *muftī* Riżā al-Dīn Fakhr al-Dīn and the *qāḍī* Keshshāf al-Dīn Terjümānī went to Moscow early in February 1925, to seek some concessions. They were well received, and some concessions were made. A meeting of the Muslim representatives in Ufa was held on 22 March 1925 with the permission of the government of Bashkiria. The account of the contacts made in Moscow pleased everybody, and telegrams of appreciation were sent to Kalinin and Stalin, and also to the Assembly of Soviets of Bashkiria, which was meeting at that time. It is not clear what was achieved after the Moscow visit and the meeting in Ufa, but it seems that the Soviet government did not rigorously suppress religious affairs. The invitation of Riżā al-Dīn Fakhr al-Dīn as a great scholar to the ceremony of the bicentenary of the Russian Academy of Sciences indicates the importance given at that time to the Department of Religious Affairs in Ufa by the Soviet academic institutions and government.

According to the decision of 30 November 1923, the Religious Administration in Ufa was given permission for religious publishing. The most important publication was the monthly *Islām Mejellesi*. This journal, which started in 1924, contains very mature articles on religious, moral and philosophical subjects. Its motto, 'The happiness of humanity can be achieved by a religion preserving its vitality, and a religious life', was exactly the opposite of Marx's and Lenin's assertion that religion was the opium of the people. It served as a guide for the men of religion, and filled the gap in religious studies. The journal was very well received by Russian Muslims and its copies were sold out, while the editors received many letters of appreciation. Its contributors were the contemporary scholars and intellectuals. It was probably closed down in 1925, when the struggle against religion that was begun by the Soviet government became harsher.

Propaganda against Islam by way of publications was emphasized from 1923. As mentioned above, one of the most important works in this field was written by Sultangaliyev. Sultangaliyev did not, however, attack Islam crudely, but tried rather to explain his own view of its nature, and sought to demolish the myths of Islam. During the period of the New Economic Policy, religion was relatively not treated harshly, but the opinion that religion was a harmful factor was maintained. The principle of struggling against religion was expressed in the Soviet constitution of 1924.

After 1924, many propagandist publications against Islam appeared. The pressure of the local Soviet organizations and their publications full of accusations against Islam aroused the people, instead of winning them. The Muslims attempted to organize meetings to defend their religious opinions, using the elasticity of certain articles in the Soviet constitution. They decided to appeal to the higher Soviet authorities, and wanted their rights to be recognized.

These decisions evoked severe criticism in the Soviet press, and were ascribed to reactionary groups working through the Department of Religious Affairs. In fact, these were the wishes and the opinions of the Muslim peasant groups themselves. The men of religion were formulating these opinions and wishes. Naturally all these were exactly the opposite of the Soviet system and the communist ideology, and severe measures were taken to suppress and to prevent this sort of movement.

Soviet policy towards Islam had an external as well as an internal aspect. The visit of a large mission to Mecca in 1926 under the leadership of the *muftī* Riżā al-Dīn is connected with the external Islamic policy of the Soviet government. This mission went to Istanbul in May 1926, and stayed there for a while. The spokesman of the mission, Keshshāf al-Dīn Terjümānī and other participants made statements that the Soviet government treated the Muslims in Russia very well, the mosques were kept open and no pressure was made against religion. One of the main reasons for sending the mission to Mecca was to have its members make such statements, in order to gain the sympathy of the Islamic world for Soviet Russia, and there were certainly Soviet agents among the pilgrims.

However, statements of this kind were not totally false; some mosques were still kept open, and the number of Muslims who prayed and fasted reached twenty million. Furthermore there were still Islamic law-courts functioning in Turkistān and Kazakhstān. In 1925 there were eighty-seven Islamic law-courts in Uzbekistān; their number came down to twenty-seven in 1926, and seven in 1927. They were all closed by 1928. Religious courts in some isolated parts of Dāghistān probably went on functioning until 1929. But these were all temporary. Parallel to the establishment of the socialist order in Soviet Russia, preparations began in 1926 to attack the enemies of the Revolution on all fronts, and in this connexion, religion as well. For this purpose 'societies of atheists' (more exactly, 'societies of the godless') were founded in Tatarstān, Bashkiria, and in the republics of Central Asia, and Islam was attacked in their publications. The head of this movement was Yemil'yan Yaroslavskiy, a well-known Communist. Yaroslavskiy's activities were against all religion. The atheists of the Tatars, Bashkirs, Özbegs and Āẕarbāyjānīs took Yaroslavskiy as a model in their fight with Islam.

The fight against Islam was intensified during the establishment of *kolkhozes* (1929–38), and reached its climax in the years of Stalin's terror (1936–8). The abolition of the Arabic script in 1928–9, and the acceptance of the Roman script in its place was a heavy blow to the culture and religion of the Muslim Turkish people. With this measure, the strongest tie with the outer world was cut off, and it became impossible for young people to read the Qur'ān and devotional literature. A campaign was launched in the Volga-Ural area by the *Komsomol* (Young Communist Organization) to collect copies of the Qur'ān. Villages were searched, and the Qur'āns that were found were burned. During the establishment of the *kolkhozes* the *mullās* were considered as part of the *kulak* group, and were burdened with heavy taxes. Many of them were forced to resign. Actually a majority of the *mullās* were poor, and they were no better off than the ordinary peasants. According to a news item in the *Yeni Köy* (*Yana Avul*) newspaper for 5 May 1930, the duties of 502 *mullās* and 363 muezzins were terminated, and 103 mosques were closed.

Thenceforth the campaigns of closing the mosques was accelerated. In a teachers' meeting held in Kazan on 31 January 1931, at which only 151 people were present, it was decided to close many of the mosques. In Kazan, where there were more than 50,000 Muslims and which was a national and religious centre for the Kazan Tatars, only one or two mosques were left for worship. According to various sources the number of mosques that closed under Soviet pressure in the years 1929–39 were as follows: 14,000 in Central Asia, 6,000 in the Volga-Ural area 4,000 in northern Caucasia and 1,000 in Crimea. Since it is known that there were approximately 8,000 mosques in the Volga-Ural area in 1917, the figures given above may be somewhere near reality.

As a result of the closure of the mosques and various restrictions on Islam, the people in certain parts of Soviet Russia showed some resistance. The most important instance was the armed rising in the Kabardino-Balkarian Autonomous Region (northern Caucasia). The Baskan area was occupied by Muslims, and severe measures were taken against the Soviet authorities, who only re-established control after sending large forces to the area. Thousands of people were severely punished, many being shot and others sent to labour camps. A rising of Muslim Georgians took place in the Adzhar Autonomous Region near the borders of the Turkish Republic in April 1929. The main reason for this was the pressure of the Bolsheviks on Islam. It was also severely suppressed, and thousands of Adzhars were removed from the border-zone and sent elsewhere. Among the Chechens there also was an armed rising against the Soviet government for religious reasons, and the fighting went on for a long time. The Muslim peoples were regarded as untrustworthy by the Soviets, and the fact that they lived in the border-zones of Turkistān, Caucasia and the Crimea was an important factor in increasing the distrust. The disastrous end that the Muslims came to after the Second World War is a bitter example of this distrust.

The suppression of Islam in Uzbekistān was also intensified. The anti-religious policy of the Bolsheviks, of some Uzbek (Özbeg) communists in particular, aroused popular fury. The clearest example of this is the events in Shahmerdan in 1928–9. Shahmerdan, in the mountainous south-east of Uzbekistān, was especially known for its religious feeling, and was the best-known Muslim pilgrimage centre. The Communist party of Uzbekistān began a campaign there. An Uzbek Communist named Ḥākim-zāde, known for his atheism, was sent to Shahmerdan in August 1928 to carry out propaganda. Ḥākim-zāde stirred the people with his words and actions to such an extent that in March 1929 he was torn to pieces by *mullās* and shaykhs, according to the Soviet account. Similar incidents happened in other parts of Uzbekistān. The armed struggles of the Basmachis, which lasted for years, were also a result of the suppression of Islam. The Basmachis killed especially those Communists who were against religion.

An aspect of the struggle against Islam in Turkistān was the campaign against women's veils. The veil was particularly worn in Turkistān, and was more or less considered to be inseparable from Islam. March 8, which is known as 'International Women's Day', was declared in 1927 to be the day for attacking the veil by the Uzbek Communist organization. On that day, 100,000 women in Uzbekistān announced that they had taken off their veils, but most of them resumed their veils again the following day. Many women were killed by their husbands or the people in Uzbekistān for taking off their veils. In spite of all the efforts of the Communist party, the campaign against the veil could not achieve any success between 1928 and 1939.

During the years of liquidation between 1936 and 1938, many of the main leaders in Muslim territories, the *'ulemā'*, the nationalists and also the Communists, were either destroyed or sent into exile. About 6–7,000 *mullās* and intellectuals from the Volga-Ural area alone were arrested and sent to Siberia or other places. In the Crimea and northern Caucasia, thousands of men of religion and intellectuals suffered the same fate. The fight against the intellectuals and the religious leaders also resulted in large numbers of victims in Āẕarbāyjān. After this movement of liquidation the religious and cultural leaders of the Muslims in the Soviet Union were wiped out. Among them was the *muftī* Keshshāf al-Dīn Terjümānī, who was accused of acting as a spy for the Japanese and the Germans. He and many of the men of religion close to him were shot. The years before the Second World War were most difficult for the Muslims in Soviet Russia.

The war, which started with the German attack on 22 June 1941, placed the Soviet Union in great danger. On the instructions of Stalin, it was decided to utilize the religious feelings of the people for the purpose of the country's defence. So the pressure against religion was relieved, and it was announced that the government would make concessions to the religious institutions. After this, Islam profited from these developments, although Muslim religious activities were subject to the directives and control of the Soviet government.

After Keshshāf al-Dīn Terjümānī was shot (1938), 'Abd al-Raḥmān Rasūl was appointed *muftī* at the Department of Religious Affairs in Ufa. Neither by his scholarship nor his personality was he qualified to occupy such a high position, but because of his father, who was a famous religious scholar, he was respected among the Muslims. The Soviet government began to exploit him as a religious leader of the Muslims in Russia during the war against Germany. In a radio speech which he made on 18 July 1941 on the orders of the Soviet government, he requested the people to defend the Soviet fatherland in the name of Islam, and pray in all mosques for the success of the Red Army. Six weeks later in another speech he requested the Muslims to pray for the Red Army. The more desperate the war became, the greater was the respect accorded to the *muftī* ʿAbd al-Raḥmān Rasūl by the Soviet government. He was regarded as the spokesman of twenty-five million Muslims, and he was treated accordingly. It was necessary for the *muftī* to make himself heard not only in Russia, but also in the Islamic world outside, whose importance had increased during the war.

In May 1942, a meeting of eighty-five *ʿulemā'* from various parts of the Soviet Union was held in Ufa. The main reason for this meeting was to stimulate the religious feelings of the Muslim soldiers in the fight against the Germans, and to find support in the Qur'ān. The *muftī* wanted the atrocities of the Germans committed in the Crimea against the Muslims to be known in Russia and the Islamic world outside, although the Germans had provided for the reopening and restoration of the mosques. In short, the *muftī* ʿAbd al-Raḥmān Rasūl performed the functions of a Soviet propagandist, and made every effort to accomplish his duty. His predecessor in Ufa during the First World War had done the same thing for tsarist Russia.

After 1943, a new *muftī*'s office, established in Tashkent, began to replace the Department of Religious Affairs in Ufa. In October of that year the religious representatives of the Republics of Uzbekistan, Kazakhstān, Kirghizia, Tājīkistān and Turkistān met in Tashkent and established the Department of Religious Affairs of Central Asia and Kazakhstān. Eighty-five-year old Ishan Bābākhān ʿAbd al-Majīd Khān, a scholar from Turkistān, who had been exiled before the war, was appointed its head. From then on, the *muftī* in Tashkent became the most important figure in the Muslim religious establishment, and began to assume a high position within the hierarchy of the Soviet government. Tashkent became a show-place for Muslim visitors of high rank. Ishan Bābākhān's son, Żiyā al-Dīn, was appointed assistant *muftī*, and subsequently succeeded his father.

Shortly afterwards, religious departments for northern Caucasia and Āẕarbāyjān were also established. This was not the case with the

Crimea, which had had its own *muftī* previously. Because the Tatars of the Crimea were accused of collaborating with the Germans, they were totally expelled from the Crimea, and sent to Kirghizia. The Karachays in northern Caucasia and certain other Muslim Circassians were similarly treated.

Thus after the Second World War there were four departments for Muslims in the Soviet Union. The Department of Religious Affairs for the European part of the Soviet Union and for Siberia, with its centre in Ufa, survived from tsarist times. It was important because of its antiquity and the high reputation of its member scholars. The Religious Department of Islam for Central Asia and Kazakhstān had its centre in Tashkent. In this way, the religious administration of Kazakhstān, which had formerly been connected to Ufa, was attached to Turkistān. The office of the *muftī* in Tashkent is most important since the majority of the Muslims in the Soviet Union (approximately fifteen millions) are found in Central Asia, and religious centres like Bukhārā, Samarqand, and the Khīva area are also situated there. Hence this department has an important place in the Soviet external propaganda. The Religious Department of Trans-Caucasian Muslims has its centre in Baku. This is the central organization for the Shīʿa in Āẕarbāyjān, whose number does not exceed two millions. However, in Āẕarbāyjān there is no difference between the Shīʿīs and the Sunnīs, and the old conflicts have been forgotten. The Religious Department of the Muslims of northern Caucasia has its centre at Buynak. The religious affairs of the Muslims in Dāghistān and the adjacent areas are run by this department.

These religious departments are under the strict control of the Soviet government. The *muftīs* and other religious leaders of high position, as well as the *imāms* and preachers of great mosques, have to serve the Soviet government with complete loyalty. During the prayers on Fridays and on feast-days, the Soviet government is praised as being 'sent by God', implying that those who disobey the government disobey God and the Prophet as well.

The Muslim areas are completely administered by the Kremlin, and form an inseparable part of the Soviet Union; hence it is impossible to consider their political history separately. The present-day political boundaries were delimited in 1924, on the basis of Lenin's Nationalities Policy. This had as its ostensible object 'the liquidation of existing inequality', but critics have seen in it nothing more than the application of the principle of 'divide and rule' by the Soviet administrators, through the separation of peoples (e.g. the Tatars and Bashkirs) who are closely related by language, religion and traditions.

There are today six 'union republics' which are or were predominantly Muslim. The Uzbek Soviet Socialist Republic, formed in 1924, is the main cotton-producing area of the Soviet Union. The capital, formerly Samarqand, was transferred to Tashkent, which has become the centre of Uzbek cultural activities, with its branch of the Academy of Sciences, its university and opera. The Kazakh S.S.R., an autonomous republic in 1920, was raised to the status of a union republic in 1936. The Russians enforced the stabilization of the nomadic Kazakhs—a policy which produced resistance and emigration to China. Large-scale Russian immigration and the founding of industrial cities have reduced the Kazakhs to a minority. A similar development took place in the Kirghiz S.S.R., which also became a union republic in 1936. The Turkmen S.S.R. was formed in 1924. Its nomadic population was sedentarized, and the cultivation of cotton developed. The Tājīk S.S.R. achieved the status of a union republic in 1929, when it was detached from the Uzbek S.S.R. The Āẕarbāyjān Republic, formed in 1920, is the oldest. Shortly afterwards it was combined with Armenia and Georgia in the Trans-Caucasian Federation, and when this was dissolved in 1936 it became a union republic. There are in addition ten 'autonomous republics' in territories which are (or were) mainly inhabited by Muslims. These form part of the Russian Soviet Federal Socialist Republic. The most important of them are the Tatar and the Bashkir A.S.S.R. In the Tatar A.S.S.R. the Tatars form only half the population, while a majority of the Tatars are to be found in other parts of the U.S.S.R. Bashkirs are also a minority in the republic which bears their name. Kazan, the capital of the Tatar A.S.S.R., has long been a centre of culture for the Turkish peoples in Russia.

CHAPTER 5

COMMUNISM IN THE CENTRAL ISLAMIC LANDS

BEFORE 1917

The period of radical reform at the end of the nineteenth and the beginning of the twentieth century was one in which all revolutionary energy was mobilized in the upsurge of the nationalist movement. It was in the wake of this movement that Marxist ideas began warily to make their way into the Muslim world. For a long time, until the Russian Revolution of 1917, socialism could only show itself as the extreme left wing of the nationalist movement.

There are two basic reasons for this slowness in the spread of Marxist ideas: the indifference of the first leaders of European socialism to the *dār al-Islām,* and the lack of receptivity to socialism offered by Muslim society as a whole.

Marxist socialism, a complex system of economic, political and philosophical doctrines, originally conceived for the industrial societies of the West, was thought to be applicable, sooner or later, to the whole world. The ideas of the founders of socialism and their successors until 1914 were, with some considerable variations in their positions, centred on Europe and the West. The Muslim East interested them only in so far as it affected their international policy. It offered no objective reasons for supposing that socialist proselytization would have much chance of success there. They regarded it as a marginal problem, dependent on the general problem of the proletarian revolution in the West. They applied to it theses designed to apply to Europe, and predicted for it the same revolutions, passage through the same economic and social 'patterns', and the same crises as the West. The 'Muslim problem' as such did not exist for them.

Marxist ideas could be reflected in the Islamic countries only by following certain well-defined channels. In fact, with a very few exceptions, the proletariat, which was small and widely dispersed, completely lacked any feeling of class, industrialization being still at a very early stage. The petty bourgeoisie, usually excellent revolutionary material in non-industrial countries, was here weak and in every instance still entirely under the influence of the ideology of the nationalist reformist movement. Finally, the peasants had in general no revolutionary traditions and were politically unorganized. Conceived as it was for the industrial societies of the West, socialism had very little hold over the East in the pre-capitalist stage of production, and it could be implanted only where certain conditions were fulfilled, namely:

1. A definite willingness by the European socialists to make the Muslims share their ideas, since socialism could not arise spontaneously in a Muslim society.

2. An atmosphere of political or religious agitation and a tradition of secrecy (such as offered by Shiʿism in Persia, for example), or of anti-feudal revolts.

3. A crisis in the nationalist movement which was beginning to lose its impetus and seemed incapable of winning the fight against the Western powers or against local despotism by force of its own ideology alone.

4. Finally, and most important, the presence of elements likely to welcome Marxist ideas, that is, in the absence of a native proletariat or petty bourgeoisie, foreign groups or active non-Muslim minorities. It has been established that the first socialist organizations in the East were in fact controlled by foreign minorities such as the Dutch in Indonesia or the Macedonians in Salonica, or non-Muslims of minority groups such as the Greeks, Lebanese Christians, and Jews in the Ottoman empire, Armenians in both the Ottoman empire and Persia, and Lebanese Christians and Jews in Egypt.

The few Muslim groups which were receptive to socialist ideas at the beginning of the twentieth century were those which, as a result of exceptional circumstances, had come into direct contact with European groups converted to these ideas. Such were the Tatar intellectuals of the Volga or of the Caucasian proletariat of the industrial region of Baku.

Thus socialist ideas could penetrate into the *dār al-Islām* only at certain points which, before 1914, were limited to Kazan and Baku in the Russian empire, Salonica and thence Istanbul in the Ottoman empire, Tabrīz in Persia, Java in Indonesia, and Alexandria in Egypt.

Kazan and the Tatar towns of the Middle Volga and Ural regions were probably the first towns in which groups of Muslim socialists appeared. There were three conditions which were favourable to this growth.

First, the special structure of Tatar society, dominated by a powerful commercial bourgeoisie and a numerous intelligentsia, which had long been in contact with the outside world, and were supported by all classes of society including the proletariat, which was numerically strong, but scattered and as yet unorganized.

Secondly, the existence, since the middle of the nineteenth century, of a powerful current of liberal reform very much in advance of the other Muslim national movements. This had removed the conservative groups from the political scene, but at the beginning of the twentieth century was already beginning to weaken and was splitting into two parts, of which the more radical left was ready to accept certain Marxist ideas.

Finally, the presence of very active groups of Russian Social Democrats and socialist revolutionaries, who as early as 1880–90 had already been trying to recruit members from the Muslim areas.

The extremist wing of the Tatar reform movement consisted mainly of students and intellectuals from the petty bourgeoisie, the majority of them being former pupils of the Russo-Tatar Teachers' Training College founded in 1876. In 1885 there had appeared the first Muslim political group which, in 1901, joined firmly in the revolutionary agitation and inspired the *Iṣlāḥ* movement which unsettled all the *medreses* of the Middle Volga. This movement, the most radical outcome of reformism, was not organically connected with the Russian revolutionary current; but it drew its inspiration from it, and was already using some of its tactics, such as strikes, mass demonstrations and even individual acts of terrorism. This was the first attempt by the Muslims at imitating the methods of the Russian revolutionaries and, as the first school of revolutionary action, it left indelible traces. All the future nationalist, socialist or communist leaders among the Tatars were to be former militant members of the *Iṣlāḥ* movement.

The influence of the Russian Marxist groups made up of intellectuals and of authentic proletarians was also very strong in Kazan, which indeed had the unusual advantage for the emergence of socialism of being at the same time a large university town and an important industrial centre. These groups very soon tried to attract Muslims and had little success among the workers because of the political inertia of the native proletariat. However, between 1902 and 1905 there were formed a few Muslim trade unions, such as that of the Printing Workers and the powerful Union of the Employees of Commerce, both of them dominated by the Social Democrats. Their militant members played a not inconsiderable part in the Revolution of 1917, and in the spreading of Communism in the East. The attempt by the Russian socialists to convert the Muslim intellectuals met with more success. In 1902, some Tatar students and writers, including Yamashev, Kulakhmetov and Akhtamov, became members of the Social Democrat group of Kazan, and in 1907 they founded the first internationalist Muslim Marxist organization. Although it was numerically small—hardly more than about a dozen militant members—this group played a very important role. It was driven from Kazan by the repressive measures of the police and re-formed at Orenburg. Here it published the first Muslim Communist periodical, the magazine *Ural,* in the Tatar language, which was confiscated after its thirty-first number, its editors being once more dispersed.

Still more far-reaching was the action of the Muslim socialist groups *Berek* and *Tañchilar*. These were attached organically and ideologically to the Russian Socialist-Revolutionary party, and were active on the left wing of the nationalist movement, adopting from Russian socialism only its methods. Their programme provides an interesting example of a combination of Russian Marxism (in its populist form) and Muslim reformism.

Gradually Marxist ideas and methods, matured on the Tatar Volga, penetrated in 1905 and 1917 into Bashkiria and thence into Russian Turkistān, but those who propagated them remained, in spite of their Marxist veneer, the heirs of reformism and sometimes even convinced pan-Turks.

The second focal point of Marxism in Russian Islam was the large industrial centre of Baku. Here there were three factors which facilitated the birth of Muslim socialist groups:

1. The existence of an authentic native proletariat consisting of workers in the large textile and petroleum industries. The industrial proletariat of the Baku region consisted in 1901 of about 36,000 workers, more than fifty per cent of whom were Muslims. It was a cosmopolitan proletariat in which Āẕarī Turkish and Persian Muslims worked side by side with Russians, Armenians, Georgians and Jews. Baku was thus a crucible in which Marxist ideas from Russia or from Europe could reach the Muslim masses. It was also a very active centre of revolutionary agitation, with a tradition of strikes and riots dating back to the 1870s. The class-struggle there took the form of actual fighting and not, as in all the other Muslim areas, of theoretical discussions by a few intellectual coteries. At the beginning of the twentieth century, Baku was the only place in the world where the Muslim proletariat could acquire a real class consciousness.

2. The liberal tradition among the bourgeoisie and the Muslim landowning upper classes, dating back to the reformist thinkers of the mid-nineteenth century, such as Feth ʿAlī Akhundov and Ḥasan Bey Melikov Zerdābī, who had been influenced both by the ideas of the French Revolution and by Russian populism. This hot-bed of young intellectuals, open to all ideas coming from abroad, including those of Marxism, played a very active part in the revolutionary movement which appeared in the Caucasus in the early years of the twentieth century.

3. Direct contact with the Russian, Armenian and Georgian Marxists. Revolutionary literature, and particularly that of social-democrat inspiration, penetrated very early in the 1880s into Transcaucasia. In 1885 the police discovered in Baku a copy of the *Communist manifesto*. In 1896 there were founded in the principal towns of the Caucasus, Tiflis, Baku, Batum and Kutais, social-democrat groups composed of intellectuals and workers, organically linked with the centres at St Petersburg, Kiev, Rostov and Moscow. In 1897, a Georgian social-democrat organization, *Mesame Dasi,* opened a subsidiary branch at Baku. In 1899 there were six Marxist groups in this town, though they still had very few Muslim members. Two years later, in 1901, these groups re-formed themselves into a central organization with Bolshevik Leninist tendencies; it was affiliated to the Russian Workers' Social Democratic party, which rapidly became one of the most active Communist organizations in Russia. Baku thus appeared at the beginning of the century as a revolutionary centre of completely 'Western' type in the heart of a Muslim region, but with its leadership still in the hands of non-Muslims —Russians, Armenians and Georgians. For the Muslims of the Caucasus, Āẕarī Turks and Dāghistānīs, this was much more a school of revolutionary action than of Marxist thought.

In 1904 there was founded in Baku the first entirely Muslim socialist group, the *Hümmet* ('Mutual Aid') party, attached to the Russian Workers' Social Democratic party, but reserved exclusively for Muslims, Āẕarī Turks, Persians and Dāghistānīs, which was a departure from the principle of internationalism rigorously applied by the Russian social democrats. Its leaders included both intellectuals and workers, and from the time it was founded the *Hümmet* was exceptionally active, publishing social literature in Turkish and Persian translations and a number of periodicals, and organizing mass-action such as strikes and meetings. *Hümmet* was a nursery for Caucasian and Persian revolutionaries, and its part in the spread of socialist ideas, and in the organization of socialist, and later Communist, groups in Transcaucasia and in Persia, was a major and a lasting one. The party brought together Marxists from every side, as well as Bolsheviks and Mensheviks; and some of these, who remained faithful to nationalist ideas, were to abandon the socialist camp after 1911, and follow the nationalist movement.

Shortly before the First World War, the socialist movement in Transcaucasia suffered a serious setback, owing partly to harsh police repression, and partly to the growing influence of pan-Turanian ideology, which was being spread by the nationalist *Musavat* party. When the Revolution of February 1917 broke out it was the latter party which seized power, while the majority of the Muslim Communist leaders were to disappear in the turmoil of the Civil War.

Outside Russia, it was at Tabrīz in Persian Āẕarbāyjān, and at Salonica in the Ottoman empire that the first Muslim Marxist organizations appeared.

Socialist ideas penetrated from Transcaucasia into Persia by way of the many Persians who went every year to Baku to work in the petroleum industry: there were estimated to be more than 100,000 Persian nationals in Transcaucasia in 1905. The first Persian Marxist (Social Democrat) cell, the *Ijtimā'iyyūni 'Āmmiyyūn* group, was founded in Baku in 1904 by some Persians, members of the Russian Workers' Social Democratic party, who after their return to Persia became most ardent propagandists for Marxism. They found there a climate favourable to their activities. This was induced by several factors: the old Shī'ī tradition of clandestine action and of conspiracy; the existence of a liberal movement hostile to the Qājār monarchy; the anti-feudal agitation of the peasants and the artisans; strong opposition to the West shown by the Shī'ī religious leaders and the native bourgeoisie, who had been ruined by European competition; and finally the separatist tendencies in Āẕarbāyjān and Gīlān. All this agitation was to culminate in 1906 in the powerful Constitutional movement and in the revolt of Tabrīz in 1908–11.

It would be a mistake to exaggerate the role of the socialist groups in these two movements, which were manifestations of the liberal revolution led by the bourgeoisie; nevertheless, the part which they played should not be minimized. It was former workers from Baku who laid in 1906 the foundations of the Persian Social Democratic party in Tabrīz, and their participation in the *anjumans* (influenced by the Russian soviets of 1905) was not negligible. Neither was their role in the associations of the *Mujāhids* and the detachments of the *Fidā'īs* who began to organize themselves in 1906–7 and who were the nucleus which directed the revolution of Tabrīz in 1908, and of Gīlān in 1909. Between 1908 and 1911 many Armenian revolutionaries (members of the socialist *Dashnaktsütün* and *Hinchak* parties), Āẕarī Turks belonging to the *Hümmet* party, Georgian Bolsheviks and even Russians, Social Democrats or Socialist Revolutionaries, came to lend their support to the Persian revolutionaries. They brought them Marxist literature and arms, and passed on to them their fighting experience and their methods of underground struggle.

The Persian Social Democratic party, whose groups proliferated throughout the whole country, was able to develop rapidly and to acquire an experience of real and often successful revolutionary struggle unique for a Muslim socialist party before 1917. But the power of the nationalist movement, and its dominant hold over the widest and most varied sectors of the population, prevented socialism from developing and from becoming a genuine mass party. The revolutionary movement at Tabrīz where Russian troops were already present was crushed in 1911 and the socialist cells were dispersed by repressive measures; but the experience of the years 1908–11 was not wasted since it inspired the more radical revolutionary movements of the 1920s.

In Turkey the systematic spread of socialism did not begin until after the Young Turk Revolution of July 1908. Before this socialist groups were found only among the non-Turkish peoples—Greeks, Macedonians or Bulgarians. The most important was the social democrat group of the workers of Edirne and Macedonia, which was founded at Sofia in 1904.

After the Young Turk Revolution, the centre of the movement shifted to Salonica, the second town of the empire and an important industrial centre, where there was founded in 1909 the Socialist Federation of Workers of Salonica, attached to the Second International and composed almost exclusively of non-Turks—Jews, Bulgarians, Macedonians and Greeks. In 1910 there was formed the Ottoman Socialist party, the headquarters of which were first at Salonica and then transferred to Istanbul, with an important section in Paris. Although a fairly large proportion of this party came from the ethnic minorities, particularly Armenians and Bulgarians, its leadership was in Turkish hands. Its press was also Turkish. This party was attached to the Second International and was genuinely Marxist, playing an undeniable part in the spread of socialist ideas in the Ottoman empire, but because of its 'minority' character and its 'Ottoman' policy (claiming equal rights for non-Turkish nationalities in the empire), it was rapidly overshadowed by the ideology of Turkism.

The party was several times prohibited by the Young Turk government and was finally dispersed immediately before the First World War and its leaders were deported or went into exile. One of them, Muṣṭafā Ṣubḥī, who was to become in 1920 the first leader of the Turkish Communist party, fled to Russia.

During this first phase of the history of Marxism in the Islamic countries, socialist ideas spread by agents of different origins—Russians, Germans, French, British in Egypt, and Dutch in Indonesia—all of whom interpreted them differently, were absorbed by different groups who made use of them for different, and often quite opposite, ends; sometimes to radicalize the nationalist movement as in Persia, sometimes, on the contrary, to oppose it as in Turkey. In places where the socialist ideas were able to amalgamate with the nationalist movement, the Marxist-inspired revolutionary groups which appeared after 1918 had little difficulty in making themselves into 'nationalist' parties which played a part in the political life of the country, e.g. in Persia and Indonesia. When, on the other hand, these ideas were rejected by the nationalist movement, the Marxist groups long remained 'minority' movements, and had great difficulty in gaining a foothold in the national life of the country.

What did 'socialism' mean before 1917 for the Muslims who embraced it? Only an extremely small minority saw in it an economic doctrine, or even a programme of class struggle, for at that time this was almost everywhere subordinated to the demands of a national struggle against the West. Socialism taught the Eastern revolutionaries techniques of agitation and of action; in its Russian form it provided them also with a number of organizational devices for the use of clandestine groups. Before 1914 few Muslims calling themselves socialists asked themselves the fundamental question: 'Is Marxism compatible with Islam?' This crucial problem did not arise until after 1917.

COMMUNISM IN THE MUSLIM LANDS OF RUSSIA (1917–24)

After 1917 this slow socialist infiltration into the Islamic world was suddenly accelerated. In October 1917, the triumph of Communism in Russia in overthrowing the tsarist monarchy, dispossessing the ruling classes, and in standing up to the intervention of the Western powers, was a stimulating example for all the Eastern revolutionaries who were engaged in the same struggle against the same adversaries.

Henceforward socialism no longer appeared in the East as a distant dream, but as an imminent reality. It was no longer a question only of the spread of ideas, but also of the action of the revolutionary groups, which, rightly or wrongly, associated themselves with Communist doctrine, and were generally attached to the Third International.

From 1917 to the present day, the growth of Communist organizations in the Muslim countries has been influenced by many factors, some of them internal: the social, economic and political situation of the country concerned and primarily the vigour of its nationalist movement. Others were external: the tactics employed at the time by the Comintern which could either help the development of local Communism, or impede it by imposing on it a line of conduct which was sometimes inapplicable; and finally, the demands of the foreign policy of Soviet Russia, which until 1960 was the only country which socialism could call its own.

The Bolshevik leaders who assumed power in Russia in 1917 were not directly interested, at least at the outset, in the problem of Islam. They were strict internationalists and considered the socialist revolution as one and indivisible in content and in form. They believed that victory in Russia would be followed rapidly by the triumph of the proletariat in central and western Europe. The East, being still at the pre-capitalist stage of development and lacking a proletariat, could only expect to be liberated by a victory of communism in the West, and to follow from afar the way indicated by the European proletariat.

In 1918, as a consequence of the Civil War in Russia, the Bolshevik leaders gradually modified their attitude. This war took place mainly in the peripheral regions of the Caucasus, the Middle Volga, the Crimea and Central Asia, all areas with a high proportion of Muslims. The need to win these populations over to the cause of the revolution, to make them allies, or at least to induce them to remain neutral while the conflict lasted, was the first reason which led the Russian leaders to take a more serious interest in Islam. The second, which ensued after the intervention of the Entente powers, was the desire to break the 'capitalist encirclement' beyond the southern frontiers of Russia, in Turkey, Persia and Afghanistan. Certainly, in calling on the colonial or semi-colonial Muslim peoples to revolt against the 'imperialist' West, the chief motive of the Bolshevik leaders was to weaken the capitalist powers. The Muslim East was not yet considered as a revolutionary subject in itself, but only as a possible temporary ally, with whose help they could more easily defeat the enemy.

In December 1917, the Council of People's Commissars of the R.S.F.S.R. (Russian Soviet Federated Socialist Republic) launched its famous appeal to the Muslims of Russia and the East, proclaiming the abrogation of the 'imperialist' treaties signed by tsarist Russia and inviting the Muslim peoples to rally to the flag of the Revolution. This first spectacular gesture was soon to take many concrete forms: on 19 January 1918 there was formed in Moscow at the People's Commissariat of Nationalities the Central Commissariat for Muslim Affairs, the direction of which was entrusted to three Tatar intellectuals, former militant members of the left wing of the reformist movement, Mullā Nūr Vakhitov, Mīr Sayyīd Sultangaliyev and Sherīf Manatov. The Commissariat dealt with all questions concerning Muslims, and in particular their recruitment into the Communist party, and the formation of a Red Army of Muslim volunteers. For two years, during the disorder of the Civil War, and while the Bolshevik leaders in Moscow were engaged in a struggle for survival with the White Armies, the Central Muslim Commissariat was able to act with a large measure of independence, controlled only very loosely by the central authorities. It set on foot an intense activity of propaganda and organization. On its initiative the Muslim Socialist-Communist party was founded in March 1918, and some months later became the Muslim Communist (Bolshevik) party.

The early years of struggle and action among the Muslim masses had a profound influence on all the later development of the Communist movement among the Muslims in Russia. It was then that the Muslim leaders made attempts to find both a means of coexistence or of symbiosis between Islam and Communism, and the most effective methods of spreading Communism in the East.

The first reactions of the Russian Muslims to Communism were varied. The majority of the Faithful were hostile to it from the beginning. For conservative Muslims, Communism was only a new form of irreligion that must be opposed, as they opposed the heresies, the secularism or the religious indifference which came from Europe; and this was completely justified by the attitude of the first Russian Marxists, who considered that Islam as a revealed religion ought to be destroyed. The anti-Islamic campaign was just one instance of the Communist opposition to all religion as 'a false and harmful ideology which lulls or confuses the revolutionary awareness of the oppressed classes, a mere survival of the feudal epoch in the socialist society now being built'.

The majority of the Muslims, unaware of the historical significance of the October Revolution and of its consequences for the future, for the most part remained neutral at the beginning of the Civil War. If, in the end, they were inclined to support the new régime, this was for opportunist reasons; the Whites, who were campaigning for a 'Russia, one and indivisible', seeming less disposed than the Reds to satisfy the demands of the non-Russians.

The intellectuals were deeply divided. Some of them, forming numerically the most important part, thought that in the Revolution they had found a unique and unhoped for opportunity to obtain their nationalist aims. They attempted to form independent Muslim states, and, attacked from 1920 onwards by the Bolsheviks, found themselves in the anti-Soviet and anti-Communist camp. A strong minority, however, among the young intellectuals, was attracted by Communism, but, with rare exceptions, without any individual conscious or reasoned adherence to Marxism. For Muslims to join the Communist party—and this was often done during the first years of the Revolution—was essentially an irrational psychological or sociological reaction, not an intellectual one. It implied neither a total acceptance of the Marxist principles nor a clear understanding of the practical corollaries of these principles. It did not involve the rejection of Muslim principles, ideas or concepts.

Having become Communists or Communist sympathizers while remaining Muslims, they attempted to discover points in common between the two ideologies and tried to reinterpret the classical ideas of Islam as equivalents of the Marxist theses, e.g. the internationalist, anti-capitalist or anti-racialist character of Islam and of Communism, without, however, feeling obliged by this attempt at harmonization to accept the dialectical materialism and the atheism of Marxism.

This group of intellectuals saw the socialist revolution as the outcome of more than half a century's struggle by the reformists for the emancipation of their peoples and the modernization of Islam. They regarded it also as a prelude to the revenge of the colonial Muslim peoples on Europe. The most typical representatives of this ideology were the Tatar Communists of the Volga, gathered round Mullā Nūr Vakhitov and Sultangaliyev, who were the leaders of the Central Muslim Commissariat. Their programme, which was the only attempt at a synthesis between Islam and Communism, can be summarized as follows:

First, the Communist revolution in the Muslim countries must be at the same time a social revolution directed against the local exploiters (feudal landowners and conservative religious leaders) and a national revolution directed against foreign domination.

Secondly, as the structure of Muslim society does not permit the simultaneous furthering of this double revolution, absolute priority must be given to national emancipation. Meanwhile, because of the weakness of the native proletariat, the leadership of the revolution must be assumed by the bourgeoisie in alliance with all the 'progressive' elements of society, including the reformist religious leaders. The revolution as conceived by the first Russian Muslim Communists was thus a revolution without class struggle. The Muslim peoples having been, under European domination, 'oppressed peoples', were therefore 'proletarian peoples'; all classes of which, with the exception only of the upper bourgeoisie and a few feudal overlords, were to enjoy the benefits of the revolution.

Thirdly, the socialist revolution in Islamic countries should not be a servile imitation of the forms of the proletarian revolution in the West. It was neither to replace the domination of the European bourgeoisie over the colonial peoples by the domination of the European proletariat over these same peoples, nor to break the cultural and spiritual traditions of Islam. Consequently, in place of the anti-religious campaign, the Muslim Communists advocated an adaptable propaganda of the 'scientific' type. Although as Marxists they were the adversaries of all religion as 'the opium of the people', they considered that Islam, being 'the youngest and the most dynamic of the religions of the world', was to have favoured treatment. They did not underestimate the attachment of the masses to their spiritual leaders and thought that any ill-advised attack on the religion of the Prophet might be reminiscent of the anti-Islamic campaigns of the Christian missionaries. Further, they recalled that the offensive against fanaticism and obscurantism had been started in the nineteenth century by the Muslims themselves. It was enough therefore to pursue this campaign for a 'laicized' and secularized Islam to cease to be an obstacle to the building of socialism, and to become, on the contrary, a factor favourable to it. Thus the Muslim Communists of the first era (1918–24) appeared, at least in Russia, as the direct heirs of reformism.

Lastly, in order to overcome European capitalism, the Third International should turn away from Europe, 'where the fire of revolution no longer burned', and concentrate all its efforts on the Muslim East. But, said the Muslim Communists, the Western revolutionaries were incapable of understanding the East and its complex problems, hence the leadership of the revolution in Asia must be entrusted to an autonomous Muslim organization, an embryo 'Colonial International' which some Muslim Communists, Sultangaliyev for example, even dreamed of setting up in opposition to the Comintern. As the first phase of the re-grouping of the Muslim revolutionaries, the Tatar Communists advocated the formation of socialist states in the Muslim regions of Russia: Tatarstān, Bashkiria, Ā͟zarbāyjān and Turkistān, which were to become models and also bases from which the revolution could spread to the neighbouring countries, Turkey, Persia and India.

Thus it can be seen that the Muslim Communists in Russia in the 1920s made use of a selection of certain themes within the Marxist doctrine which fitted in with their own aspirations. They chose only those which would serve to make more radical the reform of Muslim society and their national struggle against the West.

This programme, bold, but hardly acceptable to the Bolshevik leaders, raised the threefold problem of the autonomy of Muslim Communism in relation to the Comintern, of the status of indigenous cadres in relation to Western cadres, and of the general orientation of the strategy of the Comintern. On these three points the Muslim Communists were, after 1918, to clash with their Russian comrades. The latter rejected the principle of Muslim autonomy in the name of the monolithic structure of the international Communist movement (the autonomous Muslim Communist party was finally suppressed in March 1919 during the Eighth Congress of the Russian Communist party); they were suspicious of the Muslim cadres because of their non-proletarian origin, and in addition they did not accept the idea of the strategic priority of the revolution in Asia. They considered that the national liberation of the East was dependent on the victory of the proletarian revolution in Europe.

This initial disagreement between Western (Russian or European) and Muslim Communists appeared to a greater or less degree in all the Muslim countries and was one of the major obstacles to the spread of Communism. The difference was most striking, however, between the pre-revolutionary period of indifference by the Communist leaders to the

East and the period which began in 1918, when Muslim Asia was one of the main preoccupations of the Comintern. The strategy to be applied in Muslim countries was discussed several times between 1918 and 1920.

The first occasion was at the First Congress of Muslim Communists, held at Moscow in November 1918, at which there were created a Central Bureau of the Muslim Organizations of the Russian Communist party, and a department of international propaganda under the leadership of the Turkish Communist, Muṣṭafā Ṣubḥī. Then at the Second Congress of the Communist Organizations of the Peoples of the East, held at Moscow in November 1919, it was decided that the existing or future Communist parties in the Muslim countries should be attached to the Comintern. In particular it was discussed at the Second Congress of the Comintern at Moscow in July 1920, and at the Congress of the Peoples of the East at Baku in September 1920.

The proposals adopted at the two latter congresses admitted that the nationalist, anti-imperialist revolution in the East was an indispensable complement of the world Communist revolution, but stated that the initiative and the leadership should return to the European proletariat. They also recognized that the success of the revolution in colonial territory depended on the unity of all the local anti-imperialist forces. The Communists should therefore give their provisional and conditional support to the bourgeois democratic movements; in other words, form temporary alliances with the non-Communist revolutionary parties, in order to defeat the common enemy, while remaining organically independent of these parties. At the same time they should strive with their temporary allies in an attempt to transform the nationalist bourgeois revolution into a socialist one. According to the theses of the Second Congress of the Comintern, the victory of the democratic revolution was to mark the beginning of the decisive battle for socialism. This programme, which was difficult to apply, was for nearly ten years the theoretical basis of Communist policy in the Muslim East.

At the end of 1920, the Civil War ended in Russia. The victorious Communist régime had henceforward less need of fellow-travellers in Russia itself. The leaders in Moscow now began to encounter the opposition of their former Muslim allies, which appeared most often in the form of doctrinal deviations such as Sultangaliyevism in Tatarstān, Milli-Firkism in the Crimea, Narimanovism in Āẕarbāyjān, or in open revolts, the most spectacular being those of the Bashkirs in 1920–2 and even more those of the Basmachis in Turkistān from 1920 to 1928. The years 1920–8 were thus marked in Soviet Russia by the struggle of the central power against the centrifugal tendencies of the Muslim Communists who were trying to build socialism without Russian control. The conflict ended in the condemnation of all the Muslim deviations. For many years after this the Russian Communists were to retain a somewhat suspicious attitude, not only towards their own Muslims, but even towards the fraternal Communist parties in foreign Muslim countries, which they always suspected of falling back into nationalist deviation.

After 1918, Communist groups appeared spontaneously in nearly all the Muslim countries, e.g. Turkey, Persia, Egypt and Indonesia, but at first the Soviet government considered them of only secondary importance. Seeking above all to break the encirclement of Russia, it encouraged the advent in neighbouring countries of régimes which were independent of the West, and the internal shape which these régimes took mattered no more to it than their attitude to internal Communism. Friendly relations were established in 1921 with Kemalist Turkey, Persia and Afghanistan, in spite of the fact that their governments did not permit Communist parties to exist within their territories. Thus between 1918 and 1928 the fate of Communism in the Muslim countries depended not only on local social and economic conditions, but also on the general strategy of the Comintern and of the Russian Communist party, and finally on the foreign policy of Soviet Russia, which was pursuing parallel objectives but at different levels. During this period, the Muslim Communist parties of the East were invited by the Comintern to support and to 'push forward' their temporary allies (the democratic parties) in order to oblige them to go as far as possible along the path of the anti-imperialist struggle, while at the same time denouncing their 'inconsistent' character, and preparing to oppose them. This atmosphere, which was not very favourable to the success of Communism, explains the reason why, after a brilliant start in several countries in the years 1918–20, the Communist parties there underwent a long eclipse, which for some of them still continues.

THE ORIGINS OF COMMUNISM IN THE MIDDLE EAST (1918–28)

In 1918, of all the Middle East countries, Turkey was considered by the Comintern to be the one in which the Communist revolution had most chance of success, which would have made it the starting point for the propagation of Communism throughout the Middle East and in Africa. The 'objective' conditions there were in fact fairly similar to those which had existed in Russia in 1917: military defeat bringing with it the collapse of the monarchy and the dissolution of power, foreign occupation, economic ruin, serious unemployment among a fairly numerous proletariat (more than 100,000 workers in 1918), and finally the existence of a movement of national liberation under non-proletarian leadership, but capable, according to the theses of the Second Congress of the Comintern, of being transformed into a socialist movement. Several socialist and Communist groups appeared spontaneously in Turkey after the signing of the Armistice. In Istanbul, the Turkish Socialist party, a reincarnation of the former Ottoman Socialist party, which was closer to the Second International than to the Comintern, reappeared on the scene in February 1919. The Socialist Party of the Workers and Peasants of Turkey was formed in September 1919 by former prisoners of war who had returned from Russia, and by Turks returned from Germany, where they had come under the influence of Spartacism. This party was of Leninist inspiration and was attached to the Third International. It published a number of journals. Mention should also be made of the Workers' International Association, composed mainly of members of minority groups—Greeks, Bulgarians, Jews. The influence of these three groups did not extend beyond the capital.

In Ankara other groups were to be formed in 1920. In June a secret Turkish Communist party was established, led by two Turks and a Bashkir who had come from Russia, Sherīf Manatov. Soon after this an 'official' Communist party was formed by Tevfīq Rüshdī, without any links with the Comintern, which refused to recognize it, but with the approval of Muṣṭafā Kemāl. This party proclaimed that 'Islam contained all the elements of socialism'. Another was created in December 1920 by the leaders of the former secret Turkish Communist party, with cells in Ankara and at Eskishehir, and published periodicals. Finally there was a curious nationalist Communist party with a peasant basis, the Green Apple, which during the war against the Greeks led detachments of partisans called the 'Green Army', and which was at first tolerated but later dissolved by the government of Muṣṭafā Kemāl.

But the main attempt to implant Communism in Turkey was made from Russia, where in July 1918 Muṣṭafā Ṣubḥī organized in Moscow a

Communist group among the prisoners of war, and published the first Communist organ in Turkish, at first in the Crimea, and then in Moscow.

In the spring of 1920, Ṣubḥī settled in Baku, and from this town directed the organization of Communism in Turkey. A Central Office was formed in Baku, where in September 1920 a congress was held which resulted in the decision to amalgamate all the socialist and Communist groups in a single party. There now appeared the chief and permanent weakness of Communism in Turkey—its external if not foreign character, without any profound links with the country which at that time was completely dominated by the national problem. Kemāl's resistance galvanized all levels of the population, absorbed all the energies of the country, and subordinated everything to the demands of the struggle against the foreign powers. It is not surprising therefore that in 1919–20 Communism in Anatolia assumed some curious forms. The Green Apple party proclaimed that 'Communism is not an end in itself, but a means, the true end being the unity of Turkey' and accepted the Communist programme only as a means of buttressing the power of Turkey. It and the 'official' Communist party sought to adapt Communism to Turkish conditions, and rejected its Russian aspect which the national tradition and the Muslim religion could not 'tolerate'.

On 26 April 1920, Muṣṭafā Kemāl sent a letter to Lenin in which he proposed the opening of diplomatic relations. In the name of the Council of People's Commissars, Chicherin replied agreeing to this on 2 June 1920. In July a Turkish delegation went to Moscow and, in spite of the temporary tension between the two countries in the autumn of that year over Armenia, the first ambassador of the new Turkey took up residence in Moscow in November. The contacts resulted in the signing on 16 March 1921 of the treaty of friendship between Soviet Russia and Turkey, followed on 13 October by the treaty of Kars between Turkey and the three Caucasian Republics (Georgia, Armenia and Āẕarbāyjān) and finally, on 2 January 1922, in the treaty between Turkey and the Ukraine.

Although this diplomatic *rapprochement* was advantageous to both countries, since it helped Turkey in the struggle against the Greeks and freed Russia from the fear of encirclement of her southern frontiers, the friendship between the two countries turned out to be harmful for Turkish Communism. The leaders of the Comintern thought that the arrival of the Kemalist régime would be the prelude to its being 'overtaken' by socialism. Nothing of the sort happened. The government of Muṣṭafā Kemāl, able to rely on the support of the people, considered that there was no place for Communism in Turkey. When Muṣṭafā Ṣubḥī and fifteen leaders of the Turkish Communist party of Baku went to Anatolia, they were assassinated at Trabzon (Trebizond) on 28 January 1921. There was no immediate protest from Russia.

In spite of the Trabzon catastrophe, the Socialist Party of the Workers and Peasants of Istanbul and the Communist groups of Ankara united to form the Turkish Communist party, which in 1922 held its first congress in Ankara. This congress was broken up by the police, and the party declared illegal on 21 July 1922. The Communists then attempted to extend their activity to the trade unions, and achieved some results there. Between 1922 and 1925 they succeeded in gaining control of the trade unions of the armaments factories in Ankara, of the railway employees in Eskishehir and of some workers' organizations in the textile industry at Izmir. They were also able to infiltrate into the leadership of the General Union of the Workers of Turkey. In 1924 the Communist party resumed a partial activity, and in 1925 it held its second congress; but on 4 March 1925, the law on the stabilization of state security made it once again illegal. In October of the same year its publications were suppressed, and almost all of its leaders were arrested.

From this date, the Turkish Communist party went completely underground, and no longer played an active part in the life of the country. In 1937–8 a new attempt was made to restore it to the public scene. A Communist periodical was even able to appear, but in 1938 renewed legal action stamped it out completely.

Because of the harsh repression by the police, and even more because of the prestige of Kemalism, Communism has always encountered great difficulties in establishing itself in Turkey and in becoming a party of the masses. Its members included some brilliant intellectuals, but few workers and practically no peasants. In opposition to the nationalist movement, and thus obliged to contend with a popular régime which in addition had at the beginning the support of Soviet Russia, the Turkish Communist party was practically swallowed up by the nationalist movement.

In Persia, conditions after the 1917 Revolution seemed almost as favourable as those in Turkey, for traditionally revolutionary events in Transcaucasia had automatic repercussions in Persia. However, the first phase in the expansion of Communism there was of even shorter duration than in Turkey.

A Persian Socialist (Social Democrat) party, the '*Adālat* party, already existed in 1917 in Baku. This party was under the leadership of a veteran of the 1908 revolution at Tabrīz, Ḥaydar Khān Amū, and had several thousand members and sympathizers in the Caucasus, most of them former militant members of the *Hümmet* party. It also had cells in Tehran, Tabrīz and the towns of the province of Gīlān, and was able to provide the Persian revolution with an experienced nucleus of Communists. The internal conditions of the country also appeared favourable for the spread of Communism: the double occupation of the territory by Russian and British troops, the economic ruin of the petty bourgeoisie and the artisans, the miserable poverty of the peasant masses, and finally the traditional separatist tendencies in Āẕarbāyjān and Gīlān. The Communists could reasonably hope to turn to their profit the pre-revolutionary climate which prevailed in Persia immediately after the First World War.

The region chosen was Gīlān which since 1916 had been in the hands of the Jangalīs, a movement which was pan-Islamic, nationalist, anti-imperialist, anti-monarchist and anti-feudal. Soviet Russia became interested in it in 1919, although the leadership of the revolt of the Jangalīs was middle class and even 'clerical' (its leader Mīrzā Kūchik Khān was a *mullā*). After the conquest of Transcaucasia by the Red Army in April 1920, the revolution in Gīlān gained new impetus. In the same month a Soviet flotilla in pursuit of the retreating Whites occupied the Persian port of Enzelī and drove from it the British troops which were in temporary occupation. The Jangalīs took advantage of this to occupy Rasht, the capital of Gīlān and, making contact with the commander of the Soviet flotilla, Raskolnikov, proclaimed on 4 June 1920 the Soviet Socialist Republic of Gīlān, of which Mīrzā Kūchik Khān was elected president, his government being a coalition of Jangalī nationalist elements and Communists. The head of the '*Adālat* party, Ḥaydar Khān Amū, and the principal leaders left Baku for Gīlān. On 20 June 1920 they held at Rasht a congress of forty-eight delegates of the '*Adālat* party, which changed its name to the Communist (Bolshevik) Party of Persia.

Communism thus possessed in Gīlān a solid territorial base. But as in Turkey, after a rapid beginning, it encountered obstacles which proved insurmountable. Among the causes of its failure must be included the over-adventurous policy of the Communist party which, overestimating its strength, applied too harshly the policy of confiscating land, thus alienating its Jangalī allies. The military operations of the Gīlān Republic against Tehran also resulted in total failure. Furthermore the support of Soviet Russia very soon began to fail. The Moscow government was more interested in neutralizing Persia than in transforming it into a Communist country. It was anxious above all to obtain the evacuation of the country by the British troops, and the establishment of normal relations with a régime which would be, if not neutral like the Kemalist government, at least not overtly hostile to Soviet Russia. After several unsuccessful attempts, the two countries signed a treaty of friendship on 26 February 1921. After this the Russian rulers were no longer interested in the Soviet Republic of Gīlān. In May the British troops evacuated Persia, and in September the Russian units left Gīlān. On 29 September there was a fierce quarrel between Kūchik Khān and his Communist allies, whom he lured into an ambush and massacred. In November 1921 Persian government forces reoccupied Gīlān. The Jangalī movement was over.

Thus the only serious attempt of Communists in the Middle East to seize power ended in catastrophe. The Communist party disappeared from Gīlān; but, in contrast to what happened in Turkey, where the movement was suppressed for many years, and in the Arab countries, where it lacked the necessary social foundations, in Persia its chances of development remained strong. Destroyed in the north of the country, it almost immediately recommenced its activities in Tehran and in other large towns.

In 1922 the Communist party consisted of some 1,500 members, mostly workers and artisans. They were mainly active within the trade unions, of which they attempted, not without success, to obtain the leadership. They succeeded notably in gaining control of the Trade Unions Council of Tehran, which had been formed in 1921 combining eleven unions in the capital, and which published a periodical, *Ḥaqīqat*. The Communist party itself published or inspired a number of periodicals either openly Communist or simply 'progressive', but, as in Gīlān, it made the 'leftist' error of renouncing any alliance with the other democratic parties, and of overestimating the revolutionary possibilities of the time. After 1925 the advent of the new régime established by Riżā Shāh made the existence of Communism precarious. After 1928 particularly harsh repressive measures forced the party to go underground completely; most of its leaders left the country, its periodicals ceased (one was henceforward published in Vienna), and the Communist-dominated trade unions were dissolved. The second (secret) congress, which the party held in 1927 at Urmiyya, showed its decline, and until the beginning of the Second World War its activities outside Tehran were confined to Tabrīz and Khurāsān.

In the Arab East, the first socialist cells appeared in Cairo, Alexandria and Port Said. The Egyptian Socialist party was founded at Alexandria in 1920 by a Jewish jeweller, Joseph Rosenthal. In 1922 the party sent a delegate to the Third Congress of the Comintern and as a result changed its name to the Egyptian Communist party, which joined the Comintern. In 1924, when it was at its height, it consisted of as many as 2,000 members, eighty to ninety per cent of them nevertheless being either foreigners or belonging to minority groups, e.g., Greeks, Armenians, Jews and Lebanese Christians. In external policy, the Egyptian Communist party, following the theses of the Second Congress of the Comintern, supported the demands of the Wafd, such as the union of Egypt and the Sudan, and the nationalization of the Suez Canal; but in internal policy, it made many 'leftist' errors, attaching greater importance to the class-war than to the nationalist struggle. It was particularly hostile to the middle-class supporters of the Wafd, and made vain attempts to turn itself into a proletarian party. Its attempts to gain control of the trade unions, which in Egypt were numerous and powerful, met with little success. The Egyptian workers, still not far removed from the *Lumpenproletariat,* were more attracted to the extremist nationalist parties whose simpler and more demagogic programmes were more readily accessible to them.

In July 1924, the government of Sa'd Zaghlūl arrested the Communist leaders, notably the leader of the Communist unions, Anṭūn Mārūn, who died in prison. Further repressive measures took place in June 1925 and the Communist leaders were again imprisoned. The Communist party, was declared illegal, and disappeared for many years.

In Palestine, the Communist party which was founded in 1919, and was a member of the Comintern, remained until 1928 an exclusively Jewish party. In Syria and Lebanon the first small socialist and Communist groups were formed in 1920, chiefly among the Armenians and other Christians. The Communist party was not officially founded until 1924 and did not become a member of the Comintern until 1928. In the other Arab countries, Iraq and Jordan, Communist parties did not appear until after 1928.

The Communists in the Arab countries in the 1920s had certain common characteristics. They were generally non-Muslim intellectuals, uninterested in the nationalist preoccupations of the pan-Arab movement. Everywhere they were fundamentally opposed, not only to the governments of their countries, but also to nationalist parties, political institutions and religious traditions. Believing in the possibility of proletarian parties of the masses, they were further to the left than the theses of the Second Congress of the Comintern. To Islam they showed a systematic and intransigent hostility. All their different attempts to play a part in the political drama failed, and in 1923 a rapid decline set in, which affected all the parties equally until 1930.

In Indonesia, the Communist party was officially formed in May 1920, having grown out of two socialist groups, the East Indian Social Democratic Association (*Indische Social Demokratische Vereenining*) founded in 1914 at Surabaya by Hendricus Sneevliet (Maring) and consisting mainly of Dutch officials and employees, and the Islamic League (*Sarekat Islam*), a nationalist party founded in 1912. At the Seventh Congress of the Democratic Association, held in May 1920, there was a split and a radical group formed the Indonesian Communist party. Its three main leaders, Samoen, Tan Malaka and Ahmin, were Indonesians who for several years remained members of the *Sarekat Islam*. As a result of their efforts, an important left-wing group was formed within the *Sarekat Islam—Sarekat Rakjat* (the People's League) which collaborated closely with the Communist party. On 24 December 1920, the party joined the Comintern. Since it was recruited from the people, and thus unlike all the other Muslim Communist parties, the Indonesian Communist party rapidly became a genuine mass party, enjoying great prestige among both intellectuals and workers. After 1920 it represented an important factor in the political life of Indonesia, and reached its zenith in 1926–7, when it launched anti-Dutch uprisings in Java (1926) and Sumatra (1927). These, with the Gīlān Republic, were among the few attempts made by Muslim Communists before 1944 to conduct a real revolutionary war. The suppression of the revolts was followed by the arrest, and later the deportation, of all the leaders of the Communist party. The party then suffered a long eclipse and did not become active again until after 1945.

COMMUNISM IN THE MUSLIM COUNTRIES BETWEEN 1928 AND 1941

The political programme outlined for the Communist parties at the Second Congress of the Comintern in 1920, and applied with little success in the Muslim countries from that year on, was in 1928 officially abandoned at the Sixth Congress of the Comintern. The change was the direct consequence of the failure of the commune of Canton in December 1927, and the resulting rupture with the Kuomintang, the model which the Second Congress of the Comintern had recommended all bourgeois democratic revolutionary parties in Asia to follow.

The new strategy directed towards the colonial and semi-colonial countries which was worked out at the Sixth Congress of the Comintern put an end to the tactical co-operation of the Communist parties with the democratic reform movements, which were accused of capitulating to Western imperialism. The Communists of the Muslim countries were invited to carry out simultaneously a threefold plan of action:

First, they were resolutely to take the lead in the anti-imperialist struggle 'which could triumph only under the aegis of the Communist parties'.

Secondly, at the same time, they were to denounce the treachery of the bourgeois democratic parties such as the Wafd in Egypt, the Destour in Tunisia, *al-Kutla al-Waṭaniyya* in Syria, and Kemalism in Turkey, and to oppose them. The struggle against the nationalist movements, which henceforward were considered as the main obstacle to the revolution, thus became inseparable from that conducted against Western imperialism.

Lastly, the Communist parties, most of which were experiencing extreme difficulties, both internally from deviations and externally from police repression, were called upon to intensify the class-struggle in the country districts and in the towns, to assume the leadership of the worker and peasant classes and to fight for the control of the trade unions, accepting as allies only the semi-proletarian elements of the petty bourgeoisie and the medium peasantry.

This programme was unrealistic in the sense that it isolated the already very weak Communist parties, and obliged them to struggle openly against the parties in power, which possessed effective means of repression. The programme was modified in 1935 at the Seventh Congress of the Comintern, which inaugurated the tactics of the Popular Front. In fact, after 1933, the chief danger threatening Soviet Russia was no longer British, French or American imperialism, but Hitlerite Germany and Fascism, the ideology of which was often favourably received by nationalists in the Middle East. The anti-imperialist struggle was henceforward seen mainly as an anti-Fascist one. A new and equally difficult task was entrusted to the Communist parties in the Muslim countries—that of tactical co-operation with all the bourgeois parties which were anti-German, while refusing any organic alliances, and retaining complete ideological freedom. The narrowly proletarian policy and its over-radical demands, which had characterized the preceding period, were abandoned, as was the anti-religious propaganda.

The new direction of Comintern policy produced no positive result either in Turkey, where after 1925 Communism suffered a long eclipse, or in Persia, where the repression carried out by Riżā Shāh's government kept the party completely underground, or in Egypt, where the struggle against the all-powerful Wafd in fact annihilated the last Communist groups; on the other hand in certain Arab countries, Iraq, Syria and Lebanon, it enabled the Communist parties to obtain some results, in spite of the competition of political groups of a Fascist tendency.

In Syria and Lebanon, the leadership of the Communist party, which until then had been in the hands of Armenians, passed, in 1933–4, into those of Muslim or Christian Arabs: Khālid Bakdāsh, Muṣṭafā al-'Arīs, Niqūlā Shāwī, Fu'ād Qazān, and the whole party was arabized. From 1934 it had active groups in Beirut, Damascus, Aleppo and Ḥimṣ, and exerted a definite control over the trade unions. In 1936, the coming to power of the Popular Front in France had immediately favourable repercussions on the position of the Communists in countries under French mandate. The Communist party of Syria and Lebanon became a semi-legal party, with its own press, and controlled several organizations of fellow-travellers such as the Anti-Fascist League which was founded at Beirut in 1939. The success of Communism was due also to its flexible and intelligent policy, which was centred entirely on national liberation. The Syro-Lebanese Communist party was moreover the only Muslim Communist party to become, after the Seventh Congress of the Comintern, truly independent of that organization, and to be able to act as a really national party.

In Iraq, Communism at first appeared in the form of a Marxist club, which began in the early 1930s in the little Christian town of Nāṣiriyya. This club formed in 1932 a political group, which held a conference at Baghdād in 1934, and became the Iraqi Communist party. In its early days this party consisted exclusively of intellectuals and students, and had no connexions with the workers and peasants; and its attempts to gain the leadership of the trade union movement were without result. The majority of its supporters and its leaders were members of minority groups: Kurds, Armenians, Jews and Assyrians, and its first secretary, Yūsuf Salmān Yūsuf (called Fahd) was a Christian from Nāṣiriyya. The Iraqi Communist party was declared illegal in 1933 and suffered harsh repressive measures. It then remained inactive until the war.

When the Second World War began, the Communist parties in the Muslim countries, with the sole exception of Syria and Lebanon, found themselves in a difficult, if not hopeless, situation. The failure of their action can partly be attributed to the repression to which they were subjected, but still more to the continual changes in strategy and tactics, and to the directives of the Comintern, which were unrealistic or difficult to carry out, and which the Muslim Communists of this period followed faithfully but unimaginatively. Highly orthodox Marxists, rigid and doctrinaire internationalists, accepting every sacrifice involved, even that of being ostracized by society, they were completely lacking in flexibility. Unlike their predecessors, the pre-1917 socialists, and their successors after 1945, they openly stated the problem of whether Communism and Islam were mutually compatible, and always solved it by the outright rejection of Islam. Except in rare instances, they refused alliances, and considered Russia as the only revolutionary model, to be conformed to always and everywhere. In spite of their failure they left a romantic heritage of struggles and sacrifices, without which the more firmly based post-war Communist parties could not have developed.

COMMUNISM AFTER 1945

With the Second World War there began a new phase in the history of Communism in the Muslim countries, which for several years was to progress at an unprecedented rate.

One primary factor explains the sudden outburst of sympathy which greeted Communist ideas in the Middle East during and immediately after the war. This was the prestige which surrounded the Soviet Union after the victory of Stalingrad. After this the Middle East countries were prejudiced in favour of everything coming from Russia, while Western ideas, doctrines or methods were suspect, or stigmatized as 'imperialist'. There was, however, a great difference between the prestige enjoyed by Soviet Russia in 1945, and the attraction which the

Russian Revolution had exercised in 1920. From now on it was not the example of victorious revolution and the triumph over the wealthier classes and over foreign domination which were found attractive, but rather the economic and political success of a powerful régime, based on a totalitarian ideology, which had enabled the Russian people, who in 1917 had been technically backward, to overcome this backwardness within forty years, and to place themselves in the forefront of world progress. The attraction of the Soviet Union, and thereby of Communism itself, no longer operated, as it had formerly, on only a small number of discontented people, often of alien origin and generally on the fringe of society, but on the whole of the population, including even the elements which were hostile to Communist ideology.

From the organizational point of view the Communist parties were no longer governed by one supreme authority, the Comintern having been dissolved during the war; nevertheless their strategy was inspired by programmes worked out in the Soviet Union. The Communist parties therefore have maintained in large measure a common policy and ideology, though these are capable of considerable variation. Such, at least, was the situation until the ideological conflict between Soviet Russia and China appeared, in 1962, to threaten the unity of thought and action of the Communist world.

After 1945 the constant preoccupation of the Soviet Union was to make the Muslim world neutral, to detach it from its western alliances rather than to attach it by political and ideological links to the Communist bloc. Thus, as was the case in the 1920s, the foreign policy of the Soviet Union can be tactically different from that of local Communist parties. The support given by Moscow to certain neutralist régimes which are, however, hostile to Communism is a proof of this.

The Communist strategy, progressively restated from 1945 onwards and fixed in 1954, is that of the 'New Democracy' which advocates the formation of National Fronts broadly open to all who profess opposition to imperialism. The Communists make no claims to assume the leadership of them but are content to represent the vanguard in the national struggle against the colonialism or the neo-colonialism of the West. Without renouncing any part of their doctrine, they have attempted, generally with success, to integrate themselves in the fullest possible measure into the national life. To this end they no longer present anything beyond a minimum programme, 'rightist' as it is called in Marxist terminology, relegating social demands to the background and postponing the establishment of socialism to a distant future. They have renounced several points which were formerly considered essential, notably on the slogans of the class-struggle, and on anti-religious propaganda. Their tactics are to hold out a hand to Islam.

As with its political policy, so also the membership of the Eastern Communist parties differs greatly in its social composition from that of the 1920s and 1930s. Its members are recruited from all levels of society, but the Communist movement is pre-eminently that of the middle classes in revolt against the survivals of 'feudalism'. The majority of its leaders are intellectuals, often technicians of bourgeois origin. There are more students than workers or peasants among its militant members.

However, if consideration is confined to the internal organization and evolution of the Communist parties, the results obtained since the Second World War are somewhat deceptive. As happened after 1920, the Communist parties, in spite of a spectacular come-back, have encountered since 1950 in all the Muslim countries (outside the Soviet Union) increasing difficulties. On the other hand, in the dissemination of their ideology, the Communist parties have had some undeniable successes, with far-reaching and lasting consequences. Communism has found a place for itself, admittedly an unofficial one, in the national life. Today its doctrine is either opposed or accepted, but never unknown. The contacts between Islam and Communism, formerly difficult and infrequent, are now constant and can therefore be studied.

On the purely religious level, there is indeed an absolute incompatibility between Islam as a revealed religion and Communist ideology as a materialist doctrine, but this radical difference between them has never prevented individuals with a background of revealed religion from becoming Communists. On the contrary, on the socio-political field, the Muslim *Umma* and the Communist International are two associations of a comparable nature, both of them being totalitarian ideological movements with temporal programmes aiming at the establishment of a state under their control. They confront one another, and each may influence and sometimes penetrate the other. They are now in daily contact: Islam is prepared to take into account ideologies and values that have originated outside Islam, and is even willing to draw inspiration from them. It is thus possible to be both Communist and Muslim. On its side, Communism has since 1945 abandoned, in part at least, its intransigent totalitarian ideology, and also admits, in fact if not in theory, compatibility with other ideologies. Moreover, there are various points of contact: some of them are temporary, such as the anti-Western themes and the anti-liberal, anti-colonialist and anti-racialist reaction, others are permanent, such as the totalitarianism of both Communism and Islam, their dualist attitude towards the outside world, and finally their authoritarianism, imposing collective obligations on their adherents.

It is difficult to assess the influence exerted by Communist ideology on Muslim society. Its power and its depth should not be exaggerated. It still influences only a certain sector of the bourgeois intelligentsia, and the contacts of the masses with Communism are still only very superficial. In addition there is very often confusion between the attraction of Marxism and sympathy with the Soviet Union, with which the Muslim states are able to maintain excellent relations while at the same time persecuting their local Communists. Similarly Communism contains complex ideological strata—from Marx to Mao Tse-tung, via Lenin, and Stalin and his successors, not to mention the numerous 'heretics'—which are all current and accessible. From them Muslims can draw at will various and sometimes contradictory ideas, values and doctrines. Nowadays the term 'Communism' implies to some Muslims a whole collection of ideas, including scientific rationalism or humanist liberalism, which do not belong to Marxism but which prepare the way for the reception of Communist ideology.

Since 1945, the ideological relations between Communism and Islam outside the frontiers of the Soviet Union have rarely been those of conflict, but fit broadly into the common desire for coexistence. This is, however, difficult to realize, since true peaceful coexistence is possible only if the two doctrines are placed on an equal footing, which is the case neither in Soviet Russia, where Islam is relegated to the fringe of society, nor in the Middle Eastern countries, where life is still dominated by Islam.

The solution of coexistence allows the two ideologies to remain intact, allied to each other only for the realization of similar and often negative objectives, as, for example, the struggle against the West. But contacts may also be closer. When the considerations of the international or domestic policy of their country demand it, Muslims are tempted to seek in Communism formulas or ideas which correspond with the demands of their own ideology, quite apart from any friendship for Communism. Some even go so far as to interpret traditional Islam in the light of Communism. On the Communist side, the same willingness to discover similarities or to develop points of contact is not apparent. Thus, in the Muslim areas of the Soviet Union where the Muslims have lived for more than forty years under the Communist régime, Marxism has never taken Islamic forms, in spite of the dreams of the Muslim Communists of the 1920s. It would be impossible to discover there the slightest trace of an Islamo-Communist syncretism. Islam survives there only as a simple religious cult, the object of a very active anti-religious propaganda conducted by the authorities. Officially Islam may no longer influence in any way the life of the formerly Muslim populations, but it nevertheless retains a hold over customs and habits, and governs, in spite of prohibitions, a certain number of traditions affecting family life.

The real contacts between Communism and Islam outside the Soviet Union are of too recent a date and, for the moment, still too superficial for assessment, still less prediction, to be possible.

One may, however, ask whether the influence of Communism on Islam will in the final analysis be reduced simply to a contribution of new ideas and concepts which will finally become islamized and come to add some new techniques to the armoury of modernist reformism; or whether, as the oriental Communists of the 1920s and 1930s dreamed, Communism will finally triumph and succeed in building a new and completely de-islamized society. At present the survival of Islam in Soviet Russia does not permit of this conclusion.

Thus two essential questions remain open. The first is temporary and political. Is the Communist world or the West better equipped to gain the support of the Muslim world? The other is permanent and historical. What results may be expected from the contact between Islam and Communism, in the awareness of the social groups or of individual Muslims?

CHAPTER 6

THE POLITICAL IMPACT OF THE WEST

THE WORLD, THE WEST, AND ISLAM

The impact of the West on the rest of the world has been the most striking feature of human history in the last five hundred years. It acquired its dynamic force, ultimately, from a new attitude of mind—an avid dedication to the exploration of the unknown, an appreciation of continuity in change and of unity in variety, and a restless ambition to convert knowledge into power. This new mental outlook resulted in the progressive control of man's natural environment by means of an ever vaster and tighter division of human labour. The Western impact has been an impact of modern science, of modern technology, and of modern forms of social organization; its channels of transmission have been improved means of transport, more powerful weapons, and the desire of non-Western peoples to emulate the patterns of civilization whose effectiveness had thus been demonstrated.

This world-wide Western impact took three principal forms: overseas settlement, colonial rule and what has been called defensive modernization. The Americas were the first continent to succumb to colonial conquest; much of the indigenous population was replaced by European immigrants, whose descendants took the lead in establishing the first post-colonial states. Australia and New Zealand followed a similar course, although for them, as for Canada, independence came as the result of more gradual evolution. Today, the countries of North and South America may be considered cultural offshoots of the West, with a strong admixture of indigenous elements mainly in the Andean region from Mexico to Bolivia. Colonial rule without extensive European settlement was established in South and South-East Asia and in tropical Africa; here, the indigenous populations, having transformed their cultures to a greater or lesser extent on the Western model, at length emerged to self-government as a result of the weakening of the West in two World Wars. Russia and Japan remained strong enough to resist any attempt at conquest, but the price of their resistance turned out to be the systematic introduction, since the days of Peter I and of Meiji, of Western technology and organization. Today, Japan participates increasingly in the economic and intellectual development of the West, whereas Russian government and society have been transformed by a dissident ideology of Western origin. China has followed a pattern intermediate between the second and the third: like Africa and South Asia, she was subjected to imperial penetration, but like Russia and Japan she never lost her independence, and like Russia she has embraced a version of Marxism as her dominant ideology.

With the liquidation of the Western colonial system (in part, at least by the imperial powers themselves) after the Second World War, a fourth pattern may be discerned. What started out as the dramatic impact of a particular Mediterranean-West European culture on the rest of mankind by now has become a world-wide intellectual and social transformation that is rapidly losing its parochial Western character. Competition among Europeans, their overseas descendants in America, their heretical or orthodox disciples in Russia, Japan and elsewhere is adding to the propulsive force of this revolution of world civilization.[1]

Within this varied picture, the modern encounter of Westerners (including Russians) with Muslims has in many respects been a unique experience for both groups. It has been unique, first of all, because the Islamic Near East is particularly close to Europe in geography, history and cultural tradition. Unlike the Americas or Japan, the Near East to Europeans was always part of the 'known world': it did not have to be 'discovered' or 'opened up' by the dramatic arrival of ships at distant shores. Islam grew out of the same ancient Middle Eastern, Judaic and Hellenistic roots as did Christianity. The Arabs learned their science and philosophy from the ancient Greeks and taught them to the medieval Europeans. The Ottoman empire originated in Asia Minor, but expanded first into Europe, and only later into Asia and Africa; much of its administrative personnel throughout the centuries was recruited from Balkan Christians converted to Islam; and on that foundation it became for many centuries the most powerful, durable and extensive (hence in a sense most 'modern') realm to the west of the Himalayas. Yet, although there had been continuous contact between Islam and Christianity, a distinctive Western impact on the Muslim countries began only after Europe had attained a striking degree of military and technological superiority in the sixteenth and seventeenth centuries; and

[1] For an elaboration of these views of modernization see R. E. Ward and D. A. Rustow, *Political Modernization in Japan and Turkey* (Princeton, 1964), 3-13, and D. A. Rustow, *World of Nations* (Washington, 1967, 3-20).

even then the internal divisions and rivalries in Europe considerably delayed the full force of the impact. By the late nineteenth century, the Ottoman empire and Persia at one end of Asia, and China and Japan at the other, stood out as the two major regions never subjugated by Europe. Egypt and the Fertile Crescent were among the very last areas to be brought into the Western imperial system of hegemony. In the Arab countries and elsewhere in the Near East, therefore, the Western political impact reached its peak at a time when sections of the indigenous *élite* had already been converted to Western ideals of constitutionalism and nationalism, and when large sectors of European opinion had already turned against the colonial system. The régimes of military occupation, mandates and preferential treaties established in the Near East from the 1880s to the 1930s reflected this bad conscience of colonialism. The resistance of Arabs to these régimes reflected the ambivalent attitudes of Near Easterners to this belated impact.

For the Near Easterners, there was nothing new in receiving foreign cultural influences or submitting to foreign conquerors. Living at the crossroads of three continents and two oceans, they had throughout history been exposed to more intensive cultural interchange and more frequent invasion than the inhabitants of any other major region. But always in the past, superior culture had been balanced against superior military power. When Muslim bedouins in the seventh and eighth Christian centuries overran the Sasanian dominions and parts of the Byzantine empire, they quickly blended the Hellenistic and Iranian cultures of their new subjects with their own Muslim faith and their nomadic social organization. Later, these hellenized and iranized Muslims imparted their own faith and civilization to other nomadic conquerors such as Turks and Mongols. Now, in the Muslim experience of the Western impact, cultural and military superiority were both on the same side: for the first time in thousands of years Near Easterners were forced, slowly but inexorably, to receive and adapt the culture of outsiders who were conquering them.

After due allowance is made for these unique aspects of the Western impact upon Islam, the world-wide themes of defensive modernization, of colonial rule, of foreign settlement, and eventually of competitive coexistence, reappear. Defensive modernization began in Ottoman Turkey in the eighteenth century, in Egypt and Persia in the nineteenth, and in Afghanistan and on the Arabian peninsula in the twentieth. European colonial conquest moved concentrically from the periphery of the Islamic region to its core: Mughal India and Indonesia in the seventeenth century, Central Asia and Islamic Africa in the nineteenth and the Arab Fertile Crescent in the twentieth. Russian Central Asia, Palestine and, for a time, Algeria, have been the only Muslim territories where Western rule entailed immigrant settlement—where colonialism implied colonization. The final, competitive-coexistent, phase of the Western impact began for Turkey in the 1920s and for most other countries in the years after the Second World War.

DEFENSIVE MODERNIZATION IN OTTOMAN TURKEY

Westernizing reforms in the Ottoman empire were stimulated by military decline, and that military decline became apparent with the lifting of the second Ottoman siege of Vienna in 1094/1683. But it would be a mistake to seek the beginnings of Ottoman reform in that period; for 1094/1683 became a turning point only from a lengthy perspective of hindsight. It is true that by 1110/1699 the empire in the treaty of Carlowitz had to yield all of Hungary, Transylvania and Podolia, that this was the first major Ottoman defeat in nearly three centuries, and that the Ottomans were never to recoup these losses. But this the Ottoman contemporaries had no way of knowing. What they did know was that their ancestors had won, lost and regained extensive territories before. Their state had survived in 804/1402 the loss of its Anatolian home base and the capture of its ruler on the battlefield. Clearly, the survival of the empire depended on the continuity of a dynasty and of certain forms of political organization rather than on any identity of territory. After 804/1402, following a period of civil war and chaos, the Ottomans had restored their rule in the Balkans and then in Anatolia, and in 857/1453 they crowned their earlier military exploits by the capture of Istanbul. But they had besieged Istanbul three times before, and they had laid siege to Vienna in 936/1529 as well as in 1094/1683. Who was to say that in another century and a half, or indeed sooner, they would not return to deliver the final, decisive blow? In contrast to the petty kingdoms and principalities of Europe, barely recovering from the ravages of the Thirty Years' War and forever disputing for supremacy, the Ottoman empire represented the full embodiment of co-ordinated Muslim power. Christian and Jewish subjects as well lived under the tolerant Ottoman régime and by their industry enhanced its welfare. Within a few years after the humiliation of

Carlowitz, the Ottomans gave refuge to Charles XII of Sweden (1121/1709) and very nearly captured Peter I of Russia (1123/1711). The year 1718 inaugurated a period of fifty years of peace entirely unprecedented in all Ottoman history, and interrupted only by a brief and victorious campaign (1148–52/1735–9) in which Serbia and western Wallachia were recaptured. During this era of peaceful prosperity, moreover, there was a lively cultural interchange with the West. As European audiences read Montesquieu's *Lettres Persanes* and (somewhat later) were to watch Mozart's *Entführung aus dem Serail,* so the pashas and beys of Istanbul delighted in the colourful varieties of tulips that their gardeners were importing from Holland, and the architects of the Nūru 'Os̱māniye mosque, completed in 1168/1755, engrafted Italian baroque and rococo motifs on the Ottoman architectural style developed by the great Sinān (896–997/1490–1588). Unlike the cultural borrowings of a later period, these adaptations reflected a sense of strength and of confidence rather than of weakness and anxiety. Clearly, no event before the middle of the eighteenth century was likely to shake the Ottoman's sturdy reliance on the power of their sword, the justice of their rule or the righteousness of their faith.[1]

The idyll of the Tulip Era at Istanbul was rudely shattered by the Ottoman-Russian War of 1182–8/1768–74. The generals of Catherine II overran Moldavia and Wallachia, her political agents tried to stir up an uprising in Greece, her admirals circumnavigated all of Europe to attack the Ottoman fleet on the very shores of the Aegean. In the peace treaty of Küchük Kaynarja, the sultan was forced to cede the Crimea—the first Muslim land yielded by Ottomans to Christians—and to allow the passage of Russian ships through the Turkish Straits into the Mediterranean. The privilege retained by the Crimean Tatars to pray publicly for the sultan in his rather dubious 'capacity of Grand Caliph of Mahometanism' was balanced by the privilege newly accorded to the tsar to make representations on behalf of certain of the sultan's Orthodox subjects. In 1197/1783, moreover, the Russians unceremoniously annexed the Crimean buffer state.

Though the area yielded at Küchük Kaynarja was smaller than that surrendered at Carlowitz, the implications were far more serious. Defeat this time had been inflicted not by the Habsburg emperor, one

[1] For a divergent interpretation of the period from 1683 to 1774 see B. Lewis, *The Middle East and the West* (London, 1964), 32 f, and 'Ottoman observers of Ottoman decline', in *Islamic Studies*. I 1 (March, 1962), 71-87.

of the most powerful European rulers, but by a remote and backward country that only two generations before had itself set out on the course of autocratic europeanizing reform. The Black Sea was no longer an Ottoman lake, and Russian ships could avoid the lengthy detour via the Skagerrak and Gibraltar to sail into the Mediterranean past the sultan's very palace in Istanbul. The clause relating to the Orthodox Church opened a dreary vista of foreign interference in the empire's relations with its Christian subjects. But the defeat of 1188/1774 involved something even more precious than territory or strategy: it posed a basic problem in statecraft and in theodicy and thereby threatened the Ottoman's traditional self-confidence. The surrender of Muslims to Christian rule put into question the rationale of a state founded on Muslim conquest of Christians, and of a religious revelation that promised to the true believer prosperity and power on earth as well as salvation hereafter. It made abundantly clear the need for reform to save the state and to reassert the true faith; and the only basis of reform could be a Muslim equivalent of Satan casting out Satan.

The response to that need was the so-called New Order (*Niẓām-i Jedīd*) proclaimed in 1793 by an energetic young ruler, Selīm III (1203–22/1789–1807). The closer contacts with Europe in the Tulip Era had brought piecemeal innovations. In 1139/1727, Ibrāhīm Müteferriqa, a Hungarian Calvinist (or, more probably, Unitarian) captured during the Austrian wars and later converted to Islam, introduced the first printing press to Istanbul. A few years later, Comte de Bonneval, a French adventurer and renegade later called *Khumbarajı* (i.e. Bombardier) Aḥmed Pasha, opened the first Ottoman school of artillery. In 1187/1773, a Hungarian-French aristocrat, Baron de Tott, resumed this project. But Selīm's reforms were far more ambitious than any of these. A new army, trained and equipped in the European style, was to take the place of the Janissaries who had degenerated into a praetorian guard more inclined to cow the sultan in Istanbul and his subjects in the provinces than to fight his battles abroad. The commercial privileges long accorded to Europeans were to be cleansed of abuses. Taxation was to be tightened and extended. Diplomatic missions to major capitals were to report on events in Europe and to propose policies that might deserve emulation.

The sequel to Selīm's reform decrees foreshadowed many of the problems that were to plague the Ottomans and other Near Eastern reformers throughout the next century. These difficulties may be illustrated by a brief review of four major crises of the Ottoman state in 1798–1808, 1826–40, 1875–8 and 1908–18.

The first crisis began in 1798 with Bonaparte's landing in Egypt. Here was a thrust not just at the periphery but into the very heartlands of Islam where no European soldier had effectively set foot since the Crusades. Luckily for the Ottomans, Nelson's fleet destroyed Bonaparte's ships and cut off his supplies, and after three years the last Frenchmen were evacuated. But the crisis continued in 1804 with a Serbian uprising against the oppressive Janissaries at Belgrade, and the Russians, who once again defeated the Ottomans in the war of 1806–12, deliberately encouraged this first stirring of Christian nationalism in the Balkans, following the precedent set by the French after Campo Formio. The climax came with two successive *coups d'état* in Istanbul in 1807 and 1808. In the first, Selīm was deposed by the Janissaries and conservative '*ulemā*'. In the second, his cousin Maḥmūd II (1808–39) was installed on the throne and subsequently signed the solemn *Sened-i Ittifāq* (Deed of Agreement) in which he promised to respect the vested rights of his powerful provincial vassals. Only fifteen years after the high hopes of the New Order, the sultanate had plunged into new depths of seemingly hopeless disorder.

In the dozen years before the next crisis, Maḥmūd II undauntedly resumed his predecessor's work of reform. In complete disregard of the Deed of Agreement, he laid the basis for a strongly centralized autocratic state. The Translation Chamber at the Sublime Porte became the nucleus of the new, westernized bureaucracy. But Maḥmūd perforce concentrated on fighting conservative opposition in Istanbul and the provinces while nationalist rebellion and foreign intervention went unchecked. In 1821 the Greeks revolted in the Morea. In 1822 Maḥmūd's soldiers subdued the formidable 'Alī Pasha of Jannina a hundred miles to the north. In 1826 his new troops destroyed the obstreperous Janissaries in a major bloodbath in Istanbul, leaving the fight against the Greeks to Muḥammad 'Alī of Egypt, most powerful of the provincial pashas. In 1828, the Egyptian forces evacuated the Morea, and in 1829 a Russian invasion of the Balkans forced the sultan virtually to recognize Greek independence in the treaty of Adrianople. In 1831 Muḥammad 'Alī, in open rebellion, started marching on Istanbul, where the frightened sultan in the treaty of Hünkâr Iskelesi (1833) made his realm a virtual protectorate of the tsar. In 1839–40 renewed intervention by the great powers halted a second Egyptian attack. A few years later, in

1853, Tsar Nicholas I in contemplating the future of the sultanate uttered his famous condescending words: 'We have on our hands a sick man, a very sick man.'

The progress that the disease had made in half a century is reflected in the change of therapeutic nomenclature. Selīm III in 1793 had announced a New Order (*Niẓām-i Jedīd*) in the singular intransitive form; the reform era from 1839 to 1876 became known as the *Tanẓīmāt-i khayriye,* or Beneficent Orderings, in the plural transitive. The architects of the Tanẓīmāt were the leading members of Maḥmūd's new bureaucracy —Reshīd Pasha, 'Ālī Pasha and Fu'ād Pasha—who were eager to consolidate his work of reform and also, on occasion, to prove to the powers that the sultanate could solve its internal problems without leaving any justification for their interference. Reshīd drafted a comprehensive proclamation of reform, the *Khaṭṭ-ı Sherīf* of Gülkhāne of 1839, and 'Ālī and Fu'ād a second, the *Khaṭṭ-ı Hümāyun* of 1856, both read by Sultan 'Abd ül-Mejīd (1839–61). But beyond such solemn promises of civic equality, the Tanẓīmāt statesmen effected important changes in administrative organization. They opened permanent military and administrative schools, supplemented them by a system of public secondary education, instituted the principles of recruitment by examination and of orderly promotion in the public service and introduced the first elements of representation into a new and more uniform system of provincial administration. Their hope was to create a common feeling of civic obligation that would weld together Ottoman subjects of Christian as well as Muslim faith. But the most immediate consequence of their work was the emergence of a critical spirit among the newly trained officers and civil servants, who fully accepted the principle of europeanizing reform, but resented the autocratic and bureaucratic manner in which reform had been imposed.

This new internal force interacted vigorously with the older secessionist and foreign pressures in the third Ottoman crisis. There were Christian revolts in the Balkans in 1875 and 1876; the great powers presented their customary protests and demands; Serbia and Montenegro attacked, and when the Ottomans defeated them Russia intervened on their side. A grand diplomatic Congress at Berlin (1878) ratified the most disastrous defeat since 1774: the Ottomans lost control of most of the Balkans, of the Caucasian border area and of Cyprus, and in the remaining areas of mixed Muslim-Christian population (Macedonia and Armenia) were forced to accept a system of international supervision.

Three years later, the bankruptcy of the empire led to the establishment of an international administration for its public debt with full control over customs and certain monopolies. In the midst of these foreign troubles, the empire underwent one of its most profound internal upheavals since 1808. It was precipitated by Midḥat Pasha, the last of the great Tanẓīmāt ministers, who had built up an admirable record of effective and magnanimous administration as provincial governor first of Bulgaria and then of 'Irāq, and who sought the empire's salvation in the adoption of a written representative constitution. To attain his end, Midḥat engineered the deposition of two sultans, the spendthrift 'Abd ül-'Azīz (1861–76) and the demented Murād V. The next sultan, 'Abd ül-Ḥamīd II (1876–1909), opened the first parliament only a month before the outbreak of the Russian War, but adjourned it *sine die* before acceding to the humiliating conditions of peace. Midḥat had already been forced to resign before the parliament convened and was subsequently banished and murdered at 'Abd ül-Ḥamīd's behest. For thirty more years, Turkey reverted to autocratic reform—European-style military training, extension of telegraph and railroad networks, expansion of the school system—without the luxury of a representative constitution. Ideas of constitutionalism, however, continued to flourish among the younger members of the ruling class, particularly the military cadets, and 'Abd ül-Ḥamīd's practice of exiling the malcontents to Europe only confirmed the radicalism of the opposition.

The empire's final crisis began with the so-called Young Turk Revolution of 1908, that is, the calling of new elections after a thirty-year interval, prompted by threats of rebellion on the part of army units in Macedonia. The Macedonian conspirators, known as the Committee of Union and Progress, had been encouraged by the writings of the exiles in Paris. But hopes for orderly constitutional development, for harmonious co-operation among the empire's nationalities and for a stronger position on the international scene quickly faded. The new government's attempt to extend elections into areas of only nominal Ottoman control led to the final loss of Bosnia-Herzegovina, Bulgaria and Crete. A mutiny by conservative troops in Istanbul brought the Macedonian units to the capital and resulted in the deposition of 'Abd ül-Ḥamīd in favour of Meḥmed V Reshād (1909–18). A systematic policy of administrative centralization antagonized the hitherto loyal non-Turkish Muslim groups, notably the Albanians and later the Arabs. The Turkish-Italian and Balkan wars of 1911–13 resulted in the loss of Libya and most of the empire's remaining European possessions. They also furnished the occasion for a bitter internal struggle among civilian and military factions resulting in the establishment of a military and party dictatorship of the CUP. When the leader of the Young Turk militarists, Enver Pasha, manoeuvred the Ottoman empire into the First World War on the German side, its fate was sealed. A political revival became possible only after a protracted struggle, and then only on a much reduced scale and in the novel form of a nationalist, secularist republic committed to the principle of integral westernization.

A number of broad themes may be traced throughout this history of Ottoman reform from 1774 to 1918: the continued pressure from abroad, the empire's precarious survival amidst European power rivalries, the interplay of internal and external pressures for change, the short-range weakening produced by the reforms, the spread of westernizing sentiment, the disputes about direction of the reform and its ever-broadening scope.

The foreign pressure that stimulated the original reforms never abated. In fact, European military strength, which the Ottomans could not match in the eighteenth century, steadily increased, so that the reformers were forever pursuing a rapidly receding target. Carnot's *levée en masse* almost overnight enlarged the man-power scale of warfare tenfold; the spirit of nationalism, propagated by the French Revolution and the Napoleonic wars, created a new sense of cohesion in the countries of Europe; and the industrial revolution added powerful weapons to their arsenals. The Ottoman empire—with its polyglot and multi-religious population, its dynastic and local loyalties and its more primitive agrarian economy—could neither effectively resist nor quickly reproduce any of these developments. In the eighteenth century, the Ottomans would have done well to hold their own against the Habsburg and tsarist empires. By the turn of the twentieth, Austria-Hungary had sunk to the rank of a secondary power, and both Habsburgs and Romanovs faced the twin threats of nationalism and revolution. All that the most strenuous efforts of the Ottoman reformers could achieve was to delay the downfall of their own empire to coincide with that of its two traditional rivals.

Meanwhile, the rivalries among European powers contributed now to prevent the empire's imminent collapse, and now its more complete salvation. The British cut off Bonaparte's line of supply in 1798; a grand European alliance fought Russian designs on the Balkans in the Crimean

War of 1854–56; and the Germans reorganized and helped to command the Ottoman armies in their contest with Russian and British forces in 1914–18. But the same European powers which prevented each other from taking over the empire's legacy also conspired to thwart any resurgence of Muslim power in the Near East. They intervened on behalf of the Greeks in 1828–30, against Muḥammad 'Alī in 1833–40, and on behalf of the Balkan states in 1877–8. Time and again the European balance of power was readjusted in its kaleidoscopic combinations so as to keep the Ottomans in their twilight status as the 'sick man of Europe'.

External and internal pressures came to interact ever more stringently. The readiness of Europeans to champion the cause of their co-religionists —British philhellenism, Russian solicitude for Greeks, southern Slavs, and Armenians, and French interest in Lebanese Maronites—did much to encourage nationalism and secession. For example, the bombing of the Banque Ottomane by Armenian terrorists in 1896, which set off the first major wave of anti-Armenian persecution, was deliberately planned so as to provoke the intervention of Russia and other powers. The Tanẓīmāt statesmen, on their side, issued each of their major reform decrees at moments of external crisis so as to persuade the great powers to help those who helped themselves. Whereas the contents of the *Khaṭṭ* of 1839 and of the Constitution of 1876 reflected internal demands for reform, the *Khaṭṭ* of 1856 was largely inspired by the turcophile British ambassador, Lord Stratford de Redcliffe. Foreign crises also furnished the occasion, or at least the pretext, for Ottoman changes of government. The Russian War of 1877–8 prompted the dismissal first of Midḥat and then of the parliament; signs of a British-Russian *rapprochement* at Ottoman expense hastened the revolution of 1908; and the Libyan and Balkan wars led to several changes in factional control of the government at Istanbul. Somewhat later, the defeat of 1918 broke the power of the CUP, just as the Allied occupation of Istanbul, and Greek annexation of Izmir, threw the support of Turkish opinion behind the nationalist movement under Muṣṭafā Kemāl.

The early reforms provoked tenacious resistance from conservative forces in the state, such as Janissaries and '*ulemā*'. Partly as a result, their immediate effect was much internal disarray and a weakening of the empire in its external contest. The new army lost more decisive battles than had the Janissaries; proclamations of civic equality did not dissuade the subject nationalities from secession; and the new body of tax collectors could not forestall public bankruptcy. In fact, the growing 'social mobilization'[1] of the population through such measures as improved transport, broader government recruitment and expanded schooling did much to accentuate the latent diversity among various ethnic groups. It is a singular tribute to the pragmatic spirit of the Ottoman ruling class that these setbacks did not deflect them from their course of progressive reform.

Support for modernization spread gradually through Ottoman-Turkish society, downwards from the top of the political hierarchy and inwards from the periphery of the empire. Reform started as the command of autocratic rulers such as Selīm and Maḥmūd, was taken up in the Tanẓīmāt as the project of bureaucratic ministers, and by 1908 had become the ardent mission of organized political groups with growing support among the urban masses. In the mid-twentieth century, the transformation of society in Turkey and several other countries began to engulf the peasantry as well. The regions most accessible to Europe—the Balkans and the eastern Mediterranean—were the natural channels of its influence. Following Bonaparte's invasion, Egypt became the centre of one of the most ambitious Near Eastern attempts at westernization. Secessionist nationalism spread first to Christians and later to Muslims, first to the Balkans and then to Anatolia and Arabia: Serbs, Greeks, Bulgarians, Armenians, Albanians, Syrian and Lebanese Arabs, Arabs in the Ḥijāz and 'Irāq—in approximately that order. Being most closely identified with the imperial tradition, the Turks themselves did not turn to nationalism until the period from 1913 to 1923, when secession of the non-Turkish groups was in its final phase. Leading roles in this conversion were played by two groups of peripheral nationals, who were reacting to the upsurge of nationalism in Russia and in the Balkans. Muslim Turkish refugees from the tsarist empire provided much of the ideological rationale of early Turkish nationalism, whereas Ottoman Turks from Macedonia provided the major organizational impetus of the Young Turk and Kemalist movements.[2]

Although reform proceeded steadily, it did not proceed smoothly or without intense conflict. Even after the suppression of the provincial magnates and of the Janissaries, profound differences and bitter rivalries remained. Maḥmūd II, the early Tanẓīmāt ministers and 'Abd ül-

[1]For that term, see Karl W. Deutsch, *Nationalism and Social Communication* (New York, 1953).

[2] Cf. D. A. Rustow, 'The Army and the Founding of the Turkish Republic', in *World Politics* xi (July 1959), 527 f.; and 'Atatürk as founder of a state', *Daedalus*, XCIII, 793-828 (1968).

Ḥamīd were concerned mainly about the strengthening of the central government's power. The New Ottomans of the 1860s, Midḥat Pasha and the moderate wing of the Young Turk movement championed representation as a check on despotism and on irresponsible bureaucracy while hoping for 'harmony of the elements', that is, of ethnic groups imbued with a common spirit of Ottoman citizenship. The CUP, by contrast, came to equate Ottomanism with Turkish nationalism and representative government with party rule. From 1908 to 1918 there was an intense ideological debate, summed up rather than reconciled in Żiyā Gökalp's triple slogan of 'Turkization, Islamization, Modernization'. The Kemalists opted for the first and third of these, whereas the partial religious restoration of the 1950s reintroduced the second theme in a minor key. During the one-party period (1923–45), the republic concentrated on modernizing the urban population, whereas competitive party politics since 1945 for the first time spread the impetus to the rural areas. In sum, the Turkish public debate since 1826 has concerned not so much the principle of modernizing reform itself as the priorities among various items of reform—that is, the specific combination of tradition and modernity to be attempted at any given time.

The Ottomans' first reaction to European military superiority had been to try to borrow only the 'cutting edge' of the new instrument.[1] But by a steady and inexorable logic, the impulse of reform spread through the political and social structure. The new army required new schools for the training of officers and new financing from heavier taxes; this created a need for new administrative machinery and at length for an entirely new legal system; all this in turn added to the demand for new teachers and new public servants—and hence for more schools and more financing. Of all the nineteenth-century reforms, the new educational system most consistently proved its worth in the long run. For, amidst defeat, rebellion and bankruptcy, it was the graduates of the schools founded during the Tanẓīmāt and Hamidian periods who provided leadership in the transition from empire to republic, when reform was to be applied more intensively on a more manageable geographic scale. Yet, with the advent of the republic in 1923, reform had, in a sense, come full circle: the heirs of the new army that Selīm had founded in 1793 had deposed his cousin's grandson and pronounced a coroner's verdict on the Ottoman empire. Reform, which had started out as a selective

[1] L. V. Thomas and R. N. Frye, *The United States and Turkey and Iran* (Cambridge, Mass., 1951), 51.

expedient for the defence of tradition against the Western onslaught, had become an instrument for the wholesale transformation and even the destruction of tradition itself.

VARIATION IN EGYPT AND PERSIA

The story of Ottoman westernization was repeated with significant variations in Egypt and Persia. In Egypt, the military pressure from Europe was felt earlier and more sharply than in the rest of the empire, in Persia it was felt later and in attenuated form: the speed and intensity of attempts at reform varied accordingly in each country. Neither country had as strong an administrative tradition as the Ottomans, and both countries—Egypt through its geographical location and Persia through its subsoil resources—offered far more attractive prizes to the builders of European empires: hence Egypt and Persia could not control their own modernization to the extent that Turkey could. Egypt for a generation became a colony in all but name, and Persia narrowly avoided the same fate on several occasions; as a result there accumulated in both countries a good deal more resentment against the West than was to be found in Turkey.

While the empire of Selīm III was deprived of several outlying provinces, Egypt was itself occupied by foreign troops. General Bonaparte, moreover, landed not just with troops but also with a sizable retinue of historians, archaeologists, scientists, administrators, economists and propagandists. The French, as they had done to good effect in Belgium, Italy and elsewhere, proclaimed themselves as liberators of the common people from alien oppression; they also made much of their revolutionary anti-clericalism and its supposed affinity to Islam. On this last point, to be sure, their listeners displayed a healthy scepticism; nor did the French stay long enough to effect any lasting reorganization of administration, finances, education or agriculture. Nonetheless, three years of their presence had thoroughly shaken the rule of the Mamluk oligarchy and demonstrated what Western technology and organization might accomplish even in a Near Eastern setting. The lesson was well appreciated by Muḥammad ʿAlī, an Ottoman soldier of Albanian birth, who had distinguished himself in the campaign against the French, and in 1805 rose to the position of viceroy of Egypt.

Muḥammad ʿAlī Pasha consolidated his power by killing off his Mamluk opponents—much as Peter I had done with the Strelitsi and as Maḥmūd II was to do with the Janissaries. Once in control, he embarked on a programme of reform far more comprehensive than that of his Ottoman contemporaries. He introduced the cultivation of long-staple cotton, which found a ready market in Europe. He called in foreign military instructors, and built dockyards and ordnance factories. He sent young men to Europe to study technical subjects. And he used the proceeds of a growing export economy to finance the armies and the fleet that, in a number of brilliant campaigns, spread his power into Arabia, the Sudan, Palestine, Syria, Greece and Anatolia. In his clear appreciation of the economic base of military power, Muḥammad 'Alī differed sharply from all Turkish nineteenth-century reformers, with the sole exception of Midḥat.

European intervention in 1833 and 1840 halted his advance into Turkey, and thwarted any designs of claiming the legacy of the sultans. By the extension of European commercial privileges from the rest of the Ottoman empire to Egypt, it also withered the economic roots of Egypt's expansion. Muḥammad 'Alī's successors aggravated the plight by careless spending and by exorbitant taxes that often forced the peasants to sell their seed. The construction of the Suez Canal by the enterprising French engineer, de Lesseps, and the high demand for Egyptian cotton during the American Civil War brought a temporary reprieve. But the speculative fever of the double boom in exports and public works encouraged many sharp practices by European financiers; and, when the bubble burst, these found innumerable ways of recouping their losses and even their anticipated gains from the liberal treasury of the Khedive Ismā'īl (1863–79). In 1875 Ismā'īl was forced to sell his shares in the Suez Canal (they were bought by the Disraeli government), and in 1876 to accept foreign supervision of his finances. When a combined military-civilian opposition demanded that his successor should submit regular accounts to a parliamentary body, the European powers rallied to the protection of the foreign creditors. After lengthy deliberations, their intervention took the form of British military occupation—a *de facto* colonial régime that was to continue from 1882 until after the First World War.

Persia remained more sheltered from the main thrusts of European expansion. The Portuguese held a trading post at Hormuz in the Persian Gulf from 1507 to 1622, but the Indies offered far richer prizes to Portuguese, Dutch and British alike. Russia made contact with Persia fully a century after its first encounter with the Ottomans. In the years from 1800 to 1813 tsarist forces conquered the Persian border area between the Caucasus and the Aras river; and, for a time, Persia was drawn into the diplomatic intrigues among France, Britain and Russia. By the middle of the century, Britain had consolidated her rule in India, and Russia proceeded to the conquest of Central Asia, so that both powers took a more active interest in the intervening Persian-Afghan area. Yet none of these developments had any marked effect on the rulers of Persia, except to afford them some practice in the precarious game of playing off one great power against the other and to give them an avid taste for foreign loans at exorbitant rates.

What westernizing influence was felt in Persia in the nineteenth century, therefore, was the result of activity not by the government but by enterprising foreigners. British subjects obtained concessions for the building of telegraph lines (1865), the construction of railways and exploration of minerals (1872), the opening of a bank (1889), and a monopoly on the purchase and sale of tobacco throughout the country (1890). Tsarist officers were called to organize a Cossack Brigade (1879), while other Russians obtained concessions for the lucrative caviare fisheries in the Caspian (1888), and for a second bank (1892). Meanwhile, however, a new force for change appeared on the scene—that of popular indignation at royal extravagance and foreign influence. The tobacco concession which affected not only the growers but also all smokers and chewers of tobacco, caused particularly strong resentment. When a general boycott of tobacco, organized by the Shīʿī *ʿulamāʾ* in 1892, forced the shah to cancel the odious monopoly, the power of concerted popular action had been demonstrated. As in Turkey during the same period, newspapers written by political exiles and smuggled into the country helped keep alive the opposition spirit. By 1905 the movement had the support of the *ʿulamāʾ*, the bazaar merchants of Tehran, and large urban crowds; in 1906 these forced the shah to grant a parliamentary constitution.

Foreign influence, nevertheless, continued to play a crucial role—and that much more openly than earlier in the Ottoman empire. Britain and Russia completed their *rapprochement* against Germany by settling their outstanding issues in Asia; in a convention of 1907 they divided Persia into two spheres of influence, a Russian one in the north and a British one in the south. In 1908 the Cossack Brigade, under its Russian commander, assisted Muḥammad ʿAlī Shāh in a military *coup* by shelling the building of the parliament and its members. A counter-*coup* in 1909, led by the southern Bakhtīyārī tribe, restored the constitution and forced the shah into exile. Britain's interest had been heightened by the discovery of petroleum in the southern province of Khūzistān in 1908 and by the shift of the Royal Navy from coal to oil fuel in 1913. In 1914 the British government obtained a major financial interest in the petroleum concession first obtained by William Knox D'Arcy, an Australian, in 1901. The restored constitutional government tried to diversify its sources of foreign support by appointing Swedish officers to train a gendarmerie, and calling financial advisers from the United States. But other foreigners continued to arrive without any invitation. Between 1907 and 1921, Russian, British and German troops operated almost at will in various parts of Persia. In 1920 Soviet troops in pursuit of the routed Whites landed on the Caspian shore, and, in conjunction with local rebels, proclaimed the Soviet Republic of Gīlān. A year earlier, the cabinet in Tehran had negotiated a treaty with Britain which if ratified would have made the country into a virtual protectorate.

The full independence of the country was restored only under Riżā Khān, who as the first Persian commander of the Cossack Brigade crushed the Gīlān rebellion, seized power in Tehran (1921), had himself proclaimed shah in 1925 and in the next decade and a half inaugurated a programme that tried to match, in one rapid effort, the reforms of Maḥmūd II and Muḥammad 'Alī Pasha, of 'Abd ül-Ḥamīd and Atatürk. But the Second World War brought another period of foreign occupation by Russia and Britain, followed by further episodes of attempted secession under the Communist aegis, and of *coup* and counter-*coup* with the encouragement of Britain, Russia or the United States. From these difficulties Persia has only been extricating herself slowly since the 1950s.

Egyptians and Persians, in a variety of ways, were subject to stronger imperialist pressures than were the Turks, and their political and manpower resources for resistance were slimmer; hence among both peoples feelings toward the West were more markedly ambivalent. A characteristic early expression of this ambivalence may be found in Jamāl al-Dīn al-Afghānī (1839–97), perhaps the most colourful intellectual-political figure of the nineteenth-century Near East; and it is no accident that al-Afghānī, who spent many years of exile in Istanbul, should have exercised his most profound influence in Persia and in Egypt. Bernard Lewis has aptly described the tenor of al-Afghānī's thought:

For Jamāl al-Dīn [Islam] was a civilization, potentially a world power, and only incidentally a faith; its basic demand was for loyalty rather than for piety. The Muslims were to be united as the Germans and Italians were united, and

Jamāl al-Dīn passed his life in the search for a Muslim monarch to whom he could be a Bismarck or a Cavour. The enemy from which Islam needed to be saved was Europe, and especially Great Britain, the imperial power in India and Egypt.[1]

It is true that in Islam, from its earliest times, religion and matters of state, ethics, law and politics were blended; but al-Afghānī's emphasis on the political aspects of Islam betrays a novel, European influence. His reinterpretation clearly was not only an antagonistic response to Western encroachments but also an adaptation of Western concepts. Much as Selīm III had set out to fight the West with European-style artillery, al-Afghānī tried to fight the West with European-style ideology, with a revived Islam interpreted as a variant of modern nationalism. But whereas Selīm and his successors down to Atatürk could use the power of the state for pragmatic steps of piecemeal reform, al-Afghānī and his Persian and Arab followers had to rely on the power of the word and the pen to express popular yearnings for a dramatic and rapid improvement in the helpless condition of the Muslim community. Al-Afghānī was a moving force behind the tobacco boycott of 1890–1 and seems to have played a role also in the assassination of Nāṣir al-Dīn Shāh in 1896. In Egypt he profoundly influenced Muḥammad ʿAbduh (1849–1905), who did much to reorganize training at al-Azhar and to reconstruct Islamic theology in its two-front fight against rigid traditionalism and modern secularism.

THE TWILIGHT OF WESTERN IMPERIAL RULE

Just as Western influences such as nationalism spread inward from the periphery of the Ottoman empire, so the onslaught of European imperialism on the whole House of Islam, which Selīm and Maḥmūd were fighting with military weapons, and men like al-Afghānī with weapons of the spirit, was moving concentrically inward from an even wider circle. That circle first was drawn when Vasco da Gama circumnavigated the Cape of Good Hope and Russian adventurers penetrated across the Volga and Urals into Siberia.

The Dutch established the first system of Christian colonial rule over a large Muslim population in Indonesia in the seventeenth century. The spread of Islam to the archipelago, however, which had begun around A.D. 1200 continued, and was at times even encouraged. In the eighteenth century, the British expanded their position in India, moving inland from coastal trading towns like Bombay and Calcutta, and playing off rival local rulers. In 1803 they took Delhi, seat of the once-powerful

[1] Lewis, *The Middle East and the West*, 103.

Mughal dynasty. Thus entrenched on the subcontinent, and warned by Bonaparte's Egyptian expedition, they began to take a closer interest in the Near East, notably the Indian Ocean coast of the Arabian peninsula. They signed their first treaty with the pirate shaykhs of the Persian Gulf in 1820, and followed it up in 1853 with a permanent truce which was to give to the area the name Trucial 'Umān. They established a coaling station at Aden in 1839 to support a monthly steamer service from Egypt to India. Toward the end of the century they confirmed and rounded out their system of treaties, with the 'Umānī sultans at Masqaṭ and Zanzibar in 1890–1, with Baḥrayn in 1892, and with Kuwayt in 1899. Meanwhile, the French conquered Algeria after 1830, established a protectorate over Tunisia in 1881, and, together with Spain, another over Morocco in 1912. The British occupation of Egypt, French conquest of the Sahara, British rule over northern Nigeria and Italy's annexation of Libya in 1912 completed the European conquest of Islamic Africa. At the opposite end of the Islamic region, the Russians subdued the Mongol-descended khans of Kazan and Astrakhān as early as the mid-sixteenth century, annexed the Crimea in 1783, conquered Baku in 1806 and proceeded to expand into Central Asia, where they incorporated the khanates of Bukhārā, Khīva and Khokand between 1868 and 1876.

Nowhere in its five-hundred year history did European imperialism encounter such determined resistance as in these Muslim countries of Asia and Africa. Religious brotherhoods and nomadic tribes with their tight social organization often furnished the most effective leadership and inaccessible deserts and mountains the most favourable setting. 'Abd al-Qādir, a shaykh of the Qādirī order, fought the French in Algeria until 1847. Shaykh Shāmil, a Naqshbandī in Dāghistān in the northern Caucasus, resisted the tsarist forces for nearly thirty years until his capture in 1859; the neighbouring Circassians, Chechens and Ossetians proved almost equally tenacious. The uprising of the Mahdi and his followers in the Sudan (1881–98) involved Britain in one of its most serious colonial wars, their initial success being symbolized by the death of General Gordon and capture of Khartoum. The Pathan tribesmen of the North-West Frontier kept the British Indian army in a perpetual alert for most of a century. In Cyrenaica, the Italians encountered tribesmen of the Sanūsī order, in Morocco the Spaniards fought the Berber tribes (Kabyles) under 'Abd al-Karīm. It also seems significant in this context that Muslim Algeria, along with Indochina and Cyprus, has been one of the few areas where colonial rule was terminated as a result of guerrilla warfare; and that of the three, the Algerian war was the most protracted, and the only one fought against a large group of colonial settlers.

Despite such fierce opposition, all Muslim countries except for Albania, Turkey, Persia, Afghanistan and the Arabian peninsula had come under European domination by 1920. In some areas the colonial power acted through acquiescent local rulers, in others through its colonial officials alone. The Russians, carrying their conquests overland, generally annexed them outright, brought in settlers and assimilated some of the population. The French sponsored large-scale settlement only in North Africa and relied on direct rule except in Tunisia and Morocco. The British, with their love of precedent and of the exotic, took great pains to work out a variety of 'indirect' arrangements—with sultans in Malaya, Brunei and Zanzibar, with maharajas in the Indian princely states, with *amīrs* in northern Nigeria and with shaykhs on the Arabian coast. To give one of the more curious examples, the Sudan after 1899 was governed under what its author aptly described as a 'hybrid form of government hitherto unknown to international jurisprudence'.[1] The fiction of an Anglo-Egyptian 'condominium' was symbolized mainly by an Egyptian flag flying next to the Union Jack over government buildings. In Cairo, a 'viceroy' ruled under the deceptively unassuming title of 'British agent and consul-general'; whereas the sultan in Istanbul, who was supposedly sovereign over Egypt and perhaps the Sudan as well, had to content himself with an annual payment of tribute. None of these legalistic niceties, however, made much difference to the realities of foreign control.

A fundamentally different pattern of imperial domination developed only in Egypt and in the Arab countries of the Fertile Crescent. In these countries, imperial hegemony was established at a time when many Europeans had already developed a sensitive conscience about Europe's earlier colonial expansion and when the Near Eastern political *élite* had already been converted to such Western political ideals as liberalism, constitutionalism and nationalism. The British government announced its occupation of Egypt in 1882 as a temporary measure to protect the interests of the foreign bondholders; in 1887 it signed an agreement with the Ottoman empire promising evacuation within three years or as soon as the war in the Sudan should be terminated. In the Fertile Crescent foreign rule was established after Britain, in its wartime nego-

[1] Lord Cromer, *Modern Egypt* (London, 1916), ii, 115.

tiation with the *Sharīf* Ḥusayn, had encouraged aspirations for an independent and united Arab kingdom, and after Woodrow Wilson, in the twelfth of his Fourteen Points, had promised the non-Turkish nationalities of the Ottoman empire 'an absolutely unmolested opportunity of autonomous development'. Syria-Lebanon, Iraq and Palestine (including what later became known as Transjordan) all were made into so-called class 'A' mandates, and with regard to the first two it was specifically provided that organic laws should be framed within three years and that the mandatory power should facilitate 'their progressive development... as independent states'.

The ideas of self-determination and representative government, which Wilsonian propaganda so emphatically reiterated had found wide acceptance among Near Eastern leaders. Constitutional charters were proclaimed in Tunis, Roumania and Egypt in the 1860s. Midḥat Pasha, 'Urābī and the Persian revolutionaries of 1905–6 all had championed time-tested Western devices of representative and responsible government in an effort to restrain the financial extravagance of rulers and their consequent subservience to foreign powers. In the early twentieth century, and especially after the Balkan Wars, nationalist ideas had taken root among Turks and Arabs. When Near Eastern spokesmen after the First World War rejected foreign domination, they rejected it with liberal arguments of universal currency in the West. Other Near Easterners, nevertheless, were inclined to take at face value the statements of early advocates of the mandate system who made it sound very much like what today we call economic and technical assistance. For example, the mayor, *qāḍī*, *muftī* and other notables of Damascus on 26 May 1919, informed an American commission of inquiry headed by Messrs King and Crane that they preferred 'complete independence' in principle but that 'for financial and economic reasons, a mandate was... desirable', and that they therefore 'urged that the United States take the mandate'. On that same day Damad Ferīd Pasha, the anglophile grand *vezīr*, upbraided a speaker in the sultan's Council in Istanbul for confusing the terms 'American mandate' and 'American protectorate', allowing only the first to be discussed as a way out of the defeated empire's predicament. And a few months later, Muṣṭafā Kemāl himself, at the Turkish nationalist congress of Sivas, had to tax his ingenuity to forestall any pronouncement in favour of an American mandate.[1]

[1] Harry N. Howard, *The King-Crane Commission* (Beirut, 1963), 108; M. Tayyib Gökbilgin, *Millî mücadele başlarken*, i (Istanbul, 1959), 107; [Kemal Atatürk,] *A Speech Delivered by Ghazi Mustapha Kemal* (Leipzig, 1929), 100.

In practice the mandates were imposed by traditional techniques of military conquest, just as the 'temporary' British occupation of Egypt lasted four decades, and in parts of the country until early 1956. The Turco-Russian War of 1877–8 and the Anglo-Russian convention of 1907, coming as they did in the wake of the Ottoman and Persian constitutions, indicated that the mere adoption of Western institutions was unlikely to ward off foreign interference and military defeat. In Egypt and in Syria that same lesson was reinforced by actual occupation. In Syria, the confrontation of nationalism and colonialism was particularly dramatic: French troops occupied the hills around Damascus, and even before the expiry of a perfunctory ultimatum began shelling the city, where a nationalist assembly had proclaimed the *Sharīf* Ḥusayn's son, Fayṣal, king of Syria. In the following years, the French aggravated Arab resentment by a cynical divide-and-rule policy designed to play the Lebanese Christians, the coastal 'Alawīs and the Druzes in the mountains against the Sunnī Arab majority. In Palestine, the British outraged Arab sensibilities by including in the terms of the mandate Balfour's promise of support for 'the establishment in Palestine of a national home for the Jewish people'. In contrast to most other colonial areas, foreign rule in Palestine was to be accompanied by foreign colonization.

In view of these realities, Western pronouncements on self-determination and democracy, on temporary occupation and on the educational theory of the mandate inevitably came to have a hollow, insincere ring in Near Eastern ears. Western liberalism and constitutionalism clearly were not intended for export. 'Temporary' occupation in Egypt and mandates in the Fertile Crescent turned out to be colonial rule under another name—nothing, in fact, but colonialism with a bad conscience. For several decades after 1882 and 1920, Arab resentment and European bad conscience reinforced each other. The admittedly temporary nature of the foreign régime prevented both rulers and subjects from fully and frankly adjusting to it; hence both sides came to rely on force in dealings with each other. A perceptive observer has suggested that the British might more quickly have terminated an Egyptian occupation intended as permanent than one that was proclaimed as 'temporary' from the start.[1] In India, in more than two centuries of British rule, an indigenous class of civil servants and military officers had grown up, who effectively supported the

[1] John Marlowe, *Anglo-Egyptian Relations 1800–1953* (London, 1954), 253.

imperial system. In the Arab countries it proved far more difficult for the British and French to enlist local co-operation.

Just as Western rule had been imposed by force on Egypt and the Fertile Crescent, so it was attenuated, and at length withdrawn, in response to the threat or application of superior force. When Ottoman Turkey entered the First World War, the British were fearful of the response that pan-Islamic propaganda and the Turkish call for a *jihād* might find in Egypt. To sever Egypt's legal connexion with an enemy ruler, they converted their 'temporary occupation' into a 'protectorate', but coupled this change with a promise of full independence after the war. The Egyptian nationalist uprising of 1919 brought to the scene the Milner commission, which recommended direct dealings with Sa'd Zaghlūl (who had previously been exiled) and his Wafd party. Because of continuing disagreements over future relations between the two countries, Britain in 1922 issued a unilateral statement in which she declared Egypt independent in name, but reserved such far-reaching powers in foreign and military affairs as to deny the substance of independence. Only when Italian expansion confronted British and Egyptians with a common threat was a mutually agreed formula worked out in the treaty of 1936. In 1921 when the Hashimites assembled troops to invade Syria, the British diverted their ambitions by making Fayṣal king of Iraq, and 'Abd Allāh *amīr* of Transjordan—i.e., the eastern part of Palestine which they henceforth exempted from the provisions of the Balfour Declaration. A widespread Arab uprising in Palestine in 1937 prompted them to impose sharp limitations on Jewish immigration. Needless to say, each such concession tended to whet Arab nationalist appetites even further.

Allied policy in the Fertile Crescent in the Second World War repeated the political tactics that Britain had applied in Egypt in the First. Each tightening of control was accompanied by promises of more generous post-war treatment. Thus, the British in 1941 with some difficulty suppressed a pro-Axis *coup* in Iraq, and, together with the Free French, occupied the Levant states; at the same time, however, they issued a solemn promise of post-war independence for Syria and Lebanon and publicly offered 'support to any scheme [of Arab unity] that commands general approval'.[1] Britain's withdrawals from Palestine in 1948, and

[1] The statements were contained in the De Gaulle-Lyttleton Agreement of 7 August 1941, and Anthony Eden's speech at Mansion House the preceding 29 May; see J. C. Hurewitz, *Diplomacy in the Near and Middle East* (Princeton, 1956), ii, 231, 236.

from Suez in 1954, were prompted not only by the changed strategic situation after the loss of India and by American and other foreign pressures, but also by prolonged guerrilla warfare in both countries. Only in Iraq and in Jordan did the British succeed in establishing a friendlier pattern of co-operation with local political forces; hence by a series of treaties (with Iraq in 1930 and 1955, and with Jordan in 1946) the mandate status was converted into a more bilateral relationship. The price of such co-operation, however, was the increasing discredit of the anglophile ruling groups among the vocally nationalist segments of their own population. In Jordan, King Ḥusayn has since 1955 been able to ride out the storm. In Iraq the old order was restored through British intervention in 1941, but in the 1958 revolution it totally collapsed.

Since the end of the Second World War, the Muslim countries have fully participated in the world-wide transition from colonialism to sovereignty. At the end of the First World War, there were only six independent Muslim states (Albania, Turkey, Persia, Afghanistan, Yemen and Saʿudi Arabia—the latter formed in 1925 through the annexation of the Ḥijāz to Najd). In the inter-war period, Egypt (1922) and Iraq (1932) were recognized as independent, although their sovereignty remained in fact rather restricted until the 1950s. In the last two decades, as many as twenty states with an exclusively or largely Muslim population have been formed in formerly colonial or dependent territories. The only durable legacy of European colonialism in the Muslim region, on the other hand, is Russian rule over Āẕarbāyjān and Central Asia.

Two centuries or more have passed since the modern Western impact on the peoples of Islam first reverberated through the battle-fields of Hungary, of the Crimea and of Bengal. In that time, both Muslims and Westerners have undergone a profound transformation. Among Muslims, some were able to resist Western aggression by borrowing from the West's arsenal of artillery, of administration, of political concepts and of social ideals. Others succumbed, and had many of the same Western devices and principles more directly imposed upon them. But the distinction between defensive modernizers and colonial subjects has now disappeared: the heirs of both are engaged in propelling the modern revolution into the remote recesses of the House of Islam. Just as Muslims have won national independence, so the Westerners have lost their monopoly of power. Modern technology and modern organization which were first developed in Europe, now are shared with its descendants and disciples in North America, Russia, Japan and China, and they are ardently desired and emulated by its former subjects in Asia and Africa. Perhaps for the first time since the seventh century A.D. the historical ground thus has been cleared for a new relationship between the West and Islam—one based not on hostility or domination but on equality and co-operation. But the resentments of the past are slow to abate and emulation of Western technology and organization easily leads to new frustrations. Whether and when such a more equal relationship will grow up and what forms it will take is in the hands of future generations.

CHAPTER 7

ECONOMIC AND SOCIAL CHANGE

In the second and third quarters of the twentieth century the Muslim countries of the Middle East and North Africa began the process of breaking up an economic and social pattern that had been established, in most of them, a century earlier by a combination of European influences and native responses. The continuous display of European power from the end of the eighteenth century aroused the Muslim world to an appreciation of modern science, technology, and social and political organization. It aroused it also to self-defence through emulation of European society in order to acquire the means to overcome foreign control, or through regeneration of the traditional system of life and thought in order to withstand the intrusions. In the course of these varied responses, sometimes alternating and sometimes simultaneous, new leaders of Muslim peoples have sprung up since the early nineteenth century, changing the basis of political power and introducing reforms in the conduct of government and then in economic and social affairs. Further unplanned changes have taken place in consequence of these imposed ones.

During the nineteenth century, Europe penetrated the Muslim countries in several ways. A combination of military and political power led to varying degrees of European influence in North Africa, Egypt and the eastern portion of the Ottoman empire, ranging from outright occupation to certain preferential arrangements. Indigenous political leaders, however, still retained some power both to resist militarily and to introduce social, economic and political measures to reform their domains. They sent hundreds of students to be educated in Europe. They tried to modernize their armed forces. Meanwhile, European governments supported their nationals in economically penetrating the Muslim countries through banking, public utilities, transport and manufacturing. In several regions of the Ottoman empire the old pattern of the state's or rulers' monopoly of land ownership was ended by the creation of a landed class (with large holdings) of private individuals and families closely connected with those in political power.

It is this socio-economic and political pattern which the twentieth century has broken. European political influence in Turkey, for example, was receding in the early twentieth century, even while Europe was still to gain influence in the Fertile Crescent under the League of Nations mandates after the First World War. But in the second quarter of this century this influence too began to wane until, in the fifteen years following the Second World War, the Muslim countries achieved political independence. At first they retained the Western political structure of parliaments, parties and elections; a few years later these were abandoned in several countries. By the 1960s the Muslim world of western Asia and North Africa was largely divided between military republics and traditional monarchies, each striving to modernize in economic and social life. Such efforts have included the expansion of education at all levels and the sending of thousands of students to Europe and North America, the adoption of measures to industrialize at a faster pace, the enactment of welfare legislation, and land reform.

The state has played a leading role in these efforts, varying from encouragement of private enterprise in Turkey and Morocco, for example, to expropriation of private industry in Egypt and Algeria. Two processes have broken the economic basis of the power of foreign governments and individuals as well as of the native landed class. First, nationalization of two sorts has taken place: the transfer of capital from European governments and private individuals to native persons, and the transfer of private local capital (first that of the minorities, then of native Muslims as well) to the state. Second, in some countries more than others, large agricultural estates have been expropriated by government and sold, on easy terms, in small plots, to peasants who previously owned little or no land. Thus the pattern of economic and social power, created in the nineteenth century in both the cities and the countryside, has been broken—completely in Egypt and Algeria, considerably in Turkey, Tunisia, Iraq, Syria and Persia, and only incipiently in Morocco, Jordan, Afghanistan, Sa'udi Arabia and Libya.

The political power thus lost by foreign governments and individuals and by the native upper classes has gone to the state. At the same time, social changes have occurred which bring into question many traditional authorities, including the state. The development of secular education and the growth in the media of communication have loosened but not eliminated the control of the individual formerly exerted by religion, family and locale. Thus far, however, in most of the Muslim countries the state has been able to retain its control through force and indoctrination. All rulers face the problem of how to release the energies of the people for social and economic advance without weakening all authority. The military and civilian autocracies face the additional problem of how to release such energies without creating demands for democracy; that is, how to free individuals from 'reactionary' authority without freeing them also from the state itself.

ECONOMIC CHANGE

Even before Europe began to penetrate the Muslim world directly in the modern period, the products of Europe's developing manufactures had already, by the fifteenth and sixteenth centuries, begun to appear in the Middle East, and by the nineteenth century had become a major economic issue. Cheap textiles, especially, adversely affected native industry and crafts. Penetration became more direct when Europeans later made loans to Middle Eastern rulers and governments. In the latter part of the century European capital gained concessions for the provision of public utility services, the establishment of transport and communications systems and then some mining and manufacturing. Most of these undertakings enjoyed monopolistic privileges and hence dependable yields on capital. A half-century or more later this sequence was approximately repeated in much of North Africa.

The reaction to Europe's power and example was not long in coming, first in the centre of the Ottoman empire, and then in its outpost in Egypt. In the late eighteenth century, Selīm III introduced reforms to strengthen the empire against European incursions. Sultan Maḥmūd II ruled the Ottomans from 1808 to 1839, while in Egypt Muḥammad 'Alī Pasha won autonomy for that Ottoman territory and ruled from 1805 to 1848. Both autocrats destroyed old institutions, customs and safeguards as they forced reforms in military organization, education and administration. Muḥammad 'Alī, though nominally a subject of the sultan, was the innovator in these fields as well as in economic and social change. He established large monopolistic industrial enterprises of which he made himself the sole owner. He further weakened the guilds of masters and journeymen, as he did all independent agencies standing between himself and the masses of his subjects. In commerce he either held monopolies himself, or he gave foreign merchants certain privileges in return for their favours. His agrarian policy was to expropriate the land held by the former rulers, the Mamluks, to make it state land, and to redistribute it to the members of his own family, high officials whom he controlled, and later to peasants. He developed cotton as a commodity for export and made Egypt a one-crop economy dependent upon the world market. With the help of foreign technicians, he also developed irrigation and transport.

After the deaths of Maḥmūd II and Muḥammad ʿAlī, this impulse to modernization continued in Istanbul but flagged in Cairo. Ottoman involvement with Europe led to considerable indebtedness (especially in the effort to finance the Ottoman part in the Crimean War), and then to European financial control in the last quarter of the nineteenth century. In 1875 the Ottoman government defaulted on its foreign debt of 200 million pounds sterling. An Administration of the Public Debt was created in 1881 to safeguard the investments of thousands of European bondholders. Nominally part of the Ottoman government, the Administration was largely independent of the Finance Ministry, many of whose functions it pre-empted. It collected revenues, which it used to redeem the debt. Controlling the country's finances, the Administration was able to encourage even more European investment in Turkey. Meanwhile, Egypt was going through a similar process. In 1876 the ruler could no longer meet payments on the rising debt, then nearly 100 million pounds sterling. A *Caisse de la Dette publique* was immediately created to represent the European creditors; soon after, an Englishman was appointed to supervise the collection of revenue and a Frenchman to supervise expenditure. A European Commission of Inquiry into the country's financial condition, appointed in 1878, prepared the next year's budget. In the same year the Europeans found the 'dual control' inadequate and placed two Europeans in the Egyptian cabinet, an Englishman as minister of Finance and a Frenchman as minister of Public Works. Thus Europeans controlled revenue and expenditure while the Commission arranged for the payments to Egypt's creditors; the Commission's consent was required for new loans. In Persia, British-Russian rivalry became intense in the early nineteenth century as Britain sought to promote its commercial interests there and to protect its route to India while Russia sought territorial and financial advantage over this weak neighbour. In the last quarter of the century the familiar process of concessions and loans gave the two European powers considerable influence, which increased down to the Second World War.

Further penetration of the Middle East by European capital followed during a period of relative stability. Egyptians, Syrians and Turks gained some familiarity with Western industry, commerce and finance, although throughout the region Europeans and native Christians dominated the modern urban economy, while the land was tilled and owned mostly by native Muslims. This pattern prevailed in Turkey (and in Persia to some extent) until just after the First World War, in the Arab East until the Second World War, and in North Africa until the late 1950s, when these countries were able to control their own political and economic policy and organization.

Acting upon a century of reform recently accelerated under the régime of the Young Turks, Turkey used the First World War as an opportunity to advance its economic independence of the European powers and to promote the interests of Turks as against those of non-Muslim Levantines—Greeks, Armenians and Jews. The government ended the privileges of foreigners, and required companies enjoying concessions to keep their records in the Turkish language. Such policies opened employment opportunities to Muslim Turks. At the same time, the government called in many foreign high-level advisers, whose functions did not reduce opportunities for Turks, but were intended to increase them by increasing economic activity and efficiency. These foreign technicians now came from Germany and Austria, for Turkey was fighting against Britain and France. Finally, the government in 1915 widened a law of 1909 for the encouragement of industry, offering to native capital free land, tax-exemption for a time and freedom from certain import and export duties. It also required factories to employ only Turkish citizens, except in technical posts requiring skills that could be found only abroad. These measures were designed rapidly to change the character of both capital and labour, and hence of political and social power as well. In 1915, for example, an official inquiry revealed that Greeks and Armenians supplied seventy per cent of the capital and seventy-five per cent of the labour in the nearly three hundred factories (half in Istanbul) then accounting for most of the modern manufacturing sector.

The wartime measures were followed by the defeat of Turkey and the humiliating treaty of Sèvres in 1920. The Kemalist revolution began around the same time, sweeping away first the discredited Ottoman rulers and then the foreigners, and giving Turks, with the treaty of Lausanne in 1923, almost full control over their land. This political mastery was the basis of a resurgence of economic and social change, under Atatürk, designed to make Turkey a modern, secular, industrial country.

A similar but less extensive process of political reorganization took place a few years later in Persia under Rižā Khān, a military officer who overthrew the government in 1921 and four years later became shah. He, too, strengthened the army and tried to unify the country, stabilize its finances, introduce modern industry and social patterns, and reduce the economic influence of foreigners. The Second World War, however, brought back foreign control, as the British and Russians invaded the country to prevent the spread of German power under Hitler and to supply Russia from the south. It was not until the evacuation of all foreign troops after the war, and the government's assumption of control over oil resources, that Persia regained that full sovereignty in political and economic affairs which has enabled it to proceed with a policy of economic and social modernization.

In the former Arab provinces of the Ottoman empire—Syria, Lebanon, Iraq and Palestine—French and British influence was firmly established after the First World War, and continued by means of the League of Nations mandates and then preferential treaties and military occupation down to the Second World War. During that war they, along with Egypt, lacked the autonomy that had enabled Turkey to reduce foreign influence. Indeed, foreign control in the Arab lands (as in Persia) increased because of the Allied strategic interest in denying the area to the Germans. There was much ideological hostility to Britain and France, as well as doubt that Germany could be stopped; there was consequently considerable sentiment, especially in Egypt, for using the Allied troubles as an occasion to push for greater independence. In order to keep the area supplied and to reduce civilian hardship, which might create a favourable atmosphere for resistance if not outright rebellion, the British in 1941 established the Middle East Supply Centre. The Americans joined this economic-military venture the following year.

Each government in the area regularly sent to Centre headquarters in Cairo a list of its civilian needs. These were supplied on a much lower scale than in peacetime, and rationed according to shipping space available. Attempts were also made to increase agricultural productivity in the area, but little was done to develop local industry. The main purpose of the Allies was to keep the area supplied with the greatest economy of resources and effort; hence the authorities relied mainly upon private traders, with the result that the Middle Eastern governments and merchants made very large profits. These gains were not appropriately taxed because governments hesitated to use force to collect taxes from profiteers on a trade that was so vital to stability, and the governmental machinery in the area was incapable of that task anyway. The long-range economic effects were thus not beneficial and even the experience of regional planning was limited in value because it was tied so closely to war needs ultimately determined and executed from abroad; in any case, the co-operation did not long survive the war which had fostered it in the first place. The Centre's policy of restricting imports of finished products did, however, lead to some expansion of domestic industry.

We have just reviewed the growth of national independence in economic policy in different parts of the Middle East. Another very important process was going on during roughly the same period between the mid-nineteenth century and the two World Wars. This was the introduction of modern transport and communications, which are so necessary to modern agriculture and industry and which have also had important effects upon social life.

Modern transport and communications were often developed in the Middle East as a result of military and political considerations, and the needs of foreign powers, rather than out of purely local commercial requirements. Ports and fleets were constructed in the nineteenth century with foreign capital to accommodate increasing trade, and were gradually expanded and then nationalized following the two World Wars. The most important and fateful project was the building of the Suez Canal mainly with French and British capital. Opened in 1869, the Canal was the culmination of one era of European commercial expansion and heralded another in Africa and the Far East. Very soon it became highly profitable for its European owners as well as for the Egyptian government; even ordinary Egyptians received some benefit in the form of wages and through the money spent by European employees of the Canal. Egyptians regarded the Canal, nevertheless, as a political liability to themselves. In the midst of a political crisis the Egyptian government nationalized the Canal in 1956 and assumed full ownership, control and operation.

The first railways were constructed in the 1850s in Turkey and Egypt. In other countries the lines came only much later and after the introduction of motor and air transport, which reduced the need for rail facilities. Iraq's state railway system developed during the First World War. A railway across Persia was completed only in 1938. Jordan, Lebanon and Syria have few lines, though the one between Beirut and Damascus was constructed in the early 1890s. Egyptian railways steadily expanded in the nineteenth century and then around the Second World War, after which they were nationalized. In Turkey railways have been more highly developed than in Egypt and were also nationalized earlier, largely in the 1930s. Roads for motor transport are inadequate throughout the Middle East. Egypt and Turkey have the greatest mileage; Turkey's mileage exceeds Egypt's, but the latter's system has more first-class roads. Most countries in the region have extensive plans for building highways, but these have not been carried out rapidly enough to meet the needs of the more easily increased numbers of cars, trucks and buses. Foreign needs and activity have been especially important in road building: French in Syria and Lebanon, American in Turkey, and British, American and Russian in Persia.

Air transport was introduced in the Middle East just after the First World War, not long after its development in the West. A French-Roumanian concession established a short-lived service in Turkey in 1922, and four years later a state-supported line was inaugurated. Egypt's main airline was begun in 1933. Both these lines, as well as those of other Middle Eastern countries, have had close financial and operational ties with various Western lines. Gradually the Middle Eastern governments have fully nationalized and extended their airlines, but some still retain their connexions with Western companies.

Turkey was the first Middle Eastern country to have a telegraph service; it was introduced by the British and French in 1855, at the time of the Crimean War. In two decades or so the service reached virtually the whole of the Ottoman empire, and there were links to Europe as well. Egypt was quick to follow, and had an extensive system well before the end of the nineteenth century. A few years before the First World War a telephone service was introduced into Turkey, at first for government use only and then for private subscribers; even today, despite a great increase in use, service throughout the area is not widespread or efficient. The Turks were the first to nationalize the telegraph, by making it a state enterprise, and by making communication in Turkish possible.

Though there were a few official gazettes that functioned as newspapers in the early nineteenth century, it was only in the period 1860–80, after the introduction of telegraphic communication, that modern independent newspapers came into existence in the Middle East. The Crimean War had occasioned a desire for news both in Europe and the Middle East; telegraphy made it possible to satisfy this desire more rapidly. As newspapers became more than official gazettes, new problems arose. The unofficial press being an innovation, Ottoman rulers did not look with favour upon it in the Arab provinces. Egypt, not subject to control from Istanbul, became the refuge for enterprising, talented Arab publishers and journalists from Syria and Lebanon. In recent years the number of readers has greatly increased, but the proliferation of papers has kept the circulation of most rather low. After having gone through a long period of relative freedom of the press since the turn of the century or since the First World War, newspapers have again become, in many countries of the Middle East, little more than the government organs they were in the early nineteenth century. The difference is that the press was then largely an organ of official information, while it has now tended to become largely an organ of official propaganda.

Radio and cinema are communications media usually associated primarily with entertainment, but in the Middle East they have been operated and closely supervised by government. Introduced in the 1930s, radio has reached very large audiences only since the Second World War. Television was introduced in Egypt in 1960, and then in other countries. The importance of radio is obvious in a region with very high rates of illiteracy. It was used extensively in the propaganda war between the Allies and the Axis powers before and during the Second World War. With the cheap production of transistor sets since then, radio coverage is growing rapidly and may soon approach, at least in some countries, that of Europe. Radio transmission is extensive, and several governments take full political advantage of its appeal to the masses. As nationalism and political disputes have grown, régimes have increasingly resorted to radio as means of consolidating public opinion in their own domains and of turning it against the rulers elsewhere. The cinema has been devoted primarily to entertainment, but governments have exercised close control over it out of moral and political considerations. Most films shown to the increasing audiences are American and European. Only Egypt produces films locally in any volume.

In recent years the time-lapse between a technological innovation in the West and its introduction in the Middle East has declined. Sa'udi Arabia, for example, just being carried into the modern age by its oil economy, has telescoped the development of its media of transport and communication into a very brief space of time. When in 1945 King 'Abd al-'Azīz accepted President Roosevelt's gift of an aeroplane, he had to persuade the jurists that it was not prohibited by Muslim law. In a few years, several airports and dozens of planes were serving a number of inland and port cities. Meanwhile, in 1948, work began on the first railroad (not counting the defunct Ḥijāz Railway from Medina to the north, constructed by the Ottomans before the First World War); in 1951 the 300-odd-mile line between Dammām and Riyāḍ was opened. Around the same time modern roads were constructed between the leading cities. In 1952 a Ministry of Communications was created, which improved postal service and expanded telegraphic and telephone service. Television followed soon afterward. These projects were financed through royalties from the activity of the Arabian American Oil Company and with the company's technological aid.

On the basis of this modernization of transport and communications, achieved with varying degrees of foreign participation, the more or less independent countries of the Middle East tried to build up modern industry after the First World War. They regarded industrialization as the key to a rising standard of living and to national power, and so one country after another enacted laws for the encouragement of industry which offered tax exemptions and other advantages to native capital. Such measures were necessary precisely because conditions were not conducive to the growth of industry. Entrepreneurship, private or public, was not geared to manufacturing. Raw materials, as well as engineering and administrative skills, were lacking. Literacy was limited. Political life did not induce confidence in the future. The prevailing atmosphere thus combined with tradition to perpetuate the investment of capital in land, trade, and in substantial manufacturing ventures that were highly protected.

With the laws to encourage industry went, in some cases, the creation of special financial instruments. As early as 1917 Turkey founded the National Credit Bank, in which both administration and stock-holding were limited to Turkish nationals, in order to finance private and public enterprises. Though much was made of the few companies established with its aid, this effort was not successful. During the Atatürk revolution and as part of its policy of etatism, Turkey established the Sümerbank to help to finance industry, and the Etibank to help in mining and energy projects. In 1920 a private Egyptian bank was formed, the Misr Bank, which played a very important role in the growth of industry. By the time it was nationalized in 1960, the Misr group, already quasi-public in character, included large and flourishing enterprises in textiles, chemicals, mining, transport and insurance.

Under these influences, foreign and domestic, modern industry has advanced, as has modern agriculture to a lesser degree. In the 1920s, Turkey's contribution to world industrial production rose. In the half-decade after the Second World War its rate of economic growth was considerable, and it then declined towards the late 1950s. Industrial output increased greatly in Egypt in the 1930s, partly as a result of the application of the first protective tariff. Previously, international agreements had prohibited Egypt from imposing such tariffs. Output was expanded during and after the Second World War, mainly in already familiar lines such as textiles, cement, foods, leather and certain chemicals. Some new products were added, and an additional impetus to output came with the new régime's great emphasis upon modern industry after 1952. In most other countries, however, modern industry began on a very small scale only around the Second World War. It must be remembered, moreover, that large percentage increases are misleading because the base is so small that even a little growth yields large relative gains.

A significant and persistent feature of industry (as of all economic activity) in the Middle East is the intimate role of the state. Recent accelerated movements toward state ownership are thus not contrary to local tradition, though the extent of such trends in Egypt in the early 1960s is rather extreme even for the Middle East. State monopolies of the manufacture of tobacco, matches and alcohol, for example, are found in many countries, while in others the state owns additional enterprises not regarded in other regions as especially connected with the public interest. Private enterprise, however, did play an important role. In Egypt, for example, the first modern entrepreneurs were foreigners, foreign residents, or members of minority groups, who invested in public utilities, transport and factories to process raw materials. Before the end of the nineteenth century, native Egyptians were participating in such ventures and in banking and trade. Just before and after the First World War, the number of Egyptian entrepreneurs and investors increased considerably, turning to industry from land-ownership, politics and government service. Through all these periods, these private interests enjoyed government protection in the form of monopoly rights, tariff walls, a free hand regarding labour, and those myriad benefits of doubtful legality that accrue from the close connexion between wealth and political power. The joint-stock company in such circumstances was a more widespread and influential form of enterprise than Egypt's level of economic development would have suggested.

During the 1930s, under the impact of the world-wide depression and following the example of the U.S.S.R., Turkey adopted the policy of etatism, state direction of the economy, in order to achieve prosperity in a short time. Economists severely criticized Turkish governmental economic planning and activity, yet some impetus was given to industry by this deliberate effort. By the 1950s the share of the public sector in capital formation had fallen to, and was stabilized at, about a quarter of the total. In Egypt, meanwhile, a similar non-doctrinaire approach to economic development was adopted. The share of the public sector in capital formation rose from about a fifth to two-fifths between 1950 and 1952, even before the military revolution. After it, the public sector's share continued to grow, reaching a half in 1954 and three-fifths in 1956.

In the early 1960s, Egypt went further in the direction of state ownership and control, aiming not only to alter its own economy and society, but expecting to influence other Arab régimes to move in the same direction. As Egypt's rulers turned toward the U.S.S.R. for military and economic aid, they adopted a policy of non-alignment in international relations and socialism in domestic economy. The Suez War of 1956 and the Congo crisis of 1960 were the occasions for the sequestration of considerable assets owned by foreigners and members of certain minority groups. In 1961 came measures which affected Egyptian Muslim owners of wealth too, placing most of the economy, including trade, in the hands of the government. Private enterprise was, nevertheless, given a nominal place in the new scheme of things. Under the influence of moves towards increasing economic competition in Marxist Yugoslavia, the Egyptian theoreticians of Arab Socialism spoke of the opportunities and responsibilities of 'non-exploiting national capital' to contribute to total production and to provide healthy competition for the public sector. Little scope, however, was left to 'national capital', except in small-scale agriculture. Turkey, meanwhile, having already gone through such a period of distrust of private capital, national or foreign, was in the 1950s reverting to the encouragement of the private sector through state action.

Suspicion of the role of private capital in the Middle East has been the result of its privileged position in domestic life, and of its traditional close connexion with foreign governments, foreigners, resident foreigners and minorities. Middle Eastern governments under native

Muslim control have feared that encouragement of private enterprise would only mean the perpetuation of the economic power of foreigners and non-Muslims, who traditionally controlled banking, trade and manufacture. The new régimes, beginning with Atatürk in the 1920s in Turkey, and continuing with Nasser (Jamāl 'Abd al-Nāṣir) in the 1950s in Egypt and with new leaders in Algeria, Syria, and Iraq in the 1960s, have stressed state control and ownership. Turkey has emerged from this position as foreign economic influences have receded, and it may be that other Middle Eastern states will follow a similar path. Etatism in Turkey helped produce not only managers of public enterprises but also private entrepreneurs and managers, who, when politics became freer in the late 1940s, joined other classes in opposing the continuation of state action on the same scale. Arab Socialism, however, does not seem to be moving in this direction.

Beginning with Turkey in the 1930s, almost all Middle Eastern countries have been attracted to economic and social planning. Turkey, Egypt and Persia have had the best-trained staffs in the region, but even their planning mechanisms have revealed serious weaknesses. In Turkey and Persia, to begin with, the planning goals and apparatus have become matters of political dispute, and this has reduced their effectiveness; in Egypt, the scope for political manoeuvring has been so narrow that the planners have not been able to exert enough independent influence to become a political issue. Elsewhere, political instability has deprived planning of even a minimum of continuity. In varying degrees throughout the area, moreover, planning has lacked three important features. First, the data on which plans must be based have been far from adequate in amount and reliability. Secondly, instruments for prediction of economic and social trends have not been developed. Thirdly, there has not been enough persistence and ingenuity in the execution of plans; too often the plan itself has satisfied the desire for planning. Some lessons have nevertheless been learned. It is increasingly understood that planners must be given enough freedom to be imaginative and creative (though this degree of freedom is not yet granted), that planning calls not for the haphazard erection of factories unrelated to needs, but for the establishment of a firm basis for industrial growth in a more efficient agriculture, a healthy and educated population, and adequate transport, communication and energy sources.

The general goal of planning has been to create and direct the flow of capital necessary for economic growth. Lack of capital thus remains one of the greatest limitations upon the economic ambitions of the Muslim countries. At the same time, the continuing need for foreign capital remains a limitation upon their chief political goal, that is, complete independence. The import of foreign capital, in whatever form and from whatever source, has meant the exercise of foreign influence as well. While most Middle Eastern countries fear this influence, they still want the capital. In its National Charter of 1962 Egypt, for example, expressed the view that former colonialist powers have a sort of duty to assist the countries from which they formerly withdrew wealth. Such assistance, it was added, could take three forms, in order of decreasing desirability from the receiving country's point of view: unconditional grants, unconditional loans on easy terms, and investments where unavoidable. During the 1950s the Middle East sought all three forms of aid, including foreign investments permitting the withdrawal of profits; indeed, Afghanistan, Egypt, Persia, Iraq, Jordan, Lebanon, the Sudan, Syria and Turkey all enacted laws to encourage the investment of foreign capital, though other actions such as nationalization had the opposite effect.

Since the Second World War several billions of dollars of grants and loans have gone to the region from a variety of sources, but largely from the U.S.A. and the U.S.S.R. The former gave aid mainly to Persia and Turkey and then to Egypt, while the latter, starting later, gave aid chiefly to Afghanistan, Egypt, Syria and Iraq. The oil-producing countries of the Persian Gulf, meanwhile, received large amounts of Western private and public capital to develop their resources, which have yielded billions of dollars in profits to the investors, in tax revenues to their governments and in royalties to the local governments.

The extent of foreign aid to Turkey and Egypt is impressive. In the period 1948–62 Turkey received over eleven thousand million dollars of foreign exchange, which it used mainly to finance imports but also to repay debts. Though most of this amount came from the export of Turkish goods and sources, more than a third of it, over four thousand million dollars, came from various forms of bilateral and international grants and loans. In turn, nine-tenths of this amount came from the U.S.A. in the form of economic and military aid. From 1952 to 1962, Egypt received about one and three-quarter thousand million dollars of aid, virtually all of it from individual countries in the Western and Eastern blocs. The two largest donors were the U.S.A., which extended 700 million dollars, or forty per cent of the total, mostly in commodities since 1959, and the U.S.S.R., which since 1958 extended credits amounting to 500 million dollars, or twenty-eight per cent of the total. This aid enabled Egypt since 1956 to finance its imports of capital and consumer goods.

The emergence and expansion of the oil industry, through foreign capital and expertise, is probably the most significant economic process of this century in the Muslim world, though until now its effect upon economic development there has been limited. Not only has it tied more of the Middle East to the world economy, but it has also put the Middle East in the midst of high international politics, sometimes to the region's disadvantage. Western interest in Middle East oil began at the end of the nineteenth century, and the first rapid development of this resource took place in Persia around the First World War. An extraordinary expansion took place after the Second World War, especially in the Persian Gulf. The region's estimated reserves were a fifth of the world's total in the middle 1930s, while actual production was only about six per cent. By the early 1960s, reserves were estimated at three-fifths, while production had risen to a quarter of the world's total. Thus, owing to successful exploration, the vast increase in production has been accompanied by a vast increase in reserves. At the same time, Middle East oil has constituted a growing proportion of world trade in this commodity, reaching three-fifths by 1960. Most of this movement has been to Europe, which has relied upon the Middle East for about three-quarters of its oil. In the 1960s, North African oil became important in the world market and to that region. European and American companies have found large reserves in Algeria and Libya.

The first leading investors in and developers of this huge industry were European private interests and governments, and they were soon followed by American corporations. Gross investment reached a thousand million dollars just after the Second World War, and rapidly rose to over four thousand million dollars by 1960. Middle East oil has been profitable to foreign investors and local governments alike. The yield per well has been one to five hundred times that in the Americas, and cost per barrel has been only a tenth to a quarter of the cost in the West; prices to the buyers, however, have tended to be established more in accordance with the costs of the more dearly produced oil. The result has been that shareholders have received dividends constituting a much larger proportion of gross receipts of the companies than in other kinds of investment. To the countries in which oil has been discovered in great quantities by foreign explorers, the gains have been no less phenomenal. The leading producers (Baḥrayn, Persia, Iraq, Kuwayt, Qaṭar and Saʿudi Arabia) received over nine thousand million dollars from the oil companies in direct payments from 1948 to 1960. Thereafter these annual payments increased steadily, approaching two thousand million dollars by the mid-1960s. Several countries, moreover, themselves without substantial oil resources, receive large payments in return for the movement of oil through their waters or over their territory. For the producing countries, oil revenue makes up two-fifths to nine-tenths of their annual budgets, and provides over two-thirds of their foreign exchange. In the 1950s, a new relationship between the companies and the governments began, resulting from new sources of supply, changing demand, and a trend toward nationalization. The governments have come together in the Organization of Petroleum Exporting Countries to strengthen their position in seeking a larger proportion of the profits.

The oil-producing countries are a perfect case of a dual economy: a small highly modern sector in a broad hinterland of economic backwardness. Though the oil industry has created and transferred vast amounts of wealth, it has not had the penetrating economic impact that might be expected from enterprises of such magnitude. The industry has employed only about 100,000 persons, and this number has not been growing. In the smaller economies like Baḥrayn and Kuwayt, oil workers have made up a fifth or more of the total employed population and a very much larger proportion of those employed in industry. In Iraq and Persia, more populous, advanced and diversified, oil workers have been only one per cent of the total labour force and somewhat more or less than a tenth of all industrial workers. In recent years, native Middle Easterners have constituted an increasing proportion of the persons employed in the industry, reaching two-thirds by the early 1960s. Formerly confined to the low-paying posts requiring little skill, they have, with increasing education and training, occupied a small but growing proportion of the managerial and technical posts. Wages and other conditions of labour are in general superior to those in other industries, for the Western operating companies introduced their more favourable personnel policies, and the local governments found it easier to require or persuade foreign firms to maintain high standards than to impose enlightened policies upon native employers.

The small labour force relative to the economic importance of the oil industry indicates how difficult it has been for the Middle East to industrialize. All of the countries have found it possible to increase industrial production with varying amounts of foreign capital and technical aid, yet they have found it difficult to expand industry rapidly enough to absorb more than merely a proportionate amount of the annual increase in the labour force. Thus, for example, the index of industrial production in Egypt rose five per cent from 1952 to 1954, while the number of workers in industry rose not quite one per cent. This pattern of increasing industrial production with a stationary proportion of the labour force employed in industry has prevailed for a substantial period in the two most industrialized countries in the region. In Egypt this proportion was 8·2 per cent in 1927, varied little in the next two decades, and stood at 8·6 per cent in 1957. In Turkey the proportion was 9·2 per cent in 1935 and 9·5 per cent twenty years later. Meanwhile the number of industrial workers in each country nearly tripled during roughly the same period.

This enormous increase in the number of industrial workers has brought on the familiar three-cornered relation among labour, government and industry. Labour organization of a primitive sort appeared in the nascent modern industry of Egypt and Turkey just before and after the beginning of the twentieth century. Governments very early regarded trade unions as subversive or, what amounted to the same thing, bent upon sharing the power to determine conditions of life. It was therefore several decades before legislation was enacted to permit the formation of unions, or to require employers to improve working conditions. Such legislation came in most countries in the 1930s and 1940s, but it characteristically gave governments increasing power, which they have fully used to control the trade unions but not so fully to enforce factory laws and minimum wages.

By the 1960s there were perhaps a million organized workers in the Muslim countries of the Middle East and North Africa. Such protection as the workers have had, nevertheless, has come largely from legislation. The unions suffer from lack of professional leadership, official suspicion or solicitude, and mass indifference or ignorance. Low wages, poor health and a steadily rising cost of living have kept down initiative and energy. Low productivity has in turn been a factor in keeping wages low. Labour unrest, in these circumstances, has not been manifested in strikes, for they are prohibited almost everywhere and in any case presuppose a higher form of labour organization than exists. Instead, unrest takes the form of an individual response to dissatisfaction: inefficiency, absenteeism, rapid turnover and habitual complaining to conciliation boards where they exist. Personnel policies of management hardly recognize the benefits and incentives known in more industrial societies, such as bonuses, pensions, rest periods, sanitation and congenial working conditions. Increasingly, these are required by law, and are found in the larger factories, yet most managers in both public and private enterprises seem to assume that such non-monetary considerations are not important to workers. They may indeed be right; to workers not yet inured to industrial life and labour such benefits are remote and uncertain compared with the immediate advantage of wages in cash. Only the worker committed to this new mode of life through familiarity and the lack of alternatives is likely to regard fringe benefits as important.

As Middle Eastern governments assume increasing control over industry, their relation to labour changes. When large factories were owned by foreign capital, governments were willing to enact laws to protect native labour. Some countries, moreover, deliberately shifted to industry the responsibilities elsewhere assumed by public agencies. Thus Egypt has required large employers to provide various welfare services for their workers, including at one time even elementary education. Having satisfied (and created) such expectations, governments that have taken over much of private industry must retain an expensive welfare system. Their willingness to do so reflects their growing determination that industrialization shall be accomplished with the least possible social cost to the urban class least able to protect itself against exploitation.

This concern becomes all the more important in those countries where the massive effort to industrialize has called for attempts to prevent wages and consumption from rising too quickly. Throughout the area, then, labour is becoming more and more the object of official attention, and hence less and less able to develop independent strength in either economic or political affairs.

Another submerged class to which governments have given increasing attention is the peasantry. The exploitation and submergence of this class are proverbial. Changes in régime, new ideologies, westernization, and even alterations in land tenure, had left the peasants in their misery for centuries. In a society and economy which prized land highly, those without political influence or wealth could acquire very little of it. During the nineteenth century, the extent and value of cultivated land increased as several crops were in greater demand to supply food and raw material for both Middle Eastern and European factories. In the early part of the century, powerful rulers in Egypt and the Ottoman empire took title over vast amounts of land from private interests. Beginning around the middle of the century, rulers assigned the state lands to notables and officials. In some places these favoured classes were only agents for the collection of taxes, but they extended their rights until they were practically full and unrestricted owners. In other places, state land was given in virtual freehold to small and large holders who paid taxes directly to the state. In the late nineteenth century wealthy people in cities—merchants, bankers, manufacturers—began to acquire land, too, on a large scale. In Egypt this group included local and foreign Christians to a greater extent than elsewhere.

By the twentieth century this arrangement of large holdings in the hands of a few private owners (with vast economic power in the countryside and political power in the capital) was accepted as natural and eternal in most of the region. Changes in crops, seeds, fertilizers, tools and marketing were made as agriculture, too, responded to technological and economic change the world over. The expansion of the cultivated land and the increased use of machinery have considerably increased agricultural production. In the 1950s, for example, Egypt, Turkey, Iraq and Persia, which already employed thousands of tractors on the land, resorted to this source of power more than ever. Meanwhile, in Jordan, the Sudan and Syria, where tractors had been numbered only in hundreds, there were thousands by the early 1960s.

Social arrangements in the countryside have been more resistant to change. In the early 1950s, in country after country, two or three per cent of the landholders owned twenty to fifty per cent of the cultivated land. Meanwhile, at the other end of the scale, a large mass of smallholders owned a few acres each or, as in Persia, nearly everyone who worked the land was not even a smallholder but a tenant. In Egypt and Iraq, two-fifths of the owners held less than ten or twelve acres each; in Turkey the proportion was three-fifths, and in Lebanon nearly every owner held such small plots. In Syria there has been a more even distribution of land.

Turkey, the first Muslim country to establish its complete independence of foreign control after the First World War, was also the first to attempt land reform through redistribution in a manner that became widespread in the 1950s. Under Atatürk nearly two million acres were distributed to landless peasants. A law was passed in 1945 to speed up the process, and, after a slow start, nearly four million acres were distributed in a decade. Land reform was introduced in Iraq and Egypt in the 1940s, but it had little effect. It was not until the revolutionary régime took over in Egypt in 1952 that the Arab countries had a model of serious land reform, which has had considerable effect in Egypt, but less in Iraq and Syria. In 1951 in Persia the shah began the distribution of his private estates, and under the Land Reform Law of 1962 the government began to buy the lands of private owners above a certain maximum and to sell them to the occupying peasants. The limit set (which was later reduced) was one village.

Recent land reforms have three features. First, the government expropriates with compensation all land above a certain maximum holding, and sells small plots, on easy terms, to farmers with little or no land. Secondly, the government organizes the new owners, or encourages them to organize themselves, into co-operatives for loans, purchase of materials and implements, and for the marketing of their products. Finally, the government sometimes establishes safeguards for farm workers and landless tenants. Land reform in Egypt has had a greater impact than elsewhere. After a decade, nearly half a million acres had been transferred to about 163,000 families. Though this acreage was only eight per cent of the total amount cultivated and the number of families not quite eight per cent of all farm families, the land reform has had a political effect out of proportion to this apparently limited economic effect. It has destroyed the economic base of the old class of large landholders, whose political power over the peasants was therefore ended. At the same time, the power this class exercised in the capital was ended with the elimination of political parties and nationalization of urban enterprises. The elimination of this class has not, however, meant the commensurate growth in political and economic influence of the peasants. They have benefited somewhat economically, but the political power lost by the old landlord class has been appropriated by the government, thus reproducing the traditional alliance of soldiers and bureaucrats which prevailed before the creation of a class of powerful freeholders in the nineteenth century.

One serious problem that land reform has failed to solve is that of fragmentation, from which Egypt has suffered most. During the present century the number of farms under one acre in size and the total amount of land they have included have both doubled. Egypt and Turkey have taken hesitating steps to prevent fragmentation through inheritance, but thus far social custom and religious law have been strong enough to foil these efforts. The encouragement or enforcement of co-operatives is intended to prevent the evils of fragmentation; their success has likewise been limited in this respect.

What has been the result of a hundred years or more of economic change? The Middle East, taken as a whole and ignoring vast internal differences, has (with foreign aid) built up a modern system of communications and transport, achieved a modest beginning in industry, and has only begun to develop modern technology in agricultural production. The region has become part of the modern world economy but has thus far, in strictly economic terms, probably suffered from this relationship as much as it has benefited from it.

SOCIAL CHANGE

In selecting the social changes to emphasize in this section we shall be guided by the same principle which governed the choice of economic changes in the preceding one: to select the changes which both stemmed from and produced events and trends having a serious impact upon the lives of the peoples of the Middle East, and upon their relations with other peoples. We should mention, though we cannot discuss, the question of the relation between the economic and social changes. On this broad and complicated issue we can say here only that these two types of change are intertwined. An economic change like the growth of a transport system certainly affects a social change like the increase in migration. But the development of transport itself requires a certain social attitude and policy, and so is not purely an economic affair. Certain apparently social changes, moreover, like the position of minority groups, have a considerable effect upon the economy.

Another general question we can only touch upon is that of the relation between changes introduced by Western society and those that are more indigenous to the Middle East. Perhaps the greatest change of all has been acceptance by Muslims of the idea that change itself might be necessary or even good. This new idea has been the result of the Muslim world's realization that overwhelming Western scientific, technological and military power could be excluded, resisted or emulated only by societies somewhat similarly organized, and that, apart from matters of power, Western economic and political institutions offered the hope and means of progress along humanitarian lines as well.

The Western impact has not been uniform in its nature or effect throughout the Middle East. Some sections the West controlled directly, others it influenced from outside. Generally speaking, the direct impact of the West occurred through the introduction of, first, new economic institutions; manufacturing, trade, banking and agricultural methods; and, secondly, new means of public administration broadly conceived; civil and military service, police, public health and finance. Education was one of the few Western innovations which touched social life very directly. In response to these changes, native rulers and *élites* have, especially after achieving complete independence from Europe, introduced even more radical changes in economic and political life, and have gone further to affect social life directly by changing even religious and legal institutions. No foreign invader ever went so far as Atatürk or Nasser in seeking to impose direct and profound change. The shock and example of Bonaparte have been carried on by more determined and more effective native revolutionaries for over a century and a half. In this period the Muslim world has been transformed. It was a traditionalist, static, agricultural-pastoral society governed by an urban class of religious leaders, soldiers and bureaucrats. It is now a dynamic, nascent industrial-urban society still governed mainly by soldiers and bureaucrats, but one in which religious law no longer guides economic and political institutions.

The social changes which stimulate economic changes and are in turn stimulated by them have become familiar in recent centuries in Europe and then in other continents penetrated by Europeans. A new technology, based upon scientific thought, permits further division of labour determined by mechanical and other new forms of energy. The differentiation of occupations, for which increasing training and education are required, stimulates ambition, for new goals can be pursued with a reasonable hope of realizing them. People burst the old boundaries of birth and locale, moving to new employments, new kinds of social status, new places near or far from their origins. Formal education, awareness of the variety of human talents and social forms, and the production or importation of many new and attractive goods stimulate new tastes and desires. Family life changes, as parents no longer want their sons and daughters to follow the traditional ways, and as other institutions—schools, churches, governments—begin to share the family's task of rearing and training the young. The growth and distribution of population change with increased migration to cities and smaller families. As science and technology affect social values and people's outlook, religion becomes more an ethical imperative and a kind of social identity, less an explanation of the physical and social world. With increasing education, communication, and economic interdependence, political institutions become the concern of more social classes, whose positions and viewpoints must be considered by both despotic and democratic rulers. In varying degrees, these broad changes have begun to occur in the Muslim world too, and we shall now inquire into them in greater detail.

Muslim countries are in that stage of social change characterized by rapid population growth owing to a high and stationary birth rate coupled with a high but declining death rate. For a century or so, advances in public sanitation, and in both agricultural and industrial production, have made growth possible. In the Middle East and North Africa alone the population has probably doubled in this century, to stand in the mid-1960s at about 170 million persons. Since 1800, the population of what is now Turkey has increased about six times, and that of Egypt about nine times. The geographical distribution of this growing population has been changing. At present, density of settlement varies from less than one person per square kilometre in Libya to more than 140 in Lebanon. In Egypt, the average density is only twenty-four persons per square kilometre, but in the inhabited and cultivated areas there are nearly 700 persons per square kilometre. The cities have been absorbing more and more of the growing population. In North Africa, for example, Algiers increased its population nearly ten times in little more than a century, while since 1900 Casablanca increased its population nearly twenty times. The influence of political events is seen in further changes in Algiers. When the struggle for independence from France began in 1954, there were 300,000 Muslims and 300,000 Europeans. Ten years later the total population had increased by a third, and the balance had shifted widely; there were then an estimated 700,000 Muslims and 100,000 Europeans. Tehran, in a half century, has grown from about 200,000 to two million people, now constituting about a tenth of the entire population of Persia. In Egypt, the proportion of the urban population has steadily increased from a fifth in 1917 to nearly two-fifths in 1960.

The historical urban pattern in the Muslim world, the predominance of a few large towns over a vast hinterland, has survived modern developments. In almost every country, one or two cities tower over all others, and grow at a rate surpassing that of the lesser cities. Cairo and Alexandria, with five million people, are hardly approached in any important respect by Egypt's other cities. Baghdād stands alone as a great metropolis in Iraq. Tehran dominates Persia except for the oil industry. Beirut has a third of Lebanon's total population. These huge metropolitan areas have begun to experience problems familiar to those in other regions: insufficient housing, excessive traffic and inadequate services. Social problems of poverty, delinquency and decline of human relations also abound, though often their newness and intensity are exaggerated. On the outskirts of several large cities, migrants from the countryside have built temporary shacks that tend to become permanent settlements. City planning on a small scale was introduced in Istanbul in 1854, partly under the influence of Ottoman participation in the Crimean War. The large number of European interests and the increase in street traffic emphasized the need for improved services, leading to the establishment of a municipal commission. City planning was introduced elsewhere by Western rulers in the late nineteenth and early twentieth centuries and has been somewhat developed in recent years by Middle Easterners educated in European and American institutes of architecture and planning. Political leaders, however, have been too absorbed in national economic planning to see the importance of city planning, and its relevance to the national economy.

Demographic changes affect the material standard of living because they are an important element in the relationship between needs and resources. As regions of rapid increase of population, the Middle East and North Africa have a high proportion of young people who, though they enter the labour market early, are yet a burden on the economy. The Muslim countries as a group are not in danger of population growth outstripping the increase in resources, but some of them will face this problem if present rates of growth are maintained. Egypt is of course already in this difficult position of having to achieve a high rate of economic growth merely to maintain the existing low standard of living. In the present century, the population has doubled, while the cultivated area has increased by only a sixth and the cropped area by a third, giving Egypt the low ratio of a quarter of an acre of cultivated land per person.

Deliberate reduction of births has thus become an issue in some

Muslim countries, especially Egypt. The persistence of a high birth rate has been due not so much to a clear religious prohibition against birth control, but to traditional practice which simply has not encouraged it. In an agricultural society, men and women usually assume that they will have the number of children their natural relationship will bring. In such a society, children are not expensive to rear, and soon become economically productive, so birth control is a remote matter. A large family, it is widely felt moreover, brings social and divine approval.

The intention to keep down the size of the family comes in the cities, and among the people with higher income and formal education. In cities, children are usually not economically productive, and are expensive to rear because they attend school. Parents' aspirations for their children make each child an economic burden for a long time. Under these conditions, where status is determined chiefly by occupation, income, and education, and by one's ability to provide children with the opportunity to reach the proper level of each, ideas of voluntary birth control take hold. The few studies of fertility (the number of children under five years of age per one thousand women in the reproductive age-group fifteen to forty-nine) show that urban ratios are much lower than rural ones. An interesting difference emerges in some places between Muslim and Christian women. Among the Muslim women, urban-rural differences in fertility are negligible, but among urban women those of higher socio-economic status have a lower fertility ratio. Among Christian Arab women, however, the chief concomitant of low fertility is not higher socio-economic status, but living in urban areas. Thus urban life is associated with low fertility in both cases, but among the Muslim women the decline in fertility comes only when urban life brings with it higher income and education.

Such evidence suggests the kind of changes the Muslim family is undergoing with the changes in economic life and with urbanization. The rigid sexual code is relaxing somewhat. Young people in the cities enjoy a moderate but increasing degree of freedom both to meet and to mate. Even in the rural areas, it is more difficult to maintain the patriarchal family as young men find opportunities for employment and education in cities, and thereby escape the supervision of parents and other adult members of the family. In the cities, especially, which absorb most of the population growth, the traditional 'extended' family of several generations in one household is being replaced by the 'conjugal' family including only husband and wife and their children. Throughout

Muslim societies, the secular school, the government and the new media of communication have an increasingly important role in the rearing of the young.

The status of women, which deeply affects the nature of family life, has been changing as opportunities for their education and employment have grown. The result of uneven change is that until recently in some places women were still given as compensation to victims of major crimes, while in the cities many educated women have been pursuing independent careers in education, law, medicine and government. Polygamy has declined, though it persists in some rural and steppe areas. It was abolished in Turkey in 1926 and in Tunisia in 1956. Easy divorce by husbands has been curbed in Morocco, Iraq, Syria, Pakistan, Singapore and Persia. Elsewhere, these practices have been discouraged by official pronouncements, public opinion and economic reality. Even before Turkey outlawed polygamy (which did not end the practice in rural areas), the manpower shortages of the First World War had forced the country to employ thousands of women in factories making military clothing, and in government offices, shops and other private businesses. Following the new Civil Code of 1926 came legislation, in 1930, giving women the right to vote in municipal elections, and then, in 1934, to vote in national elections, and even to become candidates.

Surveys of opinion, attitudes and practices in the 1950s show that women strongly aspire to greater freedom. Women students do not look forward exclusively to marriage. The younger generation of women have a higher proportion than the older who are educated, employed outside the home, have shed the veil, participate in community life and were consulted by their parents in the selection of a husband. A wide gulf remains, however, between what educated women want, and what the men want for them. Women seem to want and expect fewer children than men do, are more in favour of working wives and do not express so great a need for religion as men do. Men, indeed, are ambivalent on the subject of greater freedom for women. Many men appear to resent the subjection and seclusion of their mothers, an attitude which predisposes them to favour more freedom for women. Yet the values implanted by family life and a male-dominated society predispose men to favour the old ways. It is also a question of relationships. Men may want their own wives and unmarried sisters to abide by the strict traditional code, but they may also want their sisters and daughters to have a good education, and to marry men who will be more modern. That is to say, men may be more favourable to emancipation for their women (sisters and daughters) who will one day become the responsibility of other men. The main force for emancipation is education, which has been steadily extended to girls. In the 1950s there were over a million girls attending public schools in Egypt, Iraq, Jordan, Lebanon and Syria, compared to only about 160,000 a quarter-century earlier. By 1961 even Sa'udi Arabia had 12,000 girls enrolled in schools. Education imparts a wider outlook which traditional subordination and seclusion cannot satisfy.

Modern secular education, which is spreading to all the Muslim world, has a broadening effect upon boys and young men too, of course. Western educational methods and subjects were introduced by French Catholic missionaries in the early eighteenth century, and American and British Protestants followed suit in the early nineteenth. Native rulers, especially Sultan Maḥmūd II and Muḥammad 'Alī Pasha, established secular institutions of higher education and sent many students to Europe in an effort to build up military power. Out of these foreign missionary schools and native technological institutes grew the native school system which ended the monopoly over learning long held by the religious leaders. By combining various institutes dating back, in some cases, to the mid-nineteenth century or earlier, the independent countries of the Muslim world have established national universities. Turkey created one before the First World War. The Egyptian University, founded by private enterprise in 1908, was taken over by the state in 1924. Other universities have been founded in Egypt subsequently. Syria established one in 1924, and Persia in 1934. The other countries consolidated various units into full-fledged universities only in the 1950s.

Students have sometimes played important political roles in some Muslim countries, notably Egypt, Persia and Turkey. Educated and articulate, they have taken a great interest in politics and government because of both nationalist feeling and career interests. Revolutionary leaders have often sought student support, and, indeed, have often expressed their struggle not so much in terms of social classes as in those of generations: youth against age, the modern against the traditional. As revolutionaries have assumed power, however, they have stressed the need of students to stay at their desks rather than to demonstrate in the streets. They also have tried to divert students from law and journalism, professions which had played a leading role in the nationalist revolts, to engineering and science, which are needed for the growth of modern industry.

Industrialization, changes in the family and in the distribution of population, and the advance of secular education have produced, and have been accompanied by, changes in occupations and in social classes. Before these changes, Muslim societies run by Muslims had a relatively clear class-structure. Foreigners and non-Muslims had low status and were indeed a separate group of communities. Muslims had the highest status, and among them the highest prestige and power lay with the political-religious leaders controlling the government. With the distribution of land to private owners, the growth of trade, and the introduction of modern transport, communication and some manufacturing, all of which began at various times in the nineteenth century, new classes rose. The large Muslim landowner, and the Christian and Jewish merchants and bankers, acquired more power, though only the Muslim landowner acquired higher status in a society in which people still divided themselves chiefly according to religion. A new element entered with the growing influence of the European powers, and the attendant rise in importance of the resident foreigners (the Levantines) and native Christians and Jews long familiar in the Muslim world. As Muslim countries reduced and finally eliminated such foreign and minority influences during the present century, while adopting Western economic and political institutions, another shift in social class occurred, bringing up the nationalist political leaders and the professions, such as law, journalism and the armed forces, closely identified with the nationalist struggles. The most recent changes have taken place in Egypt, Algeria, Iraq and Syria (to a certain extent), where the influence of the state, controlled through the army, has ended the power of certain classes which had thriven earlier, notably the large landowners, the independent professionals, and both Arab Christian and Muslim industrialists, bankers and merchants. In these countries the army and the higher civil service have advanced in power and prestige; the new leaders have spoken much of the dignity and importance of the mass of labourers and peasants, but thus far their position has not changed much. The new emphasis upon technology and science is intended to raise the status of occupations needed for modern industry and military power; with this emphasis goes an effort to overcome the traditional disdain of the educated class for manual pursuits, even when they are associated, as in science and technology, with higher learning.

Such changes have not been felt so deeply outside the urban areas which have been the locus of most sources of power. In the rural area, social class-differences are not so refined, and still depend mainly on the ownership of land. In the declining tribal societies of desert and steppe, any settled rural or urban pursuit is still regarded as demeaning, despite the increasing sedentarization of the bedouin resulting from economic necessity and official policy.

As in other societies, so too in the Muslim world, wealth, prestige and power do not always go together. Making the Pilgrimage to Mecca confers prestige with no difference in wealth or power. Often holy men are poor, but they still have high prestige and much influence. Businessmen have wealth and some power by virtue of it, but in many parts of the Muslim world they have little prestige, unless they associate themselves with religion by supporting it.

The basis of human association in the Muslim world has been changing and widening. Traditionally, kinship and religion exclusively fixed relations among men, covering the social-geographical area from the local community to the whole universe itself. Occupational and class affinities assumed importance from time to time in traditional Muslim society, but always in conjunction with family and religious community. In modern times associations sprang up with various unifying principles, for example, literary, benevolent, scientific, moral, and then political. More recently, occupation has been growing in importance both as a determinant of social class, and as a principle of association (where freedom to associate is still permitted). Approaching Western forms of social stratification, the modern urban Middle East has begun to reveal the coalescence, though still hardly across religious boundaries, of education, income, status and power in one's occupational position.

Vestiges of previous bases of social class, and the approach of new ones, make Muslim countries socially unstable in two senses. First, the coexistence of various systems of stratification makes it difficult to describe the Muslim world in terms of any one of them. Secondly, the changing classes themselves are unstable, because the whole economy and society are undergoing change at different rates. Within each new social class, there is thus instability too, and this applies to native capitalists, to the growing, inexperienced and poorly led working class, and to the volatile intellectuals, not firmly anchored economically or socially.

Social instability has resulted, also, from changes in the position of religion. Secularism has meant the relegation of religion to a defined place in a society in which religious ideas and obligations once pervaded all aspects of private, social and public life. Religion, nevertheless, continues to be strong among the mass of the population, persists as a very important basis of identity among Muslims, and is still a factor in political affairs.

Nationalism has been proclaimed by the leaders of most Muslim lands as the chief bond among men. This principle is a recent one for Muslims, and they have not yet fully adjusted themselves to it. Under the Ottoman *millet* system, religion defined one's relation to others in the social realm beyond kinship. It worked through the principle of tolerance of differences by avoidance of contacts except under well-defined conditions. Nationalism and the national state sought homogeneity and loyalty on less familiar grounds, but the new principle has thus far not succeeded in ordering, in a manner acceptable to all groups, the interests and relations of many communities based on a criss-crossing of religion, language, nationality and territorial origin. A vast population exchange in this century, in which about two million Turkish and other Muslims left the Balkans for Turkey while about the same number of Christian Arabs, Europeans and Jews left the Near East for Europe and America, did not remove the problem of the minority in a nationalist era.

Though the secular nationalists governing much of the Middle East and North Africa have reduced the public influence of religious leaders, some of them appeal to religious loyalty too. This has been especially true of the revolutionary leaders of Egypt, who regularly obtain the endorsement of their secular goals by the '*ulamā*'. This recognition of the religious feeling of the mass of the people has come even in Turkey, which had gone furthest in a secular direction; in the 1950s the government found it expedient not to interfere with a revival of religion among the peasants, artisans and shopkeepers.

Modernism has stimulated a certain rebirth of religious fundamentalism in both traditional and new religious brotherhoods. To many religious Muslims, to be 'modern' is to be wanton, bound by no religious or moral obligation, disrespectful of elders—in a word, libertine. The solemn authoritarian régimes bent upon industrialization have proclaimed their own secular form of austerity. They call upon the masses, in the name of national progress rather than religion, to avoid self-indulgence, and they often condemn the pursuit of pleasure as a vice of westernization and capitalism.

Many of the changes we have been discussing are registered not only in official policy, private attitudes and public conduct, but have also been codified in new legal instruments. For half a century the civil code of the Ottoman empire was the *Mejelle,* issued between 1869 and 1876, which was based on the *Sharīʿa.* Turkey replaced it in 1926 with a revolutionary adaptation of the Swiss Civil Code; the *Mejelle* continued for a time as the basic law in several former Arab provinces, but now survives only in Jordan and Israel. Egypt adopted a new civil code in the late nineteenth century, based on the *Code Napoléon,* but adopted a more indigenous code in 1948 based on both Western and Islamic concepts. This code, developed by the Egyptian jurist ʿAbd al-Razzāq al-Sanhūrī, was the basis also for those adopted after the Second World War by several newly independent Arab states. The most far-reaching transformation in the legal structure, as in so many other matters, came in the Turkey of Atatürk, which in 1926 introduced a new Penal Code based on an Italian model, and a new Commercial Code based on Italian and German models. Several other Muslim countries have modernized older penal and commercial codes, or adopted new ones since the Second World War. Changes have been made in the judiciary too. First, foreign influences stemming from extra-territorial rights were eliminated, and then the central secular judicial systems were consolidated in some countries. Thus in 1955 Egypt abolished the special courts administering religious law and transferred this function to the regular courts. A few years later Syria gave the regular courts jurisdiction over the tribes, which had until then had their own law. The importance of these changes is that they express in the legal structure the vast economic and social transformation of the Muslim world in the last century, and the determination of its leaders to continue moving the entire society in the same direction.

AN ASSESSMENT OF CHANGE

Perhaps the most significant change in the Muslim world since the eighteenth century is the growth of a favourable attitude toward change itself. The leaders of Muslim society today embrace what their predecessors abjured. Even generations after the Ottomans realized that they would have to transform their institutions to preserve them, they still could not give up the comforting idea, expressed in the *Khaṭṭ-ı Sherīf* of 1839, that their troubles could be traced to their abandonment of the precepts of the Holy Qurʾān and the great empire built upon them. Reformers of today seldom pay the past such tribute. One of the most recent recruits to modernization is Saʿudi Arabia, which early in 1964 proclaimed (in a newspaper advertisement) its determination 'to develop into a modern progressive state'. Reminiscent in tone of Ottoman pronouncements a century ago, the document spoke rather of science, industry, education and oil, than of morality, religion and God.

Apart from the effects it produces in various domains of life, change itself becomes a matter of concern—its source, rate, mode and means. It raises questions of personal and group identity which had long remained settled. It also produces its own rationale and its own subterfuge. When accused of seeking to overthrow hallowed traditions, the advocates of change often point to earlier traditions to which they say they seek to return. Thus some Muslim nineteenth-century thinkers called for a return to interest in the sciences, in which Muslim society had excelled before Europe took the lead. Similarly, the need to borrow from Europe is explained by pointing out that Muslims thereby reclaim what Europeans once borrowed from them. Or a presumed national or religious tradition is shown to be itself a foreign importation, as when Atatürk, advocating European dress, argued that the fez was Greek, and the long gown Byzantine or Hebrew. In Turkey, too, reforms that offended tradition were carried out under the banner of the need for unification; this cover protected the adoption of the Gregorian calendar and the metric system of weights and measures.

Change itself acquires a tradition. The traditional source of change for the Muslim countries of the Middle East and North Africa has been the West: Europe and then North America. Now the Muslim world distinguishes between Western Europe and North America on the one hand, and the Soviet Union and Eastern Europe on the other. Some Arab leaders now take their inspiration from the latter, and from Communist China.

A review of social and economic change inevitably exaggerates it, and (perhaps also inevitably) suggests that it has been for the better, if not in every respect then at least 'on the whole'. Change, of course, often leaves things essentially the same. Thus the recent increase in state power in many Muslim countries may only increase their resemblance today to their condition several centuries ago, though their leaders may speak the language of Marx, Lenin and Mao rather than that of the Qur'ān, the Prophet and the '*ulamā*'. Air transport is fast becoming the most frequently used means by which pilgrims go to Mecca, but the modern jets carry them there to perform a traditional rite. Change is more dramatic to us than continuity, so we tend to overlook the persistent conservatism, especially in social life, of the great mass of Muslims who still live in the countryside, or who live in urban enclaves where they pursue a traditional mode of life.

We often tend, also, to exaggerate the novelty of change, overlooking its long history. Atatürk's reforms were rooted in the Young Turk movement before the First World War, which in turn owed much to nineteenth-century Ottoman reform efforts. Much of the programme of Egypt's 'revolutionary' leadership after 1952 (except for the radical crypto-Marxism beginning in 1961) was anticipated in the previous two decades under the despised 'reactionaries'. This includes legislation and financing to encourage industry, labour and social welfare legislation, land reform, land reclamation and state participation in capital formation. Finally, we tend to exaggerate the extent of the transformation, for the Muslim world is still one in which the mass of the people are bound to religious and social tradition, government is still oppressive and not representative, agriculture predominant and modern industry still rudimentary.

TABLE I. THE UMAYYADS, 'ALIDS AND 'ABBASIDS

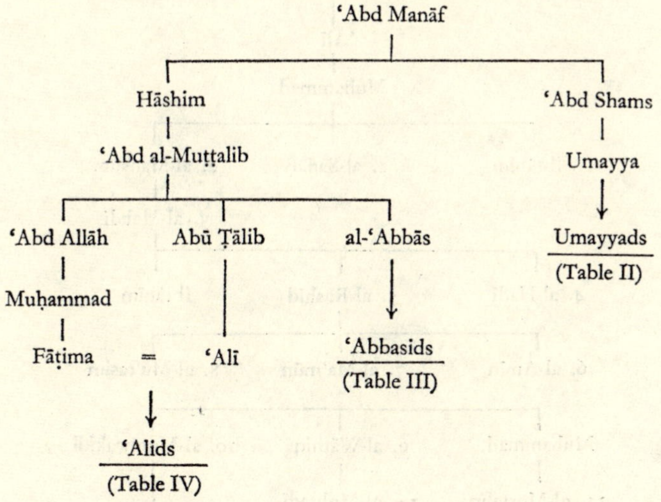

TABLE II. THE UMAYYAD CALIPHS

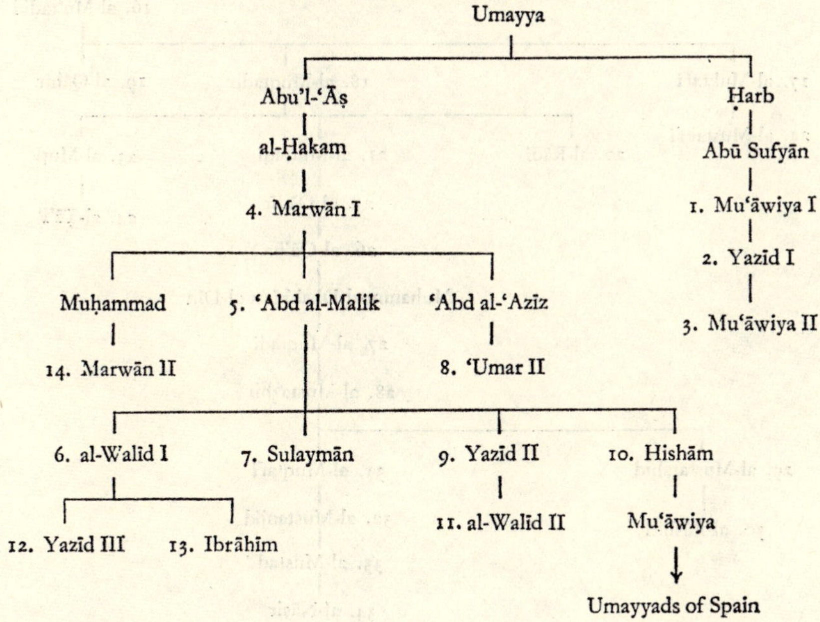

TABLE III. THE 'ABBASID CALIPHS

- al-'Abbās
  - 'Abd Allāh
    - 'Alī
      - Muḥammad
        - Ibrāhīm
        - 1. al-Saffāḥ
        - 2. al-Manṣūr
          - 3. al-Mahdī
            - 4. al-Hādī
            - 5. al-Rashīd
              - 6. al-Amīn
              - 7. al-Ma'mūn
              - 8. al-Mu'taṣim
                - Muḥammad
                  - 12. al-Musta'īn
                - 9. al-Wāthiq
                  - 14. al-Muhtadī
                - 10. al-Mutawakkil
                  - 11. al-Muntaṣir
                  - 13. al-Mu'tazz
                  - 15. al-Mu'tamid
                  - al-Muwaffaq
                    - 16. al-Mu'taḍid
                      - 17. al-Muktafī
                        - 22. al-Mustakfī
                      - 18. al-Muqtadir
                        - 20. al-Rāḍī
                        - 21. al-Muttaqī
                          - 25. al-Qādir
                            - 26. al-Qā'im
                              - Muḥammad Dhakhīrat al-Dīn
                                - 27. al-Muqtadī
                                  - 28. al-Mustaẓhir
                                    - 29. al-Mustarshid
                                      - 30. al-Rāshid
                                    - 31. al-Muqtafī
                                      - 32. al-Mustanjid
                                        - 33. al-Mustaḍī'
                                          - 34. al-Nāṣir
                                            - 35. al-Ẓāhir
                                              - 36. al-Mustanṣir
                                                - 37. al-Musta'ṣim
                        - 23. al-Muṭī'
                          - 24. al-Ṭā'i'
                      - 19. al-Qāhir
            - Ibrāhīm

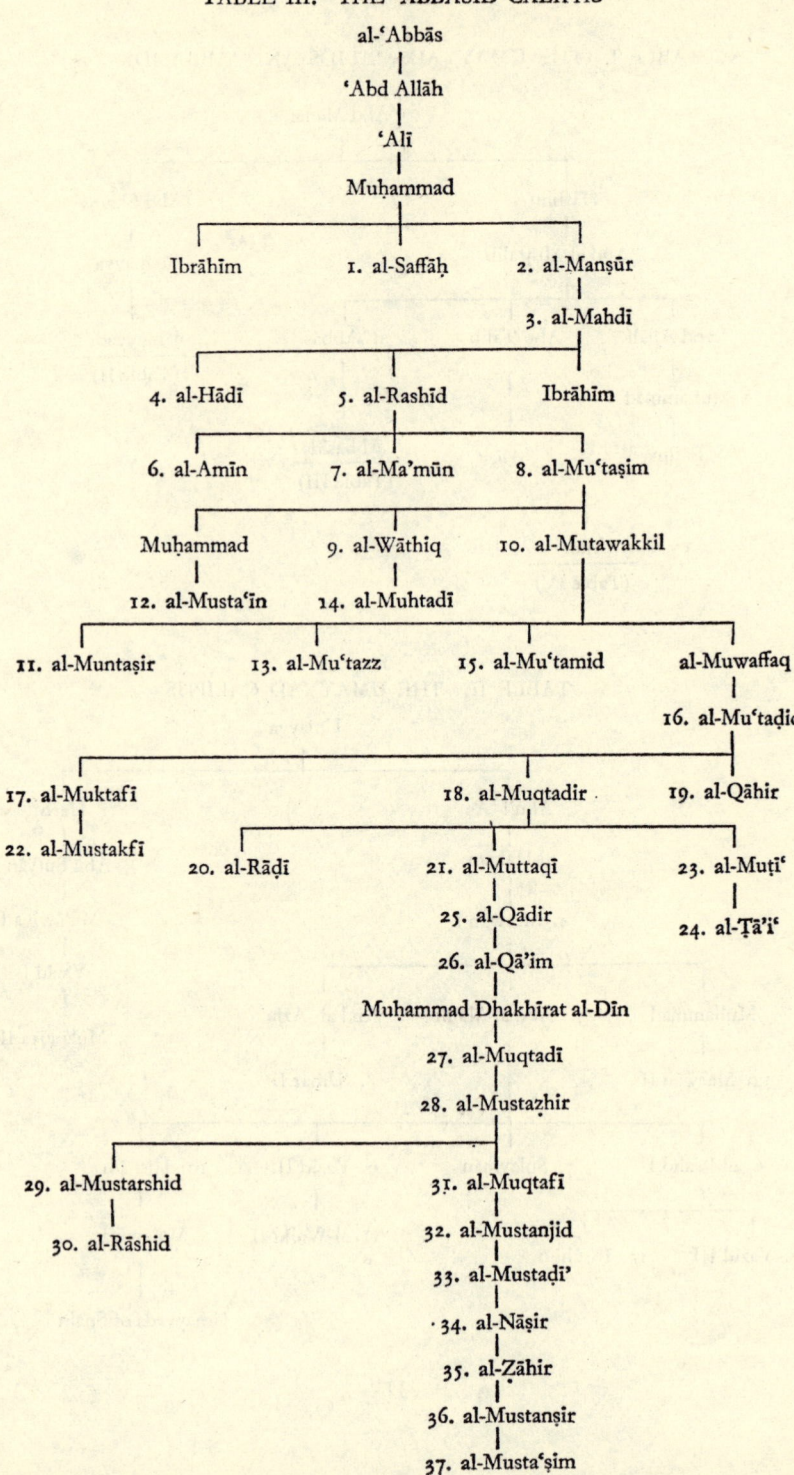

TABLE IV. THE TWELVER *IMĀMS* AND FATIMID CALIPHS

- I. ʿAlī = Fāṭima
  - II. al-Ḥasan
  - III. al-Ḥusayn
    - IV. ʿAlī Zayn al-ʿĀbidīn
      - V. Muḥammad al-Bāqir
        - VI. Jaʿfar al-Ṣādiq
          - Ismāʿīl
            - Muḥammad
              - Aḥmad
                - Ḥusayn
                  - ʿAlī al-Muʿill
                    - 1. al-Mahdī
                      - 2. al-Qāʾim
                        - 3. al-Manṣūr
                          - 4. al-Muʿizz
                            - 5. al-ʿAzīz
                              - 6. al-Ḥākim
                                - 7. al-Ẓāhir
                                  - 8. al-Mustanṣir
                                    - Nizār
                                      - *Imāms* of Alamūt
                                    - 9. al-Mustaʿlī
                                      - 10. al-Āmir
                                    - Muḥammad
                                      - 11. al-Ḥāfiẓ
                                        - 12. al-Ẓāfir
                                          - 13. al-Fāʾiz
                                            - 14. al-ʿĀḍid
          - VII. Mūsā al-Kāẓim
            - VIII. ʿAlī al-Riḍā
              - IX. Muḥammad al-Jawād
                - X. ʿAlī al-Hādī
                  - XI. Ḥasan al-ʿAskarī
                    - XII. Muḥammad al-Mahdī

Notes: I–XII. Twelver *Imāms*. 2–14. Fatimid caliphs. The first Fatimid caliph, ʿUbayd Allāh al-Mahdī, is said to have been an *imām mustawdaʿ* (trustee *imām*), not in the Fatimid line of descent.

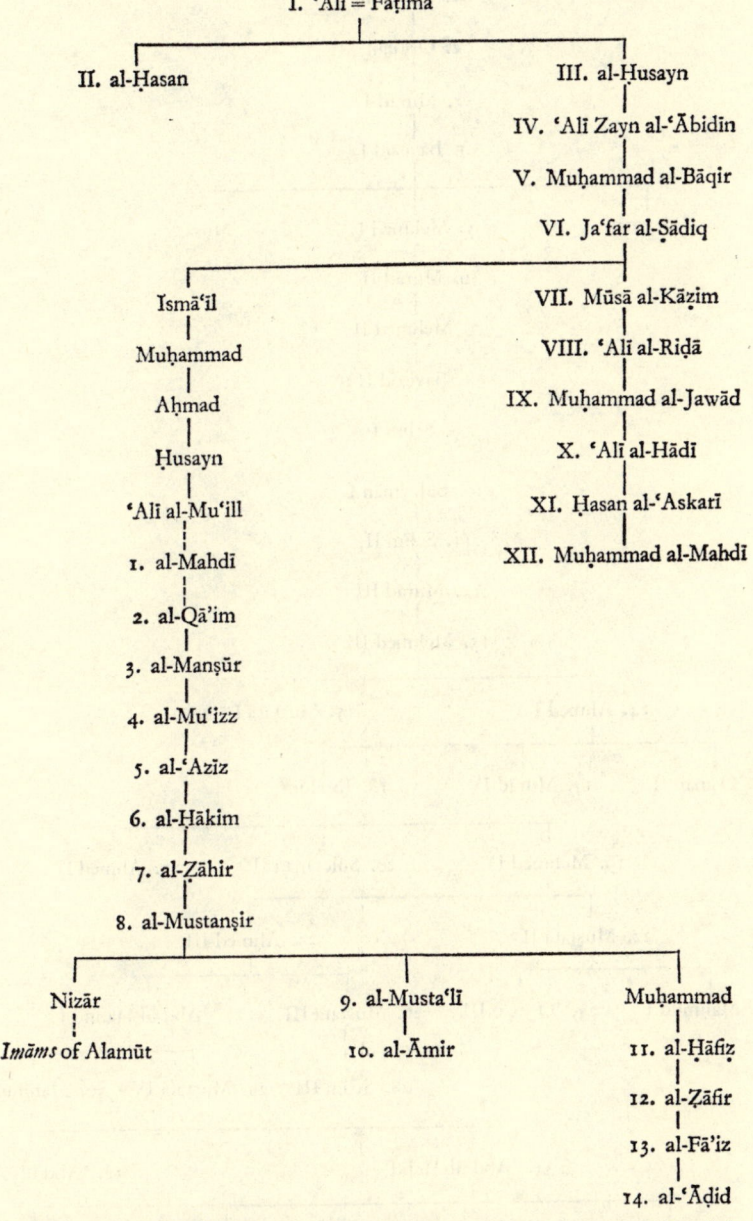

TABLE V. THE OTTOMANS

- 1. 'Osmān
  - 2. Orkhān
    - 3. Murād I
      - 4. Bāyezīd I
        - Süleymān
        - 5. Meḥmed I
          - 6. Murād II
            - 7. Meḥmed II
              - 8. Bāyezīd II
                - 9. Selīm I
                  - 10. Süleymān I
                    - 11. Selīm II
                      - 12. Murād III
                        - 13. Meḥmed III
                          - 14. Aḥmed I
                            - 16. 'Osmān II
                            - 17. Murād IV
                            - 18. Ibrāhīm
                              - 19. Meḥmed IV
                                - 22. Muṣṭafā II
                                  - 24. Maḥmūd I
                                  - 25. 'Osmān III
                                - 23. Aḥmed III
                                  - 26. Muṣṭafā III
                                    - 28. Selīm III
                                  - 27. 'Abd ül-Ḥamīd I
                                    - 29. Muṣṭafā IV
                                    - 30. Maḥmūd II
                                      - 31. 'Abd ül-Mejīd
                                        - 33. Murād V
                                        - 34. 'Abd ül-Hamīd II
                                        - 35. Meḥmed V
                                        - 36. Meḥmed VI
                                      - 32. 'Abd ül-'Azīz
                              - 20. Süleymān II
                              - 21. Aḥmed II
                          - 15. Muṣṭafā I
        - Mūsā

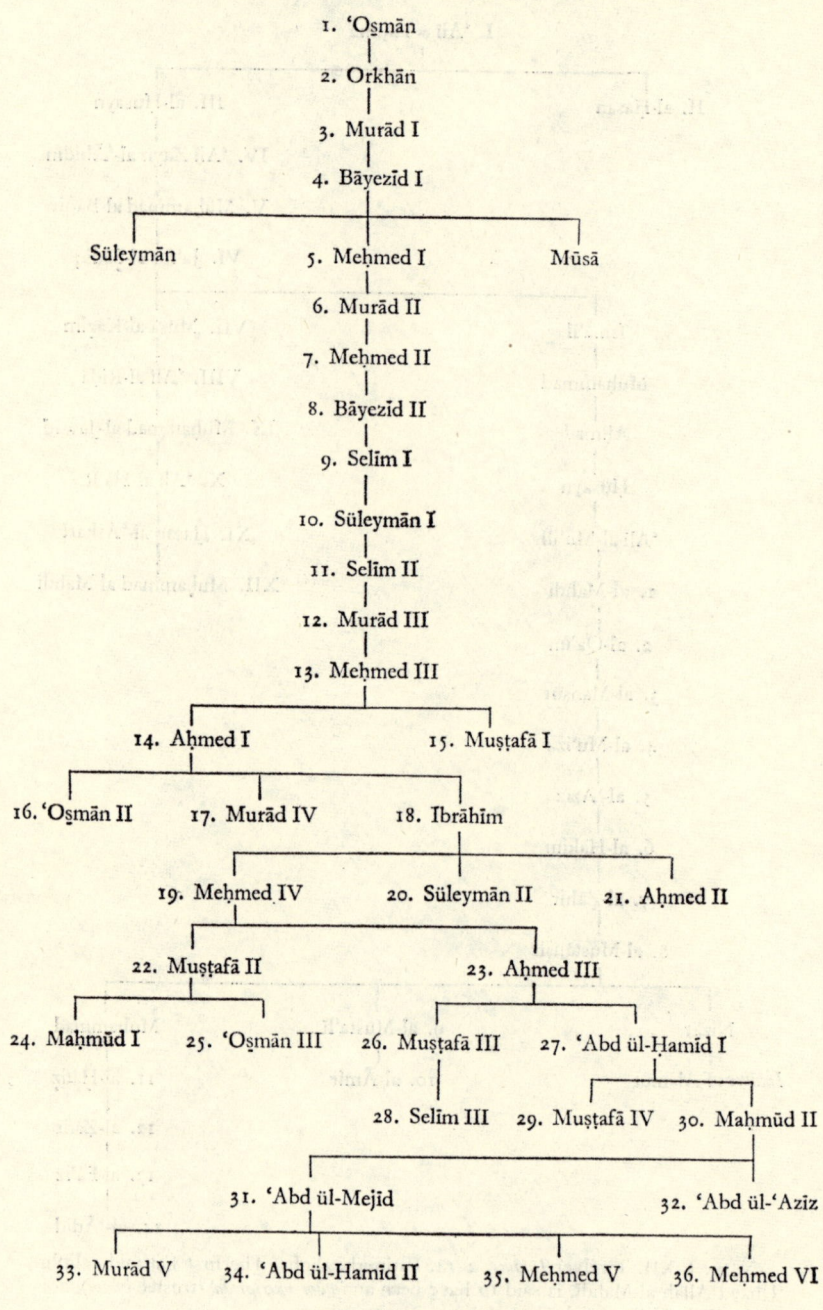

TABLE VI. THE SAFAVIDS

Ṣafī al-Dīn

Ṣadr al-Dīn Mūsā

Khwāja ʿAlī

Ibrāhīm

Junayd

Ḥaydar

ʿAlī

1. Ismāʿīl I

2. Ṭahmāsp I

3. Ismāʿīl II

4. Muḥammad Khudābanda

5. ʿAbbās I

Ṣafī Mīrzā

6. Ṣafī

7. ʿAbbās II

8. Sulaymān

9. Ḥusayn

10. Ṭahmāsp II

11. ʿAbbās III

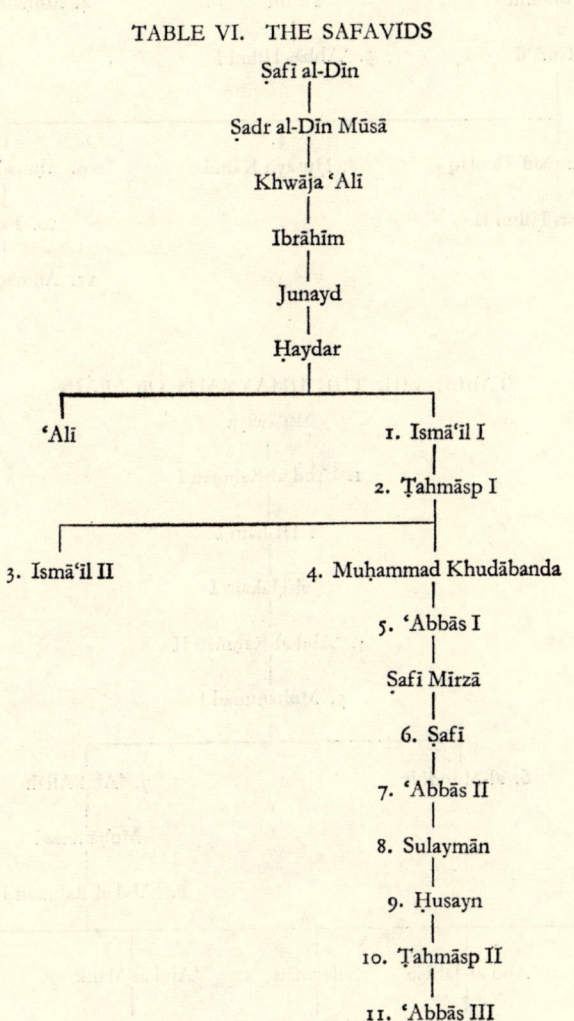

TABLE VII. THE DYNASTY OF MUḤAMMAD 'ALĪ IN EGYPT

- 1. Muḥammad 'Alī
  - 2. Ibrāhīm
    - 5. Ismā'īl
      - 6. Muḥammad Tawfīq
        - 7. 'Abbās Ḥilmī II
      - 8. Ḥusayn Kāmil
      - 9. Aḥmad Fu'ād I
        - 10. Fārūq
          - 11. Aḥmad Fu'ād II
  - Tusun
    - 3. 'Abbās Ḥilmī I
  - 4. Muḥammad Sa'īd

TABLE VIII. THE UMAYYADS OF SPAIN

- Mu'āwiya
  - 1. 'Abd al-Raḥmān I
    - 2. Hishām I
      - 3. al-Ḥakam I
        - 4. 'Abd al-Raḥmān II
          - 5. Muḥammad I
            - 6. al-Mundhir
            - 7. 'Abd Allāh
              - Muḥammad
                - 8. 'Abd al-Raḥmān III
                  - 9. al-Ḥakam II
                    - 10. Hishām II
                  - 'Abd al-Jabbār
                    - Hishām
                      - 11. Muḥammad II
                      - 14. 'Abd al-Raḥmān V
                  - Sulaymān
                    - al-Ḥakam
                      - 12. Sulaymān
                  - 'Abd al-Malik
                    - Muḥammad
                      - 13. 'Abd al-Raḥmān IV
                        - 16. Hishām III
                  - 'Ubayd Allāh
                    - 'Abd al-Raḥmān
                      - 15. Muḥammad III

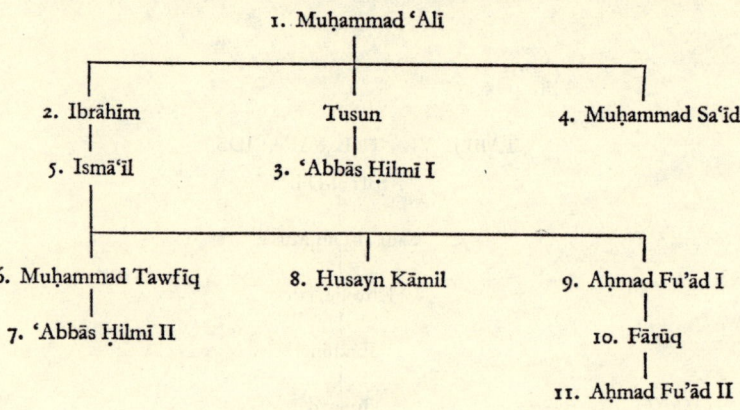

BIBLIOGRAPHY

The following book-lists are intended as a guide to further reading, and consist almost entirely of secondary sources in the principal European languages. Articles in learned journals, *Festschriften* and other collective works of the kind are not normally included; a comprehensive and systematic guide to such materials is provided by:

Pearson, J. D. *Index Islamicus 1906–55*, with its two *Supplements* for 1956–60 and 1961–5 respectively. Cambridge, 1958, 1962, 1966.

An indispensable work of reference on the bibliography of Islamic studies is:

Sauvaget, J. *Introduction à l'histoire de l'orient musulman*. 2nd edn. revised by Cahen, Cl. Paris, 1961.

An English version of this, incorporating some revision and expansion, has appeared as:

Jean Sauvaget's Introduction to the History of the Muslim East. Berkeley and Los Angeles, 1965.

A general introduction to Islamic studies is offered by:

Pareja, F. M. *Islamologia*. Rome, 1951. French edn., *Islamologie*. Beirut, 1957–63.

Numerous articles on Islamic history will be found in:

The Encyclopaedia of Islam. 1st edn. Leiden, 1913–42. 2nd edn. Leiden and London, 1960– (in progress).

There are also relevant chapters in *The New Cambridge Modern History, The Cambridge Medieval History, The Cambridge History of India,* and *The Cambridge History of Iran*.

A survey of the historiography of the Muslim Middle East is provided by:

Lewis, B. and Holt, P. M. *Historians of the Middle East*. London, 1962.

The historiography of Islam in other areas is dealt with in chapters in:

Philips, C. H. (ed.). *Historians of India, Pakistan and Ceylon*. London, 1961.
Hall, D. G. E. (ed.). *Historians of South East Asia*. London, 1962.

Amongst aids to the student, the following atlases will be found useful:

Hazard, H. W. *Atlas of Islamic History*. 3rd edn. Princeton, 1954.
Roolvink, R. *Historical Atlas of the Muslim Peoples*. Amsterdam, 1957.
Atlas of the Arab World and the Middle East. Macmillan; London, 1960.
Oxford Regional Economic Atlas: The Middle East and North Africa. Oxford University Press; London, 1960.

Genealogical and dynastic lists and tables are given by:

Lane-Poole, S. *The Mohammadan Dynasties*. Paris, 1925.
Zambaur, E. de. *Manuel de généalogie et de chronologie pour l'histoire de l'Islam*. Hanover, 1927.

The following works are of basic importance to the student of Islamic history, society and institutions. They have in different ways contributed to the corpus of knowledge about Islam, to its interpretation and understanding, and to the development of methods of research and investigation.

Becker, C. H. *Islamstudien*. Leipzig, 1924–32.

Gibb, H. A. R. *Modern Trends in Islam*. Chicago, 1947.
—— *Mohammedanism: An Historical Survey*. London, 1949.
—— *Studies in the Civilization of Islam*. Ed. Shaw, S. J. and Polk, W. R. Chicago, 1962.
Goitein, S. D. *A Mediterranean Society*. Vol. I. Berkeley and Los Angeles, 1967.
Goldziher, I. *Muhammedanische Studien*. Halle, 1889-90; Hildesheim, 1961. Eng. tr. of Vol. I, ed. S. M. Stern, *Muslim Studies*. London, 1967.
—— *Vorlesungen über den Islam*. 1st edn. Heidelberg, 1910. (French tr. by Arin, F. *Le dogme et la loi de l'Islam*. Paris, 1920.)
Grunebaum, G. E. von. *Medieval Islam: A Study in Cultural Orientation*. 2nd. edn. Chicago, 1953.
—— *Islam: Essays in the Nature and Growth of a Cultural Tradition*. London, 1955.
Hurgronje, C. S. *Verspreide geschriften*. Bonn, Leipzig, Leiden, 1923–7.
—— *Selected Works*. Ed. Bousquet, G.-H. and Schacht, J. Leiden, 1957.
Macdonald, D. B. *Development of Muslim Theology, Jurisprudence and Constitutional Theory*. New York 1903; Beirut, 1964.
—— *The Religious Attitude and Life in Islam*. Chicago, 1906; Beirut, 1965.
Schacht, J. *The Origins of Muhammadan Jurisprudence*. Oxford, 1950.
Wellhausen, J. *Skizzen und Vorarbeiten*. 2nd edn. Berlin, 1897.

Pre-Islamic Arabia

Aigrain, R. 'Arabie', in *Dictionnaire d'histoire et de géographie ecclésiastique*. Vol. III. Paris, 1924.
Altheim, F. and Stiehl, R. *Die Araber in der alte Welt*. Berlin, 1964–8.
Caskel, W. *Das altarabische Königreich Lihjan*. Krefeld, 1950.
—— *Die Bedeutung der Beduinen in der Geschichte der Araber*. Cologne, 1953.
—— *Entdeckungen in Arabien*. Cologne, 1954.
—— *Lihyan und Lihyanisch*. Cologne, 1954.
Février, J. G. *Essai sur l'histoire politique et économique de Palmyre*. 1931.
Gabrieli, F. (ed.). *L'antica società beduina*. Rome, 1959.
Grohmann, A. 'Arabien', in *Kulturgeschichte des alten Orients*. Munich, 1963.
Guidi, M. *Storia e cultura degli Arabi fino alla morte di Maometto*. Florence, 1951.
Hourani, G. F. *Arab Seafaring in the Indian Ocean in Ancient and Early Medieval Times*. Princeton, 1951.
Lammens, H. *Le berceau de l'Islam*. Rome, 1914.
—— *L'Arabie occidentale avant l'Hégire*. Beirut, 1928.
Levi Della Vida, G. 'Pre-Islamic Arabia', in Faris, N. A. (ed.). *The Arab Heritage*. Princeton, 1944.
Moscati, S. *The Semites in Ancient History*. Cardiff, 1959.
Nielsen, D. *Handbuch der altarabischen Altertumskunde*. Copenhagen, 1927.
Nöldeke, Th. *Die ghassânischen Fürsten aus dem Hause Gafna's*. Berlin, 1887.
Olinder, G. *The Kings of Kinda of the Family of Ākil al-Murār*. Lund, 1927.
Rothstein, G. *Die Dynastie der Laḫmiden in al-Ḥîra*. Berlin, 1899.
Ryckmans, G. 'Les religions préislamiques', in *L'histoire générale des religions* Paris, 1960.

Ryckmans, J. *L'institution monarchique en Arabie méridionale avant l'Islam.* Louvain, 1951.
—— 'Le Christianisme en Arabie du Sud préislamique', in *Atti del Convegno Internazionale sul tema: L'Oriente cristiano nella storia della civiltà.* Rome, 1964.
Starcky, J. *Palmyre.* 1952.
Wellhausen, J. *Reste arabischen Heidentums.* 2nd edn. Berlin, 1897. 3rd. edn. Berlin, 1961.
Wissmann, H. von and Höfner, M. *Beiträge zur historischen Geographie des vorislamischen Südarabien.* Wiesbaden, 1953.

Muḥammad

Ahrens, K. *Muhammed als Religionsstifter.* Leipzig, 1935.
Andrae, T. J. E. *Mohammed, the man and his faith.* London, 1936 (tr. from Swedish).
—— *Die Person Muhammeds in Lehre und Glauben seiner Gemeinde.* Stockholm, 1918.
—— *Les origines de l'Islam et le Christianisme.* Paris, 1955 (tr. from German).
Arberry, A. J. *The Koran Interpreted.* London, 1955.
Archer, J. C. *Mystical Elements in Mohammed.* New Haven, 1924.
Bell, R. *The Origin of Islam in its Christian Environment.* London, 1926.
Blachère, R. *Le problème de Mahomet.* Paris, 1952.
Buhl, F. *Das Leben Muhammads.* Leipzig, 1930 (tr. from Danish).
Caetani, L. *Annali dell'Islam.* Vols. I, II. Milan, 1905.
—— *Studi di storia orientale.* Milan, 1911–14.
Hamidullah, M. *Le prophète de l'Islam.* Paris, 1959.
Katsh, A. I. *Judaism in Islām.* New York, 1954. (New edn. *Judaism and the Koran.* New York, 1962).
Muir, W. *The Life of Muhammad.* Revised edn. Edinburgh, 1923.
Nöldeke, Th. *Geschichte des Qorâns.* 2nd edn. Leipzig, 1909–38.
Paret, R. *Mohammed und der Koran.* Stuttgart, 1957.
Rodinson, M. *Mahomet.* 2nd edn. Paris, 1968.
Watt, W. M. *Muhammad at Mecca.* London, 1953.
—— *Muhammad at Medina.* Oxford, 1956.
—— *Muhammad, Prophet and Statesman.* London, 1961.
Wellhausen, J. *Skizzen und Vorarbeiten* IV. Berlin, 1897.

The Patriarchal and Umayyad Caliphates

Becker, C. H. *Islamstudien.* Vol. I. Leipzig, 1924.
Butler, A. J. *The Arab Conquest of Egypt.* Oxford, 1902.
Caetani, L. *Annali dell'Islam.* Milan, 1905–26.
—— *Chronographia Islamica.* Paris, Rome, 1912–23.
Dennett, D. C. *Conversion and the Poll-tax in Early Islam.* Cambridge, Mass., 1950.

Eickhoff, E. *Seekrieg und Seepolitik zwischen Islam und Abendland.* Berlin, 1966.
Gabrieli, F. *Muhammad and the Conquests of Islam.* London, 1968.
—— *Il Califfato di Hishâm. Studi di storia omayyade.* Alexandria, 1935.
Gibb, H. A. R. *The Arab Conquests in Central Asia.* London, 1923.
—— 'Arab-Byzantine relations under the Umayyad caliphate', in Shaw, S. J. and Polk, W. R. (ed.). *Studies on the Civilization of Islam.* Boston, Mass., 1962.
Goeje, M. J. de. *Mémoire sur la conquête de la Syrie.* 2nd edn. Leiden, 1900.
Honigmann, E. *Die Ostgrenze des byzantinischen Reiches von 363 bis 1071.* Brussels, 1935.
Lammens, H. *Études sur le règne du calife omaiyade Mo'âwiya Ier.* Paris, 1908.
—— *Le califat de Yazīd Ier.* Beirut, 1910–21.
—— *Études sur le siècle des Omayyades.* Beirut, 1930.
Løkkegaard, F. *Islamic Taxation in the Classical Period.* Copenhagen, 1950.
Petersen, E. L. *'Alī and Mu'āwiya in early Arabic tradition.* Copenhagen, 1964.
Vloten, G. van. *Recherches sur la domination arabe, le Chiitisme et les croyances messianiques sous le khalifat des Omayades.* Amsterdam, 1894.
Wellhausen, J. *Skizzen und Vorarbeiten VI: Prolegomena zur ältesten Geschichte des Islams.* Berlin, 1899.
—— *The Arab Kingdom and its Fall.* Calcutta, 1927 (tr. from German).

The 'Abbasid Caliphate

Abbott, N. *Two Queens of Baghdad.* Chicago, 1946.
Arendonk, C. van. *Les débuts de l'imāmat zaidite au Yemen.* Leiden, 1960.
Barthold, W. *Turkestan Down to the Mongol Invasion.* 3rd edn. London, 1968.
—— *Histoire des Turcs d'Asie centrale.* Paris, 1945.
Bosworth, C. E. *The Ghaznavids.* Edinburgh, 1963.
Bowen, H. *The Life and Times of 'Alī ibn 'Īsà.* Cambridge, 1928.
Busse, H. *Die Buyiden im Irak.* Beirut, 1968.
Gabrieli, F. *Al-Ma'mūn e gli 'Alidi.* Leipzig, 1929.
Goeje, M. J. de. *Mémoire sur les Carmathes du Bahraïn et les Fatimides.* 2nd. edn. Leiden, 1886.
Herzfeld, E. E. *Geschichte der Stadt Samarra.* Hamburg, 1948.
Hodgson, M. G. S. *The Order of Assassins.* The Hague, 1955.
Kabir, M. *The Buwayhid Dynasty of Baghdad, 334/946-447/1055.* Calcutta, 1964.
Laoust, H. *Les schismes dans l'Islam.* Paris, 1965.
Le Strange, G. *The Lands of the Eastern Caliphate.* 2nd. edn. Cambridge, 1930.
—— *Baghdad During the Abbasid Caliphate.* Oxford, 1924.
—— *Palestine under the Moslems.* London, 1890.
Lewis, B. *The Origins of Ismā'īlism.* Cambridge, 1940.
—— *The Assassins.* London, 1967.
Minorsky, V. F. *La domination des Dailamites.* Paris, 1932.
Muir, W. *The Caliphate, its Rise, Decline and Fall.* Revised edn. by Weir, T. H. Edinburgh, 1924.
Nazim, M. *The Life and Times of Sulṭan Maḥmūd of Ghazna.* Cambridge, 1931.

Nöldeke, Th. *Sketches from Eastern History*. London, 1892 (tr. from German).
Pellat, C. *Le milieu baṣrien et la formation de Ǧāḥiẓ*. Paris, 1953.
Sadighi, G. H. *Les mouvements religieux iraniens au IIe et au IIIe siècle de l'Hégire*. Paris, 1938.
Schwarz, P. *Iran im Mittelalter nach den arabischen Geographen*. Leipzig, 1910–.
Sourdel, D. *Le vizirat 'abbāside de 749 à 936*. Damascus, 1959–60.
Spuler, B. *Iran in früh-islamischer Zeit*. Wiesbaden, 1952.
—— *The Muslim World, A Historical Survey I: The Age of the Caliphs*. Leiden, 1960 (tr. from German).
Vasiliev, A. A. *Byzance et les Arabes*. Brussels, 1935–68.
Weil, G. *Geschichte der Chalifen*. Mannheim, Stuttgart, 1846–62.

Egypt and Syria from the Arab to the Ottoman Conquest

Atiya, A. S. *The Crusade in the Later Middle Ages*. London, 1938.
Ayalon, D. *L'esclavage du mamelouk*. Jerusalem, 1951.
—— *Gunpowder and Firearms in the Mamluk Kingdom*. London, 1956.
Becker, C. H. *Beiträge zur Geschichte Ägyptens unter dem Islam*. Strassburg, 1902–3.
Cahen, Cl. *La Syrie du Nord à l'époque des croisades*. Paris, 1940.
Canard, M. *Histoire de la dynastie des H'amdanides de Jazîra et de Syrie*. Paris, 1953.
Darrag, A. *L'Égypte sous le règne de Barsbay 825–841/1422–1438*. Damascus, 1961.
Elisséeff, N. *Nūr al-Dīn, un grand prince musulman de Syrie au temps des Croisades (511–69/1118–74)*. Damascus, 1967.
Gaudefroy-Demombynes, M. *La Syrie à l'époque des mamelouks*. Paris, 1923.
Gottschalk, H. L. *Al-Malik al-Kāmil von Egypten und seine Zeit*. Wiesbaden, 1958.
Hassan, Z. M. *Les Tulunides: étude de l'Égypte musulmane à la fin du IXe siècle. 868–905*. Paris, 1933.
Kraemer, J. *Der Sturz des Königreichs Jerusalem*. Wiesbaden, 1952.
Lammens, H. *La Syrie, précis historique*. Beirut, 1921.
Lane-Poole, S. *History of Egypt in the Middle Ages*. 2nd edn. London, 1914.
Lapidus, I. M. *Muslim Cities in the Later Middle Ages*. Cambridge, Mass., 1967.
Munier, H. and Wiet, G. *L'Égypte byzantine et musulmane*. Cairo, 1932. (Vol. II of *Précis de l'histoire d'Égypte*.)
Runciman, S. *A History of the Crusades*. Cambridge, 1951–4.
Saunders, J. J. *Aspects of the Crusades*. Christchurch, N.Z., 1962.
Setton, K. M. and others (ed.). *A History of the Crusades*. Vols. I, II. Philadelphia, 1955, 1962.
Stevenson, W. B. *The Crusaders in the East*. Cambridge, 1907.
Wiet, G. *L'Égypte arabe* (Vol. IV of Hanotaux, G. (ed.), *Histoire de la nation égyptienne*). Paris, 1937.
—— *Les marchands d'épices sous les sultans mamelouks*. Cairo, 1955.
Ziadeh, N. A. *Urban Life in Syria under the Early Mamlūks*. Beirut, 1953.

The Turks in Anatolia and the Ottoman State to Selīm I

Atiya, A. S. *The Crusade in the Later Middle Ages*. London, 1938.
Babinger, F. *Mehmed der Eroberer und seine Zeit*. Munich, 1953.
Bratianu, G. I. *Le commerce génois dans la Mer Noire au XIIIe siècle*. Paris, 1929.
Cahen, Cl. *Pre-Ottoman Turkey*. London, 1968 (tr. from French).
Chalandon, F. *Alexis I Comnène*. Paris, 1910.
—— *Jean II Comnène et Manuel I Comnène*. Paris, 1912.
Fisher, S. N. *The Foreign Relations of Turkey, 1481–1512*. Urbana, Ill., 1948.
Flemming, B. *Landschaftsgeschichte von Pamphylien, Pisidien und Lykien in Spätmittelalter*. Wiesbaden, 1964.
Gabriel, A. *Monuments turcs d'Anatolie*. Paris, 1931–2.
—— *Voyages archéologiques dans la Turquie orientale*. Paris, 1936.
Halecki, O. *Un empereur de Byzance à Rome*. Warsaw, 1930.
Hammer-Purgstall, J. von. *Geschichte des osmanischen Reiches*. Pest, 1827–35; 2nd edn. 1834–6. French tr. *Histoire de l'empire ottoman*. Paris, 1835–43.
Heyd, W. *Histoire du commerce du Levant au moyen-âge*. Paris, 1936.
Iorga, N. *Geschichte des osmanischen Reiches*. Gotha, 1908–13.
—— *Histoire des Roumains et de la Romanité orientale*. Bucharest, 1937–45.
Jireček, K. *Geschichte der Serben*. Gotha, 1911, 1918.
Köprülü, M. F. *Les origines de l'empire ottoman*. Paris, 1935.
Laurent, J. *Byzance et les Turcs seldjoucides jusqu'en 1081*. Nancy, 1913.
Lemerle, P. *L'émirat d'Aydın, Byzance, et l'Occident*. Paris, 1957.
Mas Latrie, L. de. *Relations de l'île de Chypre avec l'Asie Mineure au moyen-âge*. Paris, 1879.
Melikoff, L. *Le geste de Melik Danismend I*. Paris, 1960.
Miller, B. *The Palace School of Muhammad the Conqueror*. Cambridge, Mass., 1941.
Minorsky, V. F. *La Perse au XVe siècle entre la Turquie et la Venise*. Paris, 1933.
Runciman, S. *A History of the Crusades*. Cambridge, 1951–4.
—— *The Fall of Constantinople 1453*. Cambridge, 1965.
Setton, K. M. and others (ed.). *A History of the Crusades*. Vols. I, II. Philadelphia, 1955, 1962.
Vaughan, D. M. *Europe and the Turk. A Pattern of Alliances, 1350–1700*. Liverpool, 1954.
Wittek, P. *Das Fürstentum Mentesche*. Istanbul, 1934.
—— *The Rise of the Ottoman Empire*. London, 1938.
Zinkeisen, J. W. *Geschichte des osmanischen Reiches in Europa*. Hamburg, Gotha, 1840–63; reprinted, 1962.

The Ottoman Empire from Selīm I

Anderson, M. S. *The Eastern Question*. London, 1966.
Baer, G. *A History of Landownership in Modern Egypt, 1800–1950*. London, 1962.
Bailey, F. E. *British Policy and the Turkish Reform Movement*. Cambridge, Mass., 1942.

Blaisdell, D. C. *European Financial Control in the Ottoman Empire.* New York, 1929.

Bodman, H. L. *Political Factions in Aleppo, 1760–1826.* Chapel Hill, North Carolina, 1963.

Braudel, F. *La Méditerranée et le monde méditerranéen à l'époque de Philippe II.* Paris, 1949.

Combe, É., Bainville, J. and Driault, É. *L'Égypte ottomane, l'expédition française et le règne de Mohammed Aly (1517–1849).* Cairo, 1933. (Vol. III of *Précis de l'histoire d'Égypte.*)

Davison, R. H. *Reform in the Ottoman Empire, 1856–1876.* Princeton, 1963.

Devereux, R. *The First Ottoman Constitutional Period.* Baltimore, 1963.

Dodwell, H. *The Founder of Modern Egypt.* Cambridge, 1931.

Douin, G. *Histoire du règne du khédive Ismail.* Cairo, 1933–41.

Emin, A. *Turkey in the World War.* New Haven, Conn., 1930.

Engelhardt, E. *La Turquie et le Tanzimat.* Paris, 1882–4.

Gibb, H. A. R. and Bowen, H. *Islamic Society and the West I: Islamic Society in the Eighteenth Century,* Parts I and II. London, 1950, 1957.

Hammer-Purgstall, J. von. *Geschichte des osmanischen Reiches.* Pest, 1827–35; 2nd edn., 1834–6. (French tr. *Histoire de l'empire ottoman.* Paris, 1835–43.)

—— *Die osmanischen Reichs Staatsverfassung und Staatsverwaltung.* Vienna, 1815.

Herrold, J. C. *Bonaparte in Egypt.* London, 1963.

Heyd, U. *Ottoman Documents on Palestine, 1552–1615.* Oxford, 1960.

—— 'The Ottoman 'ulemā and westernization in the time of Selīm III and Maḥmūd II', in Heyd, U. (ed.). *Studies in Islamic History and Civilization.* Jerusalem, 1961.

Holt, P. M. *Egypt and the Fertile Crescent, 1516–1922.* London, 1966.

—— (ed.). *Political and Social Change in Modern Egypt.* London, 1968.

Hourani, A. H. 'The Fertile Crescent in the eighteenth century', in *A Vision of History.* Beirut, 1961.

Hurewitz, J. C. *Diplomacy in the Near and Middle East; a Documentary Record; 1535–1914, 1914–1956.* Princeton, 1956.

Iorga, N. *Geschichte des osmanischen Reichs.* Gotha, 1908–13.

Ismail, A. *Histoire du Liban.* Vols. I, IV (all so far published). Paris, 1955; Beirut, 1958.

Kedourie, E. *England and the Middle East.* Cambridge, 1956.

Kerr, M. H. *Lebanon in the Last Years of Feudalism, 1840–1868.* Beirut, 1959.

Lammens, H. *La Syrie, précis historique.* Beirut, 1921.

Landau, J. M. *Parliaments and Parties in Egypt.* Tel Aviv, 1953.

Landes, D. S. *Bankers and Pashas.* London, 1958.

Lewis, B. *The Emergence of Modern Turkey.* 2nd edn. London, 1968.

—— *Istanbul and the Civilization of the Ottoman Empire.* Norman, Oklahoma, 1963.

Longrigg, S. H. *Four Centuries of Modern Iraq.* Oxford, 1925.

—— *'Iraq, 1900 to 1950.* London, 1953.

Lybyer, A. H. *The Government of the Ottoman Empire in the time of Suleiman the Magnificent.* Cambridge, Mass., 1913.

Mantran, R. *Istanbul dans la seconde moitié du XVIIe siècle.* Paris, 1962.
Ma'oz, M. *Ottoman Reform in Syria and Palestine 1840–1861.* Oxford, 1968.
Marlowe, J. *Anglo-Egyptian Relations, 1800–1953.* London, 1954.
—— *The Making of the Suez Canal.* London, 1964.
Masson, P. *Histoire du commerce français dans le Levant au XVIIe siècle.* Paris, 1896.
—— *Histoire du commerce français dans le Levant au XVIIIe siècle.* Paris, 1911.
Philby, H. St J. *Sa'udi Arabia.* London, 1955.
Polk, W. R. *The Opening of South Lebanon, 1788–1840.* Cambridge, Mass., 1963.
Rafeq, A-K. *The Province of Damascus, 1723–1783.* Beirut, 1966.
Ramsaur, E. E. *The Young Turks.* Princeton, 1957.
Rivlin, H. A. B. *The Agricultural Policy of Muḥammad 'Alī in Egypt.* Cambridge, Mass., 1961.
Salibi, K. S. *The Modern History of Lebanon.* London, 1965.
Sammarco, A. *Les règnes de 'Abbas, de Sa'id et d'Isma'il.* Rome, 1935. (Vol. IV of *Précis de l'histoire d'Égypte.*)
Serjeant, R. B. *The Portuguese off the South Arabian Coast.* Oxford, 1963.
Shaw, S. J. *The Financial and Administrative Organization and Development of Ottoman Egypt, 1517–1798.* Princeton, N.J., 1958.
Stripling, G. W. F. *The Ottoman Turks and the Arabs, 1511–1574.* Urbana, Ill., 1942.
Temperley, H. W. V. *England and the Near East, the Crimea.* London, 1936.
Tibawi, A. L. *British Interests in Palestine 1800–1901.* London, 1961.
—— *American Interests in Syria 1800–1901.* Oxford, 1966.
Tignor, R. L. *Modernization and British Colonial Rule in Egypt, 1882–1914.* Princeton, 1966.
Ubicini, A. *Lettres sur la Turquie.* Paris, 1853–4.
Ursu, J. *La politique orientale de François Ier.* Paris, 1908.
Wilson, A. T. *The Persian Gulf.* London, 1928.
Wood, A. C. *A History of the Levant Company.* London, 1935.
Zeine, Z. N. *The Emergence of Arab Nationalism.* Beirut, 1966.
Zinkeisen, J. W. *Geschichte des osmanischen Reiches in Europa.* Hamburg, 1840–63; reprinted 1962.

The Modern Arab States and Arab Nationalism

Ahmed, J. M. *The Intellectual Origins of Egyptian Nationalism.* London, 1960.
Antonius, G. *The Arab Awakening.* London, 1938.
Atiyah, E. *The Arabs.* London, 1955.
Brown, L. C. *The Surest Path.* Cambridge, Mass., 1967.
Edmonds, C. J. *Kurds, Turks and Arabs.* London, 1957.
Gendzier, I. L. *The Practical Visions of Ya'qub Sanu'.* Cambridge, Mass., 1966.
Haim, S. *Arab Nationalism, An Anthology.* Berkeley, Cal., 1962.
Holt, P. M. (ed.). *Political and Social Change in Modern Egypt.* London, 1968.
Hourani, A. H. *Syria and Lebanon.* London, 1946.

—— 'Race, religion and nation state in the Near East', in *A Vision of History*. Beirut, 1961.
—— *Arabic Thought in the Liberal Age, 1798–1939*. London, 1962.
Ireland, P. W. *'Iraq, A Study in Political Development*. London, 1937.
Karpat, K. H. *Political and Social Thought in the Contemporary Middle East*. London, 1968.
Keddourie, E. *The Chatham House Version*. London, 1970.
Khadduri, M. *Independent Iraq 1932–1958*. 2nd edn. London, 1960.
Kirk, G. E. *The Middle East in the War*. London, 1953.
—— *The Middle East, 1945–1950*. London, 1954.
Laqueur, W. Z. (ed.). *The Middle East in Transition*. London, 1958.
Longrigg, S. H. *'Iraq, 1900–1950*. London, 1953.
—— *Syria and Lebanon under French Mandate*. London, 1958.
Monroe, E. *Britain's Moment in the Middle East, 1914–1956*. London, 1963.
Nuseibeh, H. Z. *The Ideas of Arab Nationalism*. Cornell, 1956.
Safran, N. *Egypt in Search of Political Community*. Cambridge, Mass., 1961.
Salibi, K. S. *The Modern History of Lebanon*. London, 1965.
Toynbee, A. J. *Survey of International Affairs 1925 I: The Islamic World Since the Peace Settlement*. London, 1927.
Vatikiotis, P. J. *Politics and the Military in Jordan*. London, 1967.
—— *The Modern History of Egypt*. London, 1969.
Warriner, Doreen. *Land Reform and Development in the Middle East*. 2nd edn. London, 1962.
—— *Land Reform in Principle and Practice*. Oxford, 1969.
Zeine, Z. N. *The Struggle for Arab Independence*. Beirut, 1960.

Persia from the Safavids: Persian Nationalism

Alavi, B. *Kämpfendes Iran*. Berlin, 1955.
Arasteh, R. *Education and Social Awakening in Iran*. Leiden, 1962.
Avery, P. W. *Modern Iran*. London, 1965.
Banani, A. *The Modernization of Iran, 1921–41*. Stanford, 1961.
Bellan, L. L. *Chah 'Abbas I*. Paris, 1932.
Binder, L. *Iran: Political Development in a Changing Society*. Berkeley and Los Angeles, 1962.
Browne, E. G. *The Persian Revolution of 1905–1909*. Cambridge, 1910.
—— *The Press and Poetry of Modern Persia*. Cambridge, 1914.
—— *Materials for the Study of the Bábí Religion*. Cambridge, 1918.
Cottam, R. W. *Nationalism in Iran*. Pittsburgh, 1964.
Curzon, G. N. *Persia and the Persian Question*. London, 1892.
Ellis, C. H. *The Transcaspian Episode, 1918–1919*. London, 1963.
Entner, M. L. *Russo-Persian Commercial Relations, 1828–1914*. Gainsville, Fla., 1965.
Geyer, D. *Die Sowjetunion und Iran*. Tübingen, 1955.
Greaves, R. L. *Persia and the Defence of India, 1884–1892*. London, 1959.
Hamzavi, A. H. *Persia and the Powers*. London, 1946.

Hinz, W. *Irans Aufstieg zum Nationalstaat im fünfzehnten Jahrhundert.* Berlin and Leipzig, 1936.
Horst, H. *Tīmūr und Ḫoǧā 'Alī.* Wiesbaden, 1958.
Kazemzadeh, F. *Russia and Britain in Persia, 1864–1914.* New Haven and London, 1968.
Kelly, J. B. *Britain and the Persian Gulf, 1795–1880.* Oxford, 1968.
Lambton, A. K. S. *Landlord and Peasant in Persia.* London, 1953.
Lenczowski, G. *Russia and the West in Iran, 1918–1949.* Ithaca, N.Y., 1949.
Lockhart, L. *Nadir Shah.* London, 1938.
—— *The Fall of the Safavi Dynasty and the Afghan Occupation of Persia.* Cambridge, 1958.
Millspaugh, A. C. *The American Task in Persia.* New York, 1925.
—— *Americans in Persia.* Washington, D.C., 1946.
Minorsky, V. F. (ed. and tr.). *Tadhkirat al-mulūk.* London, 1943.
Motter, T. H. V. *The Persian Corridor and Aid to Russia.* Washington, D.C., 1952.
Ramazani, R. K. *The Foreign Policy of Iran ... 1500–1941.* Charlottesville, Va., 1966.
Roemer, H. R. *Der Niedergang Irans nach dem Tode Isma'īl's des Grausamen 1577–1581.* Würzburg-Aumühle, 1939.
Sarwar, Gh. *The History of Shāh Ismā'īl Ṣafawī.* Aligarh, 1939.
Sheil, Lady. *Glimpses of Life and Manners in Persia.* London, 1856.
Shuster, W. M. *The Strangling of Persia.* New York, 1912.
Sykes, C. *Wassmuss, 'the German Lawrence'.* London, 1936.
Sykes, P. M. *A History of Persia.* 3rd edn. London, 1930.
Thomas, L. V. and Frye, R. N. *The United States and Turkey and Iran.* Cambridge, Mass., 1951.
Upton, J. M. *The History of Modern Iran.* Cambridge, Mass., 1960.
Watson, R. G. *A History of Persia.* London, 1866.
Wilber, D. N. *Contemporary Iran.* London, 1963.
Wilson, A. T. *The Persian Gulf.* London, 1928.
Zabih, S. *The Communist Movement in Iran.* Berkeley and Los Angeles, 1966.

Westernization, Social and Economic Change

Anderson, J. N. D. *Islamic Law in the Modern World.* New York, 1959.
Ayrout, H. H. *The Egyptian Peasant.* Boston, Mass., 1963.
Baer, G. *Population and Society in the Middle East.* London, 1964.
Berger, M. *The Arab World Today.* London, 1962.
Binder, L. *The Ideological Revolution in the Middle East.* New York, 1964.
Bonné, A. *State and Economics in the Middle East.* 2nd edn. London, 1955.
Bullard, R. W. (ed.). *The Middle East. A political and economic survey.* 3rd edn. London, 1958.
Campbell, J. C. *Defense of the Middle East.* 2nd edn. New York, 1960.
Daghestani, K. *Étude sociologique sur la famille musulmane contemporaine en Syrie.* Paris, 1932.

El-Gritly, A. A. I. *The Structure of Modern Industry in Egypt*. Cairo, 1948.
Fisher, S. N. *The Military in the Middle East*. Columbus, Ohio, 1963.
Frye, R. N. (ed.). *Islam and the West*. The Hague, 1957.
Gardet, L. *La cité musulmane. Vie sociale et politique*. Paris, 1954.
Grunebaum, G. E. von. *Modern Islam: The Search for Cultural Identity*. Berkeley and Los Angeles, 1962.
Halpern, M. *The Politics of Social Change in the Middle East and North Africa*. Princeton, 1963.
Hershlag, Z. Y. *Introduction to the Modern Economic History of the Middle East*. Leiden, 1964.
Holt, P. M. (ed.). *Political and Social Change in Modern Egypt*. London, 1968.
Hourani, A. H. *Minorities in the Arab World*. London, 1947.
International Bank for Reconstruction and Development. *The Economic Development of Iraq*. Baltimore, 1952.
—— *The Economic Development of Syria*. Baltimore, 1955.
Issawi, C. *Egypt in Revolution. An Economic Analysis*. London, 1963.
—— *The Economic History of the Middle East, 1800–1914*. Chicago, 1966.
—— and Yeganeh, M. *The Economics of Middle Eastern oil*. London, 1962.
Keddie, N. R. *An Islamic Response to Imperialism*. Berkeley and Los Angeles, 1968.
Kedourie, E. *Afghani and ʿAbduh*. London, 1966.
Laqueur, W. Z. (ed.). *The Middle East in Transition*. London, 1958.
Lerner, D. *The Passing of Traditional Society*. Glencoe, Ill., 1958.
Le Tourneau, R. *Évolution politique de l'Afrique du Nord musulmane, 1920–1961*. Paris, 1962.
Lewis, B. *The Emergence of Modern Turkey*. 2nd edn. London, 1961.
—— *The Middle East and the West*. London, 1964.
Longrigg, S. H. *Oil in the Middle East*. London, 1964.
Nolte, R. H. *The Modern Middle East*. New York, 1963.
Patai, R. *Golden River to Golden Road*. Philadelphia, 1962.
Proctor, J. H. (ed.). *Islam and International Relations*. London, 1965.
Rustow, D. A. *Politics and Westernization in the Near East*. Princeton, 1956.
—— 'The politics of the Near East', in Almond, G. A. and Coleman, J. S. (ed.). *The Politics of the Developing Areas*. Princeton, 1960.
Smith, W. C. *Islam in Modern History*. Princeton, 1957.
Toynbee, A. J. *The World and the West*. London, 1953.
Yaukey, D. *Fertility Differences in a Modernizing Country*. Princeton, 1961.

Central Asia, the Golden Horde and the Tsarist Empire

Allworth, E. (ed.). *Central Asia: A Century of Russian Rule*. New York, 1967.
Barthold, V. V. *Turkestan Down to the Mongol Invasion*. 3rd edn. London, 1968 (tr. from Russian).
—— *Histoire des Turcs d'Asie centrale*. Paris, 1945 (tr.).
—— *Four Studies on the History of Central Asia*. Leiden, 1956–63 (tr. from Russian).

Barthold, V. V. *La découverte de l'Asie*. Paris, 1947 (tr. from Russian).
Bouvet, L. *L'empire mongol. 2me. phase*. Paris, 1927.
Bratianu, G. I. *Recherches sur le commerce génois dans la Mer Noire au XIIIe siècle*. Paris, 1929.
Carrère d'Encausse, H. *Réforme et révolution chez les Musulmans de l'Empire russe: Bukhara, 1867–1927*. Paris, 1966.
Czaplicka, M. A. *The Turks of Central Asia*. London, 1918.
Elias, N. and Ross, E. D. *History of the Moghuls of Central Asia*. London, 1895.
Grekov, B. D. and Yakubovsky, A. Y. *La Horde d'Or*. Paris, 1939.
Grousset, R. *L'empire mongol. Ière. phase*. Paris, 1941.
—— *L'empire des steppes*. 4th edn. Paris, 1960.
—— *Conqueror of the World*. London, 1967 (tr. from French).
Hambly, G. (ed.). *Zentralasien*. Frankfort, 1966.
Hammer-Purgstall, J. von. *Geschichte der goldenen Horde in Kiptschak*. Pest, 1840.
—— *Geschichte der Chane der Krim*. Vienna, 1856.
Holdsworth, M. *Turkestan in the Nineteenth Century*. London, 1959.
Hookham, H. *Tamburlaine the Conqueror*. London, 1962.
Howarth, H. H. *History of the Mongols*. London, 1876–88.
Kirimal, E. M. *Der nationale Kampf der Krimtürken*. Emsdetten, 1952.
Mouradja d'Ohsson, A. C. *Histoire des Mongols*. 2nd edn. Amsterdam, 1852.
Nolde, B. E. *La formation de l'empire russe*. Paris, 1952–53.
Pelliot, P. *Notes sur l'histoire de la Horde d'Or*. Paris, 1949.
Pierce, R. A. *Russian Central Asia, 1867–1917. A Study in Colonial Rule*. Berkeley and Los Angeles, 1960.
Prawdin, M. *The Mongol Empire*. London, 1940.
Schuyler, E. *Turkistan*. London, 1876. (Abridged edn. London, 1966.)
Skrine, F. H. B. and Ross, E. D. *The Heart of Asia*. London, 1899.
Spuler, B. *Die goldene Horde*. Leipzig, 1943.
—— *The Muslim World, a Historical Survey II: The Mongol Period*. Leiden, 1960 (tr. from German).
—— *Die Mongolen in Iran*. 3rd edn. Berlin, 1968.
Vámbéry, A. *History of Bokhara*. London, 1873.
Velyaminov-Zernov, V. *Matériaux pour servir à l'histoire du khanat de Crimée*. St Petersburg, 1864.
Vernadsky, G. *The Mongols and Russia*. New Haven, 1953.

Islam, the Soviet Union and Communism

Batatu, J. 'Some preliminary observations on the beginnings of Communism in the Arab East', in *Islam and Communism*. Munich, 1960.
Bennigsen A. and Quelquejay, C. L. *Les mouvements nationaux chez les Musulmans de Russie I: Le Sultangalievisme au Tatarstan*. Paris, 1960.
—— *The Evolution of the Muslim Nationalities of the USSR and Their Linguistic Problems*. London, 1961 (tr. from French).
—— *Islam in the Soviet Union*. London, 1967 (tr. from French).
Blumberger, J. T. P. *Le communisme aux Indes néerlandaises*. Paris, 1929.

Brackman, A. C. *Indonesian Communism: A History*. New York, 1963.
Ellis, C. H. *The Transcaspian Episode, 1918–1919*. London, 1963.
Eudin, X. J., and North, R. C. *Soviet Russia and the East, 1920–1927*. Stanford, 1957.
Glazer, S. *Communism in the Near East*. Washington, D.C., 1949.
Hayit, B. *Turkestan im XX Jahrhundert*. Darmstadt, 1956.
Hostler, C. W. *Turkism and the Soviets*. London, 1957.
Kahin, G. M. *Nationalism and Communism in East Asia*. Melbourne, 1956.
Kolarz, W. *Religion in the Soviet Union*. London, 1962.
Laqueur, W. Z. *Communism and Nationalism in the Middle East*. London, 1956.
—— (ed.). *The Middle East in Transition*. London, 1958.
Lenczowski, G. *Russia and the West in Iran 1918–1949*. Ithaca, N.Y., 1949.
McVey, R. T. *The Rise of Indonesian Communism*. Ithaca, N.Y., 1965.
Monteil, V. *Les musulmans soviétiques*. Paris, 1957.
Park, A. G. *Bolshevism in Turkestan, 1917–1927*. New York, 1957.
Pipes, R. *The Formation of the Soviet Union—Communism and Nationalism, 1917–1923*. Cambridge, Mass., 1954.
Rodinson, M. 'Problématique de l'étude des rapports entre Islam et communisme'. *Colloque sur la sociologie musulmane*, 1961.
Romainville, F. de. *L'Islam et l'URSS*. Paris, 1947.
Spector, I. *The Soviet Union and the Muslim World, 1917–1958*. Seattle, 1959.
—— *The First Russian Revolution, its Impact on Asia*. Englewood Cliffs, N.J., 1962.
Wheeler, G. *The Modern History of Soviet Central Asia*. London, 1964.
Zabih, S. *The Communist Movement in Iran*. Berkeley and Los Angeles, 1966.
Zenkovsky, S. A. *Pan-Turkism and Islam in Russia*. Cambridge, Mass., 1960.

Modern Turkey and Turkish Nationalism

Başgil, A. F. and others. *La Turquie*. Paris, 1939. (Vol. VII in Lévy-Ullmann, H. and Mirkine-Guetzévitch, B. (ed.). *La vie juridique des peuples*.)
Başgöz, I. and Wilson, H. E. *Educational Problems in Turkey, 1920–1940*. Bloomington, 1968.
Berkes, N. *The Development of Secularism in Turkey*. Montreal, 1964.
Edib, H. [Adıvar]. *The Turkish Ordeal*. London, 1928.
Frey, F. W. *The Turkish Political Elite*. Cambridge, Mass., 1965.
Gökalp, Z. (tr. and ed. Berkes, N.). *Turkish Nationalism and Western Civilization*. London, 1959.
Hershlag, Z. Y. *Turkey, the Challenge of Growth*. Leiden, 1968.
Heyd, U. *Foundations of Turkish Nationalism*. London, 1950.
—— *Language Reform in Modern Turkey*. Jerusalem, 1954.
Howard, H. N. *The Partition of Turkey: A Diplomatic History, 1913–1923*. Norman, Oklahoma, 1931.
Jäschke, G. *Die Turkei in den Jahren, 1935–1941*. Leipzig, 1943.
—— *Der Islam in der neuen Türkei*. Leiden, 1951.
—— *Die Türkei in den Jahren, 1942–1951*. Wiesbaden, 1955.

Karpat, K. H. *Turkey's Politics. The Transition to a Multi-party System.* Princeton, 1959.

Kazamias, A. M. *Education and the Quest for Modernity in Turkey.* London, 1966.

Kinross, Lord. *Atatürk: The Rebirth of a Nation.* London, 1964.

Lewis, B. *The Emergence of Modern Turkey.* 2nd edn. London, 1968.

Lewis, G. L. *Turkey.* 3rd edn. London, 1965.

Makal, M. *A Village in Anatolia.* London, 1954.

Mardin, Ş. *The Genesis of Young Ottoman Thought.* Princeton, 1962.

Orga, I. *Phoenix Ascendant.* London, 1958.

Robinson, R. D. *The First Turkish Republic: A Case Study in National Development.* Cambridge, Mass., 1963.

Roux, J. P. *Turquie.* Paris, 1968.

Smith, E. D. *Turkey: Origins of the Kemalist Movement and the Government of the Grand National Assembly, 1919–1923.* Washington, D.C., 1959.

Société pour l'Étude de l'Histoire turque. *Histoire de la république turque.* Istanbul, 1935.

Stirling, P. *Turkish Village.* London, 1965.

Thomas, L. V. and Frye, R. N. *The United States and Turkey and Iran.* Cambridge, Mass., 1951.

Thornburg, M. W., Spry, G. and Soule, G. *Turkey: An Economic Appraisal.* New York, 1949.

Toynbee, A. J. and Kirkwood, K. P. *Turkey.* London, 1926.

Turhan, M. *Where are we in Westernization?* Istanbul, 1965.

Ward, R. E. and Rustow, D. A. (eds.). *Political Modernization in Japan and Turkey.* Princeton, 1964.

Yalman, A. E. *Turkey In My Time.* Norman, Oklahoma, 1956.

GLOSSARY

'ĀLIM (pl., *'ulamā'*). A scholar in the Islamic sciences relating to the Qur'ān, theology and jurisprudence.

BID'A. An innovation in Muslim belief or practice; the converse of *sunna,* the alleged practice of the Prophet. *Bid'a* thus tends to be regarded as blameworthy by Muslims.

DĀR AL-ḤARB. 'The abode of war', i.e. territory not under Muslim sovereignty, against which warfare for the propagation of the faith is licit; cf. *Jihād*. It is the converse of *Dār al-Islām,* 'the abode of Islam'.

DHIMMĪ. An adherent of a revealed religion (especially Judaism or Christianity) living under Muslim sovereignty, under the protection of the *Sharī'a* (q.v.).

DIHQĀN (Persian). A member of the lesser feudal nobility in the Sasanian empire. The *dihqāns* largely retained their positions after the Arab conquest, but declined in status from the fifth/eleventh century.

FATWĀ. A formal statement of authoritative opinion on a point of *Sharī'a* (q.v.) by a jurisconsult known as a *muftī*.

FERMĀN (Turkish, from Persian, *farmān*). An order or edict emanating from an Ottoman sultan.

GHĀZĪ. A frontier-warrior, taking part in raids (sing. *ghazā*) in the Holy War (*Jihād,* q.v.) against the infidel. The term was used as a title of honour, e.g. by Ottoman rulers.

ḤADĪTH (pl., *aḥādīth*). A Tradition of an alleged saying or practice of the Prophet. A *Ḥadīth* consists of a chain of oral transmitters (*isnād*) and the text transmitted (*matn*).

ḤAJJ. The Pilgrimage to the Holy Places of Mecca, which is a legal obligation upon individual Muslims. The rites of the *Ḥajj* take place between 8 and 12 Dhu'l-Ḥijja, the last month of the Muslim year. The 'Lesser Pilgrimage' (*'Umra*) may be performed at any time.

'ĪD AL-AḌḤĀ. 'The Feast of Sacrifices', or *al-'Īd al-Kabīr* (the Great Feast), held on 10 Dhu'l-Ḥijja, to coincide with the sacrifice which is one of the rites of the *Hajj* (q.v.).

'ĪD AL-FIṬR. 'The Feast of the Breaking of the Fast' or *al-'Īd al-Ṣaghīr* (the Small Feast), held after the end of Ramaḍān, the month of fasting.

ILTIZĀM. A farm of taxes of state-lands. The tax-farmer was known as a *multazim*.

IMĀM. The leader of a group of Muslims in ritual prayer (*ṣalāt*); more specifically, the head of the Islamic community (*Umma*). The title was particularly used by the Shī'ī claimants to the headship of the community.

IQṬĀʻ. A grant of state-lands or revenues by a Muslim ruler to an individual usually in recompense for service.

JIHĀD. The Holy War against infidels, which is in certain circumstances an obligation under the *Sharīʻa* for Muslims. See also *Ghāzī*.
JIZYA. Poll-tax paid to a Muslim government by male members of the protected non-Muslim communities (see *Dhimmī*).

KHUṬBA. The sermon delivered at the Friday congregational prayer in the mosque. Since it includes a prayer for the ruler, mention in the *khuṭba* is a mark of sovereignty in Islam.

MADHHAB. Sometimes translated 'rite' or 'school', a *madhhab* is one of the four legal systems recognized as orthodox by Sunnī (q.v.) Muslims. They are named after their founders—the Ḥanafī, Ḥanbalī, Mālikī and Shāfiʻī *madhhab*.
MADRASA. A school for teaching the Islamic sciences, frequently connected with a mosque.
MAMLŪK. A slave (especially of Turkish, Circassian or Georgian origin) trained as a soldier.
MAWLĀ (pl., *mawālī*). A client of an Arab tribe; more especially a non-Arab convert during the first century of Islam, who acquired status by attachment to an Arab tribal group.
MIḤRĀB. A recess in the wall of a mosque to indicate the *qibla,* i.e. the direction of Mecca, for the correct orientation of ritual prayer.
MILLET (Turkish, from Arabic *milla*). A religious community in the Ottoman empire, usually used of the non-Muslim (*dhimmī,* q.v.) communities, which had some measure of internal autonomy.
MINBAR. The pulpit in a mosque, from which the *khuṭba* (q.v.) is delivered.
MUJTAHID. A Shīʻī *ʻālim* (q.v.), exercising the functions of a jurisconsult.
MULLĀ (modern Turkish, *molla*, from Arabic, *mawlā*). A member of the *ʻulamā'*.
MURĪD. A disciple of a Ṣūfī (q.v.) teacher.

PĪR (Persian). The Persian equivalent of the Arabic term *shaykh,* in the sense of a Ṣūfī (q.v.) teacher.

QĀḌĪ. A judge in a *Sharīʻa* (q.v.) court.
QĀNŪN. A statement of administrative regulations in the Ottoman empire.

SAYYID. Literally, 'lord'. Used to signify a descendant of the Prophet, more specifically through al-Ḥusayn b. ʻAlī. See also *Sharīf*.
SHARĪʻA. The revealed Holy Law of Islam, derived in theory from the Qur'ān, *Ḥadīth* (q.v.), the consensus (*ijmāʻ*) of the *ʻulamā'*, and analogical reasoning (*qiyās*).

SHARĪF. Literally 'noble'. Used to signify a descendant of the Prophet, more specifically through al-Ḥasan b. 'Alī. See also *Sayyid.*
SHĪ'A. Literally 'party'. Originally the supporters of 'Alī's claims to the caliphate, the Shī'a evolved into the principal minority religious group of Muslims, with numerous branches including the Twelver Shī'a and the Ismā'īlīs.
SHĪ'Ī. A member of the Shī'a (q.v.).
SIPAHI (Turkish, from Persian). In Persia a soldier. In the Ottoman state, a cavalryman, maintained by the grant of a *timar* (q.v.). From this term in Indian and North African usage are derived the English 'sepoy' and the French 'spahi'.
ṢŪFĪ. A Muslim mystic, more especially a member of a religious order (*ṭarīqa*), which has special liturgical and other practices as a means to mystical ecstasy.
SUNNĪ. A member of the majority group of Muslims (in contradistinction to the Shī'a), belonging to one of the four *madhhabs* (q.v.), which claim the authority of the *sunna* of the Prophet as transmitted in the *Ḥadīths* (q.v.).

TIMAR. The Turkish equivalent to *iqṭā'* (q.v.): in particular, the smallest type of Ottoman land-grant. See also *Sipahi.*

VILAYET. A province of the Ottoman empire.

WAQF (pl., *awqāf*). An endowment (usually of landed property) established for pious purposes (*waqf khayrī*), or for the benefit of the donor's family (*waqf ahlī*). In North Africa the equivalent term is *ḥubus*.

ZĀWIYA. A Ṣūfī convent.

INDEX

Figures in bold type indicate a main entry.

5